HAND BOOK OF PULP & PAPER, PAPER BOARD AND PAPER-BASED TECHNOLOGY

LIST OF PUBLICATIONS/BOOKS PUBLISHED BY

ENGINEERS INDIA RESEARCH INSTITUTE 4449, NAI SARAK, MAIN ROAD, DELHI - 6 (INDIA)

CHEMICALS/DYES/PETRO CHEMICALS/LUBRICANT/ ELECTROPLATING

Name of Books	Rs.	US$
* Small Medium & Large Scale Chemical Industries	375/-	60
* Industrial Chemicals Technology Hand Book	1100/-	150
* Project Ideas on All Chemicals & Allied Industries	1300/-	150
* Electroplating, Anodizing & Surface Finishing Technology	750/-	80
* Agro Chemical Industries (Insecticide & Pesticides)	900/-	100
* Technology of Synthetic Dyes, Pigments Intermediates	1100/-	150
* Petrochemicals, Lubricants, Greases & Petroleum Refining	900/-	120

GUMS, ADHESIVES & SEALANTS

Name of Books	Rs.	US$
* Technology of Gums, Adhesives & Sealants with Formulations	950/-	125
* Hand Book of Adhesives with their Formulae	650/-	100
* Adhesives Technology & Formulations Hand Book	975/-	125

SMALL SCALE INDUSTRIES/ STATIONERY/PAPER/INKS/ CANDLES & EXPORT BUSINESS

Name of Books	Rs.	US$
* Small and Cottage Scale Industries (Laghu Udyog) - In Hindi	525/-	75
* Start Your Own Export Business (How To Export)	350/-	50
* Start Your Own Small Business and Industry	350/-	50
* Candle Making Processes & Formulations Hand-Book	380/-	50
* Stationery, Paper Converting & Packaging Industries	400/-	60
* Modern Inks Formulaes & Manufacturing Industries	325/-	50
* Profitable Businesses to Start for Entrepreneurs	400/-	60
* Modern Small and Cottage Scale Industries	650/-	100
* Profitable Small Cottage Tiny & Home Industries	650/-	90

OFFSET PRINTING, SCREEN PRINTING & PACKAGING

Name of Books	Rs.	US$
* Printing Processes Technologies & Industries	375/-	50
* Hand Book of Printing Technology (Offset, Screen, Flexo, Gravure, Inkjet & Digital)	975/-	150
* Hand Book of Offset Printing Technology	500/-	75
* Screen Printing with Processes & Technology	350/-	50
* Hand Book of Packaging Industries	1300/-	150
* Hand Book of Packaging Technology	900/-	120
* Modern Packaging Technology for Food Products	600/-	90
* Hand Book of Food Packaging Technology	900/-	100

PAINT, VARNISH, COATING AND LACQUERS

Name of Books	Rs.	US$
* Paint Pigment Varnish & Lacquer Manufacturing	450/-	60
* Paint Varnish Solvents & Coating Technology	750/-	95
* Technology of Coatings, Resins, Pigments & Inks Industries	975/-	120

PLASTIC/POLYMER PROCESSING, COMPOUNDING, MOULDS, PET, RESINS & RUBBER INDUSTRIES

Name of Books	Rs.	US$
* Moulds Design & Processing Hand Book	495/-	75
* Plastic Processing & Packaging Industries	450/-	75
* Hand Book of Plastic Projects (Hi-Tech Plastic Projects)	1300/-	120
* Synthetic Resins Technology with Formulations	800/-	90
* PET Preform & Its Products (Bottles/Jar) Mfg.	1300/-	90
* Plastic Compounding, Masterbatches, PET & Other Plastics	750/-	100
* Technology of PVC Compounding and Its Applications	900/-	100
* Hand Book of Polymer and Plastic Technology	950/-	100

BAKERY & CONFECTIONERY

Name of Books	Rs.	US$
* Hand Book of Bakery Industries	350/-	50
* Hand Book of Confectionery with Formulations	600/-	80
* Hand Book of Modern Bakery Products	750/-	100

AGRO CULTIVATION, ANIMAL FARMING, AGRO PLANTATION & AGRO CHEMICAL/PESTICIDES

Name of Books	Rs.	US$
* Hand Book of Poultry Farming and Feed Formulations	450/-	75
* Hand Book of Pig Farming	400/-	60
* Agro Based H.B. of Plantation,		

Send Draft in favour of "Engineers India Research Institute, Delhi" (Postage Rs. 50/- Extra)

ENGINEERS INDIA RESEARCH INSTITUTE

Regd. Off : 4449, Nai Sarak (B), Main Road, Delhi - 110 006 (India)

* Ph: 9811437895, 91-11-23918117, 23916431, 23840361 * Fax: 91-11- 23916431 * E-Mail : eirisidi@bol.net.in

YOU CAN DEPOSIT THE AMOUNT IN EIRI ACCOUNT WITH UTI BANK LTD. CA - 054010200006248 ICICI BANK LTD. CA-022705000598 OR UNION BANK OF INDIA CA-307201010015149

HAND BOOK OF PULP & PAPER, PAPER BOARD AND PAPER-BASED TECHNOLOGY

Written By

EIRI BOARD OF CONSULTANTS & ENGINEERS

ENGINEERS INDIA RESEARCH INSTITUTE

4449, Nai Sarak, Main Road, Delhi - 110006 (India)
Ph: 91-11-23918117, 23916431, 23840361
Fax: 91-11- 2391 6431, 2391 8117
* E-Mail: eirisidi@bol.net.in
*Website: www.eiriindia.org

Also at

4/54 ROOP NAGAR, OPP. SHIV MANDIR, DELHI -110007

PRINTED & PUBLISHED BY
ENGINEERS INDIA RESEARCH INSTITUTE
4449, Nai Sarak, Main Road, Delhi - 110006 (India)
Ph: 91-11-23918117, 23916431, 23840361
Fax: 91-11- 2391 6431, 2391 8117
* E-Mail: eirisidi@bol.net.in
*Website: www.eiriindia.org

ISBN: 978-81-89765-09-5

Printed in New Delhi (INDIA)

Rs. 1150/-

Printed & Published by Sudhir Gupta for "Engineers India Research Institute", 4449 Nai Sarak, Main Road, New Delhi -110006

Preface

In India, the layered bark of the Bhoorja tree was used for writing. Bhoorja tree grows in the Himalayan ranges and is nature's own paper making plant. The leaves of the palm tree treated properly provided the engravable writing material. Cloth coated with clay and gum was used as a writing medium. Cloth formed the base for a flexible, black to gray coloured, highly polished coated surface that could be bound into books or used as single sheets.

Paper consists of a web or mat of inter meshed cellulosic fibers. The mat is formed when a very dilute aqueous suspension of the separated fibers is dried by draining off the water leaving the fibers to form a settled layer.

The term paper is derived from the word papyrus. This was a paper like material which was used for writing by the Egyptians more than 3000 years ago. Papyrus is a plant (Cyperus papyrus) that grows on the banks of the Nile. The inside of the plant was cut into thin strips and they were glued together to form a thin, semi flexible, translucent to opaque, flat material. The papyrus writings have stood the test of time for the last 3000 years.

Historically, the Chinese invented the modern paper and made it using pulp. The pulp was made from shredded cloth fibres and bamboo fibres. From China the process of paper making reached Europe via Constantinople. In the medieval period there was a huge shortage of rag as most of the paper making used rag as its basic raw material.

Many conventionally used & speciallity papers (i.e. tissue papers, toilet papers, tape papers & fire retardant quality papers) are produced out of these two cost materials.

In recent years, the emergence of mini paper plants has revealed the promise of adding new horizons to the growth & development of India paper industries. These mini plants have categorically proved to be technically feasible & economically viable and can be set-up with limited capital investment. Moreover, fully indigenous expertise, technical Know How and plant & machinery are sufficient for plant success.

The mini paper plants have contributed a lot to the manufacture of various types of speciality papers, rendering employment to a large number of persons, utilisation of agricultural wastes, paper wastes and improvement of supply conditions against risiding demands.

The book contains 60 chapters on various aspects such as:- Pulpwood Technology, Alkaline Pulping Recovery Units, Bleaching Chlorination Stage, Bleaching Alkaline Extraction, Bleaching Hypochlorite Stage, Hydrosulfite Bleaching, Peroxide Bleaching, Beating and Refining Action Upon Fibres, Consistency Control, Sizing of Paper, Dyeing of Paper, Wet Strength in Paper and Paperboard, Paper Machine - Forming Section, Paper Machine Press Section, Paper Machine - Dryer Section, Paper Machine - Automation, Calendering, Felts, Paper Machine Wires, Coated Paper, Finishing and Converting, Corrugated Containers, Boxboard, Paper Testing, Board and Hand Made Paper, Equipment Used in Paper Making Laboratory, Paper and Board Properties, Varieties of Paper Grades and their Properties, Transfer Paper, Teletape Rolls, Toilet Paper Plant, Wall Paper, Wax Coated Paper, Xerographic Paper, Paper Bags and Envelops, Paper Board Making Plant, Paper Cups for Ice-cream, Paper Cones and Tubes, Paper Draperies, Egg Tray from Waste Paper, Kraft Bag Making Plant, Note Book, Register and File, Napkins and Facial Tissues, Playing Cards, Drinking Straws, Card Board, Corrugated Board and Boxes, Grey Board, Straw Board (Manual Process), Straw Board (Automatic Process), Plant Economics of Carbon Paper, Plant Economics of Coated Paper and Board Plant, Plant Economics of Corrugated Sheet Board and Boxes, Plant Economics of Egg Tray from Pulp, Plant Economics of Exercise Note Book and Register, Plant Economics of Hard Borad from Rice Husk, Plant Economics of Hand Made Paper, Plant Economics of Paper Cones and Tubes, Plant Economics of Paper Hand Carrier Bags, Plant Economics of Paper Waste Recycling Plant and Plant & Machinery Suppliers.

This book unfolds various aspects of paper & pulp industry for the benefit of entrepreneurs & professionals.

Director

ENGINEERS INDIA RESEARCH INSTITUTE

Nai Sarak, New Delhi (INDIA)

E-Mail: eirisidi@bol.net.in

Contents-cum-Subject Index

Chapter 18

Chapter 19

Chapter 20

Chapter 21

Chapter 22

Corrugated Containers 276-314

Chapter 23

Boxboard 315-329

Chapter 24

Paper Testing 330-364

Chapter 25

Chapter 26

Chapter 27

Chapter 28

Chapter 29

Chapter 30

Chapter 31

Chapter 32

PROFITABLE SMALL, COTTAGE, TINY AND HOME INDUSTRIES
Hand Book of ICE CREAM TECHNOLOGY AND FORMULAE
Hand Book of FIBRE GLASS MOULDING
HAND BOOK OF AGRO CHEMICAL INDUSTRIES
HAND BOOK OF CONFECTIONERY WITH FORMULATIONS
MILK PROCESSING & DAIRY PRODUCTS INDUSTRIES
MODERN TECHNOLOGY OF ESSENTIAL OILS
HAND BOOK OF BIOTECHNOLO
HAND BOOK OF OILS, FATS & DERIVATIVES WITH REFINING AND PACKAGING TECHNOLOGY
MODERN BAKERY PRODUCTS
CULTIVATION PLANTATION & FARMING
HAND BOOK OF MEDICINAL AND AROMATIC PLANTS
HAND BOOK OF FOOD PACKAGING TECHNOLOGY
PRESERVATION & CANNING OF FRUITS AND VEGETABLES
HAND BOOK OF FOOD DEHYDRATION AND DRYING
TECHNOLOGY OF FOOD PRESERVATION AND PROCESSING

1

Pulpwood Technology

INTRODUCTION

The most important raw material of the pulp and paper industry is pulpwood. The continued growth and economic prosperity of the industry depends on abundant sources of wood of suitable quality and acceptable cost. The purpose of this article is to furnish basic information of pulpwood demand, resources, and qualities.

PULPWOOD SPECIES

Eastern spruce comprises three closely related species : red spruce, Picea rubra; white spruce, Picea glauca and black spruce Picea marina.The botanical range of red spruce extends from New Brunswick and Nova Soctia in Canda, southward through New England and eastern New York and along the Appalachian mountains of Georgia. It occurs chiefly on well-drained uplands and mountain slopes. Mature red spruce approximately 200 years old reaches a diameter of 18 in. and a height of 60 to 80 ft. Grown under favourable conditions, it reaches an average diameter of 9 to 10 in. and a height of about 60 ft in years.

White spruce grows from the coasts of Maine. Labrador, and Newfoundland, westward through Alaska to the Bering Straits, and as far south as the upper part of New England, New York, Michigan, Wisconsin, and Minnesota. In the U.S., white spruce commonly grows adjacent to streams and swamps. Ordinarily, mature trees are 60 to 70 ft high and 1 to 2 ft in diameter.

Black spruce, like white spruce, grows principally in Canada, with a range extending from the Atlantic coast to Alaska. In the

U.S., it grows in the Lake States, New York, New England. Pennsylvania, and as far South as West Virginia. Black spruce is primarily a swamp tree growing in poorly drained bogs where most other trees cannot survive. Swamp-grown black spruce that are 200 year old are often only 2 to 6 in. in diameter.

Spruce wood is relatively light; the average sp gr is 0.37. The tracheids, which make up over 90% of the wood volume, are among the longest and finest occurring in softwoods, and hence, are suitable for most types of paper. The extractable resin occurring in spruce range from about 0.5 to about 2.0%. Thus it is somewhat higher in resin than the firs and hemlocks, but markedly less than the pines. Wood rays comprise about 5% of the wood volume.

Spruce is readily pulped by all the conventional pulping processes. In the early days of wood pulping, it occupied a predominant position. For example, in 1920, about 50% of the pulpwood consumed in North America was spruce. This proportion has steadily decreased, because of the increased utilization of other species.

BALSAM FIR

Abies balsmea is closely similar to the eastern spruces in pulpwood properties, and hence, it is usually classed with them. Balsam fir is a small to medium sized short-lived tree. It is subject to attack by fungi that cause butt rot. Up to 40 year of age, there is usually little evidence of attack, but the percentage of defective trees increases rapidly, and the butt logs of trees 70 year old are often unfit for pulpwood. Under favourable conditions, a 40 year old tree is about 4 in. in diameter and 36 ft in height: 60 year old trees average 6.7 in. in diameter and 52 ft in height.

The botanical range of balsam fir extends from New England, New York, Pennsylvania, and southward along the Appalachian Mountains to Tennessee, and also in the northern portions of the Lake States. In Canada the growth range extends from the Atlantic coast almost to the Pacific.

Balsam fir is relatively light; the average sp. gr. is 0.34. Wood volume is composed of 94.3% tracheids and 5.7% rays. The tracheids are relatively long and slender, and hence, suitable and even superior for most papers. The annual ring is normally

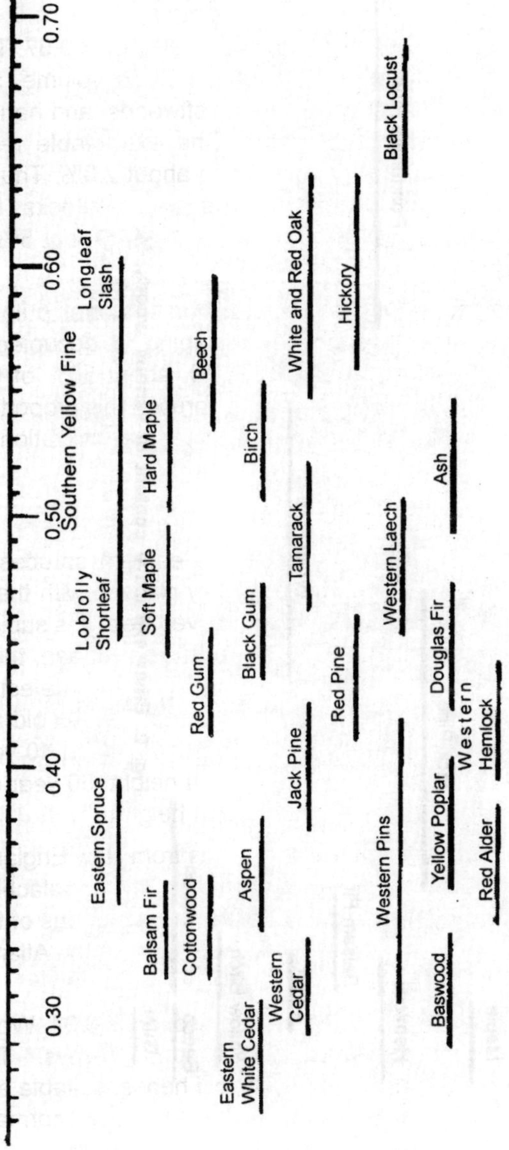

Fig. 1. Density of various wood species. Specific gravity, dry weight, green volume.

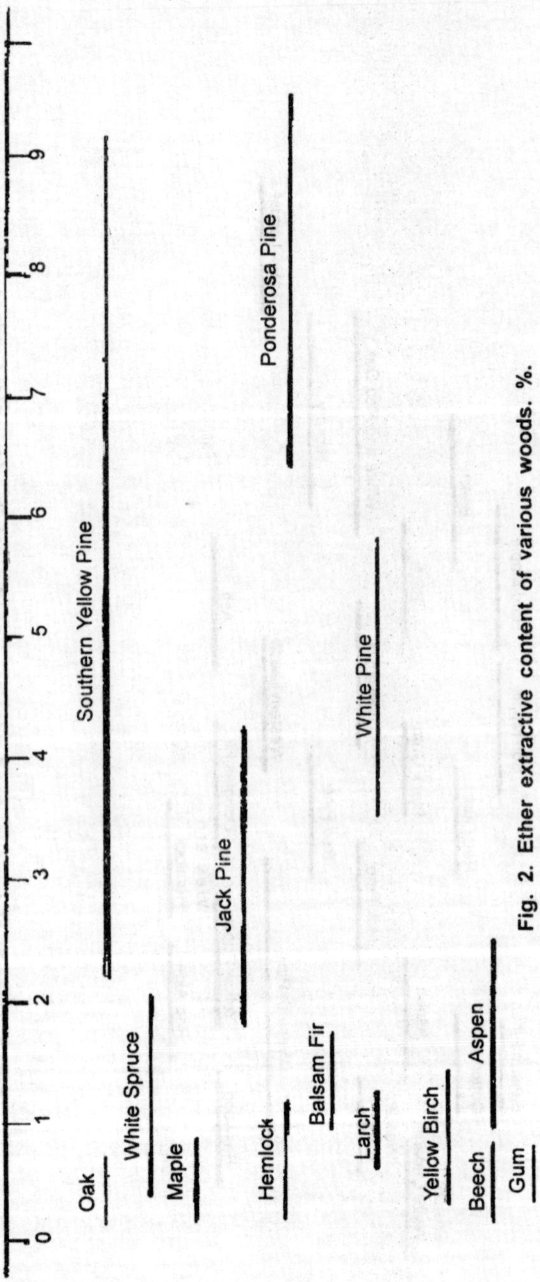

Fig. 2. Ether extractive content of various woods. %.

composed of about 2/3 springwood fibers and 1/3 summerwood. The resin content range of 1.0 to 1.8% is low, as compared with other softwoods.

Maple

There are six species of maple of commercial importance in the U.S. :

Sugar Maple	*Acer saccharum*
Black Maple	*Acer nigrum*
Silver Maple	*Acer saccharinum*
Red Maple	*Acer rubrum*
Box elder	*Acer negundo*
Bigleaf Maple	*Acer macrophyllum*

The sugar maple is the most abundant of these, and the most important both for lumber and pulpwood. Sugar maple grows from southeastern Canada and Maine to Minnesota, and south to Missuri and Alabama. The largest quantities are in the Lake States and the Northeast. Maple is not a fast grower even under favourable conditions. Timber-size trees may range from 10 to 25 rings per radial in., depending upon stand, density, and site quality. This means that a 12 in. diameter tree, grown under the most favourable conditions, would be 60 year old.

Maple fibers, comprising 61% of the wood volume, are relatively short, even for hardwood, and average 0.8 mm, with a range of 0.3 to1.3. The rays of maple are reported to be 17.9% of the wood volume, which is high even for hardwood. Ray cells are non-fibrous and of little value for papermaking. The ether-soluble extractives of maple are low 0.25 to 0.33% for heartwood and 0.23 to 0.26 for sapwood. Maple wood is relatively heavy, 0.52 sp. gr.

The poplar family comprises many species, of which the following are most important :

Eastern cottonwood	*Populus deltoides*
Swamp cottonwood	*Populus herterophylla*
Black cottonwood	*Populus triocarpa*
Quaking aspen	*Populus tremuloides*
Bigtooth aspen	*Populus grandidentata*

The wood of all aspens and cottonwoods is light in weight and colour. Under favourable conditions, the poplars grow rapidly, especially during the first 30 or 40 years, but are rather short-lived trees since they are susceptible to heartwood decay. Black cottonwood is the longest-lived of the group (See below under Pacific Coast species) Eastern cottonwood grows in small scattered stands or in mixture with other species from southern New England, west to the Lake States, and south to Florda Yields of 50 cords per acre of pulpwood from 35-year old stands are not unusual.

Swamp cottonwood grows along the Atlantic coast from Connecticut to Florida, and from Ohio and Indiana southward in the lowlands of the Mississippi valley to Louisiana and Texas.

Quaking aspen grows throughout most of the northeastern and western portions of the United States, and in large portions of Canada and Alaska. In the eastern part the range extends from Maine southward to Tennessee and westward to the Dakotas. It is found in western United States, except in the Southwest.

Bigtooth aspen grows from New England westward to central Minnesota and central lowa, and southward to Alabama and Geogria.

All members of the poplar family are readily reduced to pulp by all the commercial processes, and the various species are harvested together.

Beech

Fagus grandifolia has a botanical range from southeastern Canada and Maine to northern Florida, and westward from the Atlantic coast to Wisconsin, Missouri, and Texas.

Beech is a slow-growing tree as shown in the following table for typical trees:

Age (yr)	Diameter (in)	Height (ft)
20	0.7	13
50	3.0	33
100	7.1	57
200	15.7	84

Beech is a heavy wood with an average sp. gr. of 0.56. Fibers comprise 44% of the wood volume, and average 1.2 mm in length, a medium value for hardwood. Wood volume contains about 20% of ray volume, and 5% longitudinal parenchyma. Ether extractives of beech range from 0.3 to 0.86%.

Birch

Yellow birch, *Betula lutea* and white or paper brich, *Belula papyrifera* are the best known and commercially most important of the birch family. The botanical range of yellow birch extends from eastern Canada and New England through New York and Pennsylvania, to West Virginia, and West through Michigan and Wisconsin. The sp gr is 0.45 to 0.60.

Eastern Pines

The most important members of this group are white pine, *Pinus stroubs*, red pine, *Pinus resinosa* and jack pine. *Pinus banksiana*. White and red pine are highly prized for lumber, and hence, are relatively unimportant as sources of pulpwood. Jack pine, being less sought for lumber has become a more important source of pulpwood.

Eastern white pine grows from Newfoundland to Lake Winnipeg in Canada, southward through New England and the Lake States, and along the Appalachians to northern Georgia . Under favourable growing conditions, white pine average 1.7 in. in diameter and 7.2 ft in height in 10 year, 8.6 in. in diameter and 61 ft in height in 40 year. And 16.5 in. in diameter and 101 ft in height in 80 years.

In the U.S., red pine grows in New England. New York, Pennsylvania, and the Lake States. In Canada, its range extends from Nova Scotia and New Brunswick, westward through Quebec and Ontario to Manitoba. The growth rate of red pine is similar to the white pine.

The original extensive pine forests of the Northeastern and Lake States have been markedly reduced by heavy cutting in past years.

Jack pine grows naturally in Michigan. Wisconsin, and Minnesota, and occurs throughout larger areas and in greater quantities in Canada, where it extends in a band from Nova Scotia to the Rocky Mountains.

Jack pine occurs in mixture with other species and in pure stands. It requires an abundance of direct sunlight, more than white or red pine. Hence, it often follows fires that impoverish the soil. It also grows on "jack pine plains" where the soil is thin, bare, dry, and sandy, and where other species do not grow.

White pine is a light wood, the average sp. gr. is 0.34. Red pine and jack pine are moderately heavy, 0.44 and 0.40 sp gr, respectively. The resin content of white pine is reported as 5.6%. Red pine and jack pine are also high in resin content. For this reason, in common with other pines, these species are not preferred for the sulfite pulping process, but are acceptable for kraft. In common with other north eastern conifers, these pines have long, slender fibers that are generally considered desirable for papermaking. Wood volume is about 94% tracheids, 5% ray cells, and 0.7% resin canals.

Southern Pines

The four most important species of southern yellow pine are as follows:

(1) Longleaf pine, *Pinus palustris*, grows in the southeastern part of the United States in a belt about 150 miles wide, extending alone the Atlantic coast from Virginia to Florida, and westward to Texas. From the age of about 5 to 25 year, the growth is rapid, reaching a height of 36 ft and a diameter of 5 in 20 year, and a diameter of 11 in and a height of 82 ft in 70 years.

(2) Slash pine, *Pinus eliotti (Pinus caribaea)*, has a somewhat more restricted range than the other southern pines. It extends from the southern part of South Carolina, westward through southern Georgia. Alabma, and Mississippi to southeastern Louisiana, and southward to Florida. Slash pine grows rapidly, especially when young. Trees 10 year old, under normal conditions, average 25 ft high and 2.5 in, in diameter. At 20 year, the average height is 45 ft with a diameter of 7.5 in.

(3) Shortleaf pine, *Pinus echinata*, grows throughout most of the southeastern U.S., from New Jersey, south to Georgia, and west to Missouri, Arkansas, and Texas. Under average conditions, shortleaf reaches a height of 34 ft

and a diameter of 4.5 in. in 20 year, and a height of 82 ft and a diameter of 12 in, in 70 year.

(4) Loblolly, *Pinus taeda*, grows along the Atlantic coast and Gulf of Mexico in belt 200 miles wide, from Delaware to Texas. Many areas from which the original longleaf pine forests were cut have grown up in loblolly. The contributing factors are the abundant crop of small seeds, widely distributed by the wind, and the rapid growth and general hardiness of loblolly seedlings. Loblolly pine grows faster during the first 15 year than either longleaf or shortleaf, but not as fast as slash pine. After that, loblolly and slash maintain about the same growth rate. The loblolly average in 20 years is 7.6 in, in diameter and 43 ft in height.

Southern pine wood ranges from moderately heavy to very heavy (average sp gr 0.45 to 0.56). The tracheids comprise slightly over 90% of the wood volume, with rays about 8% and resin canals 0.8%. The tracheid fibers are among the longest and coarsest of wood fibers, averaging 4.4 mm in length and 35 to 45 μ in diameter. Southern pine contains a high content of resin, the range for longleaf is reported at 2.1 to 9.2%. The high resin content makes southern pine unsuitable for the sulfite process. Pulped by the kraft process, the resin is recovered as "tall oil", and is a valuable by-product of the industry. One of the characteristics of southern pine wood is the broad band of thick-walled summerwood fibers, often comprising half of the annual ring.

Gum

Sweet Gum, *Liquidambar stryaciflua* and *Black* or *Tupelo gum*. *Nyssa sylvatica* These are moderately heavy woods, the average sp gr is 0.44 and 0.46, respectively. Sweet gum grows from Connecticut to Missourt, and southward to central Florida and eastern Texas. Sweetgum grows in mixture with other hardwoods, and is frequently the predominant species. The best development is reached in the moist soils of hardwood bottom lands. Sweetgum that is grown in such locations along the Atlantic coast generally reaches a diameter of 15 in, and a height of 100 ft in 50 year. The ether-soluble extract is reported to range from 0.22 to 0.49. Fiber length is reported to average 1.7 mm with a range of 1.0 to 2.5. The wood volume contains 26.8% fibers, 18.3% rays, and 54.9% vessels.

Western Hemlock *(Tsuga heterophylla)*

This speciesgrows along the Pacific coast from Prince William Sound in Alaska to San Francisco Bay, and as far inland as northern Idaho and northwestern Montana. The best stands in the U.S. are found in the humid coastal regions of Oregon and Washington and in the costal regions of British Columbia in Canada. Trees 100 year old are generally 17 to 21 in. in diameter and 130 to 150 ft in height. Western hemlock usually grows in association with Douglas fir, western red cedar, and Sitka spruce. Western hemlock is moderately light (sp gr approximately 0.38).It is low in ether-soluble extractives, 0.3 to 1.3%. The fibre is somewhat longer and coarser than eastern spruce, but finer than southern pine.

Douglas fir (*Pseudotsuga taxifolia*)

Douglas fir grows in most of the forests from the Rocky mountains to the Pacific coast and from Mexico to central British Columbia. It reaches its largest size and attains its fastest rate of growth in Washington, Oregon, and Canada, in the region between the coast and the Cascade Mountains. Here, large trees 3 to 6 ft in diameter and 200 ft and more in height form dense forests.

The wood ranges from moderately light, 0.40 sp gr (Rocky Mountain type) to moderately heavy. 0.45 sp gr (Pacific Coast type). The fibre (tracheids) is relatively long and coarse, and comprises about 93% of wood volume, the remainder is ray cells. The content of ether extractives ranges from 0.3 to 2.6%. The wood is not suitable for sulfite pulping, but is readily pulped by the kraft process. Douglas fir reaches the pulp mill mostly in the form of waste from lumbering operations.

Western Pines

The principal western pines are :

Ponderosa pine	*Pinus ponderosa*
Western White pine	*Pinus monticola*
Sugar pine	*Pinus lambertina*
Lodgepole pine	*Pinus contorta*

Ponderosa pine grows in all the states west of the great plains. Because of a deep-reaching tap-root and long strong laterals, it can maintain itself on dry sites. Excellent stands occur where rainfall is only 18 in. In typical conditions of growth, ponderosa pine attains a height of 24 ft and a diameter of 4.7 in. in 50 year, and 62 ft in height and 13.2 in. in diameter in 100 year. The wood is moderately light, 0.38 sp gr.

Western white pine grows from the lower part of British Columbia southward into western Montana and northern Idaho, and along the Cascade Mountains and Sierra Nevadas through Washington and Oregon to central California. The heaviest stands occur in northern Idaho and adjacent parts of Montana and Washington. The wood is moderately light. 0.36 sp gr.

Western True firs

Included in this group are the following :

White fir	*Abies concolor*
Grand fir	*Abies grandis*
Pacific silver fir	*Abies amabilis*
Noble fir	*Abies procera*

These and other firs constitute about 14% of the softwood stand of the Pacific region, including Alaska. In the lumber trade, these species are classed together as "white fir". White fit (*A. concolor*) grows principally along the coast and mountain ranges of California and Southern Oregon. White fir grows rapidly when young, but is comparatively short lived. Under favourable conditions, it reaches an average height of 50 ft and a diameter 8 in. in 50 year. Thees over 125 years old are frequently defective.

Grand fir grows principally in western Oregon, northern Idaho, along the coast of northern Califormia, and in western and northern Washington. It also grows in western and southern British Columbia. Under favourable conditions, grand fir attains a diameter of 4 ft and a height of 200 ft. On less favourable sites, the average is 18 in. and 80 ft.

The range of Pacific silver fir extends from the southern extremity of Alaska, southward along the coast of British Columbia, through Washington to southern Oregon. In the Olympic Mountains of Washington, where the most favourable growth conditions are found. Pacific silver fir may reach a height of 200 ft and a diameter of 3 to 5 ft. but, these are exceptional. Under average conditions, mature trees are 75 to 100 ft in height and 18 to 30 in. in diameter.

Silver fir grows slowly, and trees 2 ft in diameter are often over 200 years old.

Noble fir grows principally in western and northern Washington and in western Oregon. Under favourable conditions Noble fir attains the following average growth rates :

20 year, 12 ft in height, 3.1 in. in diameter

50 year, 53 ft in height, 11.1 in. in diameter

100 year, 99.5 ft in height, 20.5 in. in diameter

200 year, 145.5 ft in height, 33.2 in. in diameter

400 year, 196.3 ft in height, 49.4 in. in diameter

The true firs are moderately light, 0.35 to 0.37 sp gr, and relatively low in extractives, 0.23% reported for white fir. All species are readily pulped by all standard processes, and yield a long fibre somewhat coarser than spruce, but equivalent to western hemlock and western pines.

Englemann spruce, *Pice engelmenni* grows from the Yukon Territory, southward along the Rocky Mountains to Arizona and New Mexico. In the United States, it grows along the upper slopes of the Cascade Mountains in Washington and Oregon, and on the slopes of the Rocky Mountains in Washington and Oregon, and on the slopes of the Rocky Mountains throughout their length. In Colorado the range extends from 9.000 to 12.000 ft in elevation. Mature trees in good situations are generally 80 to 100 ft in height and 18 to 36 in. in diameter. Engelmann spruce is often found in very unfavourable conditions, and shows extremely slow growth.

Sitka spruce, *Picea sitchensis* grows along the Pacific coast from northern California to Alaska. It is rarely found over 40 miles from the coast. In Oregon and Washington, it is commonly found in mixture with Douglas-fir, grand fir, western hemlock, and western red cedar. Sitka spruce shows comparatively rapid growth, under favourable conditions. In Washington and Oregon, the following measurements have been made : 40 years, diameter 9.5 in., height 70 ft: 60 years, diameter 15.7 in., height 104 ft. Sitka spruce is a very long lived tree. Mature trees in Washington and Oregon commonly attain an age over 400 year. And a height of over 200 ft.

Sitka spruce ranks high as a pulpwood, because of its long,

strong fibers and the ease of pulping by the sulfite kraft and groundwood processes. The fibre is somewhat coarser than eastern spruce, but is suitable for most paper products. Groundwood from Sitka spruce has standard strength and a slightly gray colour.

The two principal hardwoods of the Pacific coast region are red alder, *Alnus rubra* and black cottonwood, *Populus trichocarpa*. The natural range of red alder is along the Pacific coast from southern Alaska to southern Califormnia. The tree requires abundant soil moisture, and is confined to low elevations (because of lack of resistance to severe cold). Throughout its range, it occurs as a comparatively small sized tree in mixture with other moisture loving trees. In some bottom lands, long water courses, it forms practically pure stands.

Red alder matures in about 50 year and is considered old at 80 year. Mature trees are 14 to 18 in. in diameter and 100 ft in height.

The bulk of black cottonwood is found in western Washington. Oregon, and western Montana. It grows best at lower levels with moist soils, and is intolerant of shade. Mature trees reach 3 to 4 fit in diameter and a height of 80 to 125 ft. The early growth is rapid, but later growth is slower.

Both red alder and black cottonwood are readily reduced to pulp by sulfite or kraft process. In common with other hardwoods, the fibre is comparatively short and useful as a filler pulp, along with softwood fibre.

2

Alkaline Pulping Recovery Units

CHEMICAL RECOVERY SYSTEM

The recovery of chemical in the spent cooking liquor of the kraft process and reconstitution of these chemicals to form fresh cooking liquor is a vital part of the pulping operation in providing maximum recovery of heat and chemical values, as well as in minimizing the release of obnoxious wastes. The week black liquor from the brown stock washers goes through the following steps :

(1) Concentration in multiple-effect evaporations.

(2) Further concentration in direct-contact evaporators.

(3) Incineration in recovery furnace with addition of salt cake (Na_2SO_4) to make up loss.

(4) Dissolving smelt from furnace in water to form green liquor.

(5) Causticizing of green liquor with lime to form white liquor which, after setting and filtering, is ready for the next cooking cycle.

(6) Burning of lime mud to recover lime.

Figure 1 shows a flow diagram of the process.

MULTIPLE-EFFECT EVAPORATORS

Multiple-effect evaporators are installed in the liquor cycle between the brown stock washers and the direct-contact evaporator; these are necessary to efficiently remove large

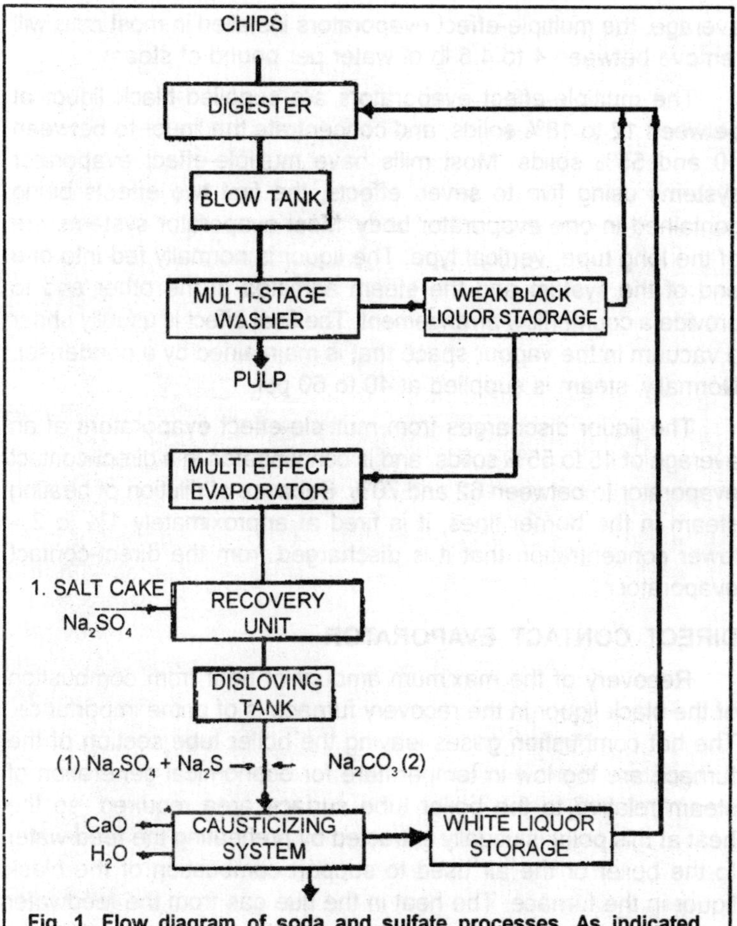

Fig. 1. Flow diagram of soda and sulfate processes. As indicated, these differ only in the make-up chemicals used.

amounts of water from the liquor so that the recovery boiler may economically produce steam from this liquor.

A multiple-effect evaporator is actually a series of evaporators arranged so that the vapour generated from one evaporator body becomes a steam supply to the next evaporator in the series. The main advantage of the multiple-effect system is the efficiency with which it evaporates the water per pound of steam suplied.

average, the multiple-effect evaporators installed in most mills will remove between 4 to 4.5 lb of water per pound of steam.

The multiple-effect evaporators are supplied black liquor at between 12 to 18% solids, and concentrate the liquor to between 40 and 55% solids. Most mills have multiple-effect evaporator systems using five to seven effects, the first two effects being contained in one evaporator body. Most evaporator systems are of the long tube, vertical type. The liquor is normally fed into one end of the system and the steam admitted at the other end to provide a counterflow arrangement. The final effect is usually under a vacuum in the vapour space that is maintained by a condenser. Normally, steam is supplied at 40 to 60 psi.

The liquor discharges from multiple-effect evaporators at an average of 45 to 55% solids, and is concentrated in a direct-contact evaporator to between 62 and 70%. Because of dilution of heating steam in the burner lines, it is fired at approximately 1½ to 2% lower concentration that it is discharged from the direct-contact evaporator.

DIRECT CONTACT EVAPORATOR

Recovery of the maximum amount of heat from combustion of the black liquor in the recovery furnace is of prime importance. The hot combustion gases leaving the boiler tube section of the furnace are too low in temperature for economical generation of steam relative to the boiler tube surface area required, so the heat at this point is usually extracted by preheating the feed-water to the boiler or the air used to support combustion of the black liquor in the furnace. The heat in the flue gas from the feedwater heater (economizer) or air heater is used to evaporate still more water from the black liquor by direct contact with the flue gas. The three types of equipment normally used are: (1) cyclone evaporator; (2) cascade evaporator; and (3) Venturi scrubber.

Direct-contact evaporation is used to further concentrate the black liquor from the multiple-effect evaporators. The liquor and gas are brought into intimate physical contact, resulting in a transfer of water from the black liquor to the gas and a reduction in the gas temperature.

The surface area of the black liquor must be extended to provide the desired heat transfer from the flue gas. If the black liquor is splashed or sprayed on hot metal, the volume must be sufficient for continuous washing. The black liquor must be agitated to prevent over-concentration, for the upper limits of solubility of the solids are being approached, which could result in a sludge that would plug the liquor handling equipment. The flue gas velocity and flow pattern in the direct-contact evaporator must be such that liquor entrainment in the gas exit is minimized.

CASCADE EVAPORATOR

A cascade evaporator consists of wheels that are partially submerged in a vat of black liquor, so that as they rotate they alternately dip into the liquor and emerge to present a wetted surface to the flue gas stream flowing through the wheel above the liquor level. The wheels are made of two circular side plates connected by tubes to provide an extended surface. The wheels are arranged in varying parallel and series configurations, depending upon the conditions of the flue gas and the quantity of water to be evaporated from the black liquor with each installation. The liquor is agitated by the paddle-wheel action of the rotating banks of tubes in the wheels. The concentrated black liquor is screened at the evaporator outlet to remove any solids that were caused by oven drying.

CYCLONE EVAPORATOR

The cyclone evaporator is a vertical cylindrical vessel with a concial bottom. The flue gas enters tangentially near the bottom, and flows in a helical patch to the top, where it leaves through a baffled outlet. Black liquor from the evaporators is sprayed across the flue gas inlet, where the liquor droplets mix with gas and are then thrown by centrifugal force to the tank wall. Sufficient liquor from the bottom of the evaporator is re-circulated to a ring of nozzles at the top of the vessel to keep the interior wall wet and to prevent localized drying on this surface. The evaporation or temperature drop of the flue gas is controlled by adjusting the quantity of spray liquor at the gas inlet.

VENTURI SCRUBBER

This device serves the dual purpose of concentrating the black liquor by evaporation and collecting the fumes from the flue gas. The Ventruri scrubber depends upon the collision of fume particles with liquid droplets, and in addition, serves to absorb heat from the flue gas to evaporate the black liquor. The flue gas a accelerated by a gradual restriction in the gas duct, and the black liquor is injected through steam atomizing nozzles at the point just before the duct tapers back to its original size. The black liquor is atomized by the steam and high-velocity flue gas, resulting in intimate mixing. The fume or dust particles collide with and adhere to the droplets, and the latter with their fume particles are centrifugally removed from the gas. Part of the concentrated liquor is recirculated to the nozzles to control the amount of evaporation. Fume collection efficiencies of 90 to 95% are continuously mintained, and a higher thermal efficiency is achieved since the outlet gas temperature can be reduced about 120°F lower than that permissible with an electrostatic precipitator to collect the fume. Offsetting this is the greater induced draft fan power required to obtain the high flue gas velocity through the throat where the black liquor is atomized.

ELECTROSTATIC PRECIPITATOR

An appreciable quantity of sodium is evaporated in the furnace in the from of salts. As the combustion gasses cooi, the sodium salts condense to a finely divided solid that is carried by the gas stream as a fume. Most of this fume is reclaimed from the heating surfaces of the recovery boiler and on the wetted surfaces of the direct-contact evaporator. The remainder, consisting of the smallest particles of sodium salts, not only would represent a costly chemical loss which must be replaced, but would also be a nuisance as an air pollutant, if allowed to escape with the flue gas. Many sulfate pulp mills are now collecting this fume from the flue gas with either an electrostatic precipitator or a Venturi scrubber.

The electrostatic precipitator operates on a principle that a particle, suspended in a gas subjected to a sufficiently strong electrostatic field, becomes charged electrically and travels toward an oppositely charged collection electrode to which it will adhere. The collection electrode is shaken periodically to remove the particles, which drop into a hopper below. The precipitator will remove from 85 to 95% of the fume. To energize the precipitator, between 50,000 and 100,000 volts are used. The voltage must be low enough to avoid sparking between the discharging and collecting electrodes. Care must be taken to see that the flue gas temperature entering the precipitator does snot get low enough to cause moisture to condense on the electrodes, which would result in fouling and rapid corrosion.

RECOVERY FURNACE

This is a completely integrated unit comprising furnace and pressure parts, superheater, economizer, shoot blowers, tubular cascade evaporator, salt-cake feeding and mixing equipment, fans air and gas systems, dissolving tank, liquor pumps, controis, and instruments. The lower structure, extending from the hearth to the sloping roof, is considered the furnace. The walls of this furnace are formed of closely spaced tubes having extended metal fins. For very high pressures, tangent tube construction is used with skin casing.

In these designs, there are no exposed refractory surfaces, except for the chrome refractory hearth. In operation, even this refractory is covered by a layer of chilled smelt as a result of the flat water-cooled hearth design. The lower section of the furnace is completely sealed by metal strips continuously welded to adjacent tube fins. The only openings below the primary air nozzle are those provided for the smelt spouts, which are located approximately a foot above the centrerline of the floor tubes. Although there is a thin layer of chrome ore over the tubes, the heat transfer rate is such that a layer of chilled smelt (from three to six in. deep) forms on the hearth. With this protective covering of hard smelt, molten smelt does not come in contact with any refractory surface, except when the initial covering layer is formed.

The lower portion of the furnace, as shown in Fig. 2, is divided into three overlapping zones between which there are no distinct lines of demarcation. In the "reduction zone", immediately above the hearth, a reducing atmosphere is maintained to burn the organic residue out of the accumulated black ash, and to secure the maximum conversion of chemical into smelt. The "drying zone" is the one in which a major portion of the moisture is evaporated from the black liquor as it is sprayed into the furnace. The heat for this evaporation process is obtained from burning the organic compounds out of the liquor in the reduction zone, and from completing combustion of unburned gas and secondary air supplied in the oxidation zone just above the drying zone.

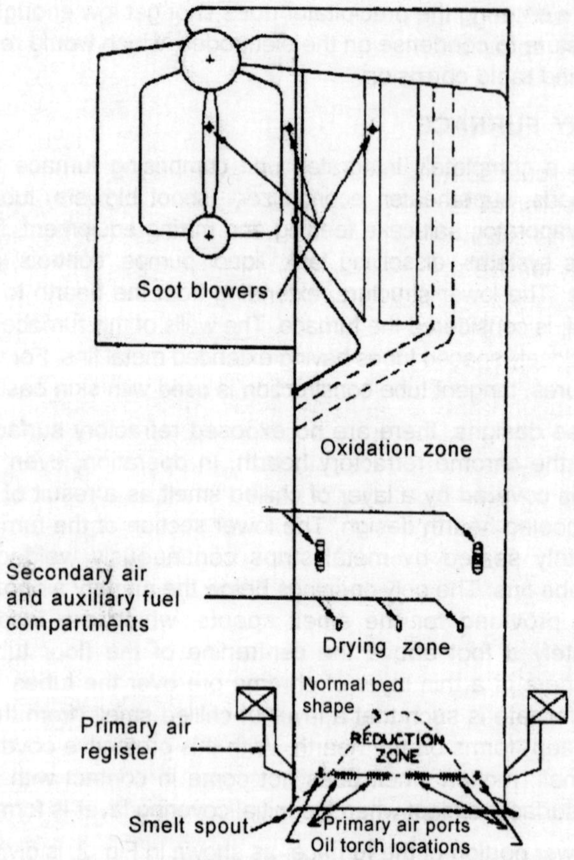

Fig. 2. Location of reduction, drying, and oxidation zones in furnace of chemical recovery unit.

Primary air is introduced near the bottom of the furnace through a single row of nozzles in each of the four walls. At this same level, there is a larger opening at each corner for the insertion of oil or gas guns. Auxiliary fuel, however, is generally required only when starting up or shutting down the recovery unit, unless the mill steam demand is such that additional seam has to be generated: the recovery unit. At a level about 15 ft above the furnace hearth, additional openings are provided for the black liquor spray guns. The number of openings varies with the size of the recovery unit, e.g., as many as twelve are used on very large units. The spray guns are mounted on rocker bars, and they oscillate in the vertical plane. They are connected by means of flexible hoses to a liquor header encircling the furnace. Secondary air is introduced at the four corners of the furnace several feet above the liquor spray openings. Specially designed registers inject the combustion air tangent to an imaginary circle in the center of the furnace. This action tends to rotate the combustion gas stream, and to create intensive turbulence in the oxidation zone of the furnace. Velocities are such that secondary air penetrates deeply into the furnace. Turbulence thus produced assures uniform and complete combustion of unburned gas origninating in the reduction zone.

The upper part of the furnace contains the screen tubes and superheater. The superheater elements consist of tubes placed tangent to each other in order to form a panel. Extremely wide transverse spacing between adjacent panels assures low draft loss through the superheater. The most important contribution of the tangent superheater design is the elimination of hand lancing, because slag does not build up to any degree on the elements.

DISSOLVING TANK

The smelt from the furnace hearth is molten and quite explosive in nature when exposed to water, primarily because the high temperature converts the water to steam so rapidly. The stream of molten smelt discharging from the furnace is broken up by a steam shower and/or a re-circulated green liquor stream to disperse the smelt so that it will not explode when it hits the liquor surface in the dissolving tank. The latter is agitated to avoid localized overheating and to maintain uniform concentration of the dissolved smelt. A large event on the dissolving tank is essential to remove both the steam and gases evolved, hydrogen (explosive) and hydrogen sulfide (posionous).

A typical green liquor composition would be 20% sodium carbonate and 5% sodium sulfide, by weight, expressed as Na_2O. The density of green liquor is 15 to 20° Baume, or 1.12 to 1.16 sp gr.

CAUSTICIZING

The green liquor is treated with lime to convert the sodium carbonate to sodium hydroxide, the sodium sulfide remaining unchanged. The resultant solution, after removing the lime sludge, is called white liquor, and is already for re-use in the digester as cooking liquor after dilution with black liquor.

Causticizing is actually divided into a number of separate functions, in addition to the above prime function of converting the carbonate to sodium hydroxide :

(1) Clarification of green liquor to remove foreign material (dregs).

(2) Washing the green liquor dregs, before disposal, to remove entrained sodium salts.

(3) Slaking lime in green liquor.

(4) Removing and washing unreacted material from the green liquor slaker.

(5) Retaining the mixture of lime and green liquor in agitated tanks to allow the reaction to be completed.

(6) Settling out and separating the sludge from the white liquor.

(7) Washing the sludge to remove the entrained white liquor.

(8) Removing excess moisture form the sludge.

(9) Burning the sludge to form reburned lime ready to use in Step 3 above repeated.

The green liquor from the dissolving tank at the recovery furnace is regulated to a uniform concentration by controlling the amount of dilution added. Weak wash water from the causticizing process is used instead of fresh water to minimize dilution of the cooking liquor. The green liquor is clarified to remove the suspended solids, such as unburned carbon, plastic chrome are and iron compounds. The solids removed by settling are called dregs. They are pumped with some of the green liquor to a washer, where they are washed with water to recover the entrained sodium carbonate and sulfide. The wash water is decanted and used as dilution at the smelt dissolving tank. The washed green liquor dregs are discharged to the sewer. In some cases the dregs are washed several times using countercurrent washing for maximum chemical recovery with a minimum of water.

SLAKER

The batch process of causticizing green liquor has been replaced by the continuous method. In so doing, separate equipment has been designed to handle each step of the process more efficiently. The re-burned lime plus any makeup line is metered into an agitated solution of hot green liquor to convert the quicklime to slaked lime. This reaction will not proceed with sufficient speed unless the temperature of the mixture is between 200 and 215°F. For this reason, steam is used to heat the green liquor feed and the reburned lime from the kiln is kept as hot as possible to ensure maximum efficiency of reaction. In some recent installations, the slaker was placed under the lime kiln discharge so that red hot lime dropped directly into the green liquor primary slaker, instead of being converyed to a surge bin. Although theoretically this would give a maximum slaking efficiency. In actual practice the discharge of lime from the kiln cannot be regulated well enough to maintain a uniform strength of white liquor. The slaker consists of a cast iron-lined steel tank to resist the abrasion of the lime, with an agitator to ensure good mixing of the lime and green liquor. The green liquor lime slurry flows by gravity to a grit removing section called a classifier. Here the unreacted particles (grit) settle out to the bottom of the tank and are raked out for disposal after washing.

CAUSTICIZERS

The overflow of liquor from the classifier flows to a series of agitated tanks with about $1^1/_2$ hour retention, where the chemical reaction of converting the sodium carbonate to sodium hydroxide takes place. Three to four tanks in series are used to minimize the possibility of the liquor short circuiting. Should the lime sludge continue to settle out of the white liquor after causticizing, a heavy build-up of lime and sodium carbonate would develop in the white liquor lines, pumps, and digesters (carryover of lime and carbonate will frequently give the bleached pulp a green coloration that can normally be traced to having used cloudy or unclarified white liquor).

WHITE LIQUOR CLARIFIER

The overflow from the last causticizer is transferred to the top and center of a vertical cylindrical tank where sufficient retention time is allowed for the lime sludge to settle out at the bottom and the clear white liquor to overflow at the circumference of the top. A large rake rotates close to the bottom of the tank to scrape the sludge to a central outlet, from which the white liquor mud is pumped to a mud washer.

As many as four settling tanks are integrally built one over the other, to conserve space, with the white liquor feed being equally divided to the different sections of the white liquor clarifier.

The size of the clarifier is dependent on the rate of setting of the lime mud. The following is a list of some of the more important variables affecting the settling rate :

(1) Strength of green liquor used, i.e., concentration to sodium carbonate and sodium sulfide. A high liquor concentration results in poor settling.

(2) Proportion of sodium carbonate and sodium sulfide. Greater amounts of the latter will require less slaking and lime sludge to settle out.

(3) Excess of lime used to the slaker. The causticizing reaction does not go to completion, and a slight excess of lime is added to obtain between 85 and 90% conversion of the carbonate to sodium hydroxide. Use of a large excess of lime will restrict the settling rate.

(4) Temperature of slaking. The temperature should be kept as close to 215°F as possible in the slaker to ensure maximum size crystal growth of the lime sludge in the causticizers for rapid settling in the white liquor clarifier.

(5) The makeup of the lime must be relatively fee of silica and iron which from a gelatinous slow setting floc in white liquor that not only makes white liquor clarification difficult, but will also aggravate operation of the lime mud washing and kiln operation.

(6) Carry-over of soap or black liquor into the slaker with the green liquor as a result of poor recovery furnace operation will seriously retard settling. In some cases starch is added to help precipitate the lime mud in the white liquor clarifier.

The white liquor overflow from the clarifier may still contain small amounts of unsettled lime mud, and incompletely reacted lime and sodium carbonate. For this reason, white liqour filters are used to remove the last traces of solids that would contaminate the pulp, particularly serious with dissolving pulp.

WHITE LIQUOR MUD WASHER

In order to pump the sludge from the bottom of the white liquor clarifier, some of the white liquor is removed with it. To minimize the loss of white liquor, the mud is washed several times countercurrently with water to minimize the amount of water used. The thick mud from the white liquor clarifier is diluted, then allowed to settle out in a vertical cylindrical tank in the same manner as in the white liquor clarifier. Since the mud will settle out quickly in dilute solution, only half of the tank settling capacity is normally required. However, the mud washer usually consists of four sections, about the same size as the white liquor clarifier, the only difference among them being that the two top trays are operated in parallel as the first wash for the mud and the two bottom trays as the second wash. The washed mud is pumped to the kiln, and the wash water is combined with the wash water wash water from the green liquor dregs to dissolve the smelt from the recovery furnace.

Some mills use the condensate from the black liquor multiple-effect evaporators to wash the mud from the white liquor clarifiers not only to economize on water consumption, but to minimize stream pollution, since this water contains mercaptans and other volatile sulfur compounds. Great care must be exercised to keep black liquor from entering this water, should operation of the evaporators become upset.

The washed mud is metered to a dewatering device before being fed to the lime kiln. This consists of either a continuous rotary vacuum filter or a centrifuge, the water removal being essential to minimize kiln fuel costs.

The vacuum filter has been recently operated with a precoat, the vacuum being left on during the full cycle of the turning cylinder. The cake of mud is washed by dilution in the filter vat and by water showers on the filter cake. The mud is removed by a doctor blade that cuts off the mud cake above the pprecoat layer. This gives a mud feed to the kiln of 60 to 65% consistency, compared to 55 to 60% when the filter is operated in the normal fashion of breaking the vacuum and blowing the mud cake off at the discharge point.

The centrifuge is a simpler piece of equipment to operate, and is capable of dewatering the mud as high as 70% consistency. Provision is made to wash the mud in the centrifuge. The wash water from the mud filter or centrifuge is used in the mud washer for countercurrent washing.

The greatest strides have been made in regulating the feed of lime mud to the dewatering devices. The first approach was to install an agitated surge tank between the mud wash and the mud filter or centrifuge using the tank to even out variation in mud density. Introduction of radioisotopes to measure the consistency of the mud has opened the door to automatic dilution control for uniform mud density. The magnetic flowmeter has proven a better means of measuring the flow of mud than orifices or displacement meters that tended to cake or were worn by the mud. A combination of these instruments is being tried to control the density of mud being pumped from the white liquor clarifier. Variations in the quantity of white liquor transferred with the mud have a decided effect on the washing efficiency, as well as the settling rate, in the mud washer. This operation is normally hand-controlled.

KILN

The lime mud is washed to remove the sodium compounds, a maximum of $^1/_4$% being allowable in order to avoid ring and ball formation in the kiln. The kiln itself is a long inclined horizontal cylinder, mounted on rollers, through which the lime flows countercurrent to the heat. The latter is normally an oil or natural gas flame. Three things take place in the kiln:

(1) Drying of the lime mud.

(2) Rise in temperature of the mud, during which I passes through a plastic stage.

(3) The high-temperature zone during which the carbon dioxide is evolved to yield reburned lime or clacium oxide.

The kiln construction is modified to accommodate these varying conditions. At the mud feed end, different means are provided to transfer the heat from the gases to the mud by providing extended surface area; this is alternately heated by the gases and then by the mud as the kiln slowly rotates, the lime tending to remain near the bottom of the kiln. The most common method of providing the extended surface is by means of steel chains attached to the kiln shell and hang in the hot gases. The temperature of the gases entering the chain section must be kept below 1000°F to avoid softening the metal.

A more recent method that was developed in Scandinavia uses sheet metal fabricated sectors that are made up of several sections. Some are fixed and others are free to rotate, but remain essentially fixed longitudinally in the kiln. As with the chain sections, precautions must be taken to avoid overheating the sheet metal which causes deformation or collapse of the sectors.

A third method is to build brick baffles in the lime any drying zone, in a trefoil pattern. Maintaining brick in a rotating kiln can be quite difficult, due to the occasional thermal shock load of cold mud on hot bricks, and the continual flexing of the long steel kiln shell, especially at the trunnions on which the kiln rides.

In the temperature rising section of the kiln following the drying of the mud, a brick lining 4 to 6 in, thick is used, made to withstand moderate temperatures. Wear is not excessive, since the lime tends to form a thin film over the face of the brick in this area. As the lime rises in temperature, it goes through a semi-liquid or plastic state. The length of time it remains in this state is dependent on the amount of soda remaining in the lime and any changes that are made in the kiln operation. The plastic lime forms pellets or balls, the size of which will very with the length of time the lime remains plastic. Under normal conditions the lime forms small pebbles up to one in. in diameter that will occasionally continue to grow in size until they reach the same diameter as the kiln. More frequently, the plastic lime will adhere to the brick and will build up a ring to such dimension that the internal diameter of the kiln is effectively reduced to a fraction of its normal size, thus acting as a dam to the flow of lime and the hot gases.

The high-temperature zone in the kiln where the carbon dioxide is driven from the lime is normally lined with 6-in. thick brick made to withstand temperatures of 2,400°F. Excessive temperatures in the hot zone of the kiln can result in fusion of the brick lining as well as the lime. Fused lime has a glasslike surface on the reburned pebbles that drastically reduces the rate of causticizing. The majority of this overburned lime is rejected to waste by the classifier following the slaker.

The gases leaving the kiln are laden with lime dust. Several methods are used to recover this dust, as well as the heat remaining in the exhaust gases. The most common methods are to use cyclones or baffled spray towers. The hot water containing the dust from these in normally used to wash the mud to the kiln.

Several kilns have been able to handle an increased amount of lime by utilizing the exhaust gases to flash-dry the mud feed before it enters the kiln. By drying the mud outside the kiln, the length of hot zone in the kiln could be extended to handle more lime without adversely affecting the heating efficiency.

The hot lime from the kiln is screened through a "grizzly" to remove large balls of lime or loose brick. The lime is either discharged direct to a primary slaker, as described earlier, or conveyed to a surge bin. The latter forms a very essential function of leveling out the variations in kiln discharge rates and causticizing lime requirements. The bin also serves as a reservoir to empty the kiln when the causticizing is interrupted.

The makeup of lime can be made as burned lime at the causticizer or as limestone at the kiln feed. The choice depends not only on the cost and availability of these materials, but on the capacity of the kiln. It is preferable to use the limestone, since hot lime will react better in slaking than cold lime.

The kiln is usually driven by a variable-speed electric motor, to permit changing the length of time the load of lime is in the kiln, as the feed rate is changed. It is common practice to install an auxiliary gasoline drive to continue rotating the kiln in event of electrical interruptions, for the kiln will warp out of shape if allowed to cook without rotating. This is especially true of kilns that could be exposed to a heavy rainfall.

The size of a kiln will vary with the pulp mill capacity and efficiency desired. Thus, kilns are made longer to move efficiently utilize the heat, and the diameter is increased to keep the gas velocities low and to increase the surface area of the lime bed in the kiln exposed to the radiant heat. An 11 ft diameter by 250-ft long kiln equipped with a chain section is capable of burning over150 tons of lime per 24 hrs.

In some countries where fuel is expensive, the air used for combusion is preheated by contracting the hot lime from the kiln. This feature has not been adopted to any extent in the United States where the emphasis has been more on increased production than fuel economy. The heat exchanging equipment is subject to plugging with the large lime balls, and the interruption in production has been a deterrent to their installation.

The gases are pulled through the kiln by the combined effect of an induced draft fan and chimney. The latter is usually quite short, being high enough to dissipate the gases which are fairly corrosive, especially when oil is used as a fuel. The location of the induced draft fan can be either before the water sprays, in which case a larger drive motor and fan are required to handle the hotter gases, or after the gases are saturated with water, in which case some difficulty is experienced with lime depositing on the fan blades and causing an imbalance.

3

Bleaching Chlorination Stage

INTRODUCTION

Chlorination, which comprises the first stage of most bleaching sequences, is intended to delignify rather than simply to decolorize pulp, and therefore constitutes an extension of he pulping process. Chlorine reacts smoothly and rapidly with the non-carbohydrate component of chemical pulps to form a highly coloured, partially water-soluble material usually referred to as "chloro-lignin". This chlorinated phenolic material becomes readily removable by the action of alkali and oxidants in subsequent bleaching stages. The ready availability of liquid chlorine at low cost is the main factor contributing to its extensive use in bleaching processes. Chlorination will continue in this dominant position as long as alternative materials such as chlorine dioxide remain substantially more expensive.

FUNDAMENTAL ASPECTS OF CHLORINATION

Chlorine-Water System

When chlorine gas is dissolved in water, a reversible hydrolysis occurs, according to the following equilibrium:

$$Cl_2 + H_2O = HOC = HCL$$

$$\rightleftharpoons$$

$$H^+ + Cl^-$$

When a base (e.g., sodium hydroxide or calcium hydroxide) is present, the additional reaction occurs:

$$HOCl + NaOH \rightleftharpoons NaOCl + H_2O$$

$$\downarrow\uparrow$$

$$Na^+ + OC^-$$

The proportion of chlorine, hypochlorous acid, and hypochlorite ion in solution depends upon the pH, as shown in the graph below:

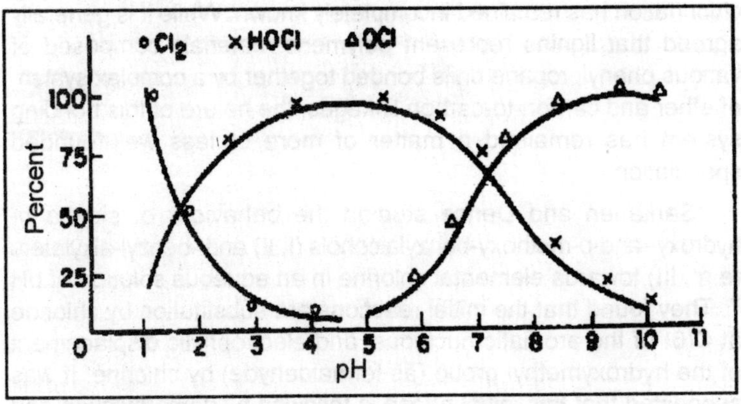

Thus, pH is extremely important in chlorine-water systems, since each of these forms of chlorine has different properties and each attack lignin and cellulose in a different manner.

One important difference is in the oxidation potential or oxidizing activity of the three forms of chlorine. Another is the manner in which each form combines with lignin, cellulose, and other materials.

Form of Chlorine	Oxidation Potential, Volts
OCl^-	+ 0.94
Cl_2	+ 1.35
HOCl	+ 1.50

Hypochlorous acid is the most active and hypochlorite the least active of the three forms. The roles played by these reactive species of chlorine during the chlorination of wood pulp will be discussed in subsequent sections.

REACTION OF CHLORINA WITH LIGNIN MODEL COMPOUNDS

The reaction of chlorine with organic compounds in general is known to proceed through addition, substitution, or oxidation. In the light of these reactions attempts have been made, from time to time, to explain the mechanism behind the chlorination of pulp. In spite of numerous investigations, the mechanism of pulp chlorination has remained incompletely known. While it is generally agreed that lignins represent polymeric materials composed of various phenylpropane units bonded together by a complex system of ether and carbon-to-carbon linkages, the nature of this bonding system has remained a matter of more or less well-founded speculation.

Sarkanen and Dence studied the behaviour of simple *p*-hydroxy- and *p*-methoxy-benzylalcohols (I, II) and -benzyl-alkyleters (e.g., III) towards elemental chlorine in an aqueous solution of pH 7. They found that the initial reactions are substitution by chlorine at C(6) of the aromatic nucleous, and electrophylic displacement of the hydroxymethyl group (as formaldehyde) by chlorine. It was suggested that this initial phase is followed by demethylation and subsequent oxidation of the resulting chlorocatechols to chlorobenzoquinones.

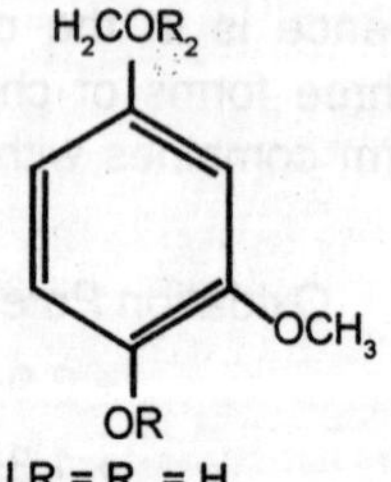

I R = R_1 = H

II R = H, R_1 = CH_3

III R = R_1 = CH_3

Singh has recently made in extensive use of high-resolution NMR spectroscopy in order to identify the chlorination products of a series of monomeric lignin model compounds of the type A. In all the cases examined, the position 2 in the benzene nucleus

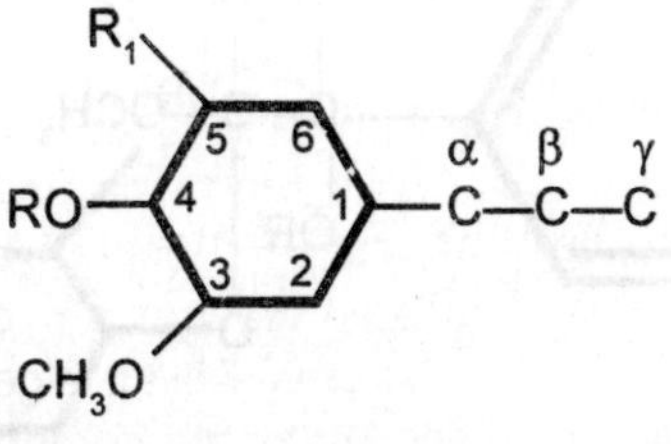

Type A $\begin{cases} R = H \text{ or } CH_3 \\ R_1 = H \text{ or } CH_3 \end{cases}$

resisted substitution, perhaps due to the steric effect of the methoxyl protons at position 3.

Chlorination of guaiacyl compounds of the Type A ($R = R_1 = H$) resulted in the aromatic substitution at positions 5 and 6, the latter was favoured at the mono chlorination level. When 4-position had no free hydroxyl group (A; $R = CH_3$ $R_1 = H$), only mono substitution occurred at position 6 of the ring. In addition to aromatic substitution, chlorine also reacted by the addition mechanism, if the model compounds contained double bonds between either α and β or β and γ positions of the side chain of the C-phenylpropane unit. Conversion of keto groups in the α-position to carboxyl group enhanced substitution of the benzene nucleus, as well as demethylation of the methoxyl group in position 3 of guaiacyl compounds.

In case of syringyl compounds (A; $R = H$, $R_1 = OCH_3$), one of the methoxyl groups became demethylated without introducing any chlorine into the aromatic nucleus. After the methoxyl group at position 5 was converted to hydroxyl group (A; $R = H$, $R_1 = OH$), substitution occurred immediately at position 6 of the ring. When chlorination was carried out in an anhydrous medium, both positions 2 and 6 became substituted by chlorine without any demethylation occurring at either of the 3 or 5 positions.

The chlorination of model compounds of the β arylether type (B) by elemental chlorine in glacial acetic acid has been studied by Gierer and Huber. These authors reported that β-arylethers

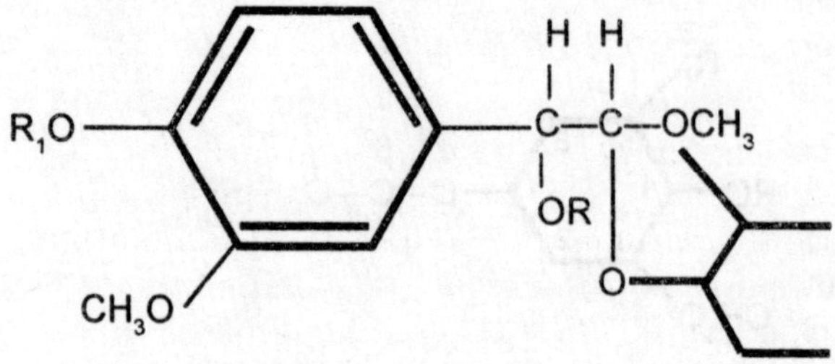

Type B $\begin{cases} R = H \text{ or } CH_3 \\ R_1 = H \text{ or } CH_3 \end{cases}$

(containing a hydroxyl group at the α-carbon atom) were readily chlorinated. The linkage between the aromatic nucleus and the a-carbon atom was split by electrophilic displacement. The resulting chlorination products (tetrachloroguaiacol, dichloroveratrole, and the dichloro-guaiacylethers of glycoaldehyde and glyceraldehyde) were isolated and characterized. Because of all the phenyl propane units in lignin, one fifth are thought to possess a free hydroxyl group at the a-carbon atom of the side chain (4), it may be expected that about every fifth lignin unit will suffer cleavage of the bond between the aromatic and the α-carbon atom of the side chain, during the technical pulp chlorination.

REACTION OF CHLORINE WITH "RESIDUAL LIGNIN" IN PULP

Under the conditions of technical chlorination, "residual lignin" in the unbleached pulp undergoes a great variety of reactions that finally lead to its degradation into water and alkali-soluble fragments. The main type of reactions observed are aromatic substitution, hydrolytic cleavage, and oxidation. These main reactions may take place at the same time or at different times, attacking the same of different reactive sites in the lignin molecule.

Attempts have been made to determine whether substitution or oxidation is the main reaction in the solubilization of lignin during technical pulp chlorination. The conclusions reached have been based on the assumption that solubilization occurs only as the result of substitution and oxidation reactions. The validity of such an assumption is questionable in the light of a strong probability of the occurrence of dealkylation reactions that degrade and solubilize the lignin polymer, without any chlorine appearing as hydrogen chloride (i.e., without substitution or oxidation).

Oxidation is the principal reaction competing with aromatic substitution in the chlorination of lignin. During technical pulp chlorination, about 50% of the applied chlorine is consumed by oxidation reactions. While the nature of the oxidation products remains to be established, the observed increase in carboxyl content (5 to 7) produced during the chlorination of lignin strongly suggests that the aromatic nucleus is ultimately converted into diabasic acid fragments. The decrease in methoxyl content generally observed during the chlorination of lignin probably represents the initial step in an oxidation sequence in which a portion of the phenolic nuclei is converted to non-aromatic products. Dence has recently obtained experimental evidence in support of this theory, and has proposed the following sequence for the oxidative breakdown of phenolic nuclei during chlorination of lignin Fig. 1.

Approximately 50% of the chlorine consumption during the chlorination stage is organically bound. The comparatively few investigations providing results pertinent to the technical pulp chlorination process indicate that chemically bound chlorine may be expected to comprise roughly 10 to 25% of the residual lignin in the pulp.

The chlorine substituents associated with lignin may be distributed between the aromatic ring (and/or its oxidation products) and the aliphatic side chain, which together comprise the basic lignin unit. The available evidence indicates that a major portion of the organically bound chlorine is associated with the aromatic portion of the lignin molecule.

In a proposed sequence for the chlorination of a sulfite lignin fragment (Fig. 2), Hibbert has indicated that chlorine substitution occurs at either the 5- or 6-position of the aromatic ring. The 5-positonis favoured when the phenolic group para to the side chain is unetherified. Ivancic and Rydholm, on the other hand, have offered a sequence for the chlorination of sulfonated lignin in which the 5- and 6-position of etherified and unetherified units both are substituted with chlorine. This sequence has been recently confirmed by Singh, using the technique of high-resolution, nuclear-magnetic resonance spectroscopy.

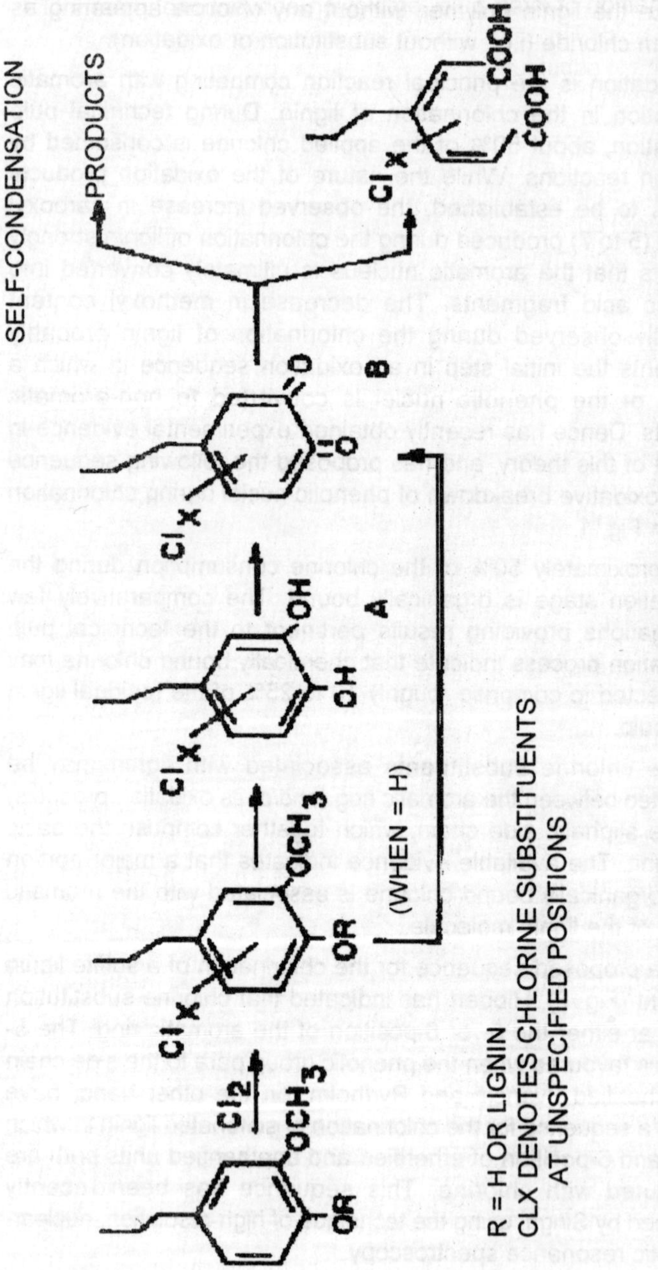

Fig. 1. Proposed sequence for the oxidative breakdown of phenolic nuclei during chlorination of lignin. After Dence.

Chlorinattion of Kraft pulp, employing conventional means of mixing the pulp with chlorine involves a heterogeneous reaction. Since aromatic substitution is one of several competing reactions during chlorination, lack of uniformity results in a varying degree for the other reactions as well. This can be illustrated by considering the demethylation pattern of kraft pulp during chlorination; under conditions where approximately 30% of the phenolic nuclei appear to be unoxidized (as evidenced by retention of their methoxyl groups), other phenolic units undergo multiple oxidation steps, ultimately yielding oxalic acid. Failure to achieve uniformity in the chlorination of pulp can be ascribed either to the inaccessibility of certain portions of the lignin in the fiber or the over-reaction of part of the lignin (as a result of high local concentrations and reactivity of chlorine).

Several factors which could conceivably account for the resistance towards solubilization of the total amount of "residual lignin" during chlorination of kraft pulp are as follows:

(1) Physical hindrance owing to the morphological structure of the fiber.

(2) A high proportion of methoxyl groups that add resistance to the solubilizing action of chlorine.

(3) Existence of chemical linkages between the thiolignin and carbohydrae components.

(4) Presence of diaryl or arylalkyl sulfides, or heterocyclic units in the residual lignin.

Most recently, Singh has demonstrated that physical hindrance, owing to the morphological structure of the fiber, is factor that results in a non-uniform chlorination involving an uneven distribution both of armoatically substituted chlorine and of demethylated aromatic nuclei. In addition to these, recent results obtained by Van Buren and Dence indicate that high local concentration of chlorine plays an important role.

Chlorination of pulp in an aqueous medium result in a loss of methoxyl groups (demethylation), leading directly to the formation of substituted O-benzoquinones. The carboxyl and carbonyl contents of the insoluble chlorinated residue are significantly higher than the corresponding values for the untreated kraft lignin. Indications are that at least a portion of these carbonyl groups

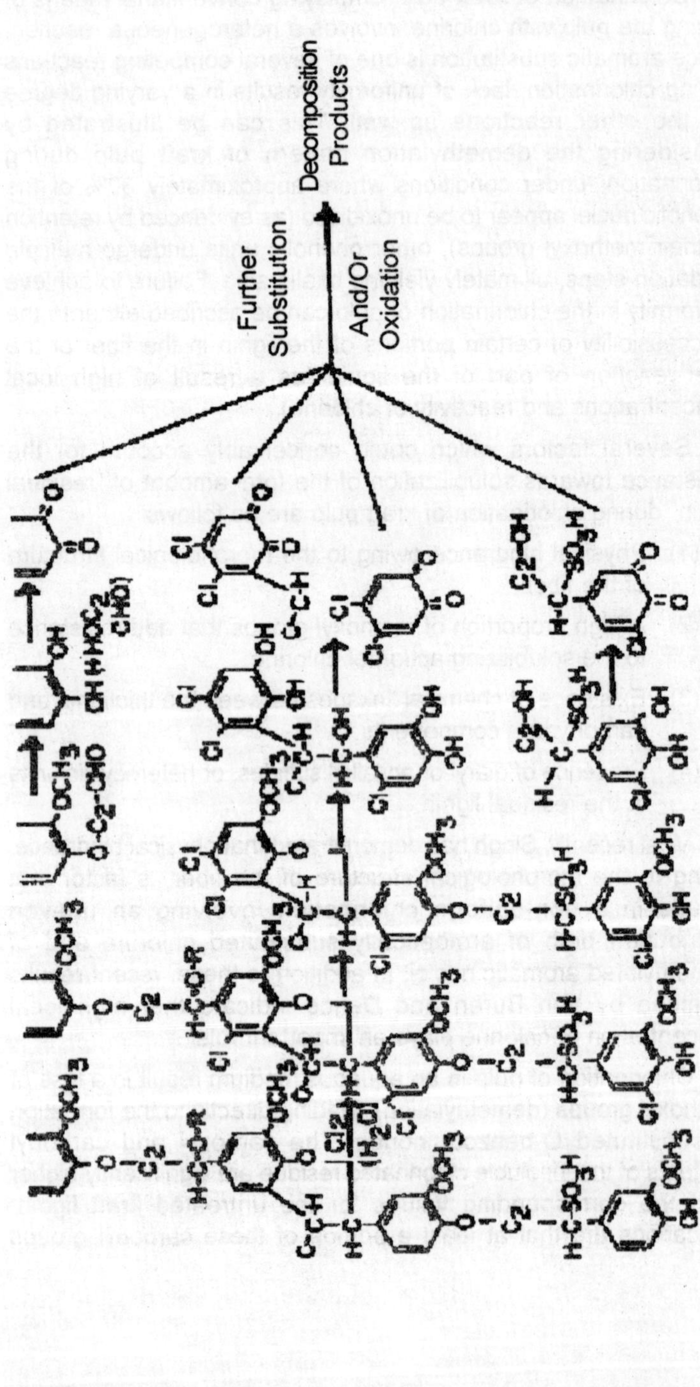

R= H OR ALKYL Fig. 2. Proposed mechanism for chlorination of a sulfite lignin fragment

are present as O-quinones or their derivatives. The increase in carboxyl contents can be ascribed to the formation of biabasic acids produced by oxidative rupture of phenolic nuclei. Experimental evidence in support of this hypothesis has recently been provided. These acids groups assist in the solubilizing of additional amounts of chlorolignin during subsequent extraction of the pulp will alkali.

Very little is known about the existence of chemical linkages between the thiolignin and carbohydrate components, although Singh has recently isolated a lignin carbohydrate complex from a sample of unbleached eastern kraft. The complex, which consisted of 78% thiolignin and 22% carbohydrate, was soluble only in sodium hydroxide or dimethyl-sulfoxide. It was insoluble in aqueous acetone dioxane or phridine which are considered good solvents for thiolignin. Electrophoresis showed that both the lignin and the carbohydrates in this material were chemically combined. While the data are insufficient to draw any definite conclusion concerning the exact nature of the linkage between the lignin and carbohydrate residues, the results indicated that such a linkage was unaffected by chlorine water, the conditions normally used in the chlorination stage. However, the linkage was easily cleaved by chlorine dioxide or hypochlorite.

In view of this, it is desirable to promote the oxidative aspects of the over-all chlorination reaction without simultaneously sacrificing the useful reactions, such asside chain displacement and dealkylation. The promising results, obtained recently through the use of sequential treatments of ClO_2-Cl_2 in the chlorination stage, may be explained as being due in part to the aforementioned useful reactions of chlorine in combination with the superior oxidative qualities of chlorine dioxide.

Reaction of chlorine with Carbohydrates in the Chlorination Stage

Under the conditions of the technical pulp chlorination, chlorine will not chlorinate cellulose; it is not specific in its oxidation reaction, and therefore will attack cellulose as well as lignin. The action of chlorine on pulp polysaccharides in the chlorination stage is by no means fully understood. Generalizations in regard to the nature of oxidations have very little justification. One may, however, state that the action of chlorine solutions on cellulose (and other polysaccharides) is not selective, i.e., they oxidize more than one functional group in the structural saccharide building units. Furthermore, oxidation may be preceded, accompanied, or followed by hydrolysis so that the effects overlap, and are difficult to separate.

One may classify the oxidations as belonging to two types, one predominantly producing carbonyl (ketonic or aldehydic) groups, and the other yielding mainly carboxyl groups in the structural sugar units of the polysaccharides (Fig. 3). Chlorine in acid solutions (elementary chlorine and hypochlorus acid) favours the formation of carbonyl groups. Apart from oxidation, cleavage of the glycosidic bonds and rupture of the ring in the oxidized saccharide building units may also take place. The proposed mechanisms for these reactions are shown in Fig. 4. Hydrolytic and oxidative cleavage of the acetal linkages in cellulose can result in a direct loss of fiber strength.

The location of the carbonyl and carboxyl groups in the oxidized units of polysaccharides present in the chlorinated pulps influences considerably their behaviour toward alkali in the subsequent extraction stage.

THE CHLORINATION OF WOODPULP

Capacity of Chlorination—In bleaching sequences, the amount of chlorine required and the degree of delignification achieved during the chlorination stage depend largely on the nature of the cooking process. Kraft pulp, for example, requires more chlorine and at the same time is less completely delignified by this treatment than sulfite Fig. 5 compares the effects of increasing amounts of chlorine upon the progressive removal of lignin from sulfite and kraft pulps, when chlorination was followed by caustic extraction. The permanganate number was slightly higher for the unbleached sulfite than unbleached kraft, yet a smaller quantity of chlorine was required for the sulfite pulp, and greater degree of delignification was achieved. The minimum permanganate number of 1.2 for the sulfite represented almost complete delignification, in contrast to the kraft pulp which reached a minimum value of 4.3 and therefore retained a minor proportion of its lignin. The reason for these differences generally is ascribed to the belief that, as compared to sulfite lignin, kraft lignin is more condensed; i.e., is comprised of larger molecular aggregates and hence,

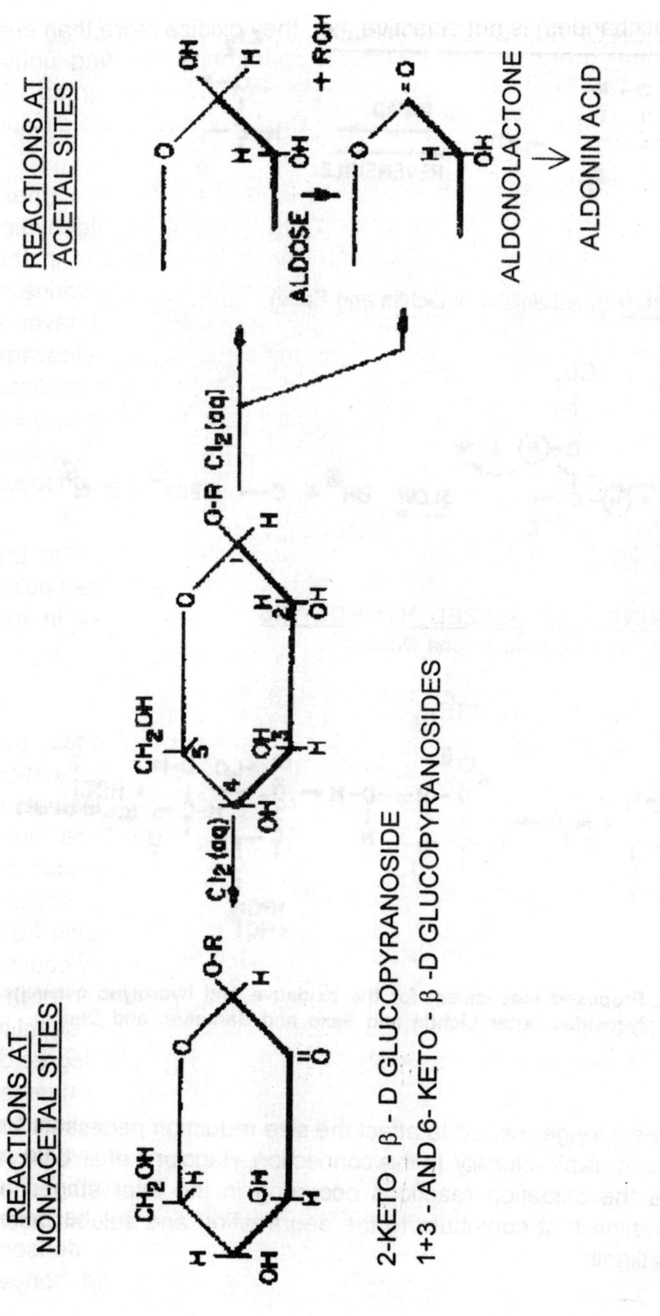

Fig. 3. Characteristic reaction of elemental chlorine with glycosides

FORMATION OF ACTIVATED COMPLEX

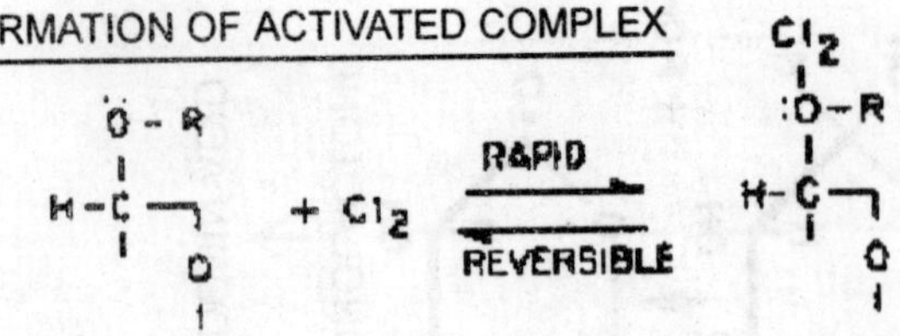

OXIDATION (Mechanisim of Lichtin and Saxe)

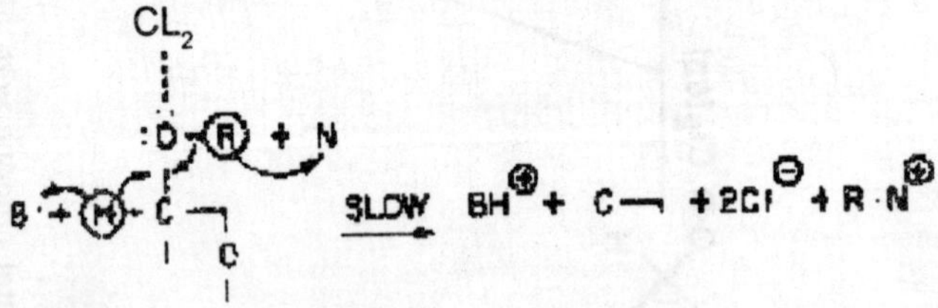

CHLORINE - CATALYZED HYDROLYSIS
(Mechanisim of Sarkanen and Dance)

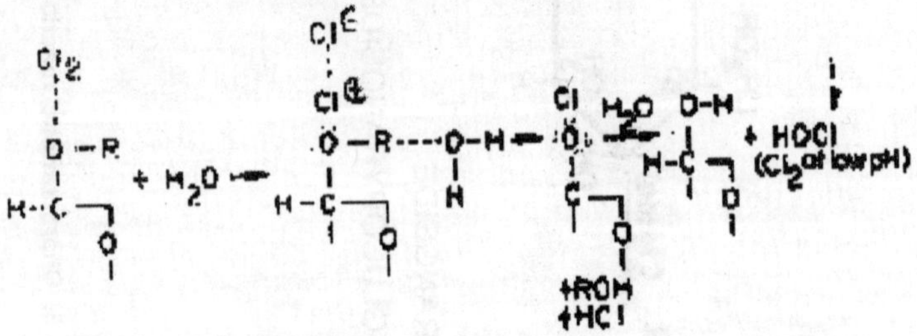

Fig. 4. Proposed mechanism for the oxidative and hydrolytic cleavage of glycosides. After Lichtin and Saxe and Sarkanen and Dence.

requires a longer period to affect the size reduction necessary for water and alkali solubility. In this connection, Hagglund et al. believe that is the oxidation reactions occurring in the later stages of chlorination that contribute to the degradation and solubilization of kraftlignin.

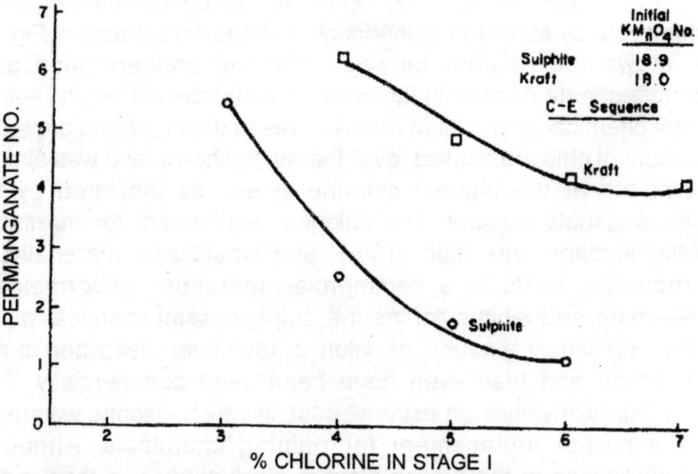

Fig. 5. Comparative effects of chlorination and caustic extraction on Permanganate numbers of kraft and sulfite pulps. Andrews, Pulp paper Mag. Can., T-92 (1964).

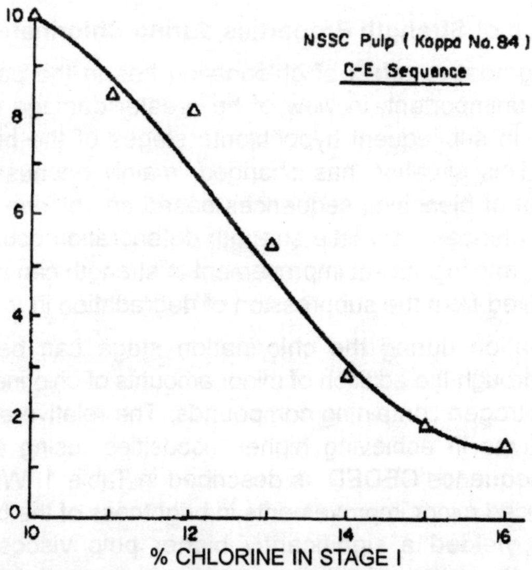

Fig. 6. The effects of chlorine concentration on the permanganate number of a neutral sulfites semi-chemical pulp. After Andrews.

Even pulps having a very high lignin content can be delignified effectively, by means of chlorination and caustic extraction. Figure 6 shows the relation between chlorine concentration and permanganate number in the case of the hardwood neutral sulfite semi-chemical pulp. Lignin removal was in direct proportion to the amount of chlorine applied, over the range shown, and was almost complete at the highest chlorine levels, as indicated by he permanganate number. The chlorine requirement for maximum delignification was high (15%), and would and materially to production costs in a commercial operation. Nevertheless, bleaching sequences for neural sulphite semi-chemical pulps involving similar amounts of chlorine have been described in the literature, and may even have been used commercially. The process exemplifies an extreme case in which chlorine was used as a partial replacement for pulping chemicals. Although delignification in the bleach plant is more expensive than in the digester, this can be offset by the greater selectivity of chlorination and caustic extraction, in terms of higher yields and better strength properties. With increasing wood costs and high strength requirements, there has been a trend towards less cooking and more chlorination.

Preservation of Strength Properties during Chlorination

The degradative effect of chlorination has in the past been considered unimportant, in view of he greater damage suffered by the pulp in subsequent hypochlorite stages of the bleaching sequence. This situation has changed, mainly because of the development of bleaching sequences based on chlorine dioxide. In these sequences, very little strength deterioration occurs after chlorination, and significant improvement in strength can therefore only be derived from the suppression of degradation in this stage.

Degradation during the chlorination stage can be largely prevented through the addition of minor amounts of chlorine dioxide or certain nitrogen containing compounds. The relative effects of these additives in achieving higher viscosities, using standard bleaching sequence CEDED, is described in Table 1. While only a few produced minor improvements in brightness of the bleached pulp, most yielded a significantly higher pulp viscosity. The difference in the degree of activity of various compounds is perhaps due to the instability of the products of reaction between these compounds and undissociated hypochlorous acid present in chlorine water.

Table 1: The Effect of Additives in Chlorination Stage on TAPPI Viscosity of Eastern Kraft Pulp.

Name of Additive In the Chlorination Stage	% on Pulp (b.d. Besis)	0.5% CEDED Viscosity (cp)
None	None	16.3
Chlorine dioxide	0.1	23.2
Ammonium chloride	0.6	28.1
Ammonium acetate	0.6	28.4
Ammonium formate	0.6	29.0
Ammonium acetate	0.6	28.4
Ammonium Aluminum Sulfate	0.6	24.3
Ammonium Chromate	0.6	24.8
Ammonium persulfate	0.6	28.5
Ammonium molybdate	0.6	25.6
Ammonium nitrate	0.6	28.2
Ammonium oxalate	0.6	29.0
Ammonium orhophosphate	0.6	27.8
Ammonium persulfate	0.6	29.2
Ammonium vandate	0.6	24.2
Acrylamide	0.6	28.0

Removal of Lignin and Carbohydrates during Chlorination Stage

Bleaching of pulp by removal of lignin obviously must reduce the yield. It the yield of bleached pulp is calculated on a wood basis, the question arises concerning the correct degree of digestion of obtaining the highest possible yield at the lowest possible consumption of bleaching chemicals.

Hagglund investigated sulfate and sulfite pulps, and found that the total yield of bleached sulfite pulps from spruce increased very little above a Roe chlorine number of 3. There is no reason to believe that lignin is removed selectively during the disgestion period corresponding to the drop in chlorine number from higher values down to 3. Hagglund's results may, therefore, indicate that a considerable amount of carbohydrates is removed in the bleaching of strong sulfite pulps. Loschbrandt, however, obtained

increasing chlorine number) than did Hagglund. Ogail found a significantly higher yield of bleached pulp when increasing the chlorine number.

Björkqvist, Gustrafsson, and Jörgensen studied the bleaching of semiichemical pulps from birch and spruce. They found that besides lignin, only non-cellulosic hexosans were dissolved during chlorination and hypochlorite bleaching, and that pentosans and uronic acids were resistant to bleaching.

Loras has made an excellent study on the removal of substance during chlorination of sulfite pulps from spruce. He reported lignin to be the major part of the substance dissolved in the chlorination process: the determination of carbohydrates in the chlorination waste liquor was somewhat dubious as only C 12% xylan, calculated on the basis of unbleached pulp, was reported.

Singh has recently carried out an extensive study on the material balance during the bleaching of kraft pulp with the sequence CEDED. He found that chlorination of an eastern kraft pulp with 6% chlorine dropped the lignin content of the pulp from 3.84 to 1.45%. Thus, over 62% of the total lignin in kraft pulp is removed during chlorination and subsequent washing. Of the lignin remaining, only a minor proportion (ca. 28%) can be removed in the subsequent extraction stage. Singh's results may, therefore, indicate that carbohydrate is the major organic component of the extraction liquor, amounting to 72% of the total residue. The lignin sample isolated from the chlorination spent liquor showed no aromatic proton peaks in its NMR spectrum. The lack of any proton signal in the aromatic portion of the spectrum clearly indicates that the aromatic components in the wash liquor after chlorination are either chlorinated in all the positions or contain hydroxyl or keto groups.

Chlorine Versus Chlorine Dioxide in the Chlorination Stage

Chlorine dioxide has become firmly established as a bleaching agent for kraft pulps. While most commonly used in the later stages of bleaching processes, as in the sequences CEDED and CEHDED, it is also used occasionally in small amounts as a chlorinating additive.

The beneficial effects obtained by replacing increasing amounts of chlorine by chlorine dioxide in the chlorination stage were first observed by Olfus, for sulfite pulps. More recent studies have indicated that, under conditions of high temperature, high consistency, and larger retention, chlorine dioxidealone can be used in the first stage of a kraft pulp bleaching sequence and will yield almost the same brightness as with chlorine (Fig. 7). Under chlorinating conditions, however chlorine dioxide is relatively ineffective, apparently because of a resistant component of the lignin residue. Chlorine-chlorine dioxide mixtures containing up to 60 to 70% of the total oxidant as chlorine dioxide are effective delignifying agents, and can be used instead of chorine under chlorinating conditions.

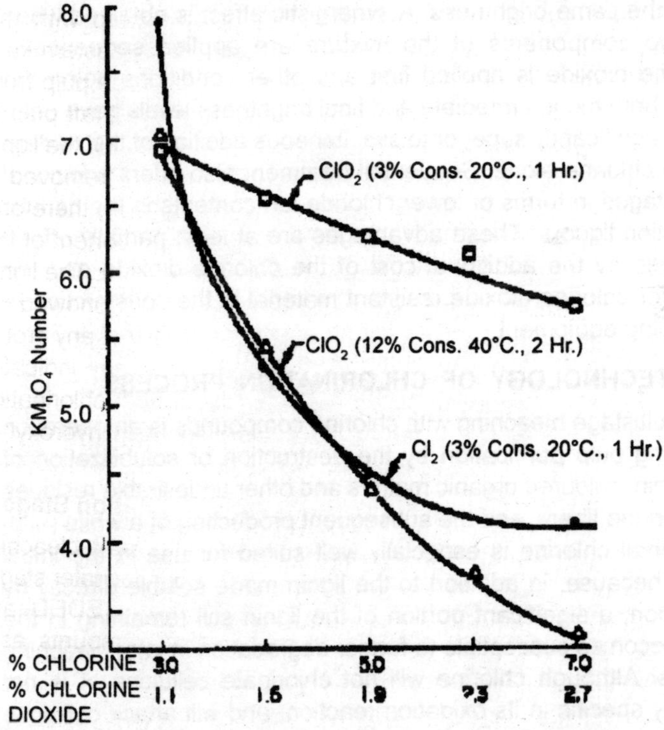

Fig. 7. Comparative delignification of kraft pulpwith chlorine at 20 °C vs chlorine dioxide at 20° and 40° after Singh and Andrews.

Singh and Andrews have found that the intermediate and final brightness of kraft pulp in a C/DEDED or CEDED sequence can be increased by increasing the amount of alkali used in the second stage, from 2.5 to 4%. In these cases, the final brightness was as high when 100% chlorine was used in the first stage as when mixtures of chlorine and chlorine dioxide were applied, although the viscosity was lower in the former case. This latter difference was almost completely eliminated, however, by the inclusion of only 0.1% of chlorine dioxide in the chlorination stage. It is apparent, therefore that the benefits of chlorine dioxide addition in the chlorination stage depend to a large extent on the conditions employed in each stage of the bleaching sequence.

Chlorine-chlorine dioxide mixtures can be used at higher temperatures than chlorine alone, without excessively degrading the cellulose, thus permitting the use of shorter retention times to effect the same brightness. A synergistic effect is obtained when the two components of the mixture are applied sequentially. Chlorine dioxide is applied first and other conditions being the same, both the intermediate and final brightness levels have been found significantly superior to simultaneous addition of the mixture and to chlorine alone. Sequential treatment also offers additional advantages in terms of lower chloride ion contents in the caustic extraction liquors. These advantages are at least partially offset, however, by the additional cost of the chlorine dioxide and the need for chlorine dioxide resistant material in the construction of bleaching equipment.

THE TECHNOLOGY OF CHLORINATION PROCESS

Multistage bleaching with chlorine compounds is an operation involving pulp purification by the destruction or solubilization of the lignin, coloured organic matters and other undesirable residues in or on the fibers, and the subsequent production of a white pulp. Elemental chlorine is especially well suited for use in the initial stage because, in addition to the lignin made soluble directly by its action, a significant portion of the lignin still remaining in the pulp becomes susceptible to further degradation in later bleaching stages. Although chlorine will not chlorinate cellulose, it is not entirely specific in its oxidation reaction, and will attack cellulose as well as lignin. For this reason, an excess of chlorine, beyond that required for chlorination of lignin, leads to rather serious

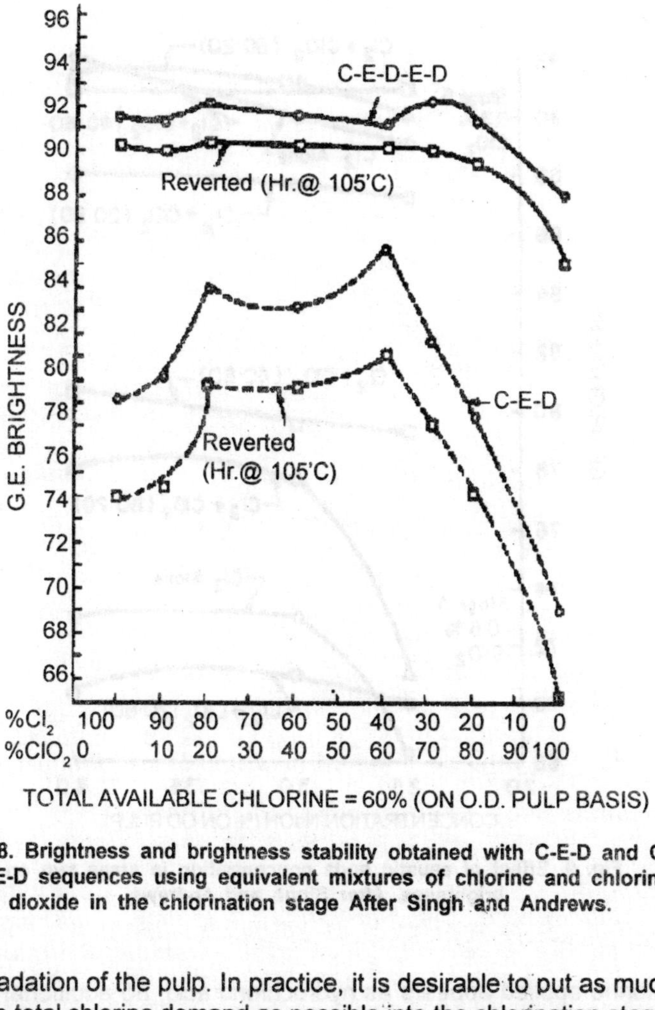

Fig. 8. Brightness and brightness stability obtained with C-E-D and C-E-D-E-D sequences using equivalent mixtures of chlorine and chlorine dioxide in the chlorination stage After Singh and Andrews.

degradation of the pulp. In practice, it is desirable to put as much of the total chlorine demand as possible into the chlorination stage. It has been found that chlorination gives more efficient lignin removal, at lower cost and with less degradation of the cellulose than oxidation with hypochlorite. The optimum amount varies from pulp to pulp but, 50 to 80% of the total chlorine demand is generally used in the chlorination stage.

The reaction is run at low consistency (3 to 4%), ambient temperature (70 to 80°F), and low pH. Since 50 to 75% of the

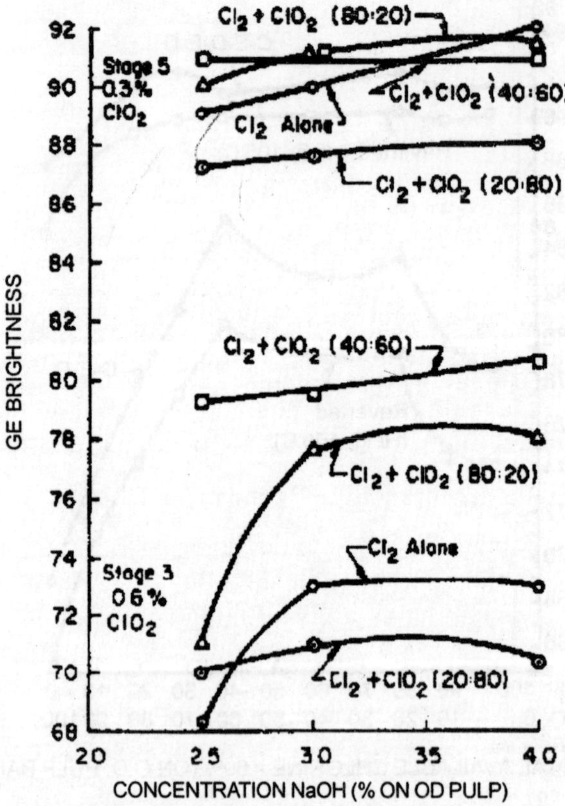

Fig. 9. Effect of caustic soda concentration in stage two on brightness. After Singh and Andrews.

chlorine applied appears as hydrochloric acid, no additional acid need be added. The pH of the slurry normally drops to about 2.0 on addition of chlorine. Present practice is to thoroughly mix chlorine gas and stock in external mixers. The chlorine mixers discharge directly at 3% consistency into the bottom of the upflow towers. At the end of a predetermined retention time, the pulp is washed to eliminate the hydrochloric acid and dissolved acidic lignin degradation products that have been formed. A major part of the lignin is washed out in this operation. Although, in principle,

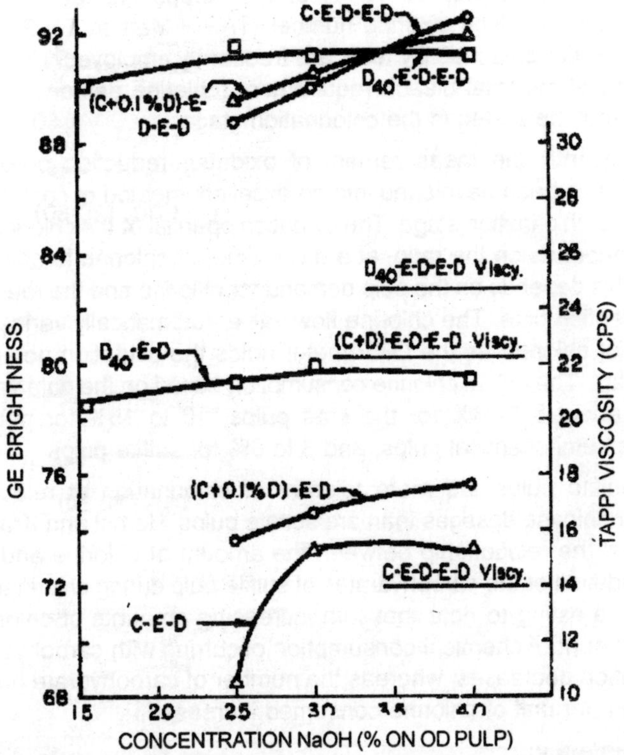

Fig.10. Relative performance of sequences involving (a) chlorine alone. (b) chlorine dioxide as an additive. (c) chlorine dioxide alone (under severe conditions) in stage 1, using varied alkalinity in stage 2 and a toral of 0.9% ClO_2 in stage 3 and 5. After Singh and Andrews.

chlorination appears to be simple operation, process variables must be carefully controlled in order ultimately to produce a bleached pulp of superior quality at minimum cost.

VARIABLES IN THE CHLORINATION PROCESS

Chlorine Concentration—The optimum amount of chlorine to be applied depends on the type of pulp and number of stages in bleaching; usually the amount of chlorine added to the chlorination stage is related to the permanganate number of the unbleached pulp or other bleachability tests. Of the several tests used to determine the bleachability of pulp, the permanganate number (TAPPI Method T214) or the Kappa Number (TAPPI Method T236). Roe chlorine number (TAPPI Method T202), and hypochlorite bleachability tests are frequently employed. From 55 to 80% of the total bleach requirement (chlorine demand of the pulp) may be added in the chlorinátion stage.

Recently the measurement of oxidation-reduction potential (ORP) has been developed into an excellent method of controlling the pulp chlorination stage. The oxidation opential of the chlorinated pulp depends on the ratio, at a given time, of chlorine to chloride ion. This depends on the pulp demand for chlorine and the reaction or retention time. The chlorine flow valve automatically varies the input of chlorine as the ORP meter holds the oxidation potential constant. The actual chlorine consumption based on the pulp varies from about 5 to 8% for the kraft pulps, 10 to 15% for neutral sulfite semi-chemical pulps, and 3 to 6% for sulfite pulps.

Sulfite pulps are more tolerant of chlorination at relatively higher chlorine dosages than are sulfate pulps. Herbst and Krassig studied the relationship between the amount of chlorine and the degradation of the carbohydrates of sulfite pulp during chlorination. It is interesting to note that with increasing amounts of chlorine, the amount of chemical consumption occurring with carbohydrate degration decreases, whereas the number of carbohydrate bonds broken per unit of chlorine consumed increased.

Consistency

The chlorination stage is usually carried out at low pulp consistencies of 3 to 4% in a continuous operation. This is done mainly because of the low solubility of chlorine in water and also because of the greater ease of mixing and pumping operation in the mill.

High-consistency gas-phase chlorination of pulp is suggested as a means of reducing pulp degradation chlorine consumption, and retention time. Thus, correspondingly smaller retention towers are required. Technically one of the principal benefits of high-consistency chlorination lies in a more uniform reaction.

Gas-phase chlorination has been studied in considerable detail by Hinrichs and Liebergott and Yorston. The former author, using kraft pulp at the optimum consistency of 30 to 35%, chlorinated for periods extending from 10 second to one hour. This produced a pulp which, in comparison to a low consistency chlorinated pulp, possessed a higher viscosity after the caustic extraction stage. The heat produced in high density chlorination resulted in only slight degradation at temperatures up to about 100°F, provided that the chlorine consumption was held constant.

Liebergott and Yorston applied chlorine (amount based on Roe chlorine number) at consistencies in the 20 to 60% range; the high range was as effective as the low. Soda and kraft pulps with Roe numbers of 1.1 and 3.8 respectively, consumed an amount of chlorine equal to 75% of the Roe number in one min. Longer retention periods did not produce a corresponding decrease in permanganate number after caustic extraction, nor was the viscosity greatly reduced. However, with hard pulps (both kraft and sulfite), the temperature rose to above 80°F. After caustic extraction, a large brightness increase resulted, but the pulp was degraded when the reaction periods were extended beyond one min, Although this appears contrary to Hinrich's result regarding the effect of temperature on viscosity, nevertheless Hinrich reacted the pulp to constant chlorine consumption, whereas Liebergott and Yorstonallowed the pulps to react to over 90% consumption, based on Roe number.

Temperature and Time

The chlorination stage proceeds freely at ordinary temperatures, and close control of temperature is therefore not as important in chlorination as it is in hypochlorite bleaching. In actual practice, the chlorination temperature is normally governed by the existing temperature of the water supply at the mill, because it is not economically feasible to cool lor heat the large quantities of water required. As the temperature of the water supply varies with the season of the year, the variables in the chlorination process are adjusted accordingly.

The rate of chlorination varies with the kind of pulp, the temperature, and the pH. Sulfite pulps are chlorinated much faster than kraft pulps, probably because the solfonated lignin in the pulp is more swollen and easily accessible and wettable by the acidic solution of chlorine than the lignin in the kraft pulp. In sulfite pulp, chlorination proceeds rapidly even at near-zero temperatures, but only a portion of the lignin in a kraft pulp reacts, and consumption of a small additional amount of chlorine will occur over a further period of 45 to 50 min. This is probably due to more highly condensed nature of kraft lignin, as compared to sulfite lignin.

Typical of many chemical process, the chlorination of wood pulp is an exothermic reaction. When one g of chlorine is reacted with pulp in strongly acid media, approximately 500 calories of heat is liberated, and stock chlorinated in 3 to 4% suspension will show a temperature rise of only 1 to 3°C. The effect of temperature on the rate of consumption of chlorine by a sulfite and a kraft pulp are shown in Figs. 11 and 12, respectively. It is apparent from these figures that the consumption of chlorine is largely dependent upon the temperature and reaction time. However, according to

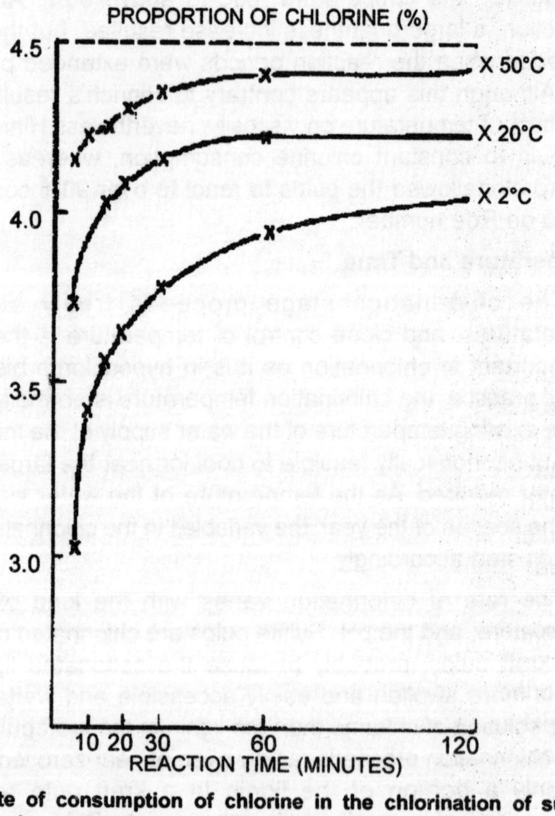

Fig. 11. Rate of consumption of chlorine in the chlorination of sulfite pulp at various temperatures. After Virkola Hentotal. Makinen, and Soila.

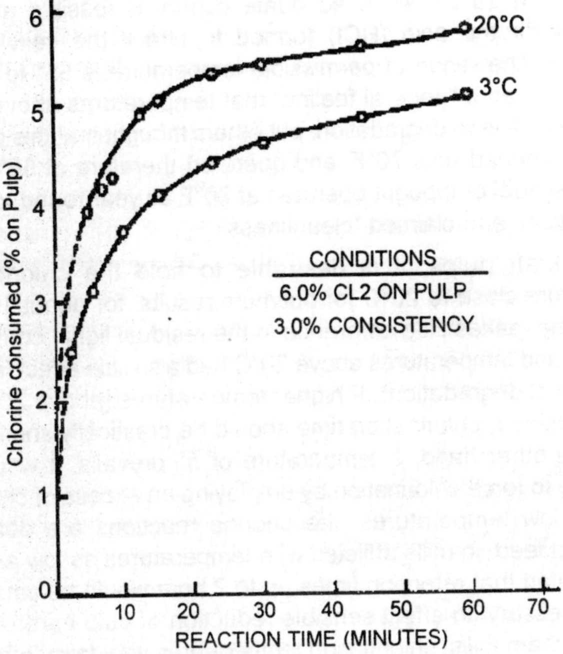

Fig. 12. Rate of consumption of chlorine in the chlorination of kraft pulp at various temperatures. After Duncan and Rapson.

Eriksson and Stockman, at constant chlorine consumption, dissolution of lignin decreases with rise intemperature. These workers investigated the influence of temperature over the range 10 to 50°C, and found it to be dependent on the amount of chlorine added. At 5% chlorine the effect was weak, but at 6.5% it was marked, in respect both to the of chorine was found to bear a linear relationship to temperature over only a portion of the temperature range. Gietz found only a slight increase in lignin removal by raising the temperature of the chlorination reaction. According to a large group of researchers, at high temperature, chlorine is merely consumed more rapidly (with no practical significance), without proportionate advantage in lignin dissolution. At equal chlorine consumption, higher temperature increased the chlorination rate, but had no effect on the final hardness.

The chlorination stage is carried out at relatively low temperature levels (20 to 25°C), since adequate control is feasible and the tendency for the acid (HCl) formed to attack the cellulose is repressed. The range of permissible temperature is 55° to 70° F. One group had a "general feeling" that temperatures above 55°F were conductive to degradation, but others thought that this danger was not reached until 70°F, and operated therefore at 65°F. Still another school of thought operated at 70°F all year round, denied degradatioin, and claimed "cleanliness".

For kraft pulps, it is desirable to hold the chlorination temperature close to 20°C for optimum results, for about 15 min. longer time makes little difference in the residual lignin content of the pulp, and temperatures above 20°C had also little effect (except for potential degradation). If higher temperatures (above 20°) can not be avoided, chlorination time should be drastically shortened. If, on the other hand, a temperature of 5° prevails, it would be advisable to force chlorination by employing an excess of chlorine, since at low temperatures, the chorine reactions are definitely slowed. Indeed, in mills afflicted with temperatures as low as 2°, it is postulated that retention times up to 2 hour would be safe, and even necessary, to effect sensible reduction of pulp hardness. In some northern mills, chlorination temperatures vary from 2 to 30°C over the year, while in southern mills, the range would be between 15 to 40°C. Since increasing the temperature results in a large reduction in pulp viscosity, it is suggested that the retention times be altered accordingly.

pH—Chlorination of lignin takes place to some extent over the entire pH range, but as might be expected, the rate is greatly increased at low pH values. In actual practice, no effort is made to regulate the pH of he chlorination stage, which assumes a value governed by the concentration of the chlorine initially present and by the hydrochloric acid formed during the reaction. Giertz found that by lowering the pH of the chlorination mixture, it is possible to enhance the chlorination (substitution) reaction while depressing the oxidation. (Fig. 13). This was confirmed by Oltus who found that by lowering the chlorination pH from 3 to 1. Up to 90% chlorine was consumed during the first 5 to 10 min of chlorination. The chlorine content of sulfite lignin and its solubility in alkali also increased significantly.

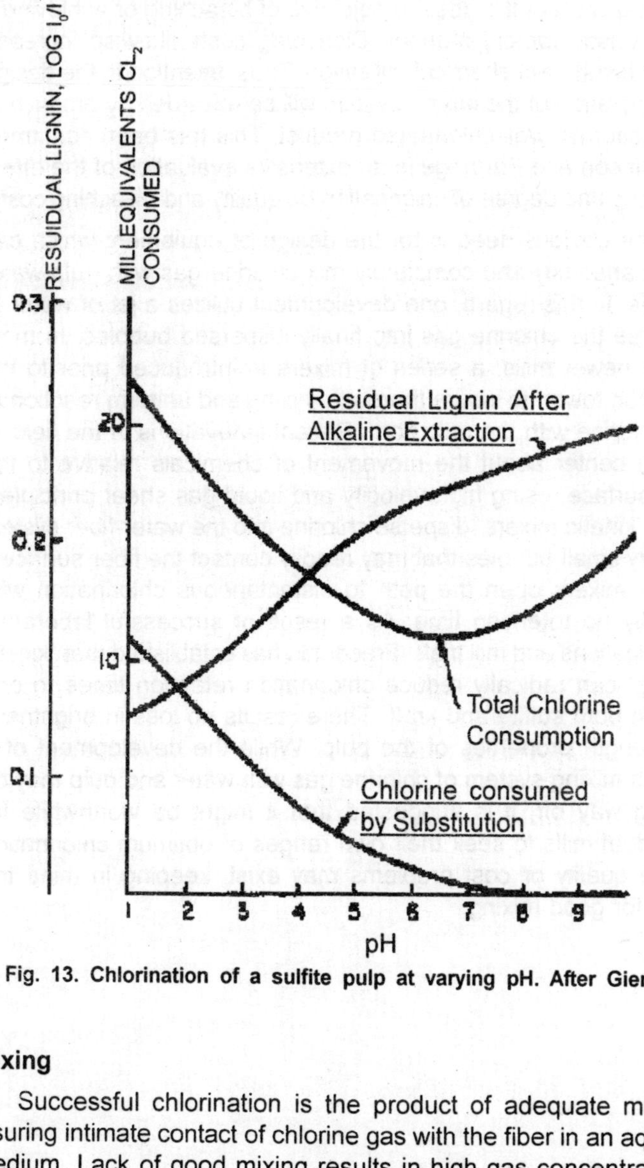

Fig. 13. Chlorination of a sulfite pulp at varying pH. After Giertz.

Mixing

Successful chlorination is the product of adequate mixing, insuring intimate contact of chlorine gas with the fiber in an aqeous medium. Lack of good mixing results in high gas concentrations in the retention tower, degradation of pulp due to "chlorine burn", and pockets of unchlorinated pulp within the tower. These cause a wide departure from the optimum, a condition which could result in falling short of the desired objective of bleaching or achieving it in an unsatisfactory manner. Bleaching costs likewise increase due to insufficient chemical utilization. Thus, attention to the design and operation of the mixing system will be rewarded by production of a uniformly well-chlorinated product. This has been confirmed by Atkinson and Partridge in an extensive evaluation of the effect of mixing and degree of chlorination on quality and bleaching costs.

The obvious need is for the design of equipment which can instantaneously and completely mix chlorine gas with pulp-water slurries. In this regard, one development utilizes a jet of water to disperse the chlorine gas into finally dispersed bubbles. In most of the newer mills, a series of mixers in introduced prior to the retention tower, to insure thorough mixing and uniform reaction of the chlorine with the pulp fiber. Recent innovations in the field or mixing center about the movement of chemicals relative to the fiber surface, using high velocity and liquid gas shear principles. Such "kinetic mixers" disperse chlorine into the water-fiber system as very small bubbles that may readily contact the fiber surfaces. These mixers open the path to instantaneous chlorination with virtually no retention time. As a result of successful laboratory investigations and mill trials. Freedman has established that "kinetic mixing" can radically reduce chlorination retention times to one min on both sulfite and kraft. There results no loss in brightness or strength properties of the pulp. While the development of a perfect mixing system of chlorine gas with water and pulp may be a long way off, it is suggested that it might be worthwhile for individual mills to seek their own ranges of optimum chlorination where quality or cost problems may exist, keeping in mind the need for good mixing.

4

Bleaching Alkaline Extraction

The alkaline extraction of wood pulps may be regarded as an integral part of the present day multistage bleaching processes. Its object is to remove those coloured components from partially bleached wood pulps that have been rendered soluble in dilute warm alkali solutions, by the action of chemicals used in partial bleaching. Quite often, more than one alkaline extraction is practiced in the widely used chlorine bleaching processes.

In the alkaline extraction stage, an extensive removal of chlorinated and oxidized lignin is attained and, as a consequence, the degree of brightness of the pulps on subsequent bleaching is enhanced, Moreover, less bleaching chemicals are required to secure a desired degree of brightness. Thus, both the economy of bleaching and retention of strength properties of the wood pulp fibers are favourably affected. In this sense, the alkaline extraction may be regarded as a bleaching stage without significant oxidation and, hence, without significant oxidative degradation of the fibers. Further benefits arising from alkaline extraction processes are associated with brightness stability, opacity, softness, and some mechanical properties of wood pulp fibers.

During alkaline extraction, usually only a limited removal of pulp polysaccharides takes place. The alkaline extraction processes are, therefore, mainly confined to the paper industry. An intensified version of alkaline extraction, known as alkaline purificaiton, is widely used in the production of pulps for the regenerated cellulose and cellulose-derivative industries. Alkaline purification also constitutes an integral part of the present-day, multistage pulp-bleaching processes. Its object is not only to remove coloured constituents, but also unwanted polysaccharides, notably those causing difficulties in cellulose regeneration and derivative manufacture. The difference between alkaline extraction and alkaline purificaiton lies mainly in the alkali concentration, temperature, and the type of unbleached pulps employed. The basic chemistry of the reactions with the pulp polysaccharides is the same in both processes. While the extent of these reactions is very moderate in the alkaline extraction, it is quite considerable in the alkaline purification. This extent of the reactions, and hence, that of the removal of polysaccharides by hot dilute alkali solutions, depends primarily on the chemical composition of the polysaccharides present in partially bleached wood pulps. The rate of the reactions is influenced by the accessibility of the pulp fibers to the aqueous alkaline solutions used and by the external conditions employed. Thus morphological and supermolecular structural characteristics of fibers, alkali concentration, temperature, pulp concentration, and period of treatment play a role both in alkaline extraction and alkaline purification.

The main objects in the stages preceding the alkaline extraction or purification are to remove the greater part of lignin from the pulps and to render the remaining portion soluble in alkali. In sulfate pulps, there are so-called "dye-like" substances that are neither removed by direct chlorination nor completely destroyed by oxidation in the subsequent bleaching treatments. They could be removed, however, by hot caustic extraction under conditions that minimize removal of hemicellulose. The use of sodium hydroxide to wash or extract the pulp after chlorination has, therefore, become a vital step in the modern bleach plants. The alkaline extraction as a stage in bleaching and purification of wood pulp results in : (1) better bleach response of the pulp to higher brightness (2) greater cleanliness and colour stability of the pulp; (3) savings in chlorine and other chemicals used in bleaching and (4) a significant improvement in strength of the fully bleached pulp.

CONDITIONS OF ALKALINE EXTRACTION

Typical conditions of the alkaline extraction stage of the bleaching sequence are as follows: NaOH, .5 to 5% basis of pulp (the higher values within this range being used for the stage following chlorination with the lower values for the stage following hypochlorite or chlorine dioxide); cosistency, 10 to 20%, depending upon equipment available; temperature of 45° to 95°C, with a value of 80°C being seldom exceeded; time, 1 to 2 hr. This relatively narrow range of conditions applies both to sulfite and kraft pulps. However, the exact choice of conditions depends on the permanganate number of the raw pulp and on the intended use of the finished pulp. Longer extraction times (as compared with sulfite pulps) at slightly elevated temperatures are needed for removal of chloro-lignin from kraft pulps. This is probably due to the existence of relatively large molecular aggregates of residual kraft lignin (after chlorination) which diffuse very slowly out of the fibre matrix.

With a consistency of 15% and with 4% NaOH basis of fibre, the concentration of the NaOH basis of water is about 0.7%. Initial pH values for kraft pulp at 12% consistency have been reported to range from 11.8 to 12.2. Corresponding final pH values were unchanged. This would indicate that little neutralization of NaOH by chemical reaction has occurred.

Relatively little data exist relating the conditions of the extraction stage of pulp properties. It has been stated that, in general, mild conditions of alkaline extraction favour the tear strength of sulfite pulps, whereas higher levels favour burst, fold opacity, and absotbency. It is probable that the range of conditions commonly practiced in pulp bleaching does not greatly influence the physical properties of the pulp.

Following a chlorination first state, the level of treatment in the alkaline stage has an important effect upon pulp brightness. The optimum alkalinity should be established experimentally for different pulps, under otherwise constant bleaching conditions.

CHEMISTRY OF ALKALINE EXTRACTION

There are many examples of reactions between ligno-cellulose and cellulosic materials and alkali. The various alkaline pulping processes are among the oldest and most widely used in that field. The production of highly purified cellulosic pulps, "alpha cellulose", makes use of the action of strong alkaline solutions. Cellulose derivatives, such as cellulose xanthate and carboxy methyl cellulose, have the highly swollen "alkali cellulose" as a first step of the process. The alkaline extraction stage of the bleaching sequence is another important example in the series of alkaline treatments.

Under the range of conditions possible in the extraction stage, the following reactions may be expected to occur to a greater or lesser degree:

(1) Dissolution and removal of chlorinated lignin.

(2) Removal of hemicellulose (pentosan) from the fibre.

(3) Saponification of fatty acids and rosin acids contained in the pulp.

(4) Degradation of the chain length of the polysaccharide component of the fibre.

The chlorination of unbleached pulp evidently results in the formation of three fractions of chlorinated lignin: (1) small molecular fragments soluble in water and removed in the wash following the chlorination stage. (2) larger molecular fragments that become soluble in alkali concentrations of 0.5 to 1.0% and at approximately a pH of 12, and (3) a refractory portion of chlorinated lignin that is insoluble even under severe treatment with alkali, and that requires subsequent oxidative stages for complete removal. Conflicting viewpoints have been reported on the removal of chloro-lignin during the extraction stage. One group of investigators have a "general feeling" that the removal of chlorolignin is a physical process in which temperature and time control the degree of solubilization. Another group have attributed the dissolution of chloro-lignin in alkali exclusively to the hydrolysis of chlorine atoms substituted on the side chain (as well as on the aromatic ring) of the lignin molecule. While the data are insufficient to draw any definite conclusion concerning the exact mechanism of the removal of chloro-lignin, it is logical to assume that a substantial part of the chloro-lignin removal is the result of a chemical, as contrasted to physical, action of the alkali on the chlorinated pulp.

Histed has reported the removal of lignin-bound chlorine, from a series of sulfite pulps, by treatment with increasing amounts of NaOH, extending from below the normal range used in the extraction stage to considerably above that range. For example, with a sulfite pulp of Kappa No. 22.7, and with the application of 4.28% NaOH in the E stage, the removal of chloro-lignin was about 83%. Although the E stage removes a large proportion of the chlorolignin present in the pulp entering that stage, because of the large amount of chloro-lignin removed in the C stage, this amount is considerably less than half of that removed by the two stages combined. Subsequent H and D stages brought the residual chloro-lignin to about 5% of that remaining after the C stage, and produced a pulp of 90.9 brightness.

The high removal of chloro-lignin in the E stage is significant in producing pulps of improved brightness, with reduced consumption of chlorine chemicals and reduced fibre degradation. It has been reported that alkaline extraction permits 5 points higher brightness than possible with hypochlorite bleachine alone.

The same reference reports the removal of pentosan at different levels of NaOH in the E stage. Below 2% NaOH, there is relatively little reduction on pentosan content of the pulp; above the point, there is a progressive increase in pentosan removal. For example, with an unbleached pulp of Kappa No. 22.7 (cited above) and E stage alkali of 4.28% the pentosan content was reduced from 4.7 to 3.6%. When alkali was increased to 12,13, pentosan was further reduced to 2.4%. It is probable that the typical E stage of the bleaching sequence has relatively little effect (through the loss of hemicellulose) upon pulp properties. For those pulps in which the preservation of hemicellulose is important for easy hydration in refining, the conditions of the E stage should be kept mild and consistent with other properties.

Unbleached sulfite pulps come to the bleach plant containing substantial amounts of resin extractives. It is probable that a major proportion of this resin remains with the pulp through the bleaching sequence. This is due both to the relatively mild conditions of the E stage, and to the fact that the resin is still largely contained within unruptured cells, and hence, is not completely accessible. Histed reports extractive content of his pulp after the E stage. A progressive reduction in extractive content is shown with increasing amounts of NaOH. In general, the resin content is reduced by about half at the levels of NaOH normally used in the E stage.

It is improbable that typical conditions of the E stage of the bleaching sequence results in substantial degradation of the cellulose component. Temperature is normally limited to about 80°C to avoid such degradation and the consequent loss of yield. Singh and Andrew report that the final viscosity of bleached pulp is relatively unaffected by increased alkali and increased chloro-lignin removal in the E stage.

It is interesting to note that so-called "alpha pulp" (over 98% alpha cellulose) cannot be obtained by increasing the intensity of the E stage. Wayman reports a maximum of 96% alpha cellulose (referred to as the "alpha ceiling"). It appears that the alpha ceiling phenomenon is due to the "stopping reaction" which interrupts alkaline degradation, and thus stops the dissolution of the impurities formed by degradation. As the alpha cellulose is raised, carbohydrate material (partly preexisting in the pulp and partly formed by alkaline degradation of cellulose) is dissolved. Values over about 93% alpha cellulose are attained only at the expense of an excessive loss of yield.

ALKALINE PURIFICATION

Production of the so-called alpha or dissolving pulps requires a degree of purification not attainable in the normal bleaching sequence. Cold sodium hydroxide solutions of 4 to 20% concentration have a much more selective dissolving action on the non-alpha cellulose components of pulp than do the more dilute, hot solutions. By cold caustic treatment, pulps of 98% alpha content are produced commercially.

Wayman and Sherk have studied the caustic treatment of chlorinated and alkali extracted sulfite wood pulp over the range from 20 to 160 gallons/liter and at temperatures from 5 to 50°C. The highest values of alpha cellulose content for a given concentration of NaOH were found at 15°C. The optimum concentration of NaOH was in the range of 117 to 142 gallons/liter, giving values of alpha cellulose of over 99% with pulp yields of 94%. This represents a 1% gain in a alpha cellulose for each 1.75% loss in yield. This contrasts with a loss of 2.67% yield for each 1% gain in alpha content with hot, dilute caustic extraction.

Pulp treated with NaOH in concentrations over 60 gallons/liter undergoes a high degree of swelling, and hence, the washing of this swollen pulp requires extensive washing equipment for the commercial production of alpha pulp.

CHEMICAL STRUCTURE OF OXIDIZED POLYSACCHARIDES IN PARTIALLY BLEACHED WOOD PULPS

It is the purpose of the bleaching operation to produce a pulp of highly purified cellulose with a minimum of reaction or damage to the cellulose itself. This can be achieved only to a relative degree, since the conditions of purification may also cause changes in the cellulose. The following brief discussion points out the nature of some of these reactions.

Wood pulps that have been partially bleached by chlorine bleaching chemicals contain several types of oxidized units in the polysaccharide components, but their nature is not fully understood. This is probably the main reason why the nature of the reactions in the hot alkaline extraction and purification of oxidized polysaccharides is also not fully understood.

It may be instructive to show by examples how the chemical structure of oxidized cellulose influences the reactions of polysaccharides with alkaline solutions. The oxidized celluloses selected are those that are likely to be present in the cellulose fraction of partially bleached wood pulps.

Oxidized celluloses with a carbonyl group on C_2 or C_3 in the glucose units represent β-glycoxycarbonyl systems. These oxidized celluloses are sensitive to alkali solutions, and the main steps in their degradation (based on the β-glycoxy elimination theory) are shown by the reaction scheme in Fig. 1. (a and b). These seps, as before, are the formation of an ion, followed by an electron shift and then the elimination of the glycoxyanion.

Oxidized celluloses with a carbonyl group on C_6 in glucose units also represent β-glycoxy-carbonyl structures. They are sensitive to alkali solutions and are degraded according to a reaction scheme shown in Fig. 2.

Cellulose oxidized on C1 in the terminal gulcose unit is comparatively resistant to boiling, dilute, alkali solution, because the endwise type of degradation is prevented or, at least, hindered. As shown in Fig. 3, the gluconic carboxyl is ionized,and the inductive effect is reversed so that the hydrogen atom on C_2 does not become sufficiently acidic to be removed by the base, a prerequisite for the β-glycoxy-elimination to take place. Thus, the

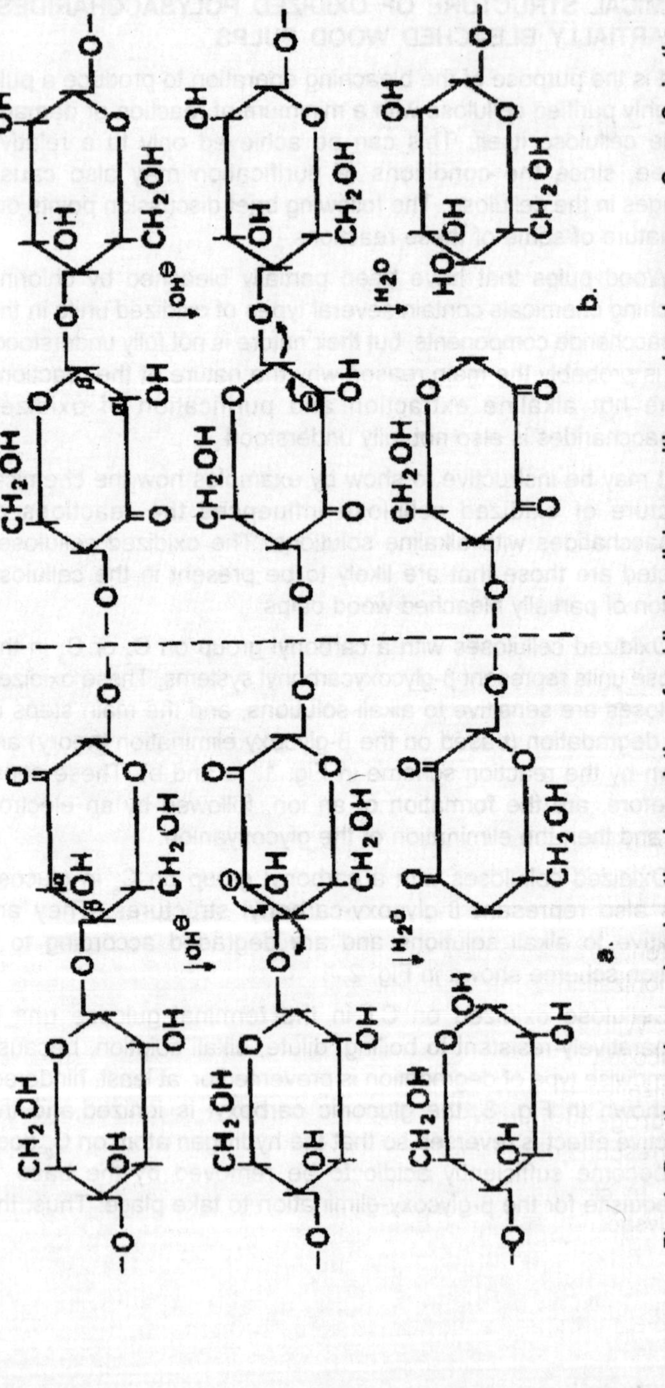

Fig. 1. Reaction scheme showing the degradation of oxidized celluloses with a carbonyl group on C_2 or C_3 in the glucose units.

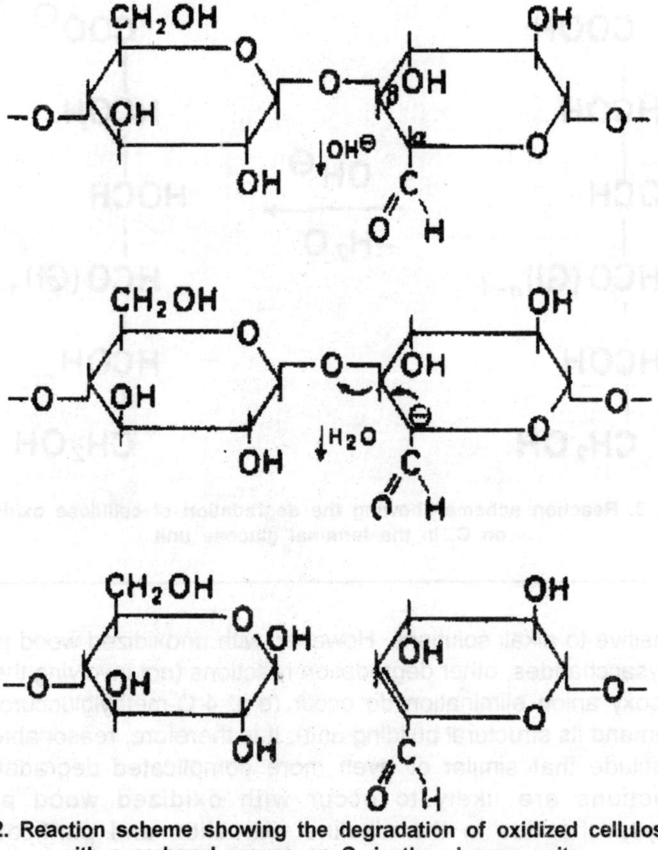

Fig.2. Reaction scheme showing the degradation of oxidized celluloses with a carbonyl groups on C_6 in the glucose units.

extent of alkaline degradation is mainly a function of the degree of ionization of the carboxylic acid.

With oxidized celluloses containing C_6-carboxyl groups in the glucose units, the situation is similar. Depending on the degree of ionization of the carboxylic acid group, some activation of the hydrogen atom at C_5 may occur. This would result in a corresponding labilization of the glucosidic bond.

In closing, it should be emphasized that oxidized wood polysaccharides that contain β-glycoxy-carbonyl structures are

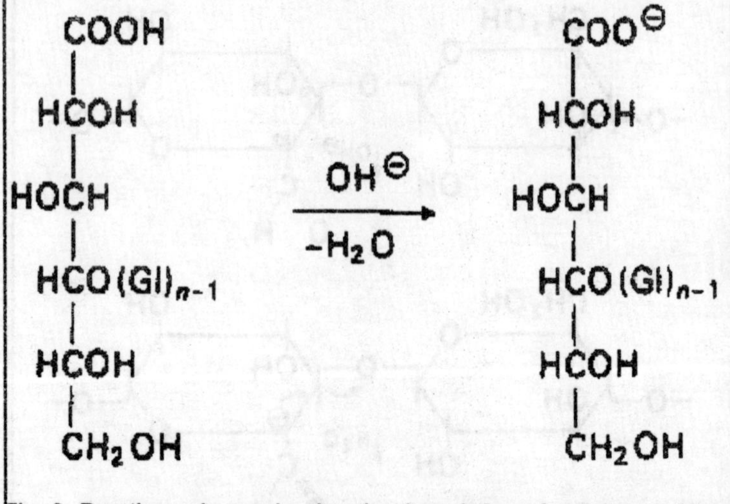

Fig. 3. Reaction scheme showing the degradation of cellulose oxidized on C_1 in the terminal glucose unit.

sensitive to alkali solutions. However, with unoxidized wood pulp polysaccharides, other degradation reactions (not involving the β-glycoxy anion elimination do occur (e.g. 4-O-methylgluccurono-xyan and its structural building unit). It is therefore, reasonable to conclude that similar or even more complicated degradation reactions are likely to occur with oxidized wood pulp polysaccharides in the alkaline extraction and purification processes.

5

Bleaching Hypochlorite Stage

THE CHEMISTRY OF HYPOCHLORITE SOLUTIONS

At first commercial bleaching powder was the standard source of hypochlorite. The usual practice today is to prepare hypochlorite solutions at the mill, from either calcium or sodium hydroxide. Chlorine is reacted with the alkali according to reactions.

$$2Ca(OH)_2 + 2Cl_2 =$$
$$Ca(OCl)_2 + CaCl_2 + 2H_2O + heat \quad (1)$$

$$2NaOH + Cl_2 = NaOCl + NaCl + H_2O + heat \quad (2)$$

Reactions (1) and (2) are reversible so that an excess of alkali is required to stabilize the hypochlorite solution. If an excess of alkali is not present, the hypochlorite solution will rapidly decompose into chlorates and chlorides, and in some cases may liberate oxygen.

$$NaOCl + H_2O = NaOH + HOCl \quad (3)$$

$$3HOCl = HClO_3 + 2HCl \quad (4)$$

$$HOCl = O + HCl \quad (5)$$

The liberated HCl in equation (4) and (5) can then attack the NaOCl thus forming more HOCl which again rearranges according to equations (4) and (5). The breakdown continues until all of the NaOCl has been converted to chlorate and chloride. Properly made hypochlorite solutions are fairly stable for about 48 hrs.

Chlorine exists largely as molecular chlorine, hypochlorous acid and hypochlorite ion in a water solution. A review of the chlorine water system. Figure 1 will show that at low pH, the

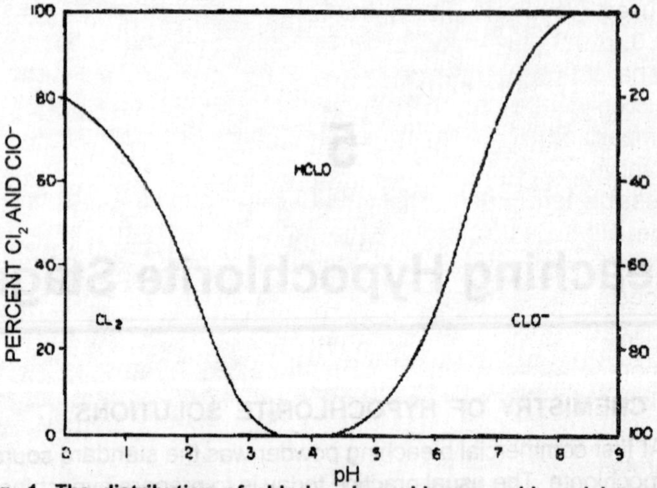

Fig. 1. The distribution of chlorine, hypochlorous acid, and hypochlorite at various pH levels on of an 0.01 *N* solution of chlorine in water (Giertz).

chlorine molecule predominates. As pH increases, the amount of hypochlorous acid increases. At pH 4 to 6, it is almost the only component present. Above a pH of 9.5 the hypochlorite ion is the only component present. The pH then is an important factor in hypochlorite solution stabilization and as will be shown later, plays an important role in bleaching reactions.

The addition of hypochlorite to bleach is based on available or active chlorine. "Available chlorine" is the term used to indicate the oxidation equivalent (expressed as weight of chlorine), and is a measure of the oxidizing power of the hypochlorite solution. The bleach liquor analysis is made by an idometric titration with thiosulfate in the presence of potassium iodide and starch. Iodineis liberated from the potassium iodide by the chlorine and is titrated with the thiosulfate to a starch end point.

EFFECT OF HYPOCHLORITE ON LIGNIN

The colour of unbleached pulp is due largely to the residual lignin not removed during the pulping process. In the multistage bleach, large amounts of this lignin are removed by the chlorination and alkali treatment preceding the hypochlorite stage, but the pulps do not become any whiter. The chlorination and alkali treatment may therefore be considered a continuation of the pulping process. Brightening of the pulp is not accomplished until bleaching agents are used. A normal sulfite pulp may have a permanganate number of 1.0 to 1.5 after chlorination and extraction while a kraft pulp may have a permanganate number of 4.0 to 6.0.This is substantial reduction in lignin compared to the original pulp, but is still sufficient to impart colour to the pulp. The remaining lignin or lignin derivatives that are less reactive, move condensed, and less accessible, are further subjected to oxidation in the hypochlorite stage. Although both chlorination and oxidation of lignin may take place in hypochlorite solution, the high pH of hypochlorite bleaching suggests that the primary reaction is oxidation.

Unlike the acid chlorination first stage where the lignin molecule is more open to attack and is rapidly removed, hypochlorite oxidation is slow. The slower rate of lignin removal by hypochlorite compared to chlorine is shown in Fig. 2. The more severe degradation of the cellulose by hypochlorite is shown in Fig. 3. Form has shown that in the bleaching of sulfite pulp, lignin removal does not take place until 20% of the bleach demand of the pulp

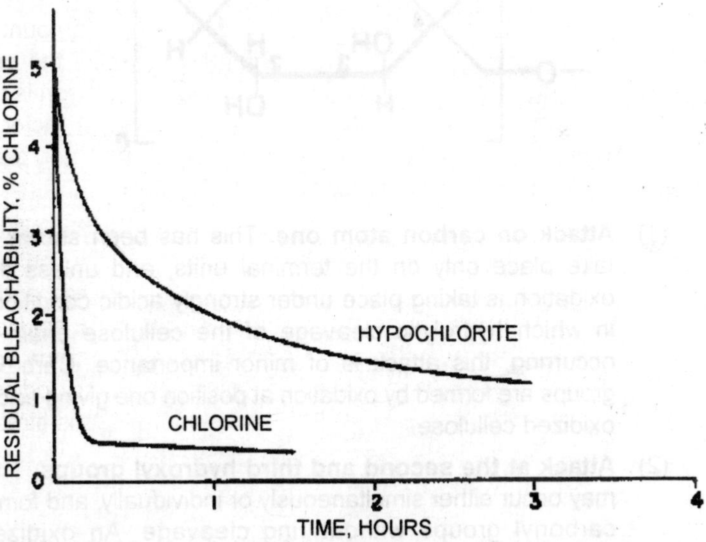

Fig. 2. Comparison of reaction rate of chlorine and hypochloriate on ligin removal (hatch).

has been satisfied. Above 20% of the bleach demand, lignin removal becomes quite rapid, until at 70% nearly all of the lignin is removed. Sulfite pulps, in which the residual lignins are partially sulfonated and are more readily solubilized by hypochlorite, may be bleached with one stage of hypochlorite, while sulfate and soda pulps require more stages of bleaching.

EFFECT OF HYPOCHLORITE ON CELLULOSE

Although hypochlorites are reasonably effective in making pulp white, they are nonspecific oxidizing agents, and will attack the cellulose molecule as well as the residual lignin. The extent of the attack on the cellulose molecule is dependent upon pH, temperature, bleaching time, consistency, and hypochlorite concentration, the attack results in two main types of oxidized cellulose, i.e., reducing and acidic. An examination of the cellulose molecule shows that six major types of attack may occur:

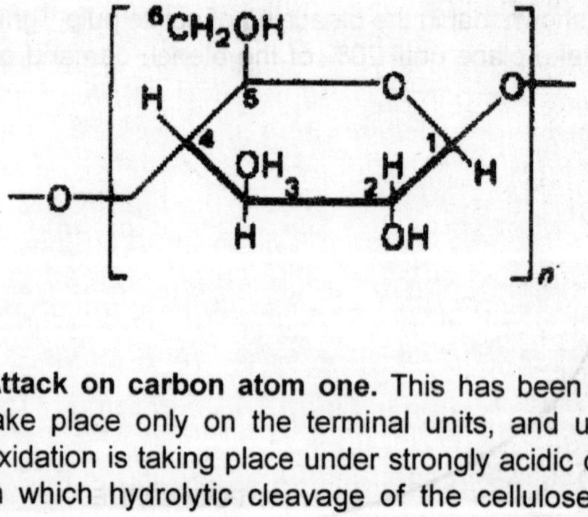

(1) **Attack on carbon atom one.** This has been shown to take place only on the terminal units, and unless the oxidation is taking place under strongly acidic conditions in which hydrolytic cleavage of the cellulose chain is occurring, this attack is of minor importance. Carboxyl groups are formed by oxidation at position one giving acidic oxidized cellulose.

(2) **Attack at the second and third hydroxyl groups**. This may occur either simultaneously or individually, and forms carbonyl groups without ring cleavage. An oxidized cellulose with a high reducing value would be produced

in this case.

(3) Attack at the second and third hydroxyl groups simultaneously to form aldehyde groups with ring cleavage. A reducing-type oxidized cellulose is thus formed.

(4) Further attack on the aldehyde groups in reaction three, converting them to carboxyl groups that given an acidic-type oxidized cellulose.

(5) Attack at position six, forming an aldehyde group resulting in a reducing-type oxidized cellulose.

(6) Attack at position six, to convert the aldehyde to a carboxyl so that an acidic-type oxidized cellulose is formed.

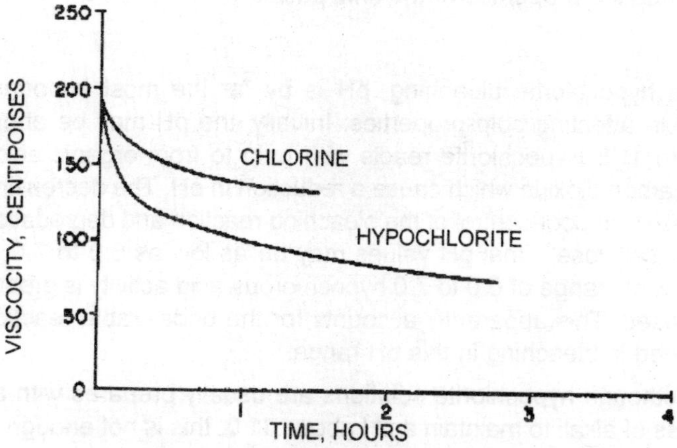

Fig.3. Comparison of carbohydrate degradation by chlorine and hypochlorite as measured by viscosity change (Hatch).

The above reactions are important in the resultant pulp characteristics. The carbonyl groups that are first formed by oxidation are rapidily hydrolyzed by alkali so that ring cleavage will occur between the second and third carbon atoms. This may be observed by a decrease in alpha cellulose content and a reduction in the viscosity. Rapson et al. have also shown that there is a relationship between the carbonyl content of cellulose and colour reversion, i.e., as the carbonyl content increases, colour reversion increases.

In the early stages of bleaching with hypochlorite, the attack upon cellulose is relatively slow, because it is protected by impurities. As the bleaching process proceeds, these impurities are removed so that the internal surface of the fibers are increased and the cellulose is in a more reactive state. Attack on the cellulose chain during hypochlorite bleaching is shown by a gradual decrease in alpha cellulose content and viscosity of the pulp. Increased copper number and hot alkali solubility are other evidences of attack on the cellulose.

EFFECT OF BLEACHING CONDITIONS

The rate of reaction and the amount of bleaching done with hypochlorite depends on the control of a number of variables that influence the properties of the final pulp.

pH

In hypochlorite bleaching, pH is by far the most important variable affecting pulp properties. Initially, the pH may be about 11.0 to 11.5 Hypochlorite reacts with pulp to from organic acids and carbon dioxide which cause a reduction in pH. The decreasing pH results in poor control of the bleaching reaction and degradation of the cellulose. Final pH values may be as low as 6.0 to 7.0 In the low pH range of 6.0 to 7.0 hypochlorous acid activity is greatly increased. This apparently accounts for the undesirable reaction obtained in bleaching in this pH range.

Although hypochlorite solutions are usually prepared with an excess of alkali to maintain a pH above 11.0, this is not enough to react with the acids formed during bleaching. Since it is desirable to bleach at a pH level in which the active bleaching agent is hypochlorite rather than hypochlorous acid, additional alkali is added for buffering at the start of the reaction to maintain the desired final pH. The desired final pH may vary with the type of pulp being bleached, kraft or sulfite, and the position in the bleach stage that hypochlorite is used. In an early stage of kraft pulp bleaching, the pH may be as low as 8.0 it may be as low as 8.5 in sulfite. In the last stage of bleaching with hypochlorite, where the fibre is more open to attack, high pH is required and in some cases, it may be as high as 10.0. The effect of pH on brightness, viscosity and yellowing at constant hypochlorite consumption is illustrated in Fig. 4.

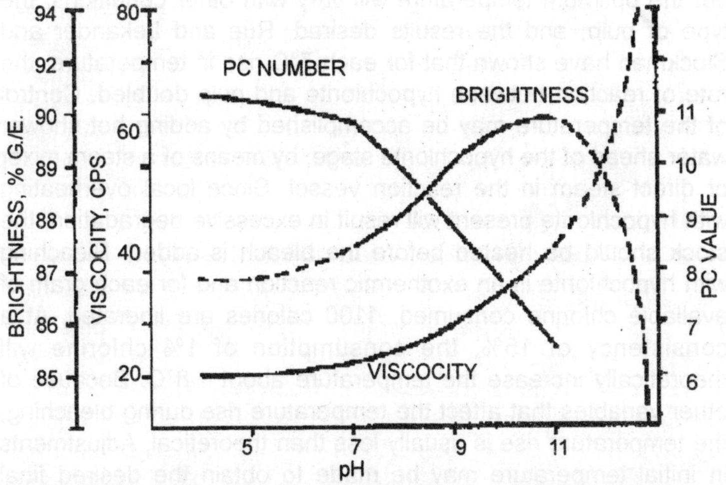

Fig. 4. Brightness, viscosity, and yellowing as influenced by pH of hyprochlorite bleaching of a paper pulp (Lekander-Stockman)

The formation of carbonyl or carboxyl groups in hypochlorite bleaching is primarily a function of pH. If sufficient alkalinity is used, most of the active chlorine will be present as hypochlorite, and the oxidized groups formed will be primarily stable carboxyls. If the pH is allowed to drop too low, hypochlorous acid becomes the active oxidant, and unstable carbonyl groups will be formed. This leads to excessive degradation and colour reversion. Too much alkalinity, however, at the start of the bleach will slow the reaction so that bleaching cannot be achieved in the time allowed. Ideally, the hypochlorite stage should be carried out at a constant pH to maintain a high rate with good control. However, no economical way to maintain a uniform pH throughout the reaction has been worked out. Attempts have been made in batch bleaching to add smal! amount of alkali throughout the bleach. This is intended to neutralize the acids as they are formed. Elaborate control of the process is required and the trend for continuous hypochlorite bleaching stages has greatly complicated the problems of adding alkali during the reaction.

Temperature

The second important variable in hypochlorite bleaching is

temperature. Bleaching temperatures may range from 30 to 60°C, but the optimum temperature will vary with other conditions, the type of pulp, and the results desired, Rue and Lekander and Stockman have shown that for each 7°C rise in temperature, the rate of reaction between hypochlorite and pulp doubled. Control of the temperature may be accomplished by adding hot shower water ahead of the hypochlorite stage, by means of a steam mixer or direct steam in the reaction vessel. Since local overheating with hypochlorite present will result in excessive degradation, the stock should be heated before the bleach is added. Bleaching with hypochlorite is an exothermic reaction and for each gram of available chlorine consumed, 1100 calories are liberated. At a consistency of 15%, the consumption of 1% chlorine will theoretically increase the temperature about 1.8°C. Because of other variables that affect the temperature rise during bleaching, the temperature rise is usually less than theoretical. Adjustments in initial temperature may be made to obtain the desired final temperature. The influence of temperature on the rate of reaction at various consistencies and on the constant charge of hypochlorite is shown in Fig. 5.

Like pH, too low a temperature slows the reaction down so that adequate bleaching is not achieved in the time allowed. If the temperature is too high, bleaching will be too fast and will be difficult to control. High temperature will also cause hypochlorous acid to give up oxygen more readily, thus reducing the bleaching efficiency by converting part of the hypochlorite to chlorate. Casey has suggested that the hypochlorite-stage temperature should be based on pulp consistency; the higher the consistency, the lower the temperature. The bleaching temperature should not exceed 40°C at 4 to 6% consistency, 38°C at 6 to 10% consistency, or 35°C at 10 to 16% consistency. For paper pulp, bleaching can be carried out at 45°C, and for viscose pulp at 50° C in order to shorten bleaching time without affecting pulp quality.

Hypochlorite concentration

The amount of hypochlorite liquor used for bleaching will depend on the chlorine demand of the pulp, the type of pulp being bleached, the desired brightness and strength required, and the position of the hypochlorite stage in the bleach sequence. In the early stage of a kraft pulp, hypochlorite addition may vary from

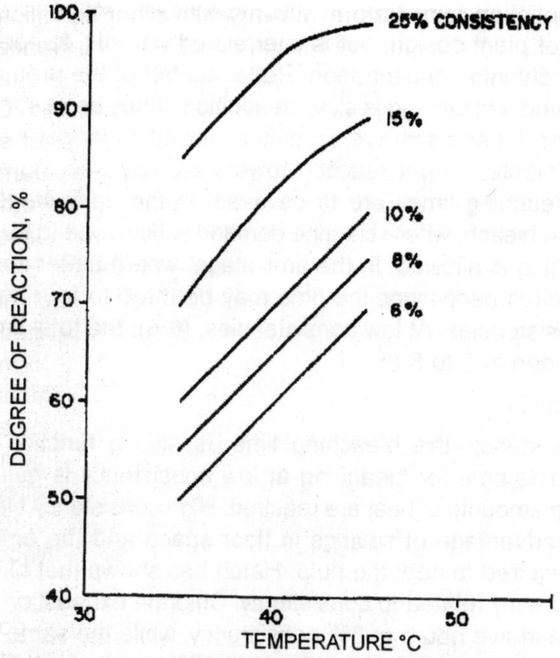

Fig. 5. Influence of temperature and consistency of the rate of hypochlorite bleaching. Constant change of 15 lbs/ton (Rydholm).

1.5 to 2.5% available chlorine. In the final stage of a multistage bleach or a sulphite bleach (where the state of purity is quite high), the hypochlorite addition may be as low as 0.5%, it seldom exceeds 1.5% available chlorine.

The rate of bleaching may be speeded up if the ratio of hypochlorite to pulp is increased, but this can result in poor control and over bleaching. Over bleaching will cause a serious loss in strength without a proportional increase in brightness. As bleaching progresses, the concentration of hypochlorite decreases and the bleaching reaction becomes very slow. For this reason, an excess of hypochlorite must be available at the end of the bleach, in order to maintain a driving force. At the end of an early bleach stage, this excess may be as high as 5 to 7 lb/ton of pulp, and at the end of a final stage, the excess may be as low as 1 to 1 lb/ton.

Time—Bleaching time in the hypochlorite stage is often a function of plant design, but is interrelated with pH, temperature, and hypochlorite concentration. Better control of the process can be achieved if bleaching is slow. In addition, it has been suggested that better dirt and shive removal is achieved by longer exposure to hypochlorite. Larger reaction towers are required, however, if longer bleaching times are to be used. In the early stages of a multistage bleach, where chlorine demand is high, one to two hours of bleaching is allowed. In the final stage, where better control of the bleach is necessary, the time may be three to four hours for high consistencies. At low consistencies, (6%), the total time may be extended to 5 to 8 hr.

Consistency

Consistency, like bleaching time, is also a function of mill design. The time for bleaching at low consistency is quite long, and large amounts of heat are required. High consistency bleaching has the advantage of savings in floor space and the amount of steam required to heat the pulp. Hatch has shown that bleaching time is directly related to consistency. Chlorine exhaustion is 90% complete in five hours at 3% consistency, while the same degree of exhaustion is complete in 45 min at 15% consistency. Too high a consistency however, may damage the fibre by mechanical action. This results in strength losses in the final pulp. The chance of overbleaching at high consistency is also greater (because of higher hypochlorite concentration) and bleaching may be less uniform than at low consistency.

Effect of hypochlorite on physical quality

Hypochlorite, when used as the sole bleaching agent or in a multistage bleach consisting of chlorine, alkali, and hypochlorite usually results in overbleaching the pulp, which has a degrading effect on pulp strength. An over-bleached pulp will generally have a high copper number, a high alkali solubility, and a low viscosity. Burst, fold, and tear will also be lower, and the pulp will hydrate more readily. Fairly good correlation has been established between viscosity and paper strength properties. Viscosity is often used in bleach plant control to note any changes in strength during bleaching. The viscosity-strength relationship will vary, however, depending on the type of pulp (kraft or sulphite) and the method of degradation. The relationship may not necessarily be used to predict the strength properties of an isolated sample.

With the demands today for high-brightness high-strength pulps for papermaking, the use of hypochlorite has diminished. Hypochlorite has been relegated to the intermediate stages where its degradative action is less pronounced. However, it is still difficult to produce a high-brightness clean pulp without hypochlorite, which, when used with other bleaching agents, is still quite effective.

6

Hydrosulfite Bleaching

BLEACHING OF PULPS WITH HYDROSULFITES

Practical interest in zinc hydrosulfite and sodium hydrosulfite as pulp bleaching agents or brighteners was noted as early as 1928. Limited commercial exploration was started around 1940, with the specific objective of raising the brightness of West Coast newsprint to equal that made in the East. Serious efforts to develop wider commercial application were begun in 1954. In recent years, applications have been developed for a variety of practical wood pulp bleaching purposes. These include bleaching of "grinder pulps", softwood "sawdust", and refiner groundwood, as well as the stripping of dyes from waste paper stocks and the improvement of the brightness levels of chemical fibres such as kraft, jute kraft and sulfite pulps. The major uses have been in the filed of mechanical pulp brightening where one of the principal advantages of the hydro-sulfites (the fact that they do not significantly affect the pulp yield) is of great importance.

Forms of Hydrosulfites Commercially Available

Both sodium hydrosulfite and zinc hydrosulfites are available as granular powders. The assay of the sodium salt is approximately 94%, the assay of the zinc salt is about 85%. Blends of sodium hydrosulfite with chelating agents, primarily sodium tripolyphosphate, are also available. Their use is beneficial under circumstances where a sequestering action on heavy metal ions, iron and copper in particular, is important.

Although hydrosulfites can be applied to pulp slurries in powder from the use of freshly prepared solution of one to five % concentration is preferable. More rapid distribution of the hydrosulfite into the pulp slurry is obtained when the agent is predissolved, and the possibility of decomposition in pockets of the moistened solid, which become acidic, is avoided.

Instead of making solutions by dissolving one of the commercial hydrosulfites, zinc hydrosulfite solutions can be prepared on the site of use, by digesting zinc dust in sulfurous acid. Solutions of approximately 5 to 8% concentrations are prepared and used either immediately, or after limited storage. Zinc efficiencies of 89% have been reported, with most of the yield loss being a result of zinc dust carry-over with the solution. For the generation of a satisfactory solution, it is necessary that considerable care be exercised in the control of pH and concentration.

Sodium hydrosulfite can also be generated by reacting sodium borohydride and bisulfite in accordance with the reaction :

$$NaBH_4 + 8\ NaHSO_3 \rightarrow NaBO_2 + 6\ H_2O + Na_2S_2O_4$$

The proper adjustment of pH, preferably at about 6.0 and the proper ratio of borohydride to sulfur dioxide and/or bisulfite are important for the efficient reduction of the bisulfite to hydrosulfite.6 This reaction can be carried out either in solution immediately prior to injection into the pulp, or *in situ*, i.e., in the presence of the pulp.

Calcium hydrosulfite, prepared by digesting iron powder with sulfur dioxide and precipitating the iron with calcium, added as lime, has recently been suggested as an agent for reductive bleaching. Under typical bleaching conditions, calcium hydrosulfite was reported to give slightly better bleaching responses than equivalent amounts of zinc hydrosulfite.

CHEMISTRY OF HYDROSULFITE BLEACHING

Bleaching Reactions

Although a large amount of work has been done on the structure and behaviour of hydrosulfites, their reactions with the colour bodies of wood pulps have not been fully clarified. However, there is little doubt but that some of the reactions involve the reduction of quinoid colour structures. These reactions are comparable to the reduction of vat dyes similar in structure to indigo. Hydrosulfites may contribute to the brightening of pulps by the reduction of soluble forms of the flavones and the reduction of flavylium salts, as well as the dissolution of chalcones to form colourless solutions.The hydrosulfites irreversibly reduce chromophoric azo groups that occur in many paper dyes. About 98% of the direct dyes used in tinted stocks can be stripped completely.

Hydrosulfite Decomposition Reaction

An understanding of the conditions leading to the maximum reducing power and efficient use of hydrosulfites is essential to their economic use. Of primary concern is the reaction of zinc hydrosulfite or sodium hydrosulfite solutions with oxygen, in which case, sodium bisulfite and sodium bisulfate results :

$$Na_2S_2O_4 + O_2 + H_2O \rightarrow NaHSO_4 + NaHSO_3$$

The reaction is extremely rapid, and from a practical standpoint, is limited only by the rate of diffusion of the oxygen into the solution. It is believed that the 20% or so of the hydrosulfite not decomposed in the above reaction forms an isomer of sulfoxylic acid, which in turn is slowly oxidized to the sulfite. The sodium bisulfate formed generates an acid condition leading to complex hydrosulfite decomposition reactions.

Probably the second most significant hydrosulfite decomposition reaction is the auto-oxidation-reduction of the hydrosulfite, which results in the formation of bisulfite and thiouslfate. The reaction increases rapidly as the pH is lowered below 7.0.

$$2Na_2S_2O_4 + H_2O \rightarrow 2NaHSO_3 + Na_2S_2O_3$$

This may be the end result of two effects in which bisulfite and sulfoxylate are formed, the latter in turn forms thiosulfate :

$$2Na_2S_2O_4 + 2H_2O \rightarrow 2\,NaHSO_3 + NaHSO_2$$

$$2\,NaHSO_2 \rightarrow Na_2S_2O_3 + H_2O$$

Under acidic conditions, the decomposition of hydrosulfite is further complicated by reactions leading to polythionic acids and colloidal sulfur. The sulfur reaction may follow the sequence indicated:

$$2\ Na_2S_2O_4 + H_2O \rightarrow S + 2\ NaHSO_3 + Na_2SO_3$$

Hydrogen sulfide precipitated as zinc sulfide has been noted as a decomposition product of zinc hydrosulfite. However, hydrogen sulfide could not be found analytically in decomposition studies with sodium hydrosulfite, although its presence is apparently detectable by odor.

At 140°F, the critical pH levels below which hydrosulfites are rapidly decomposed in the absence or pulp are 5.0 for sodium hydrosulfite and 4.0 for zinc hydrosulfite. Thus the zinc salt is the more stable of the two in acid systems. Hydrosulfites are reported to be more stable in the presence of pulp than in plain water solutions.

Practical Importance of Decomposition

It has been reported that small amounts of oxygen have a disproportionately large effect in reducing the brightness gains in bleaching. Whereas normal bleaching conditions resulted in brightness gains of 9 to 10 points with mechanical pulps, 12 points were possible by taking special precautions to eliminate oxygen completely from the system.

Further practical studies have shown that pulps are bleached best with hydrosulfites in a slightly acid medium. This closely approaches the pH of greatly increased hydrosulfite instability. The proper control of pH, the avoidance of excessive exposure to air, and the elimination of entrained air in pulp are obviously important in the successful application of hydrosulfites.

7

Peroxide Bleaching

INTRODUCTION

Hydrogen peroxide and sodium peroxide are recognized as effective and economical bleaching agents in many fields. Unlike chlorine type oxidants, they do not form chlorinated organic derivatives requiring removal and disposal. The peroxides are particularly useful in the bleaching of high-lignin wood pulps and as a final stage in chemical pulp bleaching.

THE CHEMISTRY OF PEROXIDE BLEACHING

The chemistry involved in pulp bleaching with peroxide is quite similar in every application, although the specific conditions for using peroxides will very with the type of pulp to be bleached.

The two peroxides used in pulp bleaching are hydrogen peroxide and sodium peroxide, or combinations of these two products. In solution, these two chemicals are equivalent providing suitable alkalinity adjustments are made. The ionization of each peroxide is shown below:

$$H_2O_2 + 2NaOH \rightarrow 2Na^+ + OOH^- + H_2O$$

$$Na_2O_2 + H_2O \rightarrow 2Na + OOH^- + OH^-$$

In actual use, the selection of the peroxide will depend upon the alkalinity required. This is discussed further in subsequent sections of commercial bleaching of the various types of pulp.

In peroxide bleaching systems, two simultaneous reactions compete for the available peroxide, as shown in the following three equations :

$$H_2O_2 + NaOH \longrightarrow Na^+ + H_2O + OOH^- \quad (1)$$

$$OOH + Colour \longrightarrow Oxidized\ Color + OH^- \quad (2)$$

$$2H_2O_2 \xrightarrow{catalyst} 2H_2O + O_2 \quad (3)$$

Equations one and two illustrate the generally accepted theory that it is the perhydroxyl ion that does the bleaching by solubilizing and decolourizing the impurities in the lignin and in the cellulose. Increasing the alkalinity in (1) will increase the concentration of the active bleaching agent, the perhydroxyl ion. Therefore, increasing the alkalinity will increase the rate of peroxide bleaching. However, because increased alkalinity will also lead to increased peroxide decomposition, practical conditions must be selected to give the best balance between these two effects. A similar balance exists for bleaching temperature, because higher temperatures accelerate both bleaching and decomposition. The optimum temperature must be determined for each pulp. Groundwood can not be bleached above 150 to160°F, without a sacrifice in brightness, while kraft can be bleached most advantageously, at 160 to 180°F.

Equation three represents the decomposition or peroxide, which is catalyzed primarily by compounds of heavy metals such as iron, cooper, nickel and manganese or by the enzyme, cafalase, which is the product to abnormal bacterial growth in the pulp. The fraction of the peroxide that enters into this reaction is not available for bleaching.

It becomes obvious from (1), (2), and (3) that to obtain maximum bleaching effectiveness from a peroxide solution, it is necessary to insure adequate control of each type of reaction. Steps to insure good bleaching results require:

(1) Prevention of contamination by metallic impurities or by enzyme catalysis (the latter occurs more often with mechanical pulps).

(2) Addition of chemical stabilizers or chemical pretreatments that will inactivate the decomposition catalysts.

Sodium silicate is the best stabilizer for the peroxide solution for pulp bleaching. Other nonsilicate types of stabilizers have been tried, but none is as effective as sodium silicate. In certain spray-type applications of peroxide to pulp webs (where silicate in the solution would be undersirable), the peroxide is stabilized with sodium tripolyphosphate or tetrasodium pyrophosphate, but there is a sacrifice in bleaching efficiency. Sodium silicate stabilization for maximum effect depends upon the presence of calcium and/or magnesium ions in the pulp system, in a concentration equivalent to about 50 ppm as $CaCO_3$ or $MgCO_3$. In normal operation the mill's fresh water supplies the calcium or magnesium ions to form a colloidal precipitate of calcium or magnesium silicate that deactivates the metallic ions.

In some pulp bleaching laboratories where distilled water or deionized water was used for all pulp washing operations, it was found that the addition of 50 ppm of $CaCl_2$ to the pulp (prior to thickening for peroxide bleaching) resulted in greatly improved pulp brightness response from the peroxide stage. In mill operation, it has been shown that alkaline peroxide solutions (without silicate stabilizer) when passed through a pulp-seam mixer, emerged with up to 35% reduction in peroxygen content, whereas the same solution, with the addition of sodium silicate, came through the steam mixer with a peroxide loss of only about 5%. These laboratory and mill experiences prove the need for sodium silicate pulps an adequate calcium-magnesium content in the pulp for optimum stabilization of the peroxide solution.

The rate of bleaching increases as the consistency increases over the range of 5 to 30%. As decomposition takes place throughout the reaction mixture, its rate is not accelerated by increasing consistency. Therefore peroxide bleaching efficiency increases with increasing consistency. In most cases, it is inefficient to bleach below 8% consistency; above 20% the improvement in bleached pulp brightness is small, but the chemical cost for bleaching to normal levels can be reduced by about 10 to 20%.

8

Beating and Refining Action Upon Fibres

Before sheet tormation, the water suspension of pulp is subjected to mechanical treatment that causes both a bruising and internal loosening of the fibre, as well as a cutting action. These actions occur at the same time, and predominant one depends on the characteristics of the equipment, on the conditions of beating, and on the properties of the pulp fibres.

The description or beating and refining equipment is outside the scope of this article which is limited to the response of the fibre to mechanical action and to the fibre properties affecting paper properties made therefrom.

The changes effected by beating occur mainly in the cross-wide structure of the fibre. Since the properties of fibres are measured more easily and more accurately in the longitudinal direction, most of the data on fibres are concerned mostly with the effects of stresses applied in the longitudinal direction, there is only incomplete information of the effect of stresses applied in the cross-direction of the fibre.

In order to study the phenomena taking place during beating the following two cases are examined :

(1) When the process is carried out with dry fibres of with fibres dispersed in a liquid that is non-swelling toward them, e.g. aromatic or aliphatic hydrocarbons.

(2) When the fibres are processed in water or other liquids capable of swelling the fibres.

DRY MILLING

The milling of dry fibres shows that a repeated crushing action, like that obtained in a "vibrating ball mill", causes a breakdwon of fibres, a decreased degree of polymerization (DP, and a widening of the diffraction spots in the X-ray ptterns, tending to convert the spots into haloes like that given by amorphous materials.

The failures occur in the weakest points of fibres, and the fibres fail when stressed in tension. The points of failure are located in those regions in which the structure is discontinuous, or where there are void spaces. These can be observed by the presence of bordered pits, by microscopical pits aligned in crossdirection, by nodes (which are particularly evident in Liberian fibres), and by reversal regions in the spiralling fibrils (cotton).

The decreased DP shows that failures occur also at a macromolecular scale.

The failure occurring in microfibrils probably corresponds to some organization irregularities of the cellulose polymer, in its longitudinal direction as observed in the electron microscope after treatment of the fibre with silver nitrate.

It can also be assumed that these correspond to "paracrystalline" distortions, which (according to Hosemann) represent in paracrystals in intermediate condition between solid and liquid.

Following this hypothesis, the widening of diffraction spots would be due to a comminution of the so-called crystalline regions into very small crystals, as happens in the extensive milling of some inorganic crystalline substances.

WET MILLING

When fibres are similarly milled in the presence of water, the same phenomena take place, but to a much lesser extent.

When pulp is beaten in a vibratory ball mill with various liquids (benzene, metanol water). Leopold has calculated that degradation in benzene is from 10 to 20 times larger than in water, and that the degradation in methanol is intermediate, but nearer that obtained in water than in benzene. He ascribes the different behaviour to the different plasticizing action developed on fibres by the liquids used.

The penetration of water into the regions with a lower lateral order may cause an increase in strength in the longitudinal direction, and a lateral "loosening" of the structure elements in the areas that are accessible to water.

The strength changes observed from water swelling are different from those observed in dry milling. In dry milling, the failures occur in an indiscriminate way, both in the longitudinal and cross-directions, whereas in the milling of wet fibres, the stresses tend to concentrate in the direction having a smaller strength, i.e. in the cross-direction.

PHENOMENA EVIDENT DURING "BEATING"

Under the conditions, and within the limits, of the "beating" process, phenomena occur similar to those observed in the milling of fibres in a "vibratory ball mill" in the presence of water, however, the phenomena occur to a smaller extent, because of the lower intensity of the mechanical action.

Decreased polymerization and crystallinity of the fibres occur only after intense "beating" action.

The predominant effect of "beating", kin normal papermaking processes is limited to shortening of the fibres and "loosening" of those regions of the fibre structure responsible for lateral cohesion.

Many discussions have taken place as to whether the development of the "paper making properties" of beaten fibres is to be ascribed to the "fibrillation" of the fibre outer layer or to an "internal fibrillation".

In the course of a meeting organized by TAPPI at Portland, Oregon, the current theories about evaluation of the paper pulps during beating were discussed. The different points of view gathered round two theories, which Clark called, in a very meaningful way, "boiled macaroni theory" and "fuzzy fibrillar theory".

By examining the pros and cons of the two theories, it becomes apparent that the changes brought about by beating in the fibre structure (in order to transform it into a network resembling a "boiled macaroni" or a body provided with "external fuzz") are two ways in which the same mechanism engages the outer and inner layers of fibres.

It is the loosening of the bonds that keep the different elements laterally joined together, these elements from the complex architecture of the fibrous network and they are described in the article by McIntosh.

The bonds can consist of hydrogen bridges or of molecular fringes that join microfibrils and fibrils together (according to Hearle's theory of fringed fibrils). The bonds can also consist of microfibrils which, deviating from their normal direction, could pass from one concentric layer of the fibre to the next.

The swelling action of water is due to the expansion of the spaces existing between the concentric lamellae, between the fibrils composing the fibres, and maybe between the microfibrils themselves. The swelling occurs as a consequence of the substitution of hydrogen bridges between cellulose macro-molecules with intruded water molecules.

In the expanded regions, there are still connections between fibrils (molecular fringes), and between concentric layers in the fibres. These connections can be broken by bruising or crushing action.

If the regions with lower cohesion are mainly located in the outer layer, the effect of beating favours surface splitting and the formation of external fibrillation of "fuzz". The effect on the inside layers of the fibres envolves an internal loosening of the network, i.e., what Campbell calls an "internal fibrillation." The fibre becomes more flexible and plastic, and it may be compared to a "boiled macaroni".

The present trend is to consider the loosening of the concentric layers of the fibre to be the most important effect, and Emerton has put forward this hypohthesis in speculating on the beating and refining effect of the pulp on the paper properries. He suggests that strength increase from beating depends on increases of fibre flexibility and plasticity during beating. After formation, pressing, and drying, this results in increased interfiber bonding and a denser and more transparent sheet.

Page and De Grace have recently shown an elegant microscopic demonstration of the delamination of beaten fibres. Also MicIntosh has observed swollen cross sections of beaten and unbeaten fibres, and finds subdivided concentric lamellae in the beaten fibres.

The beating process also causes the separation of the fragments of the primary wall and the breakdown of some fibre segments at the original weaker points in the structure. These points were previously weakened by cooking and bleaching treatments.

The formation of "fines" is to be ascribed to the separation and breakdown of fibres into shorter pieces. This latter effect can be increased by modifying the shape and the hardness of the beater bars.

9

Consistency Control

INTRODUCTION

One of the most important process variables in the pulp and paper industry is consistency of pulp and paper stock. Consistency is measured and regulated in practically every phase of the process to achieve uniform operation. In pulp manufacturing, consistency control is used in such areas as :

(1) Continuous digesters.

(2) Screening.

(3) Brown stock washing.

(4) Bleach plants.

In paper mill operations, it is applied in :

(1) Refining.

(2) Stock blending.

(3) Repulping.

(4) Save-all operations.

(5) Wet end of the paper machine.

"Consistency" is defined as the percentage, by weight, of dry fibrous material in any combination of pulp and water or stock (pulp and additives) and water. It is calculated by the following formula :

$$C = \frac{F}{W} \times 100$$

where C = the consistency of pulp or stock slurry expressed in percent.

W = the total weight of a particular amount of pulp or stock slurry, and

F = the weight of fibrous material in that amount of pulp or stock slurry.

Basic determination of consistency is a laboratory procedure. A measured sample of slurry is weighed the total solids are separated, dried and weighted, and the weight of fibrous material is then expressed as a percentage of the measured sample. Consistencies of less than 1% are usually considered low, those greater than 6% high. Most development of consistency control has been in ranges between these two values.

MEASUREMENT AND CONTROL

The laboratory method of spot checking consistency provides a rough guide to the addition of dilution water to achieve some degree of regulation. However, it is impossible to use this approach when consistency is changing continuously, and regulation must be based on a continuous measurement of consistency.

To date, it has been impossible to achieve direct absolute measurement of consistency on a continuous basis. Equipment available today measures various characteristics of a fibre-water suspension and relates these characteristics to consistency. This inferred consistency measurement is also affected to a degree by other variables, such as velocity of stock flow type of stock, freeness, wetness, temperature, pressure, history of the treatment of the stock type of fibres used, and broke addition. Therefore, continuous consistency devices are designed to selectively measure a characteristic that is closely related to fibre content and not greatly affected by other variables over acceptable limited spans.

These limitations have not prevented the wide-spread use of this general approach as the measurement for consistency control in the pulp and paper industry. The ability of sensing variations in consistency sufficiently satisfies the requirements, and accurate measurement of the absolute value is not as important as in other control applications. Therefore, consistency measuring and control equipment has traditionally and technically been closely related, i.e., always considered as a system and never as separate functions when applied to the process. The first continuous measuring devices developed were usually "blind" and did not even indicate the variable. The systems were little more than mechanical self-operated dilution equipment. They were directly connected to a float or some other positioning device (detecting changes in forces derived from flow, level, or other phenomenal) to control addition of dilution water.

These units were commonly referred to as "consistency regulators", and today's consistency transmitters are often referred to as "regulators", even, though they cannot actually do any regulating until incorporated in a loop with a controller and dilution valve.

Although directly connected devices are still available and a few are still in use in some mills today, new installations of this type are non-existent. The advent of modern control concepts, the trend toward centralized control centers, and the requirement to record measurement and dilution valve action have made the transmission system the most popular method used today.

10

Sizing of Paper

INTRODUCTION

The term "sizing" has sometimes been applied so broadly to paper mill processes as to indicate the addition of almost any chemical agent designed to modify the properties of the paper product. In modern usage, however, the meaning of this word is much more precise and limiting. Sizing is now defined as the process in which a chemical additive provides paper and paperboard with resistance to wetting and penetration, usually by aqueous liquids. Thus, sizing produces water repelency. This definition excludes the addition of materials (e.g., surface coatings of hydrophilic polymers) that are designed to produce other effects.

Cellulose is a very hydrophilic (water-loving) substance, and pulp fibre surfaces have a high specific energy. Thus, water readily wets these surfaces. The very porous structure of paper makes it act like a sponge in the presence of liquids. In particular, unsized (waterleaf) paper soaks up or "wicks" aqueous very rapidly and extensively. Various sizing agents have been developed to make paper reasonably water repellent. These additives provide paper with considerable resistance to wetting and penetration by liquids such as ink, water, and milk, thus leading to a product that can be used as writing paper, a water-resistant wrapping or a milk carton.

When an aqueous liquid is placed on the surface of paper, it must first wet the fibres, after which it is drawn into the sheet structure by the capillary action of the pores or spaces between adjacent fibres. In addition, the liquid tends to spread out on the surface of the paper in a process called "feathering". Liquid can also penetrate into the paper and along its surface by paths through the cellulose material itself. It is generally believed that liquid flows initially through the pores between fibres (transudation) and eventually penetrates through the cellulose material, although results obtained from certain sizing tests suggest the reverse of this sequence of envents. The rate of flow of a liquid through a very thin tube or capillary is generally represented by the Washburn equation which combines the equation representing fluid rise in a capillary tube with the Poiseuille equation for laminar flow through a tube :

$$dl/dt = (Pr^2 + 2r\,\gamma \cos \theta)/8\eta l$$

where *l* is the length of capillary filled with liquid; *r* is the capillary radius; *P* is the external pressure; γ is the surface tension of the liquid' θ is the contact angle between the liquid and the capillary wall; and η is the viscosity of the liquid. In the absence of any appreciable external pressure, the contact angle determines the driving force for liquid penetration into the paper structure. A high contact angle reduces this driving force, and for angles greater than 90°, a force resisting penetration and feathering is established. It should be noted that a rough surface can affect the apparent contact angle. In particular, a very large increase in apparent contact angle is achieved by a substrate having regularly spaced air gaps that produce the so-called "duck's back effect".

Regardless of the structure of the paper, a sizing agent should make fibre surfaces hydrophobic (water repelling) so that the contact angle with aqueous liquids will be very high. Thus, any effective sizing agent for paper must either be a hydrophobic substance or contain a hydrophobic substituent group. In the latter case, the sizing molecules must become oriented on the cellulose substrate so that the hydrophobic groups provide the eventual exposed surface. Further more the sizing agent should be applied in such a way as to become strongly attached to the fibre surfaces, so that it cannot easily be dislodged by a liquid penetrant. Finally, the sizing material should be well distributed over the fibre surface. Complete monolayer coverage of these surfaces would provide maximum sizing, but less than complete coverage is often sufficient to produce a high contact angle between a liquid and the substrate.

Papermakers use many different chemical additives to provide paper products with varying degrees of water repellency. The results of a survey of paper mills in the United States projected the 1960 consumption of sizing materials as follows :

	Tons
Rosin size	151,000
Risub (for making size)	11,000
Paraffin waxes	63,000
Wax derivatives	14,000
Wax emulsions	18.000
Asphalt emulsions	10,000
Synthetic sizing agents	8,000

The synthetic sizing agents include hydrocarbon resins, various polymers, and chemically reactive materials.

The introduction of sizing agents into the papermaking process is accomplished either by internal addition or by surface sizing. Internal addition involves adding the size to an aqueous pulp slurry at some point between the beater and the wet end of the paper machine. Materials designed for internal addition must, therefore, be water dispersible. Many sizing agents are sold to papermakers as aqueous solutions, emulsions, or suspensions. Other agents are sold in sold from, but can easily be dispersed in water just before use. Surface sizing involves addition of the agent to the formed sheet of paper or board, usually at some stage in the drying process. While internal sizing provides paper with water repellency throughout its structure, surface sizing principally modifies the surfaces of the sheet. Surface sizing agents are usually added by roll application at the size press or calender stack.

ROSIN SIZING PROCESS

The rosin sizing process was first introduced by Moritz Illing in 1807 and has since gained universal acceptance. As suggested above by the huge consumption of rosin and rosin size by the American paper industry, rosin is the primary sizing material used today throughout the world. This sizing process is cheap, reliable, and reasonably effective. It involves the internal addition of partially or completely saponified (neutralized) rosin, called "rosin size". Papermaker's alum (aluminum sulfate) is added as a co-reactant to produce rosin size precipitate *in situ*, and this precipitate becomes the actual sizing agent in the dried sheet.

Materials Used

The three main types of rosin are designated as gum rosin, wood rosin, and tall oil rosin. Modern refining processes have made them essentially equivalent from the viewpoint of sizing efficiency. Worldwide production of rosin is currently about two billion pounds per year. Half of this, mostly as gum rosin, is produced by countries other than the United States. Russia, China and Portugal are the leading foreign producers of gum rosin, while tall oil rosin is produced by several northern European countries. The largest use for rosin is as sizing agent in paper products.

In the United States, gum rosin is obtained by tapping several varieties of pine tress that grow in the Southeastern states. The collected pine sap or oleoresin is then steam distilled to remove the more volatile components, especially turpentine, from the gum rosin. Wood rosin is produced almost exclusively in this country. The mature, aged stumps of pine trees are chipped and then extracted with solvent to remove a mixture leads to a dark coloured crude rosin. Further refining of the crude product yields a lighter colored "pale" rosin. Dark rosin is used in unbleached paper and board where its colour is not objectionable, while pale wood rosin serves to size paper made from bleached pulp. Tall oil rosin is a by-product of the kraft (sulfate pulping process. Tall oil skimmings, removed from the spent liquor of the kraft cooking of softwood, contain varying amounts of fatty acid resin acid salts, together with some unsaponifiable materials. Fractional distillation of the acidified mixture permits separation of the rosin and fatty acid constituents.

For many years, gum rosin was the chief source of rosin size. In the United States, however, wood rosin has risen to challenge the utility of gum rosin in many fields, during the last 40 years. Gum rosin production is now on the decline in this country, primarily because of the high labour cost. During the last 15 years, tall oil rosin has shown a spectacular rise in production that correlates with the rapid growth of kraft pulping of Southern pine trees. Although the supply of pine stumps seems adequate to insure the availability of wood rosin for many years, the constantly increasing supply of tall oil suggests that tall oil rosin may soon become the primary ingredient in the rosin size used by American paper mills.

Commercial rosin is a glassy, amorphous material that softens at temperatures between 75 and 95°C. It consists primarily of several different monocarboxylic resin acids of alkylated hydrophenanthrene having the empirical formula $C_{19}H_{(27\ to\ 33)}$ COOH. The resin acids are divided into two general structural types, abietic and pimaric, which are illustrated in Fig. 1.These acids have varying degrees of unsaturation and chemical reactivity. Their carboxyl substituents are sterically hindered so that they are considerably weaker ($K_a = 10^{-6}$) than acetic acid. The bulky hydrocarbon portion of a resin acid provides considerable shielding of the relatively small polar carboxyl group. Thus, can serve as a very effective hydrophobic coating for surfaces. Resin acids are very soluble in most organic solvent, but essentially insoluble in water; this latter property further reduces their apparent acid strength. The resin acid component in rosin accounts for about 90% of the total material (60% in the case of dark wood rosin). The remainder consists of neutrals such as resinous alcohols, esters, ketones, fatty compounds, and various hydrocarbons.

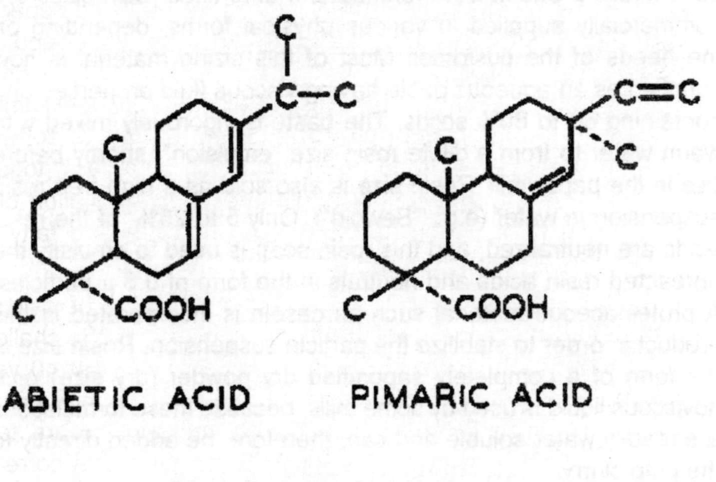

Fig. 1. Typical resin acid structures

Industrial suppliers of products based on rosin have introduced various chemical and physical modification to improve such important properties as rosin softening point, resistance to oxidation, and colour. In particular, rosin has been modified to improve the stability, handleability, and sizing efficiency of aqueous rosin size dispersions.

During the last 25 years, various chemical suppliers have developed fortified rosin sizes by incorporating a certain amount of the maleic anhydride or fumaric acid adduct of rosin in their products. This fortifier ingredient is produced by heating a mixture of rosin and maleic anhydride or famaric acid at 150 to 200°C. The levopimaric acid constituent of rosin forms a maleic or fumaric adduct which contains three acid carboxyl groups per molecule. Continued heating causes isomerization of the abietic-type acids in the rosin and thus supplies further levopimaric acid for the adduction reaction. Commercial fortified rosin sizes (e.g., "Pexol", "Mersize" and "Cyfor") are considerably more efficient sizing agents than the unfortified material, especially in certain hard-to-size systems.

Rosin size is prepared by reacting rosin with aqueous alkali. The degree of neutralization of the resin acids is varied from 5% to 100% depending on the physical state desired for the commercial product. Both fortified and unfortified rosin sizes are commercially supplied in various physical forms, depending on the needs of the customer. Most of this sizing material is now supplied as an aqueous paste having viscous fluid properties and containing 60 to 80% solids. The paste is vigorously mixed with warm water to from a dilute rosin size "emulsion", shortly before use in the paper mill. Rosin size is also sold as a high free rosin suspension in water (e.g., "Bewoid"). Only 5 to 25% of the resin acids are neutralized, and this rosin soap is used to emulsify the unreacted resin acids and neutrals in the form of 0.5 μ particles. A proteinaceous material such as casein is incorporated in this product in order to stabilize the particle suspension. Rosin size in the form of a completely saponified dry powder (dry size) or a noviscous liquid is used by some mills, because these formulations are readily water soluble and can, therefore, be added directly to the pulp slurry.

As indicated by the sizing agent consumption figures, some mills purchase rosin itself for eventual conversion to rosin size. About 7% of all rosin size consumed in the United States in millmade. Some of this material is prepared by the Delthirna process, which involves trickling aqueous alkali over crushed rosin. The resulting effluent is a completely saponified rosin size solution.

It is interesting that although rosin size is currently supplied in various physical forms(achieved by various commercial processes), all of these products perform with reasonable effectiveness in the sizing of paper. However, special environmental conditions in a particular mill's papermaking system may suggest or require the use of one of another of the various chemical modifications or physical states of rosin size (i.e., dry powder, paste, or aqueous suspension) for best results.

The rosin sizing process involves the separate addition of rosin size and alum, both as aqueous dispersions to a wood pulp slurry. Beater addition of either co-reactant is generally permissible. Addition of both chemical agents before the final pulp refining stage is not advisable, however, because fresh cellulose surfaces subsequently exposed may not become properly size. It is desirable to add the size and alum at a sufficiently early stage to provide for their uniform distribution in the pulp slurry, as well as adequate time for formation of the size precipitate. Although the addition of size, followed by alum, is the usual procedure, reversed order of addition may give better results in certain paper-making systems.

Ionic Mechanism of Precipitation

An aqueous dispersion of rosin size consists of suspended particles 0.1 to 0.5 μ in diameter, soap micelles perhaps 50 Å in diameter, and individual resinate ions. The pH of this system ranges from 8.0 to 9.5 depending on the concentration of the dispersion. Less than 1% hydrolysis of resinate ions is required to produce this degree of alkalinity. If the resin acids are completely neutralized, the suspended particles are composed almost entirely of rosin neutrals. With partial neutralization, free resin acids will also be present in these suspended particles. The particles are stabilized by a surface monolayer of resinate ions representing perhaps 2% of the total rosin size. The critical micelle concentration (cmc) for resin acids is about 0.5%. Below the cmc, as in the usual sizing process, only suspended particles and individual ions will be present.

Papermaker's alum, $Al_2(SO_4)_3 \cdot 18H_2O$, in distilled water dissociates into sulfate ions and hexahydraed, trivalent aluminum ions that then undergo three successive hydrolysis steps as represented by the following equilibria:

$$[Al(H_2O)_6]^{+3} + H_2O \rightleftharpoons [Al(OH)(H_2O)_5] + 2 + H_3O^{+1}$$

$$[Al(OH)(H_2O)_3]^{+2} + H_2O \rightleftharpoons [Al(OH)_2(H_2O)_4]^{+1} + H_3O^{+1}$$

$$[Al(OH)_2(H_2O)_4]^{+1} + H_2O \rightleftharpoons [Al(OH)_3(H_2O)_3] + H_3O^{+1}$$

The increase of acidity produced by these reactions limits the degree of hydrolysis of an alum solution. The resulting pH depends on the solution concentration. For example, a 10% alum solution has a pH of 2.5 to 3.0 as the result of less than 1% first-step hydrolysis. A 2.5% pulp slurry in distilled water, alumed to a pH of 4.5 represents a system involving perhaps 20% first-step hydrolysis. Thus, most of the aluminum in a distilled water system is in the unhydrolyzed, trivalent form. The system is highly buffered by the equilibria listed above and also by the extent to which the sulfate ion may complex with trivalent aluminum and inactivate this species :

$$[Al(H_2O)_6]^{+3} + SO_4^{-2} \rightleftharpoons [Al(SO_4)(H_2O)_4]^{+1} + 2H_2O$$

An alumed system, therefore, contains a small amount of active acidity (as represented by its pH) and a large reserve of potential acidity that is represented by the various species of incompletely hydrolyzed aluminum ions.

The precipitation of completely saponified rosin size by alum in a dilute distilled water system proceeds by the simple interaction of cationic and anionic species. According to Davision's hypothesis, the first step in this process probably involves the abstraction of a proton from the hexahydrated, trivalent aluminum ion by a resinate ion to form a molecule of resin acid and a divalent aluminum ion :

$$[Al(H_2O)_6]^{+3} + R^{-1} \rightleftharpoons Al(OH)(H_2O)_3]^{+2} + HR$$

As noted by Taube, the attachment of one hydroxyl group to aluminum reduces the binding of the remaining coordinated water molecules so that two of these can be replaced by resinate ions, thus forming a hydrated molecule of aluminum diresinate monohydroxide:

$$[Al(OH)(H_2O)_5]^{+2} + 2R^{-1} \rightleftharpoons [Al(R)_2(OH)(H_2O)_3] + 2H_2O$$

Other ionic paths of reaction would lead to the same two ultimate products, aluminum diresinate and resin acid. Since both of these molecules are very insoluble in water, they aggregate rapidly to form size precipitate particles. The suspended particles of neutrals are also precipitated by the reaction of aluminum ions with resinate ion attached to the particle surfaces.

Nature of the Precipitate

The bulk analysis of the precipitate formed from completely saponified rosin size in distilled water indicates the presence of all the neutrals, plus approximately three resinate groups per aluminum atom. The complete initial solubility of this size precipitate in benzene demonstrate the absence of aluminum hydroxide as an independent molecular species. Chemical analysis and solvent extraction work have suggested that this size precipitate is an equimolar mixture of free resin acids and aluminum diresinate. Recent infrared and thermal-pyrolysis data revealed the presence of 1.2 molecules of free resin acid, leaving a calculated 1.9 resinate groups associated with each aluminum atom in the precipitate. These results and others appear to support the suggestion that size precipitate contains resin acids and aluminum diresinate in an approximately 1:1 molar ratio, but with some hydrolysis giving less than two resinate groups per aluminum.

When rosin size is precipitated in water containing various common impurities such as hardness (calcium ions) or alkalinity (bicarbonae or hydroxyl ions), the precipitate composition reveals environmental effects that are easily interpreted by the ionic mechanism of precipitation. Thus, the addition of soluble calcium to a completely saponified rosin size solution formed a precipitate consisting largely of calcium diresinate and very little free acids. Subsequent addition of alum caused partial replacement of the calcium by aluminum in the salt component but did not increase the free acid content of the precipitate. Similarly, the presence of alkalinity in a rosin size solution resulted in a very low free acid content in the precipitate that formed when alum was added, and the salt component contained from 0.8 to 1.9 resinate groups per aluminum atom, depending inversely on the amount of alkalinity in the system. Finally, the use of an alum-sulfuric acid mixture as the precipitant led to a product containing a very high free-acid content.

The correlations indicated above between chemical environment and precipitate composition suggest that the products formed may depend on the initial ratios of the reactants. A similar observation was made by Guide during his study of size precipitates formed by the addition of perchloric acid to an aqueous solution containing both sodium abietate and sodium aluminate invarying proportions. Selective solvent extraction revealed to Guide that none of his products were stoichiometric compounds; instead, they contained varying amounts of free acid and an aluminum salt. Guide postulated the concept of aluminum hydroxide polymer-ization by means of hydroxyl bridging (olation) to include aluminum mono and di-abietate units in similar polymer chains. Thus the was able to account for a complete spectrum of size precipitate compositions, depending on the initial ratio of reactants and the degree of polymerization, DP.

It is not unreasonable to assume that polymeric products also result from the alum precipitation of a rosin size solution. However, it is not necessary to be as specific as Guide about the nature of the polymerization reactions of aluminum resinates. Free hydroxyl groups are certainly not necessary. By analogy with partially hydrolyzed alkoxides, basic aluminum acetate, and other aluminum soaps, one would expect some Al-O-Al bonds. The aluminum will attempt to assume a coordination number of at least four, and up to six if steric considerations permit. Thus, an aluminum diresinate could polymerize to a high level, if all hydroxyl groups and bound water molecules were lost. Because of steric hindrance, it is difficult to visualize a truly crosslinked, insoluble structure containing exactly two resinate groups per aluminum atom. However, if some of these metal atoms are linked to only one or even no resinate groups, there is no difficulty in picturing a three-dimensional, cross-linked structure. The aluminum atoms in such a structure would be very effectively shielded by resinate groups, so the material would be very hydrophobic. The free resin acid component of the size precipitate could be loosely associated with polymer molecules representing the aluminum salt fraction.

Precipitate Retention by Fibers

The mechanism by which size precipitate is retained by the pulp has been widely studied, following introduction of the electrostatic theory by Ostwald and Lorenz. More recently, electrokinetic studies of rosin size precipitate, wood pulp and sized fibres have been reported by Thode and co-workers, Kanamaru, Collins *et al.*, Ninck Blok, and Mason *et al.* The most recent publications involve studies by Strazdins and by Vandenberg and Spurlin.

A simplified summary of the electrostatic mechanism for the retention of size precipitate by fibres is as follows. The presence of aluminum salts on the surfaces of the size precipitate particles described earlier makes these particles positively charged in water. This has been amply confirmed by the elecrokinetic studies listed above. Some of these same studies have shown that cellulose pulp surfaces possess a negative charge in water over a wide pH range, even in the presence of alum. Since the precipitate particles and the pulp fibres are oppositely charged, retention of these particles by the cellulose can occur by simple elecrostatic attraction. The rapid growth of size precipitate particles from precipitaed molecules of free resin acids and aluminum resinate salts by frequent molecular collisions is eventually terminated by a sticking collision with a cellulose surface. This ultimate collision should be strongly encouraged by the opposite charges of the particles and fibre surfaces, since electrosatic forces operate at considerable distances, even in water. The positively charged particles of neutrals are retained by the fibres in the same manner. The sized pulp fibre surface thus appears speckled with tiny (0.1 μ diameter) roundish particles, distributed both as individuals and in clusters. This result has been confirmed by electron microscopy. The presence of larger (0.5 μ diameter) particles on fibres sized with a high free-rosin suspension plus alum has also been observed.

This simple electrostatic concept of precipitate retention is basically sound. However, recent publications demonstrate that various subtle complications must be considered in order to develop a more realistic picture of the retention process. Thus, Strazdins has shown that the presence of sulfate ion in a size precipitation systems reduces the positive charge developed on the particle surfaces and tends to prevent excessive agglomeration of these particles. This moderating effect leads to more uniform distribution of the size precipitate material on pulp fibre surfaces. Vandenberg and Spurlin have reported that various wood pulps contain up to 0.5% anionic, water soluble polyuronides that are readily absorbed by both the size precipitate and the pulp fibres. At sizing concentrations, these water solubles reduce the positive charge of size precipitate particles and exert a protective colloid action that decreases the flocculation of these particles and permits them to be more uniformly absorbed on fibre surfaces.

Opposite charge attraction is not required for the retention of precipitated particles by fibres. Strazdins notes that acid precipitation of rosin in the absence of alum forms negatively charged particles that are, nevertheless, retained by the negatively charged pulp fibres. He suggests that the hydrophobic nature of the precipitated material encourages it to escape from the water phase by adsorption on to cellulose surfaces. Adsorption occurs by a simple collision process, followed by adhesion to the cellulose substrate (due to short-range van der Waals forces). He regards electrostatic attraction as superimposed on the basic van der Waals attraction mechanism. Because of its long-range effectiveness, electrostatic attraction can then accelerate the adsorption process, depending on the magnitude of the charges on the fibres and the precipitate particles.

No matter how much the process of size precipitate retention may depend on simple physical adsorption as opposed to electrostatic attraction, permanent bonding of the sizing agent to cellulose substrates can be explained in several ways. Most pulps have a sufficient carboxyl content to permit these acidic groups to play a plausible role, either in covalent bonding or in the coordination of aluminum ions located on the surfaces of precipitate particles. It is also possible that aluminum may coordinate to cellulose hydroxyl groups. Amidst these uncertainties, however is the always prevailing fact that rosin derivatives are very tacky and readily stick to various surfaces. Thus the weak but certain van der Waals forces of attraction are the most probable source of ultimate bonding in this system, particularly when the increased area of contact after heating is considered.

Effects of Drying Sized Fibers

The size precipitate particles adhering to pulp fibre surfaces in an aqueous slurry are hydrated and swollen to some extent, depending on the amount of aluminum resinate salts present. These salts may already exist in the form of a low molecular weight polymer. The polar groups on the surfaces of the precipitated particles will be oriented outward, toward the surrounding aqueous phase.

During room temperature drying of the sized fibres, the precipitated material gradually loses most of its bound water, while undergoing further polymerization. The surface polar groups will eventually attempt to orient inward, away from air-particle interfaces that develop. To the extent that the increasing immobility of the drying particles prevents this reorientation, the surfaces of the dried material will retain a considerable hydrophilic character. Similarly, the surface of bulk rosin has a relatively low contact angle (72°) that is explained by the presence of polar carboxyl groups oriented outward from the surface.

The drying of sized fibres at an elevated temperature offers offers additional possibilities. The softening temperatures of many size precipitates are sufficiently low to permit moderate mobility of the precipitate particles during the drying of sized paper at 110 to 120°C. Increased mobility at elevated temperature permits the precipitated material to fuse, flow and spread over the fibre surfaces to some extent. This effect is demonstrated by comparing electron micrographs of sized fibres dried at room temperature with fibre dried at 15°C. In the latter example, the initially distinct boundaries of the size precipitate particles have been obliterated, and these particles have sagged to form relatively flat mounds.

Another effect of elevated temperature drying is to promote further polymerization. Probably a certain amount of cross-linking of the polymer chains also occurs, thus insolubilizing the precipitate. Furthermore, the enhanced mobility afforded during elevated temperature drying will readily encourage growing polymer molecules to reorient with their polar groups pointing inward away from the airparticle interface, thus creating a final particle surface with excellent hydrophobic character. Once the drying process is complete, these reoriented polar groups will remain relatively fixed at room temperature, due to the immobility of the large polymer molecules to which they are attached. This concept was proposed by Guide to explain the results of his experimental acid-abietate-aluminate sizing system, but should be just as valid in the more conventional rosin-alum sizing process.

Factors Affecting the Degree of Sizing

An integrated picture of the rosin sizing process is interesting but not particularly useful unless it explains the sizing phenomena that have been observed in many paper mills for years. Different parts of the broad description outlined above must now be called upon to explain specific effects that crop up in the practical application of rosin size.

In practice the presence of high alkalinity in the raw water or excessive alkalinity in the stock ends to reduce sizing development. Also calcium resinate is reported to be a much poorer sizing agent than its aluminum counterpart, and excessive hardness in a pulp slurry often reduces the degree of sizing. These adverse environmental effects have been correlated by Davison with the low free acid contents and high sintering temperatures of size precipitates prepared in either an alkaline or a hard water system. He suggests that the low mobilities of these precipitates at the elevated drying temperature reduces their tendency spread over fibre surfaces, and thus reduces sizing development. Conversely the use of an acid - alum mixture to precipitate rosin size has been found to improve sizing. A precipitate prepared in this manner was found to contain much more than the normal amount of free-resin acids and would, therefore, be much more mobile during the drying of the sized paper.

The pH of a pulp slurry during the rosin sizing process has a profound effect on sizing development. Both Wakins and Strazdins demonstrated recently that the maximum degree of sizing is achieved at a certain system pH, and that the required pH varies, depending on certain environmental factors. In particular. Strazdins found that the product of aluminum retained times the residual charge per aluminum atom correlated well with degree of sizing when this product was plotted against system pH. It is well known, of course, that a certain number of active aluminum ions needed to develop good rosin sizing in paper. Acid precipitation of rosin leads to its retention in the sheet, but the degree of sizing is negligible in the complete absence of aluminum. Similarly, the alkaline consumption of aluminum ion with the resulting production of hydrophilic aluminum hydroxide leads to poor sizing. The aluminum hydroxide may interfere with the strong adsorption of size precipitate on fibre surfaces. Thus both extremes in system pH must be avoided.

The adverse effect of high total acidity on sizing development has been discussed by Watkins. Total acidity is determined by the alkaline titration of a sample of water to the phenolphthalein end point and depends on the amount of alum that is added in order to reduce the pH to the desired level. Thus, total acidity depends on the total alkalinity introduced in the form of stock and raw water before alum addition. Continued water recycle often leads to a highly buffered system that requires much more alum to reduce the pH to the desired level. The presence of large amounts of aluminum in various stages of hydrolysis gives this system a high total acidity and detracts from the first step in the ionic mechanism of precipitation outlined by Davison. Thus, less free acid will be present in the precipitated material, and an adverse sizing effect will result, just as in the highly alkaline system discussed earlier. High total acidity is the most probable cause of those adverse sizing effects which, in the past, were blamed on high sulfate ion concentration.

Small amounts of fatty acids and their simple derivatives are sometimes found in commercial rosin. The presence of these aliphatic compounds can have a very adverse effect on the degree of sizing in most conventional systems. The poor adhesive nature of fatty acid derivatives and the converse tendency of long hydrocarbon chains to cohere readily in semi-crystalline array may result in poor bonding to the cellulose substrate. The relative mobility of these aliphatic compounds at room temperature may permit a penetrating fluid to encourage molecular reorientation, as was demonstrated by Yiannos, or even to brush aside these molecules.

The addition of the maleic or fumaric adduct of rosin as a fortifying agent has greatly improved sizing development in many paper mill systems. Various suggestions have been offered to explain this highly beneficial effect. The tricarboxylic nature of the fortifier molecules suggests that three potential bonding points per molecule are better than one, although each additional carboxyl group also increases the hydrophilic character of the molecule. It has also been suggested that the rosin adduct may serve as a scavenger to prevent aluminum hydroxide from adsorbing on fibre surfaces and thus denying these bonding sites to size precipitate particles. However, the beneficial effect of a fortifier in a distilled water system rules out this idea. The most probable explanation involves the semi-hydrophilic nature of the fortifier molecules. The presence of adduct ions during size precipitation process produces a less flocculated, more dispersed system of particles. The result is a more uniform distribution of somewhat smaller particles on the sized fibres, generally as individuals rather than in clusters. The strong tendency of aluminum to coordinate various organic anions may explain the dispersing influence of the aduct.

Many other modifiers have been added internally in attempts to improve rosin sizing efficiency. These modifiers have generally involved rather large molecules of ahydrophilic character, such as carboxymethyl cellulose, urea-tormaldehyde and other wet-strength resins, starch and natural gums. Vandenberg and Spurlin have shown that the beneficial sizing effects of materials such as gum arabic and pectin can easily be explained by the same mechanism that they employed regarding the pulp solubles (polyuronides) contained in various wood pulps. Thus, all of these additives may modify the degree of dispersion of the size precipitate in a pulp slurry and improve its distribution on pulp fibres. They may also strengthen its ultimate bonding to the dried cellulose substrate. In one sense, these modifiers may be regarded as fortifying agents that play the same role, though less efficiently, as the rosin adduct in fortified rosin size.

Sodium aluminate is sometimes employed as an additive to modify the conventional rosin-alum sizing process. The aluminate ion is actually a tetrahydroxy aluminum anion that is formed when the three-step hydrolysis of alum to form aluminum hydroxide is extended one step further by the addition of alkali.

$$[Al(OH)_3] + OH^{-1} \rightleftharpoons [Al(OH)_1 (H_2O)_2]^{-1} + H_2O$$

Sodium aluminate is generally added in place of part of the usual alum. Improved sizing development in general, or better rosin sizing a high pH, has frequently been repored for aluminate-modified sizing systems. This process modification is a step toward the experimental system employed by Guide, and his concept of polymerization by olation may have special applicability here. The effectiveness of sodium aluminate appears to depend on the environmental conditions encountered in certain paper mills.

The nature of the pulp fibres themselves has considerable influence on sizing development. An approximate correlation exists between pulp sizeability and pulp impurities content. Thus, cotton linters are relatively pure, highly crystalline, cellulose fibres containing essentially no natural resins and having a very low carboxyl content. These fibres are very difficult to size effectively. At the other extreme, unbleached pulps retain a moderate to high content of natural resins and usually have a relatively high carboxyl content. These pulps are very easy to size. The natural resins are basically a sizing agent in themselves, and thus need only a small supplement in the form of rosin size and alum. The carboxyl groups may enhance the negative charge on the surfaces of unbleached fibres, and thus provide many additional attractive sites for retention and eventual firm bonding of the sizing agent.

The effect of beating on sizing development appears to depend on the kind of sizing test employed. A sized sheet made from lightly beaten pulp usually shows better sizing with respect to resistance to liquid penetration, but its rough surface encourages ink feathering Conversely, paper made from heavily beaten pulp has a smooth surface and shows less feathering tendency. According to the Washburn equation, the smaller pores of this dense sheet should reduce the rate of fluid penetration. However, penetration sizing tests generally show a lower degree of sizing for this paper. Probably the greatly increased specific surface area of heavily beaten pulp, due to surface fibrillation and fines production, results in the sizing agent being distributed too sparsely to be fully effective. Furthermore, the initial ease of wetting may be lower for a smooth dense sheet but its ultimate absorption or an aqueous liquid may be greatly increased, due to the higher specific surface area of heavily beaten pulp.

Many paper mills have encountered severe reductions in sizing efficiency during the summer months when the entire wet and operates at a higher temperature. Cobb and Lowe have suggested that this warmer environment encourages bacterial action to produce highly coordinated organic anions that may adversely affect the sizing process. Higher temperature may also affect the surface charge and composition of the precipitated particles. It is advisable to minimize the time during which size and alum are both present in a heated stock system before sheet formation, because prolonged contact of both ingredients at elevated temperature often reduces sizing development.

It is well known that elevated-temperature drying of sized paper improves the degree of sizing obtained. This temperature effect is readily explained in terms of precipitate mobility, spreading tendency, and ability to polymerize and even cross-link. High-temperature drying leads to better fibre surface coverage by the sizing agent, a preferred reorientation of polar substituents to make the sized surfaces more hydrophobic, and a more immobile well-bonded coating on cellulose surfaces of the dried paper. Further, any hydrophilic substances that may have co-precipitated with the sizing agent can migrate away from these precipitated particles to adjacent unsized pulp surfaces during high-temperature drying. The proper drying rate and temperature profile required to achieve this sizing development (while removing water from the sheet efficiently) will depend on the production requirements, environmental conditions, and equipment limitations of individual paper mills. The most important general rule seems to be that the drying sheet should not encounter the ultimate dryer temperature until sheet solids have reached 50 to 60%. The optimum dryer temperature depends considerably on the degree of saponification of the rosin size being employed. Various modified rosin-sizing agents have been developed to cope with sizing problems encountered in mills having unusual drying process or severe drying problems.

WAX AS A SIZING AGENT

Wax is another rather common sizing material that has been used by the paper industry for many years. Large amounts of paraffin waxes are still used for coating container-stock, although polyerthylene coatings have recently provided very strong competition in this application. Although wax coatings provide very effective resistance to penetration by aqueous liquids, this massive barrier technique is not really a sizing process in the generally accepted sense.

Various types of wax emulsions are used by the paper industry, both as internal and surface sizing agents. Paraffin wax or microcrystalline wax is the main ingredient of these emulsions, although other materials such as rosin, polyethylene, and various resins are frequently included as modifiers. Rosin-wax emulsions are especially common. Wax emulsions designed for internal addition consist of negatively charged particles. They are added in conjunction with papermaker's alum as a retention agent. In some cases, wax emulsions and rosin size are both added internally, together with alum. Wax is an excellent sizing agent, but its internal addition must be limited to less than 0.5% (based on fibre) in order to prevent severe reduction of fibre-fibre bonding and eventual sheet strength. To avoid this adverse effect, wax emulsions are frequently applied at the size press as a surface treatment for paper or paperboard that has been internally sized to a moderate degree with rosin. The low melting point (50 to 80°C) of various commercial waxes allows this sizing agent to spread over fibre surfaces readily during the elevated temperature drying of the paper. However, this weak adhesive (non-tacky) nature of wax makes the treated paper more slippery than rosin-sized paper.

CHEMICALLY REACTIVE SIZING AGENTS

In recent years, various synthetic sizing agents have been introduced that react chemically with the hydroxyl groups of cellulose fibres, and thus become permanently anchored. The chemical reactivity of these additives offers several advantages to the papermaker. In principle, a mono-molecular layer of a firmly bound sizing agent with its hydrophobic substituent oriented away from the cellulose substrate should provide excellent water repellency. In practice, chemically reactive sizing agents are generally much more effective than rosins size, per pound added, because of stronger (chemical) bonding and better (monolayer) distribution. Excellent sizing is obtained at addition levels as low as 0.05%. However these synthetic materials are also more expensive than rosin. Since chemically reactive sizing agents do not require alum as a co-reactant retention aid, or bonding link to cellulose, these materials can be used in neutral-to-alkaline papermaking systems, thus reducing equipment corrosion and producing paper with better long term strength. In general, these chemical additives react with cellulose more rapidly under alkaline conditions. Those based on fatty acids make paper surfaces slippery, but various anti-slip agents can be added to the formed sheet to counter this effect. These sizing agents are generally added internally, but they can also be employed in the surface sizing of paper.

Alkyl ketene dimer ("Aquapel") is the most commonly used of the chemically reactive sizing agents. The ketene dimer molecule consists of two hydrocarbon chains, each of 16 to 18 carbon atoms in length, attached to a 4-membered lactone ring. Under neutral or alkaline conditions, the lactone ring will open and react with materials containing active hydrogen substituents. In particular, the ketene dimer will react with cellulose hydroxyl groups to form a stables ester linkage, as shown in Fig. 2.

"Aquapel" is supplied as an aqueous suspension of alkyl ketene dimer particles, stabilized by a cationic starch. The cationic stabilizer also serves as a retention aid that helps attach the particles to the anionic fibre surfaces. Although the ketene dimer molecule will also react with water, its long hydrocarbon chains apparently protect the very active lactone ring quite effectively. When added internally, about two-thirds of the retained material will react with cellulose rather than form the ineffective hydrolysis product, a ketone.

The rather low melting point of "Aquapel" (40 to 50°C) permits this sizing agent to spread over the fibre surfaces very extensively during the elevated-temperature drying of the paper. The resulting monomolecular film becomes tightly bound to the cellulose substrate by chemical reaction during the drying process. Off-machine sizing is good, but the ultimate sizing level is achieved gradually during room-temperature aging or rapidly by elevated-temperature curing. Used as an internal sizing agent, it should be added as close to the headbox as possible. Excellent sizing efficiency is obtained by the use of 0.05 to 0.3% "Aquapel" in a neutral-to-alkaline environment (pH 6.5 to 8.5). The presence of alum in this sizing system interfers with the reaction of the ketene dimer with cellulose, unless the system pH is adjusted to 7.0 or higher "Aquapel" can also be added at the size press or calender stack as a surface application. Surface sizing at the 0.5% addition level is generally effective.

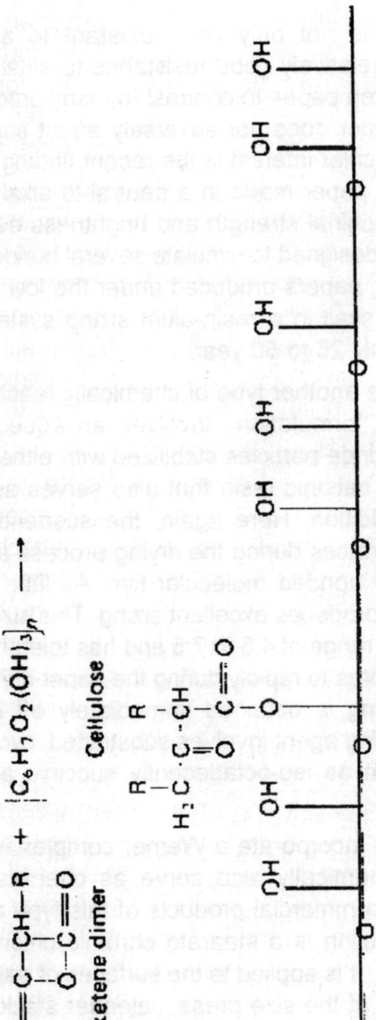

Fig. 2 Cellulose fibre surface

"Aquapel" sized paper is not only very resistant to acid penetrants, but also shows relatively good resistance to alkaline liquids, compared to rosin sized paper. In contrast to many grades of rosin, the alkyl ketene dimer does not adversely affect sheet brightness or colour. Of particular interest is the recent finding by Barrow that "Aquapel" sized paper made in a neutral-to-alkaline system retains much of its original strength and brightness even after accelerated aging tests designed to simulate several hundred years of storage. In contrast, papers produced under the low pH conditions (that generally prevail in a rosin-alum sizing system) retain these properties for only 25 to 50 year.

Fatty acid anhydrides are another type of chemically reactive sizing agent. One patented formulation involves an aqueous suspension of distearicanhydride particles stabilized with either a cationic starch or a suitable cationic resin that also serves as a retention aid for internal addition. Here again, the suspended particles melt on the fibre surfaces during the drying process and spread to form a chemically bonded molecular film. As little as 0.05 to 0.3% of this material produces excellent sizing. This sizing agent can be used over a pH range of 4.5 to 7.5 and has tolerance for alum. It reacts with pulp fibres to rapidly during the paper drying process that very good sizing is obtained immediately off the machine. A similar type of sizing agent involves substituted, cyclic, dicarboxylic anhydrides such as iso-octadecently succinic acid anhydride.

Organic compounds that incorporate a Werner complex with chromium also serve as chemically also serve as chemically reactive sizing agents. Two commercial products of this type are "Quilon" and "Scotchban" Quilon is a stearato chromic chloride dissolved in isopropyl alcohol. It is applied to the surfaces of paper or board as a dilute solution at the size press, calender stack or by spraying. The chromic chloride complex interacts with cellulose hydroxyls during the drying of the paper to produce excellent water repellency. Scotchban is perfluoro caprylic acid complex with chromium, which is also supplied as an isopropyl alcohol solution. Because of the fluorinated hydrocarbon group, this material provides paper with grease resistance as well as water repellency. It is generally applied as a surface sizing agent. Both Scotchban and Quilon are highly efficient sizing agents, because they readily from monomolecular films that become strongly bonded to pulp fibres. Both of these sizing agents have a blue-green colour, due to the presence of chromium.

MISCELLANEOUS SIZING AGENTS

A wide variety of other materials have been tried as sizing agents for paper. Many have been patented, and some are now commercial products. Asphalt is the most commonly used of these materials. Asphalt emulsions have been employed for many years to size structural paperboard products where the dark colour of the asphalt does not matter. Large quantities of asphalt are consumed in this special application, because this sizing agent is frequently used at high addition levels (up to 10% based on fibre). Asphalt emulsions are added internally, and alum is used as a precipitating and retention agent.

Fatty acid soaps are used for special applications, such as sizing photographic papers for resistance to alcholol-water mixtures. However, as previously noted, a small amount of fatty acid soap in rosin size has a very adverse effect on sizing efficiency.

Because cellulose is such a hydrophilic material, it is possible to develop reasonable water resistance by sizing paper with a vast number of relatively hydrophobic compounds that are immobile at room temperature. Thus various hydrocarbon resins have been evaluated, such as terpene resins, resinous polymers obtained from petroleum cracking, and naphthenic derivatives. More recently, various synthetic polymers of both low and high molecular weight have been developed as sizing agents. Typical examples include cationic copolymers of acrylic acid esters, hydrophoboic polyfunctional amines, and copolymers of various hydrophobic vinyl monomers with hydrophilc monomers. In the last example, the hydrophilc monomer is so chosen that it can eventually be converted into cationic quaternary ammonium sites along the copolymer, for retention purposes. Commercial products involving copolymers of maleic anhydride with vinyl monomers (such as styrene or an olefin) have been introduced recently. The immobility of a polymeric molecule and its many possible points of attachment, either weak or strong, to the cellulose fibre surfaces probably are major factors contributing to the sizing efficiency of these materials.

SIZING TESTS

An almost countless number of tests have been devised to measure the degree of water repellency of sized paper and board. In 1926, Carson listed different sizing tests, and many more have been developed since that time. Of the many different tests that are employed today, no one test is unanimously endorsed or entirely satisfactory.

A sizing test should be chosen on the basis of the intended use of the paper product. The best sizing test must either measure use requirements directly, simulate use conditions, or correlate with use requirements. The test should be adaptable for quality control of sized-paper production. The purpose of sizing is to retard the movement of an aqueous fluid through the paper, into its structural elements, or along the paper surfaces. Thus, sizing tests can be divided into three corresponding groups that measure fluid penetration, absorption, and surface movement, respectively.

Penetration tests measure the rate at which the fluid moves through paper. Those that show a sensitive response over a wide range of sizing levels are the wet break, ink flotation, photometric ink penetration, and penescope tests. The ink flotation test is convenient, semi-quantitative, and rapid. However, the sizing values obtained vary from one operator to another. The Hercules Photometric Ink Penetration Tester is an instrument designed to eliminate this subjectivity, and it gives highly reproducible results. Optical and electronic modifications have been made recently by Mashuburn. These modification have improved the ease of operation and broadened the utility of this device. The penescope test is used to test fluid penetration through paperboard samples, while the other three tests are designed to test paper. The dry indicator test (TAPPI sugar dye), the electrical conductivity test (e.g., Valley size), fluorescent dye, and the curl test also measure the rate of penetration, but are generally insensitive of high levels of sizing.

Absorption tests measure how fast an aqueous fluid is absorbed by the paper structure. These tests are used primarily for paperboard. The water pickup (total immersion) and Cobb tests measure the weight of fluid absorbed in a given time, but these tests are insensitive at high levels of sizing. The drop test measures the time required for the board to absorb a small drop of fluid.

This test is quite sensitive throughout the sizing range, but is often unreliable, because it measures the response of a very small area of sample.

The movement of a fluid along the surface of paper is measured qualitatively by an ink feathering test in which the observer notes to what extent a finely drawn ink line spreads and develops blurred boundaries while the ink is drying. This test can be made more definitive by using a standard series of inks having varying tendencies to spread of feather on the surface of sized paper.

A recent article by Reaville and Hine analyzes the various factors that may be measured by different sizing tests. They conclude that the wet break penescope, and ink flotation tests measure properties related to the penetration of fluid into the fibres, whereas the fluorescent dye. Valley size and KBB test measure some function of the transudation rate of fluid through pores between the fibres. The Cobb, water pickup, and curl tests probably measure some combined function of both fluid transudation and penetration into fibres.

It should be added hat sizing tests respond in different ways to the colour, roughness, and porosity of the paper. Tests that depend on the rate of penetration of water itself to the far side of the sheet (e.g., the dry indicator test) may be falsified by water vapour permeation, which is scarcely affected by most sizing processes. None of the conventional sizing tests gives an adequate indication of the uniformity of sizing. Nonuniformity on a scale of a few millimeters an indication of poor sizing, which can often be corrected by a change in mill conditions or by use of a modified sizing agent. Visual inspection of the specimens from an ink penetration test may be employed to judge sizing uniformity.

11

Dyeing of Paper

INTRODUCTION

The manufacture of paper is becoming increasingly scientific and so is the dyeing of paper. The art of dyeing paper is being meshed with science to an ever increasing extent. The advent of the computer and the many new colour measuring instruments will revolutionize this phase of the paper manufacturing process.

Most papers are coloured or at least tinted, and the largest percentage of coloured paper is made by dyeing the stock before the sheet is formed. The dyeing of paper is art of science of achieving the desired shade and, also meeting the necessary properties required by the end use of the paper. A paper machine represents a large capital investment, and in order to obtain a return on this investment, it must operate efficiently "Down time" is expensive, particularly on large machines. It, therefore, force the colorist to use all of his ingenuity and the help of others to get "on shade" quickly and to maintain a uniform shade for the duration of the run. The cost of dyeing paper is made up of the cost of the dye, the time getting on shade, the time lost when off-shade paper is being produced, the cleanup time, and the time required to get back in production on the next shade. The cost of the dye is often less important than the other factors. The "other factors" are the subject of this chapter and are the responsibility of the colourist.

More paper is being coloured today than ever before. Color is an important sales tool and is often the outstanding difference between two sheets of paper. Shade tolerances are being tightened, and an increasing amount of paper is being made to meet specific instrument standards.

There are two major classes of colouring materials being used to dye paper, i.e., coloured pigments and soluble dyes. Of these, soluble dyes are the most important.

COLOURED PIGMENTS

Coloured pigments are water insoluble, coloured materials. They belong in the class of fillers and loading materials, but are coloured and, therefore, are used in smaller quantities. They have no affinity for the fibre and require the strong positive charge contributed by alum to hold them in the sheet. It alum is not used, it will be necessary to use a cationic retention aid in order to retain the pigment.

Coloured pigments used by the paper industry are ground by the suppliers to fine particle size and treated with dispersing agents to improve their ease of handling in water system. The bond formed with alum holding the pigment on the fibre is a weak one. The table rolls, suction boxes and suction couch roll (as they remove water from the bottom side of the sheet) also tend to remove pigments from the bottom side of the sheet. Paper dyed with pigments is, therefore always two-sided. This is an important factor limiting the use of pigments in the colouring of paper. White pigments, such as clay and TiO_2 behave the same as coloured pigments. These are discussed in a separate chapter. There are two distinct classes of coloured pigments.

Inorganic Coloured Pigments

These include the various shades of Chrome Yellow (lead chromate), Molybdate Orange, Cadium Yellows and Reds, utramarine, burnt umber, iron oxides, and others. These pigments are relatively weak tinctorially, but have excellent lightfastness. Their use is limited to applications requiring extreme light-fastness. The Cadmium Yellows and Reds, for instance, are used to colour paper for the decorative paper-base, liminated-plastic, table tops used in the modern kitchen.

Synthetic Organic Pigments

A wide shade range of these pigments is available. They include such pigments as Hansa Yellow and Orange, the Naphthanil Pigments, Red 2B Pigments, the Phthalocyanine blues and greens, the phosphomolydic and phosphotungstic acid lakes of basic dyes, Prussian Blue, selected "vat" pigments, and carbon black. The latter colour although not strictly a synthetic organic pigment, can for practical purposes, be considered in this class.

These pigments may be very bright. The phthalocyanine blues and greens are as brilliant as the basic dyes of similar shade. Lightfastness varies, and in general, is very good to excellent, and pigments are fast to water bleeding. The Hansa Yellows may bleed in fast and oils, but they are an exception.

Pigments are always "topsided" and therefore, their use is limited. They are generally weaker than soluble dyes, and because of two-sideness, are usually, more difficult to control. Selected bright blue pigments are used for tinting while papers, both internally and in coating. They are ideal tinting colours, since they lack affinity for the fibre and, therefore, do not granite.

Soluble Dyes

Most coloured paper is dyed with soluble dyes. By the term, "soluble dye", we mean a dye that is soluble in water and colours the fibre from a solution in water. There are three important classes of soluble dyes used to dye paper. These are :

Basic Dyes

Dye hydrochlorides, sulfates, etc.

Acid Dyes

Sodium salts of a low molecular weight dye sulfonic acid.

Direct Dyes

Sodium salts of higher molecular weight dye sulfonic acids having affinity for cellulose.

Basic dyes are where the dye molecule has replaced the "basic" portion of the molecule. A solution of a basic dye is always acid.

Acid and direct dyes are dyes where the dye molecule has replaced the "acid" portion of the molecule. Since they are always sodium or related salts, the pH of a solution of these dyes is always alkaline.

Basic Dyes

The first synthetic dyes made were basic dyes. As a class, basic dyes are the brightest dyes. They are (tinctorially) extremely strong, but fugitive to light. Paper dyed with this class of colour, will fade during a short exposure under light.

Basic dyes have a strong affinity for unbleached pulps and groundwood, attaching themselves to the non-cellulosic impurities present. They have little affinity for bleached pulps. In a mixed furnish of bleached and unbleached pulps, basic dyes will jump on the unbleached fibre, resulting in a mottled appearing sheet.

These dyes are sold as dry powders or as liquid. The liquids are concentrated solutions in selected acids, such as acetic acid, or in water miscible solvents. A dilute solution of either the powder or solution type will always have a low or acid pH. Basic dyes are generally soluble in alcohol, and a dyed sheet containing basic dyes may be identified by testing the bleeding in warm alcohol.

Basic dyes are important for dyeing such ground-wood grades as the "Yellow Pages" in the classified section of the telephone directory, or "Construction Paper" used by children. The latter grades are deep brilliant shades necessitating the use of basic dyes. These dyes are also used to dye the green drug store warp and also many department store warps where economy and brilliance are desired and where lightfastness is less important.

Basic dyes may be used on bleached pulps in small quantities to improve brilliance. If deeper shades are desired, it is necessary to use mordants (either special synthetic retention aids of tannic acid) in order to retain the colour.

Basic dyes may be used in the same formula with acid or direct dyes, but solutions of basic dyes should never be mixed with solutions of either acid or direct dyes.

Acid Dyes

Acid dyes are sodium salts of relatively low - molecular weight colour acids, whereas direct dyes are similar compounds of higher molecular weight dye acids. Acid dyes, therefore, are much more soluble in water; some are soluble to over 10% in water, while others are only soluble to 2% or less. As a class, they are much more soluble than direct dyes. A water solution of an acid dye or of a direct dye is always alkaline, since they are sodium or related salts of colour acids.

Acid dyes have little or no affinity for the paper fibres. They are retained in the sheet by the chemical complex formed in sizing by the reaction of alum with rosin size. They are therefore, level dyes with little tendency to granite. This property is often important when dyes are selected to match a certain shade. Some acid dyes are so soluble that they cannot be retained in a sized sheet. The acid dye/size/alum complex may burn to the surface in deep shades, when the sheet hits a hot drier. Retention can be improved by using a retention aid. This is only used for certain special effects.

These dyes, generally, have much better lightfastness than the basic dyes. In turn, they are usually duller in shade than basic dyes, and brighter than direct dyes. The acid oranges are brighter than the basic dyes in this shade range. Lightfastness can vary from excellent to poor.

Acid dyes are usually preferred for surface colouring, because of their high solubility and their lack of preferential affinity for certain fibres. Paper, stock dyed with acid dyes, will usually blend if the paper becomes wet. These dyes should not be used to dye paper that will come in direct contact with moist or wet foods.

Acid dyes may be added before the size and alum, after the size and before the alum, and in many cases after the alum, but as with all dyes, it is generally best to add the dye before the alum.

Direct Dyes

Direct dyes, like acid dyes, are alkaline salts of dye sulfonic acids. The pH of a 1% solution of a direct dye is usually above 8.0. They differ from acid dyes, since they have an affinity for cellulose and will dye the fibre "direct" without dyeing assistants. They can, therefore, be used to dye tissue, such as facial tissue, toilet tissue and other absorbent papers, where size and alum are not used. Acid dyes would not be retained under similar conditions.

Direct days are the most important class of dyes used for colouring paper. They are somewhat duller than acid dyes, but because of their affinity for the fibre, are more versatile and easier to control. They are less soluble than acid dyes, and in many cases, a 1% solution may be colloidal, rather than a true solution. Direct dyes are available to match almost any desired shade, although some of the most brilliant shades may require the addition of basic or acid dyes. Direct dyes are available as dry powders that may be added dry to the beater or pulper of stock, and in some cases, in liquid form.

Although direct dyes are substantive, the addition of size and alum usually helps retention in medium and deep shades. The use of 5 to 10% common salt on the weight of the fibre and the heating of the pulp slurry will increase the depth of shade obtainable by improving the retention. In dyeing, an equilibrium builds up between the dye in solution and the dey going to the fibre. The use of salt and heat (120 to 140°F) changes this affinity in favour of the fibre. Salt is often objectionable, due to corrosion considerations, and heating may not be practical, since 20 lb or more of water must be heated per pound of fibre (at 5% consistency).There are synthetic retention acid thtat can be used to help retention.

Direct dyes should be added dry to the pulp that is to be coloured, or added from a cold, dilute solution. If a direct dye were added from a hot solution, it would probably "strike" and deeply dye the first fibres that it contacts, resulting in "granite" fibres. Some direct dyes have a greater tendency to granite than others; these must be handled with extreme care.

Direct dyes should always be added before alum. Some mills prefer to add the dye after the size and before the alum, others before size and alum. In either case, the dye should be added as early as possible to allow maximum time for the dye to dissolve and exhaust on the fibre. The beater should have a near neutral to alkaline pH (at the time of dye addition) to obtain optimum results, such as maximum strength, brilliance and ease of control. If a direct dye is added after the alum, it will partially precipitate before it becomes a part of the fibre, thereby resulting in weaker, duller shade that is more two-sided and more difficult to control. This is because some of the dye is converted to the aluminum salt before it is on the fibre.

At the present time, the dye industry is beginning to offer solutions of direct dyes. These solutions may be one-third to one-half the strength of the corresponding powder. They offer handling and control advantages, particularly to automated mills. These dye solutions may be metered directly into the stock system or diluted before using.

Laboratory Procedure

In order to save time getting "on shade", it is best to start the mill run with a dye formula previously developed in the laboratory.

The laboratory work should simulate the mill conditions as much as possible, particularly as far as the percentage of ingredients is concerned. These would be the percentage of each pulp previously beaten to the proper freeness; the fillers; sizing materials; and any other material used in making the mill sheet.

Preparation of the Pulp

The pulp is first beaten in a small laboratory beater to the desired freeness. The stock is drained by filtering until no free water will drain from the fibres. The pulp is then broken up into small chunks and stored in an airtight jar or plastic bag. A moisture determination is made by weighting 25 g of the wet pulp, forming this into a sheet, drying the sheet, and after weighing, calculating the amount of wet pulp needed to produce a five gram dry sheet. This weight is recorded on the jar.

Dissolving the Dye

In most mill runs, the dye is added dry to the beater. This is impractical when working in the laboratory with five gram of pulp. The dyes are, therefore, predissolved and added by pipette to the pulp slurry. By means of an analytical balance, 0.5 g of dye is carefully weighed. This is dissolved in hot water and diluted with cold water to 500 cc. Care must be taken to make sure that all of the dye is in solution. With this solution,5 cc added to the pulp equivalent to a five gram sheet is equivalent to one lb of dye per 1,000 lb of pulp.

Dyeing procedure

In the laboratory procedure, the wet weight of the furnish (equivalent to five gram dry weight) is added to a liter beaker with 200 cc of water. This is placed on a slow-speed stirrer and kept agitated. The clay or fillers, if used, are weighed and added dry. The dye solutions are measured via cc's, using a graduated pipette. After mixing five min, rosin size is added, followed by alum. The pulp is allowed to stir for 20 min and then the sheet is formed and dried. The drying must be done carefully, because overtheating can cause the dye to migrate, leading to false conclusions.

The lab sheet is then judged against the desired shade and another attempt is made with the changes deemed necessary. An experienced man can match a shade in three or four attempts; others will find they need to make more sheets before arriving at a "match". Today, it is possible by the use of colour measuring instruments and a computer to arrive at a formula in short period of time. Once the necessary standards have been established, a shade can be matched without actually making additional lab sheets. All dye suppliers maintain service laboratories and will match upon request and provide a starting formula.

The mill should start with a formula using 10 to 20% less colour than the laboratory formula calls far. This is to take care of white water, etc., that is not recovered in laboratory work.

Mill Procedure

The challenge presented to the man in charge of colouring is to translate the information developed in the laboratory to match the shade as quickly as possible. The laboratory formula is only in approximation, but it does show that the shade can be matched with the dyes used, in approximately the quantities shown. There are many factors that can affect shade control, probable the most important is to keep all the variables constant once the shade is matched. The following have or can have an important bearing on shade control:

Furnish

The furnish should be held constant. Obviously a change in pulp brightness will influence the shade. In addition, pulps very considerably in their ability to absorb dyes. In the dyeing of paper, only the surface of the fibre is coloured. The fibre from hardwood trees is shorter and wider and, therefore, has much more surface area per unit weight than softwood pulp. A given amount of dye applied to a hardwood pulp will produce a shade that will appear much weaker than on a softwood pulp. These differ from one species of tree to another; therefore, changes from one pulp to another may affect the shade.

Broke

Broke is usually an important part of the furnish. The amount and type of broke should be held as constant as possible. Broke, since it contains size and alum, usually has a low pH, and it is best to neutralize the acidity with soda ash before adding the dye.

Fillers and Loading Materials

Clay and TiO_2 (titanium dioxide) are commonly used in fine papers that are also dyed. These materials increase the amount of colour required to match a shade and can influence the two-side properties. Some dyes have a greater affinity for clay than for fibre and are, therefore, "top" colours. Others that have a preferential attraction for the fibre are "bottom" colours. TiO_2 will mask the dye, causing the shade to go weaker, therefore if TiO_2 is part of the furnish, more dye will be needed to maintain the depth. Once a formula is established, if the amount of type of filler is changed, it will probably affect the shade.

Freeness

Dyes are retained better on a beaten pulp. The lower the freeness, the better the retention. Refining can affect retention, and tightening a Jordan may, therefore increase the depth of shade.

SIZING AND ORDER OF ADDITION

Rosin Sizing

The dying of paper is generally carried out in conjunction with sizing and since most papers are sized, these two operations cannot be separated.

Acid dyes require size and alum to obtain exhaust onto the fibre. Direct dyes are usually retained better in deep shades by using size and alum. Both acid and direct dyes are sodium or related salts and have an alkaline pH. They will precipitate in the presence of alum. It is, therefore, desirable to add the dye to the beater while the pH is neutral or slightly alkaline. This will allow the dye to dissolve and exhaust onto the fibre before precipitating the colour with alum. Broke, therefore, should be neutralized before being redyed.

The optimum order of addition is to add the dye to the beater either before or after the size, and then allow sufficient time for the beater or pulper to mix uniformly. The alum should always be added last. Some colour men prefer adding the size before the colour. This is satisfactory, but it is essential to add the alum last. The same order to addition should be followed at all times.

Alkaline Sizing

Neutral or alkaline sizes are being used to an increasing extent. Direct dyes are preferred for use with these sizes. Most direct dyes are brighter at neutral or slightly alkaline pH's, and with experience, it is entirely possible that dyeing udner these conditions may be preferred. Unfortunately, the beneficial advantages of alum to aid retention is lost when these sizes are used. The dye should be added before the alkaline size of at least before any cationic retention aid is added. Time is a factor in medium and deep shades. The dye should be added as early in the cycle as possible.

pH - All dyes are more or less indicators. That is to say, shade and strength will vary with pH and total acidity. Each dye has an optimum pH. This information is available from the dye manufacturers. Fortunately, most dyes used for colouring paper have an optimum pH between 4.5 and 5.5. This is also the optimum pH for rosin sizing. Some dyes are retained better at a lower pH and others at a higher pH. Benzo Purpurine and Congo Red are two important direct reds that require a pH of 6.0 or higher to achieve the desired shade. These shades are used in paper by sizing in the normal manner, and then adding soda ash or sodium aluminate to achieve the 6.0 pH. This develops the full brilliance of the shade.

The pH should be controlled in order to control the retention of the dye and maintain the uniform shade.

Wet Strength Agents and other Additives

Wet strength agents will often precipitate dyes. They may improve retention and may increase two-sidedness. It is, therefore, essential to realize that these materials and other additives going into the system can have an affect on the shade and on shade control.

In summary, in order to control shade, the same order of addition should be followed throughout a given run, and the additives used should not be changed without compensating shade adjustments.

Stock Dyeing

The dye is usually weighed and added dry to the beater or pulper. Good circulation is desirable and usually necessary. In most cases, two to three dyes are used in a given formula to match a shade. At times, more colours are needed to balance sides, etc. The formula should be kept as simple as possible, which means using a minimum number of dyes.

The dye is followed with the size, alum and fillers. The beater is then dropped to the beater chest, pumped to the machine chest, through the refiners, and then to the headbox and the machine. The refiners will increase the depth of the shade, since they help lower freeness. The sheet may or may not be surface sized at the size press.

Judging Shades

The sheet on the dry end will be compared with the desired sample, and the adjustments necessary to match the shade are reviewed. It is important to allow sufficient time to get a truly representative sample on the machine. This means allowing the save-all to being returning white water from the new run, etc. The sheet should be allowed to cool and reach equilibrium before judging the shade. This usually takes 5 to 10 min.

Standard Lamp

The best light for judging shades is a clear north light. Since paper mills operate 24 hr a day, all judging should be done under a "day light" lamp made to simulate north light. The lamp should contain some ultraviolet light, equivalent to daylight, in order to help in judging shades containing optical brighteners.

The samples should be compared, making sure that the top sides are compared and that the machine direction is the same.

Shade Adjustments

At the start of a run, or in matching a new shade, it is preferable to start with a formula weaker than the shade. This will allow room to adjust the shade later by adding more colour. A quick adjustment is then made by adding dye to the machine chest. This is best done from a cold, dilute solution of the dye in order to minimize "graniting".

Similar adjustments are made until the shade matches the sample. A wet sample of pulp taken at this time from the headbox can be used as a standard to serve as a guide for adjusting that next beater. When the wet pulp in the beater matches the shade of pulp from the headbox producing satisfactory paper, the machine will be in equilibrium and should make satisfactory paper. The beater man or colour man should realize that changes in order of addition or any of the additives and other factors previously discussed will affect the shade.

White Papers

Despite the large quantities of coloured paper being produced, the major tonnage is still white paper. Almost all white paper is tinted to a blue white shade to counteract the slight yellow cast of essentially all bleached pulps. This is done by using a small amount of a reddish blue.

Groundwood base sheets are tinted with basic dyes. Bleached chemical pulps are tinted with bright reddish blue pigments or with selected direct dyes. Direct dyes must be handled with extreme caution for fear of graniting. The great advantage of the tinting pigments is that they will not granite.

Fluorescent White Dyes

The paper industry consumes large quantities of fluorescent dyes. The "optical brighteners" are colourless direct dyes that have the ability to convert ultraviolet light into additional visible blue white light, thereby adding brightness to the sheet. There is enough ultraviolet light in daylight that can be converted into visible light to greatly improve the whiteness or brightness of the sheet. These dyes may be better applied or surface applied. A combined beater-size press combination is frequently used. These are the only dyes that can raise the measured brightness of a white sheet.

Fluorescent white dyes work best on a bleached chemical pulp furnish. They have a negligible affect upon bleached pulps or on groundwood base papers. The brighter the furnish, the greater the effect obtainable from an optical brightener.

Two-Sidedness

The table rolls, suction boxes, and the suction couch roll on the wet end of the paper machine remove fillers, fines, and dyes, along with the water from the sheet. This results in a "two sided" effect. The difference between the top and bottom side of the sheet is particularly noticeable in a coloured sheet. The man in charge of colour must learn how to "balance the sides".

Coloured pigments and always "top-sided". The means the top of the sheet is much deeper in shade than the bottom, because the coloured pigment particles are sucked through the wire from the bottom side of the sheet.

Soluble dyes differ from pigments, since they become part of the fibre. Some soluble dyes have a preferential attraction for clay fillers, rather than for the fibre. Others are preferentially attracted to the fibre. Since clay is a pigment, and is sucked away from the bottom side of the sheet, those dyes that are attracted to clay are "top" colours. Those that have little or no affinity for clay are "bottom" colours. In running coloured filled sheets, the sides are balanced by proper colour selection and by adding a small amount of colour to the surface sizing solution applied to the bottom side of the sheet at the size press. The dye manufacturers have information on which dyes have a preferential attraction for clay or for the fibre. In unfilled sheets, the "fines" in the pulp behave as pigments. The fines come from the ray cells of the tree and contain a much higher percentage of resin impurities than the long fibres. Most dyes have a preferential affinity for those impurities which, like clay, are drawn away from the bottom side of the sheet, resulting in a top-side paper. A few paper dyes have a preferential attraction for the long fibres (purer cellulose), and these produce less, two-sided paper, or possibly a sheet dyed deeper on the bottom side.

Two-sidedness can be corrected by proper colour selection and by correcting the "sides" by addition of colour to the bottom side of the sheet at the size press. Colour selection is very important. The two-sided effect produced by coloured pigments, in most instances, cannot be corrected or controlled at the size press.

Surface Colouring

Although most papers are coloured before the wet end, some papers are coloured by applying colour to the surface of the sheet. In heavier weight paper boards, colour is often applied to the sheet via water boxes at the calendar stack. Lighter weight papers can be surface coloured by adding dye to the surface sizing solution.

Colouring at the size press is frequently used in the application of fluorescent white dyes. These are generally available in liquid form and can be added directly to the surface sizing solution. It is generally preferable to add some of the optical brightener internally and then "top" at the size press. This eliminates the marked differences in appearance between the surface and interior of the sheet.

The size press is also used to correct two-sidedness. This is done by continuously adding a small amount of dye to the size-press solution, by feeding the roll, and by applying size to the bottom side of the sheet. Acid dyes are generally used because of their excellent solubility.

Coating

Paper coating is growing rapidly. Most paper coatings are white. Tinting colours are used to counteract the natural yellowish cast of the coating. Water dispersible reddish blue pigments are generally preferred as tinting agents, although direct dyes, acid dyes, and even basic dyes are occasionally used.

Colour Selection

Colour selection requires experience and common sense. What is the end use of the paper, and what requirements must the sheet meet? This will determine what dyes should be used. If lightfastness is not important, and if the fumish contains unbleached pulps or groundwood, basic dyes should be considered. If lightfastness is important, will acid or direct dyes answer the needs, or must pigments be used?

Some key questions to consider as a basis for dye selection are: furnish to be used; lightfastness; bleedfastness; alkali fastness; acid fastness; chlorine or bleach fastness; and cost limitation.

Each mill should strive to use the minimum number of dyes in order not to end up with an excessive inventory of dyes.

Continuous Colouring

The beater, common in all mills a generation ago, is being eliminated in most newer mills and being replaced by continuous refiners. The trend, in many of the newer mills, is to eliminate all batch operations is favour of continuous processes. In the continuous process, the pulps, fillers, dyes, and sizing materials are all added continuously. The dyes are dissolved and metered into the stock stream from a cold dilute solution with the aid of a flow meter or a control feed pump. The new, liquid direct-dye solutions being introduced to the trade may be metered directly or diluted before being added to the system.

The dye solutions may be added to the intake of the machine chest, to the headbox or to the fan pump. The dye solution should be added before the alum. In deep shades it is best to add the dye as early as possible before the alum and to allow time for the dye to exhaust on the fibre.

Direct dyes are generally preferred for bleached pulps and basic dyes for groundwood and unbleached pulps.

12

Wet Strength in Paper and Paperboard

INTRODUCTION

Cellulose fibres are highly hydrophilic and are readily wetted and swollen by water. The swollen fibres are soft and plaint and when a pad of them dries, as on a paper machine, they are brought close together by surface tension forces to form inter-fibre hydrogen bonds, thus giving strength to the dry paper.

When paper is wetted the fibres reswell, the hydrogen bonds relax, and the paper loses most of its strength. Careful testing reveals that various papers may retain from about 1 to about 8% of their original dry strength, even when completely saturated with water.

WET-STRENGTH PAPER

Wet-strength paper has been defined as a paper that retains 15% or more of its dry strength, when thoroughly wetted with water. There are commercial paper products that have wet-strength in the range of 30 to 40% of the dry strength. Values higher than these are rare. To attain this degree of wet-strength, it is necessary to treat the paper or the paper stock by chemical means.

During the period of time when paper was used almost exclusively for writing, printing, and for the graphic arts generally, the need for wet strength in paper was relatively unimportant. However, as the uses for paper expanded with its growing abundance, it soon became apparent that the utility of paper would be greatly improved by having greater strength when wet.

The search for means of improving the wet strength of paper resulted in a series of discoveries, in the late 1930s and early 1940s, that certain water-soluble synthetic resins when incorporated with the paper fibre and polymerized or cured brought about a dramatic increase in wet strength. The earliest were solutions of urea-formaldehyde resins for impregnation of the paper sheet. Soon after, colloidal dispersions of melamine-form-aldehyde resins were developed that were substantive to fibre and, therefore, could be added directly to the stock furnish and be absorbed by the fibre and retained in the sheet. Substantive urea-formaldehyde resins were developed. World War II, coming on the heels of these initial discoveries, stimulated the development of wet-strangth paper and paperboard products. By the end of the war, the methods and materials were at hand, and wet-strength paper products found a large and expanding market.

Although the usefulness of wet-strength paper is fairly obvious, it may be well to outline briefly the conditions under which the property of wet-strength in paper products becomes important :

(1) **Exposure to weather.** Examples packing cases, outdoor posters, building papers, paper bags, maps and mulch paper.

(2) **Exposure to water of paper products used as drying of wiping media.** Examples; paper towels, paper napkins, windshield wiping tissue, industrial wiping tissue, lens paper, and facial tissue.

(3) **Exposure of wrapping paper to water.** Examples butcher wraps, fruit and vegetable wraps, and frozen and prepared food wraps.

(4) **Exposure to water by immersion as part of a processing operation.** Examples. Photographic paper, blueprint paper, filter paper, saturating paper, and tea bag paper.

There are a number of reasons why the wet-strength process achieved such extensive uses in a relatively short time. Wet-strength resins that could be adsorbed by the paper stock with relatively good retention and little interference with the normal papermaking process became available. Paper machines normally run at the same production rate for we-strength grades as for similar untreated grades. The amount of resin required is relatively small, normally ranging from about 0.5 to about 2.0% of the fibre furnish. The entire wet-strength process is of moderate cost. Many wet-strength grades of paper have been sold at no premium over the corresponding untreated grades.

A fortunate characteristic of the resin is that polymerization or "cure" to a final insoluble condition occurs within a few weeks of aging at normal temperatures. It is, therefore, not necessary to complete the cure on the paper machine by subjecting the paper to a high degree of heat. Also, even after the wet strength has developed, it is possible to defiber the paper by means of treatment with mild acid at elevated temperatures. The recovery of broke, therefore, becomes a relatively simple process for most grades of wet-strength paper. The degree of improvement in the wet-tensile strength ranges from 300 to 1000% of that of the same paper in the untreated state. Accordingly, the improvement is readily observed by the user of the product, and it can be easily demonstrated to buyers and prospective users.

Not only have these factors combined to bring about extensive commercial use of this process, but also the aminoplast resins (urea-formaldehyde, melamine-formaldehyee) have set standards of cost, effectiveness, and convenience that have been very difficult for other prospective wet-strengthening processes and materials to meet. Thus, although many wet-strength processes have been described in the literature, the number that the have achieved commercial use is very limited. One important development in this field in recent years has been a resin that will cure under neutral or alkaline conditions. Since urea-formaldehyde and melamine-formaldehyde require mild acid conditions for cure, it is generally necessary to run the paper machine in the range from pH 4 to 5. Under these conditions some equipment is susceptible to corrosion. In response to this problem, there has been developed a polyamide-epichlorohydrin resin that does not require acid conditions for cure.

WET-STRENGTH RESINS

Although numerous chemical agents have been proposed for producing wet-strength paper, the derivatives of urea-formaldehyde, melamine-formaldehyde, and polyamide-ephichlohydring have achieved the largest commercial application.

Urea and formaldehyde react under alkaline conditions to form dimethylolurea as shown :

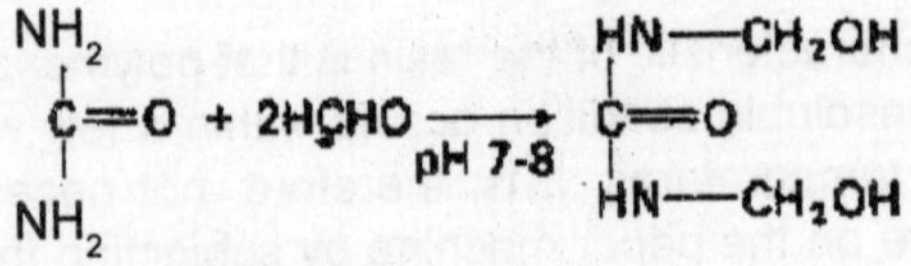

Catalysed by acid, DMU can condense with itself by several routes with the elimination of water to form three-dimensional cross-linked polymers. Beginning in 1938, polymers of this type, applied by tub sizing or other means of surface application, were used to produce wet strength.

Later UF resins, modified with sodium bisulfite, were prepared. These resins retain solubility in the "B" stage of partially polymerized condition. Such resins, when added to the stock furnish and precipitated with alum, were retained by the fibre and paper made therefrom. If a heat-curing treatment was given, they were found to have wet strength. The principle effectiveness of the bisulfite UF resins was with unbleached and groundwood furnishes.

Still later, UF resins (modified by polyfunctional amines) were developed. These resins are cationic in charge and, therefore, are substantive to fibre without the addition of alum. Of the UF resins currently used for wet strength, this class is predominant.

Melamine reacts readily with formaldehyde to form a series of methylol derivatives. The most important for wet-strength is the trimethylol derivative shown below:

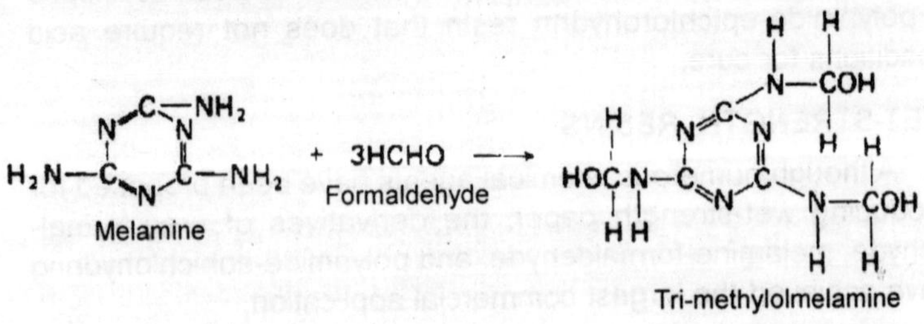

Trimethylol melamine reacts with hydrochloric acid to from a partially polmerized colloidal dispersion that a highly cationic and substantive to fibre. It is an effective wet strength agent for addition to the stock furnish. The MF colloid (introduced in 1941) was the first substantive thermosetting wet-strength resin. It has been important in wet-strength paper production since that time. In recent years, a modified form of acid colliod (using additional amounts of formaldehyde) has been marketed as HE (high-efficiency) melamine colloid.

Both UF and MF resins must be used under mildly acidic conditions in the paper machine system, pH 4 to 5. The desirability for a wet-strength resin to be used under neutral or alkaline conditions has resulted in the development of the polyamide-epichlorohydrin resins.

The resins are prepared by reacting epichlorohydrin with basic, low-molecular-weight polyamides derived from aliphatic dicarboxylic acids (such as adipic and succinic) and polyalkylene polyamines (such as diethylene triamine or tetraethylene pentamine). Sufficient epichlorohydrin is used to convert the secondary amines to tertiary and/or quaternary ammonium groups, thus imparting cationic character to the resins. This treatment leads to some cross-linking, but the extent of the cross-linking must be carefully controlled to maintain water solubility. The resulting products consist of moderately long-chain polyamide backbones with many reactive side-chains as branches. The exact structures, however are not known with certainty. One concept of the formation of this type of resin is given at next page :

As previously mentioned, many chemical agents and processes have been proposed for making wet-strength paper. Some of these have been or are being used commercially, but none have achieved the volume of use the resins discussed above. A partial list follows:

acidified formaldehyde

glyoxal

heat treatment of paper

insolubilized protein

insolubilized vegetable gums

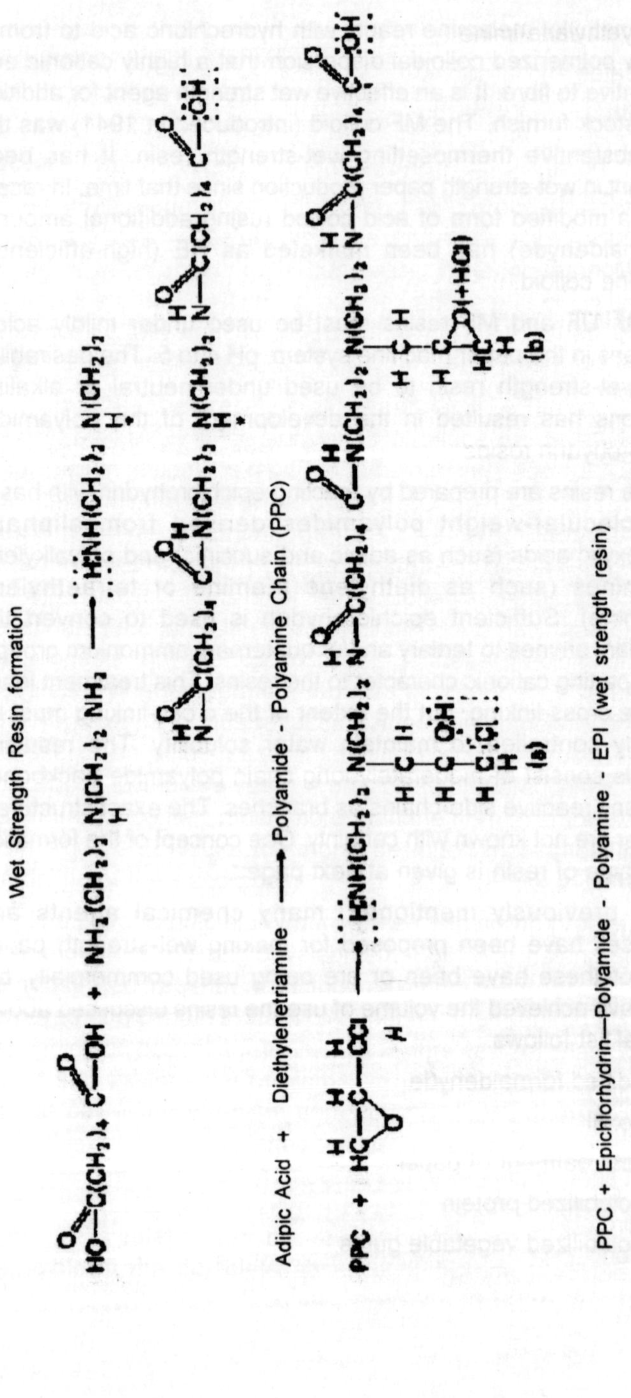
Wet Strength Resin formation
Adipic Acid + Diethylenetriamine ——→ Polyamide - Polyamine Chain (PPC)
(a)
(b)
PPC + Epichlorohydrin—Polyamide - Polyamine - EPI (wet strength resin)

polyethylene-imine
silicates and silicones
synthetic and natural latex
vegetable parchment
viscose (xanthate) solutions

A more extended discussion of these agents will be found in TAPPI Monograph 29, pp 105-125.2.

OPERATING PROCEDURES

Most commonly, the wet-strength resin is added continuously in the form of solution to the flow of furmish stock after the last refiner. The pH of the head box stock system must be maintained at the proper level for the resin being used. The flow of resin solution, in proportion to the quantity of fibre, must be closely controlled (in order to meet the wet tensile test required) without using an excess of resin. The percent resin on basis of fibre varies considerably, depending on the grade of paper and the wet strength requirement. Normally the range is from 0.5 to about 1.0%, although for special purposes it may go as high as 5%.

The paper at the reel normally has not received sufficient exposure to heat to effect complete cure of resin. For test purposes, a paper sample is heated at about 125°C for 3 to 5 min and then tested for wet tensile strength. Natural aging will develop wet-strength in the product after a few days or weeks. The relationship between the accelerated test and natural aging must be determined experimentally for each mill and product.

MECHANISMS OF WET STRENGTH

It appears that the thermo-setting wet-strength resins function mainly by protecting the existing interfiber bonds from the effects of water. This could be accomplished in the following ways: (1) covalent chemical cross-links could be formed between the cellulose and the resin, which could lead to reduced swelling and solubility; (2) the resins could absorb or penetrate the cellulosic fibres and cross-link with themselves to produce a restraining network on, or in the bounding areas; and (3) the resin could form a protective skin of polymer by either simple film formation or by strong, essentially irreversible adsorption.

Stannett has reported studies on the activation energies of urea-formaldehyde resin hydrolysis in the presence of and in the absence of cellulose fibres. Since the activation energy of both reactions is the same, it is unlikely that co-valent bonds are formed between the resin and the cellulose. Similar considerations would apply to melamine-formaldehyde and polyamide-ephichlorohydrin resins.

Formaldehyde, on the other hand, is known to react with cellulose at low pH and high temperature to form methylene cross-links as follows :

$$2\ \text{cellulose} — \text{OH} + \text{HCO} \rightarrow \text{cellulose} — \text{O}$$
$$— \text{CH}_2 — \text{O cellulose}$$

Paper treated in this way develops a high degree of wet strength. This is an example of wet strength resulting from a true reaction leading to cross-linking and reduced swelling of the cellulose structure. As would be expected, formaldehyde-treated paper is highly resistant to hydrolysis. The treatment embrittles and weakens the fibres, and hence, the physical properties of the paper are impaired. It is not clear how much of this degradation is to be attributed to the cross-linking due to formaldehyde or to the acid and heat conditions necessary for the reaction.

13

Paper Machine - Forming Section

INTRODUCTION

Paper is a web of fibres forming a three-dimensional network. The predominant method used to make this sheet involves filtration from a dilute fibre suspension in water onto an endless wire mesh that is fine enough to retain most of the fibres. The section of the paper machine performing this function is called the "forming section", and it receives the fibre suspension in a continuous jet from the heabox at 0.1 to 2.0% consistency. It then delivers a self-supporting sheet at 10 to 25% consistency to the press section. The prime functions of the forming section are to deposit the fibres so that a paper of desired quality is produced and to provide the necessary removal of water.

As the position and direction of the fibres in the sheet structure is almost entirely determined by the forming process, it follows that many of the most important quality characteristics of the paper are established here. Properties mainly determined by the forming section are formation, strength isotropy, fines distribution through the sheet, wire mark, and to a large extent, surface uniformity.

Due to the wide variation in paper properties (tissue, greaseproof, boards, etc.) basis weights (3 to 3000 lb), and speeds (10 to 5000 fpm) used in the industry, the demands on the forming section varies greatly. This has resulted in the development of a number of different types of forming methods, each with its preferred application.

For a better understanding of the present technology, a short discussion of the fundamentals of drainage and forming is needed. In addition to the forming of the mat, the forming section also compacts the sheet and removes water by suction, thus giving it sufficient strength to be transferred to the press section.

THE SHEET FORMING PROCESS

Paper is made by depositing fibres from a dilute suspension onto a fine wire mesh by filtration. The water drains through, while the majority of the fibres are retained by the wire. As the fibres are of about the same size as the openings in the wire, a large number of hem pass through in the initial phase. As more and more fibres are retained, they themselves act as a filtering medium, thus causing a progressive increase in retention. The change in retention during the sheet forming process produces a variation in structure and fibre composition through the thickness of the sheet.

During the forming process, the sheet is built up from fibres or fibre aggregrates in a generally random manner. The sheet structure is, therefore, critically dependent on the distribution of the fibres in the water suspension. Knowledge of he properties of dilute fibre suspensions is, therefore, a necessary party of understanding forming.

Fibers are flexible particles normally with a length of 1 to 4 mm, and with a length to diameter ratio mostly in excess of 100 mm. Papers are made from mixtures of fibres with greatly varying dimensions. Above a critical consistency of about 0.05%, these suspensions form three-dimensional networks due to interaction and entanglement of the individual fibres. In a flowing suspension, the network is normally broken down into aggregates varying in size between 5 to 30 mm called “flocs”. "Flocculation” is a dynamic phenomenon in shear flow with fibres moving between flocs. The tendency of fibres to floc and the strength of the fibre network increase with fibre length and consistency. Network strength is at least a third power function of consistency, as shown in Fig.1. In fluid flow, the fibre network breaks down into smaller pieces when the shear rate exceeds the yield point of the network at its weakest point. Due to the large effect of consistency on network strength, the size and density of the flocs increases rapidly with consistency. Increasing shear rate and reducing the geometrical scale will

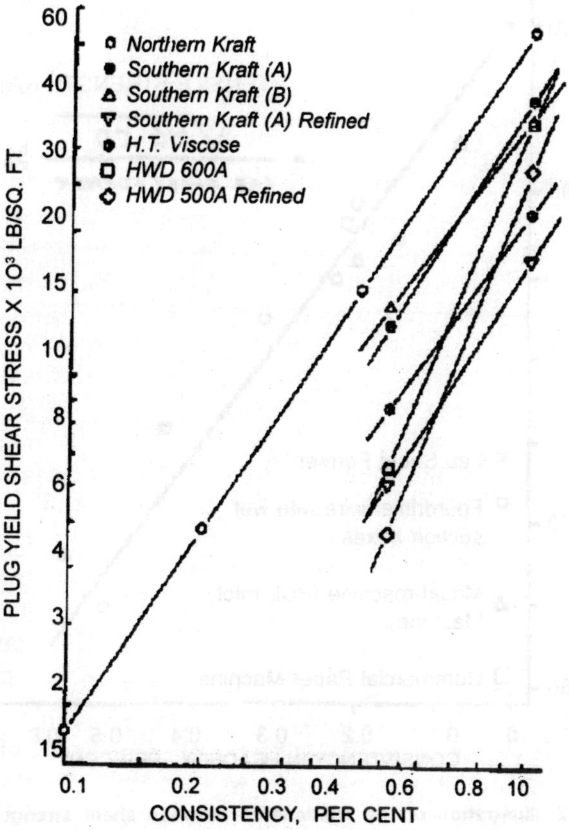

Fig. 1 Fiber network strength.

reduce the size of the flocs, but will increase their density. The uniformity of the sheet formed improves with the reduction of size and density of the flocs and is at its optimum when each fibre is free to move independently. However, in most commercial operations, it is impossible to operate at low enough consistencies, due to the limitations in drainage capacity of the forming section. Forming, therefore, occurs mainly from fibre suspensions in different stages of flocculation. Due to this, consistency is by far the most important factor in determining sheet formation. The longer the fibres, the more important low consistencies are for good formation. While bag papers are currently made at 0.15%

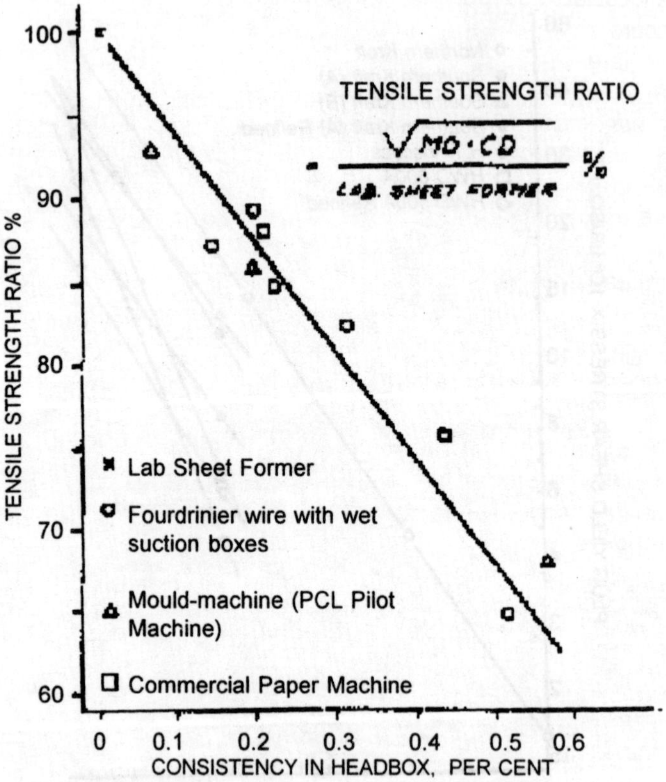

Fig. 2. Illustration of the relationship between sheet strength and forming consistency.

consistency from soft wood, kraft groundwood papers can be made satisfactorily at effective consistencies of 0.3 to 0.5%. Figure 2 illustrates the relationship between sheet formation and forming consistency. For a given set of conditions, the drainage capacity of the forming section determines the forming consistency, and thereby, the paper quality.

Turbulence breaks down the fibre networks. Increasing turbulence reduces he size of the flocs, but increases their density. The size of the flocs can also be controlled geometrically. These methods are being used in the headbox to deliver a well deflocculated suspension to the forming area. As forming normally occurs under shear-free conditions, turbulence dies very rapidly with larger flocs reformation. Only by setting the sheet close to the headbox can advantages of deflocculation by high turbulence be used to any significant degree. This method is being used in all successful applications of confined areas formers, such as suction breast roll formers and different types of twin wire formers. This makes it possible to form satisfactory sheets despite relatively high forming consistencies caused by the limited drainage capacity of these formers.

Even if the fibre flocculation in the suspension entering the forming area is the dominating factor as regard formation, there are many mechanisms in the forming process itself that have very significant effects on the paper structure. These will be further discussed under each type of former. One general remark should be stated now, as it is applicable to every process, any mechanism breaking up an already formed sheet is detrimental to the quality of the paper.

14

Paper Machine Press Section

FUNCTIONS OF THE PRESS SECTION

The press section of a paper machine has a variety of purposes. These can be expressed in different terms, but we believe that the following four functions convey comprehensively the important purposes of this portion of any paper machine.

(1) Increase the consistency (solids content) of the sheet of paper by removal of a portion of the free water contained in the sheet of paper after it has been formed.

(2) Convey the paper from the forming unit to the dryer section, without disrupting or disturbing the structure of the sheet.

(3) After the surface properties of the paper.

(4) Reduce the bulk of the paper.

The first two functions are always desirable and necessary. The influence on two-sideness of the press section may or may not be significant, depending on the specific situation and grades being made, and may or may not be desirable. Pressing always results in compaction of the sheet, and this may or may not be desirable, depending upon the grades that are being made.

TYPES OF PRESS SECTIONS

Diagrams 1 through 7 are some presently used press sections. These are not meant to represent all the kinds of press sections in use, but rather to set forth some typical arrangements. The choice of a press section is usually made dependent on the specific

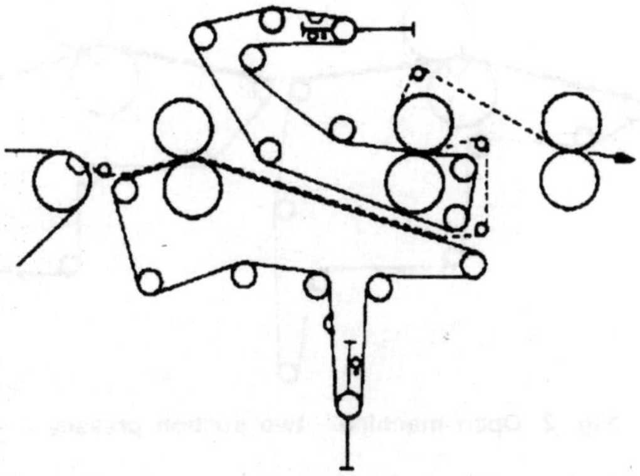

Fig. 1. Plain press-open machine, first press straight up, second press reverse, smoothing press.

desired properties of the product and the need to overcome web handling problems, particularly at high speeds.

Figure 1 is an old type of press arrangement that is used on some paper machines making fine, flat paper grades. It has the advantages of being low in cost, low in maintenance, and relatively simple to operate. It has the disadvantage of being really practical at low speeds only (below 500 fpm). Felts on plain presses often fill up rapidly with foreign material. A phenomenon called "blowing" (air between the sheet and the felt at the entry side to the nip) is prevalent on this type of press and is a limiting factor in speed and quality. The press, however, on fine papers has an offsetting advantage of producing paper that has no marks that are the result of show through of suction holes or roll grooves. Some faster machines (1000 to 1400 fpm) use plain presses in second and third press positions where water removal requirements are very low.

Figure 2 is a relatively simple arrangement from the standpoint of drives, frame and structure of the machine. It functions well on newsprint, kraft, or publishing grades up to 1500 fpm.

Problems are: a high percentage of breaks in the higher range of speeds, due to the unsupported sheet between the forming unit and the first press; the possibility of suction shell mark; and limited unit nip pressure, due to structural limitations of the suction shells.

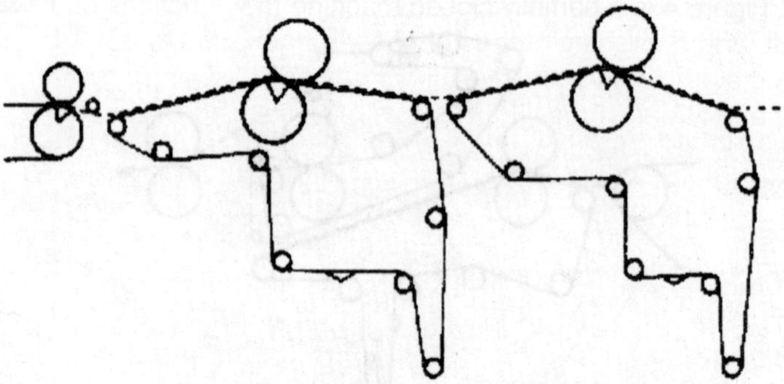

Fig. 2. Open machine - two suction presses.

Figure 3 is like Fig. 2, except the second press is inverted. It has the advantage of being self-dumping, so that when the paper breaks, the sheet will run into the pit. The press also provides bare roll contact of the wire side of the sheet to reduce two-sidedness.

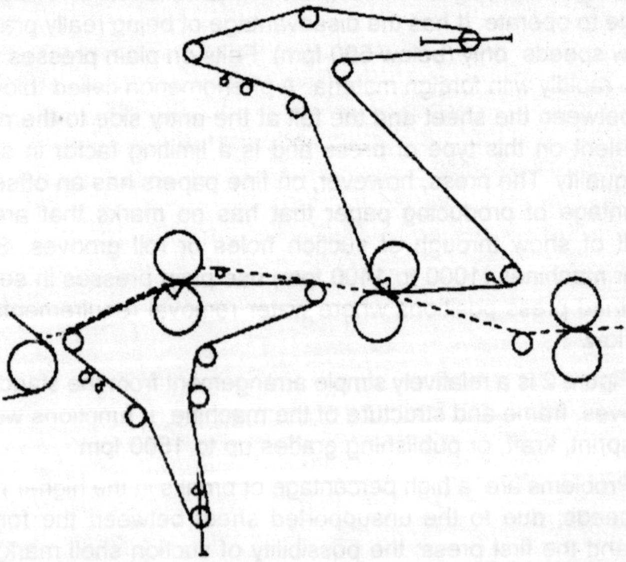

Fig. 3. Open machine - first press straight up, second press invered.

Figure 4 is a partially closed machine that functions on news, kraft, and publishing grades at speeds from 1800 to 3000 fpm. It has the advantage of eliminating the breaks between the forming unit and the first press. It produces consistencies as high as 42% entering the dryer on paper grades, with the use of the Venta-Nip Press of other hard-nip presses and high-press loadings.

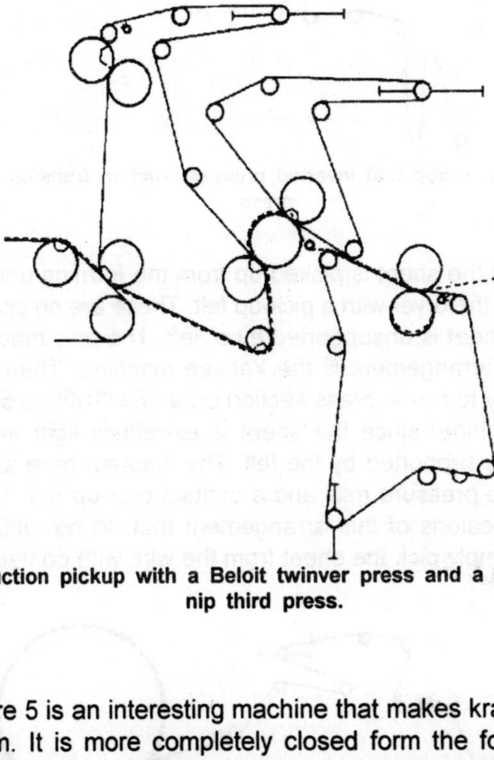

Fig. 4 Suction pickup with a Beloit twinver press and a Beloit Venta-nip third press.

Figure 5 is an interesting machine that makes kraft papers at 2700 fpm. It is more completely closed form the former to the dryer section. The machine features two inverted presses and a suction transfer to the third press. It has the advantage of no unsupported draw, except between the third press and the dryer section, and therefore, is able to operate a high speeds on light weight kraft grades with very few breaks. It has the disadvantage of being somewhat sensitive to the sheet following the inverted first and second press rolls.

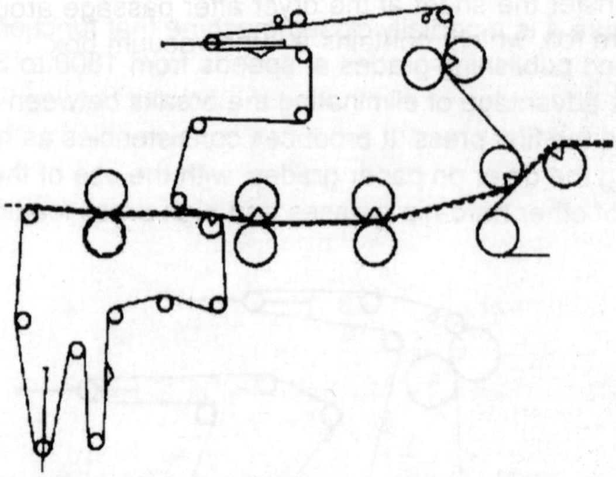

Fig.5. Suction pickup and inverted presses, suction transfer to second press.

In Fig. 6 the sheet is picked up from the forming unit and put directly onto the dryer with a pick-up felt. These are no open draws where the sheet is unsupported by a left. The only machine that utilizes this arrangement is the Yankee machine. There is really no other way to run a press section on a fast (2000 to 5000 fpm) Yankee machine, since the sheet is extremely light and fragile and must be supported by the felt. The diagram here shows two presses, two pressure rolls and a contact pick-up roll. These are other modificaions of this arrangement that do not utilize a wet felt. They simply pick the sheet from the wire with contact pick-up

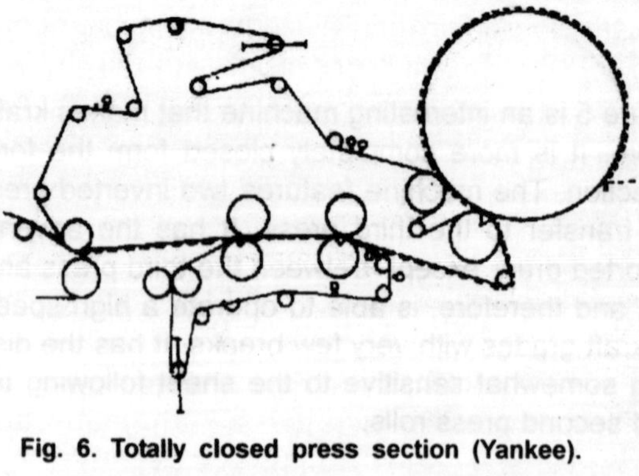

Fig. 6. Totally closed press section (Yankee).

and transfer the sheet at the dryer after passage around the first pressure roll, which contains a large vacuum box.

Another interesting press section is the Uni-Pross, which utilizes a common pick-up roll and first press nip roll. This arrangement has the advantage of simplicity, and together with a Fabric Press on the second press position. It produces extremely high dryness entering the dryer section (Fig. 7).

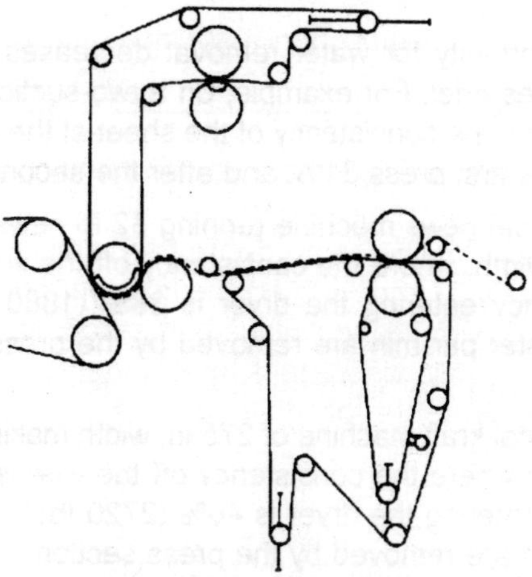

Fig. 7. KMW Uni-press.

MATERIAL BALANCE

The primary function of the press section is, of course, to remove water. The amount of water removed and the change in consistency of the sheet from its entry into the press section until it enters the dryer obviously depend on a number of things:

(1) The consistency of the sheet off the forming unit.

(2) The grades of paper being made.

(3) The speed of operation.

(4) The pressing equipment.

(5) Most particularly, the pressure per unit area in the press nips.

Consistency off the forming unit varies considerably and depends on the weight and freeness of the paper being made and the water removal equipment on the forming unit. The range of consistencies produced by paper machine formers will be in the order of 10% on the low side to 23% on the high side. Grades such as soft tissue and glassine will be in the order of 10 to 12% consistency, when formed on the wire, grades such as news and publishing grades will be 18 to 20% and kraft board will be 22 to 23 per cent.

The opportunity for water removal decreases as the paper sheet becomes drier. For example, on a two-suction press, book paper machine, the consistency of the sheet at the couch may be 20%, after the first press 31%, and after the second press 36%.

On a typical news machine running 32 lb news at 2500 fpm, 3000 in., in width, where the consistency off the wire is 18% and the consistency entering the dryer is 38% (1880 lbs/min), 226 gallons of water per min are removed by the press section from the sheet.

On a typical kraft machine of 275 in, width making 42 lb board at 16000 fpm where the consistency off the wire is 22% and the consistency entering the dryer is 40% (2720 lbs), 327 gallons of water per min are removed by the press section.

Table 1 represents water balance data on three typical press sections and shows, in the case of the kraft liner board machine, the effect of increased basis weight. The figures are expressed in pounds of water per pound of paper, pounds of water per 1000 sq ft of paper, pounds of water per min, and gallons per min.

This data illustrates not only the large difference that exists in water removal between the first and second presses, but also the effect of increasing basis weight. For example, even though the total gallons and pounds of water per pound of paper are lower when making 69 lb liner board, the pounds of water per 1000 sq ft of paper is about 45% greater than for 42 lb board. This means that the felt must press a much greater quantity of water per unit area when making the heavier weight.

NIP PRESSURE

Nip pressures are usually presented in pounds per lineal in, but the really important aspects of nip pressure is the pressure

Table 1

Position	% Cons	#W/#BD Paper	##	#/MSF	#/Min	GPM	% Cons	#W/#BD	##	#/MSF	#/Min	GPM
	Book paper 54#/3300 sq ft, 6% Moist 1200 fpm, 180" width		Water Removal				Newsprint 32#/3000 sq ft, 6% Moist 25000 fpm, 300" width		Water Removal			
Couch	20	4.00					18	4.56				
1st Press	31	2.23	1.77	27.2	490	58.8	32	2.12	2.44	25.0	1562	188
2nd Press	36	1.78	.45	6.9	124	14.9	38	1.63	.49	5.0	318	38
Total			2.22	34.1	614				2.93	30.0	1880	226

Kraft Liner

Position	% Cons	#W/#BD	##	#/MSF	#/Min	GPM	% Cons	#W/#BD	##	#/MSF	#/Min	GPM
	42#/2000 sq ft, 6% moisture 1600 fpm, 275" width		Water Removal				69#/1000 sq ft, 7% moisture 1000 fpm, 275" width		Water Removal			
Couch	22	3.55					23	3.35				
1st Press	34	1.94	1.61	63.6	2330	280	35	1.86	1.49	95.6	2190	263
2nd Press	40	1.50	.44	17.4	638	76	40	1.50	.36	23.1	530	64
Total			2.05	81.0	2968	356			1.85	118.7	2720	327

per unit area. This is, of course, influenced by the amount of loading, the diameter of the press rolls, the hardness of the press rolls, and the weight and thickness of the felts.

In has been shown by McNamara and others that the unit pressure builds from zero load on the entry side to a peak load slightly upstream of the geometrical center of the nip, and hen falls off on the exit side of the nip to zero load again.

The limitation to the peak load that a sheet can withstand before it crushes appears to be largely a function of the ease with which the water can escape as the felt and sheet are compressed in the nip. Hard-nip presses such as Beloit's Venta-Nip, the Fabric Press. Black-Clawson's HI-I Press, and the Sleeve Press all provide incompressible passways in the center of the nip, so the resistance to flour is greatly reduced and crushing occurs only at extremely high pressures.

CROWN

Any set of press rolls should be crowned for the particular pressure at which it will operate. The machine builder and roll coverer can provide the proper crown on a given roll, if they are given the details of the structure of the roll. There are some practical helps, however, which can bring a roll closer to its ideal crown:

(1) Thickness and tensile profiles of the felts after removal are helpful in indicating whether the roll is over or under crowned.

(2) Moisture profile of the paper is also helpful.

(3) Nip impressions can provide guidance in solving crown problems.

A useful formula utilizes information derived from an accurate nip impression to provide the correct crown. Although there has been doubt expressed by users that this formula is strictly quantitative, it does provide a reasonable guide to facilitate crown changes.

Nip Impression Evaluation Formula*

$$C = \frac{(N_2^2 - N_1^2)(D_1 + D_2)}{2D_1 D_2}$$

C = Necessary total crown coreection (sum of top and bottom crowns) in inches.

N_1 = Nip impression width center (in.)

N_2 = Nip impression width end (in.)

D_1 = Diameter top roll

D_2 = Diameter bottom roll

For equal top and bottom roll diameter:

$$C = \frac{N_2^2 - N_1^2}{D}$$

For instance with press having bottom roll diameter of 30 in., top roll diameter 24 in.,

$$N_2 = 2.1'', N_1 = 2.0 \text{ in.}$$

$$C = \frac{(2.10)^2 - (2.0)^2 (54)}{2(24)\,30} = +.015$$

This means total crown should be increased by .015.

When answer comes out negative, it means that total crown should be decreased by that amount.

*Raybestos-Manhattan.

Some papermakers make the changes indicated by the formula into steps. The first crown change is usually one-half or two-thirds of the amount indicated, and further corrections, if necessary, are made on subsequent grindings of the roll. In addition to the proper crown, it is usually necessary to dub or relieve the ends of the press rolls by grinding (tapering) the ends of the roll from the sheet edge out. It is usual practice to reduce the diameter of the end of the roll by 1/16 to 1/8 in. This is necessary to prevent excessive wear on the edges of the felt. Softer rolls usually require more dubbing. On machines where a wide variety of grades and basis weights are made (and it is necessary to vary the pressure on the presses to provide more bulk or prevent crushing) crown-compensated or variable-crown rolls are being used more extensively.

VACUUM

Suction presses and pressure rolls are widely used in press sections on many machines. The primary function of vacuum on a suction press roll is to retain the water that has been pressed from the felts and sheet by the nip in the holes of the suction roll shell, until the shell has rotated out of the nip region and centrifugal force discharges the water from the shell holes. The design and operation of the vacuum box, in conjunction with the speed of the machine, are controlling factors in determining whether any of the water expressed from the felt and sheet actually passes into the suction box. The factors also determine the angle around the circumference of the roll at which the water in the holes is thrown off.

A number of suction rolls, namely on board machine suction-drum rolls, single-felt Yankee machine pressure rolls, and Uni-Press rolls are equipped with very wide vacuum areas, and sufficient time is available over the vacuum, area for a large amount of water to enter the vacuum box prior to entry into the nip. These are special arrangements where the vacuum box may cover from 90 to 180° of the circumference of the roll; however, usually the vacuum box will cover only 15 to 25° of the circumference of the roll.

TEMPERATURE

Press sections operate at temperatures that range from below room temperature to 150°F. It is fairly well documented that increasing sheet temperature increases the dryness to the dryer. This is at least in part due to the reduced viscosity of the water at elevated temperatures. The level of temperatures at which a press section is operated is largely a matter of economics. In general, the hotter the sheet and felt during pressing, the more efficiently the press section will perform. Modern high synthetic felts are capable of operating at sustained temperatures of at least 150°F.

SHEET DENSIFICATION

All paper loses bulk on pressing. It is questionable whether the advantages of the increases in bulk with reduced unit press pressures can be justified, except in the case of certain products where high bulk is the most important property of the paper being made.

On any paper that is subsequently calendered, the bulk that is preserved in the press section is lost to the higher unit pressure in the calender stack.

MARKING

Felts will sometimes transfer a weave impression to the paper being pressed. The wetter the paper and the higher the unit pressure, the more likely the transfer of the weave mark becomes. These marks are referred to as warp (machine direction), filling (cross direction), and twill (weave pattern, combinations of both warp and filling) mark. Finer weaves, more permeable and smoother, heavier, and softer felts can reduce or eliminate marks. On some papers such as tissue, a crush mark is usually called a felt mark.

Shell impressions or shadow marks occur when the hole pattern in the shell is transferred to the paper. These marks are a result of the paper being pressed at a higher unit pressure over the land area than over the hole are, and also because the felt depresses into the hole, causing a lower pressure in the nip over the hole area than over the land area. Heavier, thicker felts help, as does the grinding of the roll, since grinding the roll eliminates the chamfer that occurs (because of wear) at the edges of the holes that in effect reduce the land area and increase the unit pressure over the land area.

Some marking may occur with Venta-Nip rolls, particularly on heavy weight papers. This is generally a result of the sheet being too wet, the roll in need of grinding, or the felts not being heavy enough.

OTHER PRESSING DEFECTS

Picking

Bits of stock that adhere to the felt or to a press roll cause small pits or depressions to be left in the sheet. These are called "picks." This condition is a form of incipient crush and is caused primarily because the felts or the rolls are dirty, the sheet is too wet, or the shear forces across the sheet are too great.

Crushing

This condition occurs when the formation of the sheet is disturbed druing pressing. It is a result of the sheet being too wet to withstand the impact of the nip forces. It comes about when the distance that the expressed water has to flow is so great that the hydrostatic forces developed within the sheet and the felt in the nip are excessive.

In a given press, if the machine speed is increased, at some level crushing will occur. This is sometimes called the "rush threshold." The crush threshold can be raised by providing open areas under the felt in the center of the nip (e.g., suction press, Venta-Nip press) so the water can escape. It can also be increased by freeing up the stock, by reducing the press loading, and by utilizing felts with higher vertical and lateral permeability.

Blowing

The accumulating of air at the entry side of a nip between the felt and the sheet, or in some cases, between plies of the sheet is called 'blowing'. Blow marks are folds in the paper that result because the paper is deformed on the entry side of the nip and folds over as the sheet passes through the nip. Blowing is a result of the sheet not being in intimate contact with the total surface of the felt. Air that is carried on the surface of the felt accumulates at the entry side of the nip. If the air cannot escape through the felt or through the sheet, blowing results.

Air at the entry side of the nip is also accumulated, because of the change in volume of the felt from outside to inside the nip. This volume change causes air contained in the felt voids to be pumped between the sheet and the felt.

Blowing can be reduced or eliminated by making the stock freer, by providing felts that change less in thickness as they enter the nip, and by smoother, more level felts ; also by felts that are more porous and rolls that have more open area under the felt within the nip.

TRANSFER MECHANISM FROM FORMING SECTION TO THE PRESS SECTION

Couching Process

At the end of the fourdrinier table, after the sheet is passed over the couch, the wet formed sheet is removed from the forming wire. In the open type of fourdrinier, the web is transferred across an open draw to a moving press felt that carries the sheet into the press section. The sheet is transferred at startup by cutting a narrow tail that is thrown or blown onto the press felt, and the strip is widened by moving the cut-off squirt across the sheet.

There are two types of pick-up that transfer the formed sheet from the wire to a felt. The first can best be described as contact pick-up. Here a smooth, wet, level dense felt is pressed against the formed sheet on the wire, and the sheet transfers to the felt. This type of pick-up is used for most tissue, both creped and flat, having basis weights of 5 to 30 lb on the wire. The picking-up process is aided by the fact that the wet web of fibres is attracted to the fine level capillary structure of the felt, in preference to that of the wire. Tissue type pick-up machines make use of water film and capillary forces that exist between the sheet and the felt to effect sheet transfer. Heavier basis weights can be handled with contact pick-up, but usually weights in excess of 30 lb are handled by another type of machanism.

A second type (suction pick-up) utilizes a suction roll on the roll (inside) side of a felt that has sufficient permeability so that air can be easily drawn through the felt. The resulting vacuum causes the sheet to be sucked against the felt where it adheres until it is transferred to the first press.

Suction pick-up is usually used on machines making papers having basis weights of from 20 to 40 lb. There are machines that make papers up to 130 lb that utilize suction pick-up; however, the advantages of suction pick-up on machines making only heavy weights is questionable. Once the sheet has been picked up, it remins attached to the felt, because of the capillary forces and/or the water film strength that exists between the sheet and the felt.

The principal advantage of contact or suction pick-up is in the elimination of the open draw between the wire and the first press. On any light weight (10 to 40 lb) machine, it is not unusual for more than half of the total breaks to occur between the wire and the first press. As the speed of any open machine is increased, the frequency of breaks between the wire and the first press increases.

Another type of transfer mechanism has gained widespread use in the paper industry, and although pick-up is not involved, it has been known as "Poor Man's Pick-up." In this arrangement, the sheet is allowed to run down the inclined wire after the suction couch and is pulled off the wire at an angle of take-off that reduces the sheet tension necessary to effect removal from the wire. Most kraft liner board and some paper machines utilize this method of taking the sheet from the wire. This is considered preferable to installing a more expensive pick-up arrangement.

PRESS SECTION PARTS

Pick-up Roll

In a paper machine with a suction or contact pick-up, the sheet is transferred directly from the fourdrinier wire to the pick-up felt, and the pick-up roll must be located accurately relative to the wire or couch roll. In the case of contact pick-up, sometimes a couch roll is allowed to come down onto a grooved or drilled bottom couch, and a solid nip is formed by this contact. On most modern machines, however, the pick-up roll picks up directly from the wire, and there is no backing roll. This is sometimes referred to as free wire pick-up. The top couch or pick-up roll usually varies in hardness from zero hardness to 90 or 100 P & J hardness scale. The unit pressure in the pick-up nip is important; therefore, a precise means of loading and unloading the pick-up roll is necessary. It is important that the pick-up roll be capable of being lowered so that both sides come down together. On some Yankee machines, the sheet is formed on the wire and the basis weight is adjusted. Then, the pick-up roll is lowered to contact the wire and pick-up the sheet. On other machines, the pick-up roll is left in position contacting the wire and the sheet is taken over the machine during the time the basis weight is being adjusted. On a free-wire pick-up machine, the unit pressure of the pick-up nip is a function of how far the pick-up roll is depressed into the wire and the tension on the wire.

Suction Pick-up Rolls

The suction pick-up roll may contain one or two boxes, usually a high-level vacuum pick-up box and a holding box, so that the water can be retained in the shell for a sufficient length of time and can be thrown into the Saveall pan well past the point where the pick-up felt leaves the roll. In most instances, the entire sheet is picked up from the wire by lowering the suction pick-up roll; however, in some cases, there is a gate in the vacuum box that permits the operator to pick up a narrow tail that is cut with a squirt on the wire. After the tail is through the press section, the sheet is widened out by pulling the squirt across the machine.

Suction pick-up rolls usually consist of a bronze shell and may or may not be rubber covered. On some machines, the rolls are made inter-changeable with press rolls, so that only one spare roll is necessary.

Suction Press Rolls

The suction roll consists of a bronze or stainless steel shell 2 in. or more thick, usually covered with rubber about 1 in. thick. The roll is normally drilled with 5/32 to 3/16 in. holes, and has an open area of 18 to 25%. The rolls are designed for nip pressures between 100 and 550 pli. The box inside the roll usually ranges from 4 to 8 in. wide, but can be considerably wider in special rolls for special applications. Vacuum will normally range from 10 to 24 in. of Hg. Suction box position inside the roll can be adjusted in relation to the nip. There are heads inside the box that can be adjusted and two screws (that operate from the front side) that can widen or narrow the deckle of the machine. The box is sealed against the inside of the roll by seal strips that are pressed against the roll with springs or air-loaded tubes. These seal strips are lubricated with water. The suction roll is usually surrounded by a pan or Saveall for collection of water that is thrown out of the roll.

Venta-Nip Press Rolls

The Venta-Nip press was developed and patented by Beloit Corporation. It vents the nip to the atmosphere by cutting a series of grooves in spiral fashion into the surface of the roll. The grooves are so placed that no point on the face of the roll is greater than approximately .050 from a groove. With a roll so vented, not as much back pressure is developed within the felt, the crushing is greatly reduced, and the crush threshold is raised substantially. In practice, it has been found that nip pressure can be raised 100% or more, without crushing, and with rather dramatic increases in dryness level out of the press. Depending upon the product and the rate of speed, this dryness level has been raised anywhere from 2 to 8%. Most Venta-Nip rolls consist of a zero-hardness top roll and an 8 to 12 P&J grooved roll. The grooved pattern is usually cut. 100 to .120 in. deep and .020 to .030 in. width, and the grooves are spaced approximately 8 to the inch. There are some installations of stainless steel grooved rolls where the nip is essentially zero hardness.

Solid Press Rolls

Solid press rolls are made of a hollow steel or cast iron core that is covered with rubber or rubber compounds. The rubber compound will usually vary in hardness from zero to 60 P&J.

SMOOTHING PRESS

In some press sections, particularly on machines making fine papers, a press consisting of two rolls with no felt is used to smooth out the sheet and iron out any small irregularities in it before it enters the dryer section. At this point, the sheet is still plastic and can be gently pressed. This press is intended only for leveling and smoothing a sheet and is not intended to remove any moisture from the sheet.

Doctors

The function of a doctor on a press roll is to keep the roll surface clean, to avoid buildup on either fibre or filler, to prevent impairment of the finish of the sheet, and also to prevent the build-up of any material that might tend to adhere to the sheet and cause a break at the press. In addition, the press doctor must perform the function of controlling the tail at startup or the whole sheet in the event of a break in the press section; therefore, doctors are commonly made either with a high scoop back to catch the tail of the sheet and broke, or if there is a broke conveyor installed in back of the press involved, the doctor back is expected to guide and convey broke away from the roll and on to the broke conveyor.

The blade material of the doctor must be selected properly to avoid damaging the surface of the press roll it is intended to clean. Most press roll covering materials are not very abrasion resistant, compared to metal surfaces; therefore, a top press roll doctor must be oscillated. The blade material must be very carefully aligned with the roll, so that it can be operated at minimum loading pressure against the roll.

15

Paper Machine - Dryer Section

INTRODUCTION

As the paper leaves the press section of a fourdrinier machine, it contains from 32 to 40% solids. Modern techniques in the mechanical removal of water (for example, the vented press roll, the fabric press and , most recently, the batt-on-mesh felt) have resulted in the possibility of the sheet entering the dryer part with up to 5% greater solid content than was possible before the use of these recent devices. Because of the relatively high cost of removal of water by drying, as compared with removal of water by mechanical means, it is obviously of great economic importance that the sheet should be as dry as possible when it enters the dryers. The drying of newsprint by steam is almost seven times as expensive as removing water mechanically in the presses.

The conventional method of drying is by the use of banks, generally two tiers, of cast iron steam-heated cylinders each of 48 to 60 in. in diameter. The sheet is passed round the cylinders and held in intimate contact with the heated surfaces by means of dryer felts. The number of drying cylinders and the way in which they are divided into sections is determined by the basic weight of the sheet, the weight of water to be evaporated, the speed of the machine, and the pressure of steam in the various sections.

In spite of the high capital costs and the high running costs of the conventional banks of drying cylinders, this is nevertheless an efficient method of drying paper. Despite the advances being made with accelerator hoods, through-drying techniques, straight pass dryers using high velocity air, fluid-bed drying, and infrared and micro-wave drying, new paper machines are likely to incorporate multi-cylinder drying for many years to come.

THE ARRANGEMENT OF THE DRYER PART

The dryer part of a conventional fourdrinier machine consists of from 40 to 70 paper drying cylinders, divide into from two to five top sections and from two to five bottom sections. Each section has its own dryer felt, hence the number of dryer felts on one machine can vary from four to ten. (In rare instances, machines are installed with only one top and one bottom section, each of from 20 to 30 drying cylinders.) Sectionalization is adopted in order to allow a degree of shrinkage control and to reduce the possibility of the sheet creasing and breaking. The governing factor in deciding the number of sections is generally the maximum number of cylinders that can be controlled in any one section. In cases where too many cylinders places a strain on the gears, the drive may be restricted to a proportion of the cylinders, and the felt is employed to pull round the ungeared cylinders. In most cases, partly because the felt needs to be run at a higher tension and partly because of the work the felt must do, reliance on the felt to drive the cylinders results in a lower felt life than when all the cylinders in a section are driven through the gears.

A typical dryer part of 60 paper drying cylinders, divided into five top and five bottom sections, is shown in Fig.1. The cylinder shown in the return runs of the felts in the first three sections are felt drying cylinders, and the cylinder in the main runs in the first two sections, around which no paper sheet passes are so-called Feeney dryers that assist in conditioning the felt part way in its run through the section.

At the beginning of the dryer part, there is frequently a small dryers cylinder, termed a "baby dryer," used as a lead-in from the press section to the dryer part. Also between the final dryer and the calender stack, there is often a spring or dancing roll that moves gently up and down on light springs in accordance with the tension in the web. This effectively dampens fluctuations in the draw between the dryer and he calenders thus preventing breaking of the sheet.

On slow machines (up to 500 or 600 ft\min), the sheet can be fed through the dryer part by hand, be beginning with a 4 to 6 in.

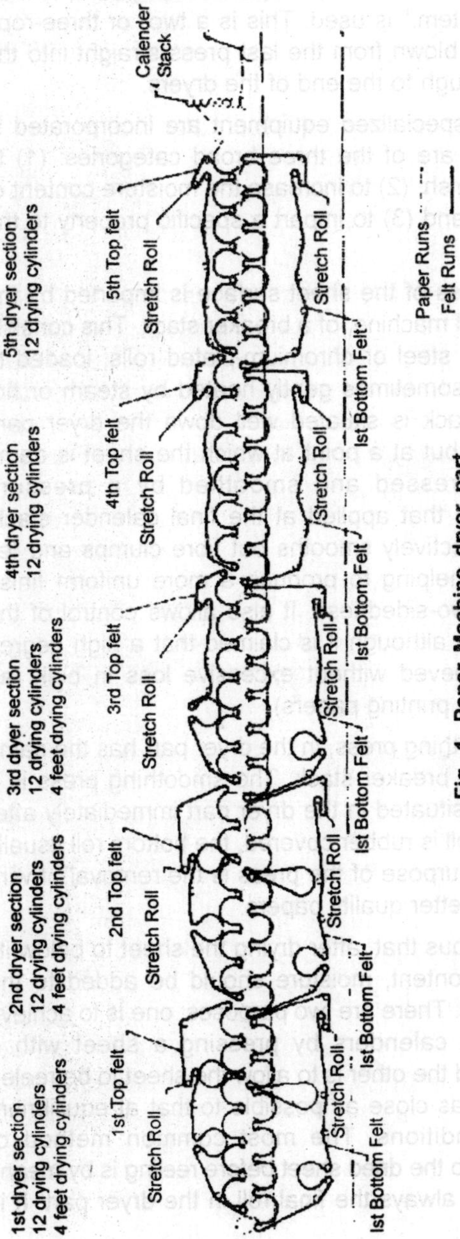

Fig. 1. Paper Machine dryer part.

tail. In the case of faster machines, a rope carrier system, termed the Sheehan rope system," is used. This is a two- or three-rope device, and the tail is blown from the last press straight into the ropes that carry it through to the end of the dryers.

Several types of specialized equipment are incorporated in the dryer part. These are of the three broad categories: (1) to improve the surface finish; (2) to increase the moisture content of the sheet at the reel; and (3) to impart a specific property to the sheet surface.

Greater smoothness of the sheet surface is imparted by the use, on certain types of machine, of a breaker stack. This consists of two highly polished steel or chromium-plated rolls, loaded to give a pressure, and sometimes gently heated by steam or hot water. The breaker stack is situated well down the dryer part, between two sections but at a point at which the sheet is damp enough to be compressed and smoothed by a pressure considerably less than that applied at the final calender stack. The breaker stack effectively smooths out fibre clumps and felt and wire marks thus helping to produce a more uniform finish and rid the sheet of two-sidedness. It also allows control of the thickness of the sheet, although it is claimed that a high degree of smoothness is achieved without excessive loss in bulk (an important advantage in printing papers).

The use of a smoothing press, in the dryer part has the same purpose as that of the breaker stack. The smoothing press is a pair of rollers, usually situated in the dryer part immediately after the presses. The top roll is rubber covered, the bottom roll usually bronze, and the sole purpose of the press is the removal of wire and felt marks in the better quality papers.

It appears anomalous that, after drying the sheet to below its equilibrium moisture content, moisture should be added to the sheet before it is reeled. There are two purposes: one is to achieve a better finish in the calenders by pressing a sheet with a dampened surface: and the other is to allow the sheet to be reeled at a moisture content as close as possible to that at equilibrium with atmospheric conditions. The most common method of introducing moisture into the dried sheet before reeling is by means of a sweat roll. This is always the final roll in the dryer part. It is unfelted and is cooled by spraying cold water into the roll. This causes vapour to condense continually on the outer surface of the roll, and this condensation is transferred to the sheet as it passes over the roll. In some instances, steam is sprayed on to the outer surface of the roll to increase the rate of condènsation and to a small extent to control the amount of water films across the roll.

The devices which are installed in the dryer part to impart specific new properties to the paper are size presses and coating units. Discussion on the use of this equipment is outside the scope of this section.

The standard paper dryer is a 5-ft diameter hollow cylinder of cast iron. Very occasionally, when high steam pressures of 100 or more psi gauge are employed, it is of fabricated steel. The cylinder is usually rough bored on inner surface, although occasionally, it is machined and ground to a mirror finish on the outside. The wall thickness must be of sufficient uniformity to give an even transfer of heat and to ensure adequate dynamic balance at high speed.

The cast iron framework supporting the drying cylinders, felt, rolls, piping, and all auxiliary equipment, is necessary extremely heavy. In spite of its ruggedness, it must be so designed as to allow accessibility to the drying cylinders for surface repairs, for sheet handling, for the installation of dryer felts, and for unobstructed flow of ventilating air that removes vapour from the felt and sheet.

The drive of the dryer section is a critical function. On the oldest machines, the drive is through an open gear train enmeshed so that each dryer in the section runs at the same surface speed. Other dryer section drives operate with chains and pinions, worms gears, or multiple gears between dryers. Modern high-speed machines employ enclosed drive gear that provide more or less unobstructed access to the back side of the dryer section.

The smooth passage of the sheet through the dryer section is closely dependent on the careful control of the draws between the dryer sections which in turn are dependent on very small speed differences between the sections. On modern machines it is possible to after the drawn at any section without affecting that at any other section.

It is customary to install doctors at least on the first few dryers often on one-third of the bottom dryer and occasionally on the majority of dryers on the paper machine. These doctors minimize build up on the cylinder surface of scale, pitch, fibre, dust etc., thus preventing the sheet from wrapping round the cylinder in the event of a break. The doctor also improves drying conditions by removing any deposit that would interfere with the intimacy of contact between the sheet and the dryer surface. The doctor assists in heat transfer by helping to maintain a polished dryer surface. The doctor blade is usually a thin strip of steel or composition material of such texture that it does not cause excessive wear of the dryer surface.

16

Paper Machine - Automation

INTRODUCTION

Paper-making is still far from being a science but as our knowledge of process fundamentals improves modern control systems are being used to adjust an ever-increasing number of critical paper-making variables. The net effect is to make an intuitive "feel" for his process les important to the paper-maker, while increasing the importance of his obtaining a true understanding of how his machine operates as a system.

Paper-making can trace its origin to antiquity; but though it is now a continuous process containing a potpourri of unit operations it is still essentially the same as it emerged some 50 to 100 years ago—the product of a group of practical, mechanically minded inventors. As demanded for greater productivity have forced increases in process throughout, stability has usually been achieved by taking steps to avoid process upsets when possible and by minimizing the response to them if they should occur. To this end, blend tanks are placed in the process, pumps are substantially oversized, and process equipment is frequently operated at a mere fraction of its true capacity. Stability results but the process is as cumbersome as an elephant (for control purposes) when it might be as quick as a cat. At presents such sluggishness is one of the most serious obstacles to the effective application of modern control methods to the paper-making process.

Until comparatively recently, the entire paper-making process was controlled manually, and the operator's eyes, ears, nose, and touch were the sensors by which process conditions were determined. Under these circumstances the control philosophy was to set key process variables at some point that made the system "operable" and then to "leave the machine alone".

More recently, the philosophy has changed to the extent analog controllers have been installed to hold some of the key variables at a specified level. This has required that not only adequate sensors for process pressures, flows, temperatures, etc., be developed but that hardware giving the required control actions be available as well. Conventional pneumatic, analog equipment able to meet just such demand has been available for quite some time and is used in the consistency regulators, temperature controller, etc., so familiar to us all.

Currently, efforts are being made to some of the finished properties of paper such as basis weight moisture content, colour, etc. Control of such factors demands special sensors and relatives elaborat, sophisticated controllers to compensate for the dynamics of the paper-making systems during upsets. The sensors required are available (in general), but the controller algorithms needed are usually too complex to implement via electronic or pneumatic analog hardward. Instead, it is more convenient to use digital computers and their availability at reasonable cost has greatly facilitated progress along these particular lines.

Finally, it is likely that attempts will be made in the relatively near future to optimize the paper-making process from an operational as well as a control viewpoint. Considerable sophistication will be required, for it will be necessary to state business as well as control objectives explicitly. Fortunately, there is a good measure of business success - profits. To measure or estimated profits for even a simple process on a real time basis is no small task. Nevertheless, the economics derivable by such an approach appear so great that such efforts for at least individual paper machines seem imminent.

SYSTEMS ENGINEERING

If an integrated approach to the problems of process operation is to be achieved, the principal of control engineering must be wed with a thorough understanding of process engineering fundamentals. This matching of control and process know-how is the essence of what shall be referred to herein as systems engineering.

The prime function of every control system is to increase process profitability by one means or another. This may be accomplished by a variety of means all of which should be kept in mind by the engineer as a system is designed. One benefit that better control can have is to reduce the use of raw materials by increasing process yield and/or reducing process recycle rate. In this case, savings are derived from both decreases in raw material costs as well as increases in throughput. Better process control can also cut cost by reducing product give away. In other words if the quality of a product can be controlled more closely, it is not necessary to have as large a safety margin between target values and the minimum properties guaranteed by the manufacture. In the paper industry, this can lead to savings derived from a reduction in the amounts of raw materials used as well as disproportionate decrease in the more expensive portion of the furnish as well. Finally process profitability can be increased by taking advantage of the greater process stability and added know-how generated as a result of the system approach. Here, saving are derived from the reductions in conversion costs brought about by increases in throughput (speed ups). Of these sources of savings, it is usually found that increases in throughput are the most successful in cutting costs because machine speed changes usually have the greater economic leverage.

If money is to be saved via the techniques of systems engineering, systems engineers must be available to practice the discipline. This cause one to ask:

(1) What is a systems engineer?

(2) What are his duties and responsibilities?

(3) What factors must be taken into account when designing a process system?

A systems engineer is best described by an enumeration of the skill of which he must be a master. In the paper industry, the first requirement is that he be an accomplished chemical or mechanical engineer with a good understanding of paper-making gained through training and/or experience. Ideally such a man should be the product of a strong engineering curricula that provides sufficient training to give a working ability with differential and integral calculus as well as linear differential equations. Such a background is necessary if the engineer is to have the conceptual tools by which control principles can be appreciated.

Secondly, the qualified systems engineer should have a good working knowledge of control theory and be acquainted with the control hardware available and of use to the paper industry. A knowledge of control and sensing hardware can only be gained and maintained by on the job experience. Control theory can only be effectively used if one has a firm understanding of the principal involved. This can seldom be learned on-the-job, but requires formal training methods and is, in fact the most serious and consistent deficiency of those practising systems engineering in the paper industry today. To have an adequate background in control theory, a systems engineer must have had at least a one semester course in automatic controls at the undergraduate level or its equivalent in formal training since graduation. Such courses are usually built around books such as those authored by Harrison and Bollinger or Coughanowr and Koppel.

In addition, at least a survey course at the graduate level covering sample data systems modern control theory, and multi-loop system design is extremely useful if digital computer control work is contemplated. A good book covering this material as well as the more fundamental concepts is the one authored by kuo.

From the above, it should be obvious that the superior systems engineer working in the paper industry should not only be a thoroughly competent process engineer, but must have a strong background in control as well. Having even great strength in one field at he expense of the other is a decided handicap.

The responsibilities of a systems engineer are three in number. First, he must see that a properly designed system is developed and specified. This requirement is accepted by most practitioners, but practiced with varying degrees of proficiency because of differences in background as far as knowledge of control principal and\or hardware capabilities are concerned. Second, a system man must make sure that the people to use it understand not only the operation of the control system but the vagaries of their process as well. This responsibility is often recognized but only met infrequently. Finally, a systems engineer must take positive steps to see that the equipment installed is used in such a way as to realized its full potential for increasing process profitability. This obligation is seldom even recognized.

In designing a system, the engineer must take several factors into account. First as much of a process as possible should be encompassed in the design of a control system. The increases the likelihood of an integrated response to upsets or set point changes in the process. It also increases the complexity of the control problem, however, for such an approach invariably leads to the necessity of having to deals with multi-loop control systems. In order to attack such problems, it is necessary to develop a good mathematical model of the system through the use of analytical and\or experimental methods. It is one thing to place an individual controller in a simple non-interacting control loop, but quite another to determine what control action is to be taken in a number of loops simultaneously in response to an upset or set point change in but one of them. In the former case, an intuitive, cut-and-try approach is acceptable, but in the latter, a model of the system must be available and controller gains must be chosen with the aid of theory simulation an intuition. This requires sophistication and know-how.

Good systems design should also take into account the magnitude and speed of response required of both the control hardware specified and the process. Care should be taken in every case to see that unreasonable demands are not placed on either portion of the system. Here the availability of the mathematic model is again an advantage for response problems can be easily simulated and, if not correctable at least taken into account.

Finally, the control scheme decided upon must be implemented through the use of demandable equipment that is installed properly. In addition, the design should be sufficiently flexible to allow subsequent systems changes in response to altered systems requirements, the development of better hardware, or simply a desire to apply more sophisticated control techniques to optimize process performance. The know-how to have this type of expertise and foresight only comes with on-the-job experience.

CONTROL THEORY

It has already been mentioned that a though understanding of control theory is a prerequisite for good systems engineering.

Even a cursory exposition of the material that it is necessary to understand in order to have a good grasp of and working ability with theory, is beyond the scope of this text. Instead, one should refer to standard texts on the subject. For instruction, the books by Harrison and Bollinger and Coughanowr and Koppel are probably best, while as a reference, Kuo's book is preferred, because of its breadth of coverage and organization.

In any case, it should always be remembered that for the process engineer, the function of control theory is to provide a framework whereby individual control problems may be reduced to their basic principles, recognized as to type, and then analyzed to determine how they may best be solved. In other words, theory should provide a method for attacking day-to-day problems, but not necessarily answers to specific questions.

Before leaving the subject of control theory altogether, it would seem wise to at least list the topics that must be understood if one is to have a sufficiently good grasp of theory for it to be an aid to him in his day-to-day work. Said topics include:

(1) *Modeling.* It is usually quite important to develop a relatively accurate model of the process being studied. This can be approached either analytically, by applying the physical laws governing the process, or experimentally, by fitting mathematical expression to experimentally derived data. There are many sources of information on this subject, but if one is primarily interest in methods for experimentally identifying important process parameters, it appears that here is no good alternative to simply digging the appropriate information out of the literature.

(2) *The Laplace and Z transformation.* These are the basic mathematical transform by which the differential and difference equation describing the behaviour of continuous and sampled data systems are converted to simple algebraic expressions (in the S and Z domains, respectively) that are easily manipulated. The theory and used of both of these transforms is well covered in texts such as the one authored by Kuo.

(3) *Block diagramming and signal flow techniques.* These are the methods by which the transformed equations describing a system may be manipulated to determine what

relation exists between various system inputs and outputs. This material is also well covered in most good control texts.

(4) *Systems transient response and compensator design.* There are quite a variety of methods for the analysis of the transient response of a system. Giving an understanding of such methods for a continuous system is usually the intent of most introductory automatic control courses. If sample data systems or more sophisticated design techniques are of interest, then advanced control courses must be taken. Texts covering this advanced material are those authored by Kuo, Langill and Dorf.

(5) *Multi-loop systems.* One need mot work as a control engineer long to realize the need for multi-loop design methods. Most of the systems encountered are, in fact, best handled by multi-loop methods. The major difference between multi-loop and single-loop design techniques is that matrix, rather than algebraic, methods are used for model manipulation. In addition, conventional design procedures are not very useful and more elaborate methods or optimal control concepts must be used. A good referance dealing with multi-loop systems is the book by Mesarovic, but one should be warned that it is a highly mathematical treatment of the subject.

TYPICAL CONTROL ACTION

Systems engineers often use unfamiliar terms to describe their work. The meaning of such terms can best be understood by the study and analysis of a simple process system such as the one shown in Fig. 1. From this schematic diagram it can be seen that the rate of flow Q to tank G is controlled by valve V. Flow Q, of course affects the level in tank G which in turn, determines the rate of efflux. Figure 1also shows that a controller C may be attached to the value of V and used to control tank liquid levels, provided it is supplied with an appropriate set point S (in this case the liquid level desired) and has an adequate signal with which to calculate control action. Finally it should be noted that a system upset can develop from two sources i.e., set point changes entered through controller C or process upsets as represented by changes in the pressure on the up-stream side of value V.

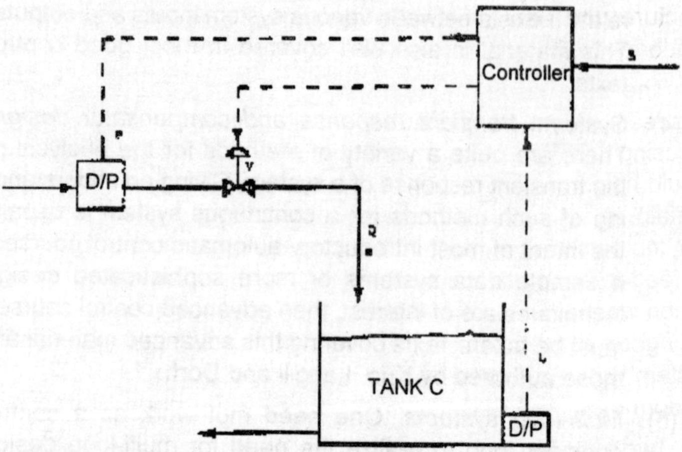

Fig. 1: A simple process system

With the system in Fig.1 in mind, lets us now examine some of the jargon so common to control language. First, the term set point: this is merely the point at which the operator would like to hold the controlled variable. Usually, set points are entered through a controller as is the case in Fig.1. The controller variable in Fig.1 is tank liquid level L and the set point is, of course, a desired liquid level.

The relative advantages of feedback and feed-forward controllers are often discussed by systems people and frequently lead to confusion on the part of the average listener. Feedback and Feed-forward controllers are differentiated, by virtue of the fact that they use different types of signals to calculate the corrective action that must be taken. The signals required by either a feedback or feed-forward controller exist in Fig. 1. A feedback controller would compare tank liquid level to set point, calculate an error term, and use it to determine the necessary adjustment to valve V. In other words, a feedback controller samples the controller variables, compares it to set point, and takes control action accordingly. The disadvantage of such a system is that some error must exist in the control variable if any control action is to be taken. The system does have a major advantage, however, and that is that only a limited amount needs to be known about the process in order to put the system under control. At this juncture, the vast majority of operating controllers are of the feedback type.

The feed-forward signal in Fig. 1 is the pressure on the upstream side of valve V. A fed-forward controller would operate by using this signal to calculate the stem position for valve V that would hold flow rate Q at a point such that tank liquid level would remain at set point. Tank level might be sampled, but it would play no part in calculating the position of valve V. The advantage of feed-forward control is that it can take immediate corrective action whenever a process upset occurs. Its disadvantage is that very good models must be available for the process or the entire system will be unstable. At present, feed-forward controllers are seldom used, unless backed up by a feed-back system.

Two other terms often used by system people that are unfamiliar to the average listener are the regulartor and the servo problem. These terms refer to the types of duty that a controller must serve. When a control man says that he is dealing with a regulator problem, he means that his controller is intended to compensate for process upsets primarily, and that it will be required to content with only modest-sized set point changes. For the case shown in Fig.1, a controller showing regulator action would be primarily concerned with compensating for upsets in pressure P.

In the servo problem, the controller in question must deal with large changes in set points, as well as process upsets. This means that in our simple case, a controller showing servo action would be required if it was expected that large programmed changes in liquid level set point were to be handed. Generally speaking, servo controllers are much more difficult to design, because the behaviour of a process is usually quite difficult to characterize mathematically in the case where large set point changes are contemplated.

When systems engineers talk about the action that they expect from their controllers they use four terms that may be unfamiliar. These terms are proportional action, integral action derivative action, and dead time compensation. Such terms usually refer to the actions expected of feedback controllers, and all of them refer to how the error term developed by the controller is manipulated in determining the control action to be taken. In the simple example shown in Fig. 1, the term proportional action merely means that the stem of valve V will be moved an amount that is directly proportional to the size of the error term. Integral action in the same system refers to the fact that the stem of value V will be moved an amount that is proportional to the time integral of the error term. In other words it will be moved an amount proportional to the area beneath a plot of the error terms *vs.* time. Finally, derivative action in our tank system would imply that the movement of the stem of valve V would be proportional to the rate of change of the error term with time or, in other words, would be proportional to the slope of a plot of the error term *vs.* time.

There is no good example of dead time in the simple system illustrated in Fig. 1, but the term is simple enough to understand. For example, consider that it takes approximately 60. sec for the paper manufactured on a fourdrinier wire travel through the dryer section of a paper machine and arrive at the real. This 60 sec to the systems engineer represents dead time. Dead time in a process system is compensated for by merely making sure that the control action taken is based on the input to the process that actually caused the output being observed. This requires that input and output data be shifted in time so that they are time-correlated before they enter the controller and are used to determine the control action necessary. Dead-time compensation was extremely difficult when only analog hardware was available, but now that digital equipment is becoming commonplace, it is not the problem that it once was.

ANALOG AND DIGITAL CONTROL SYSTEMS

The compensation discussed in previous sections can be achieved through the use of either analog or digital equipment or any likely combination of the two. Analog and digital equipment differ greatly in their construction and use, and our purpose now is to discuss and describe some of these differences. Analog systems are characterized by the fact that they are continuous. Both error detection and control actions are carried out continuously. The control action required of an analog controller is developed by applying the arror detected to an accurate electronic or pneumatic analog of the control action wanted. The output of the controller is then usually magnified and used to adjust the manipulated variable of the process.

The main advantages of analog systems are that they are rather inexpensive for small control jobs. They are usually quite simple, and their action is easily understood. Numerous engineers and technicians are familiar with the equipment, and hence, design and maintenance skill for it are readily available. Finally, the continuous actions derivable from analog equipment are quite effective in stabilizing fast-acting control loops.

Analog systems do have weaknesses, however. For example, individual controllers are not very versatile because their logic resides in specific electronic or pneumatic hardware that must be changed entirely if any substantial change in control action is desired. Secondly, it is very difficult to implement complex control algorithms, because dead-time compensation becomes quite difficult and costly if it is appreciable. Finally, it is virtually impossible to adjust the amount of proportional, integral, or derivative action derivable from an analog controller on a continuous basis. This makes it next to impossible to practice some of the more sophisticated control techniques aimed at adapting contoller response to process conditions.

Digital control systems are characterized by the fact that error detection is normally on a sampled basis, and control action is achieved through a sample and hold circuit. Control actions are developed through the use of recursion formula and because both process and controller must be characterized by difference rather than differential equations, the design procedures for digital systems are somewhat less familiar to the average control engineer. The strength of the digital approach is its versatility, as evidenced by the fact that most any control action desired can be achieved simply and altered at will. In addition, process dead time can be taken into account rather simply. These characteristics make digital equipment the logical choice for implementing some of the more sophisticated control techniques now being developed.

Like the analog system, the digital system also has its weaknesses. Usually the equipment required initially is quite expensive, and many control loops must be closed to justify its acquisition. Secondly, because more complex control laws are often used in a digital system, its actions are more difficult to predict, and troubleshooting can sometimes be very frustrating. Finally, engineers and technicians are generally considerably less knowledgeable about digital equipment than analog, and hence, design and maintenance skills are in short supply.

One hears more and more about hybrid control systems of late. A hybrid control system is nothing but a combination of analog and digital elements used in conjunction to achieve a desired control action. The hybrid approach is usually justified on the basis of economics, though in some cases, it is the only method by which a desired action can be achieved. In addition, the aim of the hybrid approach is usually to take maximum advantage of the strengths of both analog and digital equipment. While minimizing their weaknesses. Finally, hydrid systems are usually complex from both an analytic and practical standpoint. The result is that they are often difficult to troubleshoot. Also there are only a limited number of engineers and technicians qualified to work with them.

BASIC CONTROL LOOPS

There are a few simple feedback loops that appear again and again in a paper-mill system. Much of the apparent complexity of a typical millwide control system disappears if these loops are thoroughly understood. The purpose of this section is to explain the operation of the more common of these loops.

Consistency Control

Every paper mill must be able to control the consistency or solids content of the stock it processes, for unless this factor is

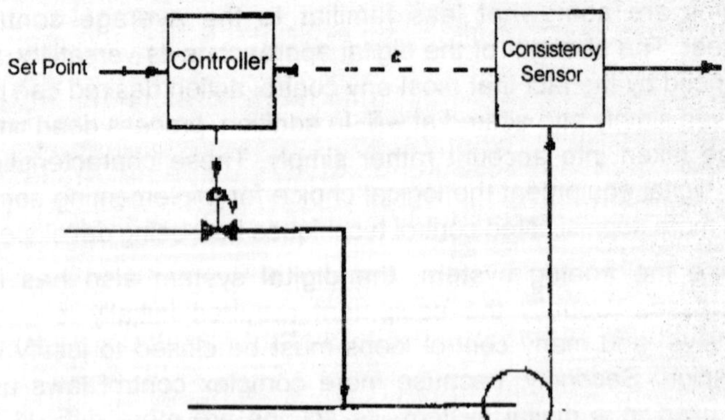

Fig. 2 A typical consistency control loop

stable, chaos results. A typical consistency control loop is shown in Fig. 2. As is generally the case in such loops, water is added to the stock immediately before a pump (P) and the fibrous slurry then is pumped through a consistency sensor and on into other parts of the process. A feedback signal (C) is obtained from the consistency sensor and sent to a controller where it is compared with a previously entered set point to develop an error term. The controller then uses said error to determine an appropriate position for the stem of the valve (V) controlling the flow of dilution water to the stock immediately ahead of the pump.

One of the more important aspects in the design of consistency controllers is to make sure that the dilution water added is well mixed with the stock before reaching the consistency sensor. Hence, the advisability of adding dilution water immediately before a stock pump or the like. Other considerations demand that the line length between the point of water addition and the consistency sensor be kept small to minimize dead time in the system. Finally, it is possible to control consistency on the basis of either a sample taken from the main stream or by making the appropriate measurements directly in the main channel of flow. At present, it appears that direct in-line sensing is preferred. This avoids sampling difficulties and risks very little in the way of breakdowns, because the in-line, at pressure, consistency sensors now available are virtually trouble-free from a maintenance standpoint.

Consistency sensors and the required regulating equipment are manufactured by a variety of companies. Most all of the popular sensors used today operate by measuring the force required to disrupt the stock suspension as it flows past a sence head. This resistance to rupture or "flock strength" is most strongly affected by the solids content of the suspension, but it is also a function of other factors such as fibre type, fibre length, pigment concentration, and flow rate past the head. The result is a measurement quite susceptible to upset, and though consistency signals are quite precise, we are far from having an accurate measure of the property. The result is that any consistency signal is suspect, whenever it changes abruptly, for one is never quite sure if solids have changed or if the measurement has been confounded by a shift of one of the other influencing factors.

In the past, consistency controllers have usually used pneumatic analog equipment with proportional plus integral control action. This may change in the future, as the cost of electronic analog and digital equipment comes down, but it is unlikely.

Flow Control

Important process flows must be under close control if real progress is to be made in closing more sophisticated loops in the paper-making process. The key to good control of process flows is the magnetic flowmeter. This device supplies the feedback signal for the flow controller which, in turn, compares the measured flow with set point and adjusts a flow control valve accordingly. A typical flow control loop is shown in Fig. 3. Flow control on a closed-loop basis is arelatively recent innovation in the paper industry, but analog pneumatic controllers with proportional and integral action have been used for the most part. As the use of digital process

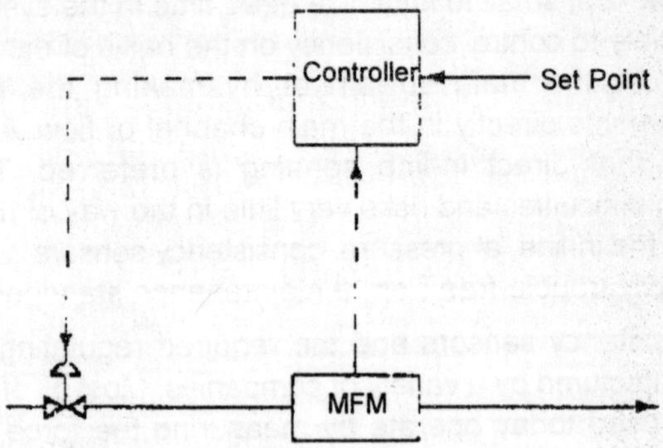

Fig. 3. A typical flow control loop.

computers has increased, however, more and more electronic analog and digital controllers are being used, particularly where mass flow rates rather than just volumetric flows are to be controlled.

Pressure Control

Pressure must be controlled at many points in the paper-making process and the controllers for this purpose have been in use for quite some time. Pressure may be sensed by a variety of

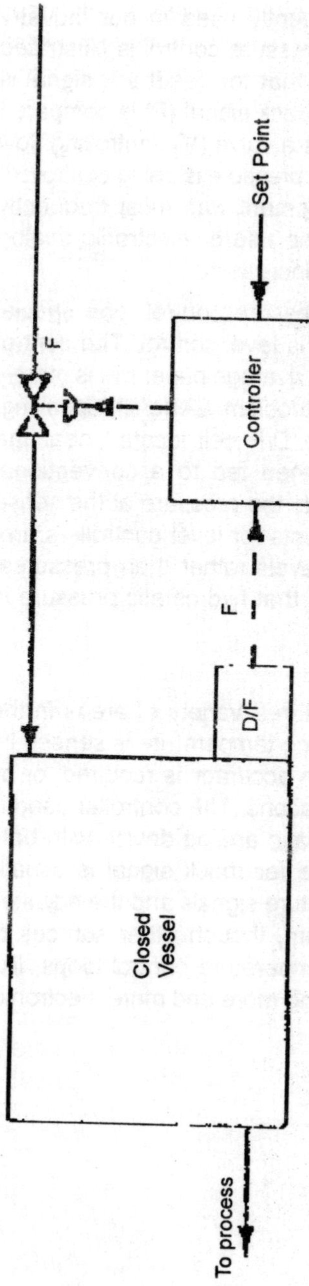

Fig. 4. A typical pressure control

methods. But one of the most frequently used in our industry seems to be the D/P cell. A typical pressure control is illustrated in Fig. 4, from which it may be seen that the feedback signal is the pressure itself. As usual, the feedback signal (P) is compared to set point, and the controller adjusts a valve (V) controlling flow to (or from) the vessel (or point) whose pressure is being controlled. In the past, pneumaticd analog equipment was most frequently used in this application, but again, the use of electronic analog hardware and/or digital controllers is increasing.

Before leaving the subject of pressure control, one special case should be mentioned, and that is level control. The control of level in the many tanks found in the average paper mill is merely a special case of the pressure control problem. Generally speaking, tank level is sensed by means of a D/P cell located near the bottom of the tank. This signal is then fed to a conventional pressure controller which merely holds the pressure at the sense point at a specified set point. Set points for level controllers are, of course, usually entered as tank levels rather than pressures, for convenience sake, but the fact is that hydrostatic pressure is controlled.

Temperature Control

Temperature control is important in a variety of areas in the average paper mill. Generally speaking temperature is sensed by resistance bulb thermometers, if high accuracy is required, or by thermocouples, in less critical applications. The controller used is again usually a conventional pneumatic analog device with both proportional and integral action. The feedback signal is usually one of the above-mentioned temperature signals and the adjusted variable is most frequently live steam, though other sources of heat are utilized upon occasion. Temperature control loops, like the rest of those discussed, are seeing more and more electronic, analog, or digital hardware used.

17

Calendering

INTRODUCTION

The principal functions of the calender in the paper-making process are to produce the desired finish and caliper (paper thickness). Finish is varied to the desired degree by increasing or decreasing the number of rolls in the calender, by loading or relieving the weight of the roll system to create higher or lower nip pressures, and by heating or cooling the rolls. (The high gloss finish produced in the supercalendering process is achieved through the use of filled or non-metallic rolls.)

Caliper is controlled by adjusting the nip load, Light loads, or fewer rolls, result in less reduction of caliper; heavy loads, or more rolls, result in greater reduction.

One of the secondary functions of the calender is to correct certain variations existing in the sheet prior to sheet entry into the calender. For example, a heavy center or edge can be corrected by, respectively, the use of over-crowned or under-crowned rolls, or crown adjustment. Not all sheet variations caused prior to the calender are curable, as, for instance, it is difficult to correct a problem such as a wet streak, due to its localized nature.

Another secondary function can be the application of sizing solution, colour or coatings. This is done in what is sometimes called the "wet" calender, because a water box (or "water docter") is used to contain the solution . Water boxes are constructed so that the flexible front lip contacts the roll surface somewhat below the top of the roll to from a dam. The solution is picked up by the roll as it rotates and is fed onto the paper at the nip.

CONSTRUCTION

There are two basic types of calender construction in use , one called the "A frame", and the other, the "openside".

The first is usually constructed in the form of a "U" shaped casting or weldment, with a cap secured across the legs of the "U" at the top. The cap serves to keep the legs from spreading when under load , and thus prevents misalignment of the ways or bearing guides. Due to the length between the base and cap, tie pieces are sometimes also needed to hold the legs of the "U" in alignment. Since the base is usually wider than the top, the structure resembles the shape of the letter "A" and thus the origin of the term "A frame". (Some calender of this type are built without a tie at the base, other than the floor plates and the bottom roll bearing housing).

The "open side" calender is designed with only a single side frame that is usually tied to the basic machine framework by the use of structural members. There are also some frames that are self-supporting. The rolls are supported or held in position by pivoted bearing housings. This type of construction is considered to be the best for efficient roll changing.

Two-roll calendars built something like a press are also used. In addition, now that controlled deflection rolls have become available, several different roll arrangements become possibilities. One would be to replace an intermediate roll, approximately halfway up the calender, with a controlled deflection roll, resulting, in effect, in two calendars on one frame. Still other possibilities include the use of a controlled deflection roll in every other position up the calender.

ROLLS - MATERIALS

The rolls are working elements of the calender and the means by which the calender functions are accomplished. The rolls of the type used in machine calendars and supercalenders are most commonly made of "chilled" iron (supercalenders use a combination of iron and filled rolls). These are cast in a vertical iron mold (or chill) to produce a hard surface or layer that is of uniform hardness throughout its depth.

Such rolls are produced with various hardness specifications, ranging from a Shore "C" sclero-scope hardness of 64 up to 80 to

85. depending on the requirement. The hardness is controlled by the carbon and alloy content. Typical unalloyed chilled iron has a chemical analysis that falls within the following:

Charbon	3.50 to 3.80
Manganese	.20 to .30
Phosphorus	.400 to .600
Sulphur	.100 to .150
Silicon	.40 to .80

The conventional chilled iron most commonly used has a hardness range of approximately 68 to 72 Shore "C" scleroscope. The other common hardness range specified is 74 minimum, which results from a aspecial alloy content. Rolls of this hardness are used for the purpose of resisting abrasion and denting in the more severe high-speed calendaring operations. Higher hardnesses and other hardness ranges are possible by varying the chemistry.

Hardened steel rolls are sometimes used, but these have been found to mark, scratch, or dent much more easily than chilled iron of equivalent hardness. The most common usage of steel rolls in in the supercalender where the rolls are not subjected to the same type of service as they are in a machine calender. However, it has been found that to give approximately equivalent service even in the supercalender, the hardness of the roll must be 8 to 10 points higher than that of a chilled iron roll.

Rubber-covered and plastic-covered rolls are also occasionally used for certain special calendaring applications. The primary purpose of this type of covering is similar to that of the filled-type roll used in supercalendering operations, i.e., to produce a gloss or other special finish requirement.

The filled rolls used in the supercalendering operation, in combination with all-metal chilled iron or steel rolls, are manufactured from a great variety of materisls, such as paper, cloth, corn husks, to name a few. This is done to produce various desired degrees of hardness and resulting paper finish conditions. This type of roll is constructed by stacking sheets of the roll-filling material on a steel core or shaft under very heavy hydraulic pressure to produce a uniform density. When the compressed mass is completed, it is locked in position by a collar, and the roll

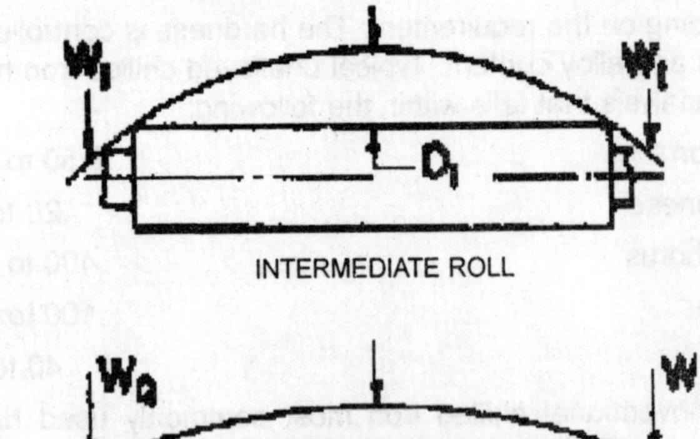

Crown for intermediate = straight.
Crown for queen = 2 $(D_1 - D_Q)$
Crown to bottom = $2[D_B + D_Q - (D_1 - D_Q)]$
Deflection (D) = 1/2C (crown)

Fig. 1. Crown analysis procedure.

is machined by turning and/or grinding to the desired dimensional accuracies.

ROLL CROWNING - THE NIP CONDITION

The working elements of a calender, namely the rolls, are really a series of round beams. These beams deflect, due to load, thus creating the need for some means of compensation for the deflection, in order to produce uniform nip pressure across the sheet and to obtain desired sheet properties and reel uniformity.

Crown is added to rolls to correct for the deflection condition and to produce the necessary operation condition.

The basic theory of roll crowning that has proved most successful inn practice is as follows. The basic deflection of all rolls in the system are calculated. The calculations must take into consideration the sheet width and all end effects that act on the roll. Calculating of roll deflections are made by the application of beam formulas, or they may be obtained from roll suppliers. The deflection values are then applied, as shown by Fig. 1. to determine crown requirement for the condition analyzed.

Various Roll Combinations

A description of the various types of roll combinations and methods used to apply additional nip pressures in connection with crown consideration is essential. Figure 2 illustrates a variety of two-roll combinations. These example are elementary, but serve as a good starting point. The illustration shows two rolls of the same size and two of different diameters, mounted vertically, horizontally, and at an angle. Additional loads are often applied to these combination for increased nip pressure.

Figure 3 shown a typical arrangement of a calender stack with all intermediate rolls of the same diameter. Six rolls suitable for five nips are illustrated, but, of course, the number of rolls might be varied from two to as many as eleven, with additional load sometimes being applied to the top roll.

Other arrangements may have the next-to-bottom or queen roll of a different size, or the queen and top-roll diameters greater than the intermediates.

Primary Objective

The primary objective in crowing rolls is to obtain a uniform pressure distribution at the roll nip. If a roll body was supported on a flat surface that had no deflected and the roll ground straight, and if the journal weight were not taken into account, uniform pressure distribution across the face of the roll would be obtained, as shown by Fig. 4.

If an additional load "W" is added to the center of the roll, a pressure distribution, as shown by Fig. 5, is produced. By removing the weight in the center and applying weight "W" on each end of

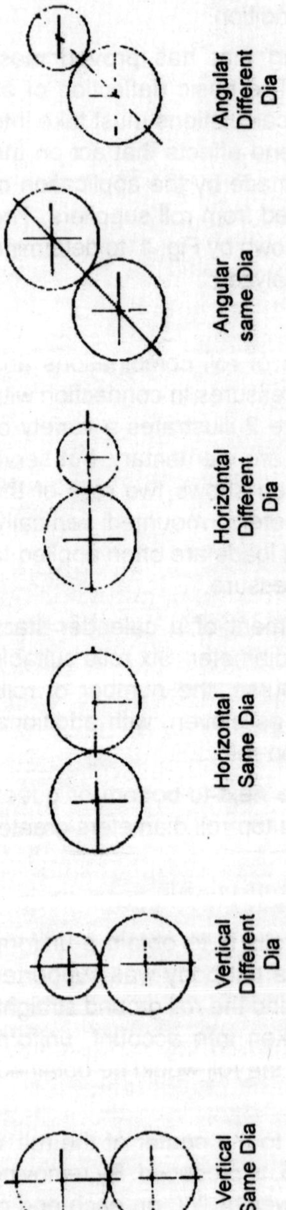

Fig. 2. Two-roll combinatins.

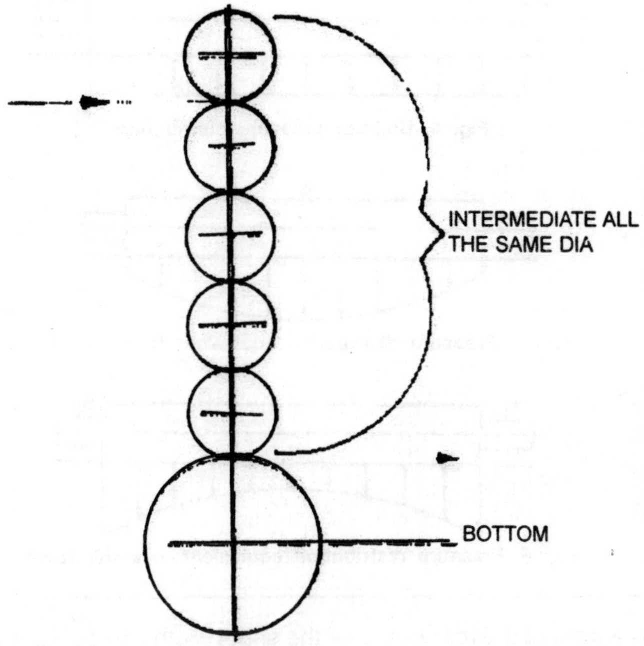

Fig. 3. Calender with all roils above the bottom one of he same diameter.

the roll at the journals, or bearing centrerlines, the pressure distribution changes, as illustrated in Fig. 6.

Crown for various Combinations

The next step is to consider proper crowns for various stock or roll combinations. First is a two-roll arrangement in which both rolls are the same diameter and weight and are mounted in a vertical position with the bottom roll fixed. In this case, the crown is calculated for the bottom roll and then for the top. The bottom roll will deflect a greater amount than the top roll, due to the fact that its deflection is caused by the weight of the top roll and its bearings, plus the weight of the bottom roll body. Since the top roll is supported by the bottom over its face length, and this has been considered in calculating the deflection of the bottom roll,

Fig. 4. Uniform pressure distribution.

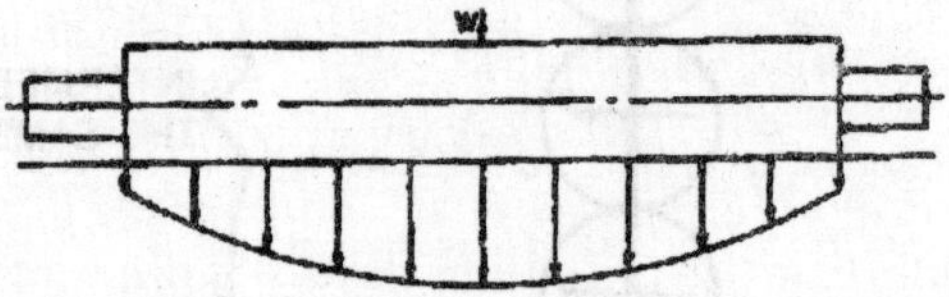

Fig. 5. Pressure distribution equivalent to overcrown.

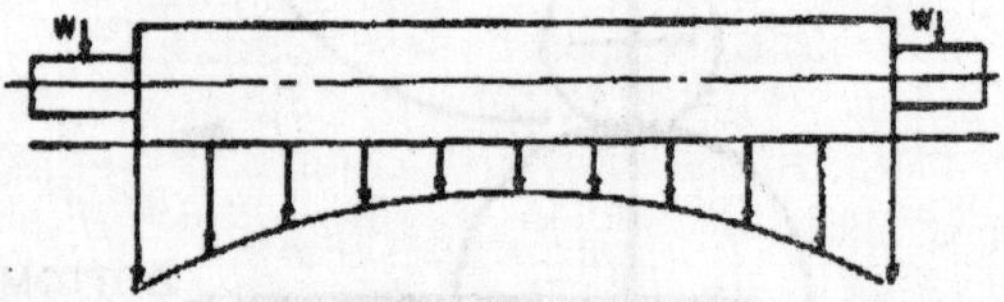

Fig. 6. Pressure distribution equivalent to undercrown.

the weight of the roll body over the sheet width can be disregarded in calculating top roll-deflection.

The bearing weights, or bearing weight plus loading, will create a variation in nip pressure. Therefore, the deflection to be considered is that caused by these loads on the top roll. These crown values are designated as basic crowns. The sum of the two basic crowns is, then, the amount of crown to be applied to the two-roll combination. The total crown can be applied to either of the rolls, or it can be split between the two in any way desired. A common procedure for a two-roll combination with identical rolls is to crown both rolls with the same amount of crown.

For two rolls of different diameters, the procedure is identical to that used when the rolls are the same diameter. In this case, however, the crown is sometimes distributed proportionately to the diameters, in order to minimize speed differentials between the center and the edges of the sheet.

In considering the two-roll combination with the rolls mounted horizontally, the only concern is with the separating force or nip pressure between the rolls; the weight of the roll bodies or bearings need not be considered. In the case of a two-roll arrangement with the rolls mounted in an angular position, it is necessary to resolve the weight of the upper roll into its component forces and thus determine the amount of nip pressure being applied by the weight of the upper roll to the bottom one. The crowns are then calculated on the same basis indicated for the vertical arrangement.

Crown for Three or More Rolls

For an arrangement in which three or more rolls are involved, the basic crowns are calculated for each roll having a different diameter or loading. Actual crowns are determined by the analysis as shown by Fig. 1, using the calculated basic deflections, D_1, D_Q, D_B.

When the top roll is a different size than the intermediates below it, the amount of crown required for this roll must be calculated and then analyzed to determine whether or not the crown required is a positive or negative crown. If the direction of the intermediate roll is greater than the deflection of the top roll, the top roll may have to be crowned with a reverse crown or concave shape. Usually, when load is applied to the top roll, the top roll has to have a positive crown, because its deflection will then exceed that of the intermediate roll.

All Weight Essential

From the analysis of the nip-pressure distribution and the roll crown for intermediate rolls, it is quite clear that any weight that is applied at the bearings on intermediate or top rolls (doctor weights, bearing weights, catwalks etc.) must be considered in the crown calculations. In openside stacks, the effects of these weights must be transferred to the centerline of the bearing, while the bearing arm is supported at the pivot point and the arm is held in a horizontal position. Doctor weights, inboard and outboard, have a very marked effect on the crown calculations in an openside stack (see Fig. 7).

In the analysis of roll crowns, it is very important that the rolls be set up in the calender and checked in the exact manner for which the crown were calculated. Again it should be emphasized

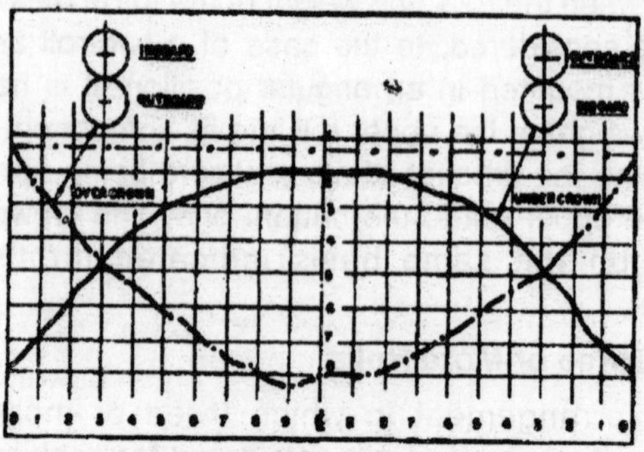

Fig. 7. Gap-test chart, illustrating effect of loading variation on identical rolls.

that any analysis of crown requirements on a particular roll combination is only suitable for the conditions specified. If any other operation condition is used, such as the removal or addition of rolls or of weight or change of sheet width, the crown combination becomes a compromise.

How to Check Nip Conditions

Various methods are used for the purpose of checking nip conditions. Carbon paper, NCR, and aluminum foil show by visual inspection the condition at the nip, but they do not provide a means for determining the amount of crown correction needed.

The most satisfactory and most illustrative impression-type check is with NCR (no carbon required) paper. This paper is a two-ply sheet (with a chemical treatment applied to one-side) that creates a blue impression when subjected to pressure. The more intense the pressure, the darker the impression. It is possible to determine the actual pounds per square inch nip pressure by first calibrating the paper being used (through the use of a known area with a known load) and then to check light reflectance, and, in turn, a curve can be plotted to indicate the relative nip pressure conditions in terms of pounds per square inch pressure. Many times, a simple visual inspection of the impression will give a very good indication of conditions that exist. Visual inspection is most effective in illustrating conditions to operating personnel.

To use this type of paper properly, the length of the sheet that is rolled through the nip should be the same length as the width of the sheet being processed, and it should be taped to the roll, outside of the nip, (as indicated in Fig. 8) and then, rolled through the nip to obtain the nip impression.

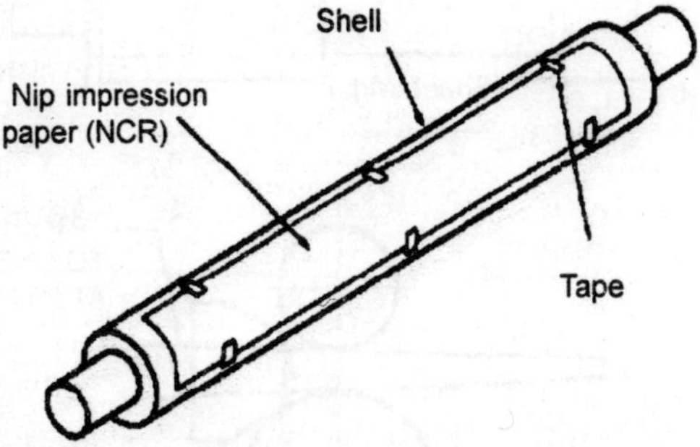

Note: Length of impression paper should be equal to the with of the sheet.

Fig. 8. Taping nip impression paper to the roll.

A quantitative method for checking the nip-pressure distribution on a calender stack is shown in Fig. 9. This is used to check the crown condition that exists with the rolls mounted in position. The procedure is to insert steel blocks, ground to precisely the same thickness, at two points along the face of the roll. The blocks are positioned in such a way that the resulting gap at the center of roll and the edge of the sheet is uniform, provided proper crowns and roll shape exists. The taper gauge is a comparator and is calibrated in .0001m divisions. From this check, it can be determined whether there is correct crown, the amount of overcrown or undercrown condition and, therefore, whether the nip pressure is uniform. Correlation of measured data with accurate calculation provides excellent data upon which correct crowns can be established.

Gap-Check Curve

The ideal chart for uniform nip would be shaped like an ox yoke. If an undercrown condition exists, the curve will be upward, and for an overcrown, the curve will be downward.

The chart in Fig.12 was made on a stack set up for three different conditions: eight rolls with seven nips; seven rolls with six nips; and six rolls with five nips. The bottom roll in this case

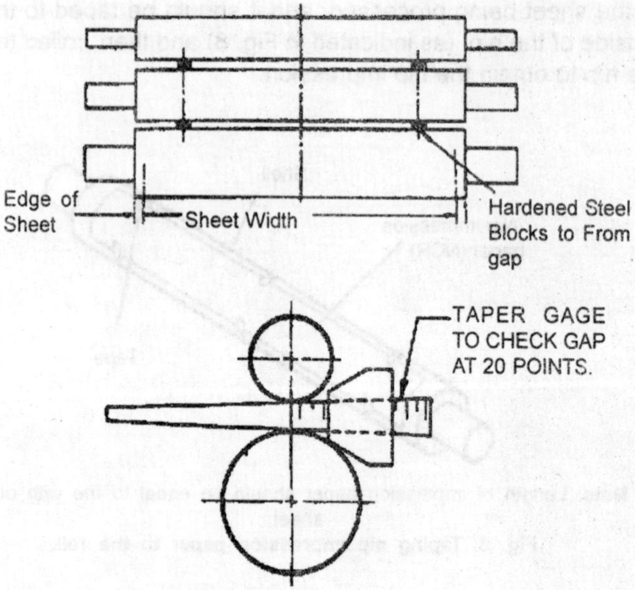

Fig. 9. Gap check for nip pressure.

had .035 inch crown. Note that, as rolls are removed, the height of the curve is reduced. This chart indicates that the crown should be increased by twice the amount indicated between the top of the curve and a straight line connecting the ends of the curve. This check will not tell where to make the correction. This must be determined from calculation and analysis, as already described.

In the case of Fig. 11, calculations indicated that there should be .045 in. crown on the bottom roll (instead of .035 in. for the eight rolls) with the intermediated all straight. Figure 12 illustrates correct crown conditions.

Figure 7 indicates the relationship existing between deflections of intermediate rolls that have variations in end effects or bearing loads. Exceptionally good correlation has been obtained with this procedure.

Target Curve

The crown shape recommended and used as a target curve is shown in Fig. 13. It is very important that the deviation of a crown shape from this target curve be held to a minimum. Minimum

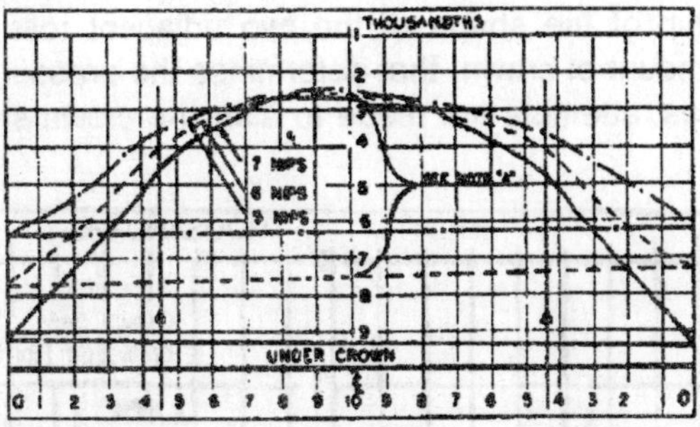

Fig. 10. Gap-check chart. Growns: bottom roll .035 inch queen roll, .0047 inch. Note "A"—Distance between curve and line represents one half required additional crown.

is used loosely here because this deviation can vary, depending on the type of paper being produced. For example, if it is a very thin sheet, a deviation of .0005 in. can be critical, whereas in running a thick sheet or board, it would be insignificant. It is also important that straight rolls be ground within close tolerances.

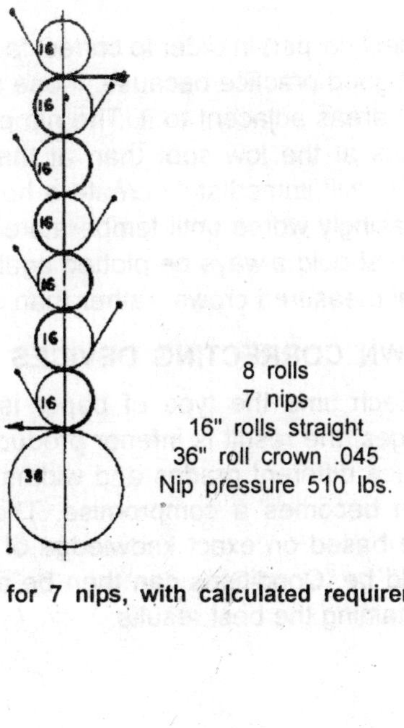

Fig. 13. Calender arrangement for 7 nips, with calculated requirements.

When a series of rolls is set up in the stack, it is really the relationship of the shape of the two adjacent rolls, as well as proper amount of crown, that determines the pressure at the nip. Sometimes, attempts are made to alter the crown shape (based

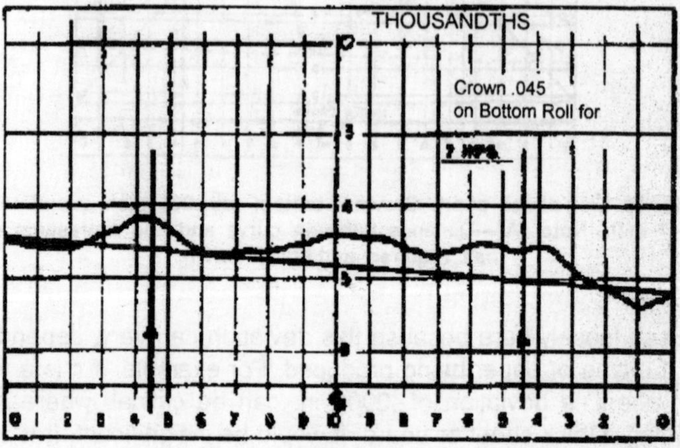

Fig. 12. Gap-check chart, showing result of correct crown. This chart is in contrast to that shown in Fig.10 for 7 nips.

on sheet caliper) in order to correct faulty operation. This, of course is not good practice because, if one area is altered, it is bound to affect areas adjacent to it. The nip pressure would, of necessity, be less at the low spot than at the high spot. A high spot, of course, will immediately create a hot spot, and this will become increasingly worse until temperature equilibrium is reached. Roll shape should always be plotted against a target curve based on actual measured crown, rather than specified crown.

CROWN CORRECTING DEVICES

Each time the type of paper is changed, or often at shift changes, the result is inferior production. Since many mills must produce different grades and widths of paper, the application of crown becomes a compromise. The best compromise can be made based on exact knowledge of what the correct conditions should be. Conditions can then be altered with greater certainty of obtaining the best results.

Devices are now available to cope with this problem; they involve the individual control of the deflection of rolls in a calender.

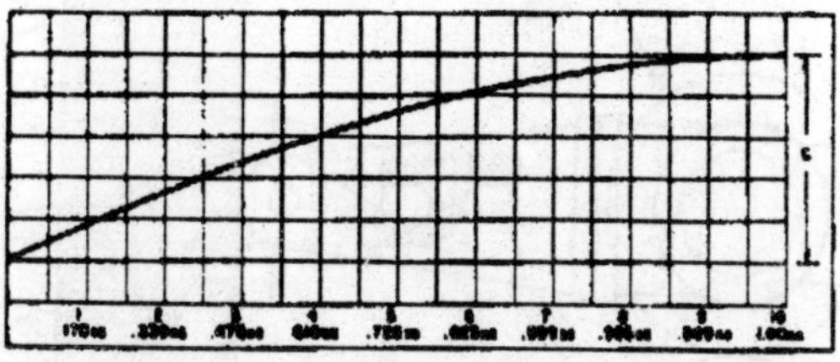

Fig. 13. Standard crown curve to produce uniform nip pressure.

These devices permit variation of the nip pressure with a given set of crowns. The types of construction are: individual roll lifting or loading; bottom and/or toproll bending; cross-axis; "Swimming Roll"™; and other types of variable deflection rolls.

Figure 14 shows a typical weight relieving system as applied to calenders. This type of unit is an effective tool, providing a means of adjustment on each individual roll in the calender or roll system. The device can be built either to load or unload and can be applied to openside or "A frame" calendars. The use of this device presents the possibility of applying a crown (to the bottom roll) that is suitable for the minimum load (pounds per lineal inch) condition. As rolls are added and the number of nips is increased, the weight relief has to be adjusted to compensate for the added weight.

Another device that has been successfully applied to adjust crowns is the one shown in Fig. 15. With this device, the roll is bent by the application of a loading cylinder on an extended journal. This permits the roll to be bent up or down, increasing or decreasing the amount of crown. The usual procedure with this device is to crown the roll for the middle loading condition, bending it up or down, as the need demands.

Another device is the cross-axis unit. The principle is shown by Fig. 16. With this unit, the roll is crowned for the minimum load condition when operating all rolls in vertical alignment. As rolls are added, increasing the number of nips, the bottom roll is crossed to increase effective crown between the rolls.

WEIGHT RELIEVING
Open-side Calender

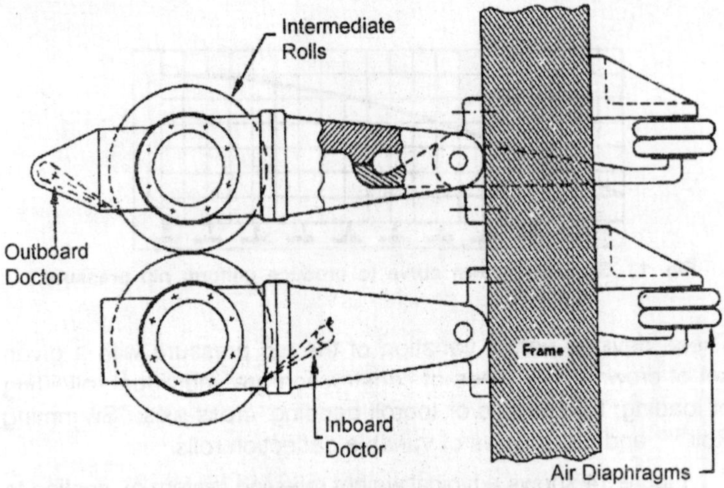

Fig. 14. Typical weight relieving system.

Adjusting Crown by Internal Roll Pressure

A device knowsn as a "Swimming Roll" (Fig. 17) is one of the most recent tools for the paper industry for adjusting crown. Figure 18 will serve to illustrate its operation. The roll consists of a stationary shaft on which are mounted two spherical self-aligning bearings at each and of a shell. The shaft rotates on the outer race of the bearings.

The end view in this illustration shows the stationary shaft in the center, with a seal projecting from the shaft in the center, with a seal projecting from the shaft to fill in the space between the shaft and the shell or internal roll surface. This provides a pressure chamber adjacent to the nip and a non-pressurized chamber opposite the nip.

The shell is completely free to deflect when hydraulic pressure is applied between the shell and the shaft. In this illustration, there is no energy in the form of hydraulic pressure in the roll system, therefore, the bottom roll deflects downward and the top roll deflects upward, due to the end effects. The top roll in this illustration is a standard type roll. You will note that under these

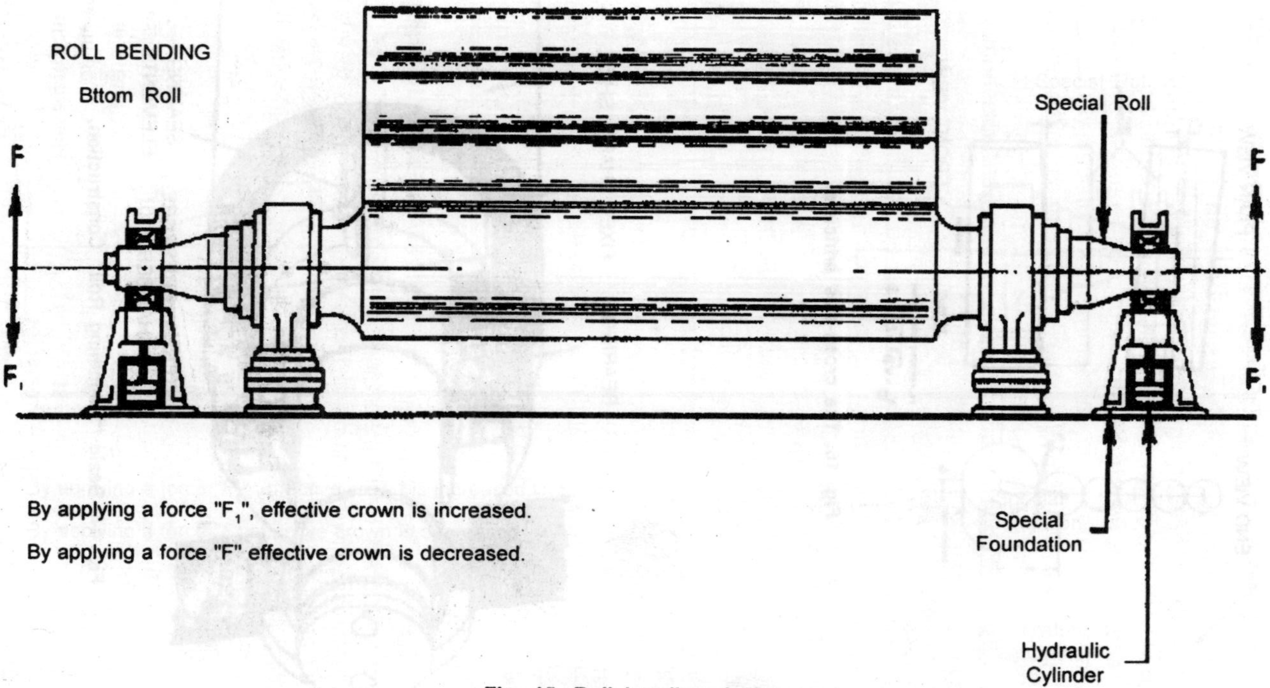

Fig. 15. Roll bending device.

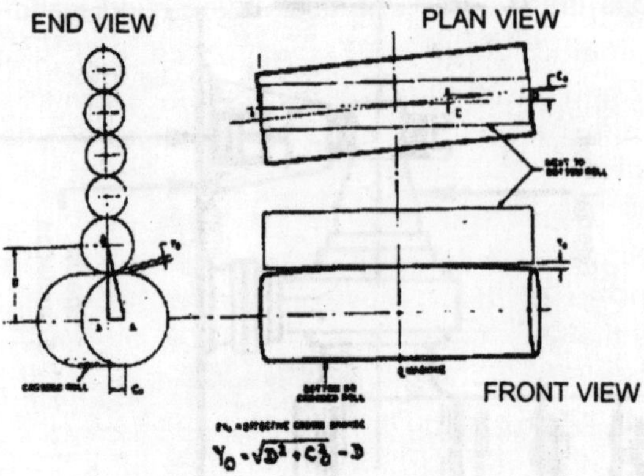

Fig. 16. The cross-axis principle.

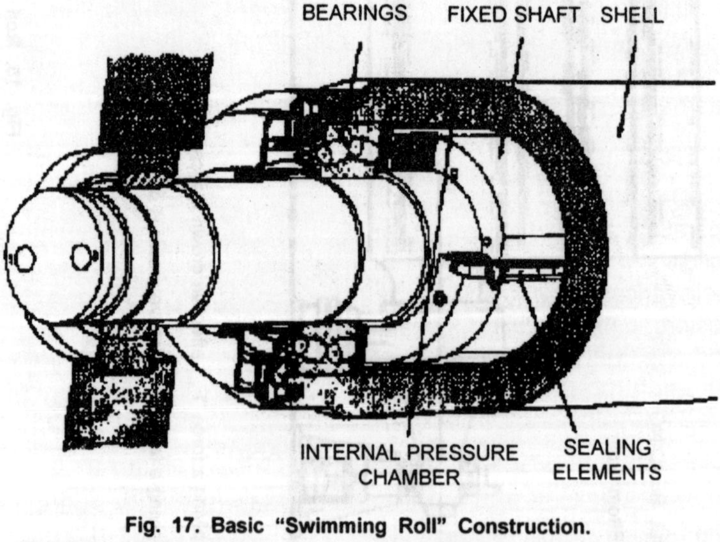

Fig. 17. Basic "Swimming Roll" Construction.

conditions the sheet will be thick in the middle and thin on the edges.

In Fig. 19, energy has been applied to the roll so that the shell is straight. This flattens out the bottom of the sheet of paper. The applied pressure in creases the deflection of the shaft, which is a stationary member.

In Fig. 20, the pressure has been increased inside the roll, which increases the deflection of the shaft, and at the same time, deflects the shell upward to match the deflection of the mating roll, thereby producing uniform nip pressure.

If it is desired to run with a flat "level" nip, as it is sometimes described, the pressure in the roll is decreased to create a level condition of the shell and a little weight relief is applied to the mating roll to take care of end effects; this creates a "level" nip as shown by Fig. 21.

In Fig. 22, where it is desired to have a nip pressure that is less than the weight of the mating roll, it is necessary to increase the weight relief and decrease the internal pressure in the roll, thereby again creating uniform nip pressure on the sheet.

If it is desired to create purposely a slight over-crown to knock down a heavy sheet in the center, or an under-crown to knock down a sheet on the edges, it is simply necessary to adjust the internal pressure of the roll.

OPERATION

One of the essential starting points for good calendaring operation is to be sure that the equipment is in first-class operating condition. Several essential parts of the calender are covered under their various headings in this chapter, such as loading systems, doctors, bearings, etc. One of the most important consideration, and one that is often neglected with respect to its relationship to the end product required, is the use of accurately ground and checked rolls.

Tolerance Related to End Product

Rolls should be held to a minimum variation in shape deviation. The actual minimum, or tolerance, that can be permitted should actually be based on the caliper tolerance for the sheet being produced.

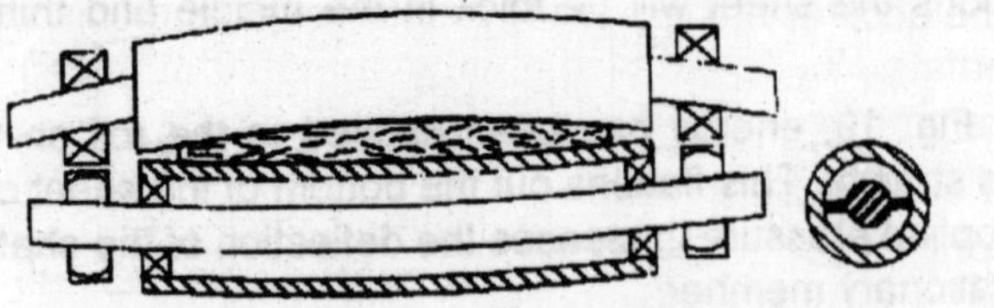

Fig. 18. "Swimming roll"—no internal pressure.

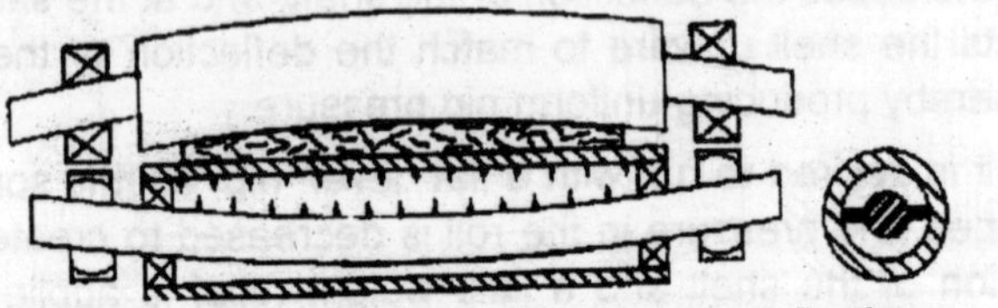

Fig. 19. Internal pressure to overcome deflection

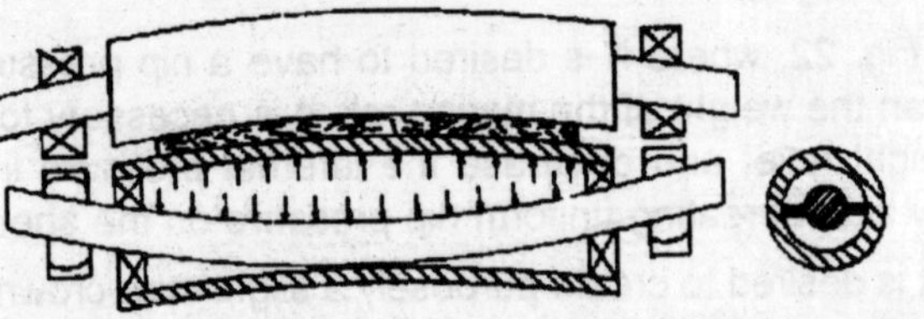

Fig. 20. Increased internal pressure to match mating roll deflection

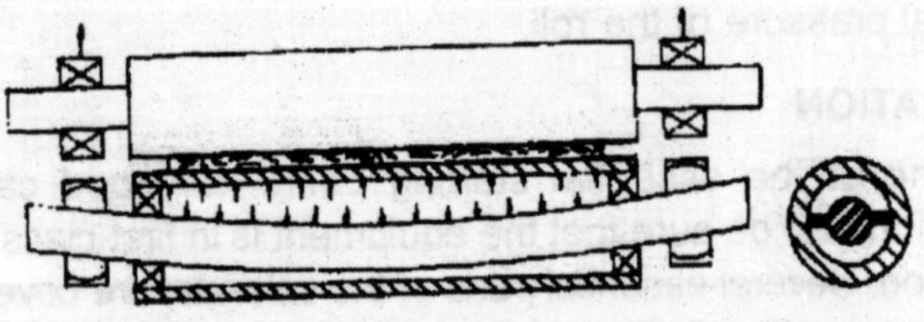

Fig. 21. Same as Fig. 19 with end effects relieved

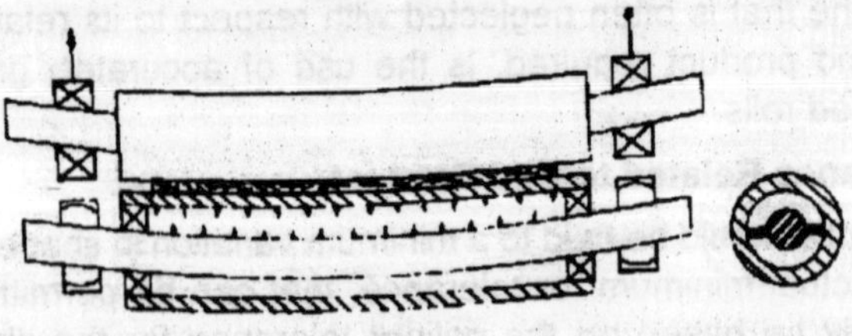

Fig. 22. Internal pressure less than Fig. 19 with additional weight relieving

The accuracy of regrinding to tolerances and finish that must be maintained is strictly a function of the relationship of requirements of the rolls to produce the end product within the quality control specifications.

For example, it does not make much sense to try to produce a sheet with a caliper variation of .0003 inch with rolls ground to an accuracy of .001 inch A very important point to keep in mind is that whenever a sheet passes through the nip in the calender, or any roll system, the sheet is feeling the effect of two rolls and, therefore, any tolerance that is required of the sheet must be devided by two, with respect to the accuracy required when grinding the rolls, to produce the sheet.

The regrinding cycle for rolls varies considerably, depending on the type of service required and the type of rolls being used. In some cases, rolls are ground as frequently as every two weeks, whereas, in other cases, rolls are reground on as much as a two-year cycle. Industry-wide, the average grinding cycle is there to six months. When rolls are changed in a calender, it is recommended that a complete set of rolls be changed, rather than changing of one at a time. The reason for this is that one bad roll in a system can affect the total system, and changing of one roll will seldomcorrect the problem, since the roll that is being replaced has, undoubtedly, affected the remaining rolls in the system.

The significant measurements, with respect to rolls operation are: roundness: concentricity; shape; station to station; taper; total crown; and roll face finish. (Cf. Bulletin 125A, Roll Measurement and Tolerances, Farrel Co.)

Other Devices Used in Calendering

There are a great many tools used by the paper-maker that are highly undesirable, since they create conditions which add to manufacturing expense. Among these tools are:

(1) The use of pads secured under the doctors for increasing rolls diameter through friction or heat. The continued use of a pad gradually wear a hole or a depression in the roll surface, and the necessary correction can no longer be obtained. This in turn creates the need for more frequent roll grinding to recondition the rolls and decreases roll life.

(2) Jacks or wedges are another form of distorting the roll combination to compensate for the lack of the ability to adjust the crown in roll systems or to correct for process variables.

The problem with these devices is that there is no way of measuring the amount of corrective force being applied and, therefore, much waste occurs when they are used.

Doctors, Which are used to keep rolls clean and free of debris, are undesirable from the standpoint of the rolls themselves. However, they are needed to keep rolls clean in many types of sheet processing. It is essential that they be kept in first-class operating condition, properly aligned with rolls, and that they not be excessively loaded, which causes both roll wear and doctor wear. It cannot be emphasized too strongly that doctors must be kept in first class condition.

One of the more common problems caused by doctors is the wearing down of the ends of the rolls due to high loading of the ends of the doctors. This is caused by the applied pressure that deflects the doctor assembly, causing heavier pressure on the ends of the roll than in the center. The doctor, so to speak, becomes a turning or grinding tool.

Doctors that oscillate help avoid roll scoring. They should be ground to fit the roll properly and should be mounted in accordance with the doctor manufacture's recommendations.

Roll Grinding

The roll grinder, although considered in most mills as a maintenance tool, is really a very necessary production machine. The following are points to be considered when grinding rolls: (1) the machine used for roll grinding should be checked periodically for proper alignment and leveling: (2) when a roll is set in the grinder, a check should be made to make sure that the bearing areas are turning concentrically : (3) it is important that the grinder be isolated from external vibration, with a suitable foundation to insure accurately ground rolls; (4) the two-wheel swing-rest roll grinder has proved to be the best type of machine for grinding rolls in the paper industry.

Rolls Grinder Tips

As with the calender, roll grinders also require careful operation and proper maintenance. The following suggestions can be helpful in the operation of roll grinding machines used in paper mills:

1. If results are not satisfactory, don't be hasty about blaming the grinder. Check first on conditions that may need correction: (a) are the roll necks round and in good shapes? (b) are the roll necks rests in good condition, and is the works properly set? (c) is the wheel in good condition ? (d) is there any unusual activity in the vicinity causing vibration of your machine?
2. Don't try to hurry roll grinding. If too much stock is hogged off at first, it is probable that more time will be lost than saved in trying to get a satisfactory surface during finish grinding. It is wise whenever possible to schedule fine work so thatthe job can be completed within one work period. Conditions overnight can vary slightly; even strong sunlight on a roll can cause sufficient metal expansion to affect a fine adjustment.
3. Unless a wheel is ideally suited to the work, occasional dressing may be required to obtain the best results.
4. It is good practice to cover the roll journals when grinding the rolls body, to keep the compound from contaminating the journal lubricant and to keep grit out of the gib or bearing area.
5. Make sure that the grinder in use is properly lubricated. A check-up by chart should be made at regular intervals.

Temperature Control

Today's increased demands for improved quality control and uniformity of paper finish, as well as higher speeds, have resulted in greater attention to the requirement for controlling rolls temperature in the calendering operation. Temperature controls is commonly accomplished either by running cold water through or introducing steam into the bore of bored rolls. Another method used for controlling temperature is use of a roll so constructed that an internal baffle is built inside of the bore, allowing more accurate control of a heating or cooling medium through controlled flow. In, addition, there is a roll built with holes drilled relatively close to the surface of the rll, immediately under the chill; passages connect these holes to a central bore, allowing the heating or cooling medium to be circulated under controlled flow rates and providing a very accurate temperature control arrangement. The roll utilize water or oil as a medium, depending on temperature requirements. In the controlled deflection type of roll, the temperature of the oil used within the roll also regulates roll temperature.

Pounds Per Lineal Inch (PLI)

A common term used in connection with the calendaring operation is "pounds per lineal inch" (PLI). This value is the result of roll weight, bearings, doctors (if they are mounted on the bearings) and any loading, such as hydraulic, pneumatic, etc., that may be applied to the roll system, and is specifically of the PLI across the sheet as the sheet passes through the calender. This value varies anywhere from 10 PLI in tissue calendering work

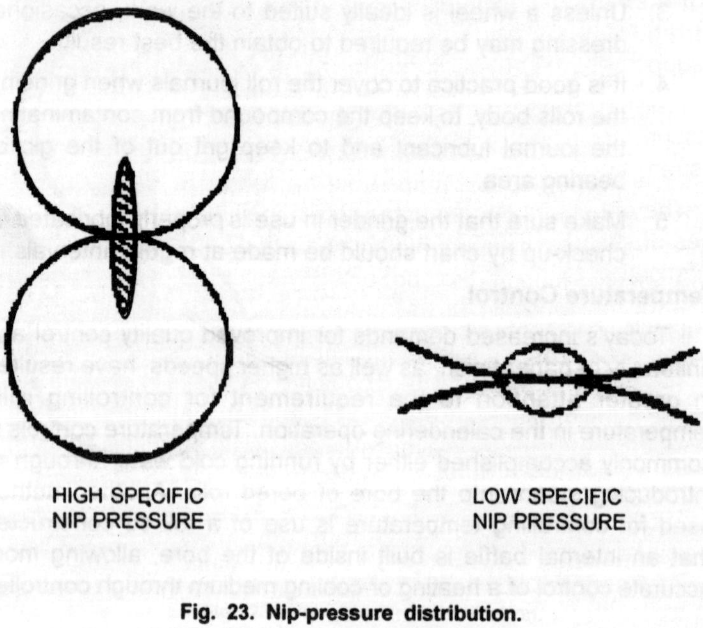

Fig. 23. Nip-pressure distribution.

up to from 100 to 600 PLI in the average or normal machine calendaring operation for paper grades, and higher for board. Supercalendering loads range from 1000 to 3000 PLI. The use of controlled deflection rolls allows an expansion of the range of loads to be obtained in connection with many calendaring operations, due to the uniform operating conditions that can be realized. Many of these rolls are being supplied for 1000 PLI use in machine calender applications.

Effective calendaring, of course, is not just a matter of PLI considerations in connection with operation, but is related to the relative roll diameters, as well as to the number of nips involved, since the rolls diameters have an effects on the pounds per square inch exerted on the sheet as it passes through the nip. There are many theories and views with respect to the need of multiple nips and/or high PLI's to produce the desired end product.

For a given PLI, the pounds per square inch pressure produced by small diameter rolls is greater than that produced by large diameter rolls. Theoretically, as roll diameters increase, it is necessary to impose a higher PLI to accomplish the same work on the sheet. As the number of rolls in the stack is decreased, PLI requirement is increased, and larger diameters are required to support the load.

It also must be realized when considering this matter that the pressure across the nip is not uniform throughout its width; this is illustrated in Fig. 23.

The effect of rolls diameter, and PLI (with respect to various types of sheet) is a field that requires much further research and investigation.

18

Felts

FUNCTIONS OF FELTS AND DRYER FABRICS

Paper machine felts and dryer fabrics serve:

(1) As conveyer belts to assist the sheet through manufacturing steps.

(2) As porous media to provide the void volume and channels for effective water removal.

(3) In the press section as textured cushions, or shocks absorbers for pressing moist sheets without crushing or significant marking.

(4) Occasionally, as marking felts to give a distinctive embossed pattern.

(5) As power transfer belts to drive non-driven rolls or parts

(6) In the dryer section, as tension bands to maintain sheet flatness and intimate contact with hot dryer surfaces.

FIBERS AND TREATMENTS USED IN FELT AND FABRIC MANUFACTURE

Fibers

The traditional fibres used in paper machine clothing are wool for wet felts and cotton for duck-type dryer canvases. Blends of wool with synthetic staple, fibres, such as nylon or polyester, have been introduced broadly into wet felts, with an increasing trend towards higher systhetic content.

Cotton core yarns plaited with yarns of asbestos fibre have long been in wide use in heavy duck-type canvases for high-temperature dryer service. Synthetic multifilament yarns are finding significant use in wet felts, usually in a plied or plaited combination with a yarn of predominantly wool content. There has been a trend toward replacement of cotton yarns in dryer clothing with synthetic multi-filament yarns which, with the introduction in 1960 of open mesh dryer fabric, began a trend toward use of 100% synthetic filaments. Such constructions are, according to use requirements, all multi-filament, all mono-filament, or partly of each type of synthetic yarn. There has been exploratory use (in open-mesh dryer fabrics for very high-temperature service) of yarns consist wholly, or in part, of special fibres and/or filaments, such as metal or spun glass.

The well informed use of synthetic even at higher price level than for the traditional products has contributed to a continuing dramatic reduction in clothing cost per ton of paper product.

Treatments

Chemical and/or heat treatments are applied to machine clothing during manufacture to improve one or more elements of performance. Wet felts have applied to them a rewetting agent to facilitate the wetting out immediately after installation. Other specific treatments are aimed at such single effects as reducing hair shedding, inhibiting bacterial or chemical attack, increasing resiliency, reducing plugging, or improving water removal. The more widely accepted "broad spectrum treatments" are almost always aimed, in part at increased resistance to abrasive wear and improved dimensional stability. In addition, they provide combinations of the improvements afforded with two or more specific treatments. Particulars are best obtained from the supplying companies.

Treatments are offered to reduce the rate of heat degradation of cotton-based dryer clothing. All open-mesh synthetic dryer fabrics in general use have had a chemical and/or heat treatment applied to stabilize the textile construction and to provide the slight rigidity that is needed for proper flatness, guiding, and running characteristics.

The judicious application of treatments has been another contributor to major reductions of clothing costs.

19

Paper Machine Wires

INTRODUCTION

Since its inception, the fourdrinier papermaking process has required a highly specialized endless belt capable of performing several functions simultaneously:

(1) Conveyor belt.

(2) Drainage belt.

(3) Sieve or screen.

(4) Power belt.

Ali these functions are to be accomplished under corrosive conditions that vary from moderately acid, low-solid waters through distinctly acid, sulphur-bearing water, including some high-solids-content waters of great chemical activity. This latter environment may be neutral or slightly alkaline. In addition, flexing occurs as the results of wraps of varying degrees and reverse bends over radii of less than $^1/_4$". As speed of machines increased, the load carrying capability required has mushroomed. This multiple challenge is to be met with a product whose uniformity has a significant effect on the quality of the paper sheet.

The initial belts were made of simple copper alloys, usually brasses, to combat corrosion. They were later hardened by the addition of tin and phosphorus to increase the wear resistance needed when machine and cloth design improved and the abrasiveness of the furnish increased, particularly as the use of groundwood and white pigment filled sheets became prevalent.

As newer materials were developed, they were tried in the laboratory. Over years of trial, the properties required in a construction material were defined:

(1) Suitable for production of fine wire strand with good formability.

(2) Suitable corrosion resistance.

(3) Sufficient mechanical properties, flexure strength.

(4) Sufficient physical properties, yield strength, tensile, and elongation.

(5) Stability within temperature range from 40 to170°F.

(6) Wear resistance under corrosion environment.

As stainless iron alloys and wear resistant platings such as chrome were developed, each was evaluated, many in the field as well as in the laboratory. Several have become construction materials. The natural organic fibres did not have properties rugged enough to meet the requirements; however, as more experience was gained with synthetic fibres or strands, some of these materials were tested and have in recent years found applications of special paper-making conditions, in ever increasing amounts. Copper alloys still are the most commonly used; they account for about 95% of all paper machine wires.

An alternate paper-making process using vats and cylinders covered with a sieve has been modified considerably in recent years by the application of some of the fourdrinier principles to the more stationary cylinder process. This results in a series of forming-type machines that for some purposes combine the advantages of each system. These formers employ screens, and in some cases, short moving belts. The construction materials for the cylinder process sieves had been primarily stainless steel, since little bending of the sieve was required, and therefore, a more chemically and abrasive resistant material could be used at the sacrifice of some fatigue resistance.

With the advent of the former system of paper-making, some return to copper alloys was required, as part of the systems clothing did require materials of better fatigue properties.

Plastic monofilament cloth may well fill the screening and sheet forming needs of the formers, where short radius bends are sometimes encountered, where the fabric's shrinking reaction in exposure to boiling water is useful in installing the screen on the cylinder, and where the load bearing demand (so necessary with the fourdrinier belt) is considerably reduced. In either process, the uniformity of the paper product is in part related to the uniformity of the screen used to cloth the wet end of the machine.

20

Coated Paper

Coatings are usually applied to paper and paper-board for the following purpose:

(1) To achieve uniformity of surface, either to the eye or to the inks, lacquers, and/or varnishes applied from a printing press.

(2) To enhance opacity (either waxed, dry, or varnished), smoothness, and the gloss of paper or paper-board.

(3) To achieve economy for base paper furnishes and to save where the brightness or functional properties of certain coatings may permits the use of mechanical pulps or unbleached pulps or waste paper.

The basic components of any coating designed for graphic art are as follows:

(1) Pigment or combination of pigments.

(2) Dispersants or a combination of dispersants for the pigment.

(3) Sometimes, but not always, an anti-foam.

(4) An adhesive or combination of adhesive either all synthetic or a mixture of synthetic and natural binders.

(5) Flow modifiers and/or lubricants.

(6) Deformers.

(7) Tinting colours.

COATING PIGMENTS

The most common pigments used in paper and paper-board are China clay, calcium carbonate, titanium dioxide, satin white and aluminum tri-hydrate. Additional information about pigments will be found in the following references at the end of this section satin white and aluminum tri-hydrate.

All pigments, except satin white, are usually delivered to the coating plant in the dry state. Exceptions to the above statement would be in the United States, i.e. clay of all grades may be obtained in tank car shipments (10,000 gal+) at about 70% solids.

Usual combinations of the above pigments in coatings are as follows:

(1) Clay 50 to 85%; Carbonate 50 to 15%

(2) Clay 65 to 90%; Titanium dioxide 35 to 10%

(3) Clay 75 to 90%; Satin White 25 to 10%

(4) Clay 65 to 90%; Titanium dioxide 20 to 5%; Al Hydr. 15 to 5%.

DISPERSANTS

The majority of the pigments listed above normally will use the polyphosphate as dispersants. Modern clay plant processes provide pre-dispersed pigments that are prepared by spray or drum drying, with the dispersants *in situ*.

The carbonate are normally dispersed with a modified sodium hexametaphosphate (CalgonT).

Because of the reactivity of the phosphates, which may slowly hydrolyze under heat or may sequester calcium ions, and because of the affinity of certain manufacture clays for the soap portion of latex dispersion, it is customary in many cases to use auxiliary dispersants that may be in the class of sulfonated naptholene formaldehydes, sodium terpolymers, phosfated potassium copolymers, and others.

Casein, soy protein, and oxidized starch are also good dispersants or adjuncts, under certain conditions.

The quantity of a dispersant to be used in preparing a pigment slurry is normally determined by titrating the pigment slurried in water with the dispersant and measuring the amount required to give the lowest viscosity. This starting point should be checked against coating colour viscosity.

BINDERS

The important blinders used in paper coatings today are:

(1) Starch (predominately corn, also potato and tapioca to a lesser extent) that has been mechanically, chemically, or enzyme modified.

(2) Casein (a protein produced from milk) has long been the standby of the coated-paper industry since 1900. It is principally produced in Argentina, New Zealand, and Australia. However, its variable quality and price fluctuations, when competing with usage in milk products, have made many mills move away from casein. Good quality casein is an excellent adhesive, but must be chemically solubilized for usage. Common alkalis used per 100 lb of casein are: sodium hydroxide 3.25 lb; ammonia 26° Be.1 gal; sodium carbonate 12 lb; borax 15 lb. These figures, taken from Cobb, are also supplemented by combinations of the above chemicals as solvents.

(3) Soy bean protein, a product obtained from the alkaline extraction of specially selected oil-free soy bean meal, has rapidly taken over as a casein replacement in the United States. Careful control and selected hydrolysis in manufacture has resulted in uniform product with wide viscocity ranges. In additional, the producers have maintained a stable price. As with casein the protein must be solubilized for use.

Brain *et al.* list the following combinations:

Soy protein	*100	100	100	100	100	100	100	100
Soda ash	12	-	-	-	8	-	-	-
Caustic soda	-	-	3.5	3	-	-	3.5	3.8
Ammonia 26° B'_{eG}	2	10	6	5.4	4	11	-	8
Borax	-	5	-	3.3	-	-	6	-

(* Figures in Pounds)

(Both casein and soy protein are subject to spoilage, borax does have a preservative action and is a good butter, however, it may cause paper embrittlement.)

(4) Animal glue has almost been completely phased out of coating usage.

(Starch, casein, and soy protein can all diverted to food usage. It is, therefore, not at all unlikely that their future industrial usage may be curtailed in the face of human needs.)

(5) The synthetic blinders:

(a) Polyvinyl alcohols were introduced to the industry in 1940 as casein was coming into short supply, due to World War II. It is produced from the hydrolysis of polyvinyl acetates. By controlling the chain length of the vinyl acetates and the degree of hydrolysis, a number of different grades may be obtained. Usually the completely hydrolyzed grades are used in paper coatings. It is a strong binder but has as yet to gain a real toehold on the coating market. In Japan and Europe, it has gained favour by replacing casein. In the writer's opinion, it may be too good an adhesive, as the low amount required for bonding (as determined in the laboratory) may not be at all adequate under conditions of adhesive migration encountered in commercial coating applications.

(b) Synthetic latices. "A synthetic latex may be defined as a dispersion of a polymer or elastomer in water, normally produced by emulsion polymerization." The main types used in paper and board coatings are:

(1) Styrene—Butadiene.

(2) Acrylics.

(3) Vinyl acetates.

All of the above latices are available at about 50% solids, they range from 0.13 to 0.2 μ particle size and are normally anionic or non-ionic in charge. Latices impart flexibility to a coating and easy calendaring. The selection of one latex over another can only be made when the formulation, the method of application, and end product are considered. Normally speaking, some formulations will show no difference in coated paper properties between latices—other will.

(c) Other synthetics are used in coatings, such as methyl cellulose, carboxymethyl cellulose, hydroxy ethyl cellulose polyvinyl pyrrolidone, etc. These are usually used as flow modifiers, or water retention aids.

The relative strength of the adhesives listed (for a publication grade paper coating) might be as follows (% on pigment):

3 to 5	Polyvinyl alcohol	12	Hydroxy-ethylated starch
8	Latex	14	Oxidized starch
9	Casein	15	Enzyme converted and acid modified
10	Soy protein		

The foregoing comments touched on the basic essentials (pigments, dispersants, and adhesives) currently in use. Let us now look at coating formulations.

The formulation of coatings satisfactory for graphic arts is still largely based on an empirical approach. The theoretical background of the various factors in coating formulation and coating application is still subjects to wide debate and speculation, so that in many cases, for example where a viscometer of a certain design may be used to define a coating, the basic proof of the definition is still the use of the coating on a coater to coat a substrate.

A dramatic coating development in the early 1930's was the so-called Massey coater. The coater consisted of a roll train (taken from a printing press) in which coating was transferred from rubber-covered roll to rubber-covered rolls and was worked and leveled, then finally imprinted on a web. Massey used an aqueous base ink to achieve an overall printing of the coating on the paper web. Because of the shear stresses involved in the transfer of coating from roll to roll at what was then regarded as high solids, much of the basic work done by Bingham, Green and others on ink rheology was impressed on paper coatings of this type. The concepts used in ink measurement to determine the rheological flow properties of paper coating introduced the need of multi-point viscometry measurement since, as can be seen from Fig.1, a viscometer is necessary to define the basic types of flow.

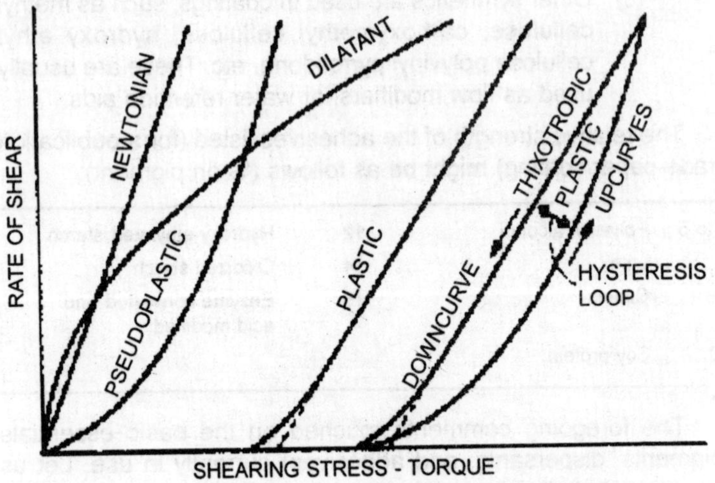

Fig. 1. Types of fluid flow in rotational viscometers

Newtonian-type flow, as is illustrated in the diagram, indicates that the rate of shear is directly proportional to the shearing force or stress.

Plastic type flow usually requires that before the flow begins, a certin amount of stress must be applied; but, once flow is underway, the rate of shear again is proportional to the shearing stress.

Pseudo-plastic type flow indicates that the rate of shear increase more rapidly than the shearing stress but, since it passes through the origin of the curve, it resembles Newtonian flow at low rates of shear, since there is no yield value.

Dilatant-type flow may be regarded as the opposite of pseudo-plasticity, since as the rate of shear is increased, the shearing stress if much greater. Dilatancy may be regarded as a hindered system in which voids are at a minimum. Generally in coating, dilatancy is often regarded as an inoperative type system; this, however, may not be wholly true.

In the systems as defined above, especially in the pseudo-plastic system, if at the top pseudo-plastic curve the shearing stress is now decreased, the down curve will be identical with the up curve. If however, the down curve in such a system does not correspond with the up curve, but produces a hysteresis loop such as is shown on the right, we say that the material is thixotropic plastic or that the basic viscosity changes are a time function, due to formation or breakdown of the internal structure. For example, household catsup is a gelled structure at rest but, if the bottle is shaken, the gelled structure is broken down and the catsup is a shaken, the gelled structure is broken down and the catsup will then pour frely is broken down and the catsup is not shaken out of the bottle, but stress is applied to break the original gelled structure, which then permits the material to flow out of the bottle. When the bottle is returned to rest, the gelled structure slowly reforms. The degree of thixotropy is usually regarded as the area between the up and the down curve.

In the so-called roll or Massey-type coasters, it has been estimated by Smith, Trelfa, and Ware that shear rates amounting to 4×10^5 reciprocal seconds can exist between the surface of the roll train of the Massey coater. In their initial work on the development of the Hercules high shear viscometer, they formed the concept of a leveling index. This dimensionless expression was the ratio of the coefficient of shear thixotropy to plastic viscosity, as a measure of coating suitability for multiple roll-type coaters. The Hercules high-shear viscometer was used in conjunction with a multiple-roll laboratory-type coater. The so-called leveling index did indicate lack of "orange peel," coating split, or the ease with which the coating smoothed itself on the surface of the sheet after it left the coating nip. A high leveling index indicated a high degree of thixotropy and low plastic viscosity. Smith, Trelfa, and Ware indicated, according to their experimental work, that coating leveling index values of .20 to .25 might be unsatisfactory and values of over .35 might indicate good performance. This paper, in many respects, was a landmark in the coating industry and, to some extent, has set the tone for much of the development work that has since transpired. It is, however, of interest to note

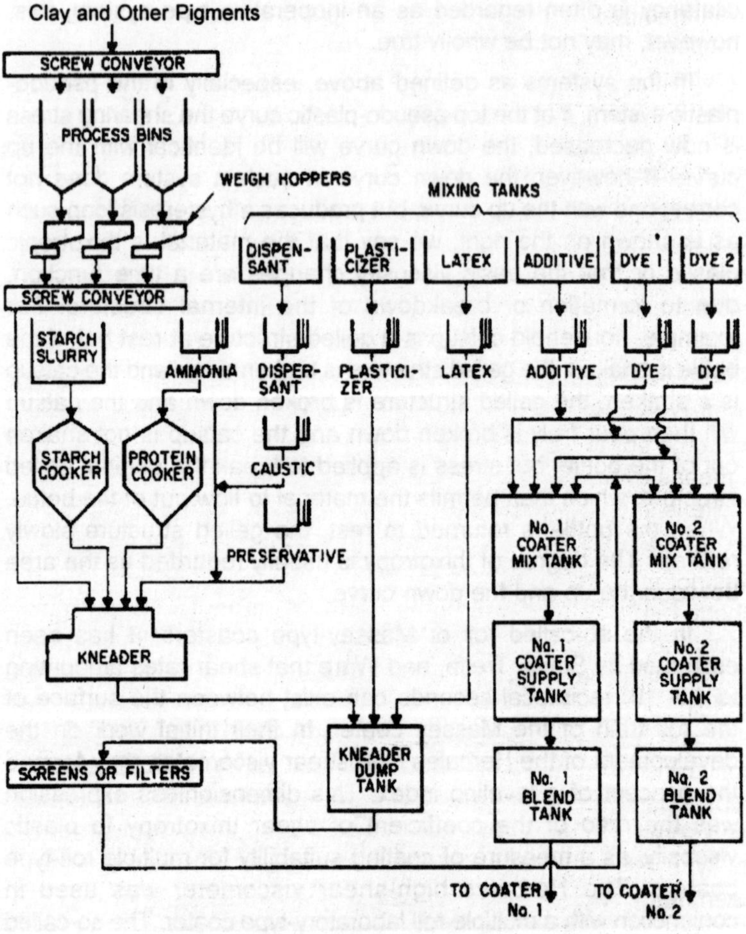

Fig. 2. Kneader colour system flow diagram

that the roll-type coaters on which this initial work was begun are no longer of the importance they were at the time the paper was prepared. Roll coaters are now used basically as precoaters (with a subsequent trailing blade application on top) or have been replaced completely by the so-called trailing-blade coaters.

The important part of the Smith, Trelfa, and Ware paper was the concept of leveling index as an inherent property of coating, i.e., it did not change with variations in the solids content of the coating mixture, and hence, defined the coating fairly well. Practically speaking, however, when coating is applied to a substrate, variations of smoothness and absorptivity of. the substrate can influence the dewatering or stability of a coating to such an extent that, although a coating may be rheologically acceptable, it will not operate.

Because the Massey coater permitted a high solids coating (usually 50 to 65%) which did not distort the web by excessive moisture and which dried easily, the technology of both pigments and adhesives were then centered around developments that could be used on the Massy or roll-type coaters. In the pigment field, this led to the use of low viscosity at high solids.

To prepare high solids coatings for the roll coaters, coating at that time enlisted the use of a sigma bladed mixer or kneader as a means of coating preparation. Such a system as described by Wolfe is shown in Fig. 2.

At the time of the introduction of Massey-type coaters, latex was not employed and was not in use in the coating industry until about 1946. Also, slurry clay did not come into general use until about the same time. The typical coating preparation as described in this diagram introduced either a cooked starch or a cooked protein, or a combination of both, into the kneader, and the dry clay and other pigments were sheared directly in the adhesives until the smooth dispersion was obtained. This material was then subsequently dumped into a storage tank from whence it was then screened into the coating blending or supply tanks. Typical roll-type or Massey-type coating formulations which might have been made in the kneader are as follows:

Offset Labal Papers—50 to 58% Solids

No. 1

100 lb	No 2 Clay
3 lb	Sod. Hexametaphosphate
200 lb	Oxidized Starch
50 lb	Dimethylol Urea
5 lb	Ammounium Sulfate
20 lb	Ammonium Strearate

No. 2

1000 lb	No. 2 Clay
150 lb	Casein
15 lb	Ammonia
3 gallons	Wax Emulsion

Publication—Letter press (50 to 58% Solids)

No. 3

850 lb	No. 2 Clay
150 lb	Calcium carbonate Pcptd.
3 lb	Sod. Hexametaphosphate
2 lb	Soda Ash
250 lb	Oxidize Starch
15 lb	Lvory Soap

2 Gallons Wax Emulation

No. 4

850 lb	No. 2 Clay
150 lb	Titanium Dioxide
50 lb	Casein (Ammonia Cut)
150 lb	Oxidized Starch
10 lb	Ivory Soap

Paper-board 52 to 55% Solids.

No. 5

1150 lb	No. 2 Clay
200 lb	Titanium Dioxide
3 lb	Sodium Tetraphosphate
5 lb	Soda Ash
200 lb	Casein
30 lb	Ammonia
80 lb	Wax Emulsion

No. 6

1150 lb	No. 2 Clay
200 lb	Titanium Dioxide
3 lb	Sodium Tetraphosphate
5 lb	Soda Ash
300 lb	Oxidized Starch
20 lb	Ammonium Stearate

Formulations No. 1 and No. 2 were designed to produce a water-resistant label for coated one side paper or a double-coated paper suitable for offset printing.

Formulas No. 3 and No. 4 are those normally used for magazine publication papers.

Formulas No. 5 and No. 6 are used on the roll coating of paper-board.

The other adjuncts (see coating components above) came to be added at this time. For example, it was found during super calendering that some coatings tended to dust, i.e., small particles of coating would flake off. In addition to the initial work done by increasing of the thixotropy, it was found that soap addition to a starch bound coating not only allowed the roll-type coating to transfer and flow better on the rolls, but it also reduced calender dusting. Hence, the introduction of either Ivory soap or ammonim stearate into these formulations to increase thixotropy and reduce dusting. The wax sizes employed at that time were basically soap stabilized and also tended to alleviate this condition. However, it was not at all unusual to have these wax emulsions break under the shearing action of the roll train; hence, they gradually were eliminated. Casein in the formulations was also a good preventative against dusting and, because of its dispersant action and protective colloid action, aided in obtaining extremely smooth and level coatings.

Dimethylol urea, the forerunner of the urea and melamine resin concentrates, was utilized at that time (about 1940) to add water resistance to starch bound coatings, since casein was in scarce supply. Ammonium sulfate was used as a catalyst, in order to reduce the pH of the coating and thus to initiate the condensation reaction between the dimethylol urea and starch. It was not unusual, when using combinations of this type, that the surface pH of the sheet would become too acid, thus imparing the drying of offset inks in the humidity printing operations.

In place of a preconverted starch, sometimes a pearl starch was "enzymes converted". Pearl starch was slurried in a starch slurry tank. It was then screened into a cooker which was usually equipped with a paddle-type agitator and a means of heating, either by direct or indirect steam. The starch concentration of the slurry was usually kept about 32% or slightly lower, since uncooked starch slurries may become dilatant at about 35% solids. The pH of this slurry was adjusted with soda ash to a pH range of 6.5 to 7.5. The enzyme, usually a bacterial alpha amylase, was introduced in sufficient concentration to provide the required viscosity at the end of the cooking cycle. As a corn starch dispersion approaches 154 to 168°F the mass will start to gell. A holding periods of about 15 to 30 min may be employed at this temperature, in which case, the enzyme acts on the starch by breaking the amylose chains at random. The amyplopectin section of the starch molecules is usually broken at the branches. After a sufficient time for liquefaction, the starch is brought up to 210° F and held for about 10 min to inactivate the enzyme. The time cycle and the enzyme concentration of the cook employed are adjusted to produced the starch viscosity range desired. The cooked and enzyme-converted starch is then incorporated into normal coating-mixing procedure.

Since enzyme-converted starch did produce a relatively inexpensive adhesive, it was adopted quite widely in the period of from 1938 to 1944. In this same period, Craig developed a technique of "converting in the presence, " wherein clay dispersion were made at relatively high solids and the required amount of pearl starch was slurried with the clay. The entire mass, usually about 65% solids + was then adjusted in pH and treated with hexametaphosephate. Enzyme was added, and the entire mass of both starch and clay were raised to the gel point of the starch, at which time, the enzyme acted *in situ*. When the coating reached the desired state of conversion, the temperature of the mass was raised to 200 + to inactivate the enzyme. While the heating of the mass of the clay along with the starch was somewhat difficult, it nevertheless produced a coating with superior properties, both from the standpoint of dispersion and the efficiency of the starch in adhesive value. Wilber and other have reported on this technique.

When the kneading mixers were used for both casein and soy protein coatings, techniques were developed where by the protein and/or casein was cut or solubilized in the presence of the clay. Techniques of this type called for the introduction of the casein and/or protein into the kneader with the necessary amount of cold water so that the added clay could produce a shearing solids concentration of about 75%.At this high concentration, the cutting agent was introduction and the casein or protein was cut in the presence of pigment. Sometimes the procedure was reversed, and the clay was dispersed at extremely high solids cutting agent added to the high-shear pigment, and the casein and/or soy protein was introduced into the high-shear mass. In either case, the cutting in the presence did have the advantages of eliminating the so called casein or protein cooker.

From 1948 to 1958, the machine coating of paper and paper-board mushroomed dramatically. These years saw the establishment of soy protein and the various lattices as factors in coating binders. It also saw the introduction of the trailing blade coater, the gradual phasing out the roll type coaters expect as pre coaters, the introduction of wet on wet coatings, air knife blade or rod combinations the roll plus blade or rod combinations, the drive towards lightweight coatings in the publication field, and the explosion of coating into bleached paper-board.

The technology accompanying this explosion is still trying to catch up and, in the field of paper and board coating, a great deal of basic equipment and technology was borrowed from both the paint and ink industries.

The widespread use of liquid or tank car shipment of clays further sparked the simplicity of coating preparation. During this period, the so-called high shear mills, such as the Kady the Abbe, the cowls, the Hochmeyer, and the Day dispersers, started to make inroads on the use of the old-type kneaders.

By intensive shearing action, on certain grades of calcium carbonate and satin white, it was found that substantial reductions in adhesive demand of these pigments could be made; and, under the need of high solids with low viscosity, the use of liquefying agent was investigated. Both urea and dicyandiamide were extensively used to liquefy both starch and protein solutions. The interest in these liquefying agents has been gradually phased out to some extent, since the amount of liquefying agent required (usually 10 to 20% of the material, based on the adhesive) was an expensive way to reduced viscosity.

Extensive work was done along the lines of attempting the waterproofing of starch through a condensation of starch with urea resins, melamine formaldehyde, and the dialdehyde, glyoxal. In the field of lactices, emphasis was placed on the development of lactices that were also capable of cross-linking with these materials, so that in many cases the latex in a latex-starch combination would waterproof the combination coating. It was, of course, also discovered that the degree of insolubility of coatings for offset printing had been substantially exaggerated and that, in many cases, a moderate water resistance would be entirely adequate to prevent "milking" or leaching on the offset blanket.

One of the most helpful concepts that came from paint technology was the idea of thinking in terms of pigments volume and adhesive volume rather than weight, or more simply, the per cent of pigment volume concentration. The percent pigment volume concentration is defined as:

$$\text{\% Pigment Vol. Conc. PVC (Dry Film)} = \frac{\dfrac{\text{Wt of Pigment}}{\text{Sp Grav of Pig.} \times 100}}{\dfrac{\text{Wt. of G.}}{\text{Sp Grav of Pig.} \times 100} + \dfrac{\text{Wt. of Adhesive}}{\text{Sp Grav of Adhesive.} \times 100}}$$

Utilizing this concept, in a dried film it much adhesive to fill the interstices or the voids between the pigments particles. The point at which the adhesive entirely filled the voids between the particles was designated as the critical pigment volume concentration (CPVC). As beck and VanLoo noted that properties of paint films, such as gloss, blistering, etc. changed quite drastically at this critical pigment volume concentration. Cobb, in a masterful paper presents in 1958, pulled together and defined the entire scope of the concept of pigment volume concentration, in terms of adhesive demand for various pigments. She demonstrated that the adhesive demand of a pigment, as far as paper coating was concerned, might be entirely independent of the specific surface and particular size of that pigment, but was governed by the per cent size of that pigment, but was governed by the percent voids of the pigment in actual use in a coating. Verwey and Overbeek, Kline, and Hemstock and Swanson also enlarged on the concept of pigment dispersion and pigment volume concentration, as well as particles shape and particle packing. Robinson, working in the liquid phase, used the concepts of relative sediments volume for viscosity and pigment dispersions. Sennett and Olivier and later Sennett, Olivier, and Morris, applied the concept of zeta potential and developed a technique for measurement in clay and coating dispersions.

It must be recognized, of course, that laboratory work to explain adhesive demand did not always fit into production operations.

The departure from the high solids roll coater, the introduction of lactices into coating formulations, and the installation of high velocity air drying on production equipment brought the knowledge abruptly to industry that the drying of paper coatings could not be regarded as an exercise in water evaporation. Attempts to push drying rates on coaters up to 10 lb/sq ft/hr in many cases produced coatings (that on printing) resulted in severe ink mottle. In exaggerated cases, particularly with air knife application, the coated surface cracked and crazed like a dried mud puddle.

Papers by Heiser and others indicated that high-velocity, high-air-tempreature type dryers caused the water portion of coatings to migrate towards the hot side, carrying with it the adhesive and leaving starved zones or a concentration of adhesive at the surface, thus producing ink mottle. Bergomi reviewed the literature on this subject.

Unfortunately in many cases a coating operation had been installed and was inoperative, due to this inadequate drying. It was easier to make attempts in correcting the coating rather than correcting the drying situations. Hence, the industry concentrated the technology on developing methods for evaluating the water holding properties or the water release properties of coatings. Studies were made to find additives for latex to make their water release more like the natural builders, thus reducing adhesive migration on rapid drying.

This water-holding capacity has been one of the reason why natural blinders are retained as part of the binder system in many of the coatings. Additional water retention aids are: the sodium alginates, the hydroxyethyl celluloses, carboxymethyl celluloses, methyl celluloses, and polyvinyl pyrrolidone. The amount of these additives used for the control of water release is a question of coating formulation, raw stock, rate of drying, method of application, etc.

In many respects, all coating formulations are interchangeable. They look essentially the same, with the major difference being the requirements for the methods of application. If, for example, a high solids coating of say 60% (being run on a trailing blade) needs 15% adhesive to give a required ink holdout or pick test, this same coating might also be used on an air knife at 40% solids, provided that the adhesive content was increased to 20%. The following is a very general rule of thumb in the coating industry in the area between 65 and 40% solids in a coating composition: as the solids content of the same coating is increased from 40 to 65% solids, for every 5% increase in coating solids, the adhesive content on the pigment may be reduced 1%. So, a coating at 40% solids that might require 20% adhesive, based on the pigment at 65% solids, would only require 15% adhesive, based on the pigment. And corresponding, if coating solid are reduced, the amount of adhesives must be increased roughly in accordance with the foregoing.

The coating formulation that follow are examples of general formulation presently used in paper and board coatings. In citing these, we have attempted to select those that illustrate the field in which they are cited, and we have stayed away from some of the formulation that are employed in special cases. These deviation as well as formulations for cast coating, thermo-swaging and bubble-type coating may be obtained from the literature cited.

Re-screen coatings on overflow from size press temperature control. Add deformer by constant addition. Above formulation may be used on Champion coaters, reducing adhesive to the 20 to 25% range with solids in 48 to 56% range.

TYPICAL COATING FORMULATIONS

Size Press Applications (35 to 55% solids) - no subsequent coats - paper

Letterpress and Grayure

1000 lb	Clay	850 lb	Clay
3 lb	Dispersant	150 lb	Calcium Carbonate (Pcpt)

200 to 300 lb	Oxidized Starch or Hydroxyethylated Starch	200 to 300lb	Oxidized or Ethylated Starch
10 lbCa.	Stearate	10 lbCa.	Stearate

Offset

As above., either pigment formulas, but any latices can be used, adjust pH to comensate for alum leaching, keep temperature down (not over 120° F), use organic dispersant.

180 lb	Starch	150 lb	Starch
50 lb	Latex (Dry Solids)	150 lb	Latex (Dry Solids)

Others

As above on pigment formulations, but as adhesives.

100lb	Protein (15% Ammonia Cut)	150 lb	Polyvinyl Alcohol
100 lb	Acrylic or SB (Latex Solids)		(non-ionic defoamer)

Web-Letterpress

In general, pigmentation varies, depending on the economics of the grades structure, the degree of ink absorbency required, and the final brightness and opacity of the coated sheet. The lowest quality coated magazine paper, probably in the No.7 Enamel category, utilizes the cheapest coating clays and most in expensive starches, usually enzyme converted.

These low quality paper are usually quite high in ground wood content, i.e., 60 to 70% and as a result, have rather low picking resistance.

Web Letterpress
(Magazine Paper - No. 7 Enamel)

Ingtredients	Parts Solids by weight
Coating grade clay, No. 2 or 3	100
Starch, enzyme converted	15
pH	8.5 to 9.0
Total solids	55%
Coating weight, lb/3000sq ft/side	4
Brightness	68
Picking resistance, IGT	Fails - No. 4 Ink
Coating method	Single blade
Basis weight, lb/3000sq ft	36

There is a great deal of activity at the present time among magazine paper producer to reduce the basis weight of the coated paper. The reason for this activity is rising postal rates that have increased the mailing costs of the magazine publishers. The publishers want lower basis weight, because that gives them more printing area per pound of paper.

Most of the paper today is about 36 lb/3 M sq. ft. but the ultimate goal is to get as low as possible. The major obstacles towards the achievement of lightweight coated paper are decrease in paper-machine efficiency and poor optical characteristics, resulting in ink show-through as the basis weight goes down.

As the quality of the coated web letterpress paper goes up, pigmentation usually changes to include precipitated calcium carbonate as a replacement for a portion of the clay. The carbonate is added to increase brightness and ink absorbency.

The binder content of the higher quality magazine paper may also change to include small quantities of synthetic latex, i.e., up to 20% of the binder. The latex, usually styrene-butadiene, improves calenderability and printability.

Most all web letterpress grades are single blade coated, either on-or-off-machine.

Web Offset Moving up the quality scale, the next major category is web offset. It lies toward the middle of the coated paper grades structure. Here, too, there is a wide variation of coating formulations, because of the broad range of papers being used in web offset. Some printers are able to get by with essentially web letterpress grades of coated paper, while others require significantly higher quality. The formulation attached is in the upper half of the quality scale for web offset.

Pigmentation for these grades trend towards the higher quality clays than used for web letterpress. Calcium carbonate may be added to improve brightness, ink absorbency, and porosity.

The binder system still tend to be predominantly starch, but of a greater variety, i.e. enzyme converted oxidized, or hydroxy-ethylated.

Synthetic latex system also find greater usage in web offset formulations, for a number of reasons. The economics of these grades structure are some - what better than the web letterpress grades, and as a result, more latex can be tolerated from a cost standpoint. Also, latex improves wet pick strength, which is frequently required by the better quality web offset printing. Higher latex levels also improve gloss ink holdout. The type of latexes usually employment are the styrene-butadienes, vinyl acetates, and acrylates.

Web Offset

(No. 4 or No. 5 Enamel)

Ingtredients	Parts Solids by weight
Coating grade clay, No.1 or 2	75
Calcium carbonte, ppt	25
Starch, enzyme converted or hydroxyethyl	8
Latex	8
pH	8.0 to 8.5
Total solids	60%
Coating weight, lb/3000sq ft/side	7
Brightness	80
Picking resistance, IGT	Fails - No. 6 Ink
Porisity, Sheffield	30 or higher
Lower wuality	Single blade
Higher quality	Size press/blade
Basis weight, lb/3000sq ft	50 or higher

Porosity is of major concern when web offset papers are printed on high-speed presses, using heat set inks. Moisture in the sheet turns to steam when the printed web passes through the high temperature ovens. Air temperatures are often in the range of 500 to 700° F, and internal web temperatures can go as high as 350° F. Unless the internal bond strength is high enough to withstand the forces generated by the steam or the coating is porous enough to allow it to escape, the sheet literally blows apart and forms blisters.

Blistering occurs most frequently in the areas where there is heavy ink coverage on the both sides of the web, although it is not necessarily confined to those areas. Coated paper printed by the web letterpress process can also develop blisters when printed with heat set inks, but the problem is more predominant with coated web-offset paper for two reasons:

(1) Web offset paper is frequently printed on blanket to blanket perfecting presses, which means that both sides are printed simultaneously. The wet ink films tend to seal off the surfaces and retard moisture transmission. Web letterpress is also printed on both sides, but usually in sequence, so that it is only necessary to heat one side at time. The other side can be in contact with a supporting drum, and thus, web temperature need not be above the boiling point of water.

(2) Web offset printing requirements are more stringent than web letterpress, i.e. higher wet and dry pick resistance, which means that binder levels and/or latex are usually higher, thus resulting in a stronger and "tighter" coating with less porosity.

Tendencies to blister usually increase as the basis weight goes up, because of the concurrent increase in the volume of moisture present in the sheet.

A number of techniques are employed in the prevention and control of blistering. One of these is a significant reduction in total moisture content below the customary 5 to 6% moisture level when the coated paper is dried. However, such reductions in moisture content make finishing on the super-calenders more difficult. There are also greater tendencies towards dusting and cracking, especially when the printed signatures are folded and collated.

These problems with finishing and dusting are two of the reasons for incorporating more latex and less natural binder in web offset coatings. Latex flexibility, in contrast to natural binders, is not affected by moisture content, and the coating remain flexible even at lower moisture levels. However, latex also tends to reduce the prosity of the coating and thus increase blistering tendencies. Therefore, proper balance must be maintained between moisture content, Z-direction tensile strength, and porosity.

Another technique is the addition of calcium carbonate to the coating formulation to maintain porosity, because calcium carbonate tends to "open up" the coating surface.

There is disagreement on the relationship between porosity tests and blistering. Some mill people claim that a reduced rate of air passage through the web does not necessarily mean the sheet will blister. Porosity measurements are made through the web. Thus, if one coated surface is porous and the other surface is non-porous, the porosimeter measurements only reflect the rate of air flow through the non-porous surface. However, during printing, internal moisture can escape through the porous side. This is why some feel the only meaningful tests are those that simulate the conditions of the freshly printed web passing through a high temperature oven. Others feel that porosity measurements, such as Sheffield or Gurely, are valid. The answer probably lies in the degree of two-sideness and the consistency in maintaining it. Published porosity values should only serve as a guide until test values can be correlated with actual printing performance, because of the influence on blistering of the balance of properties discussed eariler.

Web offset grades at the lower and of the grade scale are usually single blade coated. The higher quality grades are usually doublecoated with precoat, usually starch clay, apply at the size press. The blade top coat can be applied either on-or off-machine.

Sheet Offset

The top of the line of conventionally coated paper is the "premium" grade of enamel paper. Primary differentiation from lower grades such as No. 1 enamels is brightness, opacity and surface characteristics. Strength properties such as picking resistance are basically not too much different in any of the grades of sheet offset paper.

Pigmentation is one of the things that sets premium grades apart from the lower grades. These grades use the highest quality coating clays, i.e., better than a No. 1 grade. In addition to calcium carbonate, titanium dioxide and/or fluorescent dyes are used extensively to provide opacity and high apparent brightness. Titanium dioxide is espcially desirable as a means of maintaining the brightness and opacity of grades that will be heavily varnished.

The binder compositions also tend to be more exotic. In most cases, the major portion of the binder is synthetic latex, generally styrene-butadiene, and the balance casein or protein. Industry trends in these grades are towards completely synthetic latex binders, primarily of the alkali swellable types. These binders have the water holding properties and develop the rheological characteristics generally associated with casein or protein. Synthetic latex systems are easy to use and provide a number of property improvements. For example, coatings containing high latex levels in the binder develop high gloss and smoothness, because of the easy finishing characteristics of the thermoplastic polymer. Coating flexibility is maintained, regardless of moisture content, for good folding characteristics, without cracking or dusting. There are significant improvements in gloss ink and varnish holdout. Offset printability is excellent.

All papers in the premium grade range are double coated and in some cases, triple coated in order to achieve the high coating weights characteristic of these papers. The pre-coatings are starch/clay formulations applied by size press, roll or blade coater, or combinations of these coaters. The top coating is applied off-machine with either a spread-shaft (reverse smoothing roll) or air knife coater. Most mills producing this grade are not yet able to apply the coating weighs required with a blade coater. But many feel this situation will be resolved by equipment installation leading to the ability to apply multiple blade coats and by formulation changes made possible by high synthetic latex binder content.

SHEET OFFSET
(Premium Enamel)

Ingredients	Parts Solids by weight
Coating grade clay, better than No. 1	60
Calcium carbonate, ppt	35
Titanium dioxide*	5
Casein or protein	5
Latex	15
pH	8.0 to 9.5
Total solids	40%
Coating weight, lb/3000 sq ft/side	15
Brightness	86
Picking resistance, IGT	High No. 6 Ink

Ingredients	Parts Solids by weight
Coating Method:	
Precoat	Size press, Roll, Blade
Topcoat	Spread shaft, Air kinfe
Basis weight, lb/3000 sq ft	70 or higher

*And/or fluorescent dyes.

PAPERBOARD COATING

The single coating of paper-board is just about totally confined to the air knife. Typical formulations might be :

1000 lb No. 1 Clay or hibrite or higloss	800 lb
3 lb Dispersant	200 lb Titanium dioxide
	3 lb Dispersant
40 lb Protein (ammonia cut)	40 lb
150 lb Latex solids	150 lb
10 lb Calcium stearate (dry)	10 lb
16 lb Melamine resin (dry)	16 lb
2 lb Defoamer	2 lb

The foregoing are all purpose paper-board coatings, in many instances, the protein adhesive ratio is often increased for better gluability.

Double Coating combinations are usually empolyed for the high grade papers or board. The usual combinations are:

(1) Roll and blade or rod

The high solids roll coaters imprint a coating on the sheet that is dried, and second or leveling coat is applied by means of a trailing blade or rode-type coater.

(2) Blade or rod + blade or rod

A double coat with first a down trailing blade coat that is dried and second coated with a trailing blade or trailing rod combination.

(3) Blade or rod + air knife

A leveling base coat is applied by means of a trailing blade or rod. It is either dried or left wet and then coated by an air knife as the top coat. This combination, is usually used only on cylinder or fourdrinier paper-board coatings.

All of the above combinations whether on paper or board may be commented on as follows:

(1) The base coat adhesive content is normally run 3 to 5% higher in adhesive content than the second coat. The action of the first coat is to de-water the second applied coating very rapidly. If the additional adhesive is not in the first coat, the second coat may go dilatant and streak or be deficient in adhesive on calendering or printing.

(2) When running the same coating on both coaters, this same effect (as in 1) can be obtained by operating the second coater at slightly lower solids.

(3) When running wet on wet—blade and air knife—to insure bonding, try to keep the adhesive in both coats essentially the same. For example,

Blade or rod coat—100 lb clay—5 lb starch—15 lb latex—52 to 58% solids.

Air knife top coat—100 lb clay—4 lb protein—14 lb latex—45 to 50% solids.

(4) Since the prime coat in the above cases is a leveling or filling coat, it is customary to use No. 3 or No. 2 clays or combinations with delaminated clays as the pigment. The second coat usually contains the high grade pigments for finer particle sized pigments.

21

Finishing and Converting

INTRODUCTION

The term "converting". As used in the paper industry, refers to the processing of the raw paper, as made on the paper machine, in order to produce in improved grade of paper or a finished paper article. There are two distinct types of paper converting. The first will be referred to as 'wet converting". In this process, the paper is handled in roll form and is modified and improved by such operations as coating, impregnating, laminating, and various combinations of these processes. The second will be called "dry converting". Here, a finished product is made from the paper, such as a bag, box or small roll.

There are many different types of converting operations, and to describe them all fully is beyond the scope of this book. In this section, the principal converting operations in use for the more important paper products will be discussed.

Before describing the principal converting operations, the basic procedure used for the more important grades of paper products will be reviewed.

Packaging and warapping papers are subjected to a wide variety of converting processes to improve their usefulness. These processes include the application of various protective and waterproof coatings, and the lamination of two or more webs to increase strength and to combine qualities. These packaging papers are then further processed in order to convert them into paper bags, cartons, liquid containers, and over warp materials, in each on special machines designed for these purposes.

Another major class of paper products, the sanitary papers, are processed through highly mechanized and specialized converting procedures. Because of their low cost, this must be done with a minimum of manual labour. Toilet tissue and paper towels are rewound on continuous automatic machines from mill-size parent rolls. Paper napkins and facial tissues are similarly handled on specially designed automatic equipment that operates continuously from mill rolls and delivers a finished packaged product ready for shipment.

Building and structural papers are impregnated for waterproofness and laminated to build thickness, strength, and rigidity.

FUNCTIONAL COATINGS

One of the principal uses of functional coatings on paper is to provide a barrier to the passage of water, water vapour, and gases. These properties are of value in packaging food products and other materials which must be protected from the atmosphere or from loss of ingredients.

The oldest types of coatings used for these purposes were paraffin wax and bituminous asphalt. Subsequently, various lacquers and varnishes of both natural and synthetic resins were developed for application to paper, not only to serve as barriers, but also to give gloss and improved apperance.

Paper is also useful as a base of gummed tapes and adhesive tapes used for packaging and for a variety of other purposes. Animal glues or rubber-base. Pressure-sensitive adhesive are applied to paper in order to produce these tapes.

Greaseproof lacquer coatings and a wide variety of solutions and dispersions of modern synthetic resins are now available for use as paper coatings to accomplish almost any desired protective purpose. While paper itself is a poor barrier and has poor water resistance, a thin film of one of these coating materials greatly enhances its protective properties and expands its usefulness. The paper provides a strong low-cost base and is thus a natural complement to the higher cost and structurally weaker resins.

For applying these functional coatings to paper, there are several principal types of processes and equipment in common use.

Roll Coaters

The basic roll coater is cane of the oldest types of coaters, the coating applicator roll itself having been used in the early brush coaters and in most other types of coating machines that were subsequently developed. The single-roll coater is seldom used alone today, because of its poor control of the amount of coating being applied. The single-roll applicator is still used, however, in conjunction with more accurate subsequent metering, in the air knife coater and road coater described later in this section.

There are literally dozens of different types of multiple roll coaters, with a wide variety of roll arrangements. Among these there are three of primary importance, namely the two-roll coater, the reverse-roll coater, and the gravure print roll coater.

A typical two-roll coater is shown in Fig. 1. It consists of two rolls in a vertical arrangement with provision for adjusting both the pressure and the clearance between the rolls. For most coating operations, the paper is threaded between the rolls, although in certain cases it may pass over the top roll. With this latter arrangement, it serves as a so-called "kiss coater", the coating being metered between the nip of the rolls.

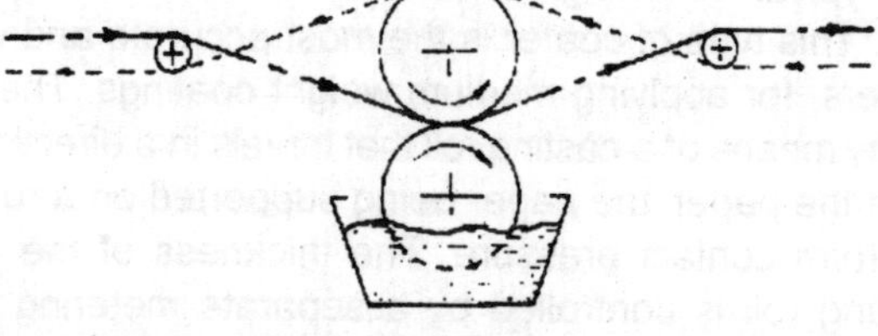

Fig. 1. Roll coater

This type of coater finds its principal usage in the waxing of paper and in the application of glue and other gums for the production of gummed tapes and label papers. The coating is contained in a pan, below the bottom roll, which may be heated in order to maintain the temperature of the wax or gum. The rolls may be made of steel or hard cast iron (chilled iron), the latter being recommended for accuracy, or there may be one rubber-covered roil and one steel roll.

Waxed paper is produced in large quantities for food packaging and for household use. For packaging, it is printed with the desired pattern prior to waxing. The wax coating operation is carried out at high speeds employing molten paraffin wax, a petroleum by-product, as the coating material. The weight to be applied is controlled by the gap between the rolls. Speeds of approximately 2.000 fpm are obtainable on modern high-speed waxing machines. The wax must be chilled quickly in order to give a glossy surface and to minimize penetration of the wax into the sheet. This chilling can be accomplished by dipping the waxed paper into a bath of refrigerated water, followed by the removal of the water with air blasts or scraper bars or both. The same rapid chilling with a different surface effect can be achieved by passing the paper over one or more specially designed cooling rolls that contain refrigerated water and have polished surfaces.

Gummed paper is traditionally made on a two-roll coater with the paper passing over the top roll in a "kiss-coating" operation. Gumming speeds are limited by drying capacity, since the gum must generally be applied as a relatively dilute water solution. Speeds as high as 800 fpm. are obtained with long hot air dryers of arched configuration.

Two typical roll arrangements of a reverse roll coater are shown in Fig. 2. This type of coater is the most accurate and versatile of the coaters, for applying medium weight coatings. The coating is applied by means of a casting roll that travels in a direction opposite to that of the paper, the paper being supported on a rubber roll to give uniform contact pressure. The thickness of the coating on the casting roll is controlled by a separate metering roll whose surface is also driven in a reverse direction. Both of these rolls are made of chilled iron and are ground to a precision of .0001 in, or better. With this type of coater, the thickness of coating to be applied depends only on the precision of the rolls and is not affected by the viscosity or film splitting characteristics of the coating or by the thickness or surface of the paper.

The reverse roll coater is widely used for applying various lacquers, varnishes, emulsions and suspensions, as well as hot melt coatings. It can apply materials with viscosities varying from slightly more than that of water up to several hundred thousand centipoises. The coating thickness that can be applied range from

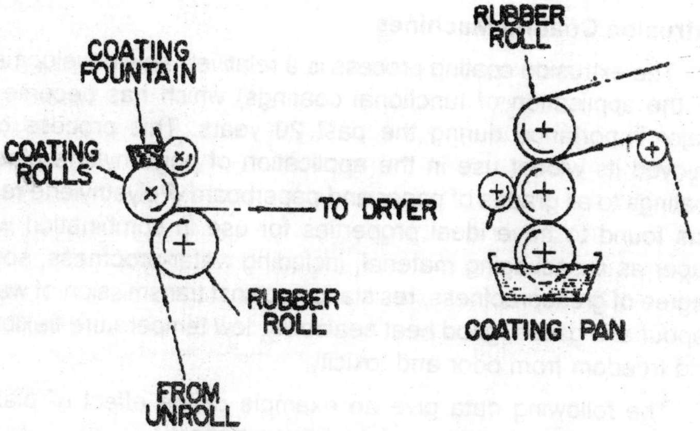

Fig. 2. Reverse roll coaters

about .001 in. minimum to .020 in., maximum wet thickness. Speeds in the range of 500 to 800 fpm can be obtained on reverse roll coaters, without encountering hydraulic difficulties.

The print roll coater is a specialized type of coater of high precision for applying very light coatings. It consists essentially of a rotogravure or intaglio printing unit in which the print roll is engraved with an over-all fine screen pattern. The print roll revolves in a pan of coating material and the excess is removed by means of an oscillating precision doctor blade. The coating is then transferred to the paper in a nip with a rubber pressure roll. The resulting coating is actually a series of small dots that may be smoothed out into a continuous film, using one or more smoothing bars or rolls. This smoothing operation may not be satisfactory, however, on certain coatings. It is also possible to use an offset gravure principle wherein the coating is transferred to a rubber roll and then to the paper. This method has the advantage of spreading the coating and blending the dots together into a continuous film, but it is, of course, limited to coatings containing solvents that do not attack the natural or synthetic rubber offset rolls. The gravure coater has the highest precision of any known type of coater, but is limited to light-weight coatings by the nature of the engraving process, and is further limited by the dotted pattern effect. It is, however used for the application of colouring lacquers, prime and release coats for pressure-sensitive adhesive papers, and for applying adhesives used in paper-lamination processes.

Extrusion Coating Machines

The extrusion coating process is a relatively new development (in the application of functional coatings) which has become of major importance during the past 20 years. This process has enjoyed its widest use in the application of polyethylene plastic coatings to all grades of paper and paperboard. Polyethylene resin was found to have ideal properties for use in combination with paper as a packaging material, including water-proofness, some degree of greseproofness, resistance against transmission of water vapour and gases, good heat sealability, low temperature flexibility and freedom from odor and toxicity.

The following data give an example of the effect of plastic coatings on the properties of packaging papers :

Coating Weight	Moisture Vapour Transmission Rate Grams/100 Sq In. per day (ASTM)	
Lb/Ream 24 × 36., 500	Low Density Polyethylene	High Density Polyethylene
7	3.2	1.6
10	2.2	0.9
15	1.6	0.6
20	0.8	0.5

Similar barrier properties are obtainable for gas transmission and grease resistance. The extrusion coating process has also been found useful for a number of other extrudable film-forming thermoplastic resins, including polypropylene, polyamides, polyvinylchloride, and polyvinylidene chloride. The volume of these materials being coated is small, however, in comparison with polyethylene, partly for economic reasons and partly because of processing problems with these other resins.

A typical extrusion coating machine is shown in Fig 3. The polyethylene resin is melted in conventional thermoplastic extruder. This consists of a driven screw within an electrically heated cylinder, which melts and compacts the resin granules and extrudes them in a continuous flow at high pressure. The resin is then discharged through a film-forming slot die consisting of a manifold

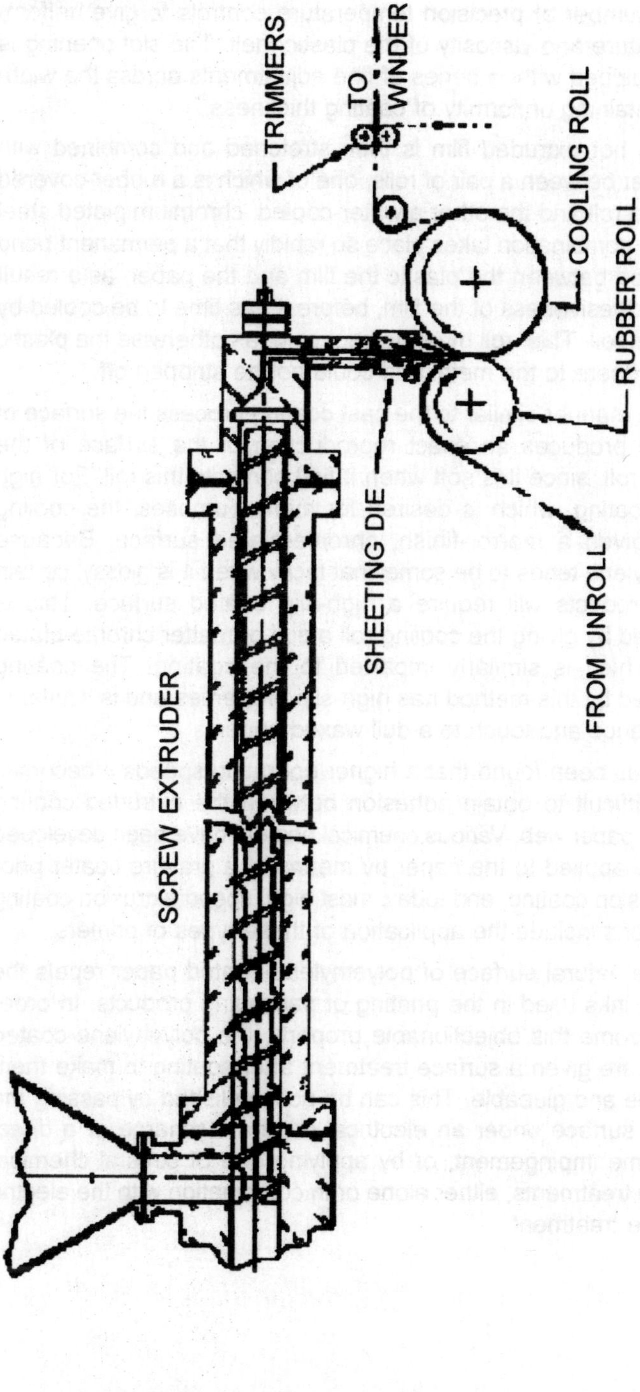

Fig. 3. Extrusion coater

with an adjustable outlet. The die is equipped with electric heaters with a number of precision temperature controls to give uniform temperature and viscosity of the plastic melt. The slot opening is also equipped with a series of fine adjustments across the width for maintaining uniformity of coating thickness.

The hot extruded film is then stretched and combined with the paper between a pair of rolls, one of which is a rubber-covered pressure roll and the other a water-cooled, chromium plated steel roll. The combination takes place so rapidly that a permanent bond is created between the plastic the film and the paper, as a result of the adhesiveness of the film, before it has time to be cooled by the steel roll. This roll must be kept cold, as otherwise the plastic would adhere to the metal and could not be stripped off.

In a manner similar to the cast coating process the surface of the film produces an exact reproduction of the surface of the cooling roll, since it is soft when it first contacts this roll. For high gloss coating, which is desired for many purposes, the cooling roll is given a marror-finish, chrome-plated surface. Because polyethylene tends to be somewhat tacky when it is glossy, certain other products will require a high-slip coated surface. This is produced by giving the cooling roll a dull or matter chrome-plated finish which is similarly imparted to the coating. The coating produced by this method has high-slip properties and is similar in appearance and touch to a dull waxed paper.

It has been found that a higher operating speeds it becomes more difficult to obtain adhesion between the extruded coating and the paper web. Various chemical primers have been developed that are applied to the paper by means of a gravure coater prior to extrusion coating, and today, most high, speed extrusion coating operations include the application of these types of primers.

The natural surface of polyethylene-coated paper repels the printing inks used in the printing of packaging products. In order to overcome this objectionable property, the polyehylene-coated papers are given a surface treatment after coating to make them printable and glueable. This can be accomplished by passing the coated surface under an electrical corona discharge or a direct gas flame impingement, or by applying one of several chemical surface treatments, either alone or in combination with the electric or flame treatment.

The extrusion coating process has one inherent disadvantage in that the plastic film tends to thicken at the edges as it is stretched between the die and the water-cooled roll. This stretching is necessary, since it has been found that the minimum practical die opening is about .020 in, while the final coating thickness is on the order of .001 in or less. The thickened edges of the coating are removed by trimming immediately after the cooling roll.

Operating speeds in the range of 500 to 1.500 fpm are commonly achieved in extrusion coating, with the upper limit being imposed either by lack of hot stretchability of the resin of lack of adhesion to the paper.

The polyethylene extrusion coating process initially found wide usage for kraft paper for multiwall bags, where it gave an excellent water and vapour barrier. It use subsequently expanded to include a wide range of food packaging papers and bags for hygroscopic chemicals and fertilizers. An important recent development is the adoption of extruded polyethylene coatings for milk containers made from bleached kraft paperboard. This product has almost completely replaced the waxed paper liquid container and is gradually replacing the glass milk bottle.

Hot Melt Coatings

A new family of coatings, which are referred to as hot melt coatings, has recently been introduced to the paper converting industry. These coatings are principally mixtures of paraffin wax and a co-polymer of ethylene and vinyl acetate, but various other polyolefins and wax-like materials may be used in their formulation. These coatings have better properties at a given coating thickness than pure polyolefin coatings, and they can also be used as heat seal and moisture repellent coatings.

Most of these hot melt coatings have viscosities which are too high for handling on conventional roll coaters (such as waxing machines or reverse roll coaters), but on the other hand, their viscosities are too low and their film forming properties are inadequate for use in the extrusion coater. Special coaters have, therefore, been developed for applying these materials, one such coater is shown in Fig. 4. The resin is melted and pumped into a slot die where it is transferred directly to the paper which is drawn over the face of the die. The amount of coating applied can be metered by controlling the rate at which it is pumped into the die,

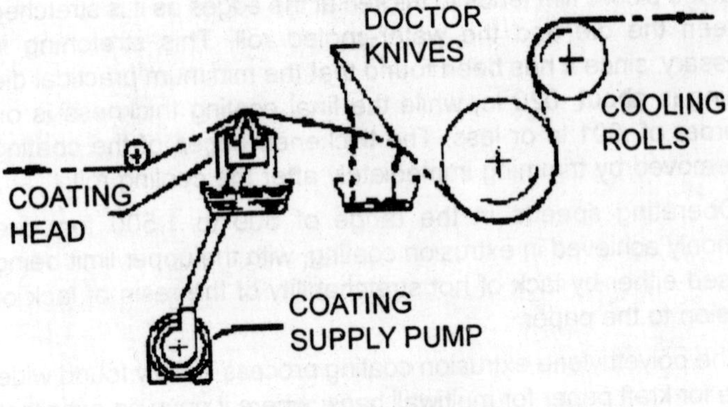

Fig. 4. Hot melt coater

by applying an excess that can then be metered by the edges of the die itself, or by a separate metering blade as shown. It will be apparent that this type of coater suffers the same disadvantages as the knife coater, with respect to streaks and lack of coating uniformity. The expansion of the use of hot melt coatings on webs has thus far been limited by the lack of a satisfactory process for applying a uniform thin coating that is free of bubbles, streaks, and pinholes.

A specialized type of coater, called the curtain coater, has been developed for applying hot melt contings to paperboard in sheet form. In this type of coater, as shown in Fig. 5, the coating is pumped into a slot die from which it is discharged vertically downward in the form of a falling film or curtain. The sheets to be coated are passed through the curtain at high speeds (1,000 to 1,5000 fpm), and the coating is deposited directly upon the sheets where it solidifies by cooling. The excess coating beyond the edges and between the sheets falls into a pan and is re-circulated.

The process has found wide usage in the application of hot melt and fortified wax coatings to corrugated cartons at the flat blank stage of their manufacture. These cartons can be used for direct packaging of moist food products, replacing more expensive containers used previously.

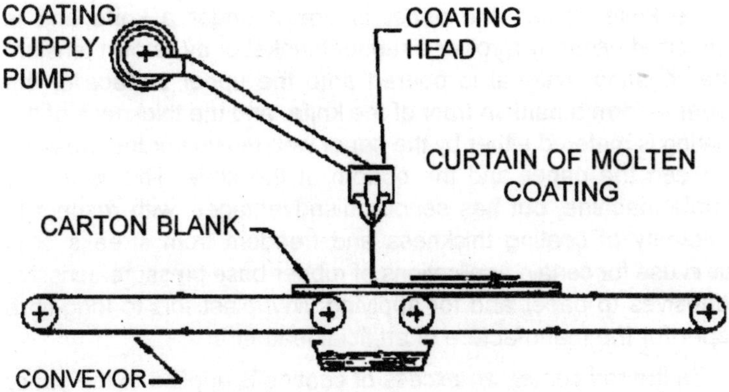

Fig 5. Curtain coater

Folding cartons used for packaging frozen foods and other food products are coated with hot melts in blank form after printing, in specially-designed pattern coating machine.

Other Functional Coating Processes

There exists a wide variety of other types of coaters used for applying functional coatings. One such machine is the air knife coater which is widely used for the application of pigmented coatings. Various plastic resin coatings can conveniently be applied to paper in the form of a water-base latex or emulsion. Polyvinylidene chloride (PVDC) in particular has found increased use in the form of a latex as a paper coating material. It is available in a relatively high solids content (on the order of 50%), and when dried, forms a good protective plastic film with excellent barrier properties.

The air knife coater has been found to be the best method of applying PVDC and similar emulsions and latices. Following the application, coatings are dried in a hot air drying tunnel, and after drying, are fused by the application of additional temperature in order to flash melt the particles deposited from the latex and to cause them to form a continuous film. It is sometimes necessary to apply two or more coats to obtain fully satisfactory results.

There are two older types of coaters that are still in use to a limited degree, and these are the knife coater and the rod coater. In the knife coater, the paper is drawn under a knife and is supported either by a roll or a rubber blanket or by its own tension. The coating material is poured onto the upper surface of the paper to form a bank in front of the knife, and the thickness of the coating is metered either by the paper web tension or the pressure between the paper and the bottom of the knife. This is a very simple machine, but has serious disadvantages, with respect to uniformity of coating thickness and freedom from streaks. It is still in use for certain applications of rubber-base pressure-sensitive adhesives to paper and for applying vinyl plastisols to long-fibre paper for the manufacture of artificial leather.

In the rod coater, an excess of coating is applied to the paper by means of a single roll applicator revolving in pan. The excess is then removed by passing the paper over a doctor bar consisting of a small diameter rod spirally wound with wire. The coating weight can be controlled by using various diameters of rod and wire. This type of coater is still in use for the manufacture of carbon paper.

OTHER WET CONVERTING PROCESSES

In addition to the coating operations already described, a number of other converting processes are carried out on paper in continuous web form, from roll to roll.

Paper and board may be impregnated or saturated with various types of resin or latex materials to make them suitable for packaging or structural purposes. Two or more webs of paper may be laminated together to give greater thickness and strength, or to give a sheet with properties derived from the combined materials.

The surface of the paper may be embossed to improve its appearance for decorative purposes, or the sheet may be creped to give elasticity and improved bursting strength.

Impregnating Equipment

One of the most important uses of impregnated paper is in the manufacture of high-pressure plastic laminates. These materials are widely used for electrical insulation, for various industrial and structural purposes, and for decorative purposes, such as table and counter tops, furniture, wall covering etc.

Although some of the industrial laminates use cloth as a base, paper is the most important fibre base in this industry. The industrial grades of laminates consist of a number of sheets of paper that have been impregnated with phenolic resins and dried, and which are then pressed together in high pressure curing presses in thicknesses from 1/16 in. up to 1 in. or more.

The familiar decorative laminates consist of a number of sheets of phenolic-impregnated kraft paper as a core with the outer sheets being made of alpha-cellulose paper impregnated with melamine resins. These are similarly pressed and cured into sheets having thicknesses in the range of 1/16 to 3/12 in. The patterns used for decorative purposes are printed by the rotogravure process on a heavy alpha sheet, prior to saturating, and a thin melamine impregnated alpha sheet, called the overlay, is then placed over the printed sheet. The overlay becomes transparent upon pressing.

A typical resin impregnating machine (referred to as a "treater" in the saturating industry) is shown in Fig. 6. The paper is unwound and dipped into a pan of resin solution, either phenol-formaldehyde or melamine-formaldehyde, with the solvent consisting of a mixture

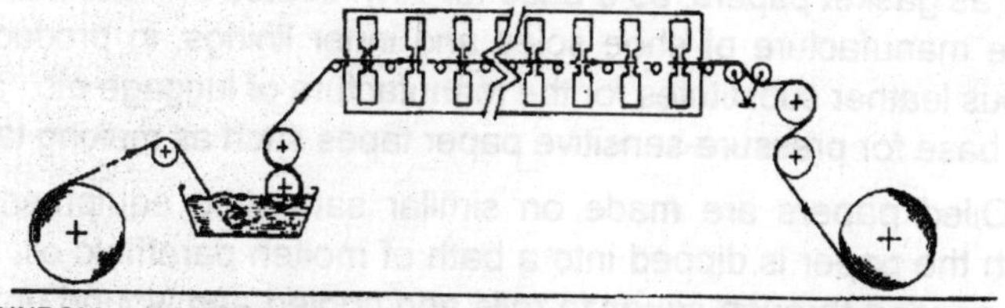

Fig. 6. Treating line

of ethyl alcohol land water. It then passes between a pair of large diameter precisely ground chilled iron press rolls. These rolls not only force the resin through the body of the paper, but also meter the final quantity of resin retained in the paper.

The sheet then passes into a hot-air drying tunnel where the solvent is evaporated and where the resin is partially cured with the release of water vapour. The phenolic impregnated kraft paper is then wound into rolls for subsequent sheeting on conventional sheeters, prior to pressing. The melamine-impregnated alpha paper is quite brittle and it is, therefore, cut into sheets as it emerges from the dryer.

A second important group of impregnated papers includes those in which various rubber-like latices are added to long-fibre papers, which then serve as a strong base paper for various products. These latices may contain either natural or synthetic rubber or a variety of synthetic resinous materials. Their purpose is to increase the internal bond strength and tear strength of the paper. The equipment used for this purpose is in general similar to the impregnator used for the treating of laminating papers. The sheet is given a longer dwell time in the pan, however, to increase the degree of saturation and penetration, since these papers are often quite thick. A longer drying time is also required to remove water from the sheet, hence, festooning dryers are still in use on heavier products of this type Lighter weight latex-impregnated paper can, however, be dried in conventional horizontal drying tunnels.

Papers that have been latex-impregnated in this manner are used as gasket papers, as a base for vinyl-coated artificial leather, in the manufacture of shoe soles and inner linings, in producing various leather substitutes for the manufacture of luggage etc., and as a base for pressure-sensitive paper tapes such as making tape.

Oiled papers are made on similar saturating equipment in which the paper is dipped into a bath of molten paraffinic oil. It is then passed through squeeze rolls and cooled and wound up; no drying is required. These papers are used for meat wrapping and also for the wrapping of machine parts.

Another important saturating operation is the manufacture of felt-like grades of paperboard for use as building papers. These materials, commonly referred to as roofing felts, consist of strong long-fibre paperboard saturated with molten asphalt. Because the penetration is rather slow, the typical roofing left saturating machine consists of a large tank with a series of dip rolls. The sheet is passed into and out of the tank a number of times over this series of rolls, and picks up a heavy content of asphalt. The sheet is then air-colled to chill the surface and reduce its tackiness and is then finally cooled on water-cooled rolls prior to winding up. This type of paper is widely used in the building industry both for roofing and as a barrier sheet in the siding of houses.

Still another saturating operation is the tub-sizing of high-grade bond and ledger papers. Although most sizing is carried out on the paper machine itself, the use of a separate continuous tub-sizing process is required for the highest qualities of writing papers. This type of saturation is carried out on equipment similar to that used for latex saturation. The paper is first passed through a rather long tub of sizing solution to give the desired dwell time, and then is passed between a pair of squeeze rolls to remove the excess and to meter the amount of size absorbed. These papers are then dried in continuous air dryers, either of the floating type of the running festoon type. It has been found desirable to use this type of drying with relaxed tension in the sheet in order to give the desired "cockle" finish on many of these grades of paper.

Laminating Processes

There are several reasons for laminating together two or more sheets of paper or board. One reason is to produce a sheet with combined properties as, for example, the lamination of a quality liner paper to a cheap grade of paperboard for making folding boxes. Here the cheap board filler provides rigidity and strength, while the liner gives the desired quality exterior surface.

Another reason for lamination is to build up the thickness and strength of board for structural purposes. Heavier grades of boxboard, for example, can be made more economically by laminating several thinner sheets together with an adhesive, rather than attempting to produce a thick sheet directly on the board machine. Heavy boards up to 1/2 in thick are made by lamination for such uses as fibre drum heads, automotive interior panels etc.

Still another use of lamination is the production of barrier paper for both packaging and structural uses. In these products, the laminant is asphalt, and it serves as a barrier material as well as an adhesive. A widely used product of this type is the so-called 30-30-30 asphalt-laminated kraft paper which consists of two 30 lb kraft sheets with a 30 lb layer of asphalt between them. The combined sheets is used in the manufacture of multiwall bags for fertilizer and similar materials.

For special purpose bags and for construction uses, two sheets of kraft paper are laminated togetehr with heavier coatings of asphalt. To give added strength, fibres can be introduced between the two asphalt-coated sheets, immediately prior to lamination. Jute fibres were formerly used for reinforcing laminated paper, but they have been largely replaced by fiberglass roving that is both thinner and stronger.

Another widely used lamination is the combination of aluminum foil and paperboard. The aluminum foil provides an ideal barrier for packaging and gives a bright glossy surface for exterior printing.

In a typical laminating machine, the adhesive is applied to the web by one of the conventional roll coaters described previously. Although in the past, the metering of the amount of adhesive was not carried out with any degree of accuracy, the trend now is to give far greater emphasis to the control of the adhesive application. This is necessary in order to maintain product quality and to economize in the cost of the adhesive consumed.

With a two-web lamination, the adhesive is commonly applied to only one web, usually the less absorbent of the two. For laminations of more than two webs, the adhesive is applied to all but a single web, to give the necessary number of adherent surfaces. Accurate control of the tension in each of the webs entering the laminator is of the utmost importance in every laminating operation. Since the sheets are permanently bonded together, any imbalance in residual tension will cause the final product to curl. This condition is corrected by applying accurate independent tension controls of each of the incoming webs.

Following adhesive application, the webs are combined in a press. For the thinner laminations, this press consists of a pair of nip rolls, pneumatically loaded, with one steel roll and one rubber roli. High pressures are not required, since the adhesives commonly used will develop the necessary bond with minimum contact pressure.

Sodium silicate solutions were once widely used as a laminating adhesive for paper and board, but these have been largely replaced by water solutions of starch, vegetable protein, or synthetic resins. Where barrier properties are desired, paraffin wax or asphalt can be applied in the molten condition as the laminating adhesive.

For sheets that are thin enough to be flexible after laminating the next step after the combining press, is to pass them over a series of heated drying cylinders. This removes the moisture from the adhesive through the sheet, and also helps to set the adhesive. Following this, these materials can be wound of sheeted.

The thicker more rigid laminated products cannot be conveniently passed around drying cylinders. For these laminations, a converted starch of highest solids content is used which will dry by absorption into the sheet and will set without further external drying. These types of products are generally laminated through two sets of press rolls that are made of steel or chilled iron. Additional pressure is required to assure a good permanent bound with thick rigid products, since they are handled only in flat sheet form after having been laminated and are not passed around a series of dryers or rolls. These products are always cut into sheets immediately after final lamination.

In the case of wax and asphalt laminations, the sheet is passed around a series of cooling rolls instead of dryers, prior to winding, in order to cool and set the adhesive.

Laminations are normally carried out in widths ranging from 40 to 120 in. Operating speeds for adhesive, wax, and asphalt laminations with flexible webs range from 1000 to 15000 fpm, put in the case of thick rigid laminated boards, the speed is limited to about 400 fpm by the heavy rotary sheet cutting equipment involved.

Embossing and Creping Processes

These two processes, although otherwise unrelated, are both used to deform the sheet of paper so that it is no longer flat.

Embossing is generally carried out for decorative purposes to give the paper a raised design on its surface. This is used extensively in making paper napkins, which will be described later, for certain grades of writing paper and papeteries, and for fancy wrapping paper and exterior box liner papers.

Embossing is a simple process carried out by passing the paper between a pair of nip rolls. The upper roll is a heavy forged steel roll that has been mechanically engraved with the desired pattern. This roll can be steam heated to help soften the paper. The bottom roll is fibre filled and is similar in construction to a supercalender roll. The patterns is impressed into this roll by running the two rolls together for a period of time before commencing the embossing operation.

Creping is a wet deforming process used to increase the stretchability of paper. Although low-stretch papers are creped in line with the paper machine, it is necessary that crepe with a high percentage of stretch be made as a separate converting operation.

To produce this type of paper, the flat sheet is first fed into tub of water containing a small amount of size to wet the paper thoroughly. It then passes through a press to remove the excess water and around a steam heated drying roll that serves as the creping roll. During drying, the size causes the paper to adhere slightly to the creping roll. The paper is then removed from the roll by a doctor blade, called the creping knife. The angle and contour of the blade and the speed and sizing conditions control the percentage of stretch and the coarseness of the crepe obtained. The paper must then be dried in a completely relaxed condition in order to avoid removing the crepe. This can be done either by carrying it on felts over a series of drying cylinders, similar to a paper machine dryer, or by carrying it through an air dryer on a slat conveyor, which avoids the application of any tension to the sheet.

These high-stretch creped papers can be used for decorative purposes, in which case, a colouring die can be added to the creping bath. They are also used as kraft paper liners for barrels and bags where the high stretch characteristics give them excellent resistance to tearing and bursting.

DRY PAPER CONVERTING

The second complete field of paper converting, called *Dry Converting* does not involve any modification of the paper web itself, but instead leads to the production of a finished article of paper from the web, which may or may not have been subjected to previous wet converting operations. These finished articles of paper include paper bags, boxes, cartons, and small rolls for household consumption, for wrapping purposes, etc.

Bag Making Equipment

The manufacture of paper bags is a large consumer of paper. The two principal classes of bags are the familiar kraft paper grocery bag or shopping bag, and the multiwall shipping sack. Various other fancy grades of single-wall bags are also made.

The basic operations performed in the manufacture of single and multi-wall bags are the same, with the exception of the number of plies. The rolls of paper are unwound at high speed on conventional unwinding equipment. Side guiding adjustment is necessary to insure accurate alignment of the webs entering the machine. Bags must frequently be printed with identification or brand markings and these markings must often be in register with the bag length. This is accomplished by the installation of single or multi-colour flexographic printers in-line with the bag-making machine.

The webs of paper are formed into tubes on a unit known as a tuber. This consists of forming shoes, over which the paper is drawn, which gradually transform it from a flat sheet into a cylindical tube. The glue is applied to the edge of each ply and the sheets are then flattened and passed through press rolls that crease the edges and seal the seams.

The finished bag is then manufactured on a bottoming machine. This is a complex automatic unit that cuts the tubes to length and folds, glues, and seals the bottom of the bag. Many bags are gusseted to provide a convenient shape for handling and filling. This is done by the installation of additional guide plates on the tuber, which tuck in the sides prior to flattening.

The finished bags are delivered a high speed from the bottomer and are ready for packaging and shipping.

Box and Carton Making

There are many designs and types of paperboard boxes and cartons in use, in addition to the corrugated carton. In general, paperboard cartons are produced by the converter and shipped to the user in the form of flat blanks. The production of these blanks is considered to be paper converting operation, whereas the actual forming, filling and sealing of the boxes is considered to be a packaging operation.

In a typical carton printing and blanking machine, the roll of paperboard is unwound and fed to single or multicolour printer. Because of its simplicity and ease of changing plates, the flexographic printer is the type most widely used. For higher quality products, however, rotogravure printing is used.

The printed board is then fed, still in printed register, to a scoring and die cutting unit. The web may be slit to produce narrower widths at this point. The cutting and scoring can be either of the rotary or flat type. The flat type involves less expense for dies and easier changeover, but it naturally results in a start-stop feeding of the board that gives lower speeds are requires accumulators for web storage.

On both of these types of units, however, the carton blanks are die cut from the web and are simultaneously scored to permit subsequent folding into carton shapes. This basic process is used for making practically all types of folding boxes, as well as for liquid containers such as paper milk bottles.

Automatic Roll Winding

A large volume of paper products is ultimately used in the form of small rolls. Because of the large tonnage involved and the necessity of producing these products at low coats, complex automatic roll winding machinery has been developed.

Toilet tissue is the largest volume product produced in the form of small rolls. Other similar products include paper towels, counter rolls of wrapping paper, household rolls of waxed paper, adding machine paper rolls, etc.

In a typical automatic roll winding machine for toilet tissue, the full mill size rolls of tissue are unwound at the machine speed of about 1500 fpm. The web passes through slitters that cut the sheet to the desired finished roll width. The finished small rolls are wound directly on a center shaft winder with automatic transfer.

Long cores are fed automatically into the machine and are cut to length on the winding mandrel. The winding mandrel then advances to the starting position. Glue is applied to assist in the transfer of the paper to the new core. Before reaching the winding station, the paper webs, such as toilet tissue or paper towels, are passed over a specially designed roll that perforates them to permit severance of the sheets when used. When a finished measured length has been wound, the unit automatically cuts the web and transfers it to the new winding core. The finished rolls are automatically ejected from the machine.

In a modification of this process, the tissue is wound to the full width rather than being slit into narrow widths on the winder. The finished roll, referred to as a "log," is then cut to the desired width on an automatic log saw.

This type of operation eliminates the necessity of matching the slit cores to the slit web on the machine. These rolls are then delivered to automatic wrapping and boxing machines for direct shipment. Mechanical handling is used throughout for efficient operation.

Automatic Cutting and Folding

The second large group of sanitary paper products is used in the form of folded sheets. These include facial tissues and paper napkins, and also such products as industrial paper wipers.

There are two different processes for making these types of products. In the first, individual or two-ply webs are individually cut with rotating knives, and are then folded. In the second process, a large number of webs, as many as 100 or 200 (the number to be contained in the finished package), are folded longitudinally in a continuous process. The resulting "log" is then saw-cut to package length.

With a single web operation, as used for paper napkins, the web is unwound and is usually first embossed to give the desired pattern, in a conventional paper embosser. This type of embosser is frequently equipped with two matched engraved steel rolls, rather than one engraved steel roll with fibre backing roll, in order to give clear-cut two-sided embossing at high speed. The web then passes through a pair of cutting knives to give the desired sheet length, and then to an automatic folder to produce the finished folded article.

In the multiple-web process, a large battery of backstands must be provided, one unwinding position for each web, corresponding to the number of sheets in the finished package. The webs are passed through continuous folders, which consists of a series of guides, to fold the sheets to the desired shape. They are then pressed flat with nip rolls to make the fold permanent.

Two principal types of folds are used, namely, the "C" type fold and the overlapped fold, continuous withdrawal of tissue from the carton. The product delivered from the folder is a continuous stack of folded sheets. The is then cut to length by means of high speed saws, and the individual bundles are ready for boxing in automatic cartoning machines.

Other Dry Converting Processes

There are numerous other paper converting processes for producing articles with less production volume than the items previously described. Paper cups are coming into increasing use as a sanitary means for serving hot drinks and carbonated beverages. These are produced from continuous webs of paper on special high-speed machinery. Paper plates for food consumption are produced by die cutting and hot pressing paper from a continuous web which has been moistened and heated in order to soften it. Envelopes are produced on automatic high-speed machinery that die cuts the envelope form a continuous web, applies glue at the seams, and folds and seals the flaps.

AUXILIARY CONVERTING EQUIPMENT

There are certain components of converting equipment that are common to many of the converting processes described herein. Thus in very case, a roll of paper must be unwound before it can be fed to a converting machine. Except for those cases where the end product is cut into sheets, the converted web must be rewound into rolls for subsequent handling. For those types of coated and impregnated papers where solvents or water are used, the web must be passed through a dryer to remove this solvent or water before the sheet is ready for winding and subsequent processing.

In addition, various web-control techniques must be employed to insure the proper handling of the paper, without side-weaving or wrinkling. These include side-guiding of the web entering the machine, application of tension control (not only to the entering web, but at various stages throughout the process), and the proper choice of drives to give the desired speed and tension characteristics, etc.

These various web processing auxiliaries will be discussed in the following sections.

Unrolls

Numerous types of unrolls are available to serve the wide range of requirements of the paper converting industry. The simplest type is, of course, a single shaft, mounted in bearings on stands, with tapered cones on the shaft to engage the paper core of the roll. A hand brake is mounted on the shaft to provide tension. This design is suitable for low-speed unwinding where the requirements for production, web tension, and side guiding are not critical. Frequently, a double stand is provided so that a second roll can be made ready for unwinding when the first one expires.

Because of the increasing demands for high-speed continuous operation of converting machines, however, the "flying-splice" type of unwind is being used to an increasing degree. Continuous operation is desirable not only for increased production, but also because speed changes and stopping to splice rolls will cause the production of off-grade material or scrap in many converting operations.

A typical turret type flying splice unroll is shown in Fig. 7. The new roll of paper is driven up to full web speed by means of a synchronized drive-motor, Gule for making this splice is applied to the leading edge of the new roll before the drive is started.

As the finished roll is about to expire, the new roll is adhered to it using a movable rubber pressure roll. On most machines, the tail of the expired roll is cut off automatically after the splice, since it is seldom possible to time the splice exactly of the end of the previous roll.

It is always necessary to apply braking to the unwinding roll

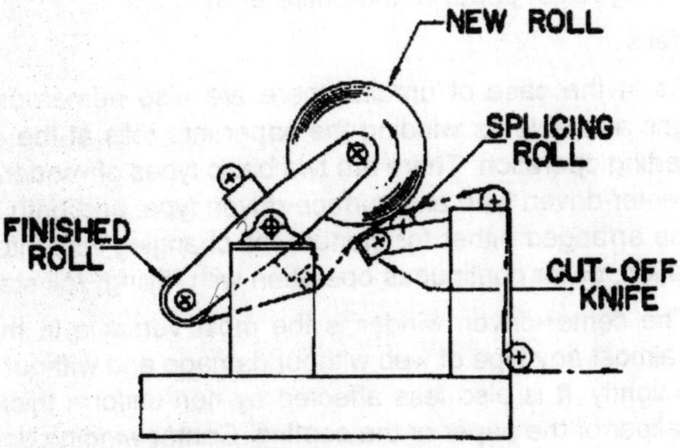

Fig. 7. Flying splice turret unwind

so that the web will be delivered under a positive tension on the converting machine. This is necessary to insure accurate alignment of the web and to avoid wrinkling. The unwinding shafts are equipped with brakes that can be of the pneumatic, hydraulic or electric type, and on the more advanced machines, these brakes are automatically controlled by a floating roll to give constant tension. In many cases, the web will then pass over a pair of driven tensioning or hold-back rolls to provide greater tension than can be conveniently obtained by braking the shaft or chucks that hold the roll core.

Many turret-type unrolls are also equipped for floor pick-up of the mill roll of paper and for automatic chucking of the roll, without the use of shafts. These features greatly reduce the amount of labour required on high-speed machines.

Side guiding is also often an integral part of the unroll. On all converting processes, it is necessary that the web be accurately aligned with the machine, and that it not be permitted to weave from side to side. Often the mill rolls have telescoped slightly, due to rough handling, and this misalignment must be corrected.

The simplest guiding arrangement is of course, a manual side adjustment of the unwinding roll which the operator performs while watching the web. On most newer high-speed machines, however, it is desirable to carry out this side guiding automatically. The location of the edge of the web can be determined by a pneumatic or a photo-electric-sensing device, and this in turn actuates a hydraulic or electric power unit that will shift either the individual unwinding roll of paper or the entire unwind unit.

Winders

As in the case of unrolls, there are also numerous winder designs available for winding the paper into rolls at the end of a converting operation. There are two basic types of winder, namely the center-driven type and surface-driven type, and both of these can be arranged either for manual roll changing with intermittent operation, or for continuous operation with "flying" roll starting.

The center-driven winder is the most versatile in that it will wind almost any type of web without damage and without winding it too tightly. It is also less affected by non-uniform thickness in the caliper of the paper or the coating. Center winding does have the disadvantages, however, of not being able to produce a very tight roll suitable for shipment, and of being limited, by drive and tension considerations and the possibility of telescoping, to a diameter build-up ratio of 6 to 1. In other words, it is not desirable to center-wind to a finished diameter larger than six times the outside diameter of the core being used, as otherwise the roll may become loose or may telescope, due to compression of the inner plies.

The simplest type of center winder is, of course, a single shaft mounted in bearings with a drive at one end and with tapered cones to engage the paper core. This design can be enlarged to comprise a two-shaft center winder, with one shaft above the other, so that a new shaft and core can be made ready for winding with a minimum of lost time during the change-over.

A more advanced type of center winder is the turret-type center winder where the two winding positions are mounted on arms on a revolving turret. This is similar to the turret-type unwind, except that each winding position is equipped with a drive rather than a break. To provide for continuous operations, the drive is arranged to bring the empty core up to full web speed. Various mechanisms are available to automatically cut off the web and to wrap it around the new core.

In order to control the speed and tension on center driven winders, many special drives are available. The simplest and oldest types are mechanical drives using up clutches or slip belts. These must be manually adjusted by the operator to give the desired tension and winding characteristics. Better results are obtained, however, by using electrical or hydraulic drives that give automatic control of speed and torque. For constant tension winding, it is necessary that the driving torque gradually be increased as the roll diameter increases and as the rotational speed decreases. For most products, however, a taper tension rather than a true constant tension is desirable in order to avoid excessive tightening of the outer layers and telescoping of the inner layers. The latest types of electrical and hydraulic drives (described later) permit any degree of taper of the tension to be obtained between the limits of constant tension and constant torque (maximum taper).

Surface winding is used on converting machines where large diameter tightly wound rolls are desired and where the product is not particularly sensitive to tension or pressure. The type of surface winder most widely used is the single drum winder that is similar to the surface winding reel used on paper-making machines. The single winding drum is driven at line speed with provisions for controlling the differential speed in relation to the last nip on the converting machine, in order to control the winding tension. The new winding core is started on top of the drum and the paper is cut and wrapped around it either by use of compressed air, a cord or tape, or an automatic cutting knife. The core is then transferred from the starting position to the running position, where it is held against the winding drum on horizontal slides during the entire winding operation. A controlled pressure is applied, either hydraulically or pneumatically, and this pressure together with the incoming web tension determine the tightness of the wind.

On some paper converting machines, a double drum winder is used for winding the product, this being basically the same design of machine as is used for slitting and rewinding. In a few cases, slitting is also done in line with the converting machine on this type of winder. Since this type of winder is basically a start-stop operation, however, it is used only where the converting process itself can tolerate intermittent operation.

Surface winders have an advantage over center winders in being able to wind much larger rolls on small cores, and to wind tighter rolls for shipment or in-plant handling. In some cases, the product would on a double drum winder can be shipped directly, without further slitting and rewinding, whereas the center wound product must always be rewound on a double drum slitter rewinder prior to shipment for any distance. Surface-driven winders require to special drives, since the winding drum operates at the same surface speed as the converting machine itself.

Dryers

Dryers are an essential part of many paper converting operations, including the application of pigmented or functional coatings, and the impregnation or saturation of paper.

Since most coating and saturating operations produce a wet surface, that cannot be touched without damaging the product, the air dryer is the most widely used type of dryer in paper converting. Heated drying cylinders, such as those used on the paper machine, can seldom be used for converted products, because the sheet will adhere to them or the coating may offset on the dryer surface.

In the early history of paper coating and saturating, the drying was carried out by merely hanging the paper in lofts or festooning chambers. The high inventory, lack of uniform quality, and high handling costs have made those methods obsolete, and have made it necessary for the industry to develop dryers that remove the water or solvent more rapidly. These requirements led to the development of the hot air drying tunnel. in its most familiar form, this consists of an insulated horizontal housing with a means for conveying the paper web through the housing, such as rolls or a slat conveyor. Air that has been heated by means of steam coils or gas burners is directed by rotary fans through a plenum system and discharge headers on to the upper surface of the paper. This produces rapid drying and efficient operation. The air is recirculated through the heaters, with a sufficient proportion being exhausted in order to remove the water vapour, and in the case of solvent drying, to maintain the concentration below the lower explosive limit.

For drying impregnated papers or double-coated papers, it is necessary to handle a sheet that is wet on both sides. One method of doing this is to pass the sheet through a vertical drying tower with hot air directed against both sides of the web. This design in limited in capacity by the height to which the paper can be carried without breaking or excessive fluttering.

Another method of handling impregnated and double-coated papers is the horizontal floater dryer. With this arrangement, the bottom conveyor and rolls are eliminated and the air is discharged through slots below the web at sufficient pressure to float the paper through the dryer.

During the past ten years, it has been found that a substantial increase in air velocity will give significant improvements in drying capacity. This makes it possible to use much shorter drying tunnels to achieve the same drying rate, and thereby to in crease production and reduce the floor space required. Many nozzle configurations are available to permit directing of the high-velocity air onto the sheet, while still providing space for exhausting and recirculating the air.

Infrared drying has been used to a limited degree in the drying of coated and saturated papers. The infrared heat can be generated either by direct gas burners with ceramic tiles, or by various types of electrical resistance elements. Although these dryers have the advantage of high-energy input per unit area, more wide-spread use of infrared heat has been restricted by its high operating cost and difficulties in temperature control, particularly with changes in web speed and during stoppages.

Since drying always involves the removal of vapours in addition to the application of heat, the most successful infrared dryers have been those using a combination of direct radiation plus recirculation of heater air.

Drives

As in the case of the paper making machine, the drive is an important part of every paper converting machine. Typical paper converting processes operate at speeds ranging from 100 fpm to 2000 fpm.

Although the trend is toward continuous rather than intermittent operation in all converting processes, these drives must nevertheless be able to accelerate from a standstill up to the operating speed, to change from one speed level to another with smooth acceleration and deceleration, and to decelerate smoothly to a stop. Quick stops are also required if emergencies develop.

The early converting machines were equipped with line-shaft drives with cone pulleys or other mechanical speed changers to synchronize the various components of the line and to control the web tension between sections. The prime mover for the line-shaft drive was either a variable speed AC motor or a constant speed AC motor with mechanical speed changer.

Line-shaft drives are still in use today and are being provided on some new high-speed machines. They have the advantage of positive control and interlocking of the machine sections. The modern line-shaft drives include accurate speed adjusting units for each section, such as PIV units in combination with differential gears, and the prime mover can be a variable speed DC motor.

The most widely used type of drive on modern converting machines is, however, the multiple motor DC drive of the variable voltage system. With this type of drive, the DC voltage is varied by the operator to control the overall speed of the machine. On older installations, the DC power was supplied by a separate motor generator set, but on most modern installations the motor generator has been replaced by a static or solid-state rectifier, such as a silicon rectifier.

The DC voltage is fed to each of the motors driving the various sections of the converting line so that they operate at approximately the same speed. A variety of means can be provided for controlling the tension and relative speed of the individual motors. The original method was to furnish field rehostats for each motor which the operator would adjust by hand. More elaborate drives use dancer rolls or tension-sensing rolls to control the individual motors, or current regulators that automatically control the motor to hold a certain tension or load. The early manually controlled rheostats have been replaced first by vacuum tube electronic control circuitry and more recently by solid-state, transistorized control circuits.

Various other electrical drives are available for converting machines, including variable speed AC motors, eddy-current clutches, etc. Hydraulic drives are also in use to a limited extent where oil under pressure is provided by a master hydraulic pump. This then drives individual oil motors on each component of the line. The same control functions are available in this type of drive as are available in the DC electric drive.

FINISHING

As used in the paper industry, the word "finishing" refers to those operations performed in the finishing room in order to make the paper ready for shipment. These operations include slitting and rewinding to produce rolls of the size desired by the customer, and cutting of the paper into sheets (sheeting) if the end product must be in sheet rather than roll form. Super-calendering, is customarily carried out in the finishing room.

Inspection of the paper is an integral part of the finishing room operations, and is carried out to some degree on the slitter-rewinder or on the sheeter. Higher quality grades of sheeted paper are subject to further individual manual inspection and counting of each sheet. Material handling and storage are major auxiliary functions of the finishing department.

The typical operations of the finishing room are carried out both on mill rolls of paper grades that are shipped without any converting operations, and on rolls of converted paper after they have been coated, laminated, etc., either at the mill or at separate converting plants.

Slitting and Rewinding

On many grades of paper, it is necessary that the rolls be slit and rewound again in the finishing room, after having once been slit and rewound on the mill rewinder at the dry end of the paper machine. This is true where the diameter or width of the rolls desired by the end user is too small for convenient operation on the large heavy equipment used in mill rewinding. On the better grades of paper, secondary rewinding is necessary for inspection of the paper, for removal of defects, proper splicing of breaks, etc.

The typical finishing room rewinder, although basically similar in design to the machine room rewinder, is smaller and more precise. It will generally accept jumbo mill rolls of about one-third or one-quarter of the paper machine trim.

The slitter-rewinder installation consists first of the backstand or unwind to hold the parent mill roll. This unit is similar to the converting unwinds described previously. The rewinding is generally carried out on a surface driven-winder of the two-drum type. Before reaching the winding station, the web passes over idler rolls and through the slitting station.

The two principal types of slitters in use are the shear-cut and the score-cut. Shear-cut slitters consist of a pair of driven overlapping sharpened blades that can best be likened to a pair of scissors in continuous rotating from. In the score-cut method, a single rotating blade is held by pressure against a hardened steel anvil roll. The blade is hardened and ground to a slight radius, rather than a true sharp point. The shear-cut method is the more versatile and can handle a wider range of weights of paper and board. It does, however, require more care in setting and maintaining the knives. The score-cut method gives a good slitting action on light to medium weights of paper with a good separation of the finished wound rolls. On heavier calipers of paper or board, however, the score-cut action causes flattering of the edges and lint formation, both of which may be objectionable for some uses.

In order to prevent interleaving of the paper after slitting, the slitters are located as close as possible to the two winding drums.

In addition, it is frequently advisable to install a bowed spreader bar or spreader roll after the slitters and before the first winding drum, to cause the webs to separate.

It is generally necessary to take a slight trim from the edges of the web at the finishing room rewinder. This results from the fact that the full roll width desired by the customer may not be an even multiple of the mill roll width, and also from the fact that the web cannot be guided perfectly into the rewinder and a slight allowance must be made for side shifting.

Paper is commonly wound on paperboard cores that are pre-cut to width and are aligned with the slitters. These cores will vary in diameter from 3 to 5 in. ID (internal diameter), for various grades of paper, and from 6 to 12 in. ID for paper-board. The winding core is supported on a shaft which in turn is held by sliding bearing housings on the machine frames. The winding roll is held down against the winding drums by means of an ironing roll or riding roll.

Pressure can be applied to the riding roll either by weights or pneumatic cylinders. It is the normal practice to reduce this pressure as the roll of paper builds up in diameter, since the weight of the roll itself gradually increases the pressure against the winding drums. The tightness or hardness of the finished paper rolls is controlled to a considerable degree by the total pressure or weight between the roll of paper and the bottom drums, and for this reason, it is necessary to compensate for the increasing diameter, by reducing the load on the riding roll. Both winding drums are driven and on the larger and wider machines the riding roll is also driven. A differential speed is commonly provided between the drums in order to tighten the paper, and thereby to wind a very tight roll, which is required so that the roll can be shipped without telescoping or flattening. This differential speed can either be a built-in fixed differential, resulting from a difference in diameter of the drums, or it can be provided by a mechanical or electrical speed variation between the drums.

Accessories commonly provided on the newer and larger reminders include a roll ejector and roll lowering table for automatic handling of the finished product. Variable speed direct-current drives that provide smooth acceleration and deceleration, as described previously, are the most popular drives for rewinding machines.

The prevention of interlaving is an important problem on slitter rewinders. This is accomplished by proper design and location of the slitters and proper tension control of the incoming web. On many machines, the winding drums are grooved with a variety of patterns to promote spreading of the rolls.

Variation in the caliper of the paper is another common cause of problems of the slitter rewinder. After the paper is slit, a thick section will tend to wind a larger diameter roll than a thin section, with the result that the rolls will attempt to turn at different angular velocities and will be wound, respectively, hard and soft. There is no good solution to this problem other than the correction of the caliper at the paper machine.

For certain specialty grades of paper, a center driven or combination type winder may be used rather than a surface driven winder. This choice is frequently made for tissue and other lightweight sheets where a tight wind is not desired. Because of the strong tendency to interleave with center winding, the general practice is to use two winding shafts, alternating the slit webs between these two shafts. The cores are permitted to slip on the shaft, using a differential friction device in order to compensate for variations in web caliper and roll diameter. With some units, the winding also rest against a surface driven drum to give a combination surface-center winding effect. If the slit rolls are not too narrow, a series of individual winding positions on alternate parallel axes across the machine can be used, instead of the two-shaft arrangement with frictional driving device.

For slitting certain very light webs, razor blades are sometimes substituted for shear-cut or score-cut slitters. These require frequent replacement, however, and are used only where rotary types of slitters cannot be used, because of difficulties with tearing, etc.

One of the important functions performed by the operator at the slitter-rewinder on many grades of paper is that of inspection. He must watch visually for holes or tears in the paper, for dirt or other imperfection, for skips in coating, etc. When any such defect is observed, the machine is quickly stopped and the defective portion cut out. The ends are then glued together with gummed tape on the rewound roll, using a carefully made splice so that the paper can subsequently pass through printing or converting operations without tearing or wrinkling. Often, it is required that the splices be marked in the rewound roll.

After the rolls have been removed from the slitter rewinder, they must be given final preparation for shipment. Wooden plugs are commonly inserted into both ends of the paperboard core to prevent its collapsing from the combined effect of high winding tension and jarring during subsequent shipment. The roll is then wrapped, with the amount of wrapping dependent on the quality and cost of the product. A simple steel strapping may be used for the cheap grades, while on better grades, the heads are covered with several layers of paper, and the outer cylindrical surface is similarly wrapped. Waterproof paper may be used if outdoor exposure is expected.

Hand wrapping is employed on the smaller rolls where a wide variety of sizes is encountered. In high-production mills where large quantities of rolls of the same general size are shipped, heading and wrapping is carried out on automatic machines designed specifically for that purpose.

Sheet Cutting and Finishing

Much high quality printing is carried out on sheet-fed, flat-bed printing presses, although long run items such as newspapers, magazines, and packaging products are printed on rotary presses. The high quality coated papers and book papers must, therefore, be delivered to the printer in sheet from, and the same is true of writing papers and ledger papers.

It should be mentioned that many of the medium to heavier grades of paperboard used in folding box manufacture, which are produced at relatively low speed on the paper making machine, are cut into sheets directly in-line with the paper machine and are never wound. In the typical finishing operation, however, mill rolls from the rewinder are fed through a high-speed rotary sheet cutter.

The mill rolls are unwound at the sheeter on a multiple reel stand or backstand. For reasons of production efficiency, a number of webs are usually fed to the sheeter at one time, with five to eight-back-stands being provided. In some cases, these are double backstands that permit the preparation of a complete second set of unwinding paper rolls, while the first set is being unwound.

Because the sheeter operates at a considerably lower speed than the slitter rewinder, the backstands are of simple design with a single shaft support for the roll and a mechanical friction brake. Manually operated side shifting is included to permit alignment of the rolls.

The paper passes from the backstands over idler rolls and spreader rolls to remove wrinkles, then passes through the nip of a pair of driven pull rolls that control the speed of the paper. On most sheeters, shear-cut slitters are provided for cutting the web into narrower widths in the longitudinal direction. The multiple webs of paper, then pass to the sheet cutter itself. This consists of a rotating fly knife and a stationary bed knife. These knives are made of heavy tool steel with carefully ground sharp edges. The rotating knife is counter-weighted for dynamic balancing. The clearance for proper cutting is obtained by adjusting the position of the bed knife. The sheet length is determined by the rotational speed of the rotating knife in relation to the speed of the paper. This speed ratio is commonly made adjustable by means of gears or any of a number of standard mechanical variable speed devices.

As the sheets are delivered from the cuter, they must be conveyed away from the knives and stakced. This is accomplished by means of a conveyor consisting of a series of parallel tapes. On high-speed units, it is advisable to use the so-called overlapping delivery system, where a first set of tapes operates at a speed slightly faster than the cutter, and the second set operates at a reduced speed to slow down the sheets prior to stopping. This results in an overlap of the sheets.

The sheets are received in a stacking device known as layboy, so-called because this operation was originally performed manually by boys. This device consists of a table with oscillating side guides that jog the sheets of paper into place. The table is automatically lowered as the pile of paper increases in height. When the full depth is reached, a set of fingers is inserted to hold the upper portion of the pile, while the bottom portion is removed without stopping the sheeter.

Since sheeted paper is commonly sold by the ream rather than by the pound, it is necessary that the paper sheets be counted. Although this was formerly done by hand, there are now reliable automatic ream counters and marking machines available.

The higher quality grades of book, writing and ledger papers are inspected by hand. The inspector manually turns over each sheet of paper in the pile to look for any unacceptable defects such as holes, dirt, specks, etc.

For products that must be delivered in sheet sizes smaller than are conveniently cut on rotary sheeters, the paper is then transferred in piles of guillotine type cutters. This type of cutter is also used where accurate trimming is required to a precise sheet size, since the precision of the rotary cutter is not sufficiently accurate for this purpose.

Following inspection and cutting or trimming, the sheeted paper is then ready for wrapping and packaging for shipment. It is normally wrapped first in paper and then packed in cartons to protect it during shipment.

22

Corrugated Containers

INTRODUCTION

In industrialized societies, the bulk of commodities and manufactured products are packaged. By far the most widely used package is the corrugated shipping container. Its functions may be summarized as follows:

(1) **Protection.** The corrugated shipping container protects the product from damage and soling as it moves through the transportation and handling environment from producer to consumer.

(2) **Storage.** It offers a convenient place and a safe method of storing a product until it is sold.

(3) **Advertising.** It can function as an advertising billboard for the user's product while the container is in transit, in storage, or on display.

(4) **Economics.** It performs the above functions at a minimal cost.

MATERIALS

A corrugated box consists of two structural elements: (1) the facings (linerboard); and (2) the fluting structure (corrugated medium). Linerboard facings are of two general types:

(1) **Fourdrinier kraft liner**. Kraft liner is made from pinewood fibres, in a continuous process from the tree to the paper web. it is occasionally referred to as "virgin" kraft, because the fibres have not been used before.

(2) **Cylinder liner**. This is often called "Jute" liner, a,misleading term, since it never contains any jute fibre. Cylinder liner is made from reprocessed fibres, generally used containers. Since 80% of all shipping containers use kraft liners, cylinder is essentially a 2/3 kraft, 1/3 medium furnish, and it is not "virgin".

The choice between these two facings is made on various considerations which may be summarized as follows. In the majority for normal shipping container uses, the two facings are interchangeable. Freight Rule requirements are based on kraft grades, and for every kraft facing, there is a corresponding cylinder facing, somewhat heavier in basis weight, but having the corresponding burst strength (Mullen). Kraft facing, grade for grade,* have better machine direction tear than cylinder facings. The cross directional tear is about the same. On shipping containers having handholes or carrying dense loads (high weight low cube), or expected to sustain more-than-normal strain on score lines, the use of kraft is indicated. Kraft facings contain a fair degree of natural sizing that is normally lost on repulping to make cylinder liner. This makes kraft boxes some what more resistant to surface moisture.

All facings have a pronounced machine direction although the difference in the ratio of machine (MD) to across directional (OD** or CD) properties is more pronounced in cylinder liner, a fact inherent in the difference between the formation of a fourdrinier *vs* a cylinder machine. Thus, because of the additional orientation of the fibres in the machine direction, cylinder liner has more machine direction stiffness than krakft. The OD stiffness is about the same. In box compression, in the end to end direction, which the carriers, consider very important, boxes made from cylinder liners give higher (by as much as 50%, depending on box size) end to end compression.

Kraft has a greater proportion of long fibres than cylinder liner, making it a somewhat coarser and more porous sheet. To give it a smoother printing surface and fill up the pores, secondary headboxes on the paper machine, containing additionally refined

---

*The definition of what is meant by grade is given in the discussion on "Grades".

** i.e. "Other Director"

(shorter fibres), are added. This gives many kraft linerboards additional two sidedness. The inherent coarseness of kraft liner can be an advantage, as for example when users desire boxes with a maximum coefficient of friction. Sometimes users ask that liner be run inside out, as the wire side tends to be rougher than the felt side. Roughness, however, is obtained at the expense of printing smoothness and cause sealing reliability.

Cylinder liner has a higher proportion of short fibres than kraft. This makes a less porous and mechanically denser web, giving a good printing and case sealing surface, It also results in a surface with a relatively low coefficient of friction, in fact some care necessary to avoid making cylinder liner too smooth, as excess slickness is undesirable.

Liners generally receive some kind of surface preparation at the calender stacks. This is known as "finish". Gums, starches, wax emulsions, carboxy methyl cellulose, and water alone, are commonly used on kraft and cylinder liners. On kraft liner one may also choose to apply no finishing material at all, this is then known as "dry finish". The choice depends upon intended use and the nature of the machine formation. For example, wax emulsions would not generally be used on cylinder liner, as this would enhance the smoothness of the sheet to the point of slickness.

"Finish" is an important property on all liners. In some handling operations, such as case sealing, the finish affects machine settings. Case sealing machines can be set to accept all of the commonly available finishes. Problems may be created when they are set to accept one kind of finish, let us say starch finish, and the liners on the shipping cases are then changed to dry finish, or *vice versa*.

Corrugating Mediums

The commonly used raw materials for corrugating medium are the following:

(a) Hardwoods, prepared by the neutral sulfite semichemical process (NSSC)

(b) Boughs (based on kraft waste)

(c) Kraft

(d) Straw

(e) Other

In the U. S., the most widely used in NSSC, known as "semi-chem." for short. These words refer to the fact that pulping of hardwoods necessitates mechanical as well as chemical defibering. Appearance and other characteristics may vary considerably, depending on the type of hardwood and the number or species used. All medium grades are more and more being made on fourdrinier machines, but can be made on cylinder machines as well. Combined fourdrinier and cylinder machine formed sheets are known in Europe. All types of forming can make good medium, quality being determined by furnish, stock preparation, and formation.

Bogus medium is made from reprocessed fibres. The name is unfortunate as it connotes (incorrectly) "imitation". When properly made, from good corrugated cutting (kraft/semi-chem), it makes an excellent medium that has good runability and flat crush.

Kraft is used as corrugating medium, when special high tear or puncture resistance is needed, but the total amount consumed for this purpose is so small that kraft for this use is generally a liner having the same basis weight. Linerboard used as corrugating medium does not corrugate well and consequently gives a relatively low flat crush (soft board).

Straw medium is still widely used in Europe, but has practically disappeared in the U.S. This has come about as a result of the cultivation of varieties of wheat, oats, and rye, which are suitable for machine harvesting and which leave little straw for harvesting. Straw has thus disappeared as a crop. It makes a good corrugating medium when admixed with 40 to 60% kraft in the form of kraft corrugated waste. Used by itself, it makes a soft medium and one very susceptible to humidity. Refining to make it harder tends to give embrittlement. Unless special (and usually uneconomical) provisions for cleaning are made, straw medium contains excessive amounts of grit that create premature water of corrugating rolls.

"Other" refers to corrugating mediums not covered by the above descriptions. In some countries outside of the United States, it is still very common to find corrugating mediums made from waste news and other inferior fibres. In Germany, such medium is known as "scherenz"* and this word has come to describe this variety of medium even if its origin is Japan of Algeria. Use of "schrenz" is dictated by economic necessity in countries that have limited or no timber resources and that wish to restrict imports of limit foreign exchange. "Schrenz" medium is soft, although additives can help. This softness is usually somewhat compensated for by additional basis weight. Corrugated boxes made in countries where this grade predominates tend to be of double will rather than double face construction.

Grades, Standard

In the United States and Canada, freight rule requirements have led to the development of standard grades of linerboard and corrugating medium. For linerboard the definition of "standard" in this context is in terms of basis weight and burst strength, based on kraft facings. Caliper is not specified for facings used for corrugated, and mills thus allow caliper to "float", which permits them to run their machines to optimize other important characteristics. For solid fibre grades, caliper is specified in the combined board and therefore, the mills run to it.

For corrugating medium, the rule calls for a minimum basis weight of 26 lb/1000 sq ft (127 g/m^2) and a minimum caliper of .009 in. (2.29 mm).+ Caliper is an important property in medium, since it influences the uniformity of flute formation as the web passes between the fluting rolls.

Flat crush is not specified in the rule, but the advent of the CONCORA Medium test (CMT)** has resulted in a further standardization in the United States, with respect to this property, so that at regular grade commercial corrugating medium in the U.S. has about the same flat crush and is completely interchangeable in common uses, regardless of the source of fibre composition.

There are some "standard" grades of linerboard and medium that are not based on the freight rule. For linerboard, this makes

*This word also applies to linerboard when made from inferior fibres.

+ Therefore, sometimes called "Nine Point".

**See TAPPI Standard T809.

it possible to furnish board constructions where the demands on the package require some grade in between the regular standards, i.e., stronger than what is called for in the rule, but not as strong as the next higher grade. Similarly, where medium of greater flat crush than is possessed by the standard No. 26 grade is needed, certain standard but heavier weights have come into use.

Table 1 lists the common grades of linerboard and corrugating medium.

Grades - Special

In addition to standard grades, numerous specialty grades are available, and new ones appear regularly, generally under trade names. We shall, therefore, limit ourselves to the major categories without attempting to list and describe them individually:

(a) In addition to the fully bleached kraft liners, there are a variety of "mottled" grades. These are made by adding to the surface, by means of secondary headbox, a small percentage of bleached kraft fibres. They give the sheet a cloudy, white appearance, creating a pleasing background effect for some types of graphics. Corresponding cylinder grades are also available. Both are made to basis weight and test specifications complying with freight rule requirements.

(b) Fully coloured and pattern coloured (such as linen-finish) linerboard grades are available.

(c) The armed services and the General Services Administration of the U.S. Government purchase so-called "V-board" grades of corrugated and solid fibre, to comply with PPP-F-320. This specification calls for caliper rather than basis weight, and wet and dry mullen, except for triple wall board, which calls for wet and dry puncture. Linerboards for this application contain wet strength treatments. "Web strength" treatment of linerboard increases the wet tensile and tear retention characteristics compared to the untreated sheet. It does not refer to stiffness or other "strength" properties.

There are also commercial or civilian applications for "wet strength" treated linears, for example in solid fibre returnable beer boxes, or corrugated boxes intended for use in some inclement environments.

Table 1: Common U. S. Grades of Linerboard and Corrugating Medium

Grade	Basis lb/MSF*	Weight g/m²	Avg. Bursting Strength psi	Avg. Bursting Strength kg/cm²	Caliper** in.	Caliper** mm.
Regular	26	127	70	4.9	.008	2.03
Fourdrinier	33	161	85	6.0	.010	2.54
Kraft	38	186	92	6.5	.011	2.79
Liner	42	205	100	7.0	.0125	3.18
	47	229	105	7.4	.0145	3.68
	69	337	135	9.5	.020	5.08
	90	439	160	11.2	.023	5.84
Bleached	38	186	84	5.9	.010	2.54
Kraft	42	205	93	6.5	.011	2.79
Linerboard	69	337	-	-	.018	4.57
	90	439	-	-	.022	5.59
Cylinder	40	195	65	4.6	.010	2.54
Linerboard	50	244	100	7.0	.013	3.30
	70	342	135	9.5	.021	5.33
	90	439	175	12.3	.028	7.11
Corrugating	26	127	-	-	.009	2.29
Medium	30	146	-	-	.010	2.54
	33	161	-	-	.011	2.79
	36	176	-	-	.012	3.05

*lb/MSF=pounds/1000 sq ft

**Linerboard calipers are averages, medium calipers are minimums for .009 and .010 in., average for the other grades.

(d) For inclement environment, packaging linerboards may be made that contain internal or surface sizing materials. Sizes are used to achieve water repellency or "roll off", but these are not film formers, and permanent contact with liquid water will wet the fibres. Sizes do not accomplish "wet strength" and are used without wet strength treatment or in conjunction therewith, but not as a substitute.

(e) Release or "adhesive" surfaces are obtained with the use of silicone, "Quilon" (stearatochromic) or similar surface treatments. These grades find application where a commodity (such as uncured rubber) would normally adhere to the facings, and some "non-stick" quality is required to release the product. Care must be taken in using such treatments, as normal water-based adhesives do not stick to such treated surfaces.

(f) In the packaging of furniture, porcelain enamel products, and the like, it is sometimes desired to impart a special finish to the facings to prevent abrasion or marring of the product where it is in contact with the package. Such coatings are generally proprietary in nature, and specially grades are available from various companies under their own trade names.

(g) Other liner specialties to obtain reduction in moisture vapour transmission rates are available, in the form of laminated liners (laminations between facings) or liners laminated to plastic films, such as extruded polyethylene. Laminants used may be asphalt, microcrystalline wax blends, polyvinyl acetate, waterproof starches, etc.

(h) In the area of corrugating medium specialties are limited to treatments imparting wet strength properties. Various suppliers have their own trade names for these grades.

Combined Board Structure

The simplest corrugated board construction is known as "single face", consisting of one facing and one corrugating medium adhered to each other. This type of corrugated has some end uses, such as wrapping for fragile products. It is not used in this form as a corrugated shipping container.

The two major types of combined board are the following:

(1) **Double Face:** one inside liner, one corrugating medium and one outside liner, as shown in Fig. 1. "Inside" and "outside" refer to the inside and outside of the shipping

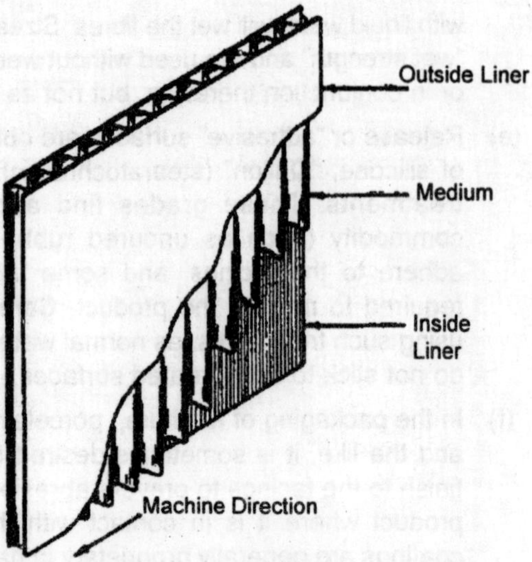

Fig. 1. Double face board

container.

(2) **Double Wall**: one inside liner, one corrugating medium, one center liner, another corrugating medium, and one outside liner, as in Fig. 2.

Double wall boards of a given "test grade" may differ in their flue structure, the convention of naming these being as follows:

Table 2

Named First OSL	Named Last ISL	Designation
A	B	AB
B	A	BA
C	B	CB
B	C	BC
C	C	CC

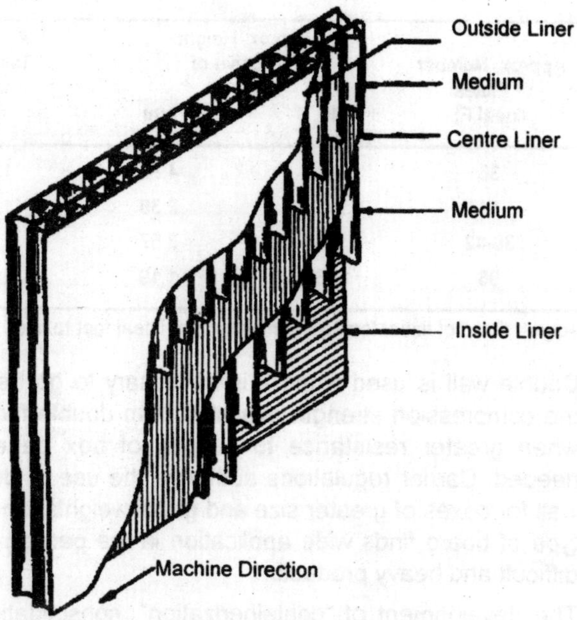

Fig. 2. Double wall board

A still heavier construction, called triple wall, has recently become available, consisting of four liners and three mediums. The convention for designating these is the same as for doubles wall, for example AAC, ABC, etc.

The common flute used for shipping containers are A, B, and C, with characteristics shown below. There is also an E-flute, which is used primarily as a consumer-type package, i.e., in the from of folding carton styles (Table 3).

Various combined board structures are chosen by matching end use requirements to the appropriate physical characteristics. The choice must be compatible with the carrier regulations. The major considerations are the following:

(1) For most shipping container applications (90%), double faced board is used. Variations in strength properties are obtainable by changing liner grades and/or selecting different corrugating mediums.

Table 3: Common Flute Contours

Flute Designation	Approx, Number of Flutes/ lineal Ft	Approx, Height Exclusive of Facings In.	mm	Approx. Take-up Factor*
A	36	3/16	4.76	1.58
B	51	3/32	2.38	1.38
C	39-42	9/64	3.57	1.50
E	96	3/64	1.19	1.30

*Take-up factor = Ratio of lineal footage of medium per lineal foot to liner.

(2) Double wall is used when it is necessary to go beyond the compression strength available from double face, or when greater resistance to bulging of box panels is needed. Carrier regulations authorize the use of double wall for boxes of greater size and gross weights, and this type of board finds wide application in the packaging of difficult and heavy products.

(3) The development of "containerization", consolidation of loads into large single shippers and large bulk shipping containers, has necessitated going beyond the strength capabilities of standard double wall boards. Two additional board structures available for such uses are:

(a) Extra or special high strength double walls. These differ from regular double will in having inside and outside liners of laminated construction, heavier than regular 26 lb medium in the smaller flute, and two mediums laminated together in the larger flute. This permits going to higher compression loads and greater puncture resistance than the best regular (600-lb test) double wall, while retaining the workability and handling characteristics of regular double wall with respect to ease of folding in case sealing or taping the box. Thickness is only slightly higher than regular double wall.

(b) For accommodating the maximum in gross weight and compression requirements, triple wall boards are made. Due to its great thickness, this construction is very stiff and requires special provisions in effecting box closure by taping.

The choice of flue configurations is based on the following considerations:

(1) The largest flute contour is "A"-flute. This configuration has the fewest flutes per lineal foot, and therefore, results in board with the lowest flat crush. This makes A-flute board the most susceptible to fabrication damage in the manufacturing operation and the most easily damaged in handling in the transportation environment. Another consequence is that scoring with the flutes is the most uncontrollable of the three common contours. At the 180° folds, damage on either side of the score is widest. Control of inside dimensions is the poorest of the three common flutes.

(2) The A-flute contour has the greatest caliper. Theoretically, A-flute board is expected to have the correspondingly greatest column crush strength and, therefore, is expected to give the highest top to bottom compression strength for vertical flute boxes. On perfectly made corrugated board, this advantage is realized, but on commercially available grades, the fragility of the A-flute is such that in practice it is no better than C-flute for top to bottom compression. For end to end compression, A-flute is the lowest of the three flutes.

(3) For use as a spacing material (interior packing) A-flute board gives the most spacing with the least amount of board consumed. On the other hand, a freight car of a given cubic volume will accommodate fewer A-flute sheets or box bundles than any other flute contour.

(4) The combination "lowest flat crush" with "greatest caliper" makes A-flute board the most advantageous to use when "cushioning" is desired.

(5) The B-flute construction has the most flutes per lineal foot. Board with this contour, therefore, has the highest flat crush (E-flute excluded for reasons stated below).

Therefore, wherever high flat crush is essential, this is the preferred flute, as in can cases, to name an example. The larger number of flutes makes for a flatter printing surface. The narrow spacing between flutes makes for the least damage on either side of a body score, and gives better control of inside dimensions. B-flute is the most resistant to fabrication and handling damage because of its high flat crush. It also has the least caliper, which makes it the least suitable for boxes requiring top to bottom compression strength. Except for boxes having the heaviest liner weights, B-flute is best for end to end compression resistance.

(6) Historically, A and B-flutes came before C-flute, which accounts for the fact that alphabetically "C" is the third flute, while its properties and characteristics place it between A and B-flutes. Its development was predicated on the hope that it would combine the best features of A (top to bottom compression) with the best features of B (high flat crush and control of inside dimensions), while eliminating the disadvantages of either. Actually, more and more corrugated boards have tended to go from. A into C-flute, but A has not been eliminated, and B-flute, continues to be used extensively. Neither users nor manufactures are inclined to lose the flexibility to tailor board construction to end use by giving up all other flutes in favour of single one. In making a choice of flute contour, one must compromise to get what is desired most, at the expense of what is perhaps also desirable, but not so essential.

(7) On double wall board constructions, top to bottom compression (materials being equal) is greatest for the thickest and least for the thinnest flute combinations. Therefore, it makes no difference whether the board is AB or BA or CB or BC. In normal operation, one gets one or the other off a given corrugator, depending on whether the A-flute (or C-flute) station is ahead or behind the B-flute station on the corrugator. If for some reason, say control of inside dimensions, it is desired to get CB from a corrugator delivering BC, the board can be reverse-scored.

We skipped over a detailed discussion of E-flute because this contour, as already indicated, is not extensively used in shipping container constructions. The reasons for this are practical. The main advantage of E-flute is the ability to offer a printing surface comparable to that of a folding carton. Such board is, therefore, printed on rotary folding carton presses. Ordinary 26 lb medium is too stiff to curve properly without breaking. Consequently, soft medium less than .009 in (2.29 mm) thick and weighing less than 26 lb/100 sq ft (127 g/m^2) is used, which rules out shipping container applications on this type of board, since this would not be in compliance with freight rule requirements on medium.

We conclude this discussion on combined board structure with some comments on symmetry—"Balanced" *vs* "Unbalanced' board combinations.

Standard grades as defined in the freight rules are based on the weight of 'combined" facings. Thus on the 200 lb test grades of double face board, a combined weight of 84 lb/1000 sq ft is called for. Accepted practice is to use two 42 lb facings. This makes for a "balanced" construction and is the preferred way. The use of a legal but "unblanced" combination, say 47 lb on one side, 38 lb on the other, is prone to warp, hence, it is more difficult to fabricate and is associated with more waste. On the other hand, it is sometimes economically desirable to run "unbalnced' double face. If something strogner than 200 lb test board is needed but the step from 200 to 275 lb test (two 42-lb sheets to two 69-lb sheets) results in unnecessary overpackaging, one may wish to run 42 to 47, or 42 to 69, none of which can be certified as 275 lb test, but all of which are better than 200 lb test. If the best appearance is desired, the heavier liner should be outside, because the heavier the facing, the less likely it is to exhibit the "wash-boarding" effect so often characteristic of the very light-weight grades. For best compression, however, the heavier sheet should be inside.

On double wall there are more options in the choice of liners, and unbalnced combinations are more common. Moreover, since combiners with two identical flue contours are uncommon (AA, CC, or BB), these grades are rare and the structure is, therefore, unbalanced with respect to flute contour, even if the same weights of facings are used throughout. The "center" liner is not really (geometrically) in the true center, i.e., at the neutral axis. Unlike the situation on double race board, these various kinds of "asymmetry" are rarely associated with warp, i.e., warp is not a problem in manufacturing. Only the effect on compression performance, depending on the nature of the board combination, remains.

On triple wall, the number of ways in which the sheet can be unbalanced in still larger than on double wall, but this is of no great practical consequence. In the U.S. only AAC and ABC (or variations thereof) are available commercially, and all current grades are unbalanced with respect to liner weights as well.

FREIGHT RULES

We have already referred in passing to the subject of freight rules, in connection with our discussion on maerials and "standard" grades, without explaining the meaning and significance of such rules to the technology of shipping containers. We take up this subject now, before continuing our discussion of shipping container structure and manufacturing of corrugated and solid fibre boxes.

A shipping container is desired primarily to carry the packaged commodity safely from the manufacturer to the consumer. While doing so, it is in the hands of a carrier (rail, truck, or air) and since it is usually not in view while in transit, it is necessary to have some means of judging whether any damage incurred is due to faulty handling by the carrier, to faulty packaging practices by the shipper, or to defective materials from the box maker. In the case of the railroads the specifications designed to serve this purpose are found in the "Uniform Freight Classification" and in the case of the truck companies the "National Motor Freight Classification". The air and ship lines do not yet have detailed specifications.

The rail and truck specifications form a part of the contract between the carrier and the shipper. In effect, they say that if the merchandise is properly prepared for shipment and if the shipping containers comply with the basic criteria, the carriers will assume the responsibility for delivering the product in a damage-free condition. All common types of containers (boxes, drums, baskets crates, etc.) must meet specifications of this kind.

The most detailed of the rules that apply to fibreboard shipping containers is Rule 41 in the Uniform Freight Classification. It governs boxes used in rail shipments*. Like all freight rules, it is written so as to apply to all containers accepted for shipment and therefore, it contains only specifications of a board general nature.

Standardization of Grades and Rule 41

One of the least understood aspects of Rule 41 is the role it has played in bringing about the standardization of grades of corrugated and solid fibre boards. This was due to a fortunate combination of circumstances and good, technically sound specification practice. Standardization was really and unintended by product of the Rule, in the sense that in setting up the specification, standardization of grades was not a consciously sought objective. Having achieved it, however, this byproduct has assumed such importance that any proposal for radical departures must invariably be examined in the light of the effect it might have on this desirable state of affairs.

In specifying facing weights, the Rule chose a criterion that is also the most convenient way to specify paperboard for purchasing purposes. Within any give, grade of type of paperboard, practically all material strength properties are either proportional to or highly correlated with basis weight. The is certainly true of such properties as tensile, tear, stiffness, rigidity, etc. Consequently those basic properties so important to package performance, yet so difficult to measure, are indirectly encompassed by this simple specification. By specifying the bursting strength, in addition to the basis weight, the rule closed any loophole that might lead to the manipulation of test criteria to the detriment of real quality. Liners could not be loaded with short fibres simply to meet the weight criterion, since they then would fail the mullen test. The basis weight requirement maintains the essential quality of one type of linerboard, while the bursting strength test does the same for other types.

This has in effect established a "floor" below which quality cannot sink. The success of Rule 41 in bringing this about is partly due to timing. It came into being when practically all goods

---

*See Section "Where to Find it" par. D. Regulations.

were transported by rail, and so the entire industry had to comply. Since the basis weights specified in the Rule are the weights of kraft liner needed to produce a desired burst level, other liners found their level at the higher basis weight needed to achieve the same burst strength level. Thus, the whole industry was able to make certain basic materials that were actually inter-changeable insofar as the freight rule requirements were concerned. This greatly facilitated the transition of the fibre box from being a substitute product to being a standard quality article in its own right. It was added in its acceptance by consumer industries which enable purchasing agents to buy their boxes from any number of box makers with the assurance that equivalent class stamp grades would indeed provide adequate boxes. This has been such an economic boon to the box industry, as well as to the customers it serves, that any change in the Rule must always be viewed with respect to its effect on this standardization of grades.

The detailed provisions of the rule can be found in the current issue of "Uniform Freight Classification", which is reissued annually. A very complete discussion of the relationship of freight rules to packaging specifications has appeared in the literature, and we recommend this reference to all reders. This limited review is intended only to explain the function of freight rules and indicate their central importance in promoting and maintaining grade standardization.

CORRUGATED SHIPPING CONTAINER STRUCTURE

We proceed now to a discussion of the structural aspects of corrugated shipping containers.

Styles

Experience in the use of corrugated shipping containers has resulted in the evolution of a number of well defined styles. The more common ones can be found in any box company manual, or the, "Handbook of Corrugated and Solid. Fibre Boxes and Products," published by FBA. Abbreviated symbols for these styles are also common, for example, a "regular slotted container" (all flap same length, outer flaps meet) is known as an "RSC". The use of such abbreviations is not practical in Europe, because of language differences, and Europeans have, therefore, adopted a code system for box and inner-packing constructions in general use.

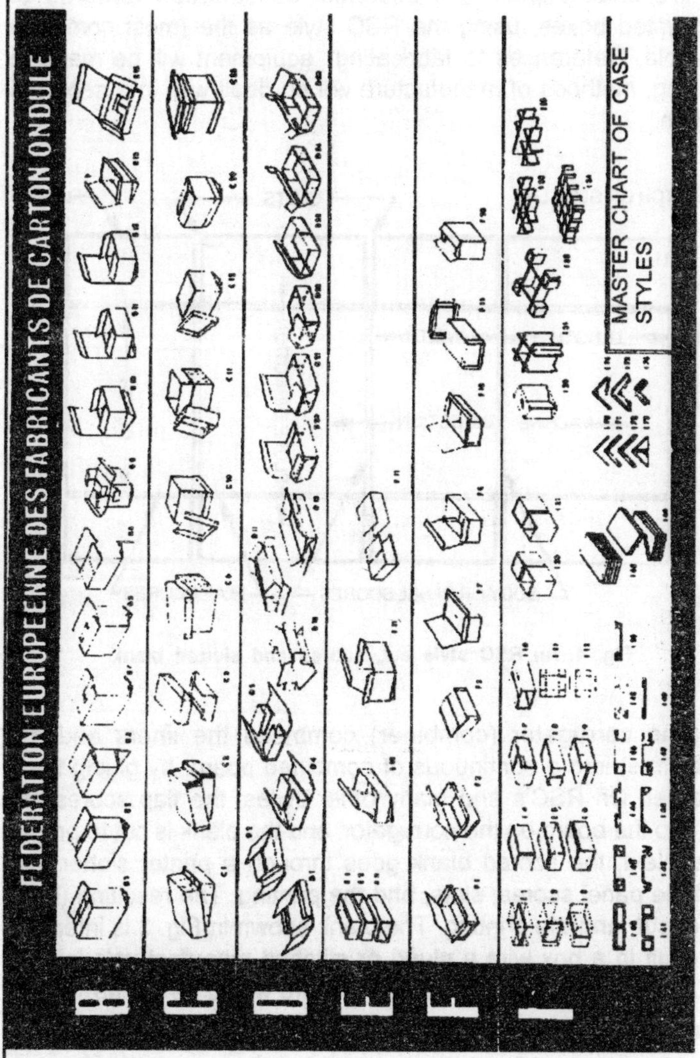

Fig. 3. Master chart of case styles

Construction Features

We shall explain the essential construction features of corrugated boxes, using the RSC style as the (most common) example. References to fabricating equipment will be made in passing, methods of manufacture will be dealt with in a separate section.

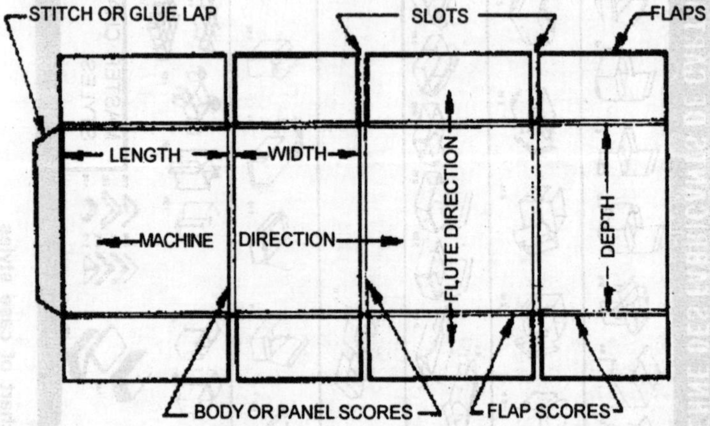

Fig. 4. An RSC style cut, scored and slotted blank

The corrugator (combiner) combines the liners and the medium(s) into a continuous of combined board, by gluing them together. On RSC's and many other styles, the flap scores are put into the board on the corrugator, and the blank is cut to proper size. Next, the scored blank goes through a printer slotter that add the panel scores, slots, and the printing. The resulting (RSC style) cut, and the printing. The blank shown in Fig. 3 is intended to result in a box with a glued or stitched manufacture's joint. It the joint was intended to be taped, there would be no lap.

Manufacturer's Joint

Rule 41 defines the "joint" as that part of the box where the ends of the sheet are joined together by taping, stitching, or gluing. The lap portion may be inside or outside. Construction details are regulated by sections 11 and 12 of rule 41. The term "manufacturer's joint" as covered by these regulations, is unclear with respect to one aspect the certificate on the box indicates that the box maker is responsible for compliance to the rule, and this includes the manufacturer's joint, which in this case should be designated the BOX manufacturer's joint. When blanks are sold to users for "wrap around", (the product) applications, the joint is not made by the box maker, the user is the "manufacturer" in this case and is responsible for forming the joint. The rule at the time of this writing fails to make this distinction.

The choice as to which joint to use depends on economics, convenience, and use. Some factors may be listed as follows:

(1) All types of joints are equivalent with respect to compression and retention of contents.

(2) A glue of stitch lap, even if crushed, tends to cause bulge when boxes are boundled for shipment. Taped boxes make flat bundles.

(3) Glue laps form strong joints over the entire area of the lap. The joint can be further strengthened through the use of extended laps. Waterproof adhesives are used. The economics of box making favour glue-lapping, since this is the fastest and also makes possible in-line operations to convert a blank to a box in a single operation.

(4) Glue lap joints are difficult to make with adequate bond if wet strength treated liners are used.

(5) Water-based adhesives to not work on curtain coated or waxed boxes. Hot melt adhesives have not developed to the point where they are feasible, economical, or readily adaptable to conventional folder gluer equipment. Therefore, unless the joint can be formed first and the box is impregnated afterward, stitching must be used.

(6) On very large and heavy boxes, stitches are preferred, particularly on flowing loads, since the strength of a glue bond is limited to the internal bonding strength of the paper. Stitching is the most positive way of forming a joint, in the sense that it lends itself readily to visual inspection. If the requisite number and type of stitches used are well clinched, there can be no question about having a proper joint.

(7) Stitches cannot be used on "bag and box" applications, since any contact of the bag with a stitch may result in a tear.

These examples could be multiplied, but in many cases, it makes no difference which type is selected; while in other cases, use, convenience, or economics favour one type of joint over another. Some use of judgement is necessary as rule 41 requirements are "minimums", and strict adherence to the rule does not necessarily result in an optimum box.

Closure

All methods of shipping container closure authorized by rule 41 are described in section 7 of the regulations. Boxes may be closed with:

(1) adhesive
(2) metal stitches
(3) wide crown staples
(4) paper sealing tape
(5) reinforced tape.

These are sometimes supplemented by reinforcement with metal strapping or wire. When such reinforcement is used, RSC boxes must still be closed by one of the methods specified in rule 41 before being shipped.

Other Aspects

In Fig. 5, we show a set-up RSC. We have now an assembled shipping container that can be regarded as an engineering structure with the following basic characteristics:

(1) **Dimensions**. Length, width, and depth are always designated in the order (L × W × D). These are always specified to be inside dimensions. On any RSC, the length can be greater than or equal to but never less than the width, by definition.

On square boxes (L = W), the inside flaps meet on other than square boxes. (L > W), there is flap gap equal to (L—W).

Depth is entirely independent of length and width. It can be greater, or smaller, or equal to either or both.

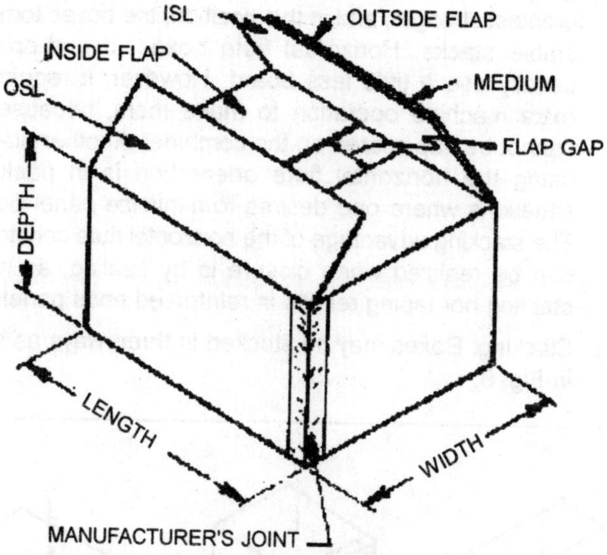

Fig. 5. Corrugated regular slotted container (RSC)

(2) **Scoring allowances**. In order to arrive at the correct inside dimensions, allowances must be made for the caliper of the board. These are known as "scoring allowances". Consequently, one must start with a slightly larger blank than would appear necessary for a two-dimensional line drawing. All manufactures have scoring allowance manuals to permit them to arrive at the correct inside dimensions for their board and flute combinations with their converting equipment.

(3) **Horizontal flute.** The use of an abbreviation like RSC always implies that the direction of the flutes is vertical. They may, however, be horizontal, in which case we specifically add, "horizontal flute RSC". or whatever the style may be.

Horizontal flute boxes are usually end-opening, and are in common usage for a few commodities, such as soaps and detergents. They are stacked, stored, and shipped lying on their side, because this is the direction of their greatest strength, and in this position, the boxes form very stable stacks. Horizontal flute boxes, if end-opening, usually use a little less board. However, it requires an extra machine operation to make them, because they cannot be flap scored on the combiner. Another place for using the horizontal flute orientation is in packaging situations where one desires to minimize panel bulging. The stacking advantage of the horizontal flute construction can be realized when closure is by sealing, as neither stapling nor taping results in reinforced ends panels.

(4) Stacking. Boxes may be stacked in three ways as shown in Fig. 6.

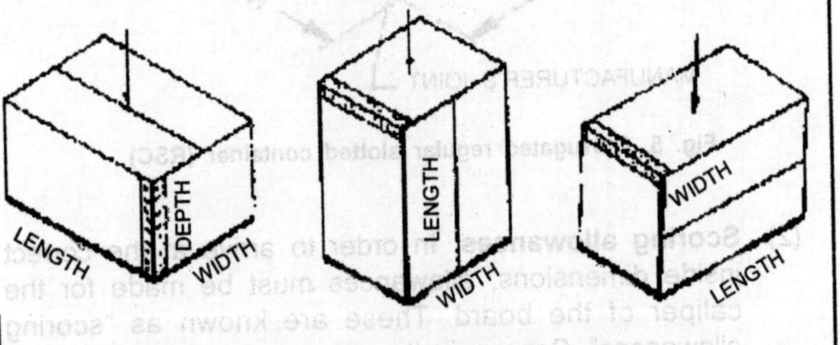

Fig. 6 The three directions of stacking

Boxes must have stacking strength in all three directions. Depending on use and the commodity packaged, one direction may have more importance than the others, but in any combination of storing plus shipping, all three directions will come into play, regardless of the box orientation. When we speak of stacking or compression strength of boxes, this refers to sealed boxes, and all published compression formulas are on that basis. Meaningful copression test values in top to bottom direction can be obtained be obtained by taping or stitching the flaps, or even without the use of any closure at all, but in the other two directions, it is necessary to glue the flaps. Referee testing should always be on a "glued flap" basis.

MANUFACTURING

This section will deal with those aspects of the manufacturing operation which are of general interest to users of corrugated shipping containers.

Structural and Graphic Design

The structural design of a box determines the extent to which the package will successfully cope with the environment and deliver the product intact to the consumer. Graphic design is an important factor in the marketing success of the product. We list below some of the considerations users should keep in mind:

(1) Structural and graphic design are creative activities, and not the place for rush and short cuts.

(2) Users should consider packaging at the same time and as part of product design. This will often eliminate the need for packaging constructions intended to overcome what are really product design deficiencies.

(3) The package designer should be given as much information as possible concerning product fragilities, the number and kinds of handlings, methods of storage, modes of transportation, and climatic environment that the package is intended to survive.

(4) No. 3 might be paraphrased to: "Use a Systems Approach" to design. The best package design is the one that considers the entire life cycle and all the functions the package is expected to perform, not just some portion of it, say "shipping." Therefore, users are well advised not to "bury the competitor's package". If the competitor's environment (manufacturing, packing storing, handling, shipping, marketing, displaying, etc.) is different, his package will not work under a new set of conditions for a different user.

(5) If at all possible, stick with standard materials or the readily available speciality grades.

(6) Users of boxes requiring many sizes will find it worth their time to devote design effort to minimizing the number of sizes in use.

(7) Structural and graphic design should be carried out with the practical and economic and economic capabilities of the manufacturing operation in mind.

(8) The graphic design and the method of printing chosen should be such that the flat crush and compression strength of the board is not impaired.

In summary, users should work with knowledgeable box makers to obtain package designs that are functional, attractive, and can be produced economically by manufacturing.

Planning and Scheduling

Corruagtor widths vary from 63 to 96 in, with 85 to 87 in being the most common. Roll widths are stocked accordingly, usually in 2-in, increments on given grades, except for known repeat and/or large orders where the exact trim desired is bought. The job of the planner is to consolidate incoming orders so as to get maximum utilization of the corrugator with minimum trim waste. He might therefore, schedule some orders two or three out for the same customer, or he might use one side of the machine to run the order for one customer, and the other side for another customer who requires a different size blank, but from the same board combination. More often than not, the width scheduled will not correspond to the exact trim of available roll stock, and therefore, the excess width must be trimmed off as waste. It is desirable for the user and box maker to provide sufficient lead time between ordering and delivery date to permit optimizing machine utilization and minimizing side trim waste.

The Corrugator

The corrugator or combiner usually has two or three single facers, generally a different flute contour at each, so as to permit the greatest flexibility in the available types of corrugated board. A cross-section of modern single facer is shown in Fig. 7.

For greater clarity, we refer to the simplified schematic drawing of Fig. 8 to illustrate the basic principles.

The operation begins by unwinding single face liner from one of the roll stands in front of the single facer and corrugating medium

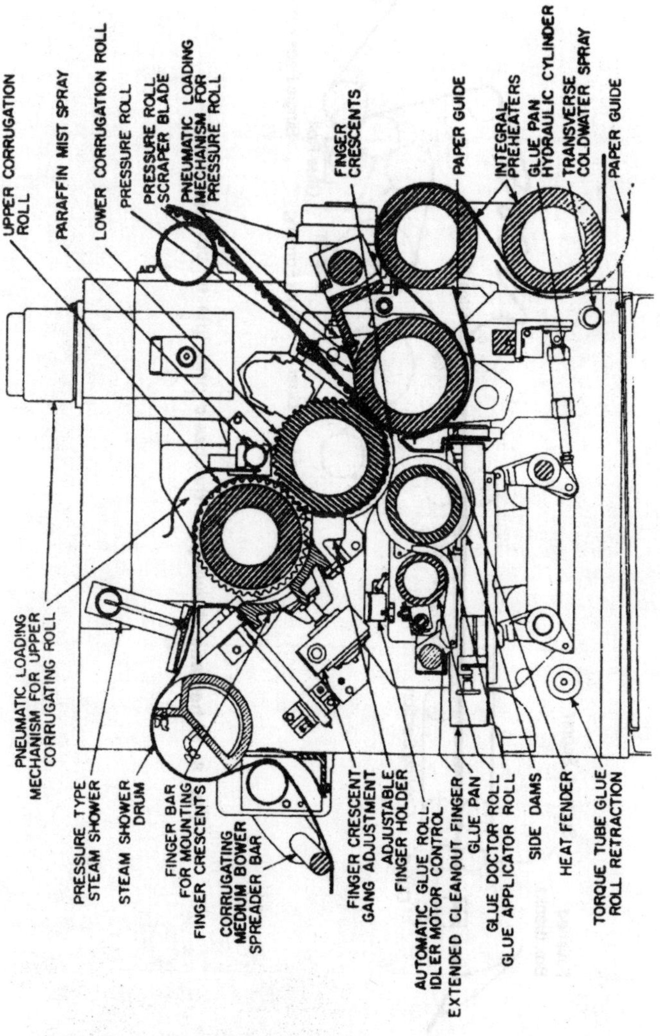

Fig. 7. Model HKE cross-section

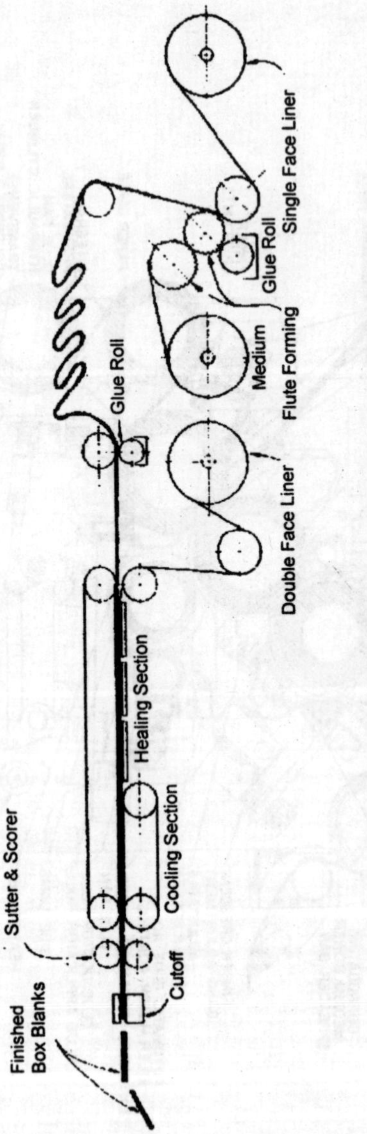

Fig. 8. Schematic drawing of the basic principle of corrugating

from a stand behind the single facer, threading the medium into the labyrinth (between the fluting rolls), applying adhesive to the flute tips from a glue roll, and bringing the liner into immediate contact to form a single face web. This web then travels to the "bridge" where it is accumulated. This step permits changing, retherading, and splicing rolls at either end without having to stop that portion of the machine that is sill running. At the end of the bridge, the single fact web is brought down past another glue roll that applies adhesive to the exposed flute tips of the medium, subsequent to which the double face liner is brought in contact with the single face web that now continues in contact between two belts as it travels through a hot plate section, to set the bond, and a cooling section. Immediately after emerging, the web goes through the slitter scorer consisting of sets of rotary scoring wheels and slitter knives. The final operation is the cut-off where the web is cut to the desired length. In order to run different sheet lengths on one side than on the other, there are generally two cut-off kinves, and two take-off stations.

The process of corrugating involves a number of complexities and controls that can only be indicated here. It is necessary to "precondition" liner and medium. This is done by threading past steamheated preconditioning rolls that move the moisture of the paper to that side intended for bonding. This "prewetting" facilitates making a proper glue bond. In addition, medium is preconditioned by steam showers. The degree of preconditioning depends on the season of the year, the kind of paper run, the moisture content, etc. The formulation of the adhesive, temperature, viscocity glue roll clearances, all have to be controlled to result in a web having a good moisture balance, otherwise, unbonded flutes, high/low corrugation, warped board, "washboarding." or other defects arise. Finally, caliper must be controlled to realize the maximum board quality.

Corrugator Adhesives

(1) **Silicate of Soda**. Sodium silicate, also known as "water glass" dries or sets by losing water. As the medium and liner absorb water, a "glassy" bond forms and holds the two together. Alone or in combination with clay or clay/protein additions, silicate was at one time extensively used in the United States, but is now limited to a very few plants.

Several problems with silicate account for this: (a) under humid conditions the bond resolubilizes, and silicate migrates through the facings, giving a streaked appearance, (b) clean-up of production equipment is difficult as assumulated silicate forms a very hard mass, (c) no satisfactory economical formulation of water-proof adhesive with silicate is available, and (d) silicate dust is an eye hazard to the manufacturer and the user.

(2) **Starch.** Present-day corrugator adhesives are based no starch, primarily corn starch. Unlike silicates, this adhesive does not dry merely by losing water. The adhesive solids require curing or setting by heat on the corrugator, thus converting the raw or partly cooked starch into a gel. Formulations and application systems differ, but all overcome the basic problems with silicate: (a) the bond does not resolubilize and starch does not migrate; (b) there are no special clean-up problems, and (c) any degree of water-resistance from slightly weather-resistant to complete waterproffness can be formulated by the addition of resins. The development of a waterproof bond requires sometime, generally 72 + hr. Consequently, the water-proffness of a sheet cannot be checked on blanks fresh off the corrugator.

Printer Slotters

The printer slotter is usually the next converting machine after the corrugator. It takes a blank sheet of corrugated board, previously cut to size and flap-scored on the combiner, adds the body scores to form the length and width panels, cuts the front and back slots for flap separation, prints in one or more colours, and cuts the stitch or glue lap, all in one operation.

Essentially the operation proceeds as follows. Blanks are laid on a feed table provided with a kicker feed mechanism and front and side gauges. The blank then proceeds through the machine by means of feed and pull rolls, and printing copy is added from sets of letter-press rubber dies. Before emerging, the printed sheet is scored by rotary scoring wheels and slotted from rotary slotter heads. After this operation, the blanks are accumulated until they form a stack, which is then moved by various means to the next converting operation.

Printer sloters very from one colour to four colour and come in various sizes, the most common ones being 28 × 68, 38 × 80, 50 × 113, 60 × 144. And 85 × 185 in. Most box shops have at least two sizes to accommodate the size varieties dictated by their business mix. Printing inks are of the flat or glossy oil-based type that dry by oxidation or moisture, or steam set inks that require no driers and set by contact with moisture from the air and in the paper stock or by applying live steam. Moisture set inks are based on glycol, which losses its solvency for resin and pigment in the presence of water and causes them to precipitate. Such inks are faster drying.

The choice of inks depends on many factors, some of which are listed below:

(1) Oleoresinous "oil" inks, particularly the glossy kind have the best rub resistance. They are also slow drying and, therefore prone to offset. Many customers like the appearance of glossy printing.

(2) Moisture set inks dry far more quickly, which is an advantage in box plants with space limitations. Apart from this, more rapid drying facilitates processing and diminishes or eliminates off-set blanks. Conversely, wet-rub in particular is poor and may give rise to consumer complaints, under some conditions. Such inks are also flatter in appearance.

(3) When solvent-based coating are applied, moisture set inks may be preferred, since solvents also dissolve the resin binders in oleoresinous inks. Moreover, such coatings overcome the problem of poor wet-rub and can restore a glossy appeararice to the printed copy if this is desired.

Finishing Operations

Following the printer slotter, the next operation is generally the forming of the manufacturer's joint, followed by bundling, or palletizing.

Stitching

In its simples from, a stitcher consists of a stitching head, a clinching anvil, a frame to hold these parts in proper position, and a mechanism that provides motion to the stitching head. Stitchers may be entirely manual or hand fed, or fully automatic, in which case, the operator keeps the hopper supplied with blanks, but the machine folds the blanks,. Squares them in both directions, feeds them into the automatic stitching machine, indexes and drives a row of uniformly spaced stitches, and automatically delivers the stitched blanks to counter-stacker or a bundling table.

Taping

On semi-automatic tapers, the operator works from the top of a pile of box blanks that are periodically replenished. An elevating or lifting device keeps the top blanks at the correct height for feeding. The operator folds the blank and squares it up. It then feeds it into a tape-dispensing section where micro-switches regulate the cutting knives so as to dispense the right tape length. The blank then travels through a belt section that keeps the tape in contact with the board long enough for the tape to dry sufficiently to form a bond.

Taping can also be done on automatic folder-tapers that are high-volume machines delivering boxes that are automatically folded and taped. Such machines do not, however, completely replace the semi-automatic machines, with their short setup time and versatility in processing small or extra large boxes, specialty items, and die die cuts. Most box plants have one or more machines of each type.

Gluing

Analogous to taping, glue lapping can be done on manual and semi-automatic machines, although not much equipment of this type is made any more. In most cases, existing taping machines are modified with attachments that convert them to folder gluers. In general, glue lap boxes are made on fully automatic folder gluers. These machines are made possible by the formulation of adhesives that have delayed tack properties. This permits the box blanks to go through automatic squaring devices before the bond sets permanently.

Automatic folder gluers may be broadly divided into two groups, those with belt-type feeders without any timed sequence, and those with feeders that engage blanks in a definite timed relationship with other machine functions. A further differentiation of type may be made according to method of folding the panels, i.e. upward of downward with the advent of flexographic printing, the operation of forming the closure can be combined with printing, slotting and scoring and even some die cutting, making container manufacture a two-step operation the first being corrugating.

The combination of box forming and flexographic printing is relatively new and still the subject of study and development. Flexographic printing permits a degree of sharp definition even with small printing, unmatched by the other available methods already discussed. Inks are water or alochol based and dry almost instantaneously. Wet rub is poor, though no worse than on moisture set inks used on conventional printer slotters, and colours are flat. There are also some other problems that cannot be discussed here. A complete displacement of other methods of printing by "Flexo" is not very likely in the foreseeable future, the variety of demands made on packaging is too great for one single method to encompass.

Tying and Strapping

The final finishing operation consists of counting, tying and strapping. For each of these operations the box maker has semi are fully-automatic equipment available. In recent years, materials handling methods have fostered the growth of unitizing knowked down ("KD'd") corrugated boxes to speed up shipment and facilitate handling by the user. The increased output of the box maker resulting from automated equipment has also aided the trend towards shipping unit loads instead of individual bundles. Hand-operated unitizing machines are available, but the trend has been to automatic equipment that compresses as well as straps the load automatically.

Some general comments seem appropriate before leaving the subject of converting. The automation of the box making process exerts some subtle influences on box quality. The box maker is compelled to demand greater uniformity in the materials he uses. In turn, he must control all aspects of his operation and the tolerances of the product he is making within much narrower limits than formerly. Payout of automated equipment is based on high-volume usage. Failure to make a product to close tolerances jams up automatic equipment and causes down time. This emphasis on greater uniformity benefits the user as well. On the other side of the ledger, many of the automated procedures and new strains and demands on the structure of the box. To move a box blank mechanically from on operation to another involves the application of pressure. Feed rolls, pull rolls, and pressure belts, are examples.

Specialty Operations and Equipment

Box making involves a host of specialty operations that will be briefly discussed below, not necessarily in the order of greatest importance:

(1) **Scorer score**. The are a number of situations requiring a separate slitting/scoring operation e. g., flap scoring orders that are too small to be set up on the corrugator, most horizontal flute boxes, the production of slit scores (board scored on one side and partially slit on the other side), and partitions and many types of incidental work.

(2) **Die cutters.** There are many applications that call for die cutting: (a) irregular or odd-shaped boxes, partitions, or parts: (b) boxes calling for various shaped holes or cut-outs; (c) store and window displays, and (d) very small boxes that can't be processed on conventional printer-slotters, to mention only a few.

There is a great variety of the die-cutting equipment available, ranging from hand-fed, flat-bed platen presses to automatic die cutters with simultaneous stripping. Increasing use is made of die cutting for several reasons; it results in the greates dimensional uniformity in the piece produced; and scoring with the bar scores results in a more accurate and reliable fold than rotary scoring.

(3) **Flap cutters.** Semi and fully automatic flap cutters are available. One type cuts flaps on blanks before they are folded, another cuts flaps on folded and jointed boxes. This equipment is used particularly in producing center special slotted containers (CSSC), boxes other than square shaped with inside and outside flaps meeting, or boxes where it is desired to have the outer flaps overlap. This is generally a slow and expensive operation.

(4) **Partition assemblers.** May users purchase assembled partitions that can be dropped into a set-up container without being first assembled by the user. Partition assembly requires a large amount of labour and space

and is particularly costly in fairly large quantities, but not large enough to justify the expense of installing automatic partition assemblers.

(5) **Overhung eccentric slotters.** For many products, blank sizes are required which cannot be slotted on rotary machines. Eccentric slotters and corner cuters can produce such blanks economically, particularly when used in conjunction with slitter scorers.

(6) **Coating equipment**. Box manufacturers employ a variety of coaters, primarily for the application of wax coatings. Such coating are used on boxes and pads to give water repellent surfaces, reduce scuff or rub in the packaging of products with surfaces susceptible to marring or scratching and the like.

The simplest coaters consist of a pressure and a coating roll, the latter rotating in a tank of hot wax or wax blend. The blank to be coated is passed between the two rolls. More sophisticated equipment is equipped with doctor blades for metering or controlling coating weights and controls for holding melt temperatures at the desired level. Heat controls are important, since waxes are often used in contact with food products that cannot tolerate the oxidation products and rancid odors inevitably resulting from overheating of waxes, even those stabilized with anti-oxidants.

Roll coating has a number of distinct limitations:

(1) Passing corrugated between steel rolls results in caliper loss, with the attendant performance penalties.

(2) The hot melt blend tends to strike into the board, giving partial impregnation rather than a surface film and discolouring the board.

(3) The viscosity range of hot melts is limited to relatively thin coatings. Blends are therefore, restricted to low-molecular-weight polymers. The desirable properties of resins, however, are not obtained until the molecular weight is raised, but this makes the coating viscous, unworkable, and results in stringing and "hen tracks".

(4) Coat weights are limited to 3 to 4 lb/1000 sq ft.

These deficiencies are overcome by "Curtain" coaters that have come into fairly wide use in recent years. Being gravity or pressure-fed and of hot melt, ambient or solvent type, the coating falls on the blank as it passes under a curtain of coating. In the case of hot melts, the coating dries instantaneously as it strikes the cool board surface, forming a true film with practically no impregnation. This enhances the appearance of the blank in that the film imparts gloss, and the discolouration resulting from impregnation is avoided. Since rate of flow as well as blank speed are controlled, accurate coat weights and weights greater than 4 lb/1000 sq fit can be obtained, sufficient to make pin-hole-free films. This in turn, combined with greater flexibility in blending with higher-molecular-weight polymers, permits attainment of barrier properties not possible with roller coating.

Summary

Our treatment of the equipment and the manufacturing operation has been necessarily brief and over simplified. We are indebted to the S & S Corrugated Box Manufactuer's Handbooks for subject matter in this section and recommend this reference to readers interested in more detail in this area, particularly with respect to construction details of box-making machinery. Box users are also urged to visit a box supplier's plant, to get a better understanding of what the operation involves. Our treatment should be adequate to convey the following. Unlike many other mass produced industrial products, corrugated boxes are also a tailor-made product, made to fit the particular needs and requirements of each individual user, be he large or small. Box making is an art as well as a technology, or to put it differently, it is a very technical process, but not always entirely scientific.

TESTING

Methods of testing for paperboard and shipping containers are issued by American Society for Testing and Materials (ASTM) and the Technical Association of the Pulp and Paper Industry (TAPPI) as follows:

(1) ASTM Standards Part 15 paper, Packaging, Casein, etc., Reissued annually.

(2) TAPPI Standards. Looseleaf bound; revisions are made only when needed. Methods pertaining to paperboard are in the T400-T599 series; container testing methods are in the T800-T999 series.

A discussion of the purpose and meaning of various tests in general use is found in reference three, parts 4, 5 and 6. A chapter on "Testing" is found in reference five. Additional references recommended are No. six and seven.

Some tests are used only in connection with Government. Specifications for example "ply Separation". applicable to corrugated and solid fibre weatherproof (V-board) grades, see PPP-F-320. Such tests are "standard", but are not found in ASTM or TAPPI.

SOLID FIBRE

Previous sections of this chapter have already dealt with some facets of solid fibre as part of the general subject of shipping containers. We turn now to those aspects which are particular to this type of board construction:

(1) **Definition.** "Solid Fibre" is a type of paperboard made by "laminating two or more plies of containerboard". This definition from section14 of Rule 41 is correct, but not very "definitive". Thus, two 42 lb/MSF kraft liners laminated together are used as one facing in some double wall corrugated boards and are not thought of as solid fibre. A more descriptive definition would add the following: (a) generally consists of three or more plies; (b) caliopers morethan 0.040 in. (1.016 mm).

Board constructions combining solid fibre and corrugated are also known and sold under various trade names. These consist of double face corrugated board with the outside liner made up of a heavy chip and a kraft liner laminated together.

(2) **Composition.** In the United States, we distinguish currently between three types of compositions:

(a) Outside and inside facings consisting of kraft liners, middle plies consisting of chip. Both facings and chip components may contain varying amounts of sizing and wet strength additions, depending on end use requirements. Cylinder liners are no longer used as facing sheets, with very rate exceptions:

(b) All components consisting of kraft liners, some of which may contain degrees of sizing and wet strength treatments depending on intended end use;

(c) Solid fibre V-boards made to varying thicknesses to comply with Government Specification PPP-F-320, which includes requirements of wet Mullen after a 24-hr immersion. Inside plies may be chip or kraft so long as test requirements are met.

(3) **Properties and end use.** All end uses of solid fibre are based on the fact that this construction is "tougher" than corrugated. Solid fibre has no flute structure that can be crushed and impair the board structure. It is, therefore, more flexible and withstands considerably higher forcers of tensile, tear, and puncture. Its greater capacity for flexing is an advantage in very severe handling environments, but it also accounts for the one characteristic in which it is inferior to corrugated, it is not as "stiff" in terms of column rigidity.

In the civilian sector, solid fibre is used in multi-trip beer, soft drink, and meat boxes. In addition, there are a number of specialty applications such as pet carriers, gift shippers, tote boxes, tool boxes, waste baskets, and many more, where a tough but inexpensive and disposable material is called for.

For military applications, solid fibre is used on boxes expected to withstand extremes in inclement environments, rough handling, and storage for prolonged time periods and under adverse conditions.

It is clear from the foregoing that the products that go into solid fibre are either of themselves load bearing, or else compression is a very secondary consideration.

(4) Specifications and Tests:

(a) Solid fibre grades are specified in terms of caliper. These range from 0.60 to .120 in. (1.52-3.05 mm), with .080 and .090 in. (2.03 and 2.29 mm) the most common.

(b) Rule 41 plays a lesser role in solid fibre boxes. The end use requirements are such that the boxes generally far exceed the test requirements called for by the rule, hence, the facing weights and burst test levels called for in rule 41 are not indicative of current commercial practice.

(c) For Government use, the test requirements for each grade call for dry and wet mullen (burst) and for resistance to play separation as defined in the standard, to assure the use of waterproof adhesive.

(5) **Box Styles**. Many common box styles used in corrugated shippers are also used for solid fibre boxes, such as RSC's, full and partial telescope boxes, double cover styles etc. For some industries, primarily beer and soft drinks, special styles have been developed to permit aoutomatic forming or box assembly and automatic filling, and to provide reclosure features, etc. all tailored for the specific and special handling and transportation environment in which these packages move.

(6) **Surface Coatings.** Beverage cases are frequently supplied with a solvent based resin coating to protect the boxes against deterioration by moisture, to reduce scuffing of the exterior, especially the printing and to improve and preserve the appearance.

Wax coating is used mainly in the meat industry as a barrier between the container and the natural moisture of the meat. This also helps to combat the effect of humid conditions around the plant and in the cooling rooms.

(7) **Manufacturing**. Solid fibre is made on a "Paster." This may be a machine especially manufactured for the purpose or a corrugator modified to permit laminating into a multi-ply sheet.

The front section of the paster consists of a series of roll stands. As the components unwind, they pass an adhesive applicator, or else are joined in an adhesive flooded nip, after which they are pressed together between several nip rolls to secure lamination over the entire area. No heat is applied; the moisture escapes through the board as it dries. The sheet is trimmed and cut at the take-off end, but no scores are applied at the paster.

The next operation is generally the solid fibre printer slotter. This equipment differs from corrugated presses in several ways: (a) printing is from metal as well as rubber dies; (b) chain scores are used to from the panels, and (c) bar scores are used to form the flaps.

It will be recalled that corrugated printer slotters do not apply flap scores. Rotary scoring wheels such as are used on corrugated presses would not be adequate to score solid fibre. Solid-fibre, printer-slotter scores have the bead on the outside of the fold.

Frequently, the blank is not only printed on the printer slotter, but scored, and generally also die-cut on a rotary or flat bed die cutting press. Beverage cases are run this way. Die-cut scores have the bead on the inside of the fold.

Beverage cases, printed (and often coated) go through a folder fluer operation. This equipment is generally designed by the box maker to accommodate boxes of his own design. These box styles have tuck flaps and also side panels reinforced by glued folds, and it is these glued folds that the folder gluers are designed to form.

The manufacturer's joint is generally formed by stitching. Some efforts are under way to introduce glue-lapping, especially on V-board boxes; but this has not as yet become common practice.

23

Boxboard

INTRODUCTION

Paperboard as a packaging material has been in use for over a century. Some of the earliest examples of packages were tobacco wraps, wooden match cartons, and soap cartons. Although John Dickinson invented the first cylinder vat in England in 1809. Thomas Gilpin is generally credited with the development of the earliest version of a cylinder machine producing heavy paper from rages (about 1816 in the United States). In 1967, the production of paperboard in the U.S. was 22.8 million tons, compared with a production of paper of 10.3 million tons. Paper and paperboard consumption has generally been regarded as an indicative index of the American economy, and industry growth has papalled other important segments of expansion.

TYPES OF PAPERBOARD

Two common classes of paperboard have been produced for packaging end use in the twentieth century - namely, cylinder and fourdrinier. Cylinder machine paperboard made from either primary virgin and/or secondary reclaimed papermaking cellulose fibres is the older type. This multilayer structure is formed on a series of screens rotating in successive vats of differing fibre-water compositions called "furnishes". The layers of fibre are deposited as a series of plies on a wet felt that wraps the top sector of the forming cylinder, and are subsequently dewatered between woolen felts or between felts and smooth hard covered rolls in conjunction with pressure and/or vacuum. When the wet fibre web has been reduced to 35 to 45% dry by sufficient pressing, it is further dewatered to 96% dry over a series of high-pressure, steam-heated steel cylinders. Subsequent smoothing or polishing of the web by pressure between a stack of finely ground steel or chrome-plated steel rolls with intermitted doctoring of moisture results in a structure generally referred to as multiply cylinder paperboard.

Fourdinier paperboard, made from all pure bleached or unbleached cellulose fibres, is generally a single layer structure formed on an endless wire. This wet web is dewatered by suction boxes, table rolls and plain presses or suction rolls without felting to 40 to 45% dry. The partly most web is further dried to 95% dry like the cylinder paperboard on steam-heated drying drums, but is usually treated in the middle of this drying process with a size press application to improve smoothness and fibre laydown. The dry web is also polished and smoothed further between finely ground, pressure-loaded rolls with suitable moisture or sizing application to provide a homogeneous structure generally called fourdrinier solidblached (unbleached) sulfate.

Cylinder multiply board is made normally in weight ranges from 50 to 220 lb/thousand sq ft (IB/MSF). The nominal caliper or thickness range corresponding to these weights is 0.12 to 0.60 in, with densities varying from 3.1 to 4.8 lb/MSF/.001 in. (National Paperboard Association Boxboard Standards).

Fourdrinier solid board is made in weight range from 35 to 120 lb/MSF (105 to 360 lb/24 × 36-500 sheet ream) with a corresponding caliper range of .010 to .030 in. Densities vary at the same caliper from 3.3 to 4.5 lb/MSF/0.001 in. or 10 to 13.5 lb/24 × 36—500/.001 in.

COMPOSITION OF MULTIPLY PAPERBOARD

Cylinder machine paperboard is formed from a series of different stock furnishes deposited from as few as two, as many as nine, successive vats. Many cylinder machines use seven or eight vats in order to form uniform, thin weights of fibre for optimum economy, quality, and functionability of plies. Generally, four separate stock systems are used to produce a typical paperboard, and these systems are classified as:

(1) Top or outer liner

(2) Under or inner liner

(3) Filler

(4) Back or bottom liner.

In order to determine the selection of fibres used in each stock system, a description of the grades of paperboard available is necessary. Normal grades used in packaging consist of paperboards of non-bending to full bending top liner, dark to light top and/or bottom liner, uncoated or coated top and/or bottom liner, and all combinations of above with either weak or strong filler stocks. Density, quality, and functionability of each grade influences the selection of fibres, especially from cleanliness or lack of contaminants in secondary or reclaimed fibres.

Research work on cylinder paperboard conducted under auspices of Boxboard Research and Development Association indicated that many paperboard characteristics such as stiffness, bending quality, tear strength, and crush resistance were related to strength of surface plies. Other properties such as tear strength, puncture resistance, and rigidity were possible with strong filler furnishes. These facts permitted the design of grades with varied end use characteristics, and allowed the development of optimum sheet properties with the most economical selection of raw materials.

Non-bending paperboard, such as plan chipboard, news lined chipboard, or white vat lined chipboard is made from predominately low-strength, clean, secondary fibres. A typical topliner furnish for each of the grades mentioned would be as follows:

Plain Chip	News Lined Chip	White Vat Lined Chip
25% Double Lined Kraft	20% Doble lined Kraft	35% Semi-Bl. Kraft. Cutts.
45% Clean news	45% News blanks	35% News blanks
30% Boxboard cuttings	35% Clean news	30% Ctd. Pub. Blanks

A typical topliner furnish for a white lined board for folding carton use would be as follow:

25% Bleached sulfite

20% Unbleached Sulfite of semi-bleached kraft

40% Hard whites or envelope cuttings

15% Soft whites or coated blanks.

Percentages of these raw materials vary with the caliper of the board, surface brightness, opacity of formation, and degree of bending quality required. Most cylinder mills would apply 3 to 6 mills (.003-.006 in.) of this furnish for normal coverage and appearance, and would use one or two vats to form the stock, depending on the type of vat available.

A typical underliner or subliner furnish for a white lined folding carton grade would be as follows:

15% Unbleached sulfite or semi bleached kraft rolls

30% Tab cards or de-inked ledger

40% Soft whites or coated blanks

15% Printed ledger or printed blached kraft boxcuts.

Percentage of these materials again would vary with the board caliper, degree of coverage and formation, and relative strength or stiffness of board required. Most cylinder mills apply 2 and 1/2 mills (.0025-.0035 in.) of this stock on one vat for normal board characteristics.

A high percentage of folding carton board is still manufactured with a news or gray back. A typical back or bottom liner furnish with normal bending characteristics for average carton work would contain the following fibres: 25% double lined kraft; and 75% clean news.

Manila and/or white back folding carton stock with average bending characteristics would contain the following percentages of fibre in the back liner furnish:

Manila (50 Brightness)	White (70 Brightness)
25% Unbleached sulfite	15% Bleached sulfite
40% Ctd. pub. blanks	25% Hd. wh. env. cuts
35% Uncoated blanks	60% Coated pub. blanks

These ratios of virgin to secondary fibres may change, depending on the caliper, formation or appearance, and degree of stiffness required in the finished board.

Filler stock usually contains a predominate percentage of overissue and institutional news for conventional cylinder paperboard. Degree of sorting and cleaning of the center ply of paperboard fibres determines the associated secondary material that comprises filler furnish. Cuttings, trimmings, reclaimed broke, and rejected cartons from folding carton converting and finishing operations (termed boxboard cuttings) are generally used with news. Reclaimed corrugated containers, mixed and or certified mixed waste from retail or wholesale.

Merchandising areas are extensively used as filler stock in conjunction with Asplund defibrator and asphalt dispersion equipment. Typical filler furnishes for news back board would be :

15% News corrugated	60% # Mixed
35% Boxboard cuttings	40% Old corrugated
50% Inst. news	
(without Asplound equipment)	(with Asplund equipment)

Paperboard requiring extra strength properties for functional characteristics is made with a different type of filler and/or backliner furnish. Carrier stock, automobile panel board, hardware or metal parts cartons, oil can or tube winding stock, and other types of non-bulge, non-deformible packaging materials use predominately new corrugated and/or double lined kraft or unbleahced kraft pulp as filler stock. Wet strength and dry strength melamine-formaldehyde, urea-formaldehyde, and phenolic resins may be incorporated into this filler for additional wet tear, wet handling, environmental stability, or sustained rigidity under extremes of storage and shipping. Although many of these extra strength grades, such as white lined kraft back, solid kraft, or clay coatedkraft back boards, are made in cylinder mills, increasing tonnages are being made on fourdrinier machines equipped either with special secondary headboxes or dry-end coating equipment, as appropriate.

Due to the greater availability of secondary fibres as well as more extensive cleaning equipment and/or de-inking methods, an increasing variety of raw materials are being used by cylinder mills. Printed and coloured paper stocks, magazines and books, as well as newspapers, are being de-inked in order to provide economical fibres for pulp substitutes. High quality liner furnish materials for subsequent coating, colouring, or laminating are being generated by good mechanical dirt and contaminant separation of such materials as plastic tabs, rubber bands, paper clips, adhesives, asphalt, polyethylene, or other extruded films. Excellent use of reclaimed fibres is possible with suitable collection and processing, and allows more suitable use of high quality pulps for more expensive paper commodities, while at the same time conserving natural and newly created forests for other industry segments.

PAPERBOARD TREATMENTS

Many types of surface treatment are used on paperboard to modify or change properties for specific requirements. Smoothness, water repellancy, grease repellancy gloss ink holdout, mold inhibition, fluorescent brightening, slickness, and other properties may be imparted to paperboard webs by treatments near the dry end of the machine.

Calender Stack Applications

Water solutions of starches, gums, or modified polymers or similar chemicals may be applied to either surface of paperboard by pressure doctoring after the web leaves the drying section. These solutions are pumped to a box positioned on the periphery of a polished steel calender roll, which is one of series of rolls mounted vertically in a heavy supporting frame commonly called a "stack". The web, which wraps the rolls in alternate nips from top to bottom, doctors a thin film of solution from the surface of the applicating roll as it enters the nip. Excess material doctored at the nip flows out the ends of the box and is recirculated for continuing application. Viscosity of these solutions is normally between 1 and 200 centipoise and the temperature may very between 55 and 185° F, depending on the material.

Dilute solutions (1 to 6% solids) of low-viscosity: modified corn or potato starch are used generally to provide smoothness and to lay down surface fibre fuzz normally present after drying the web to 4% moisture content. In addition to the smoothing action provided by the wet calendering, these materials provide control of curl, especially on sheeted stock where dissimilar furnishes are used on either surface of the sheet. In some cases, exaggerated curl must be built into paperboard for subsequent lamination, extrusion, or coating in roll form to counteract the effects of the post board converting operation.

Moderate to high concentration solutions (7 to 20% solids) of low to medium viscosity oxidized, chlorinated, or hydroxyethylated corn and/or potato starches may be used as calender stack treatments for improvement of smoothness, reduction of porosity, and slight grease resistance or improved gloss ink holdout. Dilute solutions (1 to 5% solids) of film forming polymers, such as polyvinly alcohol, carboxymethyl cellulose, sodium alginate, or carboxylated, styrene-maleic anhydride, are used for comparable properties. Most of these compounds form intimate bond with cellulose and provide a smooth lyophobic surface that resists ink and solvent penetration for improved depth of graphics reproduction.

White lined paperboard is manufactured to a given brightness by selection of bleached pulps and clean secondary fibres of appropriate quality. In some cases, a white surface may be improved in brightness and appearance, especially under fluorescent lighting by surface treatment with a water solution of flourescent whitener. This material absorbs radiation in the near ultra-violet region of the spectrum and re-emits this radiation in the visible region as a reenforcing contribution to normal brightness.

Slickness, water shedding, and release characteristics may be imparted to paperboard surfaces by calender treatment with materials such as wax emulsions, modified stearates, alkylketene dimers, or zirconium wax complexes. These materials form excellent bonds to cellulose and are printable or gluable coatings. They provide resistance against water or cold water waxing treatments.

Coating Applications

White pigmented dispersions of clay in a suitable carrying adhesive were applied to paperboard surfaces for printing quality upgrading during the 1940's. Clay coating applications were made with metering rod and print-on roll coaters for the most part. The advent of the air knife coater brought about a dramatic revolution in coating technology, in the 1950's, and resulted in a different approach to the production of white-surfaced paperboard. Coat weights in the range of 3 to 8 lb/MSF (10 to 25 lb/ream 24 × 36—500) with appreciable opacity and brightness now became possible at speeds comparable to uncoated papermaking grade production. Medium and high-velocity hot air impingement ovens together with infrared or steam cylinder drying of these water based coatings and subsequent dry calendering produced smooth, white, glossy paperaboards with unsurpassed printing quality, compared to white lined grades.

Economies of clay-coated paperboards have been well documented, due to the material saving by replacement of virgin bleached pulps with reclaimed secondary fibres. As a result, the topliner furnish of a typical 75 brightness coated paperboard is substantially different from an uncoated topliner.

Topliner Coated Board	Topliner Uncoaed Board
25% Semi biea, kraft or unbl. sulphite	25% Blea, kraft or blea, sulfite
35% Wet lap or de-inked tab cards	35% Blea, kraft Cuttings
20% Hard whites or blea, sulfite	20% Hard whites or blea, hardwood kraft
20% Soft whites or coated blanks	20% Soft whites

Coating formulations used in typical knife coaters very to some degree relative to type of adhesive and solids content, but brightness increase and coat weight are usually related to the viscosity and rheology of the formula used. Natural, water-soluble pigment binders are widely used in conjunction with the synthetic emulsion latexes to provide smooth, glossy, printable, and gluable coatings. Since most boxboard coatings are applied with air knife equipment, low solids and relatively low viscosity formulations are necessary to provide the proper coat weight and functional properties. The functional requirements, in addition to brightness and appearance, are pick resistance, ink receptivity, wet rub or handling resistance, dry marking or scuff resistance, and resistance to crazing or peeling on bending and gluing. A typical air knife coating formulation used by an on-machine operation to produce 75 brightness board would be as follows:

Air Knife Coating for 75 Brightness Bass Stock 60 Brightness, 3 lb. MSF

75 Parts	#1 Spray dried predispersed clay
7 Parts	Water-dispersible titanium dioxide
8 Parts	Styrene-butadiene latex
8 Parts	Soya protein
0.65 Part	Ammonia
0.6 Part	Defoamer
0.7 Part	Lubricant
0.05 Part	Insolubilizer

Such a formulation would be applied at a viscosity of about 100 to 300 centipoise and at approximately 40 to 45% solids. This coating would provide normal ink receptivity, gloss and varnish holdout, excellent pick resistance, and good wet rub or marking resistance. With adequate drying and calendering, this coating provides good flexibility and adhesion for bending and gluing in normal folding carton work.

A significant percentage of fourdrinier solid bleached sulfate board is used for food cartons for dry and humid cold storage. For the cold water wax, hot melt, modified paraffin, and curtain coatings applied to carton blanks for water shedding, board is usually treated with varying amounts of titanium dioxide in either the pigment coating and/or base furnish to provide waxed opacity. The change in refractive index to incident light entering the oiled or waxed cellulose sheet by titanium dioxide provides less apparent deopacifying or darkening, compared to an untreated board.

The off-machine carton blank coatings referred to provide not only water shedding protection and a glossy, scuff proof coating over printing inks, but provide varying levels of water vapour transmission resistance, grease resistance, and some gas or odor permeability resistance. Special hot melt coating equipment is essential to apply these materials, however, since the melting point range is 300 to 450°F. Some cartons may be coated both sides or overall for subsequent heat scaling on appropriate closing equipment. Other cartons are register coated with appropriate application pads to permit normal wet adhesive closing and economical use of the resin-wax coatings, but only where necessary.

CONVERTING OF CYLINDER PAPERBOARD

Printing White

Lined and clay-coated cylinder paperboard is currently being printed predominately on lithographic offset multicolour presses. Prior to the 1960's a high percentage of folding carton graphics was done on letterpress, but with the development of long-run, deep-etch plates and improved halftone fidelity, lithography rapidly displaced the relief process. Gravure has played a subordinate role in the total volume of boxboard printing, but is becoming increasingly popular for standard folding carton work. Letterset or dry offset and flexography are used to print somewhat less detail copy, but the volume remains comparatively low, relative to lithography, gravure, and letterpress.

A high percentage of folding cartons is printed in three or more colours and varnish. Paperboard is suitable for this type of decoration if it is smooth, lint and dirt free, has high surface strength and good ink receptivity and is square and flat for a high-speed, sheet-fed press. Printing speeds on paperboard sheet stock vary from about 1500 to 6500 sheets per hr, depending on the type of equipment used. Since the bulk of paperboard printing on sheets is done with the machine direction or grain of the stock parallel to the axis of the printing cylinder, thickness or caliper uniformity is of paramount importance. Pressure transfer of colours from the inked form of a relief plate or planographic blanket can be carried out at optimum quality only if paperboard uniformity provides a good makeready and minimum through-the-run lot adjustments. Multicolour overlapping forms require inks with good tack for rapid setting to provide maximum colour density and minimum distortion of copy. As a result, paperboard should have high surface strength and good cleanliness to prevent picking of any material and subsequent ink and print distortion. Further, ink receptivity and surface absorptivity should be relatively constant to provide uniform colour control for optimum customer acceptance in a retail display. Gloss inks and/or overprint varnishes are used to provide maximum detail, compared to photographic reproduction, and these materials must be balanced for adhesion to a uniformly absorptive paperboard surface to provide constant scuff and abrasion resistance.

High-speed, sheet-fed printing of paperboard requires flat, stable, non-wavy loads with a moisture content in approximate equilibrium with the press room environment. Pack-up or loss of moisture content by a cellulosic sheet in order to reach equilibrium results in curly or wavy or dished contours. Such stock will not feed through automatic feeders, end and side guides, and transfer grippers without erratic register and/or wrinkled printing copy. The misregister and wrinkling problems are most commonly found on multipress and/or offset operations under the above non-equilibrium conditions.

Paperboard sheets after multicolour printing should deliver into a pile with suitable anti-setoff spray protection on the wet ink film to provide a smooth, block-free, set-off free unit without marred printing (prior to cutting and creasing). Dry starch sprays deposited from electrostatic rollers as the wet sheet leaves the last printing unit separate the partially set inked image from the back of the next depositing sheet. By virtue of their spherical nature, starch sprays prevent ink setoff without impairing ink drying. Non-uniform, curly or wavy paperboard stock may cause an uneven pressure distribution and induce ink setoff, unless the height of the printed pile is restricted to small lifts. Rapid setting inks at low ink film thicknesses in conjunction with rapid absorption coatings may minimize setoff, but high ink gloss after drying is usually compromised. Infrared heating bars and dielectric or microwave heat absorption units are being investigated to promote more rapid ink setting, but have not gained wide acceptance in paperboard printing. Uncoated paperboard stocks immobilize inks more readily than coated boards, but generally require higher ink film thicknesses for colour density, and do not provide the high reproduction fidelity of the coated boards.

Rotogravure printing of paperboard is gaining greater acceptance for folding carton work, especially on large volume runs of standardized copy and style. Roll fed presses 20 to 48 in, in width and from three to eight colour (including back side printers) stations are capable of producing flat, blanked, printed cartons ready for gluing or filling in the minimum period of time after press makeready. Resin-solvent colours may be applied to paperboard from intaglio cylinders and dried on a moving web at speeds from 100 to 100 ft/min. Speeds up to 350 ft per min are possible with in-line reciprocating blanking and stripping directly after multicolour close register printing. Higher printing seeds are possible in conjunction with in-line rotary blankers and multiple carton deliveries. Maximum printing speeds are accomplished by rewinding the decorated web, followed by off-line reciprocating blanking and stripping at slower speeds.

Flexographic presses are beginning to occupy more board volume for relatively low quality carton work. These roll-fed presses print alcohol and/or water based inks from rubber or synthetic composition plates, and operate in a manner similar to rotogravure presses. A dry print is produced from a web in a very short period of time after ink transfer by solvent evaporation. Ink application is from a relief rather than intaglio plate, and usually the halftone fidelity is coarse, compared to rotogravure reproduc-tion. Flexographic plates are made up to 100-line screens copy, but rotogravure cylinders, by most engraving methods, provide plates in rulings from 150 to 300-lines per in. The superiority of the rotogravure method for detail in quite apparent, although the paperboard smoothness requirements for flexographic are not as demanding as for intaglio printing.

Although most relief printing on paperboard is conducted on sheet-feed presses, a significant portion of letterpress work is done on web-fed presses followed by in-line carton blanking. The use of quick set solvent-oil inks, and minimum ink coverage on creases facilitates quality carton work in a minimum period of time. Dry blanked, stripped shells are ready for conversion into glued, filled cartons for shipment in corrugated containers within three to five hr after printing. Faithful halftone printing is accomplished in screen rulings from 85 to 120 lines per in, on this equipment with good quality, clay-coated paperboard.

Improved production at less cost on short run folding carton work has resulted from the use of photopolymer printing plates on existing rotary letterpress equipment. These strong, lightweight, chemically-hardened relief plates are quickly prepared and rapidly mounted on modified printing and inking cylinders for fast makeready and production running. Rapid step and repeats eliminate individual plate strike-in and register, although very fine halftones cannot be printed at letterpress ink films with very good fidelity. Chemical etching does not provide exceptionally sharp image shoulders and sufficient relief to allow inking rollers to be set without feathering on printing copy.

These same types of photoplymer printing plates may be prepared for use on rotary offset equipment for rapid makeready and running. These thin aluminum plates, with very fine background or non-print area etched below the image area, provide the basis for ink transfer from plate to blanket cylinder, without the use of the normal offset fountain solution. Halftone fidelity again is not as sharp as that on conventional offset, due to the lack of sharp separation of image from non-image area in the etching process. However, makeready is rapid, and less sophisti-cated copy may be reproduced with good quality on a wide range of paperboard stocks.

A recent innovation in the paperboard folding carton is the laminating of pre-printed paper to a dark or chipboard base stock. Light weight papers (20# to 80#: 24 × 36-500) are printed in rolls by the gravure or flexographic process. These papers are then combined in a laminating nip with a dextrine or wax laminant, and immediately diecut, blanked, and stripped in register with the printed copy on a reciprocating in-line blanker. Although this method is not as economical as conventional paperboard conversion, maximum advantage is taken of the printing, strength, and opacity characteristics of the paper stock before lamination. In addition, on wax laminations of coated litho or lining paper, water vapour barrier for packaging hygroscopic materials is a valuable by product. An even more valuable barrier is obtained by casein-latex adhesive lamination of foil or foil-paper to chipboard for water vapour solvent and grease barrier properties, as well as a highly decorative printed effect.

Cutting and Creasing

Paperboard for the most part is cut and creased into carton blanks in off-line, sheet fed operations, Flatbed cylinder creasers, reciprocating platen creasers, and rotary cylinder creasers are used to process printed, sheet-fed image into flat carton blanks. Since a high percentage of cartons are folded and side-seam glued prior to shipment to the packer, good bending or folding quality is essential so that creases do not rupture. Appropriate creasing conditions to provide score profiles with minimum top liner tension on paperboard after folding are essential in order to minimize waste in the cartoning operation.

In order to provide a suitable material for cutting, creasing, and forming into folding carton blanks, cylinder paperboard must have:

(1) adequate top liner tensile and elongation in the principle (MD) or grain direction as well as non-principle (CD) or cross direction.

(2) adequate back liner tensile and elongation in both grain directions.

(3) suitable tendency of top liner to delaminate from underliner, or filler plies in paperboard within scoreline under standard creasing parameters or shearing stress.

(4) moisture content over 4.5% but not over 8.5%.

Extensive research and development work, performed in conjunction with a project by Boxboard Research and Development Association, resulted in a standard TAPPI test (T-495 *su* 64) for evaluating the bending quality of paperboard. Results of extensive investigation by A.D. Little. Inc. verified the theoretical value of the standard test and creasing parameters in actual practice. Conditions of male rule width, female crease width, depth of rule penetration, and crease width to board thickness ratio were found to coincide with factors necessary to produce minimum topliner tension on both cross-grain as well as with-grain creases after folding.

Standard test conditions recommended in TAPPI T-495-*su* 64 are designed to duplicate low relative humidity (RH) or equilibrium moisture conditions generally found in unconditioned converting plants during winter. Bending quality has been shown to pass through a minimum at 35% RH as equilibrium relative humidity is reduced from 65% to 20% RH. Converting plant conditioning to standard conditions on a year round basis would eliminate much carton waste currently generated by non-equilibrium environments.

Although principles of cutting paperboard with hardened steel knives against metal jackets or platens have not been well documented, uniform moisture gradients in paperboard provide the soundest basis for sharp, lint-free cutting. Thickness, liner strength and/or moisture variation are the most prevalent causes of poor cutting when a cutting makeready is applied correctly in conjunction with good creasing parameters. Metal to metal contact of hardened steel knives against softer steel jackets or platens produces undue edge dulling in a small number of impressions, unless some care is taken to provide spotting softness, under the jacket or platen, with paper to equalize cutting pressure distribution.

A recent development in high-speed creasing techniques is the Harris-B11 rotary cutting press developed in conjunction with American Can Co., Research and Development Department. This press uses male and female dies composed of photographically etched steel elements wrapped around geared cylinders in perfect register and synchronization. While creasing parameters are similar to those in conventional equipment, cutting is accomplished by the scissors shear approach of two steel lands to each other on the matched steel plates. Paperboard is reduced in thickness to less than one-third of its original thickness, and the resulting compaction explodes the paperboard apart, during element separation, with less than normal lint and with a sharp, square edge.

Automatic trim removal devices, generally called pin strippers, are being used extensively after cylinder or platen creasers to facilitate flat carton blank delivery. These strippers pick board trim between cartons in the (after cutting) to eliminate hand or air hammer stripping. The boxboard cutting waste is fed into a pneumatic collector tube, and conveyed either directly to baler to reclamation as secondary fibre, or dropped directly into a continuous extraction hydrapulper for immediate repulping and use in further cylinder paperboard manufacture.

Gluing and Sealing

Although styles of folding cartons vary widely, depending on the nature, size, and weight of the product packaged, many are sealed on at least one seam prior to shipment to the packer. Most rectangular style cartons have at least four panels and side seam, so that at least four creases (scores) are folded in the closing operation. Folding cartons shipped in a flat glued from are usually processed through a straight line side seam gluer. In this operation, the first (or side seam) score and third score are prefolded 160° from the horizontal toward the back side of the board, then flattened to original position. Immediately following, the second and fourth scores are folded 180°, and the side seam is glued.

24

Paper Testing

Paper and paperboard are used in a great variety of forms, distinguished by a wide range of properties to satisfy many different use requirements. The identification and expression of these differences require the application of standard test methods. Transactions between producer and user of paper products, the control of the manufacturing process, and the development of improved products and more efficient techniques all depend on reliable test methods.

The testing of paper and the definition of the properties are noteworthy for several characteristic features. Most of the properties that determine the usefulness of paper are not physical absolutes, but depend on the instrument or equipment used and on the details of testing procedure. For example, such a simple property as tensile strength depends both on the rate of load application and on the length of the test specimen, since a longer span increases the chance of finding a weak area. This is also true with other important properties such as brightness, gloss, tearing strength, folding endurance, stiffness and permeability. The property is defined in terms of instrument and method.

The diversity in the uses of paper has led to a great proliferation of test methods. Practically all paper manufactures, as well as converters and large buyers of paper, have developed test methods to evaluate properties of paper of special interest to themselves. Some of these tests have remained intramural others have been adopted widely and have been recognized as standard methods.

STANDARD TEST METHODS

The most authoritative body of test methods for pulp and paper is that published by the Technical Association of the Pulp and Paper Industry (U.S.) in losse-leaf form as Tappi Standards. A closely related body of standards is published by he American Society for Testing and maerials (Philadelphia, Pa.). Part 15 of the 1968 Book of ASTM Standards contains the methods relating to paper, packaging and cellulosic materials. The Tappi and ASTM standards closely correspond to each other in essential details.

The Testing Division of Tappi comprises 18 committees covering all aspects of testing of importance to the pulp and paper industry. The responsibility for each of the methods contained in the Tappi Standards Book is assigned to the appropriate committee. Among the important duties of each of these committees is a periodic review, at least every five years, of the methods under its jurisdiction.

Overall responsibility for the Tappi Standards rests with the Standards Committee which is composed of the chairman and 12 other members appointed by the President of Tappi, with the advice and consent of the Executive Committee. Four members are appointed annually to serve three-year terms. The Standards Committee approves or disapproves standards on the basis of a consensus of those substantially concerned with technical content and editorial quality. A consensus implies much fuller agreement than a simple majority, but it does not necessarily imply unanimity.

The Tappi Standards Books contains Standard Methods, Methods (until recently called Tentative Standards) and Historical Methods. A Standard is defined as a method that the responsible Technical Committee and the Standards Committee believe to have qualities of accuracy and precision suitable for referee use. A Suggested Method is one that the responsible committee considers the best available for its intended purpose, but not having known accuracy and precision required of a Standard. A Suggested Method is approved by simple majority vote of the Standards Committee. A Tappi Standard or Suggested Method no longer in general use, but which retains usefulness as a literature reference, is retained as a Historical Method by action of the Standards Committee.

The technical committees of Tappi are responsible for drafting new or revising existing test methods. Any committee may initiate such action in accordance with applicable Tappi regulations. The proposed method of revision is to be developed by a "task group" appointed by he committee chairman. The method as developed by the task group is submitted to the responsible technical committee for letter ballot. Approval by three-fourths of the voting members of the committee is required. After approval by the appropriate committee and division chairman, the proposed or revised method is submitted to the Standards Committee.

Relative Humidity in Relation to Paper Properties

It is appropriate to introduce the subject of paper testing with a discussion of the effect of moisture content on the properties of paper. Cellulosic fibres are hygroscopic, i.e., they are capable of absorbing water from the surrounding atmosphere. The amount of absorbed water depends on the relative humidity and the temperature of the air in contact with the paper. Further, under the same humidity and temperature conditions, a sample of paper may have different moisture contents, depending on whether the sample approached these conditions from a more dry state or from a more moist state (hysteresis). Finally, most physical properties of paper undergo change as a result of variations in moisture content.

Water has the effect of plasticizing the cellulose fibre and of relaxing and weakening the interfibre bonding. Hence, the moisture content has a marked effect upon many paper properties. Paper becomes notably stiffer and less flexible under dry conditions. Such properties as folding endurance, tearing strength, and stretch reach maximum values at relatively high humidities (80 to 90% RH) and decrease at low humidities when the fibres become more stiff and brittle. Tensile strength reaches maxmum value in the region of low humidity and steadily decreases with increasing moisture content, presumably because of the weakening effect on the interfibre bonding. Most of these changes in paper properties due to changes in moisture content are fully reversible, however, there are some that are not. For example, some papers undergo a permanent loss in gloss when exposed to humidities above 85%.

The above considerations apply to the moisture range from completely dry to that prevailing at about 95% RH and at room temperature. Any additional wetting leads to the presence of free water in the sheet, resulting in the more profound and permanent effects.

Hysteresis

Figure 1 shows moisture sorption isotherms for a typical paper formed from relatively pure cellulosic fibres.

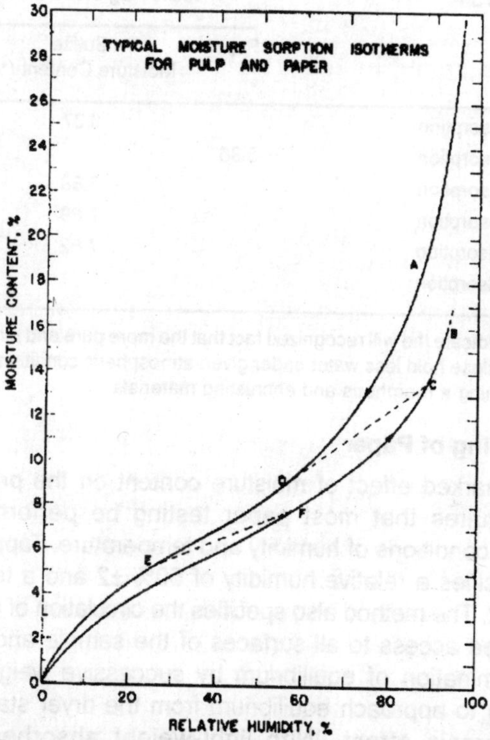

Fig. 1. Typical mosture sorption isotherms for pulp and paper.

The desorption of cellulose that has never been dried is shown in curve A. The corresponding adsorption is shown in curve B. These curves outline the boundaries of the equilibrium area. Partial absorption to a relative humidity corresponding to point C, followed by desorption, results in the course of line CD and, similarly, partial desorption to point E, followed by adsorption, results in the course shown by dotted line EF. All cellulosic materials so far is known exhibit hysteresis and similar sigmoid shape isotherms.

Table 1 shows moisture content values of several types of paper at various relative humidity values.

Table 1: Moisture content values of several types of paper at various relative humidity values

Temperature 73°F	100% Rag Paper	Bleached Sulfite	Ground Wood
	Moisture Content (%)		
52.4% RH desorption		8.37	
52.6% RH desorption	5.86		
52.4% RH adsorption		7.88	
48.0% RH desorption		7.89	
48.0% RH adsorption		7.62	
50.0% RH adsorption			9.70

The figures indicate the will recognized fact that the more pure and more crystalline forms of cellulose hold less water under given atmospheric conditions than do the forms containing a morphous and encrusting materials.

Conditioning of Paper

The marked effect of moisture content on the properties of paper requires that most paper testing be performed under controlled conditions of humidity and temperature. Tappi Standard T402 specifies a relative humidity of 50% ±2 and a temperature of 23°C ±2. The method also specifies the circulation of conditioned air with free access to all surfaces of the sample and describes the determination of equilibrium by successive weighings. It is customary to approach equilibrium from the dryer state to avoid the hysteresis effect. With light-weight absorbent papers, equilibrium is reached relatively quickly, 15 to 30 min. As density and weight of paper or paperboard increases, equilibrium requires a much longer time, because of the slow rate of diffusion of moisture to the interior the sample.

Moisture in paper is normally determined by loss in weight when dried at 105°C ±3 (T412-OS63)*. The method is satisfactory

*Designations of this type refer to Tappi methods. OS means official standard and the final number refers to the year of latest revision.

for papers not containing volatile or fusible components. For such papers, a toluene distillation method is described in T484.

Conditioning of paper is also of importance in many printing and converting operations. In addition to the effect of moisture content on physical properties, it also determines the build-up of static of the paper sheet subjected to pressure (piezo-effect) and to friction. The tendency for paper to develop static becomes greater with increasing dryness.

Because of the importance of instantaneous and continuous measurement of moisture content of paper, extensive effort has been devoted to the development of "moisture gauges". The electrical resistance and the dielectric constant of paper both vary with moisture content. Scanning instruments have been devised to indicate moisture content of paper continuously at a location during its travel through the paper machine. Practical difficulties of measurement have limited the usefulness of such gauges. The absorption and reflectance of certain bands of infrared and micro-wave radiation by paper are affected by its moisture content, and this has been used as a basis for a moisture gauge system.

DIMENSIONAL STABILITY OF PAPER

An important consequence of the sorption and desorption of water by paper is the change in dimension that usually accompanies changes in moisture content. Such changes in dimension may seriously affect register in printing processes and interfere with the use of such items as tabulating cards. Uneven dimensional changes cause undesirable cockling and curling. For these reasons, much study and effort have been devoted to elucidating the causes for shrinking and expansion of papers and to devising means for increasing dimensional stability.

Dimensional changes in paper originate in the swelling and contraction of the individual fibres. It has been observed that cellulosic fibres swell in diameter from 15 to 20% in passing from the dry condition to the fibre saturation point. It is impossible to be precise about the degree of this swelling because paper-making fibres differ considerably in this property, and because the irregular cross-section of fibres creates difficulty in defining diameter. Moreover, the definition of fibre saturation point is not exact. However, in contrast to the considerable expansion in fibre diameter in the lateral dimension, the longitudinal expansion is practically negligible, being estimated at no more than 5% of the lateral swelling.

Even though the swelling of fibre is the cause of expansion and contraction of paper, there is no direct relationship between the two phenomena. Paper samples made from the same fibre and presumably having the same fibre swelling characteristics may exhibit either, negligible or maximum dimensional changes, depending on conditions of stock preparation and conditions of sheet forming and drying. The following factors are considered to be most important in dimensional stability of paper.

(1) **Shrinkage during drying.** It is well recognized that a freshly formed wet sheet of paper, allowed to shrink freely during drying, undergoes a considerable degree of contraction and also shows a high degree of hygro-expansivity upon rewetting. Likewise, when such a sheet is constrained from shrinking during drying, the hygro-expansivity is reduced. In fact, there is fairly direct relationship between shrinkage during drying and the hygro-expansivity for paper made from the same stock and under otherwise similar conditions.

In machine-made paper, it is obvious that the tension acting to pull the sheet through the machine tends to constrain shrinkage, whereas in the cross direction, there is no corresponding force. At a result, machine-made papers shrink more in cross direction and show from two to three times greater hygroexpansivity in the cross direction than in the machine direction. In addition to the effect of greater shrinkage in the cross direction, the tendency of fibres to be preferentially oriented in the machine direction also contributes to greater cross direction hygroexpansivity, because of greater lateral swelling of the individual fibres.

It is impossible to give exact figures for the amount of expansion and contraction undergone by paper because of the many factors which contribute to this property. However, it is common for papers to show dimensional changes from somewhat less than 0.5% to about 1% in the cross direction in passing from a very dry atmosphere to a very moist atmosphere. Corresponding changes in the machine direction could range from negligible to about 0.5%.

(2) **Degree of interfibre bonding.** It is well recognized that paper made from highly beaten, slow stock shows a high degree of shrinkage during drying and a high degree of hygroexpansivity. Paper made from free stock shows less shrinkage during drying and greater dimensional stability. It has been shown that the equilibrium moisture content of highly beaten fibre is only very slightly greater than that of unbeaten fibre and, hence, cannot afford an explanation for greater hygroexpansivity. However, the greater inter-fibre bonded area of sheets made from highly beaten stocks or from pulps high in hemicellulose results in a condition where changes in dimensions of fibres are communicated directly to the rigid structure of the sheet.

In contrast, fibres in a lightly bonded sheet are more free to move and hence, their dimensional changes have less effect on the structure as a whole.

(3) **Cross-linking of cellulose.** Since the origin of dimensional instability of paper lies in the swelling characteristics of fibre, a reduction in that swelling should be beneficial. The swelling of cellulosic fibres when exposed to moisture may b e reduced by chemical means, such as cross linking of the cellulose structure by formaldehyde or by resins. Moderate improvement in dimensional stability may be achieved by such treatment, (similar to the development of wet strength in paper), but elimination of swelling in cellulose fibre by chemical means is accompained by drastic changes in fibre properties that would be detrimental to tear strength and folding endurance. The subject of reduction of swelling by chemical means is reported in a recent article by Stamm.

(4) **Non-swelling fibre.** Again, since fibre swelling is the origin of dimensional changes, the use of a non-swelling fibre such a nylon, polyethylene, or glass suggests itself. Papers made of such fibres do show dimensional stability, and if the higher cost is permissible, they represent a solution to the problem. Considerable benefit has also been reported from incorporating small amounts of non-

swelling synthetic fibre in wood furnishes. In this connection, a note of caution should be sounded. Since non-swelling fibres are also non-bonding, it may be that improvement in dimensional stability is due to reduced interfibre bonding (see above) and can be accompanied by considerable loss in strength.

The interested reader will find further information on dimensional stability in recent review articles by Brecht, Rance and Nordmann.

SUBSTANCE AND QUANTITY MEASUREMENT OF PAPER

Basis Weight

The weight or substance paper unit area is obviously fundamental in paper and paperboard products. From the earliest use of paper in the printing trades, it has been measured in reams, originally comprising 480 sheets (20 quires), but now also used to signify 500 sheets (long ream). Hence. "ream weight" is a common term to signify the weight of a lot or batch of paper. It happens that the printing trades use a variety of sheet sizes, and hence, there can be numerous ream weights for paper having the same basis weight depending on sheet size and count. The most common "standard" reams are :

24 × 36 × 480 = 414.720 sq in.

24 × 36 × 500 = 432.000 sq in.

25 × 40 × 500 = 5000,000 sq in.

In the paperboard industry, the most common method in North America of expressing substance is in pounds per 1000 sq ft.

In most European countries, and increasingly throughout the world, basis weight is reported in grams per square meter. This is the recommended expression of basis weight in TAPPI Standards. Conversion factors from g/m to other common basis weights are as follows:

to lb 24 × 36 × 480 ream, multiply by -0.59.

to lb 24 × 36 × 500 ream, multiply by -0.615

to lb 25 × 40 × 500 ream, multiply by -0.71

to lb/1000 sq ft, multiply by -0.205

The determination of basis weight is described in TAPPI Standard T410. The sample to be tested in brought to equilibrium under standard conditions. The specimens of paper to be weighed shall consist, whenever possible, of 10 sheets, each of at least 100 sq in of area.

The nature of the paper-making process is such that perfect distribution of fibre and of other constituents of the sheet is difficult to attain. Hence, the uniformity of basis weight is often as important as the average weight. The search for greater uniformity in weight distribution (both across the width of the paper machine and in the length-wise direction of the sheet) has led to the use of scanning devices to monitor paper weight continuously during manufacturing. These devices normally use the absorption of radiation, such as beta rays, as a measure of sheet substance. Proper functioning of such a system is highly dependent on particular mill and machine conditions and require close cooperation between equipment supplier and the paper manufacturer.

Thickness and Density of Paper

The thickness of paper or paperboard is the caliper (in thousandths of an inch) of a single sheet when placed under a steady pressure of 7 to 9 psi, between two circular and parallel plane surfaces, the smaller of which has an area of 0.25 sq in. (160 sq mm). In metric units, the thickness is expressed in mm, and the pressure limits are 0.49 to 0.63 kg/cm^2. Details of the apparatus and method will be found in Tappi Method T411.

The density of paper or paperboard is the weight per unit volume or specific gravity g/cm^3. Density is calculated from basis weight and thickness as follows :

$$D = \frac{W_1}{T_1 \times 18.08} = \frac{W_2}{T_2}$$

where

W_1 = basis weight in pounds (25 × 40 = 500)

W_2 = basis weight in g/m

T_1 = thickness in mils (.001 in.)

T_2 = thickness in microns (.001 mm)

The thickness of paper at constant basic weight, hence the density, may range over relatively wide limits. For example, the density of glassine may be as high as 1.4 as one extreme, while that of creped wadding may be as low as 0.1. The density of paper is increased by the use of pulp that is characterized by fine, easily hydrated fibre and by extensive beating. Fibres that tend to remain stiff in the wet state, such as groundwood and some high yield pulps, produce papers that are bulky and less dense. Subjecting the sheets to wet pressing or calendering obviously increases the density. Physical treatments, such as creping and some types of embossing, reduce the apparent of paper.

STRENGTH AND DURABILITY PROPERTIES OF PAPER

The resistance to rupture when subjected to various stresses in an important property in practically all grades of paper. Most papers require a certain minimum strength to withstand the treatment received by the product in use, but even where the use requirement for strength is not severe, the paper must be strong enough to permit efficient handling in the various papermaking, converting, or printing operations involved in its manufacture. ***Tensile strength*** is the maximum tensile stress developed in a tension test carried to rupture under prescribed conditions. The stress is expressed as the force per unit width of test specimen, the recommended units being kilograms per centimeter; however, pounds per inch is still commonly used in this country. A variety of machines are available for the measurement of tensife stress. Some of these machines are equipped to measure total elongation of the specimen and to draw a stress-strain curve from which the elastic modulus can be calculated.

The following precautions are important in the tensile test:

(1) **Sampling**, There is some non-uniformity in the best of papers, and hence, samples must be sufficient in number and adequately distributed to give an accurate test.

(2) **Conditioning**. Tensile strength of paper is sensitive to moisture content, and hence, due regard must be given to proper conditioning of the sample.

(3) **Cutting of Specimens**. The width of strip for tensile testing is normally either 15 mm or 1 in. Specimens must be cut to correct width and with parallel sides.

(4) **Rate of Loading.** Paper exhibits plastic properties when stressed, and hence the ultimate strength is appreciably affected by rate of loading. For practical purposes, it is sufficient to adjust the rate of load, or time to break, to avoid excessively fast, slow, or uneven loading TAPPI Standard T 404 specifies that the load applied in any second shall not exceed that applied in the previous second by more than 10%. It has been recently proposed in TAPPI Committee Assignment 8188 that the rate of law separation in tensile testing shall be 25 ± 5 mm/min.

(5) **Grain.** Machine made paper has "grain", i. e., it shows different physical properties in the two directions. Hence, tensile testing must be performed in both the machine direction and the cross-machine direction of the paper. The ratio between these two values of strength is an important property of paper.

Factors Affecting Tensile Strength

The tensile strength of paper is determined by the combined effect of the following factors: (1) the strength of the individual fibres of the stock furnish. (2) the average length of the fibre. (3) the inherent bonding ability of the fibre surface both in terms of bonded area and of strength per unit of bonded area and (4) the structure and formation of the sheet.

The great importance of the interfibre bonding in paper has led to the belief that this is the predominant factor in tensile strength, which fibre strength playing a secondary role. A study by J. A.Van den Akker, in which the percentage of ruptured fibres in a paper break is determined, showed that fibre strength is a substantial component of fibre strength. Also it is well recognized that fibre may be chemically degraded and weakened in the pulping and bleaching processes. Such fibre produces weak paper, not only because the fibre is easily ruptured in the testing of the paper, but also because the fibre cannot withstand the beating and refining action that is an essential preliminary to paper manufacture.

A long fibre is essential for making strong paper, and no papers of high strength are made from short-fibred furnishes. However, there is a limit to which longer fibres will contribute to paper strength, because they result in sheets with "wild" and uneven formation. A poorly formed sheet with thick and thin areas will have poor strength. The limit of fibre length for most paper making is in the order of 1/8 to 1/4 in. This value varies considerably, due to such factors as ratio of fibre length to diameter, head box consistency, and presence of colloidal (surface-active) agents.

The inherent bonding ability of the fibres of a paper stock is of outstanding importance in paper strength. It is well recognized that some pulps have a strong tendency to form interfibre bonds while others have only a slight tendency to do so. The beating and refining action has the effect of swelling the fibre by increasing the imbibition of water, of rupturing and fibrillating the fibre surface, and of rendering the fibre more flexible and better able to mat and contact neighboring fibres. All these effects enhance the interfibre bonding ability of the stock. Pressure exerted upon the wet sheet is also an important factor in promoting bonding. The bonding ability of a paper stock is increased by the addition of adhesive agents that can be adsorbed by the fibre surface and act as a cementing agent between fibres.

Stretch of Paper

It is common in performing the tensile test to determine the elongation of the test specimen while it is undergoing the test. This elongation is usually expressed as per cent stretch to rupture. The tensile machine may also be equipped to draw the load-elongation curve. The importance of the stress-strain curve is becoming increasingly recognized in predicting the durability performance of many paper products. The area under the curve resulting from plotting stress vs elongation is a measure of the work done or the energy absorbed in breaking the paper.

Tensile energy absorption (TEA) is expressed in the metric system as g-mm/mm^2 according to the equation:

TEA = 100 A/LW.

A = area under load-elongation curve in kg-cm

L = initial test span in cm

W = specimen width in cm.

For many uses, the energy absorption is more important to durability than is the tensile strength. There are numerous paper-making factors that influence the stretch of paper, such as fibre elasticity and strength, the density of the paper, formation, and the conditions of drying, particularly whether the sheet is allowed to shrink during drying or is held taut. For papers in which a high degree of stretch is sought, it is necessary to perform a physical disruption of the sheet subsequent to its formation, usually a type of creping by blade, roll, or belt or by special types of embossing. It is also possible to obtain high values of stretch in paper by using elastomeric bonding agents (rubber) as the principal cementing agents between fibres.

The stretch of normal flat paper does not usually exceed 5%. Special multiwall bag stock is being made with stretch over 10% and creped papers can be made with over 100% stretch in the machine direction.

Wet Tensile Strength

Because some paper products are subjected to wetting by water in their normal use, wet tensile strength testing has become of importance and is described in TAPPI Method T456. This test is essentially the same as the dry tensile test, except that the test specimen is watted to complete saturation over a prescribed distance between the jaws of the tensile tester. This test is primarily for absorbent papers, such as paper towels, sanitary tissues, filter paper, and the like, which readily become wet and whose strength when wet is of importance. It is important to distinguish between the strength of paper in the wet state and the retention of strength by a paper, because it resists wetting. Practically any paper will become wetted eventually if soaking is sufficiently prolonged. Paper that has not been especially treated for wet strength shows a value in this property of from 4 to 8% of its dry strength. By treatment of the paper by small quantities (1 to 5%) of thermo-setting aminoplast resins, it is possible to increase the wet strength to about 40% of the dry strength.

Zero Span Tensile Strength

This method, described in Tappi Methods T321 and T481 provides means for determining an index of the average ultimate strength of individual fibres either in a pulp test handsheet or in a commercial paper sample. Also, it may be used to indicate the degree of bonding between the fibres of a sheet, by the ratio between normal and the zero span breaking lengths of the test sheets with randomly oriented fibres.

The means for accomplishing this test are a specially constructed pair of supplementary jaws that are inserted in the jaws of a conventional tensile testing machine. They are so designed that they clamp adjacent areas of the test strip with zero jaw separation at the start of the test.

When this test is properly conducted, the strength obtained will always exceed the normal tensile strength of a paper sample, usually by a substantial amount. It has been estimated that the zero span test is about 3/8 of the ultimate fibre strength of the fibres composing the sheet.

Transverse Tensile Test

Normally we consider a paper sheet to have two directions of strength, namely, the machine direction (x axis) and the across-machine direction (y axis). Another direction of strength exists at right angles to the plane of the sheet (z axis or transverse tensile strength). The importance of sheet strength or coherence in this direction has long been recognized in the printing industry where picking of fibres from the surface of the sheet is an undesirable paper quality.

The time-honoured method of determining the resistance of paper to picking consists in depositing upon the surface of the paper a series of waxes having graded degrees of adhesive strength and in determining which wax will just lift off fibres from the paper surface (Tappi Method T459su-65). This a valuable as a practical use test, but the results are obviously only approximate and are of limited usefulness in determining the structure of paper.

Bursting Strength of Paper

One of the oldest and most widely used of the strength tests for paper and paperboard is the bursting test, usually called the Mullen test from one of the early instruments used for its determination. Tappi Method T403 defines bursting strength as the hydrostatic pressure in pounds per square inch (psi) required to produce rupture of the material when the pressure is applied at a controlled increasing rate through a rubber diaphragm to a circular area, 1.20 in, in diameter of the material under test. The area is initially flat and is held rigidly at the circumference, but is free to bulge under the increasing pressure of the test. The method is designed to measure the bursting strength of paper and paper products have a strength of .250 psi and in the form of flat sheets not over 0.25 in thick.

The primary function of the bursting test is to indicate the resistance of a paper product to rupture in use. It is quick and easy to perform and one test is sufficient for both directions of machine-made paper, whereas average tensile strength requires testing in both principal directions of the paper. For these reasons, the burst test has found almost universal use throughout the paper industry even for the testing of laboratory had sheets where the purpose of testing is to determine fundamental relationships rather than to predict in use performance of the particular paper. The bursting test is the result of a combination of factors. Obviously the amount of interfiber bonding and individual fibre strength is of predominant importance in bursting strength, as it is in tensile. However burst is also affected by the ratio of machine and cross-direction strength and by the stretch of the paper, and probably by other properties. The tensile and burst curves in the beating cycle of pulp are roughly parallel, but they also show divergences that can be only approximately explained. A recent article reports data for various strength factors of pulp, including burst and tensile, under various beating conditions.

A number of investigators have found that the correlation of burst tests among different laboratories and using different instruments leaves much to be desired. These reports emphasize the importance of vigilance in keeping the instrument in good condition and the testing procedures carefully controlled.

Tearing Strength

Another test of significance in determining the resistance to rupture of paper is that for tearing resistance. TAPPI Method T414 is designed to determine the average force in grams required to tear a single sheet of paper after the tear has been started. The results obtained by this procedure are usually designated simply as "tearing resistance." More properly, the results should be called "internal tearing resistance", as distinguished from "initial" for "edge" tearing resistance described in TAPPI method T470.

The most common form of instrument for determining tearing resistance is the Standard Elmendorf tear tester. This apparatus comprises a stationary clamp and, suitably aligned therewith, a second movable clamp carried on a pendulum (formed by a sector of a wheel or circle) that is free to swing on a substantially frictionless bearing. The pendulum carries a circumferential scale, graduated from 0 to 100 to read against a pointer that shows the retarding effect on the swing of the pendulum of the tearing of the paper speciment.

It will be noted that the retarding of the pendulum swing is a measure of work done, that is, the product of the force and the distance through which it acts. However, the scale is so calibrated as to indicate the average force required to tear one sheet of paper when the tearing test takes place through a standard distance. The standard sample is specified as sixteen sheets of paper each to be torn through a distance of 4.3 cm. When a sheet of paper is torn a certain distance, one sector having held fast while the other sector moves, the force acts through a distance twice that of the tear. Hence, the total distance of the teat test is 16 × 4.3 × 2 = 137.6 cm. Accordingly, if the reading on the scale after performing the test is 50, then the work done is 50 × 137.6 = 8800 g-cm.

It is essential that each instrument be calibrated to make sure of the correct ratio between scale reading and work done. It is unnecessary to repeat the calibration of the instrument, providing it is kept in adjustment and no parts become changed or worn. The tearing distance from the point of the initial slit and the edge of the sheet should be frequently checked. The instrument must be level.

The results are reported as grams force required to tear a single sheet. Since the scale readings are made 1/6 the actual values, this is calculated by multiplying the average instrument reading by 16 and dividing by the number of sheets tested. The force required to tear a sheet or paper is indication of its performance in use. Heavier papers will naturally have more tearing resistance than light papers. It is often important to determine the inherent tearing quality of fibre, independent of the factor of sheet weight. In Tappi Method T220, Physical Testing of Pulp Handsheets, a tear factor is determined from the equation:

Tear factor = 100 e/r

where e is the force in grams to tear a single sheet, as described above, and r is the basis weight in grams per square meter. This factor, which has been called the "tearing area", is equivalent to the number of square decimetres (100 sq dm = 1 sq metre) of paper, the weight of which, if applied to single sheet, would cause a tear to progress. Thus, it is analogous to the concept "breaking length" in tensile strength testing.

Factors Influencing Tearing Strength

As with many performance tests of paper, tearing strength is the result of a number of factors that are incompletely understood. The tearing test is very sensitive to the physical properties of the fibre. It is traditional in the industry that alkaline-cooked pulps have higher tear than corresponding acid-cooked pulps, even when other durability tests are quite comparable. Any degradation of fibre in cooking or bleaching shows up dramatically in loss of tear. It is assumed that acid-cooked pulps suffer greater fibre degradation that do alkaline-cooked pulps. The tearing strength of finished paper is reduced, by such influences as heat and acidity, to a much greater degree than is tensile strength.

Fibre length and interfiber bonding are both important factors in tearing strength. That longer fibres improve tear strength is well recognized. The explanation is straight-forward; longer fibres tend to distribute the stress over a greater area, over more fibres and more bonds, while short fibres allow the stress to be concentrated in a smaller area. The role of interfiber bonding is more complex. A low degree of interfiber bonding gives low tear, because the fibres pull apart easily. As the inerfiber bonding increases, the tear value rises to a maximum and then decreases. The phenomenon is often exhibited in beating cycle of a pulp. In the "beating curve", the increased inter-fibre bonding is accompanied by reduced fibre length, which adds to the reduction in tear value.

The tensile-tear relationship is an example of the situation often confronting papermakers in which two desirable characteristics are mutually contradictory and some degree of compromise is necessary. If a papermaker goes "all out" to get maximum tensile strength from a given stock, the resulting sheet will be low in ter. Conversely, a sheet formed at maximum tear value of the stock will be low in tensile.

One of the important consequences of this problem is the use of artificial bonding agents that permit the development of high levels of tensile strength with less beating and refining of the stock than otherwise would be needed. As a result, the fibre length of the furnish is preserved. Among the artificial bonding agents widely used at the present time are starches, proteins, natural gums, synthetic resins, and latices.

Folding Endurance

A widely-used and time-honoured test relating to the resistance of paper to repeated stress is that of folding endurance described in Tappi method T423.

Two different from of apparatus are in current use: (1) the Schopper type, for papers not more than 0.25 mm (.001 in.) in thickness and (2) the MIT (Massachusetts Institute of Technology) type which can be adjusted for paper of any thickness. Although T423 provides for the use of either of these, there is no constant relationship between test values obtained by the two instruments. TAPPI Committee Assignments are under way to provide separate methods for the two instruments.

Both testers mechanically produce double folds, repeated at the same point of specimen strips, and subject the strip to tension after each fold. The result is expressed in the number of folds before rupture at the crease. The tension in the Schopper tester is 1 kg.; that of the M.I.T. tester can be adjusted from 0 to 1.5 kg. Folding endurance is actually a measure of rate of tensile strength reduction form its original value to that applied by the instrument by repeated creasing.

Folding endurance has a double significance. Some papers such as wrapping, envelope, and cover stock are subjected to folding in use and the test indicates performance. It is also a sensitive measure of influences tending to degrade fibre. Hence it is used to indicate aging properties of paper.

Abrasion Resistance

Another index of the durability of paper is the resistance to abrasion. For wrapping and packaging paper and paperboard, this is usually referred to as "scuff resistance". For writing and drawing papers, the property of erasibility is of importance. Rubbing resistance is of importance in towelling and wiper paper, and in this instance, wet rub is of special importance. It is obvious that dense, well-bonded paper shows greater abrasion resistance than a soft, lightlybonded sheet. It also appears that the character, as well as the amount, of interfiber bonding influences abrasion resistance. Papers impregnated with elastomers, as additive interfiber bonding agents, show greatly improved abrasion resistance as compared with normal paper at the same tensile strength level. Papers requiring an extraordinary degree of abrasion resistance are normally coated or surface-laminated with plastic resins.

Method T476 describes a procedure and apparatus for testing abrasion resistance of packaging materials. This apparatus has also been adapted to rub testing of a variety of papers, textiles, and other materials. Abrasion testing is an exceedingly complex subject. A variety of instruments and procedures exist. Test conditions must be adopted to the use requirements of the product.

PAPER PROPERTIES PRIMARILY EVIDENT BY TOUCH

Rigidity, Stiffness, and Softness of Paper

The resistance of paper to a bending force is evident in all the various operations of its manufacture and in the manifold uses of paper. The range in this property extends from very soft, flexible tissues to rigid boards. It is obvious that thicker and heavier sheets tend to be stiff and rigid while soft, flexible papers are light and thin. However, even among papers of the same weight there can be considerable differences in flexibility, due to the structure of the sheet.

The rigidity of a paper is property of resisting an applied bending force and is proportional to EI where E is Yong's modulus and I is the moment of inertia.

The rigidity factor is proportional to the modulus of elasticity (E) or modulus of rigidity, which is a measure of the rigidity of the structure of the sheet, being a specific property of the material and the way it is put together inside the sheet.

The stiffness of paper is its ability to support its own weight, the inverse of flabbiness or limpness. It is proportional to EI/W, where W is the basis weight.

Softness is the subjective property of paper exhibited by the feeling of softness when a sheet is crumpled in the hand. This depends on the ease of crumpling (flexibility), together with the absence of sharp edges in the crumpled sheet. It is inversely proportional to the rigidity modified by a function of the thickness of the sheet. With two sheets of the same stiffness, the thicker of the two feels softer.

Methods of measurement

Numerous methods have been proposed for the measurement of stiffness in paper. These generally fall into three categories: (1) the bending of a strip of paper under its own weight when suspended at one end as a cantilever; (2) the effect on the period of a torsion pendulum of the torque-producing type in flexing a sample of paper; and (3) the deflection produced by an externally applied bending moment or, conversely, the bending moment reureged to produce a certain deflection. Tappi Method T451 utilizes (1) to determine "critical length}, (L), which is the overhang of a test strip that will fall from one side to the other when the holding clamp is rotated through an angle of 90°.

The flexual rigidity of a strip of paper (or beam) is the bending moment required to produce unit curvature of bend. Rigidity as a property of paper is its ability to resist in applied force and is determined fundamentally by the flexural rigidity per unit width of sheet.

The equation for deflection of uniformly loaded cantilever is as follows:

$$Y = L^4 w/8EI$$

where:

y = deflection at end of a cantilever, due to its own weight

w = weight per unit length of the cantilever

L = overhanging length

EI = flexural rigidity

E = Young's modulus

I = moment of intertia of section of strip.

The radius of curvature r, is proportional to L and may be expressed r = KL. Likewise, the horizontal distance from the point of support to the center of gravity of the cantilever, a, is proportional to L and may be expressed as a = k2 L.

The bending moment is expressed as:

$$M = aLw$$

and also from basic theory to bending :

$M = EL/r$

therefore :

$aLw = EI/r$

EI (flexural rigidity) = aLwr

then,

$EI = k_1 k_2 L^3 w$

where w is proportional to W (basis weight). Clark Rigidity, $L^3/$ W1000 (cf T-451 m 60), is therefore proportional to EI.

Flexural rigidity in dynes per square centimeter per centimeter of sheet width may also be derived from the torsion pendulum test. This device is a symmetrical mass suspended from a wire, its vibration is rotational about a vertical axis coincident with the torsion wire. The period, T, of such a pendulum is determined by the moment of inertia of the suspended mass, I_0, and the restoring torque per unit of angular displacement, r. If a paper strip is clamped to the suspended mass in such a fashion that the strip is bent when rotation occurs, the added restoring torque caused by the bending of the strip causes a reduction in the period of rotational vibration. The flexural rigidity of the strip may be computed from the periods T and T_0 of the pendulum with and without the test strip.

$$EI = 4^2 I_0 [b^3 / b(b+a)^2 \times \left[\frac{1}{T^2} - \frac{1}{T_0^2}\right]$$

Flexural rigidities determined by this method were found to be proportional to Clark rigidities.

Factors Influencing the Stiffness of Paper

The bending of a sheet of paper may be compared to the bending of a beam. In the mathematical treatment of deformation, it is usual to treat the deformed body as being composed of homogeneous material. In contrast, paper is a structure composed of discreet elements (fibres) that may differ from each other in size, shape, and elastic modulus. The structure exists only because it is welded together by bonds that have properties such as area strength per unit area, and frequency.

When a beam is bent by an applied couple, the structure of the beam is compressed in the region nearest the inside of the curve and extended in the region nearest the outside (Fig. 1). The filament, which experiences no change in length when the curvature is applied, is termed the neutral filament or neutral axis (A-A in Fig. 1). It is clear that stiffness in a sheet of paper is actually resistance to deformation, both in elongation and compression. Further, to the extent that paper is anisotropic, the stiffness can be increased or decreased, compared with an isotropic structure. For example, if paper is considered to have a laminar structure, the lamina near the surface are more significant than the lamina near the center in contributing to stiffness.

Fig. 1. Bending of a beam

The stiffness of a beam of rectangular cross section varies as the third power of the thickness. This is approximately true of paper, although some deviation is to be expected, because of the practical difficulty of keeping all other properties of paper constant while varying thickness. In any event, thickness has such a profound effect on sheet stiffness that, in making observation on other factors, thickness must be most carefully measured and taken into account. It may be assumed that the flexibility of individual fibres affects sheet flexibility and that fibre flexibility is the combined result of the geomerty of the fibres and their average elastic modulus. This relationship of fibre-sheet flexibility remains obscure for several reasons. No reliable method for determining a quantitative index of fibre flexibility is available. Further, fibre flexibility has a profound effect on interfiber bonding, and this change in bonding may have more effect on sheet flexibility than does the change in fibre properties. In a qualitative sense, it is well recognized that strong, well-bonded sheets are less flexible than lightly bonded sheets. Because of the many other factors that also influence flexibility, there is no direct relationship between strength and sheet stiffness.

Finally, the relationship between sheet density and sheet stiffness is anomalous. It is common to associate density with stiffness; however, with paper, several contradictory factors come into play Generally, paper to high density also has a high degree of interfiber bonding, and this increases stiffness. However, at the same basis weight, a dense sheet has a lesser thickness, and this tends to decrease stiffness. If the density of sheet is increased by compression in the dry state (calendering), no appreciable increase in interfiber bonding occurs, the decrease in thickness markedly decreases stiffness, and the denser sheet is also the more flexible.

The method commonly for paperboard is described in TAPPI Method T489. The test measures the flexural rigidity or stiffness of paperboard by determining the bending moment in gram-centimeters necessary to deflect the free and of vertically clamped specimen 1.5 in, wide a distance 15° from the center line when the load is applied 5 cm from the clamp.

Significance of Paper Stiffness

Stiffness is a highly desirable characteristic of many paper products. The protective quality of many packaging papers and paperboard stocks is dependent on stiffness or rigidity. In many instances the basis weight is determined by the stiffness required and means to increase stiffness would permit lower basis weight and saving of material. Stiffness is an important characteristic of tabulating cards, index cards, mounting paper, paper cups and many other items. The stiffness or "rattle" of bond, ledger, writing and similar stocks is taken as a sign of quality or "character" of the paper. Conversely, sanitary papers, towels, napkins and similar papers require cloth-like properties and a maximum of flexibility Glassine paper is frequently required to conform to the shape of other objects, and plasticizers are often used to increase its flexibility.

Surface Texture of Paper

In most of the uses of paper, the character of the surface is of great importance. It is common to say that paper has a "smooth" or a rough texture. The terms "finish" and "patten" are frequently used in describing the contour or appearance of paper surfaces. Formation and compressibility, although not strictly surface characteristics, have an important effect on the behaviour of the paper surface in such processes as printing.

The surface requirements of printing papers are highly varied. In order that the type or other printing surface make complete contact with the paper, a certain minimum degree of smoothness is required. Half-tone illustrations which may have up to 300 lines per in, require smoothness of a high order. The finest printing papers result from a compromise of various qualities in relation to printing conditions and use requirements. A printing paper of perfect smoothness, such as that of polished optical glass, would probably be disappointing, because printing presses depend on some roughness to carry paper through the presses and to aid in keeping the printing in register. Compressibility is a desirable feature in printing papers, because it aids in obtaining intimate contact between the paper and the printing surface. However, highly compressible papers also tend to stretch easily, which is detrimental to good register. Although various physical tests, such as smoothness, are useful guides in the evaluation of printing paper, there are no tests or combinations of tests that can determine the "printability" of paper. For this reason, this property is usually determined by actually performing test printing.

In other paper products, the surface is important in permitting "slip" fortrouble free passage through sorting machines, e.g., tabulating cards. The easy travel of pen or pencil over the surface is significant in writing and envelope papers. With paper stock for shipping sacks too much slip is undesirable, since it permits slippage of bags piled together. For this reason, bag stock is sometimes treated to increase surface friction.

In the area of sanitary and absorbent papers, the surface should be pleasing to the touch, it should not have an abrasive feeling, but should have a surface contour and texture similar to cloth and quite distinct from the smoothness of a film. It is obvious that surface contour can have many meanings. One surface may be rough, sharp, jagged, and hard, while another may be rounded, undulating and soft. Even though the two surface may have the same depth of profile, the surface "feel" of the two would be quite different.

Methods of Measuring Surface Texture

Both direct and indirect methods may be used in measuring the surface texture of paper. Direct methods employ a tracing or profile of surface irregularities, whereas indirect methods make use of some over all effect presumed to be related to surface smoothness, such as air flow, light reflection, friction, or electrical capacitance.

Tappi Method 479, "Smoothness of Printing Paper" covers the determination of smoothness by three different instruments. Bakk. Gurely Hill S.P.S. and Willams. The basic principle of all three instruments is the flow of air along the surface irregularities of the paper.

The Bekk smoothness tester consists of a mercury manometer connected by three way valve to a vacuum pump a glass anvil, and the atmosphere. The anvil, where the sample of paper is mounted is made of optically flat plate glass (in the center of which is a tapered hole with a diameter of 11 mm at the top and 1 mm at the bottom). The manometer shows in millimeters of mercury the difference between the pressure in the chamber and the atmospheric pressure. Two chambers are provided to cover different ranges.

With the air chamber at reduced pressure, the valve is turned to the position connecting the anvil with the manometer and air chamber. Now a pressure differential exists between the opening at the center of the anvil and the outer edge, and air will flow between the surface and a sample of paper clamped thereto at a rate depending on the roughness of the paper surface and the pressure difference. In operation, an average pressure difference of 370 mm (0.5 atmosphere) is used. The pressure on the paper is 1 kg/sq cm and the air chamber is so designed that a flow of 10 cc of air into it will cause a drop in pressure of 20 mm. By definition, the smoothness is then taken as the time for 10 cc of air to pass between the 10 sq cm of polished glass and the paper surface under an initial pressure of 370 mm. (The paper is subjected to a pressure of 1 kg/sq cm.) The smaller of the two chambers is so designed that flow of 1 cc of air will cause a pressure drop of 20 mm.

In the Gurely-Hill S-P-S raid smoothness test, eight thicknesses of paper are perforated held between the upper orifice plate and a solid lower plate that house an annular ring stated to be optically flat. The test does not differentiate between felt and wire side smoothness, but gives an average value for sixteen surfaces. By means of the lever arm, unweighted, a pressure of 3 psi is provided over the contact area of 1 sq in. The smoothness value is defined as the time in seconds for 50 cc of air to pass.

In the Williams instrument , although the air-flow principle is employed, the truly flat test surface is dispensed with, and the air is passed between two surfaces of the paper to be tested. Compressed air is applied to the center of clamp holding a folded test specimen of the paper under standard pressure. The time in seconds required for the passage of 25 ml of air is determined.

Table 2 shows smoothness values for a series of typical printing papers. It will be noted that there is a general relationship between sheet density (thickness at a given basis weight) and smoothness. In the series, mineo, machine-finished book and super-calendered book, the progressive increase in calendering shows up in markedly increased smoothness. The prime purpose of the coating of paper is to improve finish beyond that possible by calendering. Note the marked increase in smoothness of coated book, as compared with super-calendered book without any reduction in caliper.

PENETRATION OF PAPER BY FLUIDS

Because paper is composed of a randomly felted layer of fibre, it follows that the structure has a varying degree of porosity. Thus, the ability of fluids, both liquid and gaseous, to penetrate the structure of paper becomes a property that is both highly significant to the use of paper and is also capable of being widely varied by the conditions of manufacture.

In the early history of paper making, when the product was used exclusively for writing and printing, the need to limit the spreading of ink resulted in "sizing" the paper with gelatinous vegetable materials which had the effect of sealing or filling the surface pores. Later, the term "sizing" was applied to the treatment of paper stock, prior to the formation of the sheet, with water-repellent materials such as rosin or wax (engine sizing, internal sizing). As the use of paper was extended to wrapping and packaging, additional requirements were encountered in protecting the contents of the package from the effects of fluid transfer through the paper wrapping. In some instances, this has resulted in the demand for complete impermeability of the package to the transfer of any liquid or gas.

Table 2: Smoothness of Various papers

Paper		Basis Weight (lb)	Caliper (0.001 inch)	Bekk Smoothness (sec)
Mimeo				
(17×22-500)	A	21	5.60	11.3
	B	21	4.58	18.1
	C	21	4.94	16.5
	D	21	4.63	16.3
	E	17.5	5.47	8.1
Newsprint				
(24×36-4000	A	32	5.56	47.4
	B	32	3.52	47.4
	C	32	3.87	27.6
	D	32	3.96	58.4
	E	32	3.61	56.3
Machine finish book				
(17×22-500)	A	50	3.33	182.4
	B	45	3.60	78.2
	C	43	2.85	290.5
	D	62	4.12	155.6
	E	40	2.87	146.2
Supercalendered book				
(25×38-500)	A	60	3.33	589.5
	B	40	2.48	538.9
	C	40	2.54	403.3
	D	50	3.00	448.5
	E	60	3.37	270.5
Coated book				
(25×38-500)	A	70	3.57	862.5
	B	70	3.39	1129.0
	C	70	3.43	1576.8
	D	70	3.34	640.7
	E	70	3.37	928.7

In another direction, the use of paper as an absorbent medium for wiping up liquids, for filtering, and for saturating has created a demand for maximum wettability and permeability toward water and other liquids, as well as toward air and other gases. All this in turn has brought about the need for a variety of tests to indicate these properties.

By way of background, it is important to remember that cellulosic fibres are by nature hydrophilic, that is, they are readily wetted by water and they readily absorb and transmit both liquid water and water vapour. Thus, a sheet of paper formed from pure fibre and water, with little or no beating (waterleaf paper), is found to be highly absorbent toward water and other low-viscosity liquids.

Swanson has reviewed the factors governing the penetration of liquids into porous structures (such as paper) and derives the equation:

$$\Delta P = \frac{2\gamma / L \cos\theta}{r}$$

where ΔP is the pressure differential across the liquid interface and is the force causing the liquid to advance into the capillary. γ/L is the specific free surface energy of the liquid. θ is the contact angle between the solid and liquid and "r" is the radius of the capillary, assuming a perfect cylinder.

The rate of penetration is given by the Wash-burn equation.

$$\frac{dl}{dt} = \frac{ro \cos\theta}{N 4 l}$$

where

dl/dt = rate of penetration of liquid,

r = radius of capillaries or pores,

o = surface tension of liquid,

θ = angle of contact between liquid and solid,

N = viscosity of liquid, and

l = depth of liquid penetration

The contact angle θ, between a solid and liquid is illustrated in Fig. 2. If θ is zero, perfect wetting of the solid by the liquid occurs.

When q is finite, the attraction between the solid and the liquid is less than the attraction between the molecules of the liquid. At a value of θ of 90°, the solid-liquid attraction is only one-half he cohesional attraction within the liquid itself. A 180° contact angle is obviously impossible. This would imply no attraction between the solid and liquid molecules. It has been established that all molecules and atoms attract others to an appreciable extent.

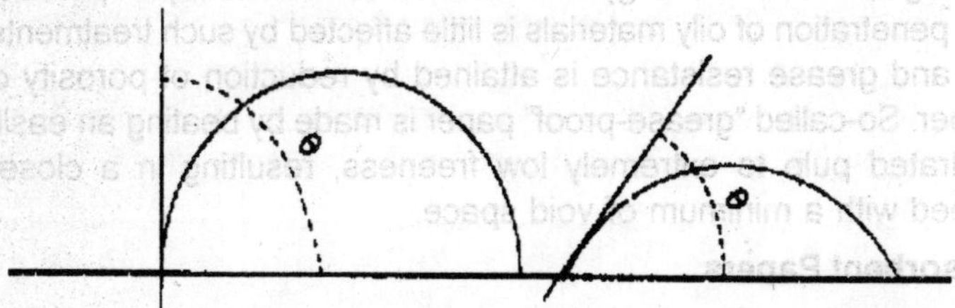

Fig. 2. Contact angle between liquid and solid.

The actual measurement of contact of contact angle is usually limited to those solids that have a smooth uniform interface with the liquid. Because of the relatively rough and heterogeneous nature of paper, it is more satisfactory to measure the rate of penetration directly. Even though the component factors of the above equation are seldom measured directly, it is important for the technologist studying the penetration of liquids into paper to differentiate among the effects due to these various factors.

Factors Influencing Water Resistance of Paper

A pure cellulosic surface is hydrophilic and easily wettable, i.e., it forms a very low contact angle with water, hence, the natural condition of a paper composed of such fibres would be highly absorbent. Actually this condition seldom prevails, since much of paper and paperboard production is treated with sizing additives to increase the resistance to penetration of water. Also, paper-making pulps contain materials other than cellulose, some of which may be adsorbed upon the fibre surface. When so adsorbed, they create a hydrophobic condition, i.e., a high contact angle between the surface and water.

Oil and Grease Resistance of Paper

In some instances, the rate of penetration of liquids other than water is the property to be measured. The permeation of paper by oil-base printing ink is determined by Tapi Method T462. The grease resistance of paper is determined by the rate of penetration of turpentine (Tappi Method T454).

Whereas the resistance of paper to the penetration of water is greatly affected by surface treatment of the fibres by materials having low surface energy and with little or no effect upon porosity, the penetration of oily materials is little affected by such treatments. Oil and grease resistance is attained by reduction of porosity of paper. So-called "grease-proof" paper is made by beating an easily hydrated pulp to extremely low freeness, resulting in a closed sheed with a minimum of void space.

Absorbent Papers

Grades such as towelling, sanitary tissue, blotting, and filter paper are commonly tested for absorbency according to TAPPI Method T432. A 0.1 ml drop of water is placed on the surface of the paper, which is supported in a manner so that the support does not touch the paper opposite the point of application of the drop. The time is measured from contact of the drop with the paper until the disappearance of the reflection from the drop surface, indicating complete absorption. For light-weight tissues, the size of drop is reduced to 0.01 ml.

It is customary to subject absorbent papers to "accelerated aging" tests in combination with the above absorbency test. This consists of exposing the sample to some elevated temperature, usually 110°C, in an oven or on a hot plate. The purpose is to simulate the well-known "self-sizing" effect (see above) that often occurs with absorbent papers. Although the correlation between the accelerated test and natural aging is not perfect, it still constitutes a useful guide in the manufacture of absorbent papers.

As pointed out previously, in the manufacture of absorbent paper it is important to keep the presence of resins, fatty acids, and other hydrophobic materials in the pulp to minimum. Maintaining a high degree of porosity in sheet and a textured surface are essential to high absorbency. Here again, the paper maker is confronted with contradictory properties, both of which are desirable. A high degree of absorbency in paper calls for low density and high porosity, which means a low degree of interfiber bonding and consequent low strength.

Since absorbent papers are expected to become wet in normal use, the strength property when wet is of prime importance. Methods have been discovered for modifying the interfiber bonding, with thermosetting synthetic resins, to increase wet strength with little effect on the total bonded area or porosity of the paper. It is also likely that the wet strength resin has relatively little effect on absorbency. However, there is a marked tendency for wet strength resins to co-precipitate with natural hydrophobic fatty acids, and thus to reduce absorbency.

It is also common to add "rewetting" agents to absorbent papers. Numerous such maerials are offered to the paper industry. There are two ways in which a rewetting agent may act : (1) by dissolving in the advancing water film, thereby reducing its surface tension: and (2) when bound to fibre surface, by increasing the free surface energy, and thus reducing the contact angle.

PERMEABILITY OF PAPER TO GASES

Air permeability of paper and other sheet materials is the ability to allow the flow of air through the structure of he sheet under a pressure differential. It depends upon the number, size, shape, and distribution of the pores of air passages within the sheet structure. "Porosity" is often used interchangeably with air permeability. This is not strictly true, since in a specific sense, the word porosity means the ratio of pore volume to total volume of the material. Likewise, "density", meaning weight per unit volume, although bearing some relationship to air permeability, is far from being equivalent. Density is affected by the specific gravity of the solid fraction as well as closed or nearly closed air cells or pockets that contribute little to permeability.

The usual method of test for air permeability is the measurement of the volume of air that flows in unit time through unit area under unit pressure difference. A method and apparatus for this measurement is described in TAPPI Standard Method T460.(ASTM Designation D-726). The instrument consists of an outer cylinder that is partly filled with oil and an inner cylinder sliding freely in the outer cylinder. Air pressure for the test is provided by the weight of the inner cylinder. The instrument is arranged to furnish air pressure to the paper specimen held between clamping plates having a circular orifice with an area of 1.00 sq in. The movable inner cylinder is graduated in units of 50 ml. It is 10 in. high with a total range of 350 ml. The average number of seconds required for the passage of 100 ml of air through 1 sq in. of paper is reported as air resistance.

Because of the ease and rapidity of the test, air permeability is widely used as an approximate indication of the permeability of paper to other fluids, such as oils and other organic liquids. It is also useful to indicate weight uniformity during manufacture and processing of paper.

It is used as an indirect means of estimating the filtering characteristics of industrial and analytical filter papers, of evaluating the impregnating qualities of saturating papers, and of indicating of ink penetration and spreading in printing papers.

Air permeability is of direct importance in bag papers for use on automatic filling machines where the displaced air must escape through the paper, and in building papers that must prevent air infiltration.

Moisture vapour permeability (MVP) is of great importance in many packaging papers and paperboards. With many commodities, it is important that the packaging material prevent the entrance of moisture vapour from the atmosphere and preserve the contents of the package in a dry state. In other instances, it is required that the packaging material prevent the loss of water from the contents by evaporation. Either way, a paper or paperboard packaging product may be required to present a barrier to the passage of moisture vapour.

Cellulose, even when formed into a film that is impervious to air (cellophane), is still not a barrier to the passage of moisture vapour. This results from the hygroscopic nature of cellulose that causes it to adsorb atmospheric water vapour. The sorbed water migrates readily through the cellulose structure and will evaporate from the opposite surface of the film or sheet, provided the atmosphere on that side is less humid than on the first side. Thus, cellulose in the form of fibre or film will act as a conductor of water vapour from a more humid to a less humid atmosphere.

Even though a paper is made "closed" and dense with very little pore space, it still does not have barrier properties toward water vapour.

When paper is required to have moisture vapour barrier properties, it is processed by one of the following methods : (1) impregnated with wax, normally paraffin; (2) coated with a solution, emulsion, or hot melt of a hydrophobic solid material such as resin, latex, wax, or asphalt; and (3) laminated with a continuous film or foil is impervious to moisture vapour and capable of strongly adhering to the paper surface (examples: polyethylene film and aluminium foil).

Water vapour permeability of paper is measured by sealing a specimen of the paper to be tested in the form of a cover to a dish containing a desiccant. The increase in weight of the desiccant represents the moisture transmitted by the paper sample. Successive weightings are made until a constant rate of gain is attained. The water vapour permeability is reported as grams per square meter per 24 hr with the test apparatus exposed to a relative humidity of 50% and a temperature of 73°F. Complete details of the test method will be found in TAPPI Method T448.

The influence of temperature and humidity on the water vapour transmission of most sheet materials is often nonlinear. Hence, results obtained at standard paper test conditions (50% relative humidity 73°F) cannot be extrapolated to predict water vapour transmission under hot, damp conditions. Tappi Method T464 gives the details of the water vapour-permeability test at 100°F and 90% relative humidity.

It is normal for wrapping and packaging maerials to undergo creasing during the packaging operation. Since creasing may have a disruptive effect on the barrier film or layer, the moisture vapour permeability of the creased material is of more significance than the test of the flat sheet. TAPPI Method T465 provides a standard method of creasing of paper products prior to the permeability test.

Fibre Analysis of Paper and Paperboard

It has always been of considerable importance to be able to determine for a sample of paper the fibres of pulps used in its manufacture. Some papers are bought with a specification of pulp furnish: with others, fibre analysis is of interest in interpreting physical tests.

Fibre indentification is accomplished by: (1) distinctive colour reaction of various pulp fibres when exposed to certain dyes and to a variety of stains based on iodine; and (2) by morphological characteristics observed in a microscope. A systematic procedure for fibre identification is described in Tappi Standard T401. The distinctive colour reactions of fibres when exposed to stain depends on the chemical and physical experience undergone by the fibre during the pulping and bleaching processes. With the many innovations that have occurred in wood pulping in recent years, it is essential that fibre analysis be performed with constant reference to known samples of presently available pulps and by a microscopist of sound judgment and experience. This is also true in forming judgements of fibre morphology where identification depends on familiarity with microscopic appearance of the fine structural details.

25

Board and Hand Made Paper

BOARD MAKING

Board technically is a variation of paper with the following characteristics and differences:

1. Board is thicker – has a higher grammage. This is in excess of 120 gsm.
2. Board generally is opaque. There is no special process necessary to ensure opacity.
3. Board is generally stiffer.
4. Inferior quality pulp may be used in making boards as printability or ability to write is not very important. However boards may be used uncoated in some packaging applications.
5. Techniques are available for making multiply boards i.e. boards with different interiors than the outer surfaces.
6. Boards are generally made on smaller deckle and slower machines. The large amount of pulp that has to be delivered to a small area makes the invention of new technologies very different.

Conventional fourdrinier is used mostly direct as a tissue forming machine. However most of the quality paper is made on the duo formers. A substantial amount of paper is made from machines that operate as board making machines. The inverform machine may be used as it is for making boards.

The pulp making for board generally follows the same procedures as paper. The volume of water that has to be drained is much larger. More fibres have to be deposited in the mat than in the case of paper. Hence the pulp is only lightly beaten or refined. If pulp from waste paper is used almost no refining is needed, only a thorough cleaning and disintegration is ensured.

The cylinder machine for board manufacture was patented by John Dickinson in 1809. A wire screen cylinder revolves in a vat containing diluted pulp. A layer of wet pulp is formed on the cylinder. Water drains off on breaking the surface and is transferred to the underside of a moving felt belt. The belt is pressed on to the cylinder by rubber rollers. In the multi-vat machine as many as eight cylinders may be used. The wet layers bind themselves to each other forming a single web of board. It is possible to have different constitution for each of the layers of board. E.g. the top and bottom layer may be a strong chemical pulp with some loading to provide a white opaque surface, the middie layer may be of poor strength such as gray waste water pulp. The principle of operation is generally simple, a rotating drum made of wire, picks up stuff either in the direct flow or in the counter flow machine. The mat formed on the wire covered mold is transferred to a felt carrier which moves it to the next cylinder mold. This process is repeated till a multiply board of several plies is obtained. The felt picks up the first ply of paper and the wet fibre mat picks up the next ply. It is possible to construct board with different layers of different physical properties over each other. Low grade waste paper pulp can be used as the stuff for the inner plies while good quality pulp can be used for the outer plies. Wet paper always adheres to the smoother surface and as both the surfaces of the felt and the fibre mat are smoother than the wire the transfer of paper is nearly complete. There are two distinct ways in which the cylinders operate. The contraflow was the standard technique till recently and the alternate method of uniflow is being used.

The drying follows the same pattern as in paper. However the major amount of water is sucked off at the earliest to reduce the amount of heat required. The drying section has a few calender stacks to provide a good surface finish. The inverform process introduced in the sixties was an important development in making paper boards. The stock is sandwiched between an upper and

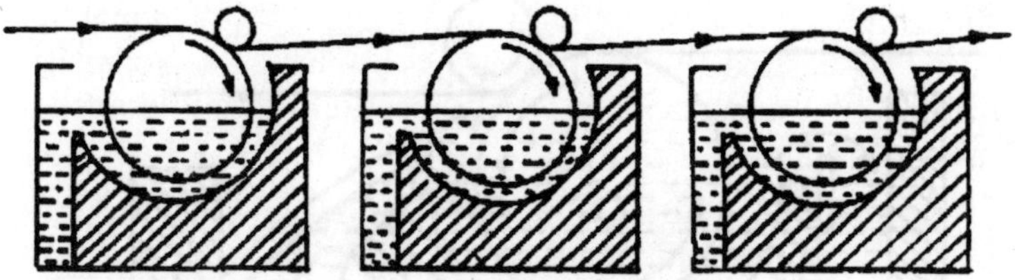

Fig. 1. Multivat board making.

lower wire under a forming roll as soon as it leaves the head box. A stiff scraper blade held Inside the wire known as the auto slice scrapes off the water. Suction boxes take-off more of the water. Several of such inverform units are combined to get boards of desired quality. The couch if assisted by vacuum removes a sizable amount of water form the mat before it is transferred to the drying section. The vacuum assisted couch compared to the pressure couch gives a larger working life to the wire as well. The transfer may be assisted with a small blast to compressed air of in some cases the drying unit may be placed very close to the wire section.

Fig. 2. Counter flow vat.

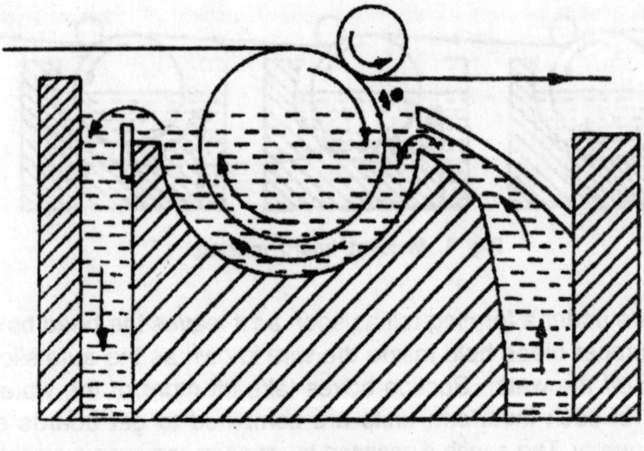

Fig. 3. Uniflow vat.

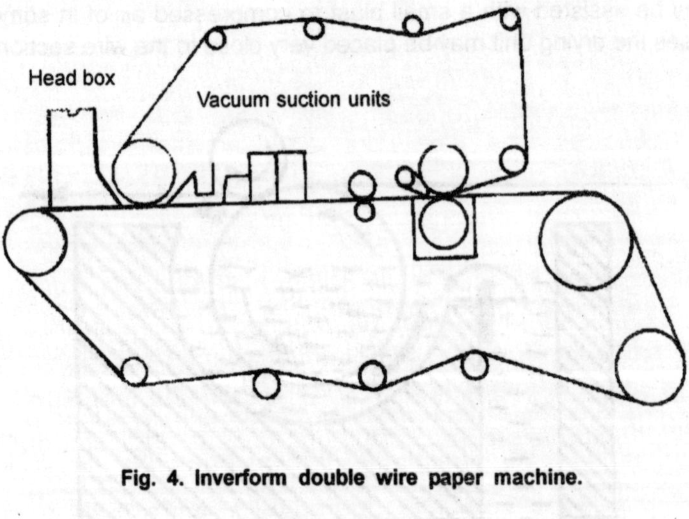

Fig. 4. Inverform double wire paper machine.

The inverform process introduced in the sixties was an important development in making paper boards. The stock is sandwiched between an upper and lower wire under a forming roll as soon as it leaves the head box. A stiff scraper blade held Inside the wire known as the auto slice scrapes off the water.

Suction boxes take off more of the water. Several of such inverform units are combined to get boards of desired quality.

HAND-MADE PAPER

Making paper by hand was the only paper making process till the invention and adaptation of the paper machines during the 18th and 19th century. Paper making in India flourished in the Mughal period and gradually declined in its importance. Hand-made paper is made now only in small quantities compared to the machine processes. This is considered a luxury item. When properly handled, hand made paper has:

1. An exquisite and elegant writing surface.
2. Has much better resistance to tear and has very good strength.
3. Has unmatched textures for the artist to use.
4. Can be made in many varieties and with many decorative inclusions.
5. Has high tensile, bursting, tearing strength.

Drawing paper for artworks, permanent document paper, card sheets, deckle edged stationery, unique carry bags, watermarked certificate papers, are but a few variations that can be made by hand.

The entire process starts with the preparation of the pulp. Generally unprinted paper wastes from printing unit are used for paper making. However high grade deinked paper may be used. If available pulp from paper mills may also be used.

All fibre used for making paper must be free of mechanical and chemical contaminants and foreign matter. The pulp must also be homogeneous.

The main difference between the machine made paper and hand made paper is in the alignment of the fibres. In the continuous process of casting pulp to paper the fibres align themselves length-wise in paper. The fibre bundles are difficult to break lengthwise but can easily be separated width wise. Hence paper properties vary strongly in the grain direction and the cross direction. In the hand made paper the grains are randomly oriented. In fact this randomness adds to the strength of paper in all directions.

Deckles and molds are made to the proper size. Usually the molds are square or rectangular. A mesh is attached to the wooden frame with panel pins along all the four sides. The mesh must be left taut.

Pulp is kept agitated in trough after ensuring that there are no lumps and the mixture is uniform. The frame is dipped into the trough full of pulp in proper dilution at an angle. When the frame is fully submerged it is kept horizontal and given a gentle shake sideways, forward and backward so that the fibres are evenly dispersed on the mesh. The frame is pulled slowly with shaking to ensure that no ripples are formed. The frame is held over the container for sometime to allow all the water to drain away.

The deckle is removed from the mold carefully. The paper now may be dried. The paper may be dried by leaving it on the mold for sufficiently long time or the paper may be transferred on to cloth for drying.

26

Equipment Used in Paper Making Laboratory

PULP FREENESS TESTER

The freeness of pulps can be measured in a pulp freeness tester. The principle involved is to find the resistance offered to a mechanical handling in a dynamic condition.

Pulp is taken in a well cleaned calibrated container. The lids are sealed and the calibrated nozzle and screen plates put into commission.

Pulp is tested to the specifications as:

ISO 52672

CPPA C1

BS 6035/2

LABORATORY HAND SHEET PRESS

These systems let prepare hand made sheets form a given batch of pulp. The properties such as colour and tint, density and chemical properties can be reasonably projected after measurements on the hand sheet.

The sheets may be pressed as circles or rectangular sheets. The equipment may be pneumatically operated or may be manual. Heaters may be built into the units to estimate the drying time requirements.

LABORATORY CALENDERS

Generally built as 3 roller calenders - width typically 300 mm. Hydraulic cylinders permit application of large pressure - as high as 100 kg per linear centimeter. Heating with thermostat control is sometimes done.

LABORATORY COATERS

The equipment are built to conduct lab experiments on coating compositions and find the suitability on the substrate. Coating is applied by metering rods but blade coating attachments are also available.

The substrate is placed on a large horizontal table and coating applied under many varied conditions. The coating material may be heated prior to application. The table may be moved automatically. There are models that have built in drying chambers or infra red heating units to make possible quick drying.

27

Paper and Board Properties

Printability and print quality are two properties associated with paper but note well-defined. In offset or gravure the printability would mean a measure of the missing dots.

Printability is defined as the extent to which properties of the paper lend themselves for true reproduction of a copy. Printability is not measurable in numbers as an absolute value as can be done in case of colour or brightness of paper.

The property can be considered as a resultant of the pulp properties and the formation parameters. The properties due to pulp are the ones such as porosity, scattering, opacity and absorbency. The properties that change due to formation are the ones such as the bulking thickness, surface smoothness, filler content and machine based variables.

The resultant is seen as:

1. Ink show through.
2. Image clarity.
3. Ink requirement.

The result of the above variants can be approximately called printability.

Print quality is the degree to which the properties of the constituents including paper combine to obtain the desired result.

The following table summarises the result of printing on a few surfaces with specific inks. To an extent this id directly related to the property of the ink as can be seen as the requirements of two different grades of ink. Generally it is possible to standardise on some type of ink and get a subjective and objective idea about printability.

Grade of stock	Type of ink	
	Black	Opaque Orange
Enamel	360	250
Litho Coated	300	180
Label	240	160
Dull Coated	205	130
Newsprint	150	140
Antique finish	135	115
Machine finish	180	140

The table above indicates the approximate area of paper of the mentioned stock covered by a fixed weight of the given grade of ink. This gives an oblique measure of ink mileage that depends on the paper and ink properties. The results are obtained using a sheetfed offset machine.

DESIRABLE PROPERTIES OF PAPER FOR VARIOUS APPLICATIONS

Printing Papers

Printing is the action of successfully placing ink on paper by various mechanical techniques. The paper has to adapt itself to the mechanical strain of handling as well as the chemical strain of ink.

Ink on paper has an important behaviour pattern. This concerns the ability of ink to set as solid on paper. Ink is a solution/colloid/dispersion of dyes/pigments in liquid vehicles. The vehicles may be water based or oil based. The process of drying is when there is a phase change in ink. The transferred ink turns solid by any one of the processes such as evaporation, absorption or fusion. These processes are indicated in the figure below.

Ink is placed on paper in many ways. The most common procedure is to directly let the ink flow on the substrate through small diameter tubes. The fountain pen or the quill are such examples.

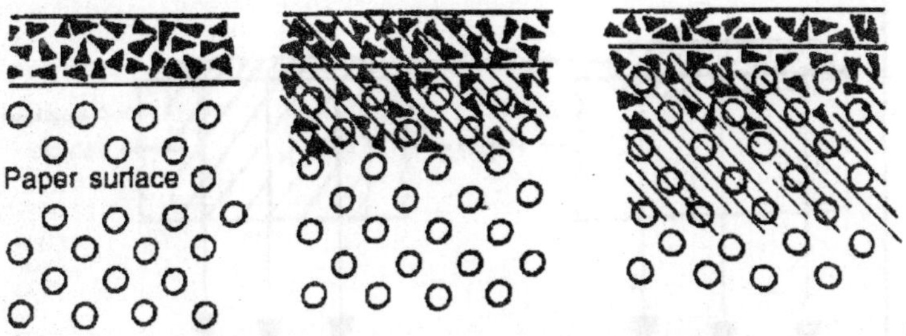

Fig. 1 Drying of ink on paper by absorption.

Printing is transferring ink on to the paper or substrate surface with the help of a large printing surface - either directly or thorough a rubber blanket as in offset printing. Printing usually means direct transfer of ink on the surface by physical contact. In all the contact techniques, the ink is shared between the printing surface and the printed surface. There are chances that the printed surface may not accept ink due to certain problems of the surface. There are also techniques by which ink is squeezed on to the surface as in screen printing. The ink jet printing and similar processes place ink on the surface by non-contact techniques. In such cases the transfer of ink is direct and metered by the printing unit. All ink is either accepted or rejected by the printed surface.

The electro-transfer techniques depend on charging the printed surface and then expect the charged areas of paper to accept ink. The transfer is 100% but the ink need to be fused into the system. After transfer the ink undergoes the drying operation.

The ink may also dry by precipitation or reaction with the substrate.

There may be errors in the process of transfer from the printing surface or in the process of acceptance of ink by the substrate. The errors may result in loss of image transferred or may involve spreading or similar effects making the image an inaccurate reproduction. In some cases effects known as strike through and see through take place. Ideally a printed sample should completely be blocked by a sheet of paper. This process is explained in the figure.

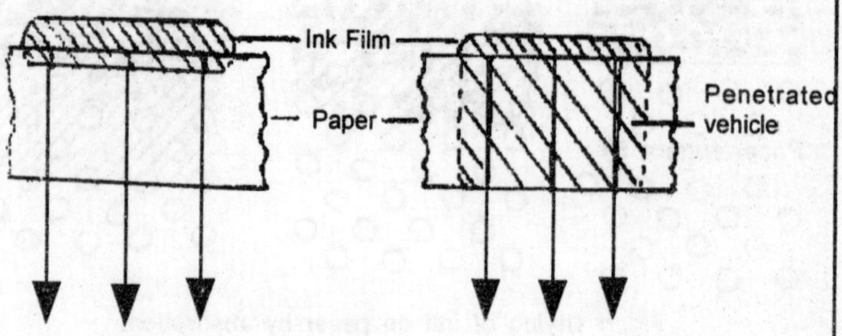

Fig. 2. Showthrough and strikethrough.

There is also the possibility that paper may be picked or torn by the ink which may be like a paste. The offset process in particular uses inks which are very tacky and is used in very thin films. In such cases the paper may stick to the blanket and when pulled may be damaged on the surface. In limits the coating may pull off or in uncoated papers the strands of fibres may be pulled off - contaminating the ink as well as producing an unsatisfactory print.

Ink dries on paper by any one or a combination of the following mechanisms:

1. **Absorption:** The pores in paper provide capillaries in which the liquid portion of the ink is absorbed. The vehicle tends to change its composition as it seeps through the thickness of paper. The insoluble constituents of ink are left on the surface. In rare cases the surface of dried ink may unbind itself from the ink vehicle and form loose powder. This also may lead to a dull printed surface. The effect is most common in moderate to low beaten paper.
2. **Evaporation:** The vehicle sometimes has many volatile compounds. When they are applied on paper or substrate that do not absorb, such as heavily coated or glazed papers, metals and non porous plastics ink loses its vehicle by evaporation. The rate of evaporation can be increased by application of moderate amounts of heat.
3. **Oxidation/Polymerization:** One of the major mechanisms of drying of ink is by polymerization of the constituents to

hard masses. In linseed oil based vehicles the polymerization occurs due to oxidation of the ink in air.

4. **Chemical Polymerization**: In synthetic plastic inks the hardener may be a constituent of the ink itself.
5. **Precipitation**: One of the processes of drying uses inks that turn dry by precipitation. The precipitation is triggered with moisture and the mass turns dry.
6. **Fusion**: In case of toners transferred to paper or similar substrate the ink is in fine powder form either as a powder or finely dispersed in no polar solvents. The toner particles are deposited on the paper surface by electrostatic attraction and are thermally fused into paper.
7. **Dye Transfer**: Dye sublimation process is used in thermal printers to transfer ink on to paper. The process directly heats and sublimes the dye in its vehicle. Paper is supposed to receive the ink as vapour and immediately have it set as solid.

Evaporation	**Oxidation/Polymerisation**
Gravure and flexography On non-absorbent stock Gravure Flexography Letter press heatset Web offset heatset	Letter press and litho on non-absorbent stock Letter press Litho
Moisture set Steam set	News inks Book inks Non-heatset web inks
Precipitation	**Absorption**

Fig. 3. Printing process and process of drying.

The quality of the paper used and the ink selected should be such that there are no undesirable print effects and should not cause any problems while printing.

Process-wise Demands

A listing of the process and the mechanism of drying commonly found as listed as below:

Printing Process	*Major Drying Mechanisms*
Letter Press	A, O, E, P
Litho Printing	O, A, C, E
Flexo, Gravure	E, A
Screen Printing	E, O, C
Dye Transfer	D
Laser Printing	F

Flexo

Ink is transferred from anilox rollers to the printing surface. The anilox roller cells have to be filled properly hence low tack ink is used. As a result picking of paper does not happen. Other surface properties are not very important. The ink generally dries by evaporation as solvent based inks are generally used. In cold countries heaters are used making it necessary to have good thermal stability for paper. Average mechanical properties needed.

Gravure

The ink is directly driven into the cells of the cylinder. The paper is pressed on. Hence pin point smoothness and absence of pits and voids is a critical requirements. Softness and compressibility are essential. Web should unwind smoothly.

Letter Press

Smoothness is important for complete image transfer. Paper surface must be ink receptive. Water resistance not important. Pick strength important.

Screen Printing

Dimensional stability and bulk are important requirements, others not very important.

Sheetfed Offset

Higher surface and bonding strength is essential as inks used are very tacky. Water resistance is important as the paper would come in contact with moistened rubber blanket. Excessive moisture might introduce curl and dimensional changes. Long grain paper is required.

Web Offset

The properties required are identical to sheetfed. The paper must have better tear resistance than as required by other processes. Ability to maintain uniform tension must exist to avoid wrinkles.

Writing Papers

It is necessary that all writing papers must be well sized to avoid spreading of ink. The surface smoothness is also of importance. Papers moderately calendered but of good whiteness are generally used. In special applications papers such as vegetable parchment are used. Specially cast papers such as onion skin finish may be used.

The paper must be well sized as the ink should not spread and also should dry as fast as possible. The inks used are mostly liquid inks and often water based hence the choice is very critical. The surface should also be reasonably smooth and show through should be at its lowest.

Packaging Papers

General printability, moisture and liquid resistance important. Must have good burst strength which is an approximate measure of the load bearing capacity. Must have good printability at least on one side. When white, must be bright enough to accept colours for the product. Folding strength is also important as packages may have to have some creasing and folding requirements.

Papers for corrugated packages must have good mechanical strength and adhesive acceptance properties. The outer side must have water resistance properties as defined for standard glazed surfaces.

Electrical Applications

Paper is a good electrical insulator. Specially made papers are used as electrical insulators in capacitors, transformers, motors and chokes. In such applications the electrical properties turn more important than others. The paper is usually immersed in mineral oil. Hence oil absorption should not affect the properties of paper especially the mechanical strength. As oil absorption properties are difficult to measure directly, water absorption and retention is used as the guide. Printability and similar properties are not important but the surface properties such as finish and smoothness are known to improve the electrical properties.

PAPERS FOR OTHER APPLICATIONS

Paper for ink jet printing has desirable characteristics very similar to the writing papers. However the inks used are very thin and the major process of drying is absorption. Precipitation has also been tried as a drying technique in ink jet printing when the paper is specially treated or manufactured to set instantaneously. The paper need not have surfaces as smooth as for writing as the printing is done without direct contact.

Paper for xerox printing and copying also need be special in that the process of drying is melting in. The paper sheet has to stand fusion at higher temperature, which requires that the fillers or coatings must be resistant to heat.

Paper for packaging food articles may have to have some very special properties. These include toxicity, smell, bleeding of colours, grease and water resistance. Some of these properties are not quite measurable but are of great importance both as requirements of law and hygiene.

The physical properties measured generally indicate the physical condition of the paper sample. To quite an extent this indicates the printability of paper as the condition of the surface and the bulk are defined in these variables. The print quality depends on these properties to quite an extent.

The various properties of paper can be put into a few categories such as:

- Bulk properties
- Surface properties
- Optical properties
- Mechanical properties, and
- Others.

Bulk Properties

Bulk properties are mainly a set of properties acquired in selection of pulp and fillers/additives. They correspond mainly to the density of paper and to an extent the thickness of paper. The thickness of paper is a manufactured property and in most of the applications has to be reasonable. The bulk of paper is specific to the application. The selection of paper or board is decided entirely by the application. For the same grammage of paper one may have different thicknesses. A reasonable thickness or bulk gives a sense of good touch and feel in a book compared to very thin pages. SGW papers are generally have a higher bulk. Dictionary and encyclopedia like large volumes of books have low bulk paper.

Surface Properties

The surface properties especially of uncoated papers may have lot of variations. The mechanism of drying, the ink requirement and many such properties depend entirely on the surface. Calendering and coatings affect the surface properties quite considerably. The manufacturing method employed in making paper decides to some extent the surface properties. The surface properties are an important parameter in selection from the point of view of printability. Selection of the printing process may also depend on the surface available. The surface properties of coated papers are decided almost entirely by the properties of the coating material.

Optical Properties

Optical properties are of two categories. The bulk optical properties such as colour, transparency/opacity (see-through) and the surface properties such as gloss, reflectance etc. Depending on the application one may have to choose the right values. The properties are a function of the beating, choice of pulp, additives and surface treatment.

Mechanical Properties

Mechanical properties are a function of the formation and selection of fibre. They are not affected by normal surface treatments but are affected by lamination and similar processes. They are of great importance in packaging applications but are significant in choosing the right printing process.

It is possible to consider the mechanical properties in two different ways. The first is the mechanical properties of the thickness of paper and other the length and breadth of paper.

The properties of the thickness are the binding of paper, variation in property because of the variations in composition over thickness such as two sidedness and fluff on surface. The length and breadth properties are the tear and pull strength, burst strength and properties related to grain direction.

Other Properties

Properties such as moisture resistance, porosity, smell, taste, resistance to heat etc. are important in specific requirements.

28

Varieties of Paper Grades and their Properties

The properties of paper as explained earlier depends on the following factors:

- **The composition of the pulp.** The chemical constitution which in turn depends on the origin and the process of pulping.
- **The physical condition and treatment of pulp**. The amount of hydration and refining that takes place.
- **Additives** such as fillers and sizing agents and other pulps of different physical and chemical properties blended with the main pulp.
- **Formation parameters.** The amount of pressure applied. The design of the machine or the process employed on forming paper.
- **Calendering** or other mechanical treatment of surface of paper.
- **Application of sizing agents** or similar treatments to get desired chemical properties of the surface.
- Coating composition.

The various combinations of the above parameters lead to a variety of papers normally recognized by their trade names.

By using hardwork kraft pulp of providing bulk, with minimal beating and a slight hydration blotting papers are made. Soda pulp and cotton linters may be used. The product is bound to be bulky, porous and absorbent.

Antique paper is produced using hardwood kraft pulp for providing bulk. A small amount of sulphate ands sulphite is used for better sheet formation. Sometimes mad entirely from soda pulp.

If a smaller amount of soda pulp is used and more of chemical fibre is included then the bulk is reduced. The beating may be increased to make papers of lesser bulk but of higher strength.

By increasing the beating and hydration further and using larger amounts of sulphite or sulphate pulp leads to a paper of better smoothness and firmness known popularly as English finish.

Increasing sulphate and sulphite and more of refining leads to a further better formed paper. This is strong enough and moisture resistant enough to be handled on litho machines and hence known as litho English fiinish paper.

Bond paper is produced using all sulphite or hard wood kraft pulp. The pulp is well beaten and well hydrated. The resultant paper will have a crackle and have a very high burst strength.

Coated body is produced with no regard for surface finish (as this would be obtained by coating any way) and hence use a high percentage of soda pulp. The sulphates may be added just enough to give the basic strength.

Coated or uncoated publication paper, tablet, litho, copying, business, cover stock, photographic, machine glazed and modified finish tissue, one-time carbon and other speciality grades are generally made using two and three press open draw fourdriniers. Plain, suction grooved, inverted, reversed and shrink sleeve presses are normally used alone or in combinations. Generally synthetic press felts must be used to reduce the breakages.

Kraft paper and bag, kraft liner board are made using softwood pulp which has long fibres. Machine speeds are similar to fine papers pick up felts must be open enough to resist filling. The second and third presses must have uniform pressure distribution to prevent base strike through.

Boards including food board, milk carton, cup, bristol, vellum, tag grades are manufactured on 2 and 3 press open draw fourdriniers. Bulk and good finish are the most desirable properties. Made from 3 plies of board, the liner, the filler and the black. The liner is usually coated with white fillings of good quality.

Newsprint and offset paper are lighter weight papers and must run at higher speeds. Stock for newsprint is primarily SGW and is characterized by short fibres and a percentage of long fibre chemical pulp is added for additional strength. Machines used are similar to fine papers. Pick up felts must be permeable and should not fill.

Single felt units are used in making tissue papers including toilet, facial napkin and toweling tissues. Yankee fourdrinier with two felts is traditionally used.

SOME SPECIALITY PAPERS AND BOARDS

Adhesive coated papers

Made from different paper bases such as glassine, coloured, glossy coated, cast coated, low gloss coated etc. foil mounted ton paper is also used. Gummed papers are more prone to curl and hence carefully handled. Adhesives could be heat seal, pressure sensitive and water based.

Blanks

Thick paper board with thickness 0.4 to 1.25 mm made on cylinder machines. It is designated by ply number.

Excessive bending and ink tact must be avoided. Used generally as backing material.

Cards and boards are generally made from chemical pulp. Grammage between 140 and 350 gsm. Because of the thickness it is possible to attain a variety of finishes. When rag content is increased a variety known as index bristol is produced which is ideal for index cards, erasable cards etc. Postal bristol is used for making post cards. Coated bristols are used in making base material good fort picture post cards.

45 to 90 gsm paper is used in making business forms. The business forms are printed on web machines hence the paper must have good physical strength. Dimensional stability to stand collating and registration and computer print out is also an important criterion.

Papers for making carbon less papers have to stand the specific chemicals on the back of the top sheets and the front of the bottom sheet. Care is taken in printing so as not to damage the coated surfaces and not to use excessive pressures or folds.

Embossed papers made with engraved rollers.

Gummed Paper

Paper with gum or adhesive coating on one side. The adhesives may be pressure sensitive or water soluble.

Hand-made Paper

Stress free and grain direction free paper made on the deckle. Traditionally 3 finishes: (1) **Hot Pressed** (Zinc plates are placed between sheets and passed through rollers to give some glaze); (2) **NOT** meaning not hot pressed: When paper is dried by pressing 3 or 4 times between felts; and (3) **Rough** when only one pressing is done and the surface is fairly rough.

Kraft

The wrapping brown paper made from sulphate pulp has long strong fibre. MG is common often with a pattern on the glazing cylinder. Can be bleached white with difficulty and can also be made in colours.

Marbled Paper

Used mainly as end papers of books. Original is always made by hand. Various liquid pigment colours float on a viscous gum solution and skilled craftsman weave patterns. Uncoated good quality strong paper is dipped sheet by sheet into the bath. Artificial marbled paper is produced by offset printing.

Coated Papers

A light pigment coating of the order of 4 gsm may be applied as a preliminary coat. Sizing is a substitute for light coatings. The higher end is the cast coated board. Between the two there are a wide variety of coated versions. Blade coating produces a matt finish. Calendering is done to get a satin smooth finish. Kuster rolls placed at the finishing end of paper machine can improve the finish. Coating can be applied to all kind of paper or substrate.

Art Paper

Heavily coated paper with high gloss. Three or so coats and super calendering done to obtain better finish. The first coat is usually on the paper machine itself. The next about 8 gsm may be off machine and blade/roller/air knife coated. Super calendering done to obtain desired finish. Expensive because of multiplicity of processes.

Bill Blade

A technique of coating in which both sides of the paper are coated with about 10 gsm of coat material. The coating is applied with rubber backing roll and blade.

Blade Coated, Cast Coated

Techniques used for coating. Both produce material with 80 to 400 gsm substance. Cast coating gives exceptionally high gloss.

Chromo Paper

Generally one-sided art paper. Used specially for colour proofing. Made from good quality material and well finished and coated matt or bright white. If chromo has to be used fort litho printing the coating as well the bulk must be reasonably water proof.

Light Weight Coated

Papers with substance of about 60 gsm. Used generally for journals.

Machine Coated

Coating done on paper machine. Generally a cheaper alternative, hence used in educational books.

Matt Coated Art

Art paper may be matt or gloss finished. Used for expensive colour printed books. Easier to read as light does not reflect directly from surface. Glossy ink can produce excellent results.

Pigment coated, Roll coated, Size press coated.

Truflo

A high gloss paper with above average bulk. Super calenders are not used. Both sides of a two wire paper is coated to a gloss finish. 115 to 170 gsm is common.

Cover papers

Are specially made coated or uncoated for books (case bound or limp bound). The substance range is around 100 gsm. Grain direction is important. Book binding cloth is rarely used now and paper with textures is the common material being used. Sold by meters.

May be unglazed and fancy finished.

Boards

Coated Boards (Art Board)

Used for covering paper backs and limp books. After printing the board is laminated substance range 200-500 gsm.

PVC

Incorporated into a base paper or applied as a coating produces a material between paper and cloth. 250 gsm is typical weight.

Uncoated paper between 150 and 500 gsm also could be used. Some are good as book and papers. Book Jackets normally coated on one side only with strength durability and high gloss-around 120 gsm.

Substance over 220 gsm. Display boards and Grayboards (usually straw or waste paper).

Ivory Board

Very smooth board for business cards, invitations and greetings.

Pulp Board uncoated wood free board-usually a single ply for paper back covers-need lamination.

Uncoated Papers

Acid Free Paper

Uses chemical pulp pH 7.07 or more. Lignin is acidic hence it has to be lignin free.

Antique Laid

Paper made with a laid dandy roll to get a pattern of noticeable parallel lines or chain lines. Other patterns also may be laid with dandy roll.

Antique Wove

They are sold as 14 to 25 vol i.e. 14 or 25 mm for 200 pp at 100 gsm. Lower vols known as book woves. 70 gsm vol 21 paper will be less expensive than 80 gsm vol 19. Eucalyptus pulp (traditionally esparto pulp) which has opacity and bulk because of short fibres are pulped CTMP to get the grade. Lower vol have a smoother surface compared to higher vols. Up to vol 21 generally produces good quality prints. Novels, children books, fax editions etc. are produced with antique wove. The colour generally is cream. Are trough or matt finish.

Bank Note Paper

Made by hand or mold. Selected linen cuttings and added ramie fibres used to get strength. Long and prolonged heating is necessary to get the most fold resistant paper.

Bank papers are rag papers normally tub sized. Thin and strong papers generally not glazed.

Bible Printing

As it is thin may have problems of pin holed and see through. Folding and holding large sheets may be a problem. India paper was used by OUP. Smooth but not very polished surface. Generally all rag or rag and wood. Loated with chalk to about 30% and a small amount of titanium dioxide.

Bleached Mechanicals

Chemically bleached and sometimes super calendered. Light weight coateds can be used for newspapers.

Bond

Classified as writing papers. Must have permanence that is durability in handling, erasing, folding etc., enough surface hardness for pen and ink writing, typing, stiffness as required for letter heads etc., generally made from chemical wood.

Cotton content bond papers with cotton (used to be called rag content) between 25 to 100 p.c. They are made on slow paper machines with air drying and well formed papers. They have added strength and a cockle finish. Due to the hard surface the right ink must be used.

High quality papers are used for policies, deeds etc.

Laid finishes are also possible and may be in colour.

Weight range 60 to 80 gsm. Alum and rosin are common sizes. Engine, surface and tub sizing may be done. Very similar to Bank paper but is stronger and thicker.

Book Woves

Low bulk antique woves.

Bulky MF Mechanical

This is pure mechanical or bleached mechanical with a semi smooth machine finish, ideal for paper backs. The fibres are shorter than chemical fibres and hence have a bulk and opacity. It has a creamy off white shade with a brightness between 70 and 75. The brightness enhanced by having an extra peroxide bleaching. Substance is between 40 to 80 gsm and thickness 70 to 125 microns. They are supplied in reels. Generally by length and sometimes by weight.

Bulky news

Same as above a non sizing and lesser smoothness good for bad paper backs.

Cartridge

Weight between 90 and 220 gsm. Used mostly in litho printing. Most popular type of printed surface. Unbleached or semi bleached made from manila, jute and kraft pulp.

Copier paper

Higher dimensional stability desired. Should not curl or jam in copier should stand the heat in copier and should be made with duo formers. Substances 70-160 gsm.

Heat set web offset

This grade may be exposed to open flames and hence moisture contend should be low – about 5%.

Light weight printing

Uncoated wood free MF used in dictionaries and the like.

Mechanical printings

Superior newsprint with engine or surface sizing.

MF

Used extensively for magazines and general printing work. Generally made from wood free and mechanical fibres and are surface sized, finish depends on calendering.

Neutral Sized Paper

Alum is acidic and if the loading is mostly calcium carbonate it may be possible to get paper pH 7.5.

Newsprint

Brightness 60 ISO, discolours quickly made almost entirely from ground wood, may be calendered to print colours, screens over 100 not ok. Standard substance is 45 to 50 gsm.

Offset Cartridge

Paper over 90 gsm specially made for litho printing. Particularly suited for children books and colour work. Surface sized, uncoated and are usually wood free. CTMP pulp may also be used. Paper is bright white may be acidic with pH 5 but must be vary flat.

Offset printing

Weight less than 90 gsm but similar to the one above. Both wood free and mechanical are available and are classified as much. Used extensively in educational books etc. of longer life.

Opaque Printing

Generally surface sized, lightly coated less than 90 gsm.

Part Mechanical

With more than 10% mechanical pulp. (Not wood free) CTMP and TMP based pulp combinations are good for most of the jobs.

Permanent Paper

Paper made from rags and cotton in Europe and America have stood the test of time. They have remained almost unchanged even after four centuries, the only visible change is the colour within too changes only when paper is exposed to sunlight or ultra violet light. The degradation that occurs in paper over time is that it turns brittle and crumbles with time. Wood pulping got introduced into paper making in the later half of the nineteenth century. It was this paper which had a problem with its life. The problem was identified as the presence of rosin and alum as either sizing or digesting agents used in pulping. With reaction with air the materials yield an acidic ambient which degrades the bonding of paper. The problem persisted with chemical wood pulps and was sometimes even more severe. Since 1950 there is a clear tendency to move from acidic to either neutral or alkaline paper making processes.

The negative effects are more predominant in wood pulps than other sources of pulp such as rags. It is assumed that the mechanism of degradation is related to lignin and hence wood pulps free of lignin are known as wood free pulps. Paper counting less than 10% ground wood is considered wood free. (American National Standard for permanent paper - ANSI Z39 1984) pH 7.5, should contain an alkaline reserve such as Calcium Carbonate, a furnish of entirely wood pulp or ideally rag fibres, a specified tear resistance and a specified fold resistance.

Pure Paper

Meaning contains less than 10% wood pulp.

Twin Wire Paper

Has much better formation on top. Depends on manufacturing process.

Water Mark

Used from dandy roll as a security measure and also as a trademark. Cutting to sheets with register is difficult hence product more expensive.

Wood free

Paper made from fibres separated by chemical processes, free from lignin and other woody parts. May contain up to 10% wood fibre.

Web Sized Offset Paper

A cheaper substitute for the light weight coated paper used in magazine applications-SC process used in making.

A FEW VARIETIES AND KINDS OF PAPER AND BOARDS

Bible Printing	25-35 gsm
Lightweight Printing	35-60 gsm
Printings	60-90 gsm

Cartridges	90-220 gsm
Boards	Over 220 gsm

SUBJECTIVE TESTS IN GENERAL ON PAPER WHILE ACCEPTING FOR PRINTING

Estimation of:

- Capability of reproducing the image elements of the original
- Cause a minimum of printing problems.

The important parameters are:

- Print uniformity.
- Relative print density.
- Colour rendering.
- Ink requirement.
- Ink setting, set off, smearing.
- Print through, (show through and strike through)
- Rub off properties.

Newsprint

The only three tests done in a newspaper plant are:

1. **Grammage**: 52 g was a std. Till 70. It has reduced to 49.8 g, 45 and 40 g and 36 and 28 g for air mail editions.
2. **Moisture**: Usually between 5 and 10%. About 1% moisture is introduced in each printing unit. Less than 7% is not very acceptable.
3. **Ash content**: generally less than 2%. In German products may reach 10 to 12% due to fillers. Tolerance and acceptance limits are not specified.

Structural Characteristic

- Felt marking and wire marking to be avoided for better quality print.
- Sheet density and thickness not specified.
- Surface smoothness is expressed as the ml of air escaping per minute with and air supply pressure of 1.471 kPa and at the edge 98 and 490 kPa.

- Smoothness should fall in the range 75 to 175 ml/min (Bendetsen 98 kPa). Higher values preferred by offset and lower by letter press.
- Bekk smoothness 45 to 75 seconds.
- No general recommendation exists for compressibility, air permeability, hardness, oil absorption and water absorption.
- Shade values: As measured on STFI master Elrepho 2000 instrument on 40 to 48 gsm.
- Y-Value 64.5%, Dominant wavelength-576.5 nm, Excitation purity 7.5%
- L *84.2, a* –0.4, b* 6.9
- Opacity: 94 to 90%

Problems in Web

1. Mechanical Defects

- Edge damage.
- Body damage.
- Head damage: Damages to the side of the reel may be mechanical or due to moisture absorption.
- Out of roundness.
- Calender cuts: Cuts in the machine direction caused in calendering.
- Slime hole: A hole on papar produced by resin or fungus.
- Water drop hole: Hole in web caused by dropping water before complete paper formation
- Plucking hole: produced by paper sticking to rollers on paper machine.
- Silver, shiver: Unseparated bundle of fibres in paper
- Hair cut: Cuts caused by thin foreign material such as hair.
- Winder wrinkle.
- Burst in reel.
- Uneven winding.

- Convex or concave winding.
- Run together at core.
- Loose paper.
- Edge cracks.
- Rough edges.
- Protruding splice.
- Stuck splice.
- Soft end, Baggy end.
- Rope marking.
- Core defects: Protruding, slipped, damaged.

2. Running Defect - Runnability of Webs

1. Web break at press start:

Before printing unit	Mechanical problems of early knife activation or baggy parts on roller.
	Tension control not ok in or after printing unit.
	Too tacky ink.
	Water in cylinder gap.
	Improper start up sequence.
2. Web break during Reel change	Improper glue.
3. Web break in run	Transport damage in reel.
	Too high winding tension.
	Too high tension on outer layers.
	Imperfect mill join.
	Out of roundness of reel.
	Holes in the web, shives in web.
	Too much too tacky ink.
	Water, ink or foreign object on web.
	Creases on the web.
	Wandering web.

Sheetfeed problems

- Double sheets – due to many problems.
- Sheets sticking and separation problems - hand jogging needed often.
- Sheet defects - incorrect edges, damage in transit and others leading to transport in machine problems.
- Mechanical strength problems - softness, tearing strength etc.
- Paper strength problems, paper sticking to roller and tearing.
- Compressibility and surface strength - marking by grippers, tear at grippers.
- Problems due to static electricity. Generally sticking together of paper sheets and hence double sheets.
- Uneven moisture on different areas due to many causes - can be cured sometimes by leaving the packet of paper to adjust to room ambient.
- Tail end hook.
- Caused by the paper sticking to the blanket too tightly when pulled off. Can be remedied by using heavier paper or adjusting ink tack.
- Wavy edges are caused by stack of paper at lower moisture level than atmosphere.
- Tight edges reverse of above. The center of the sheets goes baggy.
- Creasing further aggravated because of water.

General Problems in Print Reproduction due to Paper

Printability:

- Paper colour, inability to print some colours.
- Gray on faint print, insufficient ink, ink/water imbalance.
- Colour variation throughout stopping and starting during run, ink/water imbalance.
- Shadows filling in on photos - print too dark, over absorbent paper, excess printing pressure, over exposure of plate.

- Unprinted spots on paper-picking, ink toto tacky, too soft paper, wrong blanket.
- Spots on printed areas - hickies, paper fibres or dried oink blobs adhering to paper or blanket.
- Blurred colour photos - misregister, paper stretch due to many reasons.
- Surface smoothness problems.
- Loss of image - low spot, indents on blanket.
- Faint image outline marks on solid - repeat - ghosting, trapping, poor ink film adjustment.
- Smudge on non-image - scumming, plate corrosion, improper dampening.
- Faint tint on non-image areas - tinting, contamination of fountain solution.
- Faint pattern over print - damper marks, excessive pressure.
- Random image smudge - set off, excess ink, undrying ink.
- Distortion.

STANDARD PAPER SIZES

Standard sheet sizes of paper

- Crown: 15" × 20" at 8vo 5" × 7-1/2".
- Demy 17.5" × 22.5" at 8vo 5-5/8" × 8-3/4". Used as writing paper.
- Royal 20" × 25" at 8vo 6.25" × 10". Used as cover paper.
- Foolscap 13.5" × 17. 5" at 8vo 4-3/8' × 6-3/4"
- Medium 18" × 23"
- Bond, writing, ledger, manifold 17" × 22"

In British and American sizes the size is often referred as the basic size and the number of pages made from it e.g. crown octavo.

Metric Sizes, also ISI

- A0 = 841 × 1190 mm (Area = 1 sq. meter – All types of textbooks, magazines, newspapers, periodicals, etc.)

- A1 = 594 × 841 mm
- A2 = 420 × 594 mm
- A3 are direct further half-divisions of A2
- B0 = 1414 × 1000 mm (Large size posters and calendars)
- C0 = 1297 × 917 mm (Envelops, small pocket size books, brochures, folders, etc.)

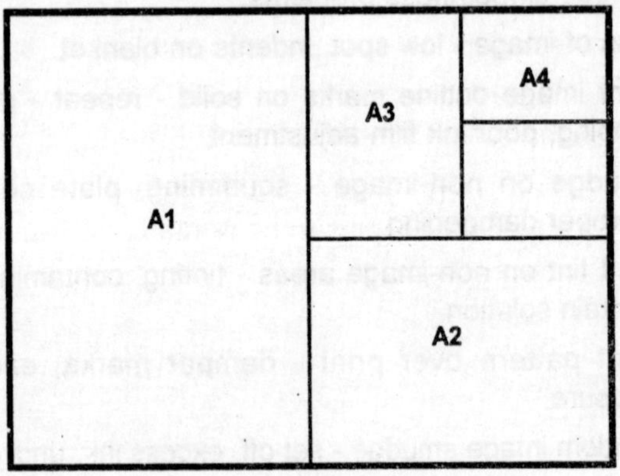

A0
Sub-divisions of A0 paper

Fig. 1. Paper subdivisions in metric sizes.

Untrimmed sizes are made available which carry the prefix R and contain 5% more area of paper as trimming allowance. The division is identical as in A0.

- RA0 = 860 × 1220 mm
- RA1 = 610 × 860 mm
- RA2 = 430 × 610 mm.

The untrimmed stock is especially useful in creating publications whose pagers are in the A range.

PAPER CALCULATIONS

Calculating the Paper Requirement for a Typical Publication to be Printed

Section is defined as a part of a book that generally is produced from one sheet of paper. The standard size of paper selected is organized into the forms and the pages are arranged as per the imposition scheme. The paper wasted in between the page layout need not be taken into account for calculating the paper requirement as the cutting allowance as well as design wastage is accounted for. The number of pages in a section hence allow a direct calculation of the paper required for the book. In case of web machines the cut off length (And the width of web) can be considered as the equivalent length of a section.

P = number of pages per section
(The number of pages per section is a design parameter and is known at the pre printing stage)

n = number of pages in the book

c = number of copies to be printed

1 ream = 500 sheets

Hence number of sheets of paper required $s = (n \times c) /p$

Add to this number the wastage and the spoilage allowance. (This may be simplified as a multiplication factor such as 1.05 – see end of this section for actual calculation. The spoilage allowance depends on the number of copies and the number of colours and also depends on the printing house.)

S = S (1 + spoilage allowance)

Number of reams to be ordered = S/500

Example: To print 1000 copies of a book which contains 144 pages and made from 16 pages sections arranged on 24" × 32" sheets:

The paper required is $s = \dfrac{152 \times 1000}{16} = 9500$

S = S × 1.05 = 9975 (Spoilage assumed as 5%)

Number of reams of paper needed $= \dfrac{9975}{500} = 20$ reams

Calculating the Weight of a Ream of Paper: If the paper is of any the of the 'An' series of sizes then

the weight of 1 ream$= \dfrac{\text{gsm rating of paper}}{2 \times 2^n}$ kilograms

Example: The weight of a ream of 60 gsm paper that is in A2 size is,

$$= \frac{60}{2 \times 2^2} \, 15 \text{ kg}$$

If the paper is untrimmed a 5% extra has to be added. For example, the weight of a ream of RAO sheets of 75 gsm rating is

$$= \frac{75}{2 \times 2^0} \times 1.05 \text{ kg} = 39.38 \text{ kilograms}$$

For the American or British sizes the following formula can be applied:

$$\text{Weight of a ream of paper} = K \frac{\text{gsm rating}}{2} \text{kg}$$

K is a conversion constant and is equal to

Bond = 0.241

Demy = 0.248

Royal = 0.3225

Crown = 0.194

For other sizes K = 6.4516 X 10^{-4} × Length × Width

(Length and width to be expressed in inches)

Example: The weight of a ream of Demy sized paper in 45 gsm is

$$\frac{0.248(K) \times 45}{2} = 5.58 \text{ kg}$$

Calculating the length of a reel of paper

Weight of the reel = w kgs

Width of the reel = c cm

Substance of paper = g gsm

$$\text{Length of paper in the reel} = \frac{w \times 10^5}{c \times g} \text{ metres}$$

Example: The length of paper is in a reel 67 cms wide and weighing 200 kgs is 3732 meters if the paper is 80 gsm.

Calculating the Length of a Reel of Paper (Approximate method)

For a roll of paper let the outer diameter be RD and the core diameter CD. Let it have a width of W centimeters. The weight of the roll is approximated depending on the type of paper used. The weight is calculated as:

Weight of the roll of paper = F × (RD^2 – CD^2) × W kg

Here RD and CD are expressed in cm and F is a factor depending on the kind of paper.

F has a value:

For newsprint	0.443×10^{-3}
For Antique finish	0.498×10^{-3}
For MF, off set, bond	0.747×10^{-3}
For SC, one side coated	0.830×10^{-3}
For 2 side coated	0.941×10^{-3}

Example: A roll of offset paper wound on a 10 cm core with an outer diameter of 100 cm and a width of 75 cm well weigh:

$0.747 \times 10^{-3} \times (10^4 - 10^2) \times 75 = 554.7$ kg

SPOILAGE ALLOWANCES

Sheetfed Work

Quantity	Printer's allowance	Binder's allowance	Total spoilage
1K to 2K	4%	2.5%	6.5%
2K to 5K	3%	2.0%	5.0%
5K to 10K	2.5%	1.5%	4.0%
10K +	2.5%	1.0%	3.5%

Add 2% per colour to printer allowance for multicolour work.

Webfeed work

Quantity	Printer's allowance	Binder's allowance	Total spoilage
10K to 15K	11%	1%	12%
15K to 25K	9%	1%	10%
25K to 75K	7%	1%	8%
75K +	5%	1%	6%

Add 3% per colour for multicolour work.

LAMINATION

Certain number of prints are required in excess for setting up laminating and UV curing units.

The spoilage may be estimated as follows:

Up to 5K	5% Overs
5K +	3%
100K +	1%

If relative humidity is 50 to 55% and surfaces are supplied flat anything can be laminated with film. When very rough, absorbent and pregrained surfaces exist, a proofing may be necessary. Rough matt coated boards are not suitable for lamination. When UV coating is done the substrate surface properties are even more critical and hence selections should be done more cautiously. (Surface oil absorbency test should have value in excess of 60 seconds is desirable.)

Ink Selection for Lamination

Warning: Colours may look different after lamination.

The formulation should be such that:

1. They dry quickly with low residual solvent.
2. Have minimal wax, polyethylene and silicone and other surface active agents. They are added to introduce slip which prevents scuffing.
3. Should be tinctorially strong.
4. Pigment should be resistant to solvents as per BS-3442 (Test method 4).
5. UV cured inks are preferred.
6. Metallic inks may get affected by immigration of lubricants to the inks surface preventing adhesion of the lamination. (Avoid laminating metallic ink-coated surfaces.)
7. Poor bonding to metal flakes in metallic inks leading to delamination. (Avoid laminating metallic ink coated surfaces.)
8. If foil stamping is to be done subsequently check.

29

Transfer Paper

The transfer papers are specially coated, which allows the built up film or print to be transferred to the substrate to which it is to be applied.

Long ago the technique used was a lithographic impression on a sheet paper which had been coated with water soluble coating. More often a coating of white pigments such as titanium dioxide, zinc oxide etc. sprayed over to visualize its background. When this print is pressed onto the substrate (Varnished) and moistened then the substrates get printed by transfer mechanism.

The 'transfer mechanism' is otherwise called "decal comania." Now-a-days by successive research work on this field, the decal comania is the result of a highly specialized process.

The base paper may be a single sheet to which the coating and printing are applied.

If tissue papers are to be used then, they are laminated to a heavier paper to avoid curl and dimensional changes. The lamination of heavier paper also provides ease of printing and registering operations.

REQUIREMENTS

(a) Should be absorbent.

(b) Should possess uniform colour.

(c) Should have high wet strength.

COATING MATERIALS

The base coat on the bottom side of the paper usually composed of binding agents such as albumen, glycerine and starch, starch and gum arabic, egg albumen, starch and dextrose (water soluble coatings). The base coat provides a smooth printing surface.

This type of coating sheets have low moisture resistance and when moisture penetrates in, the paper may curl badly. This creates problem while printing.

The curling should be avoided as far as possible. It is better to coat finished transfer paper by coating consisting of 10% of gelatin and 90% of mixture, containing water and methyl alcohol (3:2). It is observed that this coating balance the stresses in the sheet and retards moisture penetration.

There are two types of transfer sheets, according to method of application. When the transfer papers are applied to the desired surface, either by moisturing the gum on the inner face and pressing the sheet onto the object or substrate. Otherwise a varnish film may be applied to the surface and pasting the face on the substrate. These types of transfer sheets are called Direct transfer types.

In other type the print gets separated from the sheet when kept in water for 15 seconds and the print is applied to the substrate either by self; adherence or by the use of adhesives. These are called 'slide off' transfer type.

30

Teletape Rolls

Teletape rolls are magnetic recording paper or tape, a very recently developed metallic coated paper that serves to supplement or replace wire as a medium for recording sound. Such paper is coated with a magnetically reactive metal powder which acts in the same manner as the wire in becoming activated in a magnetic field and recording and reproducing sound effects. This is used for recording or taping sounds from telephones. While using these magnetic papers and tapes for the purpose of recording and reproduction of sound, the tape is coupled with the suitable transducers, which convert electrical energy into the corresponding fields of varying intensity and *vice versa*.

There is a vast scope for the production of such papers in small scale industry.

PROCESS OF MANUFACTURE

The actual medium upon which the magnetic modulation are impressed is a layer of finely powdered crystalline magnetic articles uniformly coated on a paper base. For example, paper of about 1.5 miles in thickness or even thinner medium is desirable. The density of the sheet must be absolutely uniform and the surface must be as smooth as possible to obtain the best results.

A knife over-all machine may be used for applying the coating. This however, does not give the highest degree of coating-accuracy. A direct gravure print coater can also be employed for producing coatings of constant weight.

The metallic coating must be bound firmly to the paper surface and the film must be flexible and absolutely uniform. Synthetic resin adhesives are generally used to bind the pigments to the paper surface. The denser the coating, the better the fidelity in recording.

Straight-pass driers are used for drying the solvent, the tapes are wound into a single roll and slit into the desired narrow width as a subsequent operation.

31

Toilet Paper Plant

INTRODUCTION

Development of raw materials and the invention of paper machines have ushered in an era of high quality and mass-production and paper is now called the symbol of culture.

Toilet paper is in large and increasing demand and its manufacture can easily be embarked upon by small industry and parties who have had little experiences in paper making.

The mass-producing mills generally use wood pulp as the raw material for toilet paper. But smaller mills use wood pulp and waste paper together, or use waste paper 100 per cent. Waste paper is recovered at a high rate and selection of quality is well controlled.

Wood resources are not distributed uniformly in the world. There are many countries which are poor in wood resources.

MANUFACTURING PROCESS

Broadly speaking, there are two methods for processing waste paper, namely, continuous and batch systems. In general, the process is recommended when the daily production capacity of the mill is five tons. Introduced here is a five ton/day batch system plant using waste paper as raw material. In this plant, besides toilet paper, other kinds of sanitary paper may be produced.

Toilet paper is packed 100 rolls to a case of corrugated board for delivery to the primary wholesaler.

The Japanese standard of toilet paper is:

Roll width : 114 mm ± 1mm.

Inner dia. of winding core : 37-39 mm.

*1. Finished measured length: 45, 55, 64, 75 m.

**2. substance of paper (crepe) : 21-23 g/cm^2

The manufacturing process begins when waste paper is moved upto the sorting yard above the digester by elevator.

The sorted waste paper is fed into the global digester. Simultaneously with the feeding, sodium sulphite, soda ash, etc are sprinkled thoroughly over the waste paper.

After stuffing of the digester has been completed, the gut for the digester is tightly closed. Steam is blown into the digester as it is rotated.

The next step is the charging of the material into the blow pocher.

Circulation is performed by a propeller agitator, and the digesting chemicals are thoroughly washed in the washing drum.

When the washing is over, the material is transferred into the dump chest, from where it is moved up into the head box by pump. Water is added for dilution in the head box.

The material is then sent through the silver screen and Johnson screen for removal of dust. The material which comes out of the screen is transferred into the extractor for washing and clickering.

The material coming out of the extractor is stored in the bleaching chest.

When a chest becomes full, bleach liquor is added.

After the material has been left in the bleaching chest for a fixed time following the bleaching, it is flow-fled into the mixing chest, in which bleach liquor is thoroughly washed away.

Washing takes place in the washing drum. After the washing, fluorescent dye-stuff or rhodamine is applied for colouring as may be required by consumers.

Now that this process has been completed, it is dropped into the stock chest, and sent into the machine chest.

Out of the machine chest, the stock is fed into the head box for flow-fed into the mixing tank at a regulated feed level.

In the mixing tank, the stock is diluted with white water coming out of the wire part, of which more hereafter, and then sent on to the vertical screen.

On the vertical screen, stock with a comparatively larger specific gravity and non- digested stuff are removed.

The material which has passed through the vertical screen goes into the tank and, via the high-pressure pump, is fed into the cleaner, with only accepted material fed into the paper making machine.

Name of machine	**No.**
Extractor, two-stage cylinder type	1
Bleaching test (tank capacity: 35 m^3)	2
Conveyor pump (capacity: 1.5 m^3/min.)	1
Mixing pocher (tank capacity: 35 m^3)	2
Stock chest (tank capacity: 68 m^3)	1
Conveyor pump (capacity: 300 1/min.)	2
Machine chest (tank capacity: 10 m^3)	1
White water pump(capacity: 1.5 m^3/min.)	1
Material feed equipment	
Vertical screen (bed size: 926 × 1,466 mm.)	1
Tail screen (silver type)	1
Tail pump (capacity: 0.3m^3/min.)	1
High pressure pump (capacity: 2.5m^3/min.)	1
Super clone (passing volume: 2,0001/min.)	1
Paper making equipment	
Wire parts (wire cloth of 1,735 mm. × 10.7m. of endless wire)	1
Nozzle slice	1
Deckle device made of brass plate	1
Breast roll of 418 mm. dia. × 1,840 mm. face length	1
Formation box	1

Name of machine	No.
Table roll (172 mm. dia. × 1,840 length)	5
Deflector	4
Suction box	3
Wire roll	3
Shower pipe	3
Hand guide	1
Hand stretcher	2
Bottom couch roll	1
Top couch roll	1
Save-all device	1
Edge cutter	1
Frame and sole cutter	1
Nash pump (aperture: 100 mm.)	1
Back water pump (aperture: 200 x 200 mm.)	1
Wire pit pump (aperture: 150 x 125 mm.)	1
Press part	
Top press roll (510 mm. dia. x 1,785 mm. length)	1
Bottom press roll (410 mm. dia. x 1,785 mm. face length)	1
Frame and pressure device	1
Press doctor device	1

The accepted material goes into the flow box of the paper machine, out of which a fixed amount flows out into the wire parts in consistency of about 0.15-0.2 per cent.

The stock which flows out is dehydrated by the table roll and suction box for transformation into a wet web, which is sent into the press part over a blanket. The wet web is dewatered under the pressure of the roll and pushed against the Yankee dryer.

The wet web is dried by the heat of steam inside the Yankee dryer. At the outlet of the dryer, the web is creped by a special crepe doctor, after which it is wound into rolls.

The base paper of the toilet paper, which has been ruled, is cut into the fixed width by the slitter on the slitting napkins, machine and wound into rolls in the required length.

The above plant can be easily extended, and it may be constructed in large numbers as a common enterprise.

LOCATIONAL CONDITION

1. It is absolutely necessary to ensure a supply of good quality water as well as to have a good drainage system available.
2. As the products of the plant offered are necessaries for the home, if the secondary expenses, such as forwarding charges, are too heavy, the end selling price would be affected. The plant should also have access to locations where raw materials and electric power supply are easily available.

ANNEXURE I

MACHINERY AND EQUIPMENT

Name of Machine	No.
Digester	
Global digester (3,965 mm. dia.)	1
Material Preparation	
Blow pocher (agitator dia; 610 mm.)	2
Conveyor pump (capacity: 1.5 m^3/min.)	1
Dump chest (tank capacity: 50 m^3)	1
Conveyor pump (capacity : 0.5 m/min.)	1
Head box	1
Silver screen with vibrator and transmission equipment	1
Jonsson screen (nominal size: 1 × 2m.)	1
Squeeze roll (300 mm. top roll dia. × 1,785)	2
Squeeze frame and pressure device	1
Felt roll (160 × 11,800 mm. dia)	8
Felt guide, pneumatic type	1
Felt stretcher	1
Suction box	1
Shower pipe	3

Name of Machine	No.
Mash pump (75 mm. aperture)	1
Dryer part dryer (3,050 mm × 1,876 mm).	1
Steam joint, rotary type	1
Dryer gear, helical	1
Dryer bearing and housing	1
Dryer doctor cleaning and crepe	3
Dryer ventilator, centralized type	1
Ventilator Fan	
Touch roll (410 × 1,876 mm.)	1
Touch frame and pressure device	1
Squeeze roll (300 mm. top roll dia. × 1,785 mm.)	2
Squeeze frame and pressure device	1
Felt roll	9
Felt guide, pneumatic type	1
Felt stretcher	1
Shower pipe	2
Paper roll (100 × 1,875 mm.)	2
Dryer and lubrication apparatus	1
Frame and role plate	1
Hand rail and platform	1
Operation air panel, desk type	1
Calender machine (460 × 1,742 mm.)	1
Toilet reel	1
Transmission apparatus	1
Air compressor, automatic unloader type	1
Finishing equipment	
Slitting machine	7
Fresh water pump (capacity, 3,75 m^3/min.)	1
Steam drain pump of LPDG type	1
Bleach liquor pump (100 1/min.)	1

Name of Machine	No.
Electric hoist (2 and 0.5 tons)	2
Tubular boiler, type BC-20	1
Transformer and accessories	1

DAILY REQUIREMENT OF RAW MATERIALS AND UTILITIES

Raw material	Standard	Quantity
Waste paper High grade	(70%)	6 ton
Waste paper Limitation	(30%)	2.5 ton
Wire net for wire part	1,735 × 10,700 m.	per sheet
For blow chest drum	1,500 × 3,600 m.	for 2 sets
For mixing pocher drum	1,500 × 3x600 m.	for 4 sets
Extractor	1x500 × 2x800 m.	2 sheets
Wet blanket	1,700 × 19,00 m	1 sheet
Top blanket	1,800 × 15,800 m	1 sheet
Soda ash		43 kgs.
Sodium Sulphite		300 kgs.
Fluorescent dyestuff		6 kgs.
Rhodamine (dyestuff)		0.6 kgs.
Bleach liquor Ca $(ClO)_2$ (8%)		600 kgs.

UTILITIES

Electric Powder, fuel for boiler – Grade (C) Heavy oil – 2551

Water – underground or river water – 4600 tonnes.

32

Wall Paper

INTRODUCTION

Wall papers are essentially the type of resin-treated or coated paper specialties, used chiefly due to their enhanced decorative value. In the western countries the wall paper has been a commodity of common use for long. During the post World War II period the wall paper industry suffered a set-back. At present time, the momentum has been regenerated and the industry emerging today bids fair to make these wall coverings as popular again as it once was. This world-wide growing preference for wall papers is expected to make significant impact on an appreciable section of Indian community. In India, the market position of this item is very high. The demand is already increasing with its uses.

PROCESS OF MANUFACTURE

The manufacture of wall papers include same phenomena such as plastic coating, printing, embossing and trimming. In the industry, by far the largest tonnage of raw-stock used today falls in basis weights ranging from 40-60 lbs/ream (24 × 36-500). The furnish usually varying between 70-75% ground wood with supplementary amounts of semi-bleached kraft-fibres. For greater wet-strength, the bulk of the tonnage consumed in wall-paper manufacture is treated with either melamine or urea formaldehyde resins.

The principal requirements for a suitable hanging stock is that it should be as uniform as possible, especially in colour, sizing and texture. The finished products be free from shedding. It is one of the factors of paramount importance in the wall covering industry.

PIGMENTS AND PIGMENT BINDERS FOR WALL-PAPER COATINGS

The white pigment is air floated filled clay primarily used in the wall paper industry today. This pigment fills the basic requirements of chemical innerness, soft texture and low cost. Calcium sulphate (Ca So_4) and calcium carbonate (Ca Co_3) are no longer used in any quantity owing to their reactivity with the proteinaceous binders. It is commonly used in the industry. The titanium dioxide is another white pigment employed in any quantity. It is specifically used in coating formulations for the so called soil-proof wall-coverings.

Some important pigments which are used in the manufacturing process are given below:

Table for Pigments

S. No.	Colours	Name of the Pigments
1.	Reds	Napthol reds, phthalocyanine reds, red oxides, cadmium red.
2.	Browns	Iron oxide brown.
3.	Blacks	Iron oxide black, carbon black, bone black.
4.	Greens	Pigment green B, Phthalocyanine green.
5.	Yellows	Chrome yellows, cadmium yellow, yellow iron oxide.
6.	Blues	Thin blue, Phthalocyanine blue.

The pigment binders which are used in the wall paper manufacture today include a long list of adhesive materials. Ranging from water soluble colloids (Casein & Soya protein) to a host of other latices and synthetic resin emulsions. The soya protein is mostly used in wall-paper Industry as a adhesive.

SYNTHETIC RESINS FOR COATING

In the coating process various synthetic resin emulsions are used such as polyvinyl chlorides, polyvinyl acetates, styrene butadiene and acrylic emulsions. Resin emulsions are also used as the sole pigment binders in some formulations but mostly formulations contain mixtures of protein and a compatible emulsion.

In modern time, the styrene butadiene emulsions are used in the wall paper formulations. They are still widely employed for this purpose. Styrene butadiene after blends with soya protein, it provides good wet rub resistance. It also provides good flexibility in coatings. In the manufacture of soil proof wall-paper varieties the polyvinyl chloride emulsions are used. Emulsions of polyvinyl acetate offer improved resistance to yellowing upon exposure to heat and light and great flexibility in coating formulations.

Generally the coatings have less wet rub resistance which are prepared from polyvinyl acetate emulsions in comparison to those made with styrene butadiene resins and polyvinyl chloride. Acrylic emulsions are also used in the coating formulations. These are highly expensive.

MANUFACTURING OPERATIONS

In the first operation of the manufacturing process, before the paper web is subjected to any treatment, it is the preparation of the desired pattern and its installation in the printing machine. All the wall papers manufactured today are printed by the raised surface printing method and much less frequently, wall paper is made by silk-screen printing or engraved roll methods.

The newly discovered surface printing methods employed rollers with the patterns tediously copied by hand on to a wooden cylinder and subsequently outlined with thin brass strips and filled with felt. The print rolls were later replaced by aluminium alloy rollers. In these rollers the design still had to be transferred to the roller by cutting the pattern into the metal with the help of routing tools. This method is much faster in comparison to the old method. The finished roller was more stable to moisture than the wooden roller.

A method of acid etchings designs into magnesium sleeves has been perfected, more recently. The magnesium sleeves, subsequently fitted with ends, and chrome plated. These have proved to be a tremendous improvement over the routed rolls. They have the advantage of being able to reproduce indicately detailed designs at far low cost when compared to the routing process. By the routing technique, simple designs can still be produced more cheap. The acid-etched rolls essentially dominate this field.

After the completion of a set of roller comprising a design is ready for use. It is taken to the print room and now fitted with shafts and a gear of a size to correspond with the repeat of the design. Under the bottom half, the impression of cylinder may have as few as four or as many as twelve printing stations spaced. It can be raised to separate the impression cylinder from the print rolls for threading of the web or for idling periods because the top half is unencumbered. Register is controlled by gears on the shafts of the print rollers. It is filled to a master drive gear of the same size as that of the impression cylinder. Mostly the impression cylinder is covered with a rubber jacket. Colour is furnished to the print roll with the help of felt sleeve from a colour pan. The tension is controlled either by suction boxes or by tension rolls. While the pattern is being installed in the printing machine, all the supporting equipments remain idle.

The colours for designs are being mixed when the print rolls are being installed and fitted in the printing machine. The colour mixer matches the various shades i the design and mixes very close to the proper amount of printing colour from a palatte of 12 to 16 colours. It is necessary for the given run.

After all colours have been matched the print pattern is in register, the actual production of wall-paper begins. Most of the wall-papers are manufactured by "tandem" operation. In this process the web of raw stock is fed and is machine-coated with an opaque ground, dried, printed and dried again by driers. Usually plastic-coated without the webs ever being broken in this sequence, embossing and cutting operations are also sometimes coupled.

Now the web has been coated and printed. The entire face is over coated by a conversion bath consisting of aluminium acetate. Aluminium acetate used either alone or in combination with a non-ionic resin emulsion. The protein faction of the binder insolublize by the aluminium acetate, whereas, the resin faction lays down a clear, hard film over the surface. After dry to the coating, the usual practice is to put up the web reels and to transfer them for embossing and trimming to a finishing department.

FINISHING (EMBOSSING AND TRIMMING)

In the wall paper manufacturing process, the embossing and trimming are the final finishing operations. In the wall paper industry today most of the embossing is simple pressure embossing which employs a steel roll and a paper bowl made of paper discs compressed on a shaft. The wall paper web is run is between when the rolls are pressed tightly together. When more heavily embossed papers are required, the improved embossing techniques are employed.

In the final trimming of the finished wall-papers, several different practices are used.

The process flow sheet for wall paper is given below:

The trimming of the finished wall-papers, is done in many cases. The edge is fully trimmed right at the printer or some times it is only score-cut. It is the recent development is which consists in printing a trimline on at sevage in register with the pattern, which is subsequently picked up with the help of an electric eye. In to stationary knives, that guides the trimming knives or may guide the web.

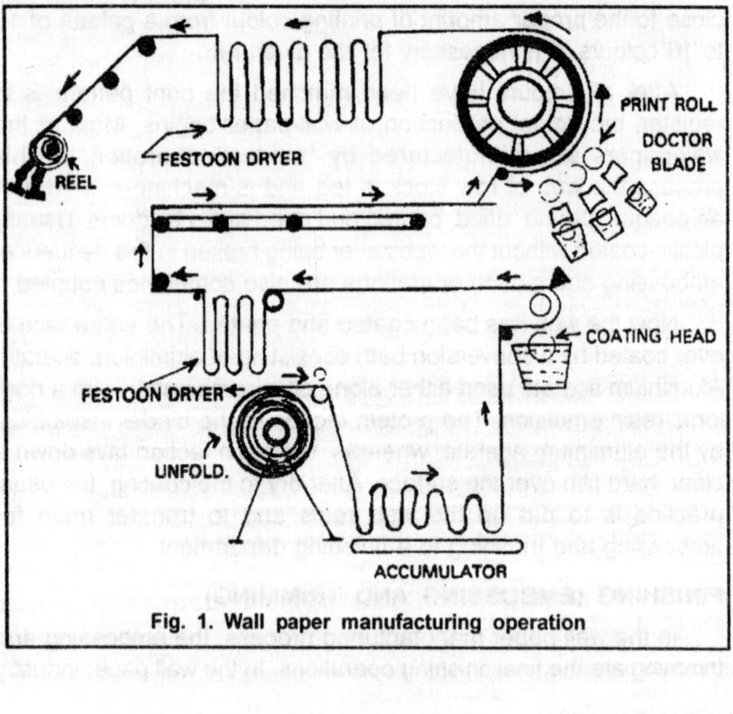

Fig. 1. Wall paper manufacturing operation

33

Wax Coated Paper

INTRODUCTION

Wax coated papers are widely used in packaging of various articles. In food packaging industries wax papers are widely used for packaging of food stuffs, because wax coated paper prevents moisture to penetrate in and does not allow the fragrance to escape out. Wax coated paper are used in metal goods industries (auto parts, razor blades etc.). In textile industry too waxed paper is used for wrapping thread, rayon and nylon etc. The waxed paper is also used for sanitary sheets, wraps for surgical instruments etc.

Wax coated paper also finds application in soap industries, cold drink straw industries, and many others such as cake glue, chewing gum, shrubs and rubber heels etc. can be wrapped in waxed papers.

There are four general types of waxed paper:

(a) Dry waxed

(b) Wet waxed

(c) One side waxed

(d) transparent papers.

DRY WAXED PAPERS

The wax is applied in such a way that it is confined entirely within sheet. The wax in dry waxing is applied by roll coater to one side of the paper. More than 10% wax must be applied to get uniform film. Although 20 to 25% wax can be used for commercial papers (wax unit).

The paper to be coated is fed through the rip between the two rolls. The bottom roll is partly immersed in molten wax. The web is waxed on either top side or bottom or both the sides. The sheets are passed over the chill rolls to get cooled.

The paper used for dry waxing should have a low, but even finish. The moisture content should be as low as 7%.

Formulation

Paraffin wax	74%
Rubber	6%
Gum Dammer	20%

Wet Waxed Papers

In case of wet waxed paper enough wax penetrates the paper to assure adequate bond.

The paper is coated on either one side or both sides. In case of both sides coating, the paper is passed through the bath and then through squeeze rolls.

Chilled iron roll, and then passed over cooling rolls or through water bath. Water is drained from the paper by scrapping blowing suction, or squeezing. The finish of the paper depends on the cooling.

(a) Very slow cooling reads to transparent film.

(b) Rapid cooling leads to gloss and opaque film.

(c) Very rapid cooling leads to unoriented wax crystals, with numerous small defects.

The moisture content of the original paper should be 7 to 9%. The paper should be clean, dry and free from dirts.

Wet waxed papers are self sealing and have good moisture resistance. Mostly wet waxed paper is used as wrapping and for baked foods, such as breads, cereal liners, soap wraps frozen food wrappers, etc.

For maximum transparency the sheet is dripped or passed between a steel roll and a rubber covered roll at a nip pressure of about 30 psi and while hot wax at 65°C is carried into the nip by the steel roll. The sheet is wounded up hot. In the next step the sheet is passed through a second bath of wax, the excess of wax is drained off and air at 10°C is passed over the sheet to bring down the temperature. Again the sheet is passed around coaling drum at 30 and 15°C. The total wax is around 40 to 50%. The second coat usually patches up the surface defects and reduces the air penetration.

34

Xerographic Paper

The paper for Xerographic is not a plain paper. The paper is specially designed to its performance under conditions of the process employed. The paper for Xerographic should have following properties:

(a) Free from Contamination

The paper should be absolutely free from those chemicals (amines) which affect the function of xerographic photo conductor. Waxes, adhesives, resins, might stick to the surface of the drum during transfer process. This may develop a defect that printing will occur in non-image areas. Such material like resin, waxes, adhesives and certain pigments which definitely affect the process, so these materials should be avoided.

(b) Smoothness

During the transfer process, the toning sets on the top of the hills of paper surface and this leads to poor fusing. On the other hand, if the paper is too smooth then poor adhesion of toner takes place. One must be careful enough so that the paper must not be too smooth or rough. The most acceptable case is papers that range from bond to duplicator smoothness.

(c) Stiffness

The paper should make intimate contact with the photo-conductor during transfer of the developed image and so this needs the paper should possess sufficient stiffness. The paper for xerographic is meant for 70 to 80 g/m^2 weight paper.

(d) Opacity

The paper for xerographic should have sufficient opacity in order to avoid the show through information copied on the other side.

(e) Level of Moisture

If the level of moisture is too low then it leads to static problem and very high level of moisture results in poor imaging. These defects are developed due to incomplete toner transfer. The moisture level should be kept at 4.5 to 6 per cent.

(f) Conductivity

Poor conductivity results in poor toner transfer on to the paper. Papers that are too resistive leads to static clinging.

Generally the surface resistivity should be between 0.01 to 10 T Ohm. If the surface resistivity is below 0.01 T Ohm then significant loss of image density occurs.

On the other hand if surface resistivity is above 10 T Ohm then transfer of toner particles takes place to non-image areas.

(g) Curl

The paper for xerography should be free curl. As moisture induced curl, wavy edges, or tight edges can lead to problems, with jam during duplexing, during collecting and stacking of finished copies.

(h) Co-efficient of Friction

The coefficient of friction of the xerography paper should be high and uniform from sheet to sheet to check multi-feeding on devices that feed the paper by friction wheels. Certain defects line static clinging curl and lack of stiffness will contribute to poor feeding in xerographic systems.

(i) Finishing

The final finishing of the paper is very important. The roll fed paper must be cut into prescribed size and wound on cores of the correct size. The paper must be free from dust and contamination of photo-conductive material. The ragged edges should be minimized.

The desired properties of the paper are bulk and surface conductivity, frictional property, solvent hold out, free from chemical contaminants.

In production of xerographic paper, photo-conductive insulator such as ZnS, CdS, TiO_2, Arsenic-triselenidide, lead oxide, mercuric-oxide, arsenic sulphide, medium-trisulphide. The binder used as are polystyrene, silicone resin, chlorinated rubbers, alkyd resin, acrylic resins etc. more often to shape up the desired properties such as flexibility etc. Plasticizers such as phthalates phosphates and adipates are used.

Roll coaters and knife coater may be used for coating process.

35

Paper Bags and Envelopes

INTRODUCTION

Paper Bags are the oldest forms of packaging item and is very popular and common now a days. Paper bag is a flexible container which is open at one end. The hand made paper bags are most important packing media. The hand made paper bags have been a commodity of common use since long. However, the introduction of machines for the manufacture of bags is fairly recent-around middle of 19th century, since then manufacture of paper bags has become on important industry by self. Paper bags are light in weight and cheapest forms of packing. They cover least space during storage and transport both in conditions of being empty and filled. However they have short span of life due to low strength. Lamination of the base paper with jute, cloth, or other reinforcing materials may increase the cost of bag.

The hand made bags of paper have been a commodity of common use since long and there are still many kinds of paper bags made by hand, such as the large ones for laundry and millinery trades etc. However, making paper bags has only become an industry of consequences since the introduction of machinery in their manufacture.

Paper pages are made of the variety of papers both bleached and unbleached. Craft papers are the most commonly used papers for the bags manufacture. Paper of other varieties that are commonly used are brown wrapper or white papers, manila papers etc. However selection of type of paper entirely depends upon the requirements of the product to be packed, consumers demand etc. The choice of type of bag to be used is made with reference to the cost and benefit ration pertaining to the intended applications.

Bursting strength of the paper has importance in paper used for making bags, and wrappings also, it is important in boxboards, utility and insulating purposes.

There is a vast scope for this item to be manufacture in cottage scale industry. Government has recognized its importance and is determined to give necessary protection to cottage scale manufacturers.

TYPES OF BAG

There are numerous type of bags, which can be made from the paper. These type of bags differs in their style of construction but also in the number of plies. There are four general types of single walled bags.

(1) Flat bags are simplest in construction and cheapest to make. In its manufacture the web of paper is formed like way a tube and glued lengthwise along the overlap. The tube is cut to the required length and the end is folded over and get pasted to make the bottom of paper bag.

(2) Square bottom of Pinch bottom bags, having side gussets or bellow folds and having bottoms similar to flat bags. These side gussets reduce the width of the bag without reducing the capacity. On filling up the bags the bottom of the bag squares-up with less bulging.

(3) Automatic self-opening square (S.O.S) bottom type bags. These bags have a flat base and side gussets. When these type of bottom bags are filled they make a neat, squared-up package with stable base. Such type of bags have advantages of both types of bag have square bag and the satchel bottom bags. These bags are very easy for opening.

(4) Satchel bottom type bags have a flat base when contents are filled in it. These bags are without gusset and forms a neat package with the stable base.

As far as number of piles are concerned, bags are available as single, double and multi-walled bags. Since small paper bags are under low stress during their service life, hence they are commonly single walled, a two ply bags is generally named as duplex construction.

Paper bags are made in variety of the sizes. Usually flat bottom bags are of smallest size among all available types e.g., medicine bags used by doctors. Satchel-bottom bags are most common type, general purpose bags. Gussets are provided to increase the capacity within same dimensions, depending on quantity of products.

USES AND APPLICATIONS

The paper bags are the major packing requirement for packaging of various type of items purchased by the customers. Paper bags are required by each type of shopkeepers in large stores, general merchants, street shopkeepers and others. These bags are generally used for packaging of the grocery items, garment and hosiery goods, chemists sundries and the common articles of the daily requirement. Generally these bags are not closed or if closing is necessary the open mouth is simply folded and pinned or stappled. The permanent closing may be done by the gumming or stitching.

Large number of domestic use articles are being packed by their manufacturers or dealers as the case be in the small paper bags. Double ply, bags (Paper-poly) are used commonly for the packaging of many food products. Paper bags have found wide use in office and commercial communications. They are used for handling of magazines, drugs, cosmetics, seeds, units of electronic industry confectionery sausages, bacon, dried fish, sausages, sandwitches, etc.

MATERIALS REQUIRED

The main raw material required is very known by its name i.e., paper. Selection of paper standard paper is essential, in order to meet the requirements. Apart form the paper the other matters like adhesive, threads etc. for sealing the end of bags are essential material required. If the multiwall bags are desired then suitable ply matter should be selected.

DESIRED PROPERTIES OF PAPER

Bursting strength and tear factor are the main physical properties required to be noticed while manufacturing this product.

The degree to which a paper sheet can expand without being torn is important in paper used for packaging.

Longer fibre length stronger bonding by appropriate beating, better sizing, better pressing conditions, gradual and moderate drying and proper moisture content in the sheet increase the bursting strength of paper. Excessive beating sudden drying or heating the paper, more fillers, improper pressing and more moisture in paper adversely affect the bursting strength.

Bursting strength of the paper has importance in paper used for making bags, and wrappings also, it is important in boxboards, utility and insulating purposes.

PROCESS OF MANUFACTURE

The manufacturing process of paper bags is grouped into two categories:

(i) Paper is fed to the machine in the form of rolls. The paper is handled very simply in this form.

(ii) Paper is fed to the machine in form of paper sheets. The process is carried out for greater speed of production. They are generally adapted for the manufacture of flat variety of bags.

In the roll feeding process the paper is fed at one end into the reel-fed machines. Initially the paper is cut into the desired size, at this stage paper is in form of flat sheet. Further the paper is sent to Folding section. Here the paper is folded in steps at different positions, according to the type of paper bag to be prepared. Later on the folded edges are pasted suitably. The process of gumming is done in a very controlled manner. An excessive as well as less application of adhesive may effect the quality of the bag. After gumming the folded paper units are subjected to the pressing so that gum used may hold two surfaces properly. The pressing is carried until the bag is taken out at the other end of the machinery.

Another process of bags preparation involves flat sheet feeding to the bag-making machines. Initially the paper is cut into the suitable size and these pre-cut sheets are piled over feed table. A suction feed takes the under-most sheet or upper-most according to the arrangement in machine. The paper sheet in turn is passed forward through a series of rollers and the various processes i.e., pasting folding etc., are carried out, until finished bags emerges out. It is necessary to cut the paper properly before it is fed to be machine.

Several versions of the machinery, used in different stages of bag making, are employed. There is a different class of machine used for making open paper bags as used by packers of cereals, tea, coffee etc., and other general items. It consists of an outer printed wrapper cut from the sheets with inner lining paper taken from the rolls. Both papers are folded and gummed separately and finished bag consists of two distinct bags one inside the other. Conventional satchel or flat bag making equipments involves the drawing of paper from the reel subjected to pasting operation on the seam. The paper is thus formed into tube of the paper of required width. The required length of paper tube is cut by a revolving serrated cutters. The tube is folded and pasted. The finished bags are passed round a heated cylinder where it is pressed, dried and later delivered out.

Paper bag machines may be coupled from their delivery unit to the printing machine according to the desired specifications. Special arrangements and machines are procured for the heat sealed bags made of paper-plastic or other specially coated or laminated.

LIST OF EQUIPMENTS

Paper bags making plant consists of following equipments and machines:

Unwinding stand.

Length Gumming Device

Former Plate

Pulling draw rings.

Cutting knife unit or separating rings.

Bottom Gumming device

Folding Device

Transporting Drum

Counting Device

Collecting Base

PAPER ENVELOPES

Paper envelopes are known to all persons. Various types and sizes of envelopes are now used quite extensively. These envelopes find applications is Posts and Telegraph Departments, offices and in all commercial communications. Some of the pocket envelope varieties are particularly suitable for all manner of contents such as seeds, powders, hair nets, postage stamps, wedges, wireless parts, violin strings, gramophone needles and such small articles. Most popular sizes of envelopes include 15 cm. × 9 cm., 18 cm. × 13 cm., 23 cm × 10 cm., 26 cm. × 12 cm.

At present, most of this item is being manufactured in cottage scale industries. Exact data of number of units engaged in this trade is difficult to give. However, there is a great potentiality for this item as cottage base production, as its demand is bound to increase with time.

PROCESS OF MANUFACTURE

Envelopes are made by Rotary Sheet Fed, envelope making machine. In a typical sheet fed envelope making machine, blanks are put on the feeding table in high stacks, the flap point downwards. While the machine is running additional blanks can be put on the table. A sucking device takes the blanks from below and carries them to the receiving cylinder. After that inside and outside of the blank is printed. The printing attachments are slewable and can be stopped individually. The operation of flap-gumming then follows. The blank is conveyed through 2 turning cylinders and then brought rapidly to the format pit where it is aligned. Folding of the blank is achieved by folding rules, where after the finished envelope falls into the drying chain.

After the drying process, the envelope is conveyed by means of sucking discs to the receiving table where the finished envelopes are stacked up and counted by 25 or 50 envelopes.

The papers used for envelopes include manila, brown, wrapper or white paper. White coloured or brown wrapper is usually employed for various types of bags. Gum arabic or locally available gum is generally used as the common adhesive, although pastes made from tapioca flour are also used to a lesser extent.

36

Paper Board Making Plant

INTRODUCTION

Paper board, which is the most basic among paper boards, is used for a wide range of purposes, including folding boxes, black board for writing pads, etc.

As yellow board is made from rice straw and treated with small amounts of lime milk, soda ash, etc., available at low cost, its manufacturing cost is cheap.

Yellow board is a kind of paper board, which can be turned into white board if bleached pulp is added as a surface layer in the process of manufacture. It has a good appearance, and can be used for the packaging of foodstuffs and cosmetics.

However, as the manufacturing of white board involves heavy expenditures for equipment and high cost of materials, It is recommended that a yellow board manufacturing plant be established to being with. After the plant operator has become skilled in making the yellow board, he may advance to the field of higher grades, such as the manufacturing of white board and surface coated boards.

PROCESS DESCRIPTION

Generally speaking, the fourdrinier paper machine is used for printing and writing paper. In making yellow board, however, the cylinder mould machine is used which does not involve a large expenditure in spite of easy maintenance and operation.

A stationary spherical digester is used for digestion of straw, because its operation is to be carried on in a batch system, without requiring complex instruments. The above type of digester provides easier operation than the continuous digester.

Straw pulp comes in two kinds - yellow pulp and white pulp. in making yellow pulp, lime is used as stated above. There are cases where it is used with soda ash.

However, in the cases of white pulp, it is made by various processes - caustic soda, sulphate and chlorine processes. whatever the process, it is complex.

PRETREATMENT OF STRAW

The rice straw, which has been collected and stored, is cut to a suitable uniform length by a cutter, and it is sent to the duster via a belt conveyor. The dusted straw is carried to the next process on another conveyor.

COOKING

The straw stored in a chip bin is put in a digester at the rate of about 2.5 tons of done dry straw at a time.

The above operation is performed on the second floor.

when the above operation is over, a fixed amount of lime solution is added, after which digestion continues for several hours (6-8 h/cycle) with steam under a pressure of 4-6 Kg/cm^2.

The cooked material is blown into a blow pit/and waste liquid is washed away by a beater placed in the lower part of the pit.

STOCK PREPARATION

The raw material made available from the above operation is fed into a dilution box with a pump. Fresh water is added to the box to provide consistency to suit the following beating process.

Nodes and sheaves are eliminated by the inclined screen to drop the stock into the next beater, in which it is treated for an appropriate number of hours so as to make it suitable for paper machining, as well as provide a good quality for the finished paper.

Stock which has been subjected to the beater process is stored in the beater chest, out of which it is sent into the head box by the pump. Then it is fed into the next process, Jordan's engine, maintaining to fixed head for uniform cutting of fibres.

The stock which leaves the Jordan's engine is sent into the mixing box by the pump in order to provide the consistency necessary for paper making by adding back water from the machine box (fresh water, if necessary).

The stock goes out of the above equipment into the selective screen, where it is dusted, for transfer to the distributing box and head box.

CHEMICAL PREPARATION

This is an independent section, in which the lime for digestion is dissolved to the stipulated concentration and stored.

The process so for described constitutes the first half of the paper making process, namely the section for manufacturing of raw materials.

PAPER MACHINE

The raw materials in the head box, flow into the paper machine. The paper machine consists of wire, press, dryer parts, calender and paper cutter. Paper is continuously made in the order of the above parts.

WIRE PART

One or several (fine, in this plant) cylinder moulds rotate in each vat. The stock which has been fed is scooped up by the rotating cylinder mould machine for formation of sheet.

When cylinders go out of the stock liquid, the surfaces of the cylinders are covered with wet paper which constitutes fabric.

The number of cylinders is decided according to the thickness of paper to be made. The thicker the paper, the larger the number of cylinder.

PRESS PART

The bottom felts, which rotate endlessly, pass the crest of the cylinders one by one to pick up the paper layer formed there.

After passage of the second press roll, felt and paper are separated, with felt resuming its advance to the cylinder after water has been squeezed out of the felt by the squeeze roll, and paper proceeding towards the next dryer part.

DRYER PART

The paper which comes out of the final press roll has been smoothened by the smoother. It is dried when it comes into contact with the surfaces of the fourteen paper dryers (cylindrical, with steam inside), one after another.

Canvas or dry felt is employed to ensure good contact with cylinders.

CALENDER

The calender comprises chilled rolls, the surfaces of which are hardened. Paper gains glaze as it passes between the rolls through the slip action of heat and pressure.

CUTTER

Paper is finally cut into the required size by the cutter, thereby ending the continuous paper making process.

When paper is specially required in a smaller size, it is cut by a guillotine cutter which is provided separately.

RAW MATERIALS UTILITIES

Consumption of rice straw for making one kg. yellow board is 1.8-2 kg. (bone dry straw). If the straw contains 50 per cent moisture, 3.6 to 4 kgs. is required.

Accordingly a 5 tons/day plant needs 9-10 tons of bone dry straw a day. The success or failure of enterprise largely depends on the costs of collection, transport and storage of straw.

Especially in a case where crops of rice straw are concentrated once or twice a year, consideration should be given to the risk of decomposition which may occur during the storage of a large quantity of straw to meet the yearly need.

Lime is required as a chemical to process straw at the rate at 260-270 kgs. per ton of straw board, or 1,340 kgs/day for daily output of 5 tons.

Utilities involve water, steam and electric power, and it is desirable to have water as clean as possible. A large volume of water is required for making yellow board, some 1,500 m^3 per day of 24 hours for a 5 ton plant.

One of the conditions essential for location of the plant site is that pure water is available at a low cost.

One and a half tons of steam are required per hour, and it a fuel oil boiler is used, oil consumption will be 3.36 kl/d.

If some fuel cheaper than fuel oil is available, the manufacturing cost would be that much cheaper. However, in view of the expenditure for equipment, it is desirable to burn fuel oil in a low cost package boiler.

Electric power consumption will be 250 kw at a maximum and 170 kw on an average.

As the monthly consumption of electric power is 4,080 kwh, it is necessary to have a service cable for more than 440 V.

REQUIRED MACHINERY AND EQUIPMENT

Pretreatment Section	:	Straw cutter, Belt conveyors, Straw duster, Dust fan.
Cooking Section	:	Spherical digester, Washing beater, Stuff pump.
Stock Preparation Section	:	Inclined screen beater, Beater chest, Conveyor pumps, Jordan's engine, machine chest, gate valve, Selectifier screen.
Chemicals preparation section	:	Lime dissolving tank, liquor transport pimps, lime storage tank.
Paper machine section of wire Parts	:	Wire cylinder mould, Vat, Couch rolls, Back water pump. Belt rolls, Belt stretcher, Belt guide, Wringer roll, Belt squeeze roll, Belt whipper guide, Shower pipe, Main water pipe, Frame sole plate. Baby press roll, Press roll, Paper roll, Stairs hand rail.
Dryer Part	:	Smoother, Paper dryer, Metals and gears, Canvas dryer, Canvas roll, Canvas guide, Canvas stretcher, Dryer doctor, Spring roll, Frame sole plate, Platform stair hand rail. Steam joint piping.

CALENDER PART

Cutter Part	:	Frame, Roll.
Guillotine's Cutter and Others	:	Guillotine's cutter, Knife grinder, Slitter knife grinder.
Driving equipment	:	Main, Floor cone.

37

Paper Cups for Ice-cream

INTRODUCTION

Cups of paper are made in variety of sizes and shapes according to the amount of material to be filled. Cups are designed and processed in the variety of ways depending on the matter to be handled by them. Icecream cups are made such that they are resistant to the fats, acid and alkaline liquid. The paper of cups is selected carefully so that contents may not be contaminated and may affect the odour of contents. Paper cups can be divided into two type –

(1) Light duty and
(2) Heavy duty.

Light duty containers are made of the three pieces: (1) The body, (2) Bottom and (3) Lid. The bottom is held to the body by means of an adhesive. The lid is removable and is either inserted in a groove at the top of the body. This type of cup is used to keep product for a long period. Also the cups are made in one piece. In these type the lid is just fit over the top of cup and these icecream cup are used for a short period. Heavy duty cups are made with heavy bodies of single or double wrap. They are coated with wax so that they may be impermeable to water or any other substances.

Another popular type of paper cup is a long cylindrical type with a lid that fits on the top of the body and gives a perfect seal. They are very strong and used for packaging of variety of food products like icecream, dairy products etc. These cups have sufficient strength and can be reused again. Generally icecream cups are disposable in nature.

Wax coated paper cups are preferably used for cold food and the drinks. Simple paper is used for hot food and drinks, prepared meat, vegetable and quick frozen food. Another purpose of paper cups are for drinking water. uncoated paper cups are preferred for beverages. These paper planted cups have capacity of 100 – 200 ml. However the size and shape of cups may vary.

Also, paper crimped cups and curd cups are used in railway catering services etc., are same as ice-cream cups. The equipment installed for the manufacture of ice-cream cups can be used to produce these varieties during off-season periods. Paper crimped has now achieved popularity mainly because the confectionery trade being used in increasing quantity to hold the better-class sweet-meats, crystallised fruits, etc., crimped cups made from grease-proof paper are also used considerably as baking dishes for small cakes.

PROPERTIES OF PAPER CUPS

Paper cups are resistant to acidic, alkaline medium. They are tasteless and odourless in nature. They cannot be contaminated from the outside. These cups may contain several types of food e.g., ice-cream etc.

Wax coated cups are used for keeping the cold substances like icecreams, cold, drinks, and freezed food etc. The bacterial contamination is non existant as paper containers because of only using once. They are always free from the sieve, spot and discolouration. They are made of the chemical which is non-poisonous in nature. Adhesives employed in the fabricating and sealing of the paper cup are free from toxic odours or injurious substances. They must be easily decomposable, non-permeable, non-soluble in liquids and must be moisture resistant. Printing and labelling of brand, manufacturer's name, design, trade mark, etc. must be easily embossed.

USES AND APPLICATION

Paper cups have found a wide range of applications in icecream industry. They have very wide field of application. Paper cups are used for keeping the cold drinks, icecream and fruit juices etc. Another special type of cylindrical paper cups are made which keeps the hot and cold beverages and rare provided with the handles.

Paper cups are also used for keeping the cold refrigerated milk. Paper cups are made into variety of cross-sectional cylindrical shapes like square shape, tetrahedral shape etc. Beside using for the above mentioned purposes they can be reused again for general house hold items.

PROCESS OF MANUFACTURE

The production of ice-cream cups is seasonal i.e., in summer time. The equipment installed for the manufacture of ice-cream cups can be used to produce other varieties during the off season period. The other type of paper cups are- paper crimped cups, curd cups etc.

The process of manufacture of ice-cream cups consists of the two steps as:

(1) Forming of cups and

(2) Waxing of cups.

Forming of the cups involve the formation of complete cup including base, walls, folding edges from the plane sheet of paper. The sheet of the paper is inserted in the machine by laying on pins and the carriage of the press with the shaft carrying the inner folding device is lowered. Both the inner folding mechanism that is in the shaft and the outer folding mechanism in the wall of machine combine automatically to press the sides of the cup into overlapping plates to form the wall. The mechanism also turns over the edges into a folded rim which enables the cup to be nested. The first operation deals with a preliminary casing, in the second operation tightening of the crease is done and simultaneously the top edges are turned over.

Waxing of the formed cup is very important step. It involves the application of additional pressure on the crease under heat in order to dissolve the wax to stick the plates together. The final finishing operation involves pressing of the plates together that fits the upper part with a flange so that a lid can be placed over it. Further step involves the packing of the cups. The packing is done with care to prevent any damage of the cups during handling and transportation.

LIST OF PLANT AND M/C

(1) Cutting and creasing platen press with motor

(2) Paper cutting machine with motor

(3) Screw press (hand operated)

(4) Wax coating machine

(5) Printing press with motor

(6) Miscellaneous equipment-tools, dies etc.

38

Paper Cones and Tubes

Paper Cones and Paper Tubes are required by the textile industries for winding of thread. The demand for these items is increasing very rapidly due to the expansion of the Art Silk Industries in the country as well as sanction of new units.

Paper Cones should be of uniform weight, size and strength, such paper cones are in great demand in the textile and rayon industries as it would be possible to determine the weight of the thread after winding. The indigenous production, except a few units which have installed batch-type machinery, is not very suitable as the cones are not of uniform weight.

The demand for Paper Cones and Tubes has been steadily increasing and some of the units are working additional shifts to meet the demand. Based on the performance of the existing units, it is clear that there is a good scope for the product. Moreover with the sanction of new textile units in U.P. and other states, the demand for Paper Cones and Paper Tubes will cope with such demand. In addition to above, one should foresee replacement of plastic cones with the paper cones in the very near future because the plastic industry in India is heavily dependent upon overseas development of plastics and related products would have to suffer a withering spell of inflationary pressure due to high-priced crude.

WORKING PROCESS IN ORDER OF MACHINERY REQUIRED

Punching Device

Punching machine is used for punching out kraft paper into fan shape according to proposed size of paper cone.

Bevelling Device

Bevelling machine is used for bevelling one side to punched paper in the above process at its back surface to get smooth level on surface of paper cone when winding up the paper into paper cone.

Embossing Device

Embossing machine is used for making emboss on outside surface of paper cone aiming to prevent yarns from slipping down when it is wound up into paper cone.

Winding Device

Gluing machine is used for winding up glued paper into paper cone shape. Wound paper should be dried well and then delivered into top curling machine.

Gluing Device

Gluing machine is used for gluing bevelled and embossed paper and glued paper should be delivered to winding machine continuously. Gluing machine should be complete with ½ HP motor switch and standard accessories.

Top Curling Device

The top curling machine is used for cutting bottom of paper cone and curling top of paper cone. It is a semi-automatic machine. Some cones are sometimes cut at its top prior to curling the top. One shaft type can only can Bottom cut and top curling. Two shaft type can bottom cut, and top curling including Top cut prior to top curling.

Notching Device

Notching machine is used for cutting a notch at bottom side of paper cone where an end of yarn is handed on.

Printing Device

Printing machine is used for printing a name and/or mark at bottom surface of paper cone.

Top Colour Painting Device

Top colour painting machine is used for colouring top of paper cone. This machine only need 2 labourers for one machine. One worker does painting only and the after does putting on and from painting mandrel.

Velvetting Device

Velvetting machine is used for blowing paper powder onto paper cone which is already pasted. This process is chiefly adopted for such paper cones as used for winding synthetic yarn on it.

Brushing Device

The brushing machine is used for brushing of velevetted paper cones for smooth finish.

39

Paper Draperies

INTRODUCTION

The paper draperies are essentially the type of resin-treated or coated paper specialties used chiefly due to their enhanced decorative value. Products of paper draperies include e.g. decorative window curtains or hangings made from paper. In the field of paper converting industry, the advent of paper draperies is a fairly recent development, as contrasted with that of wall papers. The first time, papers draperies were manufactured in 1938 in the United States. This, however, picked-up later particularly in the post world war period while the consumer acceptance was slow in the beginning. Paper draperies are not so popular in India but is more popular in the Western world today. Due to its low price and high decorative value, this product will undoubtedly attract the attention of a wide cross-section (C.S.) of Indian community if it is introduced in the market in attractive shades and designs.

MANUFACTURING PROCESS

The manufacturing process of paper draperies can be divided into following three major steps:

1. Plasticzing the base sheets.
2. Printing the plasticized paper.
3. Fabricating the drape from the printed paper.

Plasticizing the Base Sheet

The plasticizing process of the base sheet is usually one of impregnation, and it imparts to the base-sheet the cloth like qualities. The web is unwound from the roll, to accomplish this. Now it is allowed to pass through a bath containing a softner in water solution.Thus the web impregnated is then allowed to pass between a pair of squeeze rolls so that the excess of plasticizer is removed Now the web is finally passed over drying drums. The excess of water is removed with the help of these drums. The finished paper is then rewound in roll form. Now the base paper contains the predetermined amount of plasticizer. It is usually calculated as a percentage by weight of the web. On the paper machine, the process is sometimes carried out as a tub size operation. But it is more often run as a secondary converting procedure. When tension is applied in handling a limp sheet of this kind, extreme care is essential because of the tendency to form wet wrinkles which normally corrects this tendency by the use of spreader rolls or bars.

For drape manufacture, the plasticizing agents are employed. It should essentially be hydroscopic and water soluble and in addition it should possess certain other desirable characteristics which are given below:

1. A narrow humectant range.
2. Non-volatility.
3. Freedom from objectionable odour.
4. Non-toxity.
5. Lack of colour.

For this purpose, glycerine has been the best known, most effective, and most readily available plasticizer and despite its limitations such as with respect to humectant range. In this industry, it has been used quite successfully. Some of the glycerine substitutes or extenders have also found considerable application fairly recently, some glycerine substitutes are e.g. sorbitol, ethylene glycol, invert sugar, potassium acetate and sodium lactate etc. A fairly new development has been the incorporation into the web of a flame retardant to retard or prevent the propagation of flame. In the paper drape, a stable and non-volatile flame retardant is essential. It is never subjected to dry cleaning or laundering.

During impregnation, the introduction of flame retardants is usually combined with the plasticizers. Therefore, the combination of substances or substance used must be compatible with the plasticizer. The various flame retardants are employed for this purpose, for example aluminium sulphate, borax, diammonium phosphate, ammonium sulphate and the ammonium salt of sulfonic acid etc.

Printing the plasticized paper

After the plasticizing of the paper it is printed in the next step. In case of paper drapes, this step is very crucial and calls for a perfect blend of skills on the part of the artist and the printer as well. The choice of design and colouring is of paramount importance, in as much as the visual appeal of the product is a major determining factor in selling. Although it is destined for a shorter useful life.

40

Egg Tray From Waste Paper

Waste	Water		
Cutting	Pulp Making		
Water	Pulp Dilution	Moulding	
Product	Sun Drying	Pressing	Water

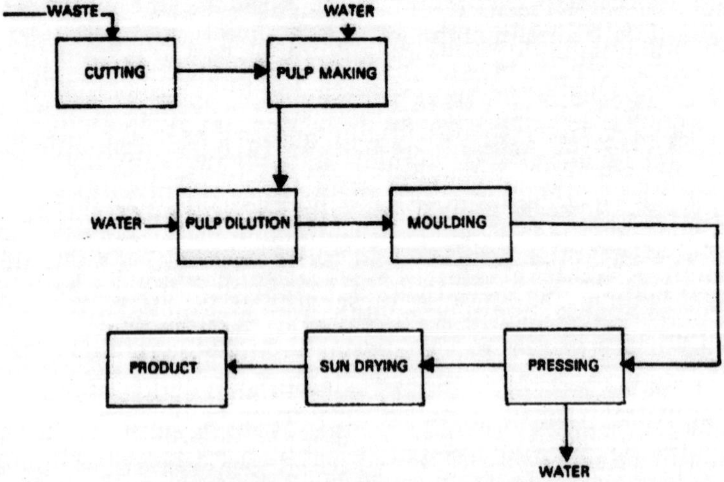

Fig. 1. Flow diagram for manufacturing egg trays

RAW MATERIAL REQUIREMENTS

The main raw material for the manufacture of egg trays is the waste paper and fibrous materials.

Basis : 25,00,000 trays per month.

1. Waste paper and fibrous materials—1,37,500 kgs.
2. **Caustic:** It is required very rarely and in very little quantity.

In fact it is used when the raw material is very hard and it is not possible to convert it into pulp.

PROCESS

The waste paper and fibrous material is first prepared before processing it. In preparing step, the waste paper is beaten with a stick and any dust and undesired material is removed. After preparing, the waste paper is cut into pieces of not more than 3 inches. This cutting is done on a cutting machine. This cutting machine is available in two types. One is manually operated and the other is electrically operated. Electrically operated machine is more costly and is more complicated and so it is not used is small scale industries. .Hand operated machines are widely used. A hand operated machine consists of long sharp edged blades. These blades are loaded with a compression spring. The prepared paper is put beneath the blade and then blade is pressed with instantaneous force.

The paper is cut in the single stroke and the cut paper falls down. Now the paper is slided and the operation is repeated. At one time as large number of cutting machines are used. Normally

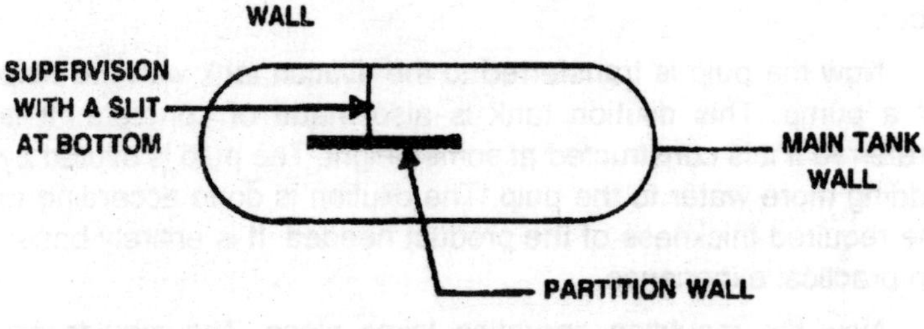

Fig. 2. Diagram of manufacturing egg trays from waste paper

for a production of 10 ton pulp, 10 to 15 cutting machines are sufficient.

Now the cut pieces of paper are transferred to a beater. This beater consists of a tank, knife drum, drum platform and motor. The tank is purchased ready-made and is made of cast iron sheet. But if it has to be made then, it is preferred to make it of concrete and preferably underground. The shape of the beater is shown below:

The knife drum is made of wood with a large diameter. A number of sharp edged knives are fixed at the circumference of the drum of equal distances. The distance between two consecutive blades is normally kept 1/2 inch. This drum is supported on two bearings horizontally and attached to a motor and gear arrangements. Below this drum a drum platform is kept. This platform is also made of wood. A slight upward curvature is given to this platform.

Alongwith cut pieces of waste paper water is introduced into the beater. The amount of water should be sufficient to make the pulp flowable. After the introduction of water, the beater is switched on. The direction of the rotation of the drum and platform knives and due to rubbing effect, the fibres of the papers are separated and the paper is then pushed back through the bottom slit. Thus the next pieces come under and the process is carried on.

This beating is done for about 4 hours. This time of duration depends upon the quality of the waste paper. If the waste paper is of soft quality then time will be less and if its is of hard quality, then it may be more than 4 hours. The pulp thus is stored for sometime. Caustic is added at this stage if needed. After adding the caustic the beater is again switched on after a period of one hour.

Now the pulp is transferred to the dilution tank with the help of a pump. This dilution tank is also made of concrete. It is preferred if it is constructed at some height. The pulp is diluted by adding more water to the pulp. The dilution is done according to the required thickness of the product needed. It is entirely based on practical experience.

Now the moulding operation takes place. The moulds are made of wood. The bottom is false which can be removed when

stirred well using a stirrer. A wire gauge mould is fixed at the bottom of the wooden vats. The shape of the wire gauge is similar to the egg tray.

When the pulp solution is stirred well, the bottom of the mould is removed. The water in the solution passes through the mesh and comes out and the fibrous materials deposit on the mesh evenly and take up the shape of the egg tray. The tray is then dried alongwith the wire mesh. In order to remove the number of meshes, the tray is pressed a little to remove the adhering water and the tray is dried, after removing the wire mould. Sun drying can easily be sued here. Sometimes it is better to use steam drier. This drying is done at about 100°C. Sun drying consumes more time.

The dried trays are then cut into proper sizes and marketed. One tray capacity is 30 eggs. This capacity may be changed according to the desire by using different wire meshes moulds.

Uses

(a) They are used for packing eggs.

(b) They are employed for space saving.

(c) They protect the eggs from damage by shocking.

Miscellaneous

Sometimes these egg trays are also made of plastic, but due to their smaller flexibility, they are not so much popular. Moreover plastic trays are costly.

Market Potential

At present there are many manufacturers of these trays, but the production is not sufficient to meet the demand. Apart from some big units, there are so many small scale manufacturers of these trays. Their exact production is not available since most of them are not registered with any industrial institution. There is a further scope for such trays as they are required for replacement because of breakage and tearing during handling.

41

Kraft Bag Making Plant

Multi-wall kraft bag is a large- size multiply paper bag made up of more than two sheets of strong kraft paper (normally 3-4 ply) for the purpose of holding heavy matter over 10 kgs.

It is the most suitable container for certain amounts of cements, fertilizers, rice, barley, wheat flour, sugar, salt, pelletized resin and other industrial chamicals in powder, groin and small lumps for transport or storage.

It comes in the following four types to suit the shape of the material to be contained:

(a) One and machine-sewn.

(b) Both ends machine-sewn.

(c) One end pasted.

(d) Both ends pasted.

When air-tightness is required, an anti-moisture paper bag is available by the insertion of pitched kraft or such moisture prevention paper such as polyethylene-laminated paper, etc., in between the kraft papers of (c) or (d) type bag.

Pitched kraft, which is also called tarpaulin paper, is a piece of kraft paper, one side of which is coated with asphalt, over which another piece of kraft paper is attached to organize, so to speak, an asphalt sandwich.

In the case of the cement paper bag, if it contains 50 kgs. 20 Bags are required per ton. Accordingly, the larger the output of cement in a country the larger the demanded for kraft bags.

As already stated, moreover, there are favourable prospects for increasing the demand for paper bags for fertilizers and other materials.

The scope of the consumption of multi-wall kraft bags is extremely large, with the demand increasing by 6 to 10 per cent year after year.

Multi-wall paper bag is pasted into a cylindrical shape on tubing machine with both ends cut. Both ends or one end of the bag is either machine-sewn or pasted.

In the case of cement bags, the pasted type is overwhelmingly used in Europe, while in Japan and southeast Asia sewn type bags are mostly used.

The design and letters on cement on the surface, at the side or back of paper bags, can be printed simultaneously with tubing because a mono-colour or multicolour printing press is attached to the tubing machine.

In the case of cement bags, mono-colour (generally in black) printing with water ink is common. However, two or three colour printing is necessary for fertilizer, sugar and other bags.

In selecting a suitable location for the plant, it is necessary to look for a lot, offering convenience in transporting raw materials into the plant, ant still be close to consumers so as to economize on expenses in forwarding bags.

It is understood that the plant should be located where it is easy to obtain supplies of electricity, water and labour.

From the technical point of view, the manufacturing of kraft bags is not especially difficult. On the business side, management may not be so difficult because of the fact that the consumers and the quantity required are comparatively stabilized.

Therefore, multi-wall kraft bag manufacturing may be recommended as a promising example for smaller enterprises

MANUFACTURING PROCESS

There are two kinds of multi-wall paper bags, one with gussets on both sides (mainly machine-sewn type paper bags) and the other without gussets (mainly pasted type paper bags.)

However, through exchange of the shaping plate on the tubing machine, it is possible to turn out the above two kinds of bags on the same tubing machine.

Here is an outline of the manufacturing process of multi-wall paper bags mainly made by the sewing process:

(1) Kraft paper is put on the tubing machine, placing the number of sheets corresponding to the required number of ply, for simultaneous tubing and printing with a press inter-locked with the tubing machine. The length of the paper bag depends on the order, but it is generally cut to 43-20 inches. The length of the bag may be adjusted through exchange of gears on the tubing machine.

(2) Paper tube manufactured on the tubing machine is machine-sewn on an automatic both-ends sewing-machine, after the shaping of valve (normally done manually).

(3) The manufactured paper bags, which have been sewed, are packaged on a packing press by 100 to 150 pieces. The packages are stored in the warehouse, from which shipment is made as may be required.

When manufacturing pasted bags, in case the quantity is small, it will be advantageous to paste both bottoms manually.

In case, however, the quantity is large, it will be advantageous to use an automatic bottomer

In such a case, a high level tubing machine has to be used.

REQUIRED MACHINERY AND EQUIPMENT

1. Tubing machine(complete with 2-colour press, hoist and 1 beam) — 1 set

   Length of bag 20-43" width of bag 14-23½ " (through exchange of shaping plate) width of gusset 0-5" Body paper. width upto 48", Dia. Upto 39" upto 6 ply. — 2 sets

   Manufacturing capacity 120 bags/min.

2. Both-end sewing machine, length of bag 24 ½ -36 ½ ". — 2 sets
3. One-end sewing machine, Length of bag 25 ½ -36 ½ ". — 2 sets

Manufacturing capacity 1,500 bags/min.

4. Packing machine, 100-150 bags per bale capacity :
   50 bales/h. 1 set
5. Compressor 7-10 kg/cm^2 1 set
6. Paste making machine 1 set
7. Inspecting machine 4 sets
   (for elongation, tearing point, permeability of air, weighing).

MONTHLY REQUIREMENT OF RAW MATERIAL AND UTILITIES

Items	*Quantity (tons)*
Kraft paper	1.86
Crepe paper	7
Sewing thread	1.5
Filter code	1.5
Paste	1.5
Ink	1

MARKET POTENTIAL

The Kraft bags are used for packing cement, fertilizers, rice, barley, wheat flour, sugar salt, pelletized resin, industrial chemicals, minerals and miscellaneous materials.

As the economy rises, the competition will rise and which in turn would necessitate the importance of product appeal. So there would be vast demand for packaging material for better product appeal.

Now the export potential is backed up of government and this would be rather possible if the quality of packaging is improved to match the international standards.

The gunny bags which were previously used for packing carious items have been discarded due to enough loss of materials during storage and transportation. Now-a-days kraft paper bags are universally adopted to minimize the losses during transportation etc.

Hence the production of kraft bags will increase to bridge the gap between demand and supply.

42

Note Book, Register and File

INTRODUCTION

Paper books, Register and files are the essential domestic items with the growth of education and literacy among the masses and industrialisation within the country the demand of stationery items - notebook, register and file covers for the writing purpose has been increasing at very tremendous rate.

In the developing countries like India there is sharp growth of population. People of all classes, whether higher or lower income group tends to make their wards educated. The school/college going children use either note-books or registers for noting down the study matter and the writing purposes. Since the awareness of education in urban as well as rural area is growing day by day, The demand of these stationery items is also increasing.

Note-books are mainly used by students, teachers, housewives, businessmen and office going people-students use them for noting down their class lessons, notes and important information.

Note-books are widely known and vastly used day-to-day products. Registers are also known as long note-books. Registers have larger page size as compared to the note-books and are more common to college students and upper age groups. File involves the sheet of loose papers tagged or punched altogether so that they can be collectively stored at single place. Files may have different type of papers grouped in it. Nature of papers can be made variant in the files, while in note-books and registers where papers are binded the quality throughout remains same.

Files are used on account of fact that its contents pages can be taken out when needed and then secured back in the proper position. Files can be provided with either lined pages, different sheets and printed pages according to the requirements.

It is quite difficult to obtain the exact production and consumption data regarding these products due to their largely scattered small scale manufacturers. However the per capita consumption of these essential stationery commodities may be regarded as the barometer of industrial, educational progress and prosperity of the society. The growing education among the peoples and industrialization within the country, has increased the utility of these items. Other factors like population growth, compulsory primary education, Government incentives to the schools regarding free supply of stationary items and concessions to their manufacturers etc. have largely increased the demand. Now they are considered as need of hour and are very common item of daily life.

USES OF NOTEBOOKS, REGISTERS AND FILES

Note-books, Registers and files are used by people of all classes and in various different fields. Note-books and registers have common use by school going children, college students, office peoples, business men and others. Students use them for noting down their class lessons, notes and other important information related to their subject of studies. These written work in note-books can be used in future at suitable time when needed. Files are very common to the business houses, offices; in banks in corporate offices; in post offices; in railway department; in factory offices and in every type of the government departments. These items are used to keep the record of daily activities of offices, maintaining the accounts and other necessary information. Various records in files can be maintained for a longer period in the files. Basically note-books, registers, files utilizing the paper for communication purposes, are very important media for development of society. These stationery items are one of the basic source for formal education and conveying and recording the ideas by writing. The contents can be preserved for long time to be used in future when needed.

The demand of these paper based stationery products has increased many-folds during the past few years because of spread of education, growth in other social activities and developments of industrial complexes. Increasing population and in turn the need of education to children as well as to illiterate adults has rapidly increased the demand.

It can be noted that the production of note-books, registers and files depends upon the availability and production capacity of the paper throughout the country. A new entrepreneur can well venture into the field by installing units for manufacturing of paper note-books and registers or files to satisfy present and future demand.

RAW MATERIALS REQUIRED

The main raw material required for the manufacture of note-books, registers and files, is the proper standard writing paper. This paper is available in form of reams. In addition to the writing paper, cardboard or thick paper for binding is also taken up from the paper industry. Materials used in binding up and finishing like – cloth, gum, staple pin etc. and packaging of finally prepared products are the other requirements in he manufacturing process.

MANUFACTURING PROCESS

They are available in variety of dimensions and number of pages. Generally note-books are of smaller size around 10 inches long and 6 inches in breadth, while the registers commonly are approximately 18 inches by 9 inches size. Sizing of the note-books and registers however are different and depends on the manufacturer. Number of pages in them are mainly dependent on demand, normally note-books have 96, 120, 144, pages while registers are made of 76, 120, 144 pages normally.

The process of manufacture of the note-books and registers has following steps:

(1) Cutting of papers

(2) Ruling (line Printing)

(3) Printing of covers

(4) Stapling (Punching)

(5) Binding

(6) Finishing.

CUTTING OF PAPER

The paper is available from the manufacturers/dealers in form of rims. However the government provides paper at concessional rates as rates books are aid in literacy programmes of government. The paper of desired quality and fineness is available in large dimensions. It is cut down ti the required size and trimmed from edges, with sharp cutting edges cutter. The trimmed sheets are then packed according to size and sent for further processing.

RULING

The paper after cutting to the proper dimensions is sent to the ruling machines. The paper is ruled in the ruling machines because the note-books are generally ruled. Registers are also ruled suitably as desired. Selection of proper ink is very essential as the clear appearance is desired. Files do not involve any ruling but they are pressed to facilitate the folding at different positions, in order to provide different thickness limits.

PRINTING OF COVERS

Covers are provided to the note-books and registers in order to prevent the book from deterioration during handling. Covers for note-books and registers are made from the materials like hard boards, hard and thick paper, ordinary papers. Files on the other hand may also be made of plastic sheets in different colours and varieties. Covers are printed suitably giving the name of manufacturer and brand name/trademark etc. Also space is provided for writing the particulars of authorised persons. Various designs etc may also be printed to improve the appearance of covers.

STAPLING AND STITCHING/PUNCHING

The paper obtained after the cutting and ruling operations is then bonded together either by stapling or stitching and for improved finish both. Each unit of note-books and registers consists of certain specific number of pages and they are priced accordingly. In order to make thick note-books, two or more stapled note-books are being combined accordingly. Care is essentially to be taken as any minor mistake may lead to loosening of the pages. Files involve the punching of perfectly sized holes for providing clips and the laces.

BINDING

It the note-books and registers are to be bound by ordinary or hard papers, then such printed paper covers are directly stapled or stitched. In case of thick covers, card board covers and stapled books are placed between the properly sized board and the printed cover is pasted to it with some gummy substances. The inside pages are get pasted to the inside of board at both the sides.

After binding the finished products are ready for dispatch in the market.

LIST OF PLANT AND MACHINERY

(1) Paper slitter

(2) Printing Machine (Ruling)

(3) Printing machine (for covers)

(4) Stapling Machine

(5) Binding and Finishing Unit

(6) Folding Equipment

(7) Miscellaneous.

43

Napkins and Facial Tissues

These papers are light weight sanitary tissues. Facial tissues and paper napkins are soft loosely fitted for absorbency so that they may absorb moisture and hold it. The sheet is creped to increase the softness and absorbency. The paper must be clean and should have pleasant odour. On the other hand paper should have sufficient wet strength and should not leave any residue on the face or hand.

These papers, are manufactured in India by very limited firms. These papers are very popular in big hotels, restaurants, Indian airlines etc. due to their light weight, high absorbency, hygienic nature and attractive printing.

The manufacturing process begins when the waste paper is moved upto the sorting yard above the digester by elevator.

The sorted waste paper is fed into the global digester simultaneously with the feeding. Sodium sulphate, soda ash, etc. are sprinkled thoroughly over the waste paper.

After stuffing of the digester has been completed the gate of the digester is tightly closed then steam is blown into the digester as it is rotated.

The material is then sent through the silver screen, and the Johnson screen for removal of dust. The material which comes out of the screen is transferred into the extractor for washing and dichering.

The base paper which has been reeled is cut into the fixed width by the slitter on the slitting machine and wound into rolls in required length.

These rolls are fed to a two colour flexographic printing machine wherein these are printed and cut with the help of an attachment fitted there. The softness, strength and smoothness is obtained by passing the tissue through a nip formed between a brush roll and patterned baking roll.

These tissues can be treated with wetting agents to improve wet strength imparting resins such as UF and melamine resins. More often additional wetting agents are employed in the wet strength tissue to maintain its absorbency.

44

Playing Cards

In the modern age of living, the most appealing and alternative playing cards are made on PVC coating paper. The advantages of these playing cards is: (1) Better look, (2) Non-effective on water, (3) Long lasting, an (4) Protection from dust. Although these type of playing cards are somewhat costlier than ordinary playing cards.

Play card is a source of interesting and educational game if it is properly used. It is used for playing a number of games such as:

1. For gambling i.e. Flash, Mang-patta etc.
2. For Rummy, Coast Peace, Seep etc.

Apart from the above, there are various other games from playing cards. Sometimes, in the magic show, the playing cards are sued.

MANUFACTURING PROCESS

First of all, thick sheet of good quality paper is taken and print design is marked on one side of the sheet. Next the sheet is cut into 54 sheets of equal sizes. As we know that one set of playing cards normally contain 54 cards including 2 jokers. Now each sheet is printed with numbers and design as desired. This operation is also carried out in another printing press having changeable printing blocks. It is, at this stage, PVC coating operation starts. Before coating PVC coating compound is made in a mixer. Now, this coating compound is fed to the hopper of a roll coater. Paper sheet is passed through the coating machine twice for coating of both faces of sheet. Same operation is observed with other sheets of paper also. After coating of both faces, paper sheets are required to be cut in equal sizes of actual playing card. Every corner of playing card is also rounded off in the same operation of cutting. Now the cards are carefully packed with each number in every pack and two jokers. The packing box should either be printed on coated paper or in plastic.

PLANT AND MACHINERY

Consists of such as Printing machine, Cutting and Corner forming machine, PVC solution reservoir, Playing cards box making machine, Packing machine, Blocks, other ancillaries, installation and erection etc.

45

Drinking Straws

Drinking straws as the name suggests, are used for drinking liquid food products, aerated drinks, beverages and fruit juices. Drinking straws are made from various materials paper, drinking straws which are wax coated, rubber drinking straws and plastic drinking straws. These straws made from different materials serve the same purpose. There is a slight disadvantage in using paper-drinking straws because sometimes they get plugged due to bending during the aerated drinking-straws overcome this problem. But on the other hand, the paper-drinking straw is considerably cheaper than plastic drinking straw.

The technique of manufacturing drinking-straw is very easy, consisting of gluing, rolling and cutting operation. Drinking straws are produced in our country mostly by the small scale sector. This being a consumer product a small industrialist has to depend upon local market only for its marketability.

The basic qualities which a good drinking-straw should have are:

1. It must not be leaky.
2. It must not become successively wet and absorbent with the liquid so that it may become pasty solid and plug the way from the bottle to the mouth.
3. It should be chemically inert to the aerated drink, fruit juice or to whatsoever drink it is being used.
4. It should not be costly also.

In these days, people are changing their habits rapidly and the consumption and production of aerated and carbonated drinks is increasing day by day.

MANUFACTURING PROCESS

The technique of manufacturing of drinking straw is very simple and can be produced by using hand-operated as well as power operated machines.

The raw materials required for manufacturing 10,000 straws/day.

PVC	5 tonne/year
Glue	1 tonne/year

The stepwise process of producing plastic drinking-straw is as follows:

1. Selection of Plastic
2. Sheet-cutting to required width
3. Gluing
4. Winding
5. Hot air Blowing (Drying)
6. Straw-sizing.

46

Card Board

Packing may be defined as a means of protecting contents from ordinary handling, providing ease in packing and unpacking and simultaneously providing a means for publicizing the contents.

Against the above background, the card board box is replacing the conventional wooden boxes steadily attracting a worldwide demand.

Card board is an important grade of paper board. It has wide ranging application which includes its use in manufacture of card board boxes. Other important applications include book binding.

Card board is made by overlapping two or more plies of kraft paper. The major raw materials for manufacture are rice straw, lime, soda ash etc. The board is also made from bagasse, but the cost of production is more in this case. Other raw materials used are straw of wheat, maize, barley etc. which are available in abundance in many parts of the country. In several areas, substantial quantities of these are surplus after meeting the requirements for cattle fodder, but not large enough to set up large scale card board or paper factories. Large amounts of water are required in the board manufacture. An ideal location for the production plant is a place where the rice straws and plenty of water are easily available. As compared to Fourdinier machine, commonly used in paper making use of cylinder mould machine is found more suitable in board manufacture.

The prospects of card board industry appear to be good and the demand is expected to rise with the rapid industrial development of our country.

MANUFACTURING PROCESS OF CARD FROM PULP AND WASTE PAPER

The raw material used for the manufacture of card board are pulp and waste paper in the ratio of 1:3 respectively.

Initially in a tank containing water, raw materials are introduced and mixed thoroughly. The pulpy mass thus prepared is then fed to the roller beater.

While the entire pulp is rotating in the beater, a jet of steam may be injected and the pulp is subjected to cutting under the knives. After about one hour or more depending upon the desired consistency of the pulp obtained, the pulp is then transferred to the stock chest where all the heavier particles are allowed to settle while keeping the pulp rotating or it may be passed through a screen to remove the undesirable substances coming alongwith the pulp. It is then refined in the refiner.

Then it is transferred to a MS tank while inter-connected with another M.S. tank and in both these tanks, stirrers are fixed in order to stir well the pulp to which water is added from a tank.

When the desired consistency is accomplished, it is subjected to Board Forming Machine, though a stock circulating system cylinder or vat machine is usually employed for this purpose.

The components of a vat machining comprise the cylinder mould covered with wire mesh and is particularly submerged in the stock suspension contained in the vat when the cylinder mould is rotated, water drains through the wire cloth leaving the fibre deposited upon its surface as long as difference in water level exists to promote flow in that direction. The fibres clinging to the wire surface are carried out of the water and under a couch roll by the rotation of the mould. Water is removed from inside the mould. The sheet of the board formed on the cylinder surface is couched by the hydraulic press with the help of a hydraulic pump. The board thickness depends on the inflow consistency.

It is then subjected to drying operation. The board so formed is sent for either sun drying or multiple deck platoon dryers or tunnel dryers.

Subsequently the card board sheets are cut by a cutter or slitting machine into desired size and of desired gsm., depending upon the thickness of the board.

After the visual tests, the sheets are sent for packing. Sheets of uniform size and thickness are packed in a bundle. Hundred sheets are counted, weighed and packed in a bundle, which are then sold on weight basis.

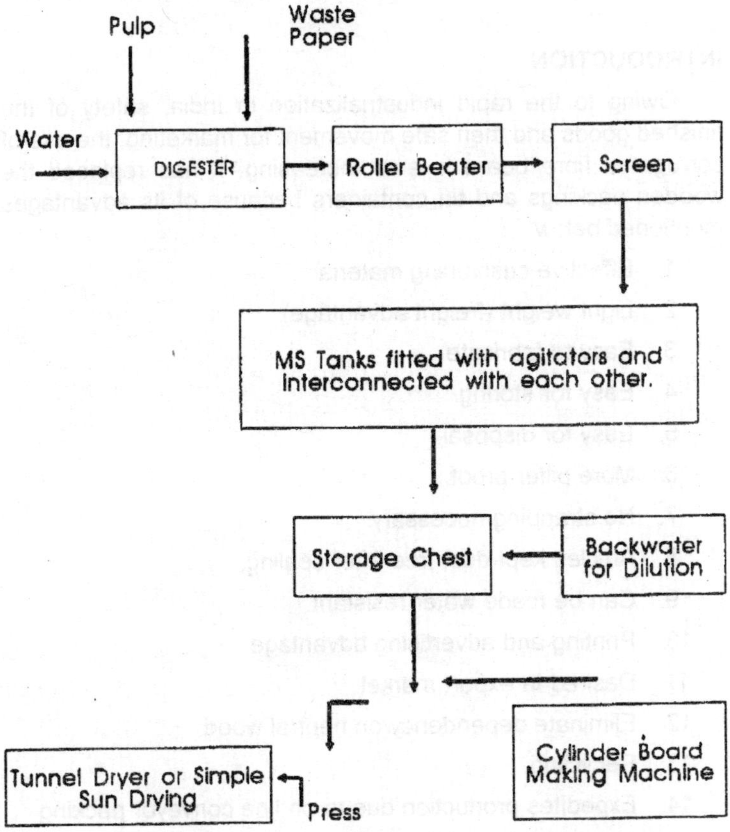

Fig. 1. Flow sheet for manuafcture of card board

47

Corrugated Board and Boxes

INTRODUCTION

Owing to the rapid industrialization in India, safety of the finished goods and then safe movement for marketing, the use of corrugated fibre board is ever increasing. It has replaced the wooden packings and tin containers because of its advantages mentioned below:

1. Effective cushioning material.
2. Light weight (freight advantage).
3. Easy to fabricate.
4. Easy for storing.
5. Easy for disposal.
6. More pilfer proof.
7. No strapping necessary.
8. Articles kept dust free after sealing.
9. Can be made water resistant.
10. Printing and advertising advantage.
11. Desired in export market.
12. Eliminate dependency on neutral wood.
13. Recycling.
14. Expedites production due to on line conveyor packing.

A recent survey has revealed that 75% to 80% packing is now being done by the paper corrugated board.

USES

At present, it is extensively used in breweries, glass-wares, cigarettes, pharmaceuticals, soap and cosmetics, biscuits, milk and milk products, tea and coffee, hosiery and foot-wears, toys, photographic equipments, electric goods, bicycle and auto-parts, rubber products, cashewnut industry, synthetic fibres.

Fig. 1. Single face corrugating machine

PROCESS OF MANUFACTURE

Corrugated Board

Corrugated board is made with a corrugated sheet of paper attached to the facings of flat paper, usually kraft, by adhesives. It is formed on single face *Corrugating machine*.

SINGLE FACE CORRUGATING MACHINE

Corrugated roll formed on this machines. The corrugating machine consists of a set of corrugating rolls with heating arrangements and glue applicator rolls. One kraft liner paper and corrugating medium paper are fed into the machine. Before the medium paper enters the corrugating rolls, the later will be heated using heating arrangement fitted therein, to produce a surface temperature of 320-340° F. These rolls will heat the corrugating medium when it comes in their contact. This heat treatment makes the paper soft and pliable so that uniform flutings are produced. On leaving the corrugating rolls, the corrugating medium comes out to meet a glue applicator roll which applies adhesive to tips of fluts formed by the rolls. Immediately after the application of glue, the first liner is brought into contact with the glued tips and then wound to roll. The resulting board is known as a single face corrugated roll. Double Face corrugated Board is produced by gluing second liner to the open side of the S.F. Corrugated Board and further piles of the board can be, increased by glueing the boards together as required. The glueing is done by the pasting machine.

Technical Data

Length of corrugating roll	62"	52"	42"
Width of paper	60"	50"	40"
Speed per mm	30-50 ft.	30-50 ft.	30-50 ft
Required H.P.	5 H.P	3 H.P	3 H.P
Length of Machine	21 ft.	15 ft.	15 ft.
Width of Machine	102"	92"	82"
Height of Machine	6'	6'	6'
Net Weight (approx)	4000 kg.	3300 kg.	2800 kg.
Gross Weight (approx)	4500 kg.	3800 kg.	3200 kg.

COMBINED ROTARY SLOTTER CREASER

The only heavy duty machine designed specifically for the special corrugated boxes low tonnage. High Profitability. More the production hail the cost total accuracy. The functions of the machine are creasing slotting and corner cutting to corrugated board simultaneously and quickly. The machine can be used for mass production which cannot be achieved by eccentric slotter. This machine is the best among chainfed slotters manufactured with vast experience and excellent skillness. Durability of the machine and its perfect slotting and refined creasing are guaranteed. The salient features of the machine are appended below. Slotter shaft and creases shaft can be adjusted up and down by the handle attached on operation side with graduated marks. Speed controlled at operation side. Sheet rack attached on the feeding table. Less noise and long durability. Very easy to operate and a skilled worker can operate to top speed for maximum output.

The printing can be done directly on the ready-made sheet without effecting the flutes with rubber stereos by using letter press inks. This process is known as flexographic printing. The machine (Fig. 8) for this purpose comprises of a main cylinder and an ink section working over it. The ink rollers are so designed that the ink gets evenly spread and ground before being transferred to the rubber stereo affixed on the main cylinder. The sheets are piled on a table and are placed one by one on the feed table by hand. The strikers moving on the table, feed the sheet into the printing area as per adjustments. After getting the print impression, the sheet travels on a conveyor to get proper dying, whereafter it piles up on the ground. The machine prints single colour at a time.

PASTING MACHINE

This machine is used for glueing the fluted side of the board. It can be pasted paper to board as well as board to board. Single face board fabricated in the corrugating machine is cut into the required size and fed into this machine with the result that the glue is applied on the tips corrugated board. Such board is brought in contact with the second liner and both paster together.

Specifications

Size	62"	72"	82"
Speed	150 r.p.m	150 r.m.p.	150 r.m.p.
Power Required	1/2 H.P.	1/2 H.P.	1 H.P.
Floor Space	82" × 30"	92" × 32"	104" × 36"
Height	50"	50"	50"
Gross Weight	500 kg	600 kg	700 kg

Fig. 2. Pasting machine

SHEET PRESS

This machine is used for setting corrugated sheets straight and even, after being processed on the pasting machine. This is achieved by keeping the pile of sheets pressed between the lower and upper plates of this machine. The upper plate is moved up and down by means of an electric motor.

Specifications

Size of Machine	45" × 65"	66" × 75"
Press Area (approx.)	43" × 63"	63" × 73"
Press Height (approx.)	0-48 ft.	0-84 ft.
Height of Machine	78"	84"
Floor Space	50" × 75"	70" × 85"
Weight (approx.)	1000 kg	1600 kg
Power Required	2 H.P.	3 H.P.

Fig. 3. Sheet press

BAR ROTARY CUTTING AND CREASING MACHINE

This machine performs simultaneously the functions of cutting and creasing in the manufacture of boxes. Whereas creasing is required in the manufacture of folders of interior packing, cutting is required to cut sheets to size to form stips or blanks.

Technical Data

Size of Machine	45"	85"	75"	95"
Speed (per min.)	400 ft.	400 ft.	400 ft.	350 ft.
No. of cutters	4	4	4	4
No. of creasers	4	4	4	4
Min. distance between two dies	3"	3"	3"	3"
power required	1 H.P.	105 H.P.	2 H.P.	2 H.P.
Height	48"	48"	48"	48"
Floor space	65" × 40"	86" × 58"	106" × 63"	123" × 63"
Gross weight (approx.)	800 kg.	1500 kg.	2000 kg.	2500 kg.

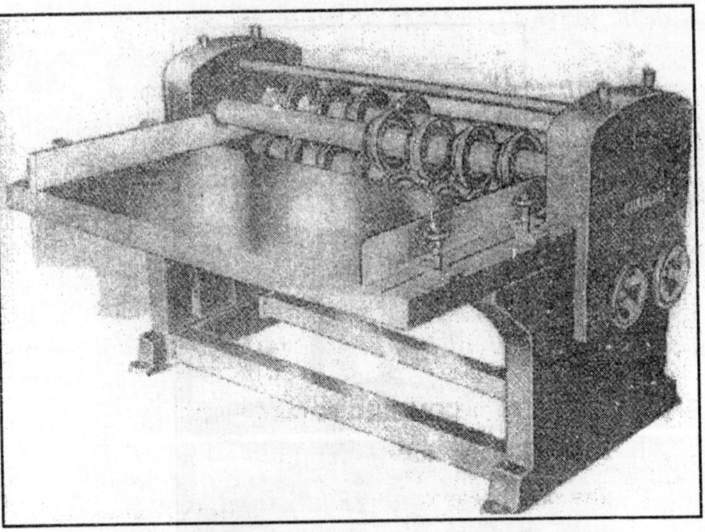

Fig. 4. Bar Rotary cutting and creasing machine

Fig. 5. Combined rotary slotter creaser

COMBINED ROTARY SLOTTER CREASER

The only heavy duty machine designed specifically for the special corrugated boxes low tonnage. High profitability. More the production half the cost total accuracy. The functions of the machine are creasing slotting and corner cutting of corrugated board simultaneously and quickly. The machine can be used for mass production which cannot be achieved by eccentric slotter. This machine is the best among chainfed slotters manufactured with vast experience and excellent skillness. Durability of the machine and its perfect Slotting and refined creasing are guaranteed. The salient features of the machine are appended below Slotter shaft and creaser shaft can be adjusted up and down by the handle attached on operation side with and graduated marks. Speed controlled at operation side. Sheet rack attached on the feeding table. Less noise and long durability. Very easy to operate and a skilled worker can operate to top speed for maximum output.

Specifications

Size	60" × 85"	60" × 100"	60" × 120"
Capacity (Shts/Min)	30	30	20
Maximum Sheet size	55" × 80"	55" × 95"	55" × 115"
Minimum sheet size	25" × 25"	25" × 25"	25" × 25"
Minimum slotting interval	6"	6"	6"
Minimum creasing interval	6"	6"	6"

BOARD CUTTING MACHINE

This is a manual operated machine utilized for cutting all classes of board and paper etc. It is equipped with adjustable front and back guides and a foot operated clamp that holds the sheet flat while being cut. The cutting blades are made of knife steel and precision grounded to secure clean and accurate cutting.

Specifications

Size (cutting length)	42"	52"	62"
Working table width			
Maximum adjustable -	42"	42"	42"
Distance of the front guide	22"	22"	22"
Floor space	70" × 50"	85" × 50"	100" × 50"
Approx. Net weight	450 kgs.	550 kgs.	600 kgs.

Fig. 6. Board Cutting Machine

Fig. 7. Corrugated sheet printing machine

CORRUGATED SHEET PRINTING MACHINE

The most advanced and speedy process of printing the paper board, is now with rubber stereos and is called the flexographic printing. The advantage of this process is that the printing can be done directly on the ready-made sheet without affecting the flutes, by using letter press inks.

Specifications

Machine size	42" × 80"
Print Area	40" × 76"
Feeding system	Chain feeding
Printed speed	1000-1500 sheets/hour
Floor space	16" × 16"
Power Required	2 H.P.

48

Grey Board

The recent trend in business style packaging of finished products has its own importance. The quality of the product is measured with the show of packaging and packaging material. That is why the demand of Grey board is increasing rapidly.

Grey board is an important grade of paper board. The importance of paper board as an essential commodity is constantly increasing with the expansion of education among the people. Further in a progressive society, the consumption of paper is closely linked to its economic, social and cultural activities.

The consumption of grey board, is for various purposes viz. for making cartons for medicines, pharmaceutical packagings, making boxes for shoes, hosiery and other items for book-binding making registers for flat files, sale of textile goods etc.

Grey board is a superior packaging material and due to rapid industrialisation is in very good demand.

Grey board is a homogenous board made usually of mixed waste paper with or without screenings and pulp on a board machine.

Grey board is used where stiffness rather than printability is required.

Plenty of raw materials for making of the boards is available in India.

Grey board has the advantage of light weight, easy to fabricate, keeps the articles dust free after sealing and has the advantage of attractive printing, thus making the packed item more eye-appealing for sale.

PROPERTIES OF GREY BOARD

The resistance of grey board extends from very soft, flexible tissues to rigid board.

It is obvious that thicker and heavier sheets tend to be stiff and rigid while soft, flexible are light and thin.

Grey board is one whose thickness is not greater than 1 mm.

The weight of grey board is commonly expressed in g/m^2 (gsm.).

MANUFACTURING PROCESS OF GREY BOARD

Rags and gunny bags are introduced in a digester; Straw is cut upto short lengths and charged into a separate rotary spherical digester. The mass is treated with 10-15% of chemicals (Lime, Soda Ash or Caustic Soda) are added. Contents are heated by direct stream between temp. of 140°C to 150°C and a pressure of about 40-50 psi.

After the cooking is completed, the pulp is blown into a receiving tank or blow pit provided with a perforated false bottom through which the liquor is drained from the pulp.

The pulp is then washed in a washing potcher and is held in a pulp storage tank at a consistency of about 5%.

The above pulp is then introduced in a beater. After about one hour, the charge is transferred to the stock chest. Waste paper, however, is not cooked and is put into the pulper. This pulp is then transferred to the beater for further pulping. This is then transferred to the stock chest and mixed with the rag pulp in proper proportions.

The pulps are then refined in the refiners and are put in the head box of separate machines. The sizing chemicals are added in the beater. In the head box the consistency is regulated to about 1% of the bone dry weight of the fibre.

BOARD FORMING

The pulps are cleared in a vibrating flat strainer and are fed to the board forming machine through a stock circulation system. A cylinder or vat machine is usually employed for this purpose.

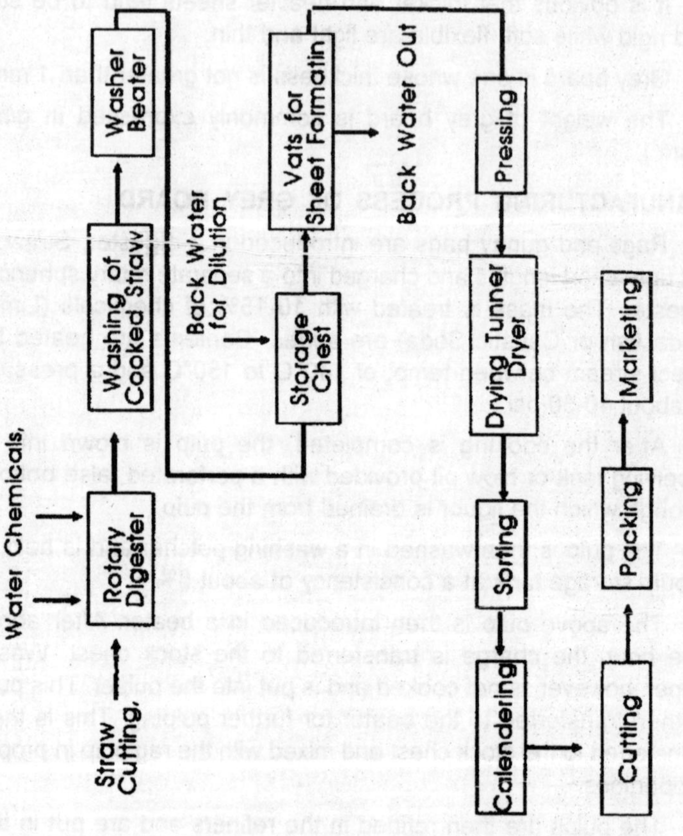

Fig. 1. Flow sheet for the Manufacture of Grey Board

Cylinder mould and vat constitute the basic components of a vat machine. The cylinder mould is covered with wire mesh and is partially submerged in the stock suspension contained in the vat. When the cylinder mould is rotated partially submerged in the stock suspension, water drains through the wire cloth leaving the fibres deposited upon its surface. The fibres clinging to the wire surface are carried out of the water and under a couch roll by the rotation of the mould. Water is removed from the inside of the mould.

CYLINDER MACHINE OPERATION

The above stock is passed through a regulating box where it is diluted to the desired consistency which then flows through screens to the head box in which it is kept at such a level that flow through pipe will keep the stock in the vat at the desired level.

When the cylinder mould revolves partially submerged in the vat, the stock sticks to the wire of the cylinder mould, while the water goes through the wire mesh to the suction pipes and is returned to the regulating box for the purpose of diluting more stuff. The sheet of board formed on the cylinder surface is couched by the hydraulic press. The thickness of the board depends upon the inflow consistency.

Capacity and the amount of flow maintained and the pick-up capacity. One squeeze press (Baby Press) is usually provided to draw out the water taken by the felt from the couch.

DRYING OF THE BOARD

The board so formed under the hydraulic press, is sent for drying in either multiple-deck dryers or tunnel dryers.

For the boards, stationary multiple deck platoon dryers are the simplest form of dryers, usually heated by steam. There many be twenty mounted one above the other. The sheets of wet board are carried by an adjustable elevating conveyor or a tipple to one sheet after another in a stationary rack, then transferred to a movable rack from which the boards are slit into the dryer press,

49

Straw Board (Manual Process)

For the purpose of making straw board, pulping of the raw material is conducted slowly in stationary digester. The object of digestion is to remove dirt, grease and other accompanying impurities and to cause softening of the materials. It is followed by beating which is done slowly and carefully. The purpose of beating is to increase the sheet formation properties without sacrificing strength.

SHEET FORMATION

For the purposes of sheet formation, the pulp is held in vats. Vats may be of stone, copper or wood lined with metal. Extending the full length of the vat, at the bottom is a paddle wheel known as a 'hog,' which runs at a low speed to keep the pulp in motion. The sheet is formed by immersing the mould in the vat containing the pulp which is diluted with the required amount of water.

As stated earlier, the mould essentially consists of a metal or wooden skeleton frame to suit the size of the sheet required; on the surface is stretched a fine copper wire gauze cloth which hold the pulp and simultaneously allows the water to drain through in a manner similar to the action of a sieve.

After the mould has been immersed in the vat containing the pulp of desired consistency, it is shaken horizontally to produce a well-felted sheet. A film of pulp is thus set by the draining away of the water through the wire gauze. The deckle is then removed

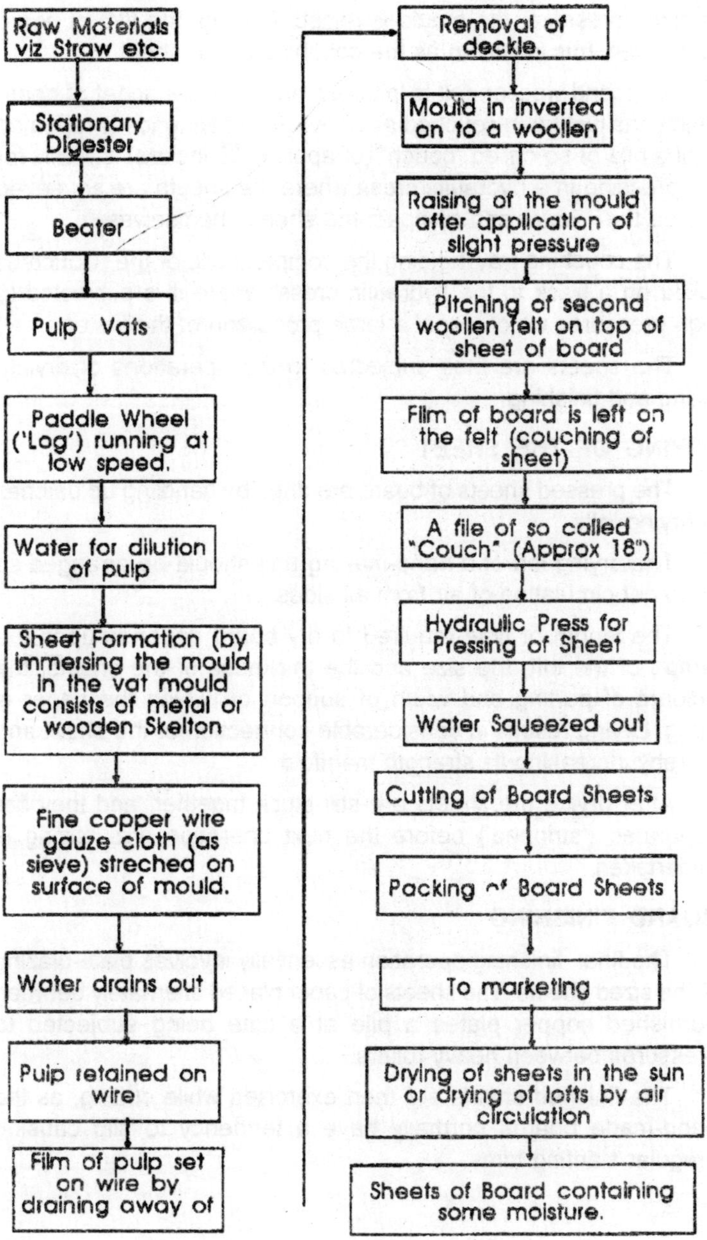

Fig. 1. Flow diagram of manufacture of starw Board (manual process)

and the mould is inverted on to a woolen felt. After the application of slight pressure, the mould is raised, leaving, the film of board on the felt, this is known as the couching of the sheet.

A second woollen felt is 'pitched' on top of the sheet of board which has just been couched as above. The sequence is repeated until a pile of so-called "couch" (of approx. 18 inches) is ready for the pressing in a hydraulic press where the sheets are squeezed to free the water and compact the sheets themselves.

The couching tray, holding the complete pile or the "Couch" is rolled on a track to the hydraulic press, where it is subjected to high pressures which expel a large proportion of the water.

The sheets are then subjected to the operations of drying, sizing and finishing.

DRYING OF THE SHEET

The pressed sheets of board are dried by handling up batches in drying lofts.

The drying loft of a hand-making unit should be arranged so as to get circulation of air from all sides.

The length of time required to dry board depends upon the temp., of the loft, the size and the thickness of the sheets, the amount of parting and width of support on which the paper is hung. Drying results in considerable contraction of the sheet and thereby increasing its strength manifold.

After drying the sheets are still stuck together, and they are separated ('stripped') before the next operation, viz., sizing is undertaken.

BOARD FINISHING

The final finishing operation essentially involves plate-glazing of the sized sheets. The sheets of paper placed alternately between burnished copper plates a pile at a time being subjected to pressures between heavy rollers.

The finished sheets are then exercised while cutting, as the hand-made boards normally have a tendency to slip causing irregular slanting trims.

50

Straw Board (Automatic Process)

Straw Board is an important grade of paper board. It has wide range of applications which include its use in manufacture of card board boxes, cartons and similar packaging materials. Other important application is in book binding. It is made from partially cooked straw, bagasse, or grass or a mixture of these. However, the major raw materials for its manufacture are rice straws, lime and soda ash. Though the board is also made from bagasse, but the cost of production is more in this case. Large amounts of water are required.

for the production of Straw Board, the ideal location is a place where rice straws, and plenty of water are easily available.

As compared to fourdrinier machine commonly used in paper making, use of cylinder mould is found more suitable in board manufacture.

Straw board is made in two grades, namely A and B. The specifications are given below:

	Grade A	*Grade B*
Moisture content as receiving percent, max,	10	10
Breaking length in metres, min.		
MD	1150	1150
CD	750	750
Burst factor, min.	5.0	5.0
Stiffness factor, min	20	20
pH	—	5.5 to 8.5

	Grade A	Grade B
Ash percent, max.	—	20.0
Water soluble chlorides (as NaCl) percent by weight, max	—	0.05
Water soluble sulphates (as Na_2 So_4) percent, by weight, max.	—	0.25
Fatty and/or similar acids (as $C_{17}H_{33}$ CooH), percent by weight, max.	—	0.25

A tolerance in thickness of ± 10 per cent on average thickness and tolerance on substance of ± 5 per cent is allowed.

However, in general, Straw Board is thicker, heavier and less flexible than the conventional paper.

The weight of straw board is commonly expressed in gm/m^2.

The demand and utility of paper board is increasing at a high rate and the industry has good market potential.

MANUFACTURING PROCESS

The straw is cut into shorter lengths and charged into spherical rotary digester and the mass is treated with requisite amounts of chemicals (lime, soda ash or caustic soda). Contents of the digester are heated by direct steam to a pressure of about 30-40 psi and the cooking carried out for about 4 to 6 hours. However, the exact conditions of cooking, e.g. amount of chemicals, steam pressure, duration of cooking etc. are governed by the nature of raw materials.

Subsequently, the cooked material is blown into a blow tank and the waste liquid is washed away.

The cooked and defibrised material is fed into a dilution box and the pulp consistency is adjusted by addition of water.

It is then subjected to the beater operation and the resulting stuff is then stored in the beater chest from where the pulp is pumped to the head box. It is then fed into Jorden Engine and from there it is pumped to the mixing box. Here, once again the consistency of the pulp is adjusted by the addition of back water from the machine box.

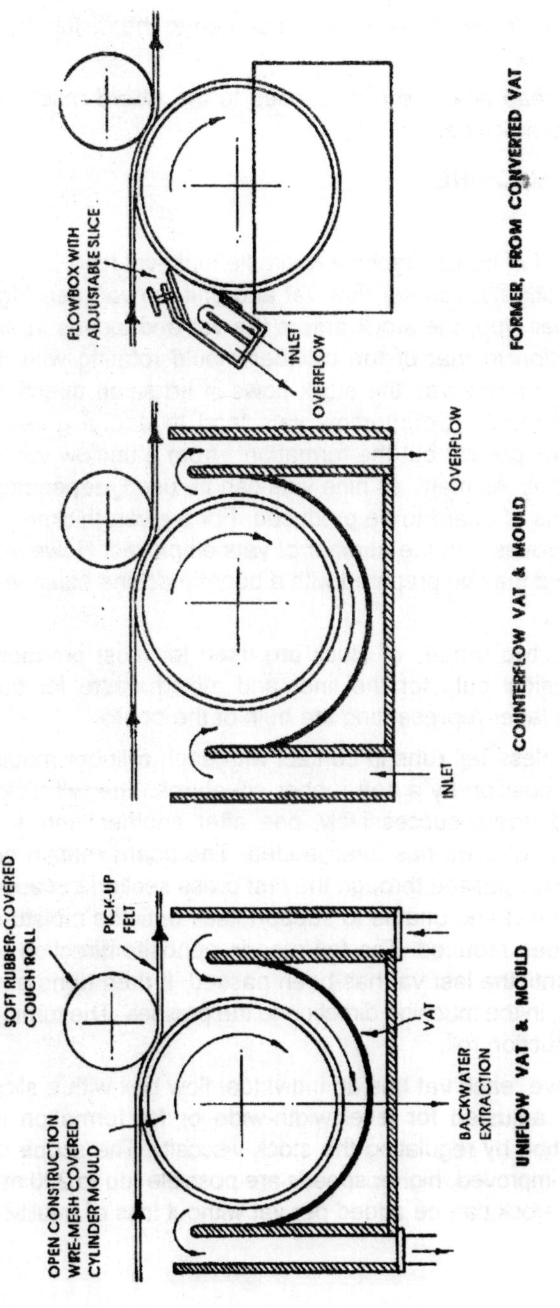

Fig. 1. Types of vat and former

The pulp stock then passes via the screen to the distribution box and head box.

From the head box, the pulp passes to the Board machine (cylinder mould machine).

THE BOARD MACHINE

Formation

The wet end of board machine is simple multi-vat type. There are two types of vats: counter flow vat and uniform vat (see Fig. 1). In the former type, the stock enters the vat and moves in an opposite direction to that of the cylinder mould rotating with it, whereas in the uniflow vat, the stock flows in he same direction as taht of the mould. Counterflow vats tend to add a greater quantity of stock per vat but the formation from a uniflow vat is superior in quality. As many as nine vats can be used, depending on the thickness of board to be produced. For a given thickness, the quality improves with the number of vats employed. However, fair quality board may be prepared with a board machine equipped with six vats.

In general, two grades of stock are used for most products bleached chemical pulp for the liner and mixed waste for the remainder, the latter representing the bulk of the board.

A long, endless felt runs in contact with each cylinder mould and is held in position by a soft rubber couch roll. The felt picks up the formed layers successively, one after another, until the desired number of plies has been added. The board remain on the felt until it has passed through the first press section because it is heavy and wet and unable to suppprt itself until the moisture content has been reduced. The felt runs in opposite direction to the machine until the last vat has been passed. It then turns and runs overhead, in the machine direction to the presses. The turning roll can be a suction roll.

In the above, each vat has an individual flow box with a slice which can be adjusted for level width-wide or for formation in machine direction by regulating the stock viscosity. The scope of the vat is thus improved; higher speeds are possible (up to 200 m.) min and more stock can be added per vat without loss of quality.

Board Pressing

As board is normally heavy in substance (upto 450 gm.^{2} or more), it carries more moisture than paper per unit length. Furthermore, the water is more difficult to remove; pressure must be applied gradually in order to avoid crushing. For this reason, more presses may be needed than in the case of paper. The production of a board machine is usually limited by its drying capacity, which is strongly influenced by the press section. Ply-adhesion, is another important quality consideration which is also influenced by pressing "Baby-presses," which are small, plain presses with light loading, are often incorporated with the long felt in the vat section in order to bring the board to a condition suitable for the main presses. Plain, grooved or suction presses can be used. However nip pressures are normally lower than for paper and the moisture content is seldom higher than 65 per cent.

Figure 2 shows the flow diagram of a board machine with a capacity of 5 tonnes per day.

Board Drying

Drying section of a board machine is similar to that of paper machine, but control may be different. Board is predominantly sheeted, and the sheets should stay flat in order to avoid problems with carton making. For this reason, board machines may have separate steam system for the top and bottom dryers because curl is a function of the drying rate from the board surfaces. Board may also differ from paper in relation to MG finishes. Pre-dryers and after-dryers are normally used to increase the output determined by the capacity of the MG cylinder. The finish required can be obtained by having the board go on to the cylinder at a 60 per cent dryness, and leave 85 per cent dry.

Reeling, Winding and Sheeting

Board machines, other than MG machines, usually have two calender stacks in order to obtain the finish required and to control the bulk or thickness of the sheet. It is common, for the first stack, to use "water-doctors," or shallow wooden trays with an open side touching one or more calender rolls, thus adding water to the sheet. The de sired board finish can thus be obtained without undue pressure, which would reduce bulk or thickness and consequently stiffness, which is a desirable board quality.

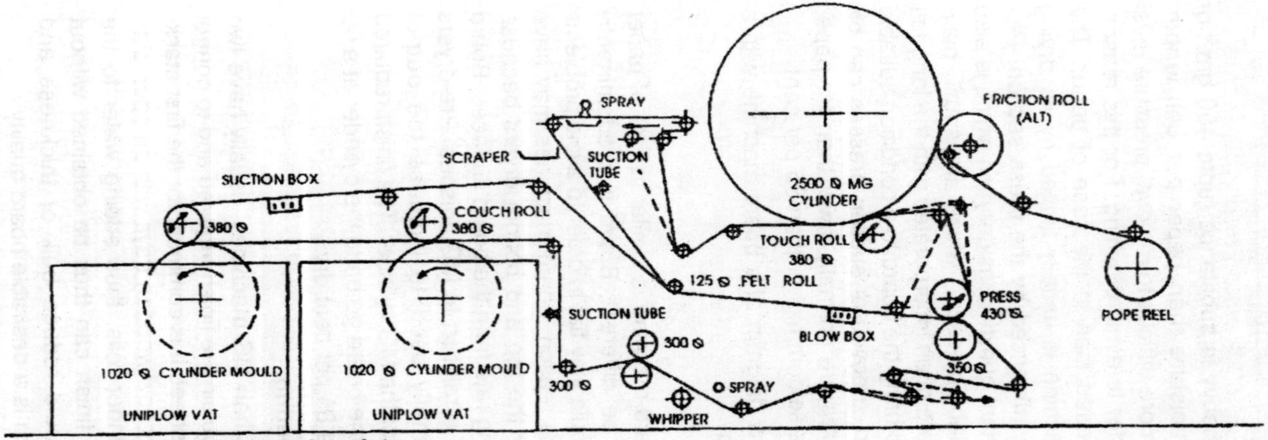

Design andoperation data

Type of machine	:	Cylinder mould (M.G.)
Capacity (gross)	:	4.5 to 5 tonnes/day
Substance range	:	40 to 120 G.S.M.
Operating speed	:	12 to 70 m/min
Trimmed width	:	1500 at reel
Mould width	:	1750 (effective)

All sizez are in mm.

Fig. 2. 5 TDP capacity paper machine with two cylinder moulds and M.G. cylinder

The board machine reel is similar to that of the paper machine. However, small mills seldom use a separate winder because the bulk of the production is sheeted. If reels are welded, they can be slit to width on the machine reel or produced from a very simple and inexpensive rewinder.

CUTTER

The cutter is the most important finishing machine. It is usually full-width. A double ,synchronised fly-knife cutter is used for the production of sheets of standard sizes. Small mills may use a simpler and less expensive technique which involves two operations: cutting followed by guillotinizing.

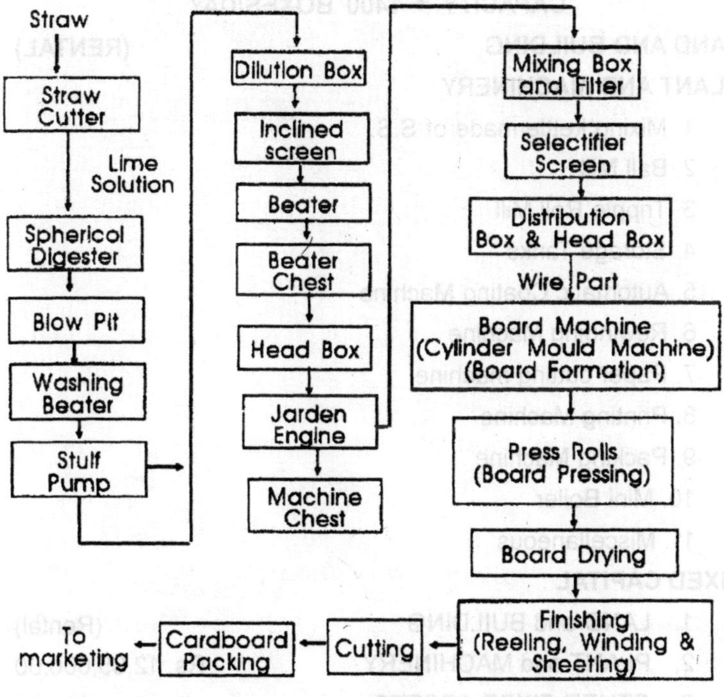

Fig. 3. Process flow sheet for straw board

51

Plant Economics of Carbon Paper

CAPACITY = 1400 BOXES/DAY

LAND AND BUILDING **(RENTAL)**

PLANT AND MACHINERY

1. Mixing kettle made of S.S.
2. Ball Mill
3. Tripple Roll Mill
4. Storage Tanks
5. Automatic Coating Machine
6. Rewinding Machine
7. Paper cutting machine
8. Printing Machine
9. Packing Machine
10. Mini Boiler
11. Miscellaneous

FIXED CAPITAL

1.	LAND and BUILDING	(Rental)
2.	PLANT and MACHINERY	Rs. 12,65,000.00
3.	OTHER FIXED ASSETS	Rs. 2,15,000.00
	TOTAL	Rs. 14,80,000.00

RAW MATERIALS

1. Tissue Paper
2. Carnauba Wax
3. Candellia Wax
4. Paraffin Wax
5. Light Mineral Oil
6. Oleic Acid
7. Carbon Black
8. Methyl Violet Blue
9. Victoria Blue Black
10. Packing Material inculding Boxes

TOTAL WORKING CAPITAL/MONTH

1. RAW MATERIAL	Rs. 2,64,359.00
2. SALARY and WAGES	Rs. 83,125.00
3. UTILITIES and OVERHEADS	Rs. 45,500.00
TOTAL	Rs. 3,92,984.00

TOTAL CAPITAL INVESTMENT

TOTAL FIXED CAPITAL	Rs. 14,80,000.00
TOTAL WORKING CAPITAL FOR 1 MONTH	Rs. 3,92,984.00
TOTAL	Rs. 18,72,984.00

TURN OVER/ANNUM

By Sale of 420000 boxes	Rs. 58,80,000.00

PROFIT SALES RATIO = Profit / Sales x 100 = 10%

RATE OF RETURN = Operating profit / T.C.I x 100 = 33%

BREAK EVEN POINT (B.E.P) = 65%

52

Plant Economics of Coated Paper and Board Plant

CAPACITY : 198 Coated Art Paper and Chromo Paper/Annum
310 Coated Art & Chromo Board/Annum

LAND & BUILDING
(LAND AREA REQUIRED = 350 Sq.Mtr.) = RS. 15,65,000.00

PLANT & MACHINERY

1. Coating mixer
2. Stainer
3. Stainless steel storage tanks
4. Metering Machine
5. Kiss Coating machine (fitted with coating pan and accessories)
6. Cutting machine fitted with access.
7. Testing equipments
8. Miscellaneous

FIXED CAPITAL

1. LAND & BUILDING	Rs. 15,65,000.00
2. PLANT & MACHINERY	Rs. 21,30,000.00
3. OTHER FIXED ASSETS	Rs. 1,65,000.00
TOTAL	Rs. 38,60,000.00

RAW MATERIALS

1. Paper (white ordinary paper)
2. Board (ordinary)
3. Coating Formulation (for white glazed finish)

TOTAL WORKING CAPITAL/MONTH

1. RAW MATERIAL	Rs. 29,68,000.00
2. SALARY & WAGES	Rs. 92,125.00
3. UTILITIES & OVERHEADS	Rs. 2,50,500.00
TOTAL	Rs. 33,10,625.00

TOTAL CAPITAL INVESTMENT

TOTAL FIXED CAPITAL	Rs. 38,60,000.00
TOTAL WORKING CAPITAL FOR 3 MONTHS	Rs. 99,31,875.00
TOTAL	Rs. 1,37,91,875.00

TURN OVER/ANNUM

1. Coated art paper with white glaze finish
2. Coated chromo paper with white glaze finish
3. Coated art board with white glaze finish
4. Coated chromo board with white glaze finish — Rs. 5,21,86,000.00

PROFIT SALES RATIO = Profit / Sales x 100 = 19%

RATE OF RETURN = Operating profit / T.C.I x 100 = 74%

BREAK EVEN POINT (B.E.P) = 28%

53

Plant Economics of Corrugated Sheet Board and Boxes

CAPACITY = 2650 KGS/DAY

LAND AND BUILDING (LAND 750 SQ.MTR) = RS. 20,15,000.00

PLANT AND MACHINERY

1. Corrugated Sheet Making Unit
   Single Face paper Corrugating Machine
2. Two Board Cutters
3. One reel Stand, Light model
5. One sheet pressing machine
6. One eccentric slotter
7. One 4-Bar Rotary cutting and Creasing
8. Two stitching machine
9. One Partition slotter
10. One slotting machine (700t operated)
11. One vertical Bending machine
    (Heavy duty, motorised with starter)
12. Corner cutting machine (700t operated)
13. Two colour Board Printer
14. Laminating M/c. for lamination of
    Printed Corrugated board.
15. D.G. set

FIXED CAPITAL

1. LAND and BUILDING	Rs.20,15,000.00
2. PLANT and MACHINERY	Rs.13,59,000.00
3. OTHER FIXED ASSETS	Rs. 4,85,000.00
TOTAL	Rs. 38,59,000.00

RAW MATERIALS

1. Kraft Paper in Rolls
2. Glue (Starch)
3. Stitching wire
4. Printing Ink
5. Polyethylene film

TOTAL WORKING CAPITAL/MONTH

1. RAW MATERIAL	Rs.23,36,375.00
2. SALARY and WAGES	Rs. 1,26,390.00
3. UTILITIES and OVERHEADS	Rs. 1,27,950.00
TOTAL	Rs.25,90,715.00

TOTAL CAPITAL INVESTMENT

TOTAL FIXED CAPITAL	Rs. 38,59,000.00
TOTAL WORKING CAPITAL FOR 2 MONTHS	RS. 51,81,430.00
TOTAL	Rs. 90,40,430.00

TURN OVER/ANNUM

By sale of 7,95,000 Kgs. of Corrugated Board and Boxes Rs. 3,81,60,000.00

PROFIT SALES RATIO = Profit/Sales x 100= 14%

RATE OF RETURN = Operating profit / T.C.I x 100 = 61%

BREAK EVEN POINT (B.E.P) = 34%

54

Plant Economics of Egg Tray from Pulp

CAPACITY = 6000000.00 NOS/ANNUM

LAND & BUILDING

(LAND REQUIRED 2000 SQ.MTS) **Rs. 27,50,000.00**

PLANT & MACHINERY

1. Pulp dilution and treatment machine
2. Forming section.
3. Automatic tray stamping machine.
4. Drying section (Continuous Conveyor) belt dryer with hot air blowing arangement)
5. Oil fired, 100 PSIg
6. Water treatment section
7. Tray Cutting Machine
8. Instrumentation & Process Control equipments
9. Laboratory Equipments and other

FIXED CAPITAL

1.	LAND & BUILDING	Rs. 27,50,000.00
2.	PLANT & MACHINERY	Rs. 20,70,000.00
3.	OTHER FIXED ASSETS	Rs. 4,25,000.00
	TOTAL	Rs. 52,45,000.00

RAW MATERIALS

1. Grey Paper Pulp
2. Binding Agent, starch glue etc.
3. Others Consumables

TOTAL WORKING CAPITAL/MONTH

1. RAW MATERIAL	Rs. 1,07,000.00
2. SALARY & WAGES	Rs. 71,250.00
3. UTILITIES & OVERHEADS	Rs. 1,05,500.00
TOTAL	Rs. 2,83,750.00

TOTAL CAPITAL INVESTMENT

TOTAL FIXED CAPITAL	Rs. 52,45,000.00
TOTAL WORKING CAPITAL FOR 2 MONTHS	Rs. 5,67,500.00
TOTAL	Rs. 58,12,500.00

TURN OVER/ANNUM

By sale of egg trays 6000000 Nos. Rs. 66,00,000.00

PROFIT SALES RATIO = Profit / Sales x 100 = 26%

RATE OF RETURN = Operating profit / T.C.I x 100 = 29%

BREAK EVEN POINT (B.E.P) = 58%

55

Plant Economics of Exercise Note Book and Register

CAPACITY = 2520.00 NOS/DAY

LAND & BUILDING
(LAND AREA REQUIRED = 454 SQ.MTR.) = Rs. 17,23,693.00

PLANT & MACHINERY

1. Automatic double set rulling machine
2. 2 Bar rotary cutting creasing, sorting and perforating machine
3. Paper cutting
4. Shifting attachment
5. Extra set of blades
6. Wire stitching machine complete\with Iron stand wooden table, stiching
7. Hand operated gumming machine
8. Dab press
9. Electrification and installation charges
10. Miscellaneous items tools and implements

FIXED CAPITAL

1.	LAND & BUILDING	Rs. 17,23,693.00
2.	PLANT & MACHINERY	Rs. 5,26,000.00
3.	OTHER FIXED ASSETS	Rs. 30,000.00
	TOTAL	Rs. 22,79,693.00

RAW MATERIALS

1. Paper white for excercise Notebook
2. Paper white for Register
3. Grey board, Card board, stitching wires
4. Stiching wires, ink, glue, thread, cloth etc.
5. Packing expenses
6. Miscellaneous items

TOTAL WORKING CAPITAL/MONTH

1.	RAW MATERIAL	Rs. 5,88,276.00
2.	SALARY & WAGES	Rs. 82,327.00
3.	UTILITIES & OVERHEADS	Rs. 22,500.00
	TOTAL	Rs. 6,93,103.00

TOTAL CAPITAL INVESTMENT

TOTAL FIXED CAPITAL	Rs. 22,79,693.00
TOTAL WORKING CAPITAL FOR 1 MONTH	Rs. 6,93,103.00
TOTAL	Rs. 29,72,796.00

TURN OVER/ANNUM

1.	By selling of 600000 excercise book	Rs. 90,00,000.00
2.	By sale of 156000 Registers	Rs. 21,84,000.00

PROFIT SALES RATIO = Profit / Sales x 100 = 20%

RATE OF RETURN = Operating profit / T.C.I x 100 = 76 %

BREAK EVEN POINT (B.E.P) = 33%

56

Plant Economics of Hard Board from Rice Husk

CAPACITY = 1.67 TON/DAY

LAND AND BUILDING

(LAND AREA 800 Sq.Mtrs) **Rs. 15,85,000.00**

PLANT & MACHINERY

1. Blender
2. Mat forming line for forming mate of Rice Husk
3. Hydraulic Hot-press complete with motors and instruments
4. Double Dimension Saw 3' * 4' Heavy duly with cutting length 2,500 mm cutting width1,300 mm cutting
5. Wide Belt Sander
6. Glue Spreader
7. Resin Kettle
8. Glue Mixer
9. Boiler
10. Diesel Generating set

FIXED CAPITAL

1. LAND & BUILDING	Rs. 15,85,000.00
2. PLANT & MACHINERY	Rs. 12,05,000.00
3. OTHER FIXED ASSETS	Rs. 1,20,000.00
TOTAL	Rs. 29,10,000.00

RAW MATERIALS

1. Rice Husk
2. Resin
3. Packaging Materials & Miscellaneous

TOTAL WORKING CAPITAL/MONTH

1. RAW MATERIAL	Rs. 1,97,500.00
2. SALARY & WAGES	Rs. 1,21,320.00
3. UTILITIES & OVERHEADS	Rs. 61,500.00
TOTAL	Rs. 3,80,320.00

TOTAL CAPITAL INVESTMENT

TOTAL FIXED CAPITAL	Rs. 29,10,000.00
TOTAL WORKING CAPITAL FOR 1 MONTH	Rs. 3,80,320.00
TOTAL	Rs. 32,90,320.00

TURN OVER/ANNUM

By Sale of 500 tonnes of Hard Board Rs. 70,00,000.00

PROFIT SALES RATIO = Profit / Sales x 100 = 23%

RATE OF RETURN = Operating profit / T.C.I x 100 = 49%

BREAK EVEN POINT (B.E.P) = 51%

57

Plant Economics of Hand Made Paper

CAPACITY = 1.00 TON/DAY

LAND & BUILDING (LAND AREA 450 SQ.MTR) Rs. 13,50,000.00

PLANT & MACHINERY

1. Paper shredding machine
2. Washing tank (M.S.Rubber lined)
3. Beating drum (M.S.epoxy lined)
4. Spreading system (S.S.type)
5. Hydraulic press.
6. Drying chamber, fitted with air heater & blower
7. Moulds.
8. Calendering machine.
9. Water storage tank (PVC tank)
10. Chemical preparation tank.
11. Boiler
12. Pipes, pumps, and miscellaneous fittings.
13. Laboratory testing equipment.
14. Miscellaneous equipments.

FIXED CAPITAL

1. LAND & BUILDING	Rs. 13,50,000.00
2. PLANT & MACHINERY	Rs. 11,65,000.00
3. OTHER FIXED ASSETS	Rs. 6,45,000.00
TOTAL	Rs. 31,60,000.00

RAW MATERIALS

1. Waste paper
2. Caustic soda
3. Sizing Chemical Resin
4. Bleaching Chemical H_2O_2
5. Others, packaging material.

TOTAL WORKING CAPITAL/MONTH

1. RAW MATERIAL	Rs. 1,98,025.00
2. SALARY & WAGES	Rs. 1,73,500.00
3. UTILITIES & OVERHEADS	Rs. 1,52,500.00
TOTAL	Rs. 5,24,025.00

TOTAL CAPITAL INVESTMENT

TOTAL FIXED CAPITAL	Rs. 31,60,000.00
TOTAL WORKING CAPITAL FOR 2 MONTHS	Rs. 10,48,050.00
TOTAL	Rs. 42,08,050.00

TURN OVER/ANNUM

Receipt by selling 300 ton of Hand Made Paper Rs. 1,14,00,000.00

PROFIT SALES RATIO = Profit / Sales x 100 = 37%

RATE OF RETURN = Operating profit / T.C.I x 100 = 101%

BREAK EVEN POINT (B.E.P) = 36%

58

Plant Economics of Paper Cones and Tubes

CAPACITY = 20000.00 NOS/DAY

LAND & BUILDING **= Rs. 16,60,000.00**

FIXED CAPITAL

1.	LAND & BUILDING	Rs. 16,60,000.00
2.	PLANT & MACHINERY	Rs. 15,00,000.00
3.	OTHER FIXED ASSETS	Rs. 3,25,000.00
	TOTAL	Rs. 34,85,000.00

RAW MATERIALS

1. Paper (Cone quality)
2. Glue
3. Other Misc.

TOTAL WORKING CAPITAL/MONTH

1.	RAW MATERIAL	Rs. 2,99,500.00
2.	SALARY & WAGES	Rs. 1,09,250.00
3.	UTILITIES & OVERHEADS	Rs. 64,800.00
	TOTAL	Rs. 4,73,550.00

TOTAL CAPITAL INVESTMENT

TOTAL FIXED CAPITAL	Rs. 34,85,000.00
TOTAL WORKING CAPITAL FOR 1 MONTH	Rs. 4,73,550.00
TOTAL	Rs. 39,58,550.00

TURN OVER/ANNUM

Receipt after sale of 6000000 paper cones of diff sizes at the average	Rs. 1,08,00,000.00

PROFIT SALES RATIO = Profit / Sales x 100 = 38%

RATE OF RETURN = Operating profit / T.C.I x 100 = 104%

BREAK EVEN POINT (B.E.P) = 31%

59

Plant Economics of Paper Hand Carrier Bags

CAPACITY = 200000.00 NOS/DAY

LAND AND BUILDING

(LAND REQUIRED 1500 SQ.MTR.) **Rs. 18,75,000.00**

PLANT & MACHINERY

1. One complete Plant & Machinery Set-up for automatic One-colour flexo-printing, Paper cutting, sides sealing, folding, eyeletting and tagging unit for paper carry hand bags of various with complete accessories
2. Automatic plant
3. Tools, jigs, fixtures
4. Gen set.

FIXED CAPITAL

1. LAND & BUILDING	Rs. 18,75,000.00
2. PLANT & MACHINERY	Rs. 16,20,000.00
3. OTHER FIXED ASSETS	Rs. 5,15,000.00
TOTAL	Rs. 40,10,000.00

RAW MATERIALS

1. Kraft paper
2. Printing Inks (Various desired Colours)
3. Packaging Materials
4. Tags, Eyelets

TOTAL WORKING CAPITAL/MONTH

1. RAW MATERIAL	Rs. 17,64,440.00
2. SALARY & WAGES	Rs. 1,11,321.00
3. UTILITIES & OVERHEADS	Rs. 1,61,500.00
TOTAL	Rs. 20,37,261.00

TOTAL CAPITAL INVESTMENT

TOTAL FIXED CAPITAL	Rs. 40,10,000.00
TOTAL WORKING CAPITAL FOR 3 MONTHS	Rs. 61,11,783.00
TOTAL	Rs. 1,01,21,783.00

TURN OVER/ANNUM

1. By sale of 1,80,00,000 Nos. Paper Carry Bags	Rs. 45,00,000.00
2. By sale of 1,80,00,000 Nos. paper Carry Bags	Rs. 72,00,000.00
3. By sale of 1,80,00,000 Nos. Paper Carry Bags	Rs. 1,35,00,000.00
4. By sale of 60,00,000 Nos. Paper Carry Bags	Rs. 60,00,000.00
TOTAL	Rs. 3,12,00,000.00

TURN OVER/ANNUM

PROFIT SALES RATIO = Profit / Sales x 100 = 15%

RATE OF RETURN = Operating profit / T.C.I x 100 = 45%

BREAK EVEN POINT (B.E.P) = 43%

60

Plant Economics of Paper Waste Recycling Plant

CAPACITY = 12.00 TON/DAY

LAND & BUILDING
(LAND REQUIRED = 5000 SQ.MTR. = Rs. 1,55,50,000.00
PLANT & MACHINERY

1. Shredder/Cutting machine for reducing large size waste paper sheets
2. Dust Separator/Cyclone Separator
3. Fiberization Unit for pulping of waste paper with accessories.
4. Belt Conveyor.
5. Pit Potcher
6. Pump
7. Conical Refiner
8. Hollander Beater
9. Johnson type Strainer
10. Decker Washer
11. Washing & Bleaching Protcher
12. Pump
13. Johnson Type Strainer
14. Hydropulper

15. Chlorine feed system complete with accessories.
16. Pump
17. Mixing Chest (fitted with agitator)
18. Blending chest with agitator and drive.
19. Conical Refiner
20. M.C. Chest 7 chemical mixing Chest
21. Pump
22. Head Box
23. Centricleaner
24. Cylinder mould
25. Couch Roll
26. Squeeze Press upper roll
27. Centricleaner
28. Rotary Vacuum Thickener
29. Centrifugal pump for back water with electric drive.
30. Chlorine handling system complete in all respects
31. Booster Pump
32. Squeeze Press Bottom Roll
33. Main Press upper roll
34. Main Press lower roll
35. M.S. Belt rolls & Guide rolls
36. Nash type Vacuum pump
37. Vacuum Box
38. Machine Frame
39. MS/MG Dryer & Cylinder
40. M.G. Touch Roll
41. Rewinding Reel
42. Paper Cutter Machine

43. Rolls for winding reel
44. C. I. Foundation Rails
45. Back Water Pumps
46. Reduction Gear
47. Pressure Screen
48. Boiler 1 Ton/hr. Steam generating
49. Hypochlorite stage tower agitator
50. High density pump.
51. Three stage centricleaner system.
52. Pollution Control Equipment
53. D. G. Set
54. Lab equipments
55. Instrumentation & Process Control Equipments
56. Miscellaneous, pipe fittings & others

FIXED CAPITAL

1.	LAND & BUILDING	Rs. 1,55,50,000.00
2.	PLANT & MACHINERY	Rs. 1,28,82,000.00
3.	OTHER FIXED ASSETS	Rs. 28,25,000.00
	TOTAL	Rs. 3,12,57,000.00

RAW MATERIALS

1. Waste Paper
2. NaOH
3. Alum
4. Rosin
5. Starch
6. Liquid
7. Packaging materials

TOTAL WORKING CAPITAL/MONTH

1.	RAW MATERIAL	Rs. 34,24,250.00
2.	SALARY & WAGES	Rs. 5,24,400.00
3.	UTILITIES & OVERHEADS	Rs. 9,55,000.00
	TOTAL	Rs. 49,03,650.00

TOTAL CAPITAL INVESTMENT

TOTAL FIXED CAPITAL	Rs. 3,12,57,000.00
TOTAL WORKING CAPITAL FOR 1 MONTH	Rs. 49,03,650.00
TOTAL	Rs. 3,61,60,650.00

TURN OVER/ANNUM

By sale of 3600 MT of Paper = Rs. 9,36,00,000.00

PROFIT SALES RATIO = Profit / Sales x 100 = 28%

RATE OF RETURN = Operating profit / T.C.I x 100 = 72%

BREAK EVEN POINT (B.E.P) = 38%

LIST OF THE READY AVAILABLE DETAILED PROJECT REPORTS

AUTOMOBILES, MECHANICAL & METALLURGICAL

1. AGRICULTRAL EQUIPMENTS
2. AGRICULTRAL EQUIPMENTS INCLUDING THRESHERS
3. AIR BRAKE HELICAL COIL
4. AIR COOLER
5. AIR FILTERS(FOR SCOOTER CAR & EXCAVATORS ETC.)
6. ALUMINIUM & ALUMINIUM ALLOYS FROM ALUMINIUM SCRAP TO MAKE UTENSILS (INDUCTION FURNACE MELTED)
7. ALUMINIUM ALLOY WHEELS
8. ALUMINIUM ALLOYS FROM ALUMINIUM SCRAP TO MAKE UTENSILS (INDUCTION FURNACE)
9. ALUMINIUM HOT & COLD ROLLING MILL
10. ALUMINIUM BOTTLE MANUFACTURING (COLD EXTRUSION OF ALUMINIUM)
11. ALUMINIUM/COPPER CABLE LUGS
12. ALUMINIUM CANS FOR BEER PACKAGING
13. ALUMINIUM CANS FOR CAPACITORS
14. ALUMINIUM CAPS FOR INJECTION VIALS
15. ALUMINIUM EXTRUSION
16. ALUMINIUM FURNITURE & HARDWARE
17. ALUMINIUM SHEET ROLLING MILL
18. ALUMINIUM UTENSILS
19. ALUMINIUM UTENSILS & SCHOOL BOXES
20. ALUMINIUM WIRE DRAWING AND SUPER ENAMELLING FOR WINDING
21. ANODISED ALUMINIUM UTENSILS
22. ANODIZING OF ALUMINIUM
23. ANTIMONY OXIDE FROM LEAD SCRAP
24. ARC WELDING FILTER GLASS
25. ALUMINIUM FOIL CUTTING & ROLL MAKING
26. AUTO FLAPS FOR TRUCKS & BUSES
27. AUTOMOBILE WORKSHOP (GARAGE & SERVICE CENTRE)
28. AUTO GEARS
29. AUTO HORNS
30. AUTO LEAF SPRING
31. AUTO TUBES
32. AUTO PISTON RING
33. AUTO PISTON
34. BAKERY AND BISCUITS EQUIPMENTS FABRICATION
35. BALL POINT PEN REFILLS
36. BALL ROLLER & TAPER BEARING
37. BAND SAW BLADES
38. BARBED WIRE
39. BICYCLE SPOKES
40. BRAKE LINING ASBESTOES/ RESIN BASED & ASBESTOES FREE
41. BRASS ARTWARE/HOLLOW WARE CASTING (WITH THE HELP OF PHENOLIC RESIN)
42. BRASS CASTING
43. BRASS PIPES FROM BRASS SHEET WITH LONGITUDINALLY WELDING
44. BRASS WARE BY CASTING METHOD (BRASS ARTICLES VIZ. BRASS POOJA LAMPS AND OTHER CASTED)
45. BRIGHT BARS
46. BUFFING AND POLISHING INDUSTRY (JOB WORK)
47. BUTT HINGE (BRASS SHEET)
48. CARBON BRUSH HOLDER & SLIP RING
49. CO_2 WELDING WIRE ELECTRODES (COPPER/ COPPER ALLOY COATED M.S.WIRE)
50. CARBON FILM RESISTORS
51. CARBURETTORS
52. CAST STEEL PANES FOR MELTING FURNACE
53. CHEMICAL ETCHING OF STAINLESS STEEL
54. CHEMICAL RESISTANT IRON & STEEL
55. COLD FORM SECTION MILL
56. COLD ROLLED FORMING OF SECTION AND OTHER SECTIONS
57. COLD ROLLING OF MS STRIP
58. COLD TWISTED DE-FORMED RIBBED STEEL
59. COMPRESSOR (HERMETIC) FOR AIR CONDITIONERS
60. COMPRESSED NATURAL GAS (CNG KIT) FOR AUTOVEHICLE
61. CONTINUOUSLY CAST STEEL WIRE RODS (5 mm)
62. CONTINUOUS CASTING COPPER WIRE RODS
63. CONVEYOR BELTINGS
64. CONVEYOR BELT, TRANSM -ISSION BELT & V BELTS
65. COOKING RANGES
66. COPPER/BRASS SHEETS, CIRCLE & UTENSILS
67. COPPER FOIL
68. COPPER INGOTS, RODS MAKING & WIRE DRAWING
69. COPPER PRODUCTS FROM COPPER SCRAP
70. COPPER SMELTING PLANT
71. COPPER WIRE RODS FROM COPPER SCRAP
72. CORRUGATED BOX MAKING MACHINERY AND OTHER THEIR PARTS
73. CYLINDER LINER FOR AUTOMOBILES
74. DOOR LOCKS/PAD LOCKS
75. DRILL BITS & TOOL BITS
76. DRUM CLOSURES
77. ERW STEEL CONDUIT PIPE
78. EARTH MOVING EQPT.
79. ENGINE VALVES FOR AUTOMOBILES
80. FABRICATION OF HEAT EXCHANGER
81. FABRICATION OF STORAGE TANKS AND M.S. DRUM
82. FERROUS ALLOY NI-HARDY I.V CASTING
83. FERROUS Mn ALLOY CASTING BY ALUMINA THERMIC PROCESS
84. FERRO ALLOYS
85. FERRO SILICON & FERRO MANGANESE FROM DOLOMITE (SMS GRADE)
86. FIRE EXTINGUISHERS
87. FLIP-TONE CANS
88. FORGED CONECTING ROD
89. FORGING UNIT
90. FOUNTAIN PEN NIBS
91. FOUNDRY SAND
92. FUEL INJECTION SYSTEM
93. GALVANIZED M.S.STRIPS
94. GALVANIZING PLANT
95. GALVANIZED IRON WIRE
96. GAS WELDING TORCHES AND NOZZLES
97. GASKET SHEET
98. GATE GRILLS & WINDOW FRAMES
99. GENERATING SET (DIESEL)
100. HARD ANODISED ALUMINIUM
101. HOSPITAL WARES
102. HOSPITAL FURNITURES
103. HOT DIP GALVANIZING
104. HOT FORGED FASTENERS
105. HOT MIX PLANT
106. INJECTION MOULDED PLASTIC COMPOUNDS WITH TOOL ROOM
107. INJECTION MOULDED PLASTIC COMPONENTS AND METAL PIPE SPINNING UNIT
108. INVESTMENT CASTING
109. IRON/STEEL WIRE GAUGE
110. IRON TAWA
111. KNIVES (S.S.KNIVES)
112. KITCHEN SINK (S.S.)
113. L.P.G REGULATORS
114. MACHINE SCREWS & SELF TAPPING SCREWS
115. MARUTI WORKSHOP CUM SERVICE STATION
116. MAGNESIUM INGOTS & BULLETS CASTING

"Detailed Project Report" Payable in advance through Draft/Cash/M.O. in favour of *"ENGINEERS INDIA RESEARCH INSTITUTE"*. 4449, Nai Sarak (D), Main Road Delhi - 110 006 (INDIA) ● Ph : 23918117, 2391 6431, 2384 0361 ● Mob : 098114 37895 ●Fax : 91-11- 2391 6431 ●E-Mail : eirisidi@bol.net.in ● WebSite : www.eiriindia.org

117. MANUFACTURE OF TIN CONTAINERS
118. MANUFACTURE OF STORAGE TANKS, PRESSURE VESSELS, HEAT EXCHANGERS
119. MARK II HAND PUMPS
120. MARUTI WORKSHOP CUM - SERVICE STATION
121. MECHANICAL JACKS
122. METAL CUTTING DIE DESIGN
123. METAL CUTTING OF AND GRINDING WHEELS (ABBRASIVE CUTTING WHEELS)
124. METAL HOOKS & CLIPS
125. METAL SEPARATION (COPPER, TIN, LEAD) FROM SPENT WASH ACID
126. METALLIC RING JOINTS
127. METALLIC GASKET (SPIRAL WOUND)
128. MICROVEE & ABSOLUTE FILTER
129. MICROWAVE OVEN
130. MILD STEEL INGOTS
131. MINI STEEL PLANT
132. MODERN VEHICLE WORKSHOP
133. MOPED
134. M.S.HINGES
135. M.S.INGOT AND HR. STEEL STRUCTURALS
136. M.S.INGOT BY INDUCTION FURNACES
137. M.S.PIPES
138. M.S. WELDING ELECTRODE
139. MUFFLERS & SILENCERS FOR THREE WHEELERS
140. NAIL CUTTER WITH FILER & MANICURE
141. NICHROME WIRE
142. NICKEL LINED SCREENS
143. NON-FERROUS ALLOY ROLLING
144. NON-FERROUS FORGING
145. NON-FERROUS FOUNDRY
146. NON PRESSURE
147. INCANDESCENT LAMP
148. NUMBER COMBINATION LOCKS FOR LUGGAGES
149. NUTS & BOLTS
150. PAPER COATED ALUMINIUM AND COPPER WIRE
151. PETROMAX CONTAINER
152. PHOTO ETCHING OF STAINLESS STEEL PLATES
153. PIPE GALVANIZING PLANT
154. PISTON RING-AUTOMOBILE
155. PLANT PROTECTION EQUIPMENTS
156. PLATINUM LABORATORY APPARATUS
157. PRESSURE COOKER & ALUMINIUM UTENSILS
158. PRESSURE COOKER (ALUMINIUM)
159. PRESSURE DIE CASTING
160. PRINTED ALUMINIUM COLLAPSIBLE TUBES
161. PRINTED TIN CONTAINERS
162. PRINTING PRESS (CYLINDER MACHINE)
163. PUMPS FOR CHEMICAL INDUSTRY (SPECIAL)
164. RAILWAY SLEEPERS (M.S.)
165. RAZOR TWIN BLADE
166. R.C.C SPUN PIPES
167. RECONDITIONING OF M.S. DRUMS/BARRELS
168. RE-ROLLING COPPER AND BRASS SHEET AND RODS
169. RE-ROLLING MILLS
170. RESIN COATED SAND
171. RESIN CORED SOFT SOLDER WIRES
172. ROLLING MILL (BY INDUCTION FURNACE) & MANUFACTURE OF BARS, ANGLES, SQUARES, TUBES AND OTHERS
173. ROLLER BEARING & FORGING
174. ROLLING OF STAINLESS STEEL PATTA
175. RUBBER INSULATED PLIERS (HAND TOOLS)
176. RUBBING COMPOUND FOR AUTOMOBILES
177. SCIENTIFIC LABORATORY EQUIPMENTS
178. SCOOTER ASSEMBLING
179. SECONDARY LEAD EXTRAC-TION BY SCRAP BATTERY PLATES, PIPES & SHEET
180. SEAMLESS M.S. TUBES & PIPES
181. SELF TAPPING STEEL SCREW
182. SEWING NEEDLES
183. S.G. IRON & ALLOY STEEL
184. SHEET METAL PRODUCTS, (FERROUS/NON-FERROUS)
185. SHIP/MARINE CONTAINER
186. SHOCK ABSORBERS
187. SHOE EYELETS
188. SHOT AND GRITS BY AUTOMIZATION PROCESS
189. SHOVELS
190. SILICO MANGANESE ALLOYS
191. SILENCERS (MUFFLERS) EXHAUST & TAIL PIPE FOR ALL TYPES OF VEHICLES
192. SINTERED BEARING
193. SINTERED BUSHES
194. SINTERED METAL PRODUCTS
195. SOFT AND HARD FERRITES
196. SPANNERS
197. SPARK PLUGS
198. STEEL PLANT (ELECTRIC ARC FURNACE BASED- EAF)
199. SPHERIODAL GRAPHITE CAST IRON
200. SPRAY DRYER
201. STAINLESS STEEL HINGES
202. STAINLESS STEEL SHEET ROLLING TO PRODUCE STAINLESS STEEL UTENSILS
203. STAINLESS STEEL UTENSILS
204. STAPLE PINS, PAPER PIN, GEM CLIPS ETC.
205. STEEL CASTINGS
206. STEEL CHAIN
207. STEEL FOUNDRY
208. STEEL FURNITURES AND ELECTRICAL APPLIANCES
209. STEEL PLANT (MINI)
210. STEEL RODS AND COILS FROM SCRAPS
211. STEEL ROLLING MILL
212. STEEL STRIPS (COLD ROLLED) SILICON WITH GRAIN RIENTED FOR ELECTRIC USE
213. STEEL TRANSMISSION LINE TOWERS & ROLLING MILL TO PRODUCE STEEL SECTION
214. STEEL FURNITURES AND ELECTRICAL APPLIANCES
215. STEEL WIRE DRAWING AND GALVANIZING
216. STEEL WOOL
217. SUBMERGED ARC WELDED PIPES
218. SUBMERSIBLE PUMP MANUFACTURING
219. SUPER ENAMELLED COPPER WIRE
220. THREE WHEELERS
221. TIE-ROD ENDS
222. TIN CONTAINERS
223. TOOLROOM AND SHEET METAL PRODUCTS
224. TRACTOR TRAILERS
225. TRANSMISSION POWER FITTING
226. TUBULAR POLES
227. SUPER ENAMELLED COPPER WIRES
228. TUBULAR POLES FOR ELECTRICAL TRANSMISSION (BY FABRICATION PROCESS)
229. TUBULAR POLES OF M.S. & HIGH TENSILE STEEL
230. VACUUM CLEANERS
231. VACUUM FLASK (STAINLESS STEEL)
232. VALVES FOR REFRIGERA TION AND AIR-CONDITION
233. VEHICLE WELDING & PAINTING
234. VENETION BLIND
235. WASHING MACHINES (AUTOMATIC & COMPUTERISED)
236. WATER CONTROLLER (AUTOMATIC)
237. WATCH STRAPS/CHAINS/ BRACELETS/BELT BRASS & STAINLESS STEEL
238. WATER COOLERS
239. WELDED WIRE MESH
240. WELDING ELECTRODES
241. WICK STOVES
242. WIND MILL WINDOW FRAME (FERROUS & NON-FERROUS)
243. WRIST WATCH

359. DI ETHYL OXALATE
360. DI METHYL ORTHOPHTHALATE
361. DI-METHYL PHTHALATE
362. DICLOFENAC GEL
363. DIOCTYL PHTHALATE (DOP)
364. DI PHENYL GLYCERINE
365. DI PHENYL OXIDE
366. DINITRO-CHLORO BENZENE
367. DISTILLED WATER
368. DODECYL BENZENE SULPHONATE
369. DUSTLESS CHALK
370. EDTA & ITS SALTS
371. ELECTROLESS NICKEL PLATING ON PLASTICS
372. ENDOSULFAN
373. EPOXY RESIN BASED COMPOUND
374. ETHYL ACETATE
375. EHTYL ETHER
376. ETHYL ALCOHOL (POTABLE LIQUOR)
377. ETHYL HEXANOL
378. EXTRACTION OF ESSENTIAL OILS BY SUGAR CRITICAL FLUID (CARBON DIOXIDE) METHOD FROM FLOWERS, HERBAL & SPICES
379. FERRIC ALUM
380. FERRO CHROME LIGNO SULPHONATE
381. FERRO MANGANESE
382. FERRO SILICONE
383. FERRO VANADIUM FROM VANADIUM SLUDGE
384. FERROUS SILICATE
385. FERROUS SULPHATE
386. FERTILIZER FROM ANIMAL BLOOD & LEATHER WASTE
387. FLUORESCENT TUBE LIGHT POWDER
388. FOAMED PVC COMPOUNDING & ITS PRODUCTS
389. FORMALDEHYDE
390. FRACTIONAL DISTILLATION OF D.M.O (DEMENTHOLIZED OIL)
391. FRACTIONAL DISTILLATION OF ESSENTIAL OIL & MEDICINAL PLANT EXTRACT
392. FRICTION DUST (LIQUID & POWDER) FROM CNSL
393. FRUIT FLAVOURS
394. FURFURAL FROM RICE HUSK
395. GARLIC ACID
396. GASKET SHELLAC COMPOUND
397. GEAR OIL
398. GIBBERELLIC ACID
399. GLASS PUTTY
400. GLYCERINE
401. GOSSYPOL (POLY PHENOL) FROM COTTON SEED OIL
402. GUAR GUM POWDER
403. HAIR FIXER (HAIR GEL TYPE)
404. H - ACID
405. HENNA PASTE MAKING
406. HEPTAL DEHYDE
407. HIGH CARBON FERRO CHROME
408. HYDRATED CALCIUM SILICATE BRICK
409. HYDRATED LIME FROM SEA SHELL
410. HYDROCHLORIC ACID
411. HYDRO FLUORIC ACID
412. HYDROGEN PEROXIDE (BY AUTO-OXIDATION PROCESS)
413. ICE PACKS (SOLUTIONS TYPE, WHITE GEL TYPE, VIOLET SEMI SOLID POLYMER TYPE)
414. IMPROVING DROP POINT PARAFFIN WAX FROM 45-50ºC TO 75-80ºC
415. INDUSTRIAL ALCOHOL
416. INTEGERATED COMPLEX OF EASTER & ALLIED PRODUCTS (D.O.P, D.B.P, ETHYL ACETATE WIRE ENAMEL & CABLE JELLY)
417. IMFL (WHISKY) & COUNTRY LIQUOR
418. IRON OXIDE FOR MAKING FERITTE
419. IRON SULPHIDE
420. JUTE BATCHING OIL
421. KESH KALA TEL (HAIR DYE LOTION) (VASMOL 33, BLACK NITE TYPE)
422. L-LYSINE MONOHYDROCHLORIDE
423. LACTIC ACID FROM WHITE SUGAR BY FERMENTATION PROCESS
424. LDPE GRANULES FROM VIRGIN (LDPE RESIN)
425. LEAD EXTRACTION FROM BATTERY SCRAP
426. LEAD OXIDE (A) LEAD MONOXIDE (B) LEAD TETRA OXIDE (C) GREYLEAD OXIDE
427. LIQUID GLUCOSE & ITS BY PRODUCTS
428. LIQUID OXYGEN BOTTLING PLANT
429. LIQUID SHOE POLISH
430. LIQUID FLOOR POLISH
431. LUBE OIL VISCOSITY IMPROVED FOR P.P.G/P.E.G
432. LUBRICANTS ASHLESS 100% COMBUSTION
433. MAGNESIUM CARBONATE AND MAGNESIUM BICARMONATE
434. MAGNESIUM HYDROXIDE POWDER
435. MAGNESIUM SILICATE
436. MAGNESIUM SULPHATE
437. MALACHITE GREEN
438. MALEIC ANHYDRIDE
439. MANGANESE SULPHATE
440. MANUFACTURING OF CARBON MONO-OXIDE WATER GAS
441. MENTHOL BOLD CRYSTALS FROM FLAKES
442. MENTHOL CRYSTAL & MENTHA OIL
443. MERCURIC OXIDE
444. METAL PRE-TREATMENT CHEMICALS
445. METHANE GAS BY SODIUM ACETATE & SODA LIME
446. METHYL ACETYL RICINOLATE
447. METOL
448. METOL FROM HYDROQUINONE & METHYLAMINE
449. MICANITE
450. MICRO NUTRIENT MIXTURE
451. MINERAL WATER
452. MINERAL WATER AND PET BOTTILNG PLANT
453. MINERAL WATER IN BOTTLES, GLASS AND POUCHES
454. MINI CEMENT PLANT (BY ROTARY KILN PROCESS)
455. MIXED FERTILIZER
456. MOSQUITO & FLIES REPELLENT AGARBATTI (INCENSE STICKS)
457. MONO CHLORO ACETIC ACID
458. MONOCROTOPHOS (TECHNICAL)
459. MOSQUITO COIL
460. MOSQUITO COIL & MAT
461. MOSQUITO MAT
462. MOTHER TINCTURE & BIO CHEMIC MEDICINES
463. NAPHTHALENE & PHENYL (INTEGRATED UNIT)
464. NATURAL MINERAL WATER BY REVERSE OSMOSIS PROCESS
465. NICKEL PLATING BRIGHTNER (PRIMARY OR CARRIER BRIGHTNER & SECONDARY BRIGHTNER)
466. NICKEL SULPHATE
467. NICOTINE FROM TOBACCO WASTE
468. NICOTINE SULPHATE FROM TOBACCO WASTE
469. NITRO BENZENE
470. NITRO CELLULOSE SANDING SEALER/LACQUER
471. NITRO MUSK
472. NITROGEN & OXYGEN GAS PLANT
473. NON-IONIC SURFACTANT (WETTING AGENT)
474. NO-CARB PASTE
475. OCTANOL
476. ORTHO NITRO PHENOL
477. OXALIC ACID FROM MOLASSES
478. OXALIC ACID FROMRICE HUSK
479. OXALIC ACID FROM TREE BARK
470. OXALIC ACID FROM WASTE VEGETABLES
471. OXYGEN GAS PLANT
472. OXYGEN GAS PLANT (AIR SEPERATION METHOD)
473. PARA-AMINO BENZOIC ACID
474. PARA-AMINO PHENOL
475. PARA TOLUENE SULPHONIC ACID
476. PECTIN FROM RAW PAPAYA
477. PERFUME (LEMON & OTHERS)

CRUDE NAPHTHA
570. TRIMETHYL AMMONIUM CHLORIDE
571. TRIPHENYL PHOSPHITE (T.P.P)
572. ULTRAMARINE BLUE (LIQUID)
573. UREA FORMALDEHYDE & MELAMINE FORMALDEHYDE POWDER
574. UNDECYLINIC ACID
575. VINYL ACETATE MONOMER
576. VITAMIN C
577. VITAMIN E
578. WASTE WATER TREATMENT PLANT FOR INDUSTRIAL SECTOR IN INDIA (ONLY MARKER SURVEY)
579. WIRE DRAWING LUBRICANT
580. WIRE ENAMEL
581. XANTHATES
582. YELLOW DEXTRIN
583. ZINC CHLORIDE
584. ZINC OXIDE
585. ZINC PHOSPHATING BY COLD PROCESS
586. ZINC SILICATE
587. ZINC STEARATE
588. ZINC SULPHATE
589. ZINC SULPHATE MONOHYDRATE
590. ACID BLACK
591. AURAMINE'O'
592. AZO DYES STUFF
593. DYE & DYE INTERMEDIATE
594. DYE INTERMEDIATES
595. MALACHITE GREEN
596. METHYLENE BLUE
597. PHTHALOCYANINE BLUE
598. PHTHALOCYANINE BLUE & GREEN
599. REACTIVE DYES
600. SULPHUR BLACK DYE
601. VAT DYES
602. WATER CHILLING PLANT
603. WADDING OIL (100%) FOR WADDING OF COTTON HOSIERY CLOTH IN THE DYEING PROCESS
604. WHITE OIL
605. WAX FLOOR POLISH

ELECTRICAL, ELECTONICS, COMPUTERS AND INFOTECH/IT PROJECTS

606. AIR CONDITIONING
607. ALUMINIUM ALLOY CONDUCTOR
608. ALUMINIUM CABLE
609. ALUMINIUM ELECTROYTIC CAPACITORS
610. AUDIO CASSETTE ASSEMBLING & RECORDING
611. AUDIO CASSETTES DUPLICATING RECORDING
612. AUDIO CASSETTES & AUDIO STUDIO
613. AUDIO CASSETTES PLANE & RECORDED
614. AUDIO MAGNETIC HEADS
615. AUDIO MAGNETIC TAPE
616. AUDIO/VIDEO CASSETTES
617. AUTO BULB/LAMPS
618. AUTOMATIC VOLTAGE STABILIZER
619. BATTERY PLATES
620. BACK OFFICE (Rs. 5000/-)
621. B/W TV & COMPUTER MONITOR PICTURE TUBE
622. BREAD BOARDS
623. CALL CENTRE
624. CAMERA (35 MM)
625. CAPACITORS
626. CARBON ELECTRODE USED FOR BATTERY CELL
627. CARBON POTETIOMETERS
628. CEILING FAN
629. CERAMIC INSULATOR
630. CHILDREN INFOTECH TRAINING INSTITUTE (Rs. 5000/-)
631. CHOKE AND PATTI
632. CHOKE AND STARTER
633. CHOKE USED FOR FLUORESCENT LAMPS
634. COLOUR TELEVISION
635. COLOUR AND BLACK & WHITE TELEVISION
636. COMPACT DISC
637. COMPACT DISC PLAYER (AUDIO/VIDEO)
638. COMPUTER EDUCATION INSTITUTE
639. COMPUTER ASSEMBLY
640. COMPUTER HARDWARE
641. COMPUTER KEYBOARD
642. COMPUTER PERIPHERALS
643. COMPUTER PRINTERS
644. COMPUTER RIBBON
645. COMPUTER RIBBON REINKING OR REFILLING
646. COMPUTER STATIONERY
647. COMPUTER STATIONERY &

IMPORTED HARDWARE PARTS
648. COMPUTER TERMINALS
649. COMPUTERISED WASHING MACHINE (AUTOMATIC)
650. COMPUTER SOFTWARE
651. CONDENSER FOR MOTOR USING MPP FILM
652. CONTENT DEVELOPMENT CENTRE (EOU) (Rs. 5000/-)
653. CONTROL PANEL BOARD
654. COOLING COIL FOR AIR CONDITIONERS
655. COPPER STRIP COIL FROM SCRAP
656. CORDLESS TELEPHONES
657. CYBER CAFE
658. CYBERKIOSK (Rs. 5000/-)
659. DATA PROCESSING CENTRE (Rs. 5000/-)
660. D.C. MICRO MOTORS
661. D.G.SETS
662. DISH ANTENNA AND CABLE T.V. NETWORK EQUIPMENT
663. DISTRIBUTION TRANSFORMERS & REPAIRS
664. DOMESTIC ELECTRICAL APPLIANCES- ROOM COOLER, WASHING MACHINE, WATER HEATER, ELECTRIC ROOM HEATER
665. E-SCHOOL
666. E-COMMERCE/BUSINESS
667. ELECTRIC ENERGY METER
668. ELECTRIC FANS
669. ELECTRIC HORN FOR AUTOMOBILE
670. ELECTRIC LAMP/GLS (INCANDESCENT LAMP)
671. ELECTRIC MIXER
672. ELECTRIC MOTORS UP TO 10 HP. REWINDING OF ALL TYPES OF MOTORS WATER PUMPS
673. ELECTRIC MOTOR WINDING (FOR FAN, MIXIES, ETC.)
674. ELECTRIC STEAM IRON
675. ELECTRICAL APPLIANCES
676. ELECTRICAL FIXTURES
677. ELECTRICAL STAMPING
678. ELECTROLYTIC CAPACITORS
679. ELECTROMAGNETIC RELAY
680. ELECTRONIC BALAST/CHOK
681. ELECTRICAL CHOKE
682. ELECTRONIC DIGITAL WATCHES
683. ELECTRONIC DIGITAL WEIGHING MACHINE
684. ELECTRONIC FIRE ALARM
685. ELECTRONIC GAS STOVE LIGHTERS
686. ELECTRONIC PRESSURE INDICATORS, ELECTRICALS, ELECTRONIC LIQUID LEVEL INDICATORS, ELECTRONIC TEMPERATURE INDICATOR, DIGITAL TACHOMETER
687. ELECTRONIC TELEPHONE INSTRUMENTS
688. ELECTRONIC TOYS
689. ELECTRONIC WATCHES & CLOCKS
690. FAX MACHINES
691. F.H.P MOTORS
692. FLOPPY DISKETTES
693. FLUORESCENT LAMP STARTER
694. FLUORESCENT TUBULAR

813. BREAD (AUTOMATIC PLANT)
814. BLACK PEPPER (SPICES)
815. BREAD AND BISCUITS
816. BREEDING FARM
817. BROILER CHICKEN
819. BUTTON MUSHROOM CULTIVATION & PROCESSING
820. CANNING OF RASAGULLAS IN METAL CANS
821. CAFFEIN FROM TEA WASTE
822. CANNING OF FRUITS & VEGETABLES
823. CASEIN AND BY-PRODUCTS
824. CASHEW FRUIT JUICE FROM CASHEW FRUIT APPLE
825. CASHEWNUT KERNEL EXTRACTION FROM CASHEWNUT FRUIT
826. CASHEWNUT SHELL LIQUID & KERNEL PROCESSING
827. CASHEW FENI
828. CATECHEU (BY CHEMICAL PROCESS)
829. CATTLE FEED FROM TAPIOCA
830. CHEWING & BUBBLE GUM
831. CHICKEN/SHEEP MEAT PROCESSING
832. CHOCOLATE (MILK)
833. CIGARETTE AND BEEDIES
834. COCOA BUTTER FROM COCOA MASS
835. COCONUT PRODUCTS & BY PRODUCTS PROCESS COMPLEX
836. COLD/SOFT DRINKS
837. COLLECTION OF MILK AND MILK MAKING POWDER
838. COLLECTION OF MILK AND PACKING IN POLYTHENE POUCH (1/2 KG. 1 KG. & 2 KG.)
839. CONDENSED MILK (SWEETNED)
840. CONFECTIONERY INDUSTRY (TOFFEE & CANDY, SEMI-AUTOMATIC PLANT)
841. COUNTRY LIQUOR FROM MOLASSES
842. CIGARETTE
843. DAIRY FARM AND DAIRY (MILK) PRODUCTS (PASTEURISED MILK, BUTTER, GHEE, PANEER)
844. DAIRY FARM TO PRODUCE MILK & PACKING IN POUCHES (50%) & CAN(50%)
845. DAIRY FOR MILK PROCESSING
846. DAIRY FARM (BUFALO)
847. DAL (PULSE) MILL UNIT
848. DEHYDRATION OF CARROT & GARLIC
849. DEHYDRATION & CANNING OF FRUITS & VEGETABLES
850. DEHYDRATION OF FIGS
851. DEHYDRATION OF FRUITS AND VEGETABLES
852. DEHYDRATED ONIONS AND ONION POWDER
853. DRY ICE BY BREAKING OF AIR
854. DRYING OF RED CHILLIES, HALDI, DHANIA, AND GREEN PEAS
855. EGG POWDER (40,000 EGGS PROCESSING PER DAY)
856. EXPORT OF PROCESSED FOODS AND MARINE PRODUCTS
857. FISH CANNING & POUCHING
859. FISH FARMING (PRAWN & OTHER MARINE PRODUCTS)
860. FISH MEAL
861. FLOUR MILL AND MUSTARD OIL
862. FOOD COLOUR & ORASTED GROUNDNUT GRAM PEAS, ETC IN POUCHES
863. FROG LEGS PROCESSING
864. FROZEN MEATS PROCESSING
865. FOOD FLAVOURS (WHISKY) VODKA, GRAPE, BUTTER SCOTCH)
866. FOOD PRODUCTS COMPLEX (DEHYDRATED ONIONS, GARLIC POWDER & FLAKES, CATTLE FEED, TOMATO POWDER, TOMATO PRODUCTS, CANNED FRUITS & VEGETABLES, TOMATO PURE, GROUN NUT OIL, REFIND OIL, DEHYDRATED GRAPES, BANANA POWDER & WAFFERS)
867. FRUIT JUICE, JAM, JELLIES & ALLIED PRODUCTS
868. FRUIT JUICE, PICKLES PROCESSING AND CANNING
869. FRUIT JUICE MAKING & PACKING IN PLASTIC CONTAINER/POUCHES
870. FRUIT PROCESSING (JAM & JELLIES)
871. FRUIT PULP & JUICE CONCENTRATES
872. FRUIT & VEGETABLE DRYING (FREEZE DRYING METHOD)
873. GOAT & SHEEP FARMING
874. GRAM DALL/PULSE MILL
875. GRAPE DEHYDRATION
876. HARD BOILED CANDY (TOFFEE & CANDY)
877. HERBAL CIGARETTES
878. HONEY PROCESSING & PACKAGING
879. ICE CREAM OF DIFFERENT FLAVOURS
880. ICE CREAM STABILIZER
881. ICE MAKING PLANT
882. INDIAN MADE FOREIGN LIQUOR (I.M.F.L)
883. INSTANT FOOD (IDLI MIX, DOSA MIX, GULAB JAMUN MIX)
884. INSTANT FOOD (INSTANT FOOD & FAST FOOD PARLOUR)
885. INSTANT NOODLES
886. INSTANT TEA
887. INSTANT TEA FROM BLACK TEA
888. INTEGERATED STARCH BAKING POWDER/YEAST INDUSTRY
889. IODIZED SALT
890. IODIZED SALT (ORDINARY MOISTURE-LESS/FREE FLOWING IN PLASTIC BAGS AND CONTAINERS)
891. JAM, JELLIES, FRUIT JUICE & ALLIED PRODUCTS
892. KATHA AND CUTCH
893. KHANDSARI SUGAR
894. KHANDSARI SUGAR & IMFL
895. LACTIC ACID FROM WHITE SUGAR BY FERMENTATION PROCESS
896. LACTOSE & BY PRODUCTS PROCESSING FROM MILK
897. LIQUID GLUCOSE AND ITS BYE PRODUCTS
898. MACRONI AND VERMICILLI
899. MALT EXTRACTION FROM BARLEY
900. MANGO PROCESSING (MANGO PULP, JUICE & SLICES)
901. MAYUR BRAND TYPE CHEWING TOBACCO
902. MINERAL WATER
903. MILK PRESERVATION & MARKETING TO WHOLE SELLERS (INPOUCH PACKING BY UHT TECHNOLOGY)
904. MILK PROCESSING AND PACKAGING OF MILK PRODUCTS
905. MILK PRODUCTS (CASEIN, LACTOSE, GHEE & WHEY POWDER)
906. MILK TOFFEE
907. MINI FLOUR MILL
908. MINI SUGAR PLANT
909. MISRI (PEARL SUGAR CANDIES)
910. MODERN RICE MILL
911. MURABBA
912. MUSTARD OIL EXTRACTION & REFINING
913. MUTTON TALLOW
914. NAMKEEN INDUSTRY (BHUJIA, CHANA CHUR ETC.)
915. NAMKEEN & SWEETS
916. NON-BASMATI RICE FROM PADDY
917. OLEORESIN, ESSENTIAL OIL, DYES & POWDER OF SPICES
918. OLEORESIN EXTRACTION FROM DIPTERO-CARPUT TURMINATUS AND PINUS KHASYANA
919. OLEORESIN EXTRACTION FROM CHILLI
920. PAN MASALA AND POUCH

Apart from the above mentioned reports EIRI is also having other most lucrative projects (as many as 30,000). You just name it and we have that report.

MAKING
921. PAN MASALA, TOBACCO, ZARDA & KIMAM
922. PANEER FROM MILK
923. PAPPAD PLANT
924. PAPAIN FROM PAPAYA (PAPAYA LATEX)
925. PECTIN FROM MANGO PEEL PECTIN FROM APPLE POMACE
926. PHYTO TEA (HERBAL TEA)
927. PICKLES AND SAUCES
928. PICKLES MURABBA ETC. (VEG. & NON. VEG. PICKLES)
929. PIGGERY MEAT PROCESS
930. PINE-APPLE JUICE PREPARATION & PACKAGING
931. POTATO CHIPS/WAFFERS
932. POTATO POWDER
933. POUCH FILLING & PACKAGING OF EDIBLE OIL & GHEE
934. POULTRY FEED
935. PROCESSED FOODS & SPICES (EOU)
936. PROCESSED READYMADE FOOD
937. PROCESSING OF FRUITS & VEGETABLES
938. RABBIT FARMING
939. RASGULLAS MAKING & CANNING IN METAL CANS
940. READY TO EAT PROCESSED COOKED FOOD
941. READY TO EAT SNACK FOOD (CRAX, ROLL & BALL TYPE)
942. RICE & CORN FLAKES
943. ROASTED/SALTED/ MASALA, CASHEW NUTS, ALMONDS & PEANUTS
944. ROLLER FLOUR MILL
945. SALT LICKS FOR CATTLE
946. SAUSAGES FOOD CASING
947. SOFT DRINKS
948. SOFT DRINKS ESSENCES
949. SOFT DRINKS (NON CARBONATED) MANGO, LICCHI, PINEAPPLE FLAVOURS FROOTI TYPE IN TETRAPACK)
950. SOFTY ICE CREAM CONES (FULLY AUTOMATIC)
951. SOFT/COLD DRINKS (COLA, ORANGE, LEMON ETC. FLAVOURS)
952. SOYABEAN PRODUCTS
953. SOYA MILK & PANEER
954. STARCH & ALLIED PROPDUCT FROM BROKEN RICE
955. STRAWBERRY CULTIVATION & PROCESSING
956. SUGARCANE JUICE PRESERVATION
957. SUGAR CUBES FROM CANE SUGAR
988. SUGAR PLANT
989. SWEET AROMA BETEL NUT
990. SYNTHETIC TALLOW
991. TAMARIND JUICE POWDER
992. TEA & COFFEE PROCESSING & PACKAGING
993. TOFFEES, GOLIES, CANDY (HARD BOILED)
994. TOMATO PRODUCTS
994. TRADING BUSINESS OF SPICES & PAN MASALA
995. TUITY FRUITY
996. VODKA FROM POTATOES
997. WINE, BRANDY, WHISKY & CHAMPAGNE
997. WINE FROM DATES
998. YEAST FROM MOLASSES
999. ZARDA, KIMAM NO. 60,90,120,160,240,300 & 400 (TOBACCO)
1000. ZARDA-ZAFRANI (BABACHHAP TYPE)

GUMS & ADHESIVE

1001. ACRYLIC ADHESIVE
1002. ADHESIVE (FEVICOL TYPE)
1003. ADHESIVE BASED ON POLYURETHANE
1004. ADHESIVE FOR BAND AID (JOHNSON & JOHNSON TYPE)
1005. ADHESIVE INDUSTRIES (LAMINATED, STICKER, DDL & OTHER TYPES)
1006. ADHESIVE FOR GASKET (LIQUID/PASTE)
1007. GUAR GUM
1008. GUM BOTTLE (PVC)
1009. GUM FOR PASTING LABELS
1010. OFFICE PASTE
1011. RUBBER ADHESIVE
1012. SURGICAL ADHESIVE PLASTER

LEATHER & LEATHER PRODUCTS

1013. HANDMADE LEATHER
1014. LEATHER AUXILLARIES & CHEMICALS
1015. LEATHER DYES
1016. LEATHER WASHERS
1017. LEATHER BOARD FROM LEATHER WASTE
1018. LEATHER FOR UPHOLSTRY (SOFA)
1019. LEATHER GARMENTS
1020. LEATHER GOODS
1021. LEATHER SHOES
1022. LEATHER SHOE & CHAPPAL
1023. LEATHER SUITCASES, BRIEFCASES & TRAVELLING BAGS
1024. LEATHER GOODS AND GARMENTS
1025. LEATHER GARMENTS, SHOE & CHAPPAL
1026. LEATHER TANNING
1027. LEATHER TANNING & GARMENTS (EOU)
1028. SHEEP SKIN PICKLING PLANT
1029. SHOE UPPER
1030. SPORT SHOES (PLASTIC)

MISCELLANEOUS PRODUCTS

1031. AGARBATTI (INSENCE STICK)
1032. AGARBATTI (Mosquito Repellent)
1033. AGARBATI BAMBOO STICK
1034. AGARBATTI SYNTHETIC PERFUMERY COMPOUND
1035. AIR FRESHNER (ODONIL TYPE)
1036. AIR TAXI
1037. AMUSEMENT PARK
1038. ANODIC ALUMINIUM LABEL
1039. AQUACULTURE PRAWN FARMING (100% EOU)
1040. AQUA CULTURE SHRIMP FARMING (100% EOU)
1041. ARTIFICIAL FLOWERS
1042. ARTIFICIAL JEWELLERY
1043. ASBESTOS YARN
1044. ASH TRAYS FOR MARUTI VEHICLE
1045. AIR BUBBLE PACKAGING
1046. ASPHALTIC ROOFING SHEET (METAL COMPONENTS)
1047. AUTOMATIC BOOK BINDING
1048. ALKYD RESIN
1049. APPLE JUICE CONCENTRATE
1050. BALL POINT PEN FEFILLS (JOTTER TYPE)
1051. BANK BRANCH BUILDING
1052. BANQUET HALL
1053. BIO-COAL BRIQUETTES FROM AGRICULTURAL CELLULOSE WASTE
1054. BOOT CREAM/POLISH
1055. BUFFING & POLISHING COMPOUND
1056. BRASS BADGES BY ETCHING
1057. BRIQUETTED FUEL FROM AGRO WASTE
1058. BRIQUETTING OF LIGNITE COAL

"Detailed Project Report" Payable in advance through Draft/Cash/M.O. in favour of *"ENGINEERS INDIA RESEARCH INSTITUTE"*. 4449, Nai Sarak (D), Main Road Delhi - 110 006 (INDIA) • Ph : 23918117, 2391 6431, 2384 0361 • Mob : 098114 37895 •Fax : 91-11- 2391 6431 •E-Mail : eirisidi@bol.net.in • WebSite : www.eiriindia.org

1193. CANDLES (SEMI-AUTOMATIC)
1194. CORN OIL (MAIZE OIL)
1195. DEHYDRATED CASTOR OIL
1196. EUGENOL FROM CINNAMON LEAF OIL
1197. EXTRACTION OF ESSENTIAL OIL (CARDAMON, JEERA, AJOWAN, GINGER OILS ETC. & PACKAGING OF GROUND SPICES)
1198. EXTRACTION OF JASMINE ESSENCE
1199. EXTRACTION OF ESSENTIAL OILS BY SUPER CRITICAL FLUID METHOD FROM FLOWERS, HERBS & SPICES
1200. EUCALYPTUS OIL
1201. EXTRACTION OF OIL FROM OIL SEED EXPANDEREXTRUSION TECHNOLOGY)
1202. FAT LIQUOR SULPHATED OIL
1203. FLAVOURS FOR FOOD
1204. GARLIC OIL & POWDER
1205. GINGER OIL, SANDALWOOD OIL AND NAGARMOTHA OIL
1206. GINGER OIL
1207. GINGER OIL & GINGER DUST
1208. INTEGERATED WAX COMPLEX
1209. IONONE FROM LEMON GRASS OIL
1210. JASMINE & LILLY FLOWER OIL
1211. LEMON GRASS OIL
1212. LIQUID PARAFFIN
1213. LUBE OIL & GREASE
1214. LUBRICATING OIL
1215. MENTHOL CRYSTALS
1216. MENTHOL OIL & CRYSTAL
1217. MICRO CRYSTALLINE WAX
1218. MUSTARD OIL (EDIBLE OIL)
1219. OIL FROM ARTEMISIA HERBS
1220. PALM OIL CRUSHING UNIT
1221. PAN MASALA
1222. PARAFFIN WAX
1223. PARAFFIN WAX FROM SLACK WAX
1224. REFINED OIL-SUN FLOWER OIL, GROUNDNUT OIL, STAFF FLOWER OIL & COTTON SEED OIL
1225. REFINED VEGETABLE OIL
1226. RECLAMATION OF USED ENGINE OIL
1227. RICE BRAN OIL (R.B.O)
1228. ROSE OIL EXTRACTION
1229. SMOKE LESS CANDLE
1230. SPICE OIL & OLEORESINS
1231. SOLVENT EXTRACTION PLANT (OIL CAKE BASED)
1232. SYNTHETIC ALMOND OIL
1233. SYNTHETIC TALLOW
1234. SYNTHETIC GHEE
1235. VEGETABLE OIL EXTRACTION & REFINING
1236. WADDING OIL (100%) FOR WADDING OF COTTON HOSIERY CLOTH IN DYEING PROCESS
1237. WAX EMULSION FOR TEXTILE
1238. WAX FLOOR POLISH

PAINT, ENAMEL, SOLVENTS, THINNERS, INKS & VARNISH

1239. ACRYLIC EMULSION PAINTS
1240. ALUMINIUM PAINT
1241. AUTOMOBILE PAINTS
1242. BALL POINT PEN REFILL INK
1243. BITUMINIOUS ROAD EMULSION
1244. BITUMEN
1245. BITUMINIOUS FELTS FOR WATER & DAMP PROOFING
1246. BITUMINIOUS ROAD EMULSION RAPID MEDIUM & SLOW SETTING
1247. BUFFING & POLISHING
1248. CEMENT PAINT FOR WHITE & GREY CEMENT

1249. DISPERSANT
1250. DRY DISTEMPER
1251. DRY DISTEMPER & CEMENT PAINT
1252. DUPLICATING INK BLACK FOR GESTNER DUPLICATOR
1255. EMULSION PAINTS (WATER BASED)
1256. HAMMERTONE PAINT
1257. INSULATING VARNISH & WIRE ENAMEL
1258. IRON OXIDE PIGMENTS
1259. INSULATING VARNISH (POLY VINYL BUTYRAL BASED, FFC GRADE)
1260. LIME COLOUR (CEMENT COLOUR)
1261. SYNTHETIC RED OXIDE FOR FLOORINGS
1262. SOLVENT & THINNERS
1263. MARKING INKS (WATER PROOF)
1264. METAL NAPHTHANATE (AS DRIER FOR PAINTS)
1265. N.C.PUTTY
1266. OFFSET PRINTING INK
1267. OIL BOUND DISTEMPER PAINT
1268. PAINT BRUSHES
1269. PAINT REMOVERS
1270. PAINT INDUSTRY
1271. PAINT & VARNISH
1272. PICTURE VARNISH
1273. POWDER COATING PAINT
1274. PRINTING INKS (OFFSET, FLEXO & ROTO GRAVURE)
1275. PRIMER PAINT & ENAMEL PAINT
1276. PUTTY & WATER PROOFING PAINT
1277. PRINTING INKS (FLEXO-GRAPHIC INK)
1278. PUTTY (METAL CASEMENT)
1279. RED OXIDE PRIMER (ANTI CORROSIVE)
1280. REFRECTORY PAINT (GRAPHITE BASED)
1281. SCREEN PRINTING INKS
1282. SILK SCREEN PRINTING INK FORMULATION FOR PLASTIC, PAPER, CLOTH
1283. STAMP & PAD INK
1284. STOVING PAINT
1285. SPIRIT SOLUBLE MALEIC RESIN
1286. TEXTURE PAINT
1287. THINNERS AND ITS ALLIED PRODUCTS
1288. TONER INK
1289. VARNISH THINNER (SOLVENT)
1290. VACUUM METALLIZING LACQUERS
1291. WOOD PRIMER

PHARMACEUTICAL, DRUGS, AYURVEDIC/HERBAL COSMETICS & MEDICINES, HOMOEOPATHIC MEDICINES, DISPOSABLE SYRINGE, DENTAL COLLEGE & FINE CHEMICALS ETC.

1292. AROMATIC PILLS
1293. ASPIRIN
1294. AYURVEDIC PAIN BALM OINTMENTS
1295. AYURVEDIC CHURAN AND TABLETS
1296. AYURVEDIC TABLETS (HAJMOLA TYPE)
1297. AYURVEDIC/HERBAL PHARMACY
1298. AYURVEDIC SHERBATS
1299. AYURVEDIC PRODUCTS
1300. BULK DRUGS (E.O.U)
1301. BLOOD BAGS
1302. CALCIUM GLUCONATE
1303. CAPSULE, TABLET & INJECTION WITH MODERN INSTRUMENTS
1304. CASHEW FENI
1305. CHLOROQUINONE PHOSPHATE (BULK DRUGS)
1306. CLINICAL THERMOMETER
1307. DENTAL CLINIC

"Detailed Project Report" Payable in advance through Draft/Cash/M.O. in favour of *"ENGINEERS INDIA RESEARCH INSTITUTE"*. 4449, Nai Sarak (D), Main Road Delhi - 110 006 (INDIA) ● Ph : 23918117, 2391 6431, 2384 0361 ● Mob : 098114 37895 ●Fax : 91-11- 2391 6431 ●E-Mail : eirisidi@bol.net.in ● WebSite : www.eiriindia.org

1308. DENTAL COLLEGE
1309. DENTAL GRADE EUGENOL
1310. DEXTROSE MONOHYDRATE, LIQUID GLUCOSE
1311. DEHYDRATED ONION & ONION POWDER
1312. DEXTROSE POWDER (ANHYDROUS FROM STARCH)
1314. DEXTROSE SALINE SOLUTION
1315. DISTILLERY (I.M.F.L)
1316. DISPOSABLE NEEDLES FOR SYRINGES
1317. DISPRIN
1318. DISTILLED WATER
1319. EMPTY HARD GELATINE CAPSULES
1320. FILLING & PACKING OF CAPSULES
1321. GLUCOSE - D - POWDER
1322. GLYCERINE
1323. HERBAL COSMETICS
1324. HERBAL SHAMPOO
1325. HERBAL HAIR OILS (AYURVEDIC)
1326. HOMOE & BIO-MEDICINES WITH MOTHER TINCTURE
1327. HOMOEPATHIC MEDICINES
1328. HYPODERMIC NEEDLES
1329. I.V. FLUIDS
1330. IBUPROFEN
1331. INFUSION & TRANSFUSION SETS (I.V. SET)
1332. INJECTABLE FOR PHARMACEUTICALS
1333. INJECTION AMPOULES PACKAGING BOX
1334. INTEGERATED SURGICAL COTTON
1335. ICE MAKING PLANT
1336. ICE & COLD STORAGE
1337. LACTOSE & BY PRODUCTS PROCESSING FROM MILK
1338. LICHEN (JATAMANSI CHARILA)
1339. LIQUID GLUCOSE AND ITS BY-PRODUCTS
1340. L-LYSINE MONOHYDRO CHLORIDE
1341. LIQUID GLUCOSE FROM POTATOES
1342. MEDICAL COLLEGE
1343. NICOTINE FROM TOBACCO WASTE
1344. OINTMENT-AYURVEDIC (YELLOW & WHITE)
1345. PHARMACEUTICAL AND FOOD GRADE GELATINE
1346. PHARMACEUTICAL INDUSTRY (TABLETS, CAPSULES, LIQUID, GEL, OINTMENT POWDER INJECTABLE)
1347. PHARMACEUTICAL UNIT (EOU) WITH FORMULA TIONS, INJECTABLES, ETC. PYRIDINE & DERIVATIVES
1348. SALT (IODIZED SALT)
1349. SALINE & INJECTION WATER
1350. SALINE WATER & DEXTROSE SOLUTION (I.V.FLUID IN PLASTIC BOTTLES)
1351. SORBITOL
1352. STARCH (MAIZE)
1353. SURGICAL ADHESIVE PLASTER
1354. SURGICAL BANDAGES
1355. SURGICAL GLOVES
1357. SURGICAL COTTON
1358. SURGICAL COTTON AND BANDAGE
1359. SYNTHETIC CAMPHOR POWDER
1360. TABLETS & CAPSULES
1361. TISSUE CULTURE
1362. TINCTURE FROM RECTIFIED SPIRIT
1363. TRIMETHOPIME
1364. VETERENARY MEDICINES (ONLY FORMULATIONS)
1365. VITAMIN 'C', SORBITOL' ANHYDROUS DEXTROSE, STARCH

PULP, PAPER, STRAW/GREY BOARD, KRAFT PAPER, PACKAGING, PAPER CARRY BAGE, PAPER FROM AGRO WASTE & STATIONERY ETC.

1366. AMMONIA PAPER
1367. AUTOMATIC BOOK BINDING
1368. ADHESIVE (FEVICOL TYPE)
1369. ALL PIN & GEM CLIPS
1370. CARBON PAPER
1371. CARD BOARD
1372. CARBON LESS PAPER
1373. CELLPHANE PAPER
1374. COMPUTER FORMS & SECURITY PRINTING PRESS
1375. CORRUGATED BOARD & BOX (PRINTED & LAMINATED)
1376. CORRUGATED BOARD AND BOXES FROM FROM CARD BOARDS
1377. CORRUGATED CARTONS FROM PLAIN PAPERS
1378. CORRUGATRED PACKING & MATERIAL (BULB & TUBES PACKING)
1379. DESK TOP PUBLISHING
1380. DEFOAMING AGENT FOR PAPER PLANT
1381. DRINKING STRAW PAPER
1382. D.T.P CUM OFFSET PRESS
1383. EGG TRAYS
1384. EXERCISE NOTE BOOK, REGISTER AND PAD
1385. FLEXOGRAPHIC INK
1386. GREETING CARD BY OFFSET PRESS
1387. HAND MADE PAPER FILTER PAPER
1388. HARD BOARD
1389. INJECTION AMPOULES PACKAGING BOXES
1390. INSULATIING PAPER
1391. KRAFT PAPER
1392. KRAFT PAPER FROM BAGASSE
1393. LAMINATED PACKAGING PAPER WITH PRINTING
1394. LAMINATION & COATING ON PAPER
1395. M.G. PAPER FROM WASTE PAPER
1396. MILL PAPER FROM WASTE PAPER
1397. MILL BOARD FROM RICE & WHEAT STRAWS
1398. MILL BOARD FROM WASTE PAPER
1399. MINI PAPER PLANT FROM SISAL
1400. MINI PAPER PLANT
1401. MULTI WALL PAPER SACKS
1402. NEWS PAPER FOR CHILDREN
1403. NEWS PRINT PAPER FROM RICE STRAW BAGASSE
1404. NEWS PAPER CHILDRENS
1405. NEWS PRINT PAPER
1406. OFFSET AND TREADLE TYPE PRINTING PRESS
1407. MILL BOARD BASED ON RICE STRAW
1408. PAPER AND BOARD FROM STRAW
1409. PAPER & PAPER PRODUCTS
1410. PAPER ENVELOPES
1411. PAPER CARRY BAGS
1412. PAPER BOARD CARTON
1413. PAPER CONES FOR LOUD SPEAKERS
1414. PAPER FROM AKRA
1415. PAPER FROM BAGASSE WITH CORRUGATED BOARD & BOXES
1416. PAPER FROM BAMBOO
1417. PAPER GLASSES FOR BEVERAGES
1418. PAPER FROM RICE HUSK & WHEAT HUSK
1419. PAPER FROM TREE BARK, EUCALYPRUS WOOD
1420. PAPER PRODUCTS
1421. PAPER PLANT (WHITE WRITING & NEWS PAPER FOR PULP & WASTE PAPER)
1422. PAPER PLATES, PAPER GLASS
1423. PAPER CONES & TUBES
1425. PAPER PLANT WITH DTP & PRINTING & PUBLISHING UNIT
1426. PAPER BASED PHENOLIC SHEET
1427. PAPER CUP FOR ICE CREAM
1428. PAPER TUBES SPIRAL WINDING COMPOSIT CONTAINER
1429. PAPER LABLE FOR BEER BOTTLES
1430. PARTICLE BOARD & BLACK BOARD WITH SANDING & LAMINATION OF PARTICLE BOARD
1431. PARTICLE BOARD FROM RICE HUSK
1432. POUCH FILLING & MAKING FOR TOMATO SAUCE
1433. POUCH MAKING &

GRAVURE PRINTING
1434. PROCESSING OF PAPER FOR FEEDING IN COMPUTER
1435. PULP FROM BAMBOO & WOOD
1436. PAPER FILES
1437. PLAYING CARDS
1438. ROSIN SIZING AGENT (FOR PAPER PLANT)
1439. SAND PAPER
1440. SANITRY NAPKINS
1441. SILICON COATED PAPER
1442. STENCIL PAPER
1443. STRAW BOARD AND GREY BOARD
1444. STRAW BOARD & MILL BOARD
1445. STRAW BOARD AND PAPER BOARD
1446. TISSUE PAPER FACIAL
1447. TISSUE MOIST TOILETERY CLEANSING TISSUE AND RELATED PRODUCTS
1448. TISSUE PAPER ROLLS
1449. TETRA PACK FOR MILK PACKAGING, GHEE & OTHER LIQUIDS
1450. TOILET PAPER ROLLS
1451. TOILET PAPER & NAPKINS
1452. WAX COATED PRINTED PAPER
1453. WET FACE FRESHNER TISSUE
1454. WHITE WRITING & PRINTING PAPER
1455. WRITING & PRINTING PAPER (PAPER MILLS)

PLASTIC, B.O.P.P, ACRYLIC, DISPOSABLE PLASTIC PRODUCTS, PET PRODUCTS, P.V.C, H.D.P.E, P.P, L.D.P.E., P.U, A.B.S, THERMOFOARMING, MASTER BATCHES, & POLYMER AND RUBBER PRODUCTS, TYRE, TUBE, ADHESIVE, SHEET, COIR & MANY OTHERS

1456. ABS GRANULES FROM ABS SCRAPS FROM OLD T.V. CABINETS, WHITE GOODS ETC.
1457. ACRYLIC BEADS
1458. ACRYLIC COPOLYMER EMULSION
1459. ACRYLIC LATEX
1460. ACRYLIC SHEET
1461. ACRYLIC SHEET & MOULDED PRODUCTS
1462. ACRYLIC TEETH
1463. AUTO TUBES
1464. AUTO FLAPS FOR TRUCKS & BUSES
1465. AUTO TYRES & TUBES
1466. BABY BOTTLES (PLASTIC) WITH WHITESILICON RUBBER NIPPLES
1467. B.O.P.P. FILM
1468. B.O.P.P. PRESSURE SENSITIVE SELF ADHESIVE TAPE
1469. BABY NIPPLE (SILICON)
1470. BABY NIPPLE (BIG SIZE)
1471. BALLOON PLASTIC ADVERTISING
1472. BLISTER FILM PVC
1473. BLISTER PACKAGING & POUCH PAKAGING
1474. BLOW MOULDING PLASTIC CONTAINER
1475. COATING ON METALIZED POLYESTER FILM/METALISED PAPER/ ALIMINIUM FOIL
1476. COATING ON PLASTIC (ELECTROLYSIS) & GLASS
1477. COIR FOAM (RUBBERISED)
1478. COLOUR COATING ON PLASTICS
1479. COLOUR MASTER BATCHES FOR VARIOUS PLASTICS
1480. CYCLE TYRES AND TUBES
1481. DISPOSABLE PLASTIC CUPS GLASSES, ETC.
1482. DISPOSABLE PLASTIC SYRINGES & NEEDLES
1483. DISPOSABLE PLASTIC SYRINGES
1484. DOUGH MOULDING COMPOUND (D.M.C)
1485. EPOXY RESIN
1486. EXPANDED POLYESTRENE MOULDING (THERMOCOLE)
1487. F.R.P AUTO, SCOOTER ROOFS & CEILINGS
1488. F.R.P PRODUCTS (HELMET, WASHBASIN SHEETS, ROOFING SHEETS)
1489. FIBRE REINFORCED PLASTIC (HIGH PRESSURE MOULDING WITH SMC BMC AND DMC)
1490. FIELD RUBBER CONVERTED TO THE 60% LATEX RUBBER
1491. FLEXIBLE P.U. FOAM
1492. FORMALDEHYDE CROCKERY & OTHER ITEMS
1493. FORMALDEHYDE RESIN (UREA, PHENOL, MELEMINE)
1494. GASKET SHEET
1495. GUM BOTTLE (PVC)
1496. GLASS BEADS
1497. HDPE COATED PAPER SACK
1498. H.D.P.E. BAGS
1499. H.D.P.E. CONTAINERS (BLOW MOULDING)
1500. H.D.P.E. CONTAINER, POLY JARS BY INJECTION MOULDING (FOOD GRADE)
1501. H.D.P.E. JERRY CANS
1502. HDPE MANUFACTURING FROM ETHYLALCOHOL
1503. H.D.P.E PIPE AND FITTINGS
1504. H.D.P.E. PIPES
1505. H.D.P.E PRINTED BAGS
1506. H.D.P.E TWINES AND ROPES
1507. H.D.P.E. & L.D.P.E PIPES AND FITTINGS
1508. H.D.P.E/PP BOX STRAPPING
1509. H.D.P.E/PP WOVEN SACKS USING PLAIN LOOMS
1510. HOLOGRAM STICKERS-3D
1511. H.M BAG PLANT WITH PRINTING UNIT
1512. HAWAI CHAPPALS (RUBBER)
1513. I.V PLASTIC BOTTLE
1514. ICE CREAM CUP (PLASTIC)
1515. INJECTION MOULDED AUTO COMPONENTS
1516. INJECTION & BLOW MOULDED PLASTIC PRODUCTS
1517. INJECTION MOULDED PLASTIC PRODUCTS
1518. INTEGERATED COMPLEX ESTER'S & ALLIED PRODUCTS (D.O.P, D.B.P, & ETHYL ACETATE, BUYTL ACETATE, WIRE ENAMELS, JELLY CABLE COMPOUND)
1519. L.D.P.E. (LOW DENSITY POLY ETHYLENE) GRANULES FROM VIRGIN (L.D.P.E. RESIN)
1520. INTEGERATED SURGICAL RUBBER GOODS INDUSTRY
1521. INJECTION MOULDED PLASTIC BALLS
1522. L.D.P.E FROM ETHYL ALCOHOL
1523. LDPE MOULDED PRODUCTS
1524. LAMINATION OF COEXTRUSION MULTILAYER FILM IN ROLL FORM
1525. LATEX RUBBER
1526. LATEX RUBBER CONDOM
1527. MASTER BATCHES (COLOURED, P.V.C, L.D.P.E, H.D.P.E, ETC.)
1528. MELAMINE FORMALHYDE RESIN
1529. MOULDED LUGGAGE
1530. MULTI-LAYER (3 LAYER BAGS)
1531. MULTI-LAYER (3 LAYER) FILM WITH LAMINATION & PRINTING
1532. OIL SEAL
1533. PET BOTTLE/CONTAINERS
1534. PET BOTTLES FROM PRE FORM
1535. PET BOTTLE & MINERAL WATER
1536. PET PRE-FORM FROM PET RESIN
1537. PET PRE-FORM CUM PET BOTTLES
1538. PET PRE-FORM PET BOTTLES CUM MINERAL WATERS
1539. POLY CARBONATE RESIN
1540. PTFE COMPONENTS
1541. PU/PVC SOLE FOR SPORT SHOE BY IMPORTED M/C.
1542. PVC BATTERY SEPARATOR
1543. P.V.C COMPOUNDS (FRESH)
1544. P.V.C COMPOUNDS (SCRAP)
1545. P.V.C ELECTRICAL INSULATING TAPE
1546. P.V.C. EXTRUSION PROFILES
1547. P.V.C FITTINGS
1548. P.V.C FLEXIBLE FUSIBLE POWDER HEAT FUSIBLE POWDER
1549. P.V.C GRANULES (FOR

INSULATION & SHEETS GRADES)
1550. P.V.C GRANULES FROM PVC SCRAPS (WITH POLLUTION CONTROL)
1551. P.V.C HOSES
1552. P.V.C LEATHER CLOTH
1553. P.V.C FLEXIBLE PIPES
1554. P.V.C PIPES AND FITTINGS
1555. POLYTHENE BAGS (PRINTED)
1556. PVC PLASTICS FILM SHEET SOFT/RIGID
1557. PVC RESIN AND COMPOUND
1558. PVC RULAR
1559. PVC STABLIZERS (SINGLE PACK SYSTEM)
1560. PVC WIRE AND CABLES
1561. PAPER BASED PHENOLIC SHEET FOR ELECTRICAL
1562. PHENOL FORMALDEHYDE RESIN
1563. PHENOLIC RESIN
1564. PLASTIC BEADS FROM PLASTIC SCRAPS
1565. PLASTIC BUTTONS
1566. PLASTIC CANS
1567. PLASTIC COLLAPSIBLE TUBE
1568. PLASTIC CORRUGATED SHEET & BOXES
1569. PLASTIC FILM AND SHEETS WITH PRINTING FLEXO & ROTO/LDPE/HDPE/PP/HM/PVC
1570. PLASTIC FILTER MASTER BATCH & OTHER MASTER BATCHES FOR VARIOUS PLASTICS
1571. PLASTIC JERRY CANS
1572. PLASTIC GRANULES OR POWDER FROM PLASTIC SCRAP
1573. PLASTIC INJECTION MOULDED T.V. CABINETS
1574. PLASTIC ITEMS MANUFAC TURE FROM POWDER MELAMINE
1575. PLASTIC GOODS
1576. PLASTIC PIPES & TARPAULINES
1577. PLASTIC SHEET FROM SCRAP
1578. PLASTIC PLANT (BLOW MOULDING & INJECTION MOULDING)
1579. PLASTIC PRODUCTS (GOLD, SILVER, NICKEL)
1580. PLASTIC TOYS
1581. POLYESTER BEADING
1582. POLYESTER FILM
1583. POLYTHENE BAGS & AUTOMATIC PRINTING
1584. POLYTHENE PRINTED BAGS
1585. POLYURETHANE FOAM AND ITS PRODUCTS
1586. PROPYLENE FILM (PRINTED) & BAG MANUFACTURING
1587. PLASTIC MATS
1588. RAINBOW COLOUR ON PVC FILM & SHEET
1589. RED MUD PVC PIPES AND FITTINGS
1590. RE-RUBBERISED OF SOLID TYPE
1591. RESIN COATED SAND REXINE
1592. REXINE CLOTH & ALLIED PRODUCTS
1593. RUBBER ADHESIVE
1594. RUBBER AUTO PARTS
1595. RUBBER BELTING
1596. RUBBER MOULDING UNIT INCLUDING LINING RUBBER SHEETING
1597. RUBBER RECLAIMING
1598. RUBBER ROLLERS FOR TEXTILE MILLS & PAPER INDUSTRIES
1599. RUBBER & PLASTIC SHEETS, MATS & FLAPS
1600. RUBBER SHEET AND ALLIED HOSPITAL RUBBER GOODS
1601. RUBBERIZED PVC GASKET
1602. RUBBERISED COIR
1603. RUBBER COMPOUND FOR AUTOMOBILES
1604. SAFETY BELTS
1605. SILVER AND GOLD PLATING ON PVC AND NYLON-6
1606. SILICONE RUBBER NIPPLES/ TEATS
1607. SPECTACLE FRAMES (PLASTIC)
1608. SPUNGE RUBBER
1609. SURGICAL EXAMINATION GLOVES
1610. SYNTHETIC PEARL COATING ON POLYSTYRENE BEADS
1611. SYNTHETIC RUBBER ADHESIVE
1612. TEFLON MANUFACTURING
1613. TEFLON TAPE
1614. TEFLON TAPES & CABLES
1615. THERMOCOLE SHEET AND MOULDED PRODUCTS EXPANDED POLYESTERENE EXTRUSION PROFILES
1616. THERMOFORMED PACKAGING (BLISTER PACKAGING & POUCH PACKAGING)
1617. THERMOPLASTIC POLYURETHANE
1618. THERMOFORMED CUPS, PLATES & GLASS WITH HIPS SHEET
1619. THERMOCOLE
1620. THERMOCOLE BASED DISPOSABLE GLASS, CUPS & PLATES
1621. TOOTH BRUSHES
1622. TOY BALLOON, DECORA TIVE & INDUSTRIAL BALLOONS
1623. TREAD RUBBER
1624. TYRE RETREADING (HOT)
1625. TYRE RETREADING BY COLD PROCESS
1626. TYRE TUBES & FLAPS
1627. TYRE & TUBES
1628. UNSATURATED POLYESTER FOR REXINE
1629. V-BELT AND FAN BELT
1630. VINYL ASBESTOS AND PVC WALL PAPER
1631. VITON (FLUORO ELASTOMER)

SOAP, COSMETICS & PERFUMES

1632. ACID SLURRY, SYNTHETIC DETERGENT POWDER
1632. ACID SLURRY
1633. AGARBATTI SYNTHETIC, PERFUMERY COMPOUND
1634. AFTER SHAVE LOTION
1635. ANTISEPTIC CREAM
1636. BETA IONONE
1637. BLEACHING POWDER
1638. BLUE DETERGENT POWDER
1639. CLEANING POWDER (VIMTYPE)
1640. COLD CREAM
1641. COLOURED FLAME & PERFUMED CANDLES (RED, BLUE GREEN FLAME)
1642. COSMETIC INDUSTRY (MODERN)
1643. COSMETIC INDUSTRY (SHAMPOO, SPRAY PERFUME, TALCUM POWDER
1644. DETERGENT POWDER (ARIEL TYPE)
1645. DETERGENT POWDER (NIRMA TYPE) FULLY AUTOMATIC PLANT
1646. DETERGENT WASHING POWDER
1647. FISH OIL SOAP
1648. GLYCERINE TRANSPARENT SOAP
1649. HAIR REMOVING CREAM
1650. HERBAL COSMETICS
1651. HERBAL SHAMPO & CREAM
1652. HERBAL/AYURVEDIC COSMETICS
1653. INCENSE POWDER, INCENSE STICKS & INCENSE CAKE
1654. OPTICAL WHITENERS
1655. ROSE OIL EXTRACTION
1656. SHAMPOOS (COCONUT OIL BASED COLD PROCESS)
1657. SHAVING CREAM
1658. SINDUR (KUMKUM)
1659. SOAP COATED PAPER
1660. SPRAY DRIED DETERGENT POWDER
1661. STAIN REMOVER
1662. TALCUM POWDER (FACE & TOILET POWDER)
1663. TOILET AND HERBAL SOAP
1664. TOOTH PASTE & POWDER
1665. WASHING DETERGENT POWDER AND WASHING SOAP
1666. WASHING POWDER LIQUID DETERGENTS, LOTION & SHAMPOO

ENTERTAINMENT CLUB WITH 4 STAR HOTEL
1779. HOSPITALS
1780. ICE CREAM PARLOUR
1781. INTERNET SERVICE PROVIDER (I.S.P.)
1782. MEDICAL COLLEGE
1783. MEDICAL COLLEGE, HOSPITAL & RESEARCH INSTITUTE
1784. MEDICAL TRANSCRIPTION CENTRE
1785. MENTAL RETARDATION HOSPITAL & CEREBRAL PALSY
1786. MOTEL/SMALL HOTEL
1787. MULTISTOREY COMMERCIAL COMPLEX
1788. MULTISTOREY RESIDENTIAL COMPLEX
1789. NURSERY SCHOOL
1790. NATURE CARE CENTRE
1791. NURSING HOME
1792. ONLINE SHOPPING MALL (RS. 5000/- REPORT)
1793. PORTAL
1794. REHABILITATION CENTRE FOR AGED & NEEDY PERSONS
1795. RESIDENTIAL CUM COMMERCIAL COMPLEX
1796. RESTAURANT
1797. RESTAURANT WITH PUB
1798. SCHOOL (PRIMARY)
1799. SCHOOL (HIGHER SECONDARY)
1800. THREE STAR HOTEL
1801. TOURIST CLUB
1802. TRAINING INSTITUTE FOR MEDICAL TRANSCRIPTION
1803. VIDEO FILM STUDIO
1804. WARE HOUSE
1805. WEBSITE DESIGN & E-MAIL REGISTERING

AGRO BASED INDUSTRIES

1806. COAL BRIQUETTES FROM AGROWASTE
1807. FURFURALFROM RICEHULL
1808. MUSHROOM CULTIVATION & PROCESSING (BUTTON)
1809. MUSHROOM GROWING & PROCESSING WITH AIR CONDITIONING
1810. MUSHROOM CULTIVATION & PROCESSING UNIT DEHYDRATION & PACKAGING OF OYSTER & PADDY STRAW MUSHROOMS
1811. ORGANIC MANURE
1812. PAPAYA CULTIVATION
1813. PAPAYA & TOMATO CULTIVATION
1814. PROCESSING & UTILISATION OF COCONUT
1815. PROCESSING OF SHEEP HAIR TO PRODUCE WOOL

BAKERY, CONFECTIONERY & FOOD PRODUCTS

1816. AGROLACTOR SOYA MILK
1817. APPLE FRUIT JUICE WITH CANNING BOTTLING
1818. AYURVEDIC SHARBAT
1819. BAKERY UNIT (PASTRIES, BREAD, BUNS, CAKE, TOFFEE ETC.)
1820. BAKING POWDER
1821. BANANA & ITS BY PRODUCTS
1822. BANANA POWDER
1823. BANANA WAFERS
1824. BANANA CULTIVATION
1825. BEER INDUSTRY
1826. DEHULLING OF JAUN FOR BEER
1827. BEER & WINE
1828. BEER, ALCOHOL, IMFL
1829. BESEN PLANT
1830. BISCUIT PLANT
1831. BREAD & BISCUIT PLANT
1832. BOTTLING PLANT COUNTRY LIQUOR FROM RECTIFIED SPIRIT
1833. BRANDY
1834. BREAD RUSKS
1835. CANNED FRUITS & VEGETABLES
1836. CANNING & PRESERVATION OF MEAT
1837. CANNING & PRESERVATION OF VEGETABLES
1838. CANNING OF MANGO PULP & MANGO SLICES
1839. CARBONATED BEVERAGS
1840. CASHEW FENI
1841. CASHEW NUT (DRIED & FRIED)
1842. CATTLE BREEDING
1843. CATTLE BREEDING & DAIRY FARM TO PRODUCE MILK
1844. CATTLE FEED FROM TAPIOCA
1845. CHEWING GINGER & AMLOKI
1846. CHEWING GUM
1847. CHILLI SAUCE
1848. CHILLI POWDER
1849. CHOCOLATE
1850. CIDER PLANT
1851. COCOA POWDER
1852. COCOA BUTTER & COCOA POWDER
1853. COCONUT SHELL POWDER
1854. COCONUT WATER
1855. COCONUT SWEET (WATERY)
1856. COCONUT MILK POWDER (DEHYDRATED)
1857. COCONUT PRODUCTS & BY PRODUCTS (INTEGRATED PLANT)
1858. COLD DRINK
1859. CURRY POWDER
1860. DAIRY FOR MILK PROCESSING (GHEE, BUTTER & PANEER)
1861. DAIRY PRODUCTS
1862. DAIRY PRODUCTS MILK PACKAGING IN POUCH (GHEE, BUTTER, ETC.
1863. DAIRY FARM TO PRDUCE MILK WITH PACKAGING (COW)
1864. DAIRY FARM TO PRDUCE MILK WITH PACKAGING (BUFALLOE)
1865. DAIRY FARM & MILK PRODUCTS
1866. DAL MOTH, CHANACHUR & BHUJIYA
1867. DEHYDRATION OF FRUITS & VEGETABLE
1868. DESICCATED COCONUT POWDER FROM COCONUTS
1869. DEHYDRATION & CANNING OF FRUITS & VEGETABLES
1870. DRY FRUIT ROASTING & PACKAGING
1871. DRYING OF RED CHILLIES, HALDI, DHANIYA, PEAS & GROUND NUT
1872. EGG POWDER
1873. FISH CANNING IN TIN & POUCHES
1874. FISH DEHYRATION (DRYING OF FISH)
1875. FISH MEAL
1876. FISH PROCESSING (BEAST FREEZING PROCESSES)
1877. FLAVOURS FOR FOOD INDUSTRIES
1878. FLOUR MILL (ROLLER)
1879. FROZEN MEAT
1880. FOOD DEHYDRATION (FRUITS & VEGETABLES)
1881. FRIED & ROASTED GROUND NUT, GRAMS, PEAR ETC
1882. FRUIT JUICE MAKING & PACKAGING IN PLASTIC CONTAINER
1883. FRUIT JUICE IN TETRA PACK (DRINKS)
1884. FRUIT JUICE, SQUASHES, SAUCE & KETCHUP, JAM, JELLY, VINEGAR ETC.
1885. GARLIC FLAKES
1886. GARLIC POWDER
1887. GHEE & BUTTER
1888. GINGER (PULVERISED)
1889. GINGER GLAZING & PRESERVATION
1890. GINGER STORAGE
1891. GINGER PROCESSING
1892. GINGER OIL & GINGER DUST
1893. GINGER POWDER (DRY) & OLEORESIN
1894. GRAPE DEHYDRATION
1895. GRAPE CULTIVATION
1896. GRAPE JUICE
1897. HONEY PROCESSING & PACKAGING
1898. ICE CREAM & ICE CANDY
1899. ICE CUBE
1900. INVERT SUGAR
1901. IDLI MIX, DOSA MIX SAMBHAR MIX, VADA MIX, GULAB JAMUN MIX
1902. INSTANT COFFEE & INSTANT TEA

1903. INSTANT NOODLES
1904. INSTANT SOUPS
1905. IODIZED SALT FROM CRUDE SALT
1906. JAM CHUTNEY PICKLES & SQUASHES
1907. KATHA MANUFACTURING
1908. LECITHIN (SOYA BASED)
1909. LEMON & ITS PRODUCTS
1910. MACARONI MANUFACTURING
1911. MACARONI, SPAGHETTI, VERMICELLI & NOODLES
1912. MAIZE & ITS BY PRODUCTS MALTING PLANT
1913. MANGO PAPPAD (AAM PAPPAD)
1914. MANGO POWDER RIPE
1915. MANGO POWDER
1916. MANGO PROCESSING & CANNING (MANGO PULP)
1917. MEAT PROCESSING (CHICKEN MUTTON)
1918. MEAT PROCESSING (BUFFALO)
1919. MENTHOL BOLD FROM MENTHOL FLAKES
1020. MILK POWDER
1921. MILK POWDER & GHEE
1922. MILK POWDER, GHEE & SPICES
1923. MILK PRESERVATION & MARKETING TO WHOLE SELLERS
1924. MILK PRESERVATION & MARKETING TO WHOLE SELLERS (IN POUCHES)
1925. MILK TOFFEE MANUFACTURES
1926. MINERAL WATER
1927. MINERAL WATER IN POUCHES
1928. MINI FLOUR MILL ATTA MAIDA, SUJI & WHEAT BRAN
1929. MITHAI/HALWAI (SWEET & NAMKEEN)
1930. MUTTON PROCESSING
1931. PAN MASALA (MEETHA, SADA, ZARDA) MAKING & PACKING
1932. PAN MASALA AND POUCH MAKING
1933. PANEER (CHEESE)
1934. PAPAD & BARIYAN
1935. PAPAD PLANT
1936. PEPSICOLA IN POLYTUBES
1937. PETHA PACKAGING
1938. PICKLES
1939. PIGGERY/MEAT/CHICKEN PROCESSING
1940. PINE APPLE JUICE CANNING
1941. POTATO & ONION POWDER
1942. POTATO & ONION FLAKES
1943. POTATO CHIPS
1944. POTATO GRANULES
1945. POUCH FILLING FOR SAUNF SUPARI ILAICHI ETC.
1946. PRESERVATION OF RAWS MANGO JUICE
1947. PROCESSED CHEESE & MARINE PDTS.
1948. PULP FROM TARMARIND
1949. READYMATE PROCESSED FOOD
1950. RICE & CORN FLAKES
1951. RICE BASMATI (TRADING)
1952. RICE POLISHING & PACKAGING IN POUCH
1953. ROASTED/SALTED/MASALA/ CASHEW NUTS ALMONDS & PEA NUT
1954. ROLLER FLOUR MILL

INFOTECH/IT PROJECTS

1955. MEDICAL TRANSCRIPTION
1956. E-COMMERCE
1957. CYBERCAFE
1958. INTERNET SERVICE PROVIDER (ISP)
1959. COMPUTER EDUCATION CENTRE
1960. PORTAL (WEBSITE DESIGN)
1961. CALL CENTRE

TERMS AND CONDITIONS

FOR INDIA

1. Please ask for Quotations/ Proforma Invoice for Each *Market Survey Cum Detailed Techno Economic Feasibility Report.* Payable in advance through Draft/M.O./Cash in favour of 'ENGINEERS INDIA RESEARCH INSTITUTE', Delhi. Delivery by Regd.Post/Courier within 2 Days. (Postage Free)

2. Ask for a Hi Tech Projects, monthly magazine. Each issue covers approx. 75 project profiles.

FOR OVERSEAS

1. Please ask for Quotations/ Proforma Invoice in US $ for Each *Market Survey Cum Detailed Techno Economic Feasibility Report.* Payable in advance through Bank Draft in favour of 'ENGINEERS INDIA RESEARCH INSTITUTE', Delhi. (Payable in India). Delivery by Regd. Air Mail Post/Courier within 3 Days. (Postage Free)

2. Ask for a Hi Tech Projects, monthly magazine. Each issue covers approx. 75 project profiles.

ENGINEERS INDIA RESEARCH INSTITUTE

4449, Nai Sarak (D), Main Road, Delhi - 110 006 (India)
Phones: 91-11- 2391 8117, 2391 6431, 2384 0361
Fax: 91-11- 2391 6431 E-Mail : eirisidi@bol.net.in Website:www.eiriindia.org
Also at : 4/54, Roop Nagar, Delhi - 110 007 (India)
Ph:. 23840361 Mob: 098114 37895

PATRON: YOU CAN ALSO DEPOSIT THE AMOUNT IN "EIRI" ACCOUNT WITH UTI BANK LTD. CA-054010200006248 OR ICICI BANK LTD. CA-022705000598 OR UNION BANK OF INDIA CA-307201010015149 AND JUST SMS US ON PH. 09811437895